Extremely Violent Societies

In this groundbreaking book Christian Gerlach traces the social roots of the extraordinary processes of human destruction involved in mass violence throughout the twentieth century. He argues that terms such as 'genocide' and 'ethnic cleansing' are too narrow to explain the diverse motives and interests that cause violence to spread in varying forms and intensities. From killings and expulsions to enforced hunger, collective rape, strategic bombing, forced labor, and imprisonment he explores what happened before, during, and after periods of widespread bloodshed in countries such as Armenia, Indonesia, Bangladesh, Nazi-occupied Greece, and in anti-guerrilla wars worldwide in order to highlight the crucial role of socioeconomic pressures in the generation of group conflicts. By focusing on why so many different people participated in or supported mass violence, and why different groups were victimized, he offers us a new way of understanding one of the most disturbing phenomena of our times.

CHRISTIAN GERLACH is Professor of Contemporary History at the University of Bern. His award-winning titles in German include *Calculated Murder: The German Economic and Extermination Policy in Byelorussia* (third edition, 2001); *War, Food, Genocide: German Extermination Policies in the Second World War* (second edition, 2001); and *The Last Chapter: The Murder of Hungarian Jews, 1944–45* (with Götz Aly, second edition, 2004).

Extremely Violent Societies

Mass Violence in the Twentieth-Century World

Christian Gerlach

CAMBRIDGE UNIVERSITY PRESS
Cambridge, New York, Melbourne, Madrid, Cape Town, Singapore,
São Paulo, Delhi, Dubai, Tokyo, Mexico City

Cambridge University Press
The Edinburgh Building, Cambridge CB2 8RU, UK

Published in the United States of America by Cambridge University Press,
New York

www.cambridge.org
Information on this title: www.cambridge.org/9780521706810

First published 2010

Printed in the United Kingdom at the University Press, Cambridge

A catalogue record for this publication is available from the British Library

Library of Congress Cataloguing in Publication data
Gerlach, Christian, 1963–
  Extremely violent societies : mass violence in the twentieth-century
  world / Christian Gerlach.
    p. cm.
  Includes index.
  ISBN 978-0-521-88058-9 (hardback) – ISBN 978-0-521-70681-0 (pbk.)
  1. Violence–History–20th century. 2. Violence–Social aspects. I. Title.
  HM886.G46 2010
  303.609′04–dc22   2010033714

ISBN 978-0-521-88058-9 Hardback
ISBN 978-0-521-70681-0 Paperback

CONTENTS

ACKNOWLEDGMENTS

All research projects are the result of discussions and exchanges between scholars and many other people. This is especially true for this study. It was conceived when I taught at the National University of Singapore, most of it written during my years at the University of Pittsburgh, and it is being finished now that I teach at the University of Bern, Switzerland. I feel deep gratitude to my colleagues at these places.

Several institutions contributed financially to works that led to this volume. The Center for Historical Studies, University of Maryland, granted me a year-long stipend and the History Department at the University of Pittsburgh an early sabbatical. I also received a small travel grant by the European Union Center and a Hewlett International Grant from the Center for Latin American Studies, both at the University of Pittsburgh, and generous support for the workshop "Famine and mass violence" by the German Academic Exchange Service (daad), New York. Many thanks to all of them.

What would we historians do without archivists? I would like to thank many of them for their invaluable help, particularly Birgit Kmezik and Sieglinde Hartmann (Politisches Archiv des Auswärtigen Amtes, Berlin), R. Schröder (Bundesarchiv, Berlin), Michael Hussey of the National Archives and Records Administration, College Park, Maryland, Jennifer Jerome (Australian National Archive, Canberra), Klaus Urner (Archiv für Zeitgeschichte, Zurich), Rosie Dodd (Oxfam), and Giuliano Fregoli (FAO). The same goes for the library staff at the Universities of Maryland, Singapore, Pittsburgh, Bern, at the University of California at Los Angeles, and at the Josef-Wulf-Bibliothek at the Gedenkstätte Haus der Wannseekonferenz, Berlin.

I am deeply indebted for critical comments and suggestions to several colleagues who took it upon themselves to read individual chapters of the manuscript: Timothy Barnard, Christoph Dieckmann, Hilmar Kaiser, Peter Karsten, Dirk Moses, Patrick Neveling, and Clemens Six. Michael Watson from Cambridge University Press and Adrian Stenton gave me countless useful hints to improve the manuscript; many thanks to them. Many other colleagues and friends were kind enough to talk with me about my work, giving me inspiration, responding critically to my ideas, or pointing me to relevant sources. Only a few can be mentioned: Yehonatan Alsheh, Andrej Angrick, Omer Bartov, Florent Brayard, Roland Clark, Raya Cohen, Christoph Conrad, Robert Cribb, Seymour Drescher, Marc Dronin, Thomas Du Bois, Moritz Feichtinger, Alexandra Garbarini, Wendy Goldman, Ian Gordon, Anna Hájková, Hilmar Kaiser, George Kent, Hans-Lukas Kieser, Edward Kissi, Tom Kohut, Paul Kratoska, Pieter Lagrou, Wendy Lower, Stephan Malinowski, Christof Mauch, Hans Mommsen, Dirk Moses, Georgios Niarchos, Fritz Ottenheimer, Claudio Pavone, Dieter Pohl, Hans Safrian, Dominik Schaller, Jacques Semelin, Helene Sinnreich, Alexa Stiller, Andreas Stucki, Gregor Thum, Christian Thorne, Tatjana Tönsmeyer, Nicolas Werth, Michael Wildt, and Madeline Zilfi. I am very grateful to all of them, as well as to those colleagues, archivists, and students who cannot be mentioned here or prefer not to be mentioned. Thanks also to the students of my classes on this topic at the Universities of Pittsburgh and Bern, especially Anthony Tantoco, Catherine Tighe, and Brett Wieviora. Also, I would like to thank Ulrich Makosch who shared his experiences as an eyewitness with me.

Over several years, many institutions gave me the opportunity to present and discuss my ideas laid out in this book, among them the University of Zurich, Switzerland; the EHESS/Institut de l'Histoire du Temps Présent, Paris; the Strassler Family Center for Holocaust and Genocide Studies, Clark University, USA; the History Departments at Williams College, USA, Keele University, UK, and the National University of Singapore; and the Asian Studies Center, University of Pittsburgh. The same chance was given to me at a number of conferences and workshops, among them the "Nazism–Stalinism Workshop," Harvard University; the conferences "Le Guerre e il Novecento," Università degli Studi di Napoli "Federico II," Naples, Italy; "Genocides: Forms, Causes, and Consequences," Berlin; "Crimes against humanity: causes, forms and prevention of genocide," organized by the Heinrich Böll Foundation and the European Network of Genocide Scholars, Berlin; "Removing Peoples: Forced Migration in the Modern World (1850–1950)," University of York, UK; "The Legacy of Simon Wiesenthal for Holocaust Studies," Wiesenthal Institute for Holocaust Studies and Institute for Contemporary History, Vienna, Austria; "From Europe to Latin America and Beyond: The Continuity of Genocidal Social Practices," at the Second Conference on Genocide, Universidad Nacional de Tres de Febrero, Buenos Aires; and at the Second European Congress for World and Global History, Dresden. Thoughts relevant to this volume were also discussed at the workshop "Famine and mass violence" that I co-organized with Helene Sinnreich at Youngstown State University in 2008. I thank all participants in these events and all the organizers: Hans-Lukas Kieser, Florent Brayard, Thomas Kühne and Debórah Dwork, Alexandra Garbarini, Christoph Dieckmann, Malcolm Murfett, Dianne Dakis, Terry Martin, Sheila Fitzpatrick, Michael Geyer, Jürgen Zimmerer and Dominik Schaller, Marianne Zepp, Claudia Haake and Richard Bessel, Bertrand Perz and Ingo Zechner, Daniel Feierstein, and Matthias Middell.

Parts of this book take up earlier publications by me that need to be acknowledged here. Chapter 1 takes up longer passages of my article, "Extremely Violent Societies: An Alternative to the Concept of Genocide," from *Journal of Genocide Research* 8(4), 2006, pp. 455–71 (see www.tandf.co.uk/journals/titles/14623528.asp). Chapter 3 includes stretches and material from my earlier chapter in a collective volume, "Nationsbildung im Krieg: Wirtschaftliche Faktoren bei der Vernichtung der Armenier und beim Mord an den ungarischen Juden," in *Der Völkermord an den Armeniern und die Shoah*, edited by Hans-Lukas Kieser and Dominik Schaller (2002, pp. 347–422). A brief version of Chapter 5, setting a somewhat different emphasis, has been published as "Sustainable Violence: Mass Resettlement, Strategic Villages, and Militias in Anti-Guerrilla Warfare" in *Removing Peoples*, edited by Richard Bessel and Claudia Haake (2009, pp. 361–92). I would like to thank Taylor Francis Group, Chronos Verlag, and Oxford University Press for their generous permission to use parts of these publications.

Unfortunately, such a project tends to take a toll in terms of social and family life. Hence I feel deep gratitude to my mother, Elfriede Gerlach, to Christina Blume, and to my daughter Nina for all their support and appreciation, for giving me strength, and for bearing with me over many years.

I would like to dedicate this book to Wolfgang Scheffler, a model of empirical rigor and intellectual sincerity, who did not live to see the publication of this study.

ABBREVIATIONS

AA	Auswärtiges Amt
ADN	Allgemeiner Deutscher Nachrichtendienst
AfZ	Archiv für Zeitgeschichte, Zurich
ANA	Australian National Archive
Baperki	Consultative Body for Indonesian Citizenship
BBC	British Broadcasting Corporation
BTI	Indonesian Peasants Front
CAVR	Commission for Reception, Truth and Reconciliation in East Timor
CIA	Central Intelligence Agency
CUP	Committee for Union and Progress
EAM	National Liberation Front (of Greece)
ELAS	People's Liberation Army (of Greece)
EPW	Economic and Political Weekly
FAO	Food and Agriculture Organization of the UN
FLN	National Liberation Front (of Algeria)
FRG	Federal Republic of Germany
FRUS	Foreign Relations of the United States
GDR	German Democratic Republic
Gerwani	Indonesian Women's Movement
HGS	Holocaust and Genocide Studies
HMI	Islamic Students Organization (of Indonesia)
IAMM	Directorate for the Settlement of Tribes and Immigrants
ILO	International Labor Office
IPKI	League of Upholders of Indonesian Independence
JGR	*Journal of Genocide Research*

JSD	National Socialist Party (of Bangladesh)
KAMI	Indonesian Students Action Front
KAPPI	Indonesian High School Students Action Front
KAP-Gestapu	Action Front for the Crushing of the 30 September Movement/PKI
KOPKAMTIB	Operational Command for the Restoration of Order and Security
MPLA	People's Movement for the Liberation of Angola
NARA	US National Archives and Records Administration
NU	Nahdlatul Ulama
PA AA	Politisches Archiv des Auswärtigen Amtes
PAIGC	African Party for the Independence of Guinea and Cape Verde
Partindo	Indonesian Party
PII	Indonesian Muslim Students' Association
PKI	Communist Party of Indonesia
PKK	Kurdish Workers Party
PNI	Nationalist Party of Indonesia
POW	prisoner of war
PSI	Socialist Party of Indonesia
RPKAD	Army Paracommando Regiment
RSHA	Head Office of Reich Security
SOBSI	All-Indonesian Labor Union
SOKSI	Central Organization of Indonesian Socialist Workers
SS	Schutzstaffeln (Protective Squadrons)
TASS	Telegraphic Agency for Communications and News (Soviet News Agency)
UN	United Nations
UNESCO	United Nations Educational, Scientific and Cultural Organization
UNHCR	United Nations High Commissioner for Refugees
UNICEF	United Nations Children's Fund
UNROD	United Nations Relief Operation in Dacca
UPI	United Press International
USAID	United States Agency for International Development
WHO	World Health Organization

1 INTRODUCTION

Extremely violent societies

This book suggests a new approach to explaining mass violence. It tries to explore what is going on in societies before, during, and after periods of widespread bloodshed, and it attempts to trace the social roots of human destruction. The study includes an outline and rationale for the new approach, probes its potential in several case studies, and offers general conclusions about processes typical of what I call "extremely violent societies."

Violence is a fact of human life. Some people may be lucky enough not to experience it. But no society is free of violence, of murder, rape, or robbery. This book, however, deals with extraordinary processes that entail unusually high levels of violence and brutality, which is why I speak of "extremely" violent societies.

"Mass violence" means widespread physical violence against non-combatants, that is, outside of immediate fighting between military or paramilitary personnel.[1] Mass violence includes killings, but also forced removal or expulsion, enforced hunger or undersupply, forced labor, collective rape, strategic bombing, and excessive imprisonment – for many strings connect these to outright murder and these should not be severed analytically.[2] By extremely violent societies, I mean formations where *various population groups* become victims of massive physical violence, in which, acting together with organs of the state, *diverse social groups participate for a multitude of reasons*. Simply put, the occurrence and the thrust of mass violence depends on broad and diverse support, but this is based on a variety of motives and interests that cause violence to spread in different directions and in varying intensities and forms.

This phenomenon differs from what many scholars and other observers see in mass violence – briefly put, a state's attempt to destroy a population group, largely for a certain reason, and often called "genocide."

To begin with, the problem mostly goes beyond the assault of just *one* victim group. Under Nazi Germany, for example, Jews were targeted for killings, but so also were disabled people, Roma and Sinti, political opponents, Soviet prisoners of war, the Polish leadership – broadly defined, and "guerrilla-suspect" rural dwellers; perhaps twelve million foreign nationals were deported to Germany as forced labor, and millions of Eastern Europeans, Greeks, and Dutch were plunged into famine. During World War I, Armenians, Greeks, Assyrians, Chaldeans, and Kurds in the Ottoman Empire died in forced resettlement and massacres, and many Turks were also killed. Under Soviet rule from the 1930s to the 1950s, wealthier peasants or individuals with suspicious 'bourgeois' origin, people uprooted by the collectivization of agriculture, political opponents, foreign prisoners of war, and citizens belonging to ethnicities who became collectively suspect, were arrested, banished, resettled, or killed. While the treatment of these various groups, and the time, duration, and manner of their persecution may have differed, as did their mortality figures and ratios and their fates afterwards, I suggest that in many ways their suffering should be examined as a whole. A scholar who would look only at the persecution of urbanites, or of ethnic Chinese, or ethnic Vietnamese, or the Cham, Lao, Thai, etc. minorities in Cambodia under the Khmer Rouge, in isolation, rather than as the outcome of a single process or of interrelated processes, would appear strange. Such a view would be an obstacle to analysis.[3] Whereas many scholars insist on strictly distinguishing between the different phenomena of violence, I am interested precisely in the links between the different forms.[4]

Many historians have attested to the "wide-scale voluntary, and indeed willing or even enthusiastic, participation" of men, whether officials or not, in mass killings.[5] Theoreticians of warfare, among them Clausewitz, have argued that the particularly destructive character of wars originates from the input of the element of "raw violence" by the mass of people, which made armed conflicts even more brutal after the beginning of mass conscription and popular participation in politics. It is this involvement that led to a "genocidal tendency in war" per se.[6] Recently, the argument has been made that "ethnic cleansing" (and sometimes "genocide") occurs under particular conditions as a perversion of democracy in the early stages of a country's experience in popular political participation.[7] Others hold that "national democracy can be compatible with war and genocide" more generally.[8] I would add to this that it is mass participation which often gives modern mass violence its ghastly pace and thrust and which makes policies of destruction actually materialize.

Each mass slaughter is multi-causal. Some genocide scholars have concluded that the interaction of a variety of factors and processes results in an escalation of human destruction – but it appears unclear how this happens more specifically.[9] If a variety of people in considerable numbers join in the organization of mass violence, they do so out of a variety of interests, backgrounds, or attitudes. Their different reasons seem to lend urgency to their use of force. To boil it down to one cause that brought them all together to participate (ideological, retributive, economic 'genocide,' etc.) makes little sense if the shocking power of violence stems precisely from a mixture of various factors. It seems more promising to ask questions about the overlap of attitudes and interests that brought them together. What did they agree upon, for how much time, and with what different purposes?[10] Such questions may enable us to explain why mass violence started or intensified at certain points and slowed down or ended at others.

Mass violence cannot be viewed as freak event, inexplicable or occurring outside of history (as some view the murder of European Jews); it requires broad contextualization. By asking which reasons brought so many different people to participate in or support mass violence, and why different groups were victimized, the extremely violent societies approach tries to place human destruction in the context of longer-term societal developments. In fact, when inquiring into what is going on in such countries, it seems less and less possible to me to neatly separate cause and effect. Instead, one should inquire into the entire social process of which mass violence is only a part, the relationships between structural and physical violence, between direct violence and dynamic shifts in inequality, and between social groups and state organs. As a historian, I seek to complement the dominant political histories in the field by a social history of mass violence.

True, to explain mass violence, it is simplistic to tell only the story of government policies and some rogue regime such as the Nazi government persecuting the Jews. But while an inquiry into extremely violent societies pays special attention to the social contexts of mass violence, this does not mean that it can disregard the role of the state. In fact, so strong are the interrelationships between state and society that they cannot be understood in terms of dichotomous, isolated units. Governments may give orders and try to manipulate people, but they also devise or modify policies according to perceived public pressure and opinion. "The state" is part of society, and reflects its rules and norms, or those of powerful groups, which it then tries to impose or stipulate in turn; and modern functionaries or officials are also citizens with their own agendas and judgment, which means that they are not just cogs that carry out government policies exactly as formulated. If anything, I expect that I will be guilty of maintaining too strong an emphasis on official policies (which my earlier works have not really neglected either). This emphasis is also to be expected because state operations are better documented in the official and other records historians tend to use. Popular involvement in mass violence inevitably leaves less of a paper trail.

By focusing more widely than just on government intentions, the extremely violent societies approach enables us to study far more actors and to take all of their intentions into account, including social and political groups, officials from various ministries, agencies, etc. The agendas of non-state actors often have a major impact on determining the targets, timing, and forms of assault. In the case of such participatory violence, it may become difficult to assign *sole* responsibility for physical violence to one authority or figure, but it is possible to assess each group's contribution. In any case, assigning responsibility for mass violence is no zero-sum game – if there is popular participation, and public-popular cooperation in violence, this need not diminish the guilt of either officials or non-officials, as the chapters on Indonesia and anti-guerrilla warfare will demonstrate, and as the historiography on Nazi Germany has shown. My approach is designed to take into account every sort of actor, from top to bottom levels, within or outside an official apparatus.

That said, this study blurs the distinction between perpetrators in a strict sense and unaffected bystanders.[11] Chapters like the one about the role of economic incentives in the destruction of the

Armenians will draw into question the very concept of the 'perpetrator,' because people whose acts would hardly be defined as murder or even criminal were in no small degree conducive to the death of Armenians. Therefore I shall rather use the more inclusive term of 'persecutor.'

If one thinks beyond government acts against one group, it may also become possible to overcome the much criticized division between 'perpetrator history' and 'victim history' as in Holocaust studies that can even let victims appear as groups somehow falling outside of society. Victims and others are part of one interactive process, in which the former are not just passive or even reactive, but seek support, alliances, or counteraction.

Results and restrictions of the genocide approach

This section explains why I do not find "genocide" a useful framework for exploring some of the phenomena at hand, and why I think an alternative framework may be fruitful. For "genocide" marks an approach – one of several imaginable ways to think about mass violence[12] – that lays specific emphasis on the history of ideas and of political systems.

A state turns against a group in society that is mostly ethnically defined – this is the story mostly told in genocide studies. The genocide approach focuses on regimes vulnerable to turning to "genocidal" acts, such as Nazi Germany, the Soviet Union, Rwanda, or Cambodia. Many argue that a turn to "genocide" happens in a crisis of the state or of government.[13] Genocide scholars concentrate on how such regimes mobilize bureaucratic machineries, armed formations, and citizens or subjects for violence, most notably through manipulation, propaganda, legislation, and orders; how a persecuted population group, on the basis of an idea of hierarchical otherness, is being excluded, discriminated, stripped of rights, denied its human character, or declared immoral and a threat to the nation. It is excluded from the "universe of obligation."[14] Using the genocide approach, scholars try to show what grounds are found or invented for rationalizing the destruction of that group (often thought of as premeditated), how mass murder is organized, and how the immoral character of the slaughter is later denied on the basis of the earlier determined rationalizations. Genocide, then, is seen as originating from a failure of a political and judicial system, as well as of public opinion. Genocide scholars often try to isolate one core motive for extermination[15] that is frequently found in the "ideology" of such a regime, mostly pertaining to racism, more rarely to class hatred or religious fanaticism. Then the cure is obvious: prevent or topple such a regime, create a less vulnerable political system, and educate the population about the need for tolerance. For genocide is an action-oriented model designed for moral condemnation, prevention, intervention, or punishment. In other words, genocide is a normative, action-oriented concept made for the political struggle, but in order to be operational it leads to simplification, with a focus on government policies.

More recent works have added that the emergence of modern nation-states has resulted in massive violence against societal groups because they seem to not belong to the majority culture and are suspected of disloyalty, undermining the mission of state policies which they do not subscribe to. This frequently occurs when states have to compete with each other in a conflictual international system; hence genocide is said to often occur in times of war. Several authors now argue that nation-states first turned to genocide during colonialism, particularly in the nineteenth century.[16] The rise of biologistic racism is emphasized as an important background of this increase in violence. As mentioned, some have also argued that the age of mass politics that began in the early twentieth century has increased rather than minimized the risk of extreme violence because populist movements have tried to overcome or circumvent political problems through violence.[17]

But thinking in terms of "genocide" means using a framework that restricts the analysis. Genocide scholars have never agreed what "genocide" actually means. The term is used arbitrarily. Many of them have remained dissatisfied with the definition in the UN Genocide Convention: "acts committed with intent to destroy, in whole or in part, a national, ethnical, racial or religious group, as such."[18] Since the 1970s, social scientists have advanced a variety of alternative definitions.[19] Semantically, the term "genocide" means "murder of a tribe." This implies that the victims of "genocide" are members of an ethnic or racial group, which appears to be the dominant popular assumption, and also the view that prevails in scholarly practice. Even religious differences are being reinterpreted as ethnic, for instance with reference to the multi-layered conflict in Bosnia (see also Chapter 7). Speaking of "genocide" then suggests a particular causation. In a primordial interpretation, ethnicity in genocide studies appears more often than not as something natural and long-standing – not historical, constructed, and fluent. In other words, race or ethnicity tend to be interpreted as a given, instead of being subject to inquiry; a point of scholarly destination instead of a point of departure.[20] Germans hated Jews, Turks hated Armenians, Hutus hate Tutsis, so they killed them: ethnicity is attributed a causality for mass violence, which may lead to a circular logic. True, if "genocide" is about ethnicity, then "genocide" is about ethnicity. What will we find out with such an "explanation"?

If genocide scholars agree on one thing, it is that "intent" constitutes "genocide."[21] This also applies to the UN Genocide Convention, and to Raphael Lemkin, the field's founding father.[22] This emphasis on "policy"[23] has led to a state focus in genocide studies,[24] for it is the state to which the "intent" is attributed and that devises policy. The following circular logic is characteristic: "Genocide is primarily a crime of the state and empirically it has not been true that it appears without intent"[25] (which rests, of course, on the premise that every act of violence or suffering inflicted unintentionally is just defined as not constituting "genocide"). As a result, genocide studies have tended to construct a monolithic actor out of people (officials and others) that to me seem to have very contradictory intentions. The focus on government rule and state intent makes it difficult to analyze the particular processes at work within societies. A scholar who wishes to prove "intent" for "genocide" might well be expected to regard later phases as mere implementations of premeditated planning, and to be less interested in the huge differences between destructive ideas or intentions and the real outcome in terms of violence.[26] This may result in neglecting or downplaying the popular contribution to the genesis of mass violence, which is crucial for the extremely violent societies approach explored in this book.

The biggest problem of genocide studies is the lack of an empirical foundation. This emptiness is obvious at every genocide conference. It may in part be due to the reductionist genocide approach with its emphasis on "proving" "genocide" (however defined) and therefore official "intent." It may also have to do with the high level of abstraction in the work of political scientists and sociologists who have had a strong position in the field. Whatever progress has been made on the topic in the past fifteen years has resulted from empirical work. For a dense description that helps overcome preconceived perceptions of incidents of mass violence, however, it is indispensable to work with a large pool of primary documents as well as secondary sources. The extremely violent societies approach is derived from empirical observation and made for analytical purposes. It is about a new way of thinking about mass violence (which is why I call it an approach). It means to raise new questions. Its value (or uselessness) will be proven by the analytical gains it precipitates. Therefore, empirical case studies on a broad source basis are crucial to this study.

State-oriented as it is, the genocide approach – while having made important contributions – still captures only some of the causations and developments relevant to mass violence. This book sets a different emphasis. It focuses on processes in the societies involved, while not ignoring government action.

Existing approaches regarding the social origins of "genocide"

While most works in genocide studies are state-centered, a number of ways of focusing more on the social roots of "genocide" have been suggested. Roger W. Smith proposed studying "genocidal societies," including a wide range of topics such as the relationship between genocide and economic systems, religious stimuli, gender differences, and the participation of younger generations, as well as the consequences of "genocide" on the politics, economy, and social structures of a country, plus the question of whether and how "genocidal societies" recover.[27] Michael Dobkowski and Isidor Wallimann called for investigations into "the history and nature of societies giving rise to mass death as human-made and thereby influenceable" and into the "social, economic and political circumstances making mass death possible."[28] Taking up some of Marx's early concepts, Tony Barta proposed explaining mass violence through objective "relations of genocide," dictated by conflicts of interest between social groups, instead of through "policies," "intentions and actions of individuals." He illustrated his case by a sketch of the relations between white settlers and Australian aborigines in the nineteenth century.[29] Daniel Feierstein tries to understand mass extermination as "social practice," as a specific mode of government-sponsored destruction and reconfiguration of social relations, which leads to the building of new identities and value principles, for example by hampering what he calls practices of solidarity, cooperation or autonomy.[30] However, his conception of changing social relations is focused directly on the fate and environment of just one victim group, and his abstract way of arguing also lets him leave aside wider social contexts and longer-term social dynamics.[31]

None of these authors have tested these approaches empirically. Some who have moved in this direction have in practice maintained an emphasis on government policies. Mark Levene has suggested a geographic focus involving the interaction between several groups over longer time periods in a "zone of genocide," but he focused on state rule over such a territory and on the relationship between state and citizens.[32] A similar contradiction surfaces in Frank Bajohr's work, which stressed the need to "understand Nazi rule not as top-down dictatorship, but as social practice, in which German society had a part in many ways."[33] Even though Bajohr promises to explore "a variety of actions and behaviors of society," he does in fact concentrate on purported popular reactions to official policies against Jews.[34] Leo Kuper has offered a book chapter on "Social Structure and Genocide," but then largely restricted the content to a discussion of colonialism and its consequences.[35]

Sources

My emphasis on empirical work warrants some remarks about the sources used for this volume. For three of the five case studies, official records are largely inaccessible. This problem is most striking for Indonesia but also applies to East Pakistan/Bangladesh (namely to Indonesian and Pakistani military records). Access to Turkish archives has become gradually easier in recent years, but permissions given are erratic, far from all records are available to researchers, and some scholars may be allowed to see more than others.[36] A few Ottoman documents have been published. Oddly, archives in Syria and Iraq have not been used in existing research.

Given the inaccessibility of Ottoman files, research on the destruction of the Armenians has rested on three pillars: records by foreign diplomats, survivor reports, and materials from foreign missionaries. They have provided for a relatively rich and detailed picture, compared to Indonesia and Bangladesh.[37] Scholarship on the Indonesian killings of 1965–66 has been based on a set of sources of exceptionally low quality, including much third-hand information, many journalistic accounts, doctored "confessions" of tortured PKI (Communist Party of Indonesia) functionaries and military officers, and anecdotal evidence. Here, almost no missionary reports and exceptionally few survivor accounts are available (though some have been published recently), and those that are available have often been affected by social and political constraints. Aside from the legal implications and censorship, there is still a lot of popular support for the 1965 murders today, with the result that many survivors assert that they and other victims were not or at most marginally involved in communist activities.[38] Witnesses are still extremely hesitant to discuss the topic at all.

Under these circumstances, records by foreign diplomats and other foreign observers can be of special value in the reconstruction of events inside a country, although so far they have only rarely been used for Indonesia and Bangladesh.[39] My chapters about these two countries make use of US, Australian, and West and East German records.[40] In the Ottoman case, my material includes correspondence by US, German, and Austro-Hungarian diplomats. For Bangladesh, a substantial amount of journalistic accounts, some memoirs by US missionaries, and additional unpublished records from various UN agencies and Oxfam were also at my disposal.

The limitations of these documents have to be acknowledged. They have their biases, like all sources, and only allow for an inquiry of medium empirical depth, rendering regional or local studies almost impossible and the reconstruction of decision-making difficult. Diplomats (and journalists) were social outsiders – especially significant among a tight-lipped culture like Indonesia's – residing in a few major cities where embassies or consulates were located. Travel was difficult, though not impossible for diplomats and journalists; cables by foreign correspondents were censored (some tried to bypass this by using diplomatic channels); the number of diplomatic personnel was limited, as was their access to official documents.[41] They relied on certain sets of partisan local informers. White foreigners suffered from chauvinist feelings of superiority on a cultural, racist, or religious basis, which could lead to the portrayal of locals as particularly savage or bloodthirsty. To a limited extent, diplomats were also actors in their respective situations, with clearly defined interests that must be kept in mind, although these are not at the center of this study. It is the job of diplomats to gather information and a clear picture of political developments in their host country. Their, in a broad sense, imperialist perspectives at times provide for sober views from outside into a foreign culture, but also reflect a limited understanding of that culture – and, for both reasons, a historian making use of them may come into conflict with prevailing narratives of national histories (see Chapter 7). In any case, although extensive work in the future with primary language government records and other materials, once accessible, will greatly enhance my findings and without doubt lead to partial corrections, I try to make a contribution, also on a factual level, on the basis of the research possible at present.

Two further case studies refer to published material only. While this author can claim to be familiar with much archival material for Nazi Germany, the situation is different for my chapter on anti-guerrilla warfare, which deals with about twenty countries across several decades. Here, I rely (except, again, for Germany) on published scholarship to study very specific mechanisms in state operation and social response to violently transform marginal rural areas by mass resettlement, militia-building, and enforced "development." Through this largely generalizing comparison, I try to offer insights into the striking international similarities, and links, but also variations.

The existing scholarship and other accounts on the events discussed in this book are dominated by competing nationalist narratives. Often these are propagandist, but this is not sufficient for me to dismiss out of hand facts presented in a source. Of course it is essential to use secondary sources from different political and cultural backgrounds, a variety of academic traditions and languages, and multiple approaches. Aside from the usual validating of the plausibility of information, evidence may be of special value if it is self-incriminatory, or confirms facts running counter to an author's apparent interests, or is from independent, non-involved observers.

Objectives of this volume

Many genocide scholars have noted in general terms that mass violence occurs during a crisis not only of a state or regime but of society more generally.[42] In a general sense, a crisis has been described by an economist as an intermediate phase of transition and trouble, with structures becoming fluid and a loss of transparency and predictability, when a new orientation becomes necessary for individuals but information is contradictory and hard to assess and the political system is becoming under pressure. What is lost in such situations is trust in the rules that govern social interaction.[43] The intention of this book is to describe more specifically the processes a crisis of society involves, how it feeds into violence, and how mass violence is linked to longer-term societal conditions and changes. Societies are not intrinsically or inevitably violent, they turn extremely violent in what is a temporary process. This can happen in capitalist and in socialist societies, in the latter in connection with pressures from the international capitalist system.[44] Indirect, structural violence is transformed into a variety of uses of direct, brute force: either by radicalization under pressure, by the diversion of pressures and aggression to prevent the outbreak of other conflicts, or by counter-violence by former victims (often allegedly to prevent other, more substantial violence). A perception of social crisis also helps to explain why the use of violence is so often not just a matter of the state, e.g. of functionaries.

The present book is not intended to offer a comprehensive history of extremely violent societies throughout space and time. It is not meant to cover the historic genesis of the phenomenon either. It does not use the extremely violent societies approach as a template, but probes the potential of the extremely violent societies approach in a variety of ways; for doing this in a number of ways, the chapters each pursue individual, specific research problems instead of following uniform questions and adhering to a common structure. As a result, the book does not aim at a systematic comparison between the countries discussed in different chapters, although it does allow for some general conclusions that are presented in Chapter 8. It does not cover all possible uses of the approach either. For example, inter-societal processes that could also be analyzed through my approach are hardly covered in this book. Yet all chapters discuss official and non-official persecutors, most deal with various target groups and their responses, and all with the broader social and political context.

The first batch of the following case studies are concerned with the participatory character of mass violence. Why do so many and such a variety of people take part in violence, and what are the consequences for the victims if they do? Chapter 2 presents the mass slaughter of alleged communists and others in Indonesia in 1965–66 as based on a coalition for violence – a coalition that originated from an overlap of interests due to a range of social conflicts, a very broad, diverse and unstable short-term alliance, which helps explain the ghastly burst of violence. This chapter is the most comprehensive of the volume, also discussing a variety of victim groups, their survival strategies, the limits to violence, and the international dimension. Chapter 3 is more limited in scope. It traces the effects of one set of motivations (economic issues) for the mass involvement in the persecution of one group, the Armenians, in the Ottoman Empire during World War I. Greed, hope for social ascent, war-related misery and despair account to no small degree for mass involvement in turning on Armenians (and other middlemen minorities in history) in many forms, from governmental confiscations to vicious robbery to extortionate "trade," from enslavement to the affectionate adoption of minors.

The second batch of case studies analyzes the societal crisis that an extremely violent society undergoes. They raise even more long-term issues about the relationship between social change and violence, including the phenomena of geographic and social mobility and the long-term impact of violence. Chapter 4 describes the path from a political conflict between elites over East Pakistan/Bangladesh to a general societal crisis that led to mass violence actively and passively involving enormous groups of people, especially in 1971, though it lasted longer. This case study also investigates the relationship between direct and structural violence as it establishes links between killings, expulsions, etc., and the massive famines of 1971–72 and 1974–75. In Chapter 5, I discuss government strategies for enforcing specific ways of social transformation in combating guerrillas in marginal rural areas by vast enforced population movements and building militias – and how this process spiraled out of control in about twenty countries from the 1930s to the 1990s. Chapter 6 tries to explore what linking the fates of the different victim groups of Nazi Germany can add to our understanding of the violence. As an example, I inquire into one country's experience: occupied Greece. How were the 1941–42 famine, the murder of Jews, bloody anti-guerrilla warfare, and various expulsions and flight movements related to each other and to a crisis in Greek society? And what connected wartime conflicts to the long trail of violence from the 1910s to the 1970s? Two concluding chapters discuss the role of nationalist narratives in the public understanding of mass violence and highlight general patterns of what is going on in extremely violent societies.

Part I

Participatory violence

2 A COALITION FOR VIOLENCE

Mass slaughter in Indonesia, 1965–66

In the Kumingan district of Jakarta, a giant pair of brazed steel-made sixes looms between high-rise buildings.[1] The '66,' in gleaming metal implying progress and modernity, is a monument for mass murder. It celebrates those who declared themselves the 'generation of 1966' in that year – university students and other youth who helped bring down the Sukarno regime, the 'old order', and did so by participating in 'crushing' the political left and murdering at least 500,000 people in 1965–66.

Young urbanites were just one of the groups that teamed up for these killings. This chapter revolves around mass participation in violence and examines in which ways it is based on multiple motives – both are important characteristics of an extremely violent society which led to a diverse coalition for violence in Indonesia. The nature of this coalition is used to explain why violence was so tempestuous, why it spread against groups other than leftists (another feature of an extremely violent society), but also why violence took different forms and intensities and where it had its limits. This question is important because most leftists survived. Moreover, the chapter explores in which organizational frameworks activities by non-state actors took place, how actions by political groups or mobs were related to forceful government policies of persecution, and how the political polarization among citizens was linked to longer-term social change. In this way, it attempts to integrate the political and social history of mass violence.

In 1965, Indonesia was a multi-party republic under a leftist–nationalist President with authoritarian structures and a coercive consensus policy ("Guided Democracy") based on the state ideologies of *nasakom* and *pancasila*. *Nasakom* meant to harmonize the three principles (and main political currents in the country) of nationalism, monotheistic religion, and communism, *pancasila* stood for five often freely interpreted principles, anchored in Indonesia's constitution: belief in one god, national unity, democracy, international humanitarianism, and social justice. Capitalist Indonesia faced an economic crisis. Internationally, it was entangled in a low-level military conflict (called Konfrontasi, or Confrontation) against Malaysia and Britain and had alienated most capitalist countries. Since the 1942 Japanese occupation, through the war of independence, suppressed regional rebellions, the communist Madiun revolt, and pro-Islamic uprisings, and after 1966 leftist insurgencies, the occupation of East Timor, decades of combating independence movements in Aceh and New Guinea, and the diverse wave of violence of 1996 to 2000, Indonesia has lived through various forms of mass violence almost without interruption. In March 1965, this had prompted the commander of the armed forces, General Achmad Yani, to remark: "Since 1940, Indonesia has never known real peace," and Freek Colombijn and Thomas Lindblat to begin their 2002 volume with the simple sentence: "Indonesia is a violent country."[2] This chapter is devoted to the most dramatic in this long string of destructive events.

On October 1, 1965, a "30 September Movement" of officers loyal to leftist–nationalist President Sukarno started a coup in the capital Jakarta, abducted and killed six of the highest-ranking generals of the armed forces, including Yani, and declared the government ousted. Minister of Defense Nasution escaped with injuries. The rebels, informed about unusual troop concentrations around Jakarta, claimed to have forestalled a right-wing coup by a "Council of Generals" (called Yani's "brain trust" by US diplomats),[3] the existence of which was later denied in Indonesia. Within 48 hours, troops under the then little-known right-wing Major-General Suharto, Commander of the Army Strategic Reserve Command, crushed the putsch, initially without much bloodshed.[4] Ongoing research controversies have unearthed that important political players had had some foreknowledge about the coup: several leaders of the Communist Party of Indonesia (PKI) including Chairman Dipa Nusantara Aidit,[5] the Air Force command, parts of the Javanese territorial Diponegoro division, General Suharto, and probably Sukarno. In the extremely charged political atmosphere, a clash was looming, and there were signs that right-wing military officers made preparations to respond to a potential leftist coup, even in a high-level meeting on September 30.[6] Yet all of the theories about various string-pullers and allegedly sophisticated coup plots have remained unsubstantiated, and leave the impression that nobody had a clear plan.[7] The focus on guessing who lay behind the coup has deflected debates about the following violence, especially inside Indonesia. In any case, although the PKI remained passive and gave only verbal support to the rebels in the beginning,[8] with not even the entire core leadership (let alone ordinary members) having advance knowledge about the coup, the army and various political parties and organizations blamed the rebellion on the communists. Mass arrests against them started in early October 1965, large-scale killings in mid-October all over Java and in most of Sumatra, and by mid-November 1965 also in Bali, where the bloodbath would be at its worst. On March 11, 1966, Sukarno handed over power de facto to Suharto, who banned the PKI the next day.

In many ways, this slaughter was the foundation of the 'New Order,' a thinly veiled, divisive military dictatorship preaching national unity, economic 'development,' and social harmony. Even though the 'New Order' ended in 1998, those mass killings are still popularly supported and aggressively defended by many inside Indonesia. After all, they argue, it was the sovereign, the people who stood up, enraged by the communists, and exerted a legitimate form of violence.[9] Helen Fein was stunned by the "lack of denial or shame" of a government (and society) that frankly and publicly admitted to have killed half a million to a million people.[10] Here, a number of murderers later liked to describe the act of murder in detail, which is unusual if one compares it to other countries.[11] With fine Australian understatement, Robert Cribb has remarked about assumptions that perpetrators of such atrocities would suffer from a mental fall-out: "Indonesia's mass killers [...] have shown little evidence that they feel this particular moral difficulty."[12]

What they destroyed was the biggest communist movement ever in a capitalist country, verbally radical but reformist in substance. In August 1965, the Communist Party of Indonesia claimed to have 3.5 million members and about 15 million in overlapping mass organizations linked to the party, namely the Indonesian Peasants Front (BTI) with 9 million, the All-Indonesian Labor Union (SOBSI) with

3.5 million (organizing more than half of Indonesia's unionized workers), the Pemuda Rakjat (People's Youth), and the Indonesian Women's
Movement (Gerwani) with 3 million each.[13] The membership of these
organizations was socially diverse, including about 20 percent women,
a minority of urban workers, small vendors, and rickshaw drivers,
many plantation toilers, squatters, sharecroppers, and small farmers,
but also teachers, artists, and some wealthier farmers, with 60 percent
overall residing in the countryside (so that some called it "a movement
of petty bourgeoisie"[14]). In the 1957 local elections, the PKI, which
was weaker on the outer islands, had drawn 27.4 percent of the votes
in Java, where more than half of Indonesians lived, and over 50 percent in some regions of Central and East Java.[15]

The murderers were equally diverse, victims varied greatly by
region in numbers, and were killed for a multitude of reasons. There
were links between these three facts. As Robert Cribb and Colin
Brown put it:

> *In Aceh, the party's followers were loathed as infidels by
> the local Muslim community; in North Sumatra they were
> hated by sections of the indigenous Batak community
> for promoting the interests of the Javanese settlers who
> worked on the state plantations [...]. In the cities of the
> archipelago, many Chinese fell victim to the PKI's close
> association with the People's Republic of China. In Bali,
> the PKI had attacked the practice of Hinduism [...]. In
> the countryside of Central and East Java [...] the PKI's
> promotion of land reform won it bitter enemies, but here
> it was especially detested by orthodox traditional Muslims
> [...].[16]*

In West Timor, "the party seemed to be all things to all
people," abhorred for anti-feudal measures or establishing old authority, supporting Christians or animists or Muslims, illiterate farmers as
well as university lecturers.[17]

In terms of party politics – aside from the military, namely army
troops – it was, above all, the Nahdlatul Ulama (NU), an orthodox
Islamic party, and the right wing of the Nationalist Party of Indonesia
(PNI), especially their youth groups, but also several others, who
called for, organized, and carried out many murders, while President

Sukarno, many cabinet ministers, some military units, and provincial governors remained opposed to the slaughter. Participation was widespread and diverse, but by no means universal. Two lines of interpretation account for this violence: leftist–liberal versions stress the role of the military, centralized organization, and the manipulation of the masses, whereas right-wing representations – including supporters of the Suharto regime – have emphasized that the people, together with the somewhat downplayed armed forces, killed communists in righteous anger about communist outrages, or in a frenzied overreaction to political and social tensions. By contrast, this chapter argues in line with the extremely violent societies approach that military and popular violence can be better understood through their interaction.

Until Indonesian military records are made available, only vague estimates about the number of people murdered in the 1965–66 violence are possible. In addition, a systematic analysis of the papers of local and civilian authorities will be required, as military records only covered the more organized part of the slaughter. Present ideas about the dimension of the massacre are based on scattered information of very low quality. The figure of 500,000 dead is the one most often cited and was also adopted by the Suharto regime from the 1970s.[18] This indicates a ghastly magnitude and speed since by far most of the murders happened within only three months from mid-October 1965 to mid-January 1966. There were two official attempts to count the victims. A Fact Finding Commission sent out by President Sukarno in December 1965 and January 1966 to Java, Bali, and Sumatra settled on a number of 78,500 that was obviously too low, marred by the attempt of the commission to appease Sukarno and by the obstruction by the military authorities.[19] A team of about 100 university students and graduates from Jakarta and Bandung, commissioned by Suharto in 1966, reported confidentially that about one million people had been killed: 800,000 in Java and 100,000 each in Sumatra and Bali. Perhaps this number was inflated in an effort to intimidate the political left; the basic findings of the report were published in the national press.[20] Noticeably, representatives of capitalist countries at the time often repeated in slightly varying phrasing that the real figure would "never be known" – even before the bulk of the killings had started.[21]

Regional accounts of the murders seem to imply higher victim numbers than half a million. For example, the British Consul in Medan estimated that 200,000 people had died in Sumatra alone, half in "official" and half in "unofficial," unrecorded murders. In East Java, an international aid organization counted 400,000 orphans.[22] The chief of police in Solo, Central Java, stated that 20,000 or 4.4 percent of the population had been slain, correcting the official figure of 11,000. This compares to estimated death rates of about 1 percent in Kediri and 0.5 percent in Jombang areas in East Java.[23] The CIA cited early estimates of 150,000 killed in Central Java.[24] In addition, a number of high figures, sometimes even over one million, have been suggested by competent sources. *Washington Post* journalist Stanley Karnow, touring in April 1966 and interviewing local commanders, police, village headmen, and hospital doctors said that at least half a million lives had been lost. The Swedish ambassador, after traveling through Java in early 1966 and talking to numerous local officials, plus tapping administrative phone lines (the Indonesian phone service was run by the Swedish company Ericsson), gloomily stated, according to diverging reports, that a figure of 300,000 dead was "dangerously low," even 400,000 "far too conservative," "quite incredible," and "a very serious underestimate." CIA agent John Stockwell placed the number killed at 800,000. Major-General Ibrahim Adjie, Commander of the West Java territorial Siliwangi division, told the Australian military attaché unsolicitedly that two million people had been killed. The former commander of the Army Paracommando Regiment (RPKAD) killing squads, Sarwo Edhie, is said to have either boasted or confessed late in his life that two or three million were murdered.[25] Many more may have died as an "indirect result of the violence because of the breakdown of family and community relations," especially among children and the elderly already destitute after the 1963–64 famines.[26] Moreover, disregarding much contradictory official data about persons in detention, later a total of about 1.8 million 'eks-tapols' (former political prisoners) were registered alive.[27]

The role of the military

Before we turn to the role of non-state actors in the mass murders, it is necessary to characterize the impact of the core government force, the military, and the limits to its influence. Without the Indonesian armed forces, the killings of 1965–66 could not have happened on anything like the same scale. The military substantiated its expressed will to destroy the PKI by fierce slanderous propaganda, it carried out mass arrests and a good deal of the murders, started the violence in Jakarta, West and Central Java as well as North Sumatra, steered the purge of official institutions, bodies, and enterprises, staged show trials, and encouraged, trained, and armed the political right to denounce, capture, or kill leftists.

The military response to the October 1, 1965 coup was carried out in interaction with the public from the beginning. Within 48 hours, the putsch was defeated in the capital, while it took until October 4 in Central Java. The recovery of the bodies of the killed generals at Lubang Buaya on Halim Air Base on October 4, staged as a media event covered by TV and radio, including a radio address by General Suharto in the evening, marked the beginning of a fierce anti-communist propaganda campaign. Army newspaper *Berita Yudha* featured it on the same day. In the face of contrary evidence, Suharto pronounced that the generals had been badly tortured and their genitals mutilated (as it was reported, by Gerwani women who had also danced naked for those members of the communist People's Youth who were present[28]). The risk of this conscious lie – as Suharto received an autopsy report by a team of frightened but conscientious military doctors that excluded mutilations[29] – only made sense if the army was already embarked on destroying the PKI. In fact, the CIA reported, without elaboration, that on October 5 the army had "made the decision to 'implement plans to crush [the] PKI.'"[30] The next steps were the solemn funeral of the murdered generals on October 5 with a speech by Nasution and, on October 8, a big demonstration by the multi-party Action Front for the Crushing of the 30 September Movement/PKI that ended in the burning of the PKI headquarters. Less publicized, the first riot against PKI buildings had occurred in Yogyakarta on October 5. Two days later, the derogatory acronym "Gestapu" had been invented for the 30 September Movement.[31]

Suharto continually emphasized how important it was for the army to be "influencing public opinion and making use of all information media."[32] This was part of the effort to gain moral hegemony. A similar strategy was adopted by the crucial army paratroopers during the RPKAD murder campaign in Central Java, where joint military–civilian propaganda units were set up and executions, sometimes combined with torture, quickly started. As the commander's adjutant recalled: "This gave the people confidence. They were not afraid of killing any more." RPKAD commander Sarwo Edhie stressed the need for mobilization through propaganda, made several press statements during his crusade, and even invited foreign journalists as well as selected local press photographers to cover their operations. The latter were not allowed to take pictures of the act of killing but could publish pictures of those killed as long as their faces were not shown, which culminated in a special exhibition in Yogyakarta in 1967.[33] In East Java, political parties seem to have set up coordinated propaganda structures independent from the military.[34]

Standard fare in the propaganda campaign were alleged communist plans to kill thousands of opponents throughout the country after a successful coup, for which lists and even mass graves had already been prepared.[35] Stories of murders by the PKI were invented, as communists were also baselessly accused of having murdered "hundreds of thousands of patriotic folk" during the Madiun revolt in 1948, when, provoked by killings of hundreds of communists, the PKI had started an insurrection on the Indonesian side during the war of independence; the uprising had been defeated and up to 30,000 suspected communists killed.[36] Communism was depicted as an ideology alien to Indonesian society and the PKI as Chinese agents, thus playing on anti-Chinese sentiments in the country. Caches of arms were presented as evidence for an imminent communist takeover, although communists very clearly did not use firearms to defend themselves and Chinese small arms shipments had all been delivered to the armed forces.[37] The military further helped to set up several radio stations run by right-wing students organized in KAMI in Jakarta, Bandung, and Magelang.[38]

While the armed forces' control over the media was absolute in Jakarta from October 2 on (with the radio being the main source of information), the picture in the provinces was different, with communist newspapers and journals still published in Yogyakarta up to October 10, some even up to October 22, and in Bali until November.[39]

As Suharto acted more in the background, it was above all General Nasution, Minister of Defense and survivor of the October 1, 1965 kidnappings but without a formal army command, who repeatedly called in public for the mass murder of communists, particularly in November 1965, asserting that the 'mistake' of Madiun (that is, to kill 'only' 30,000 leftists in 1948) was not be repeated.[40] Earlier, in 1964, Nasution had said that "Madiun [...] would be mild compared with army crackdown today" in case the PKI turned to strikes or riots.[41] Nasution's little daughter Irma had been mortally wounded during the October 1 coup. "According to an excellent source, Nasution demanded that every Communist be killed."[42] In early 1966, he made his satisfaction about the results known in an interview with Japanese journalists: "This purge was so successful that the PKI has almost been crushed. [...] We succeeded in sending almost all of them [PKI leaders] to hell, not only in Jakarta but in the entire country. In doing so, we could not pay attention to the fate of individuals."[43]

Propaganda – a mixture of half-information, persuasion, and threats – was an inseparable part of the terror against the PKI that started almost immediately after October 1, 1965.[44] By mid-October, the military announced that they had arrested 3,000 to 3,500 persons, many in Jakarta. In early November, detentions numbered 5,000 in the capital and West Java alone.[45] Every night from early October on, military and police searched poor *kampungs* in Jakarta. On October 21, US Ambassador Marshall Green cabled that, according to a PSI official, "in Djakarta area nearly 2000 PKI members have been arrested and about four hundred have been executed." The source was regarded as reliable, having run "his own 'murder incorporated'" and paid villagers for murders. Army troops at a prison in Jakarta granted prisoners food and water once per day and repeatedly allowed in Islamic students of HMI who abused prisoners at their will, attacking them with knives. Sukarno's complaint on October 23 that "hundreds" of People's Youth members had been killed probably referred mostly to Jakarta, too. In mid-December, West German Ambassador Werz wrote that of about 2,000 Pemuda Rakjat members suspected of having been on Halim Air Base, the rebels' headquarters, "supposedly hardly anybody is alive any more."[46]

The territorial commander of West Java, Major-General Ibrahim Adjie, started the crackdown on leftists equally early.[47] However, probably in agreement with the central army leadership, he refused to arm the Islamic population and unleash them against the communists because he did not trust the Muslim groups, as this region had been a center of the religious Darul Islam uprising in the 1950s.[48] Before the coup, Adjie had already designed a system under which officers of his Siliwangi division were attached to village heads, thereby curbing the PKI influence and land conflicts (except on the ground of estates and state forests) and enabling him to now hold the countryside under control. Villagers were "clearing out" leftists and handed them over to the army.[49] In West Java, relatively few cases are known in which civilians killed alleged communists. Only in the areas of Cirebon and Garut did such actions assume a mass character, based on local conflicts, a strong PKI, and incited by the local military.[50] Even so, the military killed thousands in West Java.[51]

In North Sumatra, the anti-communist campaign began on October 3, 1965, launched by General Kemal Idris, who moved a battalion to Medan against Suharto's orders and started to arrest communists immediately. Days later, Suharto allowed Idris to bring stronger forces into the provincial capital.[52] The West German Embassy described how about 2,000 communists were killed per week "in an almost stereotypical occurrence" – loaded on trucks by the army, who were stopped by an excited crowd, to whom the suspects were surrendered for killing after some symbolic resistance. The British Consul put the rate of weekly killings at 3,000. Another report mentioned 10,500 slaughtered prisoners.[53] The territorial commander Lieutenant General Achmad Junus Mokoginta, who was also All-Sumatra Military Commander, closely cooperated with right-wing political groups, especially youth organizations. "Wholesale killings," as the US Embassy put it, had already led to the destruction of the PKI as an organization in North Sumatra by early November. After all branches of the PKI and its affiliates had been disbanded, declaring oneself a member of those organizations meant that one was to be "eliminated."[54] For the North Sumatran plantations alone, findings of the British Consul as well as employment data suggest a death figure of 27,000 to 40,000 (100 to 150 per estate).[55]

Yet the military was deeply divided; aside from leftist sympathies in the air force, conflicts were manifest even in the army, which left only three battalions loyal to Suharto in East Java and a similar number in Central Java in early October 1965.[56] The remote province of West Sumatra makes the crucial role of the military obvious: anti-communist articles and graffiti started to appear after October 6, when Major Iman Suparto arrived by plane from the capital, but the regional military commander and governor maintained calm for months before being replaced in February 1966 by officers loyal to General Mokoginta, who mobilized the local population for violence. Similar initial calls for restraint could be heard in the Yogyakarta area.[57]

Aside from sending couriers, replacing commanding officers, and relying on regional units, the central military command leadership also deployed troops to politically strategic provinces, namely sections of the 50,000-strong RPKAD, an elite unit that first had put down the coup in Jakarta and then helped to start the crackdown on communists in the capital for two weeks while more of its units arrived from Borneo and New Guinea.[58] Either on Suharto's initiative or at the request of RPKAD commander Colonel Sarwo Edhie, large parts of the unit were relocated to Central Java, where PKI organizations had mostly managed to hold their political enemies in check for the time being and no major killings occurred. On October 17, the RPKAD landed in Semarang, arresting 1,000 leftists the same evening, swiftly moving troops into Magelang, Solo, and Yogyakarta, starting everywhere with a 'show of force' and rapidly organizing an all-out extermination operation by mobilizing local political groups largely made up of Islamic activists.[59] They caused wholesale destruction. During this campaign, Sarwo Edhie reported back to Suharto, whose home was Central Java, and possibly to Nasution, and in the end Suharto took a parade of RPKAD units.[60] In early December 1965, RPKAD troops were deployed to Bali, where they first helped to organize and then to bring under control the worst mass murder of the 1965–66 killings, which meant they didn't stop them, but reduced and steered them.

RPKAD units machine-gunned villagers who showed any resistance, including women (among them a group insulting them by showing them their bare behinds), as witnessed by accompanying journalists and as Sarwo Edhie, who himself at times gave the order to shoot, later admitted. Locals reported that his troops carried out most of the killing near Bojolali themselves. At other places, they killed by stabbing and throat-cutting. During those weeks, they also shot 300 prisoners every night near Prambanan. In addition, RPKAD members accompanied local Muslim youth in Central Java on nightly killing sprees. Inside a detention camp in Denpasar, Bali, they were constantly killing prisoners with automatic weapons.[61] Local territorial units and field artillery in the districts of Jember and Banyuwangi, East Java, killed suspects either near to their homes or after imprisonment over a longer period of time. In Bali, army units returned detainees to villages, instructing the entire community to kill them.[62] In 1967, the military was said to be still executing sixty prisoners per week without trial in Yogyakarta. These are only examples. Murders by the military were quite systematic. A former army officer told a friend that he had been given an unspecified quota of "communists" to be killed in a certain district.[63] Thousands of inmates of prisons and camps were executed without trial; army officers classified their prisoners locally by categories, killing them by grade.[64]

Overall, the anti-communist persecution was led by the Operational Command for the Restoration of Security and Order (KOPKAMTIB) under General Suharto. It was established on October 10, 1965, on the basis of Sukarno commissioning Suharto to restore order on October 3. It became the "'core' institution around which the 'New Order' government was constructed and the key institution for political and social control." All prisons were under its control, and KOPKAMTIB authorization enabled the military to permeate the territorial administrations throughout Indonesia.[65] Among other activities, KOPKAMTIB could therefore issue orders to purge government institutions and services from alleged communists and putschists.[66] Beyond the fact that thousands were fired, the influence of civilian authorities at local, regional, and central levels on the violence is still more or less unknown.

The military initially unleashed the murders, but then tried to continue them in a more controlled way. Where the military was strong, fewer uncontrolled killings happened.[67] The fact that the armed forces were in firmer control of persecution in big cities led to a higher proportion of long-term detentions and fewer murders compared to the countryside, as many observers noted. This was all the more striking as a large portion of urban dwellers – probably nearly 40 percent, compared to 15 percent of the population in general – were among the members of the PKI.[68] The higher rate of arrests and lower rate of killings applied to Jakarta, whereas there is conflicting evidence for Yogyakarta and Surabaya.[69]

But conditions in jails or camps were far from guaranteeing survival or safety. In overcrowded, initially often improvised, detention facilities, inmates faced brutal treatment and extremely bad conditions, including much lower provision than for criminal prisoners of even the basics, such as medical treatment and food. Daily allowances per political internee in fiscal terms were extremely low, and food rations of between 150 and 400 grams of rice have been reported.[70] For years, this resulted in a high mortality rate. Prisoners without the support of relatives were especially vulnerable. In Kalisosok Jail in Surabaja, East Java, a survivor recalled that detainees felt impelled to eat chalk from the walls, and 758 died of starvation between 1966 and 1969, while on the Nusa Kambangan prison island off Central Java, thousands perished, reportedly at a rate of twenty per day, not counting at least as many summary executions.[71] Death rates of one to four inmates per day were not infrequent. In Salemba prison in Jakarta, the monthly death rate in 1969 amounted to 1.5 percent of the prisoners. In the highly publicized Buru island camp, 315 of 10,000 prisoners died between 1969 and 1977.[72] As a reputable journalist learned, numerous suspects of the last big wave of arrests in 1969 were killed in Java prisons "because the jails are already overcrowded and the Army lacks funds to feed the additional prisoners."[73] It is safe to assume that a five-figure number of prisoners died of neglect in the custody of the armed forces.

There is no question that prisoners in army and police detention facilities were systematically physically tortured by beating, with burning cigarettes, electric shocks, near-drowning, and more. Such treatment could even extend to the children or grandmothers of suspects.[74] "Torture was the customary prelude to death" also for army prisoners, who were swiftly killed in Flores.[75] Torture against women prisoners seems to have been somewhat less common but still widespread, including brutal sexual abuses and rape. In Bali, this also frequently occurred in the context of mere questioning.[76] As well as a means of extracting information, torture was a demonstration of power, a crime without consequence, showing that the detainee had no rights whatsoever, an act meant to break her or him mentally and morally. This often succeeded but, on the other hand, also seems to have hardened some other prisoners' opposition.

However, the new military regime seemingly lacked a consistent strategy about holding trials. Show trials were obviously important for their public, not their legal, function, as a means to 'prove' communist 'treachery' and justify state persecution. However, it has to be kept in mind that the first trials (against PKI Politbureau member Njono and against the coup's leader, Lieutenant-Colonel Untung) were only held in February 1966, when most of the popular violence had come to an end.[77] A few were filmed and broadcast, yet most were hardly covered by any media at all. Some members of the PKI Politbureau, for example, were unceremoniously shot, others brought before a Special

Military Court. Out of a total of about 1.7 million people arrested, a mere 1,014 were tried before military or civilian courts. Most sentences were severe, with about 12 percent given death sentences, roughly 60 percent prison terms of fifteen years or more, and very few acquittals. Yet, while none of those sentenced to death was granted clemency, only seven official executions appear to have resulted by the early 1980s. The timing of trials appeared equally arbitrary; the first major one against Gerwani leaders only took place in 1975.[78] For those never tried, release decisions were just as unpredictable.

Despite the indispensable role of the military in the Indonesian killings, their power, and that of the army in particular, had limits. The military was divided and the central government weak. Another limitation was a lack of manpower. An archipelago of 3,000 islands spread over a width of 5,000 kilometers is not easily controlled. In late 1965, the Indonesian armed forces consisted of 400,000–500,000 troops, 250,000–400,000 of which belonged to the army. However, most of this manpower was tied up in the Confrontation in Borneo and, to a lesser degree, Sumatra.[79] In addition, in late September 1965 around 60,000 troops were concentrated in or around Jakarta, and others deployed to West Irian and Sulawesi to hold down insurgencies.[80] Hence large parts of Java as well as the Eastern Islands were stripped of military presence; and quite a few units on the ground there – namely in the Diponegoro and Brawidjaja territorial divisions of Central and East Java, respectively – as well as parts of the air force, plus some in the navy and the marines, were considered unreliable by right-wing military officers.[81] Suharto and Nasution therefore shoveled certain troops from the outer islands to Java and others in the opposite direction in October and November 1965, which took several weeks and did not resolve the lack in numbers entirely.

The other weakness of the military was lack of knowledge. Many scholars argue that the army had prepared for the destruction of the PKI before the coup. This may be true in general, but not in any systematic way. The fact alone that of all people General Parman, head of military intelligence, was among the generals kidnapped and later killed on the morning of October 1, 1965 (without any guard in front of his house; he initially believed that he was being taken to Sukarno) sheds doubt on the sophistication of army preparations.[82] Moreover, the armed forces, according to indignant US Ambassador Marshall Green, "seem to lack even the simplest overt information on

PKI leadership," which is why the US Embassy helped out by providing lists containing 5,000 names (see below).[83] After half a year, no more than four out of ten PKI Politbureau members or candidates had been killed or arrested (with three more in the remainder of 1966 and two in 1968). By 1967, less than half of the members of the PKI's Central Committee had been "arrested or knocked off." The same applied to the regional leadership in Central Java and North Sumatra.[84] Only during the crushing of the guerrilla movement in Central Java in 1968–69 would a large part of the central PKI leadership fall into military hands.[85] When Carmel Budiardjo was interrogated in Likdam prison, Jakarta, in early 1970, she noticed an organizational chart of the PKI hanging on an office wall, with many of the boxes for names of functionaries in PKI "committees, commissions and departments [...] still empty."[86] More than four years after the coup, the authorities were still in the dark about the identity of considerable numbers of central PKI functionaries! The Indonesian military, as well as some foreign observers, deduced from calculations that they had succeeded in laying their hands on only a very small fraction of the 120,000 to 300,000 PKI core functionaries.[87] Lists of communists, compiled before or after October 1, mostly originated not from the armed forces but instead from lists provided to them by political groups like NU, HMI, or IPKI.[88]

Judging from these two deficiencies, from an anti-communist point of view, or from a lack of control highlighted by the inability to apprehend many leading PKI members, it is highly unlikely that the military was in a position to comprehensively plan and control the violence that fully ensued within three weeks of the coup. To overcome its lack of both manpower and intelligence it was essential for the armed forces to cooperate with citizens and organizations willing to provide these on its behalf. The resulting manhunt created an atmosphere that sometimes prompted prisoners to turn themselves in, or to voluntarily return to prisons, because they seemed to be safer than home.[89]

Participatory violence: military encouragement, political organization, and mobs

The participatory character of violence is crucial to understanding an extremely violent society. Many military units encouraged civilian groups to join in the violence against alleged communists. In a way, this was in accordance with the traditions of the Indonesian military, which had contributed to the creation of the state of Indonesia by fighting the war of independence against Dutch colonizers through guerrilla tactics which relied on popular support. Nasution and Suharto played a major role in this. In the struggle against the various uprisings of the 1950s and 1960s and during the 'Confrontation' with Malaysia from 1963, the armed forces had developed strategies to maintain the goodwill of the populace as well as structures anchoring it territorially. The latter included the acquisition of considerable administrative and economic functions that were rationalized in early 1965 under the theory of 'dwifungsi' or the double responsibility – military and socio-political – designed by the military by chief political strategist Nasution.[90] Suharto, as the head of the neighborhood association in his Jakarta *kampung*,[91] knew first hand about the cooperation between citizens and security forces and must have shared these ideas.

Army considerations about military–popular cooperation in the violence of 1965–66 are best documented for the RPKAD's murder crusade. The Indian journalist K. Tiwari, who had spent eleven days in the first half of November 1965 with the RPKAD in Central Java, stated that:

> *Colonel Eddy [sic] estimated that before the coup about 75% of the population in the Solo-Jogjakarta area were communist. He now believed that 40% of the people were on his side and that this percentage would increase. The Colonel had also spoken of the training he was giving to Moslem groups (as yet no arms had been issued), and of his belief that mass movement should be fought by mass movement. [...] Moslem youths were acting as the eyes and ears of the Army in the region, guiding patrols and generally informing. These functions were important for forces which were unfamiliar with the area [...] but Eddy [sic] was also laying the foundations for what he saw as an anti-communist bulwark in the region which would eventually be able to operate without direct army backing.[92]*

A visiting journalist from UPI reported days later that Edhie estimated his men had "already trained nearly 25,000 young men."[93] This corroborates Edhie's later rationalizations when speaking to a journalist:

> [T]he area was too big and too crowded for him to distribute his forces effectively. "We decided", he says, "to encourage the anti-Communist civilians to help with the job. In Solo we gathered together the youth, the nationalist groups, the religious [Moslem] organizations. We gave them two or three days' training, then sent them out to kill the Communists."[94]

Edhie's adjutant Wusibono, who put the number of RPKAD losses in Central Java at just two men, described paramilitary training and the distribution of weapons in similar words.[95] The head of the former vigilante group in Solo later stated that at least 10,000 people had been killed and at least 15,000 men and women arrested in and around the city, and showed trophies from "victims of what he jarringly termed the 'final solution'."[96]

The encouragement of participatory violence was thus not only a post factum invention.[97] Civilian participants did not justify their action by orders of a central authority "but by the right of the People itself to save the nation, the country's future, religion, and so on," as Benedict Anderson has observed. This popular form of bloodshed has become a tradition in modern Indonesian history.[98] The anti-communist student organization KAMI (KAMI means 'we' or 'our' in Indonesian) defied the ban on their organization imposed by President Sukarno, arguing that their "struggle is on behalf of the people's inner sense," so they would "only obey the people's voice" – despite the fact that the organization "had no more than 10,000 members in the liberal estimates of its own leaders."[99] Diplomats from capitalist countries soon noted the popular drive for violence with amazement and satisfaction. "Anti-communist festival continued in Djakarta streets today with big parade and largest bonfire to date (communist university)," wired US Ambassador Green, while West German diplomats raved about the "anti-communist people's movement."[100] In the eyes of some, this was also what the power of the military was based on. According to a travel report by Hungarian and Soviet journalists, "the position of the army is only strong (for example, [in] East Java) where the Muslims are strong."[101] A local army officer in Banyuwangi said that 4,000 had been killed there "in what he proudly called 'a real people's war'." In 1970, the PKI exile organization admitted that the party was confronted with a situation "in which the masses of the people do not support the PKI, even on the contrary [...]."[102]

The ways in which people were killed indicate a high degree of popular participation, and extreme hatred. It seems that only a minority were shot by the military. Most were beheaded, stabbed, or had their throats slit with knives or swords (sometimes after they had been tied up), others were hacked to death, strangled, slain with clubs or rocks, drowned, or burned or buried alive.[103] In other cases, the armed forces delivered victims to their village communities for murder, sometimes starting with a public military execution of leaders, or villages traded victims in order not to have to slaughter neighbors.[104]

Partners of the military in the violence were, for the most part, political or politico-religious parties and groups, youth and student groups in particular. The small IPKI – League of Upholders of Indonesian Independence, a party affiliated to the military – their Pancasila Youth and union SOKSI (with their rabble-rousing weekly *Ampera*) were obvious allies. Their main areas of activity were Sumatran plantations, often administered by the military, where SOKSI had been established to keep the PKI in check, but they were neither regionally nor operationally restricted to that. "[T]he Pemuda Pancasila has provided the 'mass organization' in North Sumatra with the greatest numbers and the greatest will to harass the leftists," the US Consulate commented. "In many cases, with and without army sanction, it has also served as the executioner of the army's communist prisoners." In some places, the IPKI was outdoing the NU in terms of terror. Their targets included People's Youth, the BTI, the Chinese self-help organization Baperki, Chinese shop owners, and sometimes PNI youth of the left wing of that party, indicating that especially the Pancasila Youth developed their own agenda for killings.[105] The Pancasila Youth in the Medan area maintained their own execution squad, known internally as "frog force" as they leapt from village to village, driving around in vehicles stolen from Baperki and marked with signs "Youth Action Command for the Annihilation of the September 30th Movement/PKI and Its Stooges" (reminiscent of the KAP-Gestapu, a multi-party coalition to crush the PKI). They used to bring victims to their Medan headquarters, where they were interrogated and then beheaded or, later, as this caused less blood to splatter, strangled with a hot wire ("to send him back to Peking,"[106] as they called it, though the victims were not ethnic Chinese). The Pancasila Youth also led the anti-Chinese pogrom in Medan, beheading people in public, and again played a major role in the pogrom of Makassar, Sulawesi.[107] US Consul Theodore Heavner was told by two Pemuda Pancasila representatives "that their organization intends [to] kill every PKI member they can catch" and commented that their attitude "can only be described as bloodthirsty."[108]

More than any other political group, the Nahdlatul Ulama, their youth organization Ansor, and armed wing Banser (All-Purpose Units) made a mark on the mass killings throughout virtually the entire country. The NU newspaper *Duta Masjakarat* called for the extermination of communists as early as October 7, 1965. Three days later, Ansor asked the military in Sumatra for weapons for killing communists. By October 5, the NU leadership had unofficially encouraged their East Javanese members to "physically eradicate" the communists. Ansor youth from religious schools were responsible for most of the many murders in Kediri (with NU organizational efforts resulting in low survival rates in the area). They put 3,500 people to death within five days in another town in East Java and slew people near Mlaten and, under army supervision, in the district of Banyuwangi. In some areas, Ansor and Banser forced all adults to participate in the slaughter.[109] Religious schools (which students from poor families could hardly afford to attend) instigated the violence. Jusuf Hasjim, a senior NU member who had taken a leading role in setting up Banser, said in 1998 that "Hitler's Mein Kampf had provided the inspiration on how to organize the youth."[110]

Along with the NU, the Islamic mass organization Muhammadiyah and their large affiliated student organization HMI played a major part in the Jakarta demonstrations and riots. The Muhammadiyah engaged in relentless propaganda, obtained condemnations of the communists from religious scholars, and participated in the terror in Java.[111]

In some areas of Indonesia, Muslim radicals were said to have killed all alleged communists without official help. In the rigidly Islamic, traditionally unruly, province of Aceh, this is supposed to have taken place in the first days of October 1965, even before military orders arrived (around October 10, the military imposed a curfew to bring the situation under control). Soon, similar reports were received about Madura: West German diplomats estimated that 3,000 and 2,000 people had been killed, respectively; for Aceh, an army source claimed 6,000 victims.[112] However, some sources state the murders in Aceh were instigated by local armed forces, at least those in November 1965 in the Gayo highlands, where between 800 and 3,000 leftists and Javanese plantation workers were killed. The bloodshed went so far that the territorial military commander remarked in December that it made little sense to dissolve the local PKI since the province "has been entirely purged in a physical sense of PKI elements."[113]

The PNI is notorious for organizing the most intense mass slaughter of 1965–66 in Bali, where probably 80,000 to 100,000 people were killed in little more than one month – 4–5 percent of the population. The paramilitary wing of the Marhaenis Youth, called Tameng ('shield') in Bali, black-shirted like the Ansor youth, started with stoning houses and attacking individuals, then turned to systematic nightly raids during which they captured alleged leftists according to lists or denunciations, and decapitated them or slit their throats with knives or swords.[114] But in Central Java, the PNI and their Democratic Youth played a leading role in the killings, too, as they did for instance in the Banyuwangi district, East Java.[115] In Central Java, the right wing of the PNI (which was on the retreat at the national level) dominated the party's organization,[116] and in Bali the PNI represented the establishment.

Smaller parties took part in the killings as well, as PSI Social Democrats (themselves under fire in Bali) and functionaries of the Islamic student organization PII.[117] Christian vigilantes – mostly Catholic youth – participated in killings in northeastern Sulawesi, West Timor (where 3,000 people were killed) and Flores.[118]

Even women militias were formed: "My wife was trained as a member of the voluntary women's corps to wipe out the communists," a former village official from Central Java recollected of a then mother of four. At the RPKAD parade in Jakarta on January 4, 1966, after their return from the killing spree in Bali, "women paramilitary volunteers wearing distinctive commando camouflage jackets" marched along – including Sarwo Edhie's wife.[119]

It was a very broad coalition that teamed up with the armed forces, including conservative bureaucrats and youth, reaching from the conservative-Muslim parties and organizations NU and Muham-madiyah to the modernist-Islamic Masyumi, the right wing of the nationalist PNI, the army-affiliated IPKI, all the way to the (outlawed) Social Democratic PSI – and the man who conveyed lists with com-munists to be eliminated from the US Embassy to General Suharto (see below), Adam Malik, was nominally a Trotskyist. Some called this the "New Order coalition," a "loose assemblage of antagonistic political forces."[120] They did agree, above all, on one thing: killing communists.

This coalition also established an umbrella organization that has so far been given only superficial attention by researchers, the "Action Front for the Crushing of the 30 September Movement/PKI" (KAP-Gestapu). On the evening of October 1, 1965, several Islamic representatives met in Jakarta, planning to set up a Muslim anti-communist alliance of a number of organizations with the Nahdlatul Ulama. However, the political section of Army Headquarters (KOTI) under Major-General Sutjipto proposed instead a broader coalition, which led to the foundation of KAP-Gestapu on October 2 under Chairman Zainuri Echsan Subchan (NU) and Secretary-General Harry Tjan Silalaki (Partai Katolik), in the presence of Mar'ie Muhamad, Secretary-General of Muhammadiyah. (One of these three had already approached General Nasution on September 28 – before the coup – to arrange the training of anti-communist youths by the army in response to the air force training communists.) On October 2, Jakarta commander Major-General Umar Wirahadikusuma prom-ised weapons and logistic support.[121] Subchan, third deputy chair-man of NU, was a 34-year-old orthodox Muslim (*santri*) businessman from Central Java, President of the Indonesian Chamber of Commerce and leader of the Union of Indonesian Moslem Scholars, "bright and impressive," a former leader of Masyumi and unusually well con-nected to Muslims of different shades, youth leaders, and the Chinese business community, as well as the army, particularly Nasution and Sarwo Edhie.[122]

During their first rally with a few hundred supporters in Jakarta on October 4, in a statement also broadcast by radio and TV, KAP-Gestapu demanded the banning of the PKI and affiliated organ-izations and the purging from the government and state institutions of participants and sympathizers of the '30th September Movement.' But this was only the first step in what was planned as a more than week long "crescendo" of increasingly violent action. Four days later, the Action Front organized a much bigger demonstration in Jakarta, which ended with the sacking and burning of the PKI party headquarters by NU, Christian, and IPKI youths as well as physical attacks on communists. Afterwards, demonstrators reported back to Brigadier General Djuhartono at National Front headquarters, handing him a "resolution" to the National Front. By October 9, KAP-Gestapu (later renamed Pancasila Front) already comprised six parties and thirty-eight organizations (many youth organizations), compared to four parties and a total of twenty-seven organizations, largely orthodox Muslim, only five days before.[123] By November 9, all parties except the PKI had joined and were able to stage a demonstration in Jakarta with allegedly several hundred thousand participants. At that time, a Catholic Party representative praised the "unprecedented teamwork" within the association.[124] As the name 'Action Front' was to signal, the KAP-Gestapu did engage in physical attacks on communists; on December 2, US Ambassador Green wrote that this organization was "still carrying [the] burden of current repressive efforts targeted against [the] PKI, particularly in Central Java."[125]

Sectoral alliances such as those among the non-communist trade unions echoed the demands of the anti-communist coalition.[126] For university students, seventeen organizations joined KAMI (Indonesian Students Action Front), founded with strong links to the military on October 25, 1965 in Jakarta. KAMI conducted violent demonstrations against communists and Chinese; KAPPI was later added for high-school level students.[127] In early 1966, they enjoyed strong support among the urban middle class, with mothers' groups and shopkeepers organizing food supplies and neighborhood associations providing clothing and shelter.[128] Numerous student demonstrations after March 1966 and continued anti-Chinese riots – not all to the army's liking – show that they were not merely creatures of the military.

While some judged KAP-Gestapu as not particularly efficient in organizational terms because it gave local groups too much independence,[129] it was also active on regional and local levels, for example in East Java, Central Java, and North Sumatra. For some time, however, All-Sumatra Military Commander Mokoginta seems to have favored an alliance of Islamic forces only. He did assemble religious and community leaders together with representatives of the political parties from West Sumatra in mid-December 1965, urging them "to eliminate all leftist elements in their own fields and encouraged their organizations to form a united front." This resulted in mass rallies and meetings where communists renounced their party membership or dissolved their local party section.[130] In East Java, a so-called "Coordinating Body for the Vigilance Command," a short-lived alliance with similar objectives, was set up locally, perhaps rooted in an anti-communist party coalition which had been in existence since at least 1964. Just before the massacres on Bali reached their peak, almost all political organizations on the island, including PNI, NU, IPKI, the Catholic Party, and the Protestant Parkindo, together with all eight district heads (bupatis), called for the ousting of leftist Governor Sutedja.[131]

The KAP-Gestapu became a rival organization to the established National Front (a Guided Democracy organization with mandatory membership for all parties, civic groups, and professional organizations). The National Front rapidly lost influence, came under anti-communist military influence, and underwent political purges from December 1965. But on October 10, 1965, it was still possible for an all-party delegation including the PKI to be sent from Yogyakarta, Central Java, to the capital. Even later, the province's governor called for frequent consultations of the National Front, apparently to use it as an instrument to prevent full-scale violence.[132] On October 21 the government decreed that the National Front should purge itself of alleged supporters of the '30th September Movement.' In August 1966, following regional suspensions, Suharto dissolved the National Front.[133] President Sukarno understood from the beginning the need to form an alliance in order to keep society under control, calling for "unity" of political organizations and trade unions after the first post-coup Cabinet meeting on October 6. He consistently aimed at reconciliation and the containment of the violence. Recognizing the significance of the KAP-Gestapu, in January and February 1966 the President tried to have a "Sukarno Front" set up as a political counter-force, a move that worried the army for some time but was finally blocked through prohibitions by the regional commanders, beginning with Major-General Adjie, who had also been the first provincial commander to ban the PKI.[134] The National Front, the KAP-Gestapu, and the Sukarno Front represented three attempts to gain or maintain the moral hegemony in the country and to present a consensus that really did not exist.

Mob violence

There were no clear demarcations between planned violence organized by political groups and spontaneous, rather uncontrolled pogrom-like events involving large crowds that tended to commit murders indiscriminately. Given the difficulty of sourcing information, all that can be done at this stage is to search for certain indicators of unorganized popular violence which involved an even wider circle of people than organized groups.

Mob violence has featured prominently in Bali, with people chased down by village mobs and their homes torched. Whole village communities attacked others. In Pare, Central Java, and neighboring villages, people were assaulted by large crowds from other villages and some of them burned alive in their houses. Mass killings of prisoners or individuals by angry masses were reported in Madura and North Sumatra.[135] Witnesses and travelers who later passed through Bali saw either fires from such events every night or later entire neighborhoods gutted.[136] Participation in killer gangs often happened spontaneously, without any formal structure or membership, depending only on the will of the individuals involved.[137]

Another sign of uncontrolled violence can be seen in the murder of whole families, including women and children. In the "area around Surabaya," East Java, it was reported that "minors and children" were dragged out of their homes and killed with their parents, apparently in close proximity to their homes, and especially if both of the parents were communists. According to other sources, entire families were massacred at home in East Java if the allegedly communist parents refused to come out. Similar events occurred in some other regions.[138] Even entire villages were wiped out by neighboring communities or in cooperation with the armed forces in Bali, but also in Central Java and Aceh.[139]

However, children were also murdered as a result of conscious decisions by political groups. A member of a youth group in Central Java recounted how they attacked houses of 'communists' at night and knifed everyone inside: "'We had to make sure that we got everybody this time, so there would be no comeback.' [...] 'that is why we took the whole family'." An Australian report took this as a widespread practice.[140] In Flores, people told a traveling Australian Embassy official that they wished to "exterminate the PKI thoroughly (thoroughly meaning wives and children as well), as some sort of guarantee against future reprisals" or vengeance. On Roti island near Timor, the army was said to have killed about "50 communists and their families," or at least some family members, in November 1965.[141] Minors and even children could be found among female detainees in Jakarta.[142] Murders of children happened locally based on a fairly widespread discourse about what to do with the children of murdered communists that chillingly resembles Himmler's thoughts in his infamous Posen speech in 1943. Wives of generals reportedly talked about killing all children fourteen years and older of '30th September Movement' participants. Even in 1969, a businessman urged the Nixon administration in the USA to continue their support for a strong role for the Indonesian military for more than a decade because "the offspring of the executed hard core communists will grow up within the next ten to fifteen years. They will just be the same like their fathers were." For similar reasons, Nasution had in 1966 called for charity support for the bereaved of communists killed.[143] Decades later, the 'problem' would be addressed by inventing the concept that persons had to be "environmentally clean" if they were to perform politically sensitive jobs or functions such as teachers. They needed to prove that they had no relatives implicated in the 1965–66 persecution, making the latter a "permanent, semi-hereditary condition."[144]

In general, what regional studies about East Java indicate – the region where the popular participation in the murders was highest, military control was low, cruel ways of killing were common, and scores of corpses washed up on river banks, destroying the fishermen's business as nobody wanted to buy fish any more – is that even there the degree of organization by political groups was high in many areas (and that several local military units participated in the killings). This does not mean that murders were not brutal, with entire families slain, and involving mutilations with penises, heads, human limbs, or torsos being displayed at roadsides and in squares.[145] In parts of East Java, it seems that such cruelty by civilian gangs served to inspire awe in the early weeks of the massacres, while later killings happened less publicly and with fewer mutilations because these were no longer necessary to instill horror and authority.[146] Near Kediri, an Ansor squad used to lead crowds of 3,000 villagers attacking other villages. Throughout Indonesia, many of the locations of killings also indicate a degree of planning rather than uncontrolled rage, as the victims were transported (often on trucks) mostly in small groups to their deaths at sites such as forests, remote plantation grounds, wells, cemeteries, river banks, and sea beaches.[147]

The case of Bali shows the interplay between the military, political organizations, and unorganized violence. Under the influence of leftist Governor Sutedja and a Sukarnoist military commander, large-scale killings were prevented until November 1965, longer than anywhere else on the inner islands. In the following seven weeks, 80,000–100,000 people died – between 4 and 5 percent of the population.[148] This figure roughly equaled the number of members in communist organizations, but the killings were not restricted to leftists.[149] After relative calm in October, November had seen a build-up of anti-communist propaganda by the regional PNI, supported by some military officers and authorities.[150] The existing controversy over whether it was the incoming RPKAD squads who triggered full-scale mass murder or whether, as the older view had it, they brought the killings under control, appears too simplified, reflecting the notions of either strict military control or popular frenzy.[151] The RPKAD arrived on Bali in early December. An officer of the unit had publicly stated on November 24 that the killing of women, elderly people, and children as in Klungkung, Bali, had to be prevented. In fact, at that time General Suharto made general public statements against mob violence ("unrestrained anger") while military persecution ("mopping up operations") should continue, and Sarwo Edhie, too, warned against excessive killings despite having unleashed these himself.[152] But after meeting modest resistance in Bali, RPKAD started a bloodbath in Negara in which 1,506 people were reported killed.[153] What followed within the next three weeks was the peak of violence with murders and arrests by the RPKAD squads, PNI youth, and village communities combined. Actually, major uncontrolled killings as in Klungkung had already been documented for early and mid-November. Local clashes are supposed to have led to the start of some massacres by the military, and both had triggered the wholesale destruction of villages on a scale that was obviously larger than some researchers assume, in a mix of PNI-organized and much uncontrolled violence.[154] Simultaneously, the vilest anti-Chinese pogroms occurred between November 29 (before the arrival of the paratroopers) and December 7 (in their presence). The RPKAD withdrew from Central Java and Bali on December 31, 1965, where according to TASS correspondent Olga Tschechotkina, the last big massacre of locals happened on New Year's Eve.[155] Yet, because of jails crammed with political prisoners, the Tameng would still execute truckloads of them every night in February 1966 (when witnesses still saw bodies lying in the villages of East Java and in Lombok as well).[156] Neither the events in East Java nor in Bali would suggest that the military could easily control the party militias, or that the army just tried to implicate many people by having them have blood on their hands.[157] What explains the unmatched intensity and rapidity of the slaughter on the picturesque island of Bali was interlocking action by centrally deployed elite troops, local military, small Islamic groups ferried over from East Java, the regional PNI fighting their only sizable opposition with youth death squads, village communities either 'purging' themselves or attacking neighboring settlements, and individuals taking advantage of the killing spree.

Reasons for killing

As diverse as the coalition that teamed up to exterminate the communists were their motives for doing so. The 1965–66 slaughter was a complex, multi-causal event. The motivations of different groups often overlapped, and many individuals had more than one reason for participating in the violence. Many Indonesians had only vague ideas about Marxist doctrine or what it meant to be a communist; they acted instead on assumptions about what it entailed.

There is no doubt that many people acted under pressure. Some were coerced to kill – a few even forced to put to death their own family members against whom they held no grudge. Some attempted to distract suspicion from themselves or to prove that they were reliable.[158] Loyalty to their religious or village community required many men to participate when villages or cultural groups were pitted against each other. Some people were also convinced of the menace of imminent communist atrocities, though actual confrontations were restricted to the early weeks and some areas of Central and East Java. It would appear even from publications during the Suharto regime that the use of arms by the PKI and the construction of palisades by the leftists in these areas were largely defensive.[159] In other parts of the archipelago hatred was spurred by rumors and propaganda inventions about the murder of the generals or communist death lists. What amazed witnesses for the most part was how unresistant the 'communists' were who went to their death.

Violence against alleged communists was often driven by struggles about land, between individuals or communities. Big landowners organized extermination actions evidently in order to prevent future threats to the ownership of their estates, as in West Timor.[160] The houses and fields of tens of thousands of ethnic Chinese, driven away from inland West Kalimantan in 1967 for alleged communist sympathies, were taken over by local Dayaks. Enormous amounts of property such as houses, furniture, vehicles, wet and dry rice fields, fishponds, or radios were either confiscated by the authorities or appropriated by individuals, with no chance in practice for the owners to get them back later and dim prospects for ex-prisoners to return to their village.[161] However, in the longer run, land and businesses often ended up in the hands of transmigrants, supported by the military.[162] Beneficiaries of the limited land reform and land occupations before October 1965, which had been supported by the PKI and the BTI, often saw themselves forced to return the plots received, and the land reform came to a standstill. Several hundred thousand hectares were returned to the old, wealthier landowners by, given the usual distribution size, as many tenuous holders.[163] The expulsion or murder of squatters on plantations was a mass phenomenon. Even some wealthier landowners had to die for their land, which ended up in the hands of local politicians or officers. In cities, people in wealthy urban neighborhoods were sometimes arrested just so that somebody else could lay hands on their house.[164]

Religion had played a major role in violent conflicts in Indonesia since the 1950s, especially in the Darul Islam rebellion that affected multiple regions. Yet those clashes had taken place between Islamicists and representatives of the secular state, whereas communists had hardly been victimized at all. Now, the alleged despising of religion by leftists provided one of the major arguments for murder in varying contexts. Islamic leaflets blemished communists as "anti-religion and anti-god" and "devils." The killing in Pasuruan, East Java, started with incitement by the central mosque announcer. In several locations, including Kediri, East Java, the killers were blessed by Islamic leaders or a *fatwa* was issued. The fact that the majority of the – compared to land struggles – rare previous conflicts with a religious connotation on record in East Java before the coup were related to folk theatre would suggest that communist provocations were rather innocuous.[165] However, land conflicts could be interpreted as assaults on Islam, too, as many larger owners had transferred surplus land to mosques or religious schools and claims for these lands were interpreted as a direct assault on Islam.[166] Contrary to the view of Iwan Sudjatmiko (based on a press survey), conflicts over religious issues seem to have aroused Hindus in Bali against the PKI as well, following systematic incitement by Hindu priests, but again it is unclear how far this was actually the result of leftist actions. Many communists in practice continued to be pious themselves. Governor Sutedja and communist leaders did call for marriages between commoner men and brahmana women to be legalized, therefore calling into question the caste system – and with it social order. Rumors about the theft of temple relics appear less convincing, and for the mocking of religious observances by communists there is no hard evidence.[167] As with the persecution of animists and atheists, violence seems to have been based more on vague suspicions and general assumptions of hostility, and less on previous tangible clashes.

Entire professions came under suspicion. Labor organizers, fishermen, and estate workers were among the first targeted.[168] In 1966, prices for the famous woodcarvings from Bali and batik from Central and East Java soared as many such artisans, a number of whom belonged to a communist union, had been killed. In West Timor, it was not easy to get a plumber because there had been a collective suspicion against craftsmen.[169] "Most, if not all, of the members of the Balinese dance troops are numbered among the victims," an observer noted – many women among them. On Buru island, scores of shadow puppeteers and gamelan players were imprisoned.[170] Many ludruk theatre actors in East Java had their throats cut by NU murderers. Eighty percent of Central Javanese shadow players were said to have been killed. In 1988, shadow puppeteers were still listed among the sensitive professions to which the concept of 'ideological cleanness' was applied, so that former leftists could not perform.[171] In 1965, teachers were also routinely killed in many regions; others landed in prisons or fled. For the new school year, the Education Minister was missing 40,000 out of the 93,000 teachers needed.[172]

On an elite level, the persecution of leftists, and with it a profound change in the political orientation of the country, opened up career opportunities in politics, the upper echelons of the bureaucracy, and in academia. In Bali, the PNI tried to eliminate their last big opponent in regional politics. With regard to the "reign of terror" in Java, a journalist remarked that some extremists "wanted to put everybody back in sarongs [...] but the young leaders of the mass Muslim organisations do not show signs of fanaticism so much as ambition."[173] "Past and prospective purges will open many vacancies which both the Army and the political parties are anxious to fill," commented the US Embassy.[174] In the lower ranks, if right-wing artists called for the persecution of their leftist colleagues with devastating results, if university students selected and killed their communist peers, high-school students tormented theirs, and women's and police wives' organizations were urged to expel all 'communist' members and seize Gerwani kindergartens,[175] the boundaries were blurred between the mere fact that these perpetrators could best identify leftists and the advantages they gained by eliminating competition.

Many of the urban middle-class university students involved also fought for their right to party. Some student demonstrations were organized like festivals, where stylish fashion and haircuts were displayed as well as pop songs played, sung, or danced to. The PKI together with Sukarno had denounced foreign films and music and helped restrict their dissemination; the students "were even afraid to have parties" before they got rid of their Spartanic taste oppressors. Army-sponsored student radio stations gave them an opportunity to disseminate their new youth culture in 1966. One of the new measures of the Jakarta city administration after 1966 was to legalize gambling to increase revenue.[176] NU politician and KAP-Gestapu Chairman Subchan bore the nickname "dancing ulama" because of his frequenting of night clubs and public alcohol consumption.[177]

Most scholars agree that women were relatively infrequently specifically targeted for killings in 1965–66,[178] though many died when entire families were exterminated. Initially, many women seem to have been arrested; in January 1966, nearly 25 percent of the prisoners in internment centers in Sumatra were women, while they may have represented 10 percent of the remaining detainees nationwide in 1976, according to Amnesty International.[179] The question remains why – given that the pro-PKI women's organization Gerwani was so widely denounced[180] – the killings were so predominantly of men. Aside from cultural inhibitions and the underrepresentation of women in the political left (less than 20 percent of PKI and People's Youth members were female), it would seem that women appeared less as a political threat, competitors for power, or economic or professional rivals. Probably other ways were seen than killing to subjugate women, such as sexual humiliation and, last but not least, to neutralize them by making them widows, burdening them with taking care for a family alone.

Context: social change and political polarization

This section serves to contextualize the 1965–66 violence within longer-term processes in Indonesian society. It is a brief analysis of the dynamics, conflicts, and complex group identities and loyalties that existed in Indonesia in 1965, focusing primarily on the countryside, where 85 percent of the population lived and most murders happened.

According to an influential, but not universally accepted, interpretation based on works by Clifford Geertz and others, rural Java was characterized by vertical *aliran* (streams) instead of class divisions. This view distinguished three cultural and socioeconomic groups: the *santri* – orthodox Muslims, in economic terms larger landholders and merchants; the *abangan* – nominal Muslims who mixed Islam with older animist, Hindu, and Buddhist practices, identical with the rural poor; and the *prijaji* – modernist nationalists with little interest for religion or of Hindu belief, primarily state bureaucrats seldom living in villages. Reputedly, this led to great cohesion within villages belonging either to the *santri* or *aliran* stream, where people were supposed to live in shared poverty without significant social differences. Without major class tensions, the system was said to have resulted in agrarian "involution," a quiet decline through farm atomization due to population increase while people clung rigidly to tradition.[181]

Yet, despite the fact that extremely few large private estates existed, there were marked economic differences and an ongoing class differentiation in the villages. A collective study of Indonesian villages at the time questioned the "popular notion that village life is peaceful" (which is unrealistic, although it was an image also prominent in 'Western' scholarship): "land, status and prestige, differences between generations and differences between the sexes can be frequent sources of serious friction."[182] By 1963, 67 percent of all landholding peasants in Indonesia owned less than 0.5 hectares (slightly down from 70 percent in 1940).[183] A quarter held 2 hectares or more. One-third of the rural families in Lombok were entirely landless, and 42 percent of the arable land in Lombok was pawned to landlords. As in Java, 80 percent of households had to turn to sharecropping and/or wage labor, often for more than one landlord. Similarly to other regions, Lombok was in a transition from widespread tenancy to wage labor, which would become common in the early 1970s.[184] Landlessness, low rural wages, and an extremely low average calorie and rice consumption characterized the situation throughout the archipelago, with the production of corn, tapioca, and potatoes – crops for the very poor – also down.[185] Deepening and broadening poverty indirectly affected the state budget, too, as revenue from direct taxes had been falling to extreme lows since the 1950s.[186] In this protracted near-unbearable situation, traditional practices of *gotong rojong* (mutual help) and therefore cohesion in the village assumed extreme importance, while on the other hand mutual help had only a limited capacity to keep poor families from collapse,[187] resulting in class differentiation.

Rural poverty and repressive customs in the villages spurred large-scale migration. Throughout the 1960s, but especially after 1965, poorly dressed vagrants on roads were a common sight, cities received a heavy influx of unemployed peasants, and homelessness was an unexceptional fate.[188] In the "village revolution" that transformed the countryside, many traditional farmers could not continue to hold on to their land because the property – with 0.3 hectares on average – had become too small to sustain a family. While larger landowners, businessmen, and officials bought or rented their land, attracted by rising land values and product prices, former peasants moved to the cities as pedicab drivers, street vendors, coolies, servants in restaurants, or vagabonds. A few remained as sharecroppers in the villages.[189] Others rented land, practiced sharecropping, or looked for jobs in addition to working their small plots, but, given extremely adversarial sharecropping rates and low rural wages, this could make them slip into debt as well. Due to these competitive conditions, local customs often restricted moving to another village by excluding newcomers from the community, its rituals, and protective mechanisms, for years, and expelling members who faced a dire existence.[190] Given such hostility, migrants often preferred to move to the cities or to the outer islands.

Rural poverty was reinforced and change accelerated by the famines of the mid-1960s. In late 1963 and early 1964, a drought hit parts of Java as well as Bali. By February 1964, Reuters reported one million people affected by starvation in Central Java, where thousands were treated for hunger edema and malnutrition.[191] In some areas of West Java, too, people had a meal only every third day. Parts of East Java were battered as well, particularly the Ponogoro subdistrict where 80,000 suffered from hunger edema.[192] In Bali, volcanic eruptions in March and May 1963 had killed at least 2,000 people, displaced 75,000, and damaged the plots of up to 250,000 peasants, about one-third of agricultural producers, mostly in the east of the island. When the situation was aggravated by drought, a famine in 1964 left at least 18,000 people starving, affecting above all the rural population with little land. From 1964 to 1965, the price for land on Bali almost doubled.[193] In 1966, floods struck at the Solo river valley in Central Java. The Lombok famine of 1966, caused by drought, inflation, administrative failure, and a "drive for profits" from continued rice exports from the island, claimed maybe 50,000 lives.[194] An Australian traveler described some of the consequences of the famine for the "hunger belt [...] south and east of Jogjakarta" in Central Java, arriving after the worst was over in early 1965: in the case of drought, small landowners "go very hungry, the old people and little children die, and tens of thousands of others go begging in the streets of Yogyakarta, Surakarta [Solo], Semarang, and Sourabaya [in East Java]." Prostitution and criminality in the cities flourished. Destitute villagers would begin by looking for side jobs and borrowing from neighbors, then they would sell their furniture, pawn or sell their land, and finally leave when the money they had raised ran short because there were few miserably paid rural jobs and an overabundance of cheap labor. Some even sold their children, the sign of utmost despair in a famine. In towns and cities, at least they would have access to water, some to government-run emergency rice kitchens, or they could find some junk, search for and sell scrap, or live with friends.[195] Despite a record rice crop in 1965,[196] famines served as a catalyst; a lot of land would change hands, village elites would make a gain, and not all refugees would be in a position to return, even if they wanted to. Locally, they could also trigger charismatic religious movements, some of whose members later turned against communists.[197]

The rural landless and urban poor, even parts of the urban middle class, were squeezed by another redistributive process, the hyperinflation of 1965–67. In 1965, prices rose by 500 percent, and by 650 percent in 1966.[198] Staple food price inflation was even more drastic, with rice prices skyrocketing by 900 percent in 1965 and rationing protecting only government officials, employees of state firms, armed forces personnel, and some city dwellers. Rice prices almost quadrupled from August to late September 1965, when the black market rate of the US dollar reached record levels. Next to the violence, what ordinary Indonesians would remember decades later about 1965 were economic crisis, inflation, and high food prices.[199] Although inflation was worst in Jakarta, in general the average daily calorie intake was down to around 1,800, with rice consumption falling by 17 percent in 1964–65; for those below median income it decreased by 40 percent,[200] in part substituted by cassava or corn.

No wonder that young men were the prime group involved in the killings, both as perpetrators and victims. The career of young adults in this situation was blocked: they were specially hit by landlessness, since the family land tended to remain with the parents and there was too much competition for the few wage labor jobs. Coming from a self-confident post-colonial generation fed with stories about past oppression overcome by the successful struggle for independence, with the highest literacy rate and often speaking Bahasa Indonesia fairly well (not only regional languages), but frustrated, they played the most active role in village community life. They placed the most emphasis on the practicing of traditional mutual help (now strengthened and transformed through new channels such as peasant organizations and labor unions), and were politically the most active.[201]

In a slowly, but over time radically, changing rural environment the traditional roles of women were being challenged too. They increasingly entered the public sphere; many had to engage in wage labor and others engaged in politics. If religious and other men (and probably some women) fiercely and sometimes violently opposed alleged sexual liberties taken by women, as during the anti-communist propaganda campaign, they did so because such liberties appeared both as a symbol of social disorder, and also as a sign of a change they did not accept.[202] Not only did the upheaval lead to massive physical violence against women but also to specific long-term oppression and exploitation, making the female half of the population the losers of 1965.[203]

The misery of the growing number of rural poor and the pressure by the communists led the government to react with limited land reform. According to the Basic Land Law of 1960, land exceeding a ceiling of 5 hectares for irrigated and 6 hectares for rain-fed land (big landholdings by Javanese standards) was to be redistributed. It also established conditions for individual land ownership to replace traditional rights to collective landholdings or use.[204] Although the land reform could at best provide land ownership for 6 percent of the county's four to five million sharecroppers, there was fierce opposition that shows that the Indonesian communists – though far from being revolutionary – overstretched the openness of influential elites to even mild reform. The wealthier farmers reacted by inventing or deliberately complicating existing traditional rules, or creating local amendments or legal hurdles, or organizing fake transactions. Such resistance, and its backing by the Suharto regime, meant, for example, that less than half of the limited land designated for redistribution in a Balinese district had been handed over by 1996. Countrywide, only 200,000 hectares were officially turned over by September 1965.[205]

Under massive pressure from their membership base, the PKI supported the land reform by so-called 'unilateral actions' trying to overcome owners' resistance, that is, spectacular land occupations often involving the support of hundreds of people. Some of them went beyond the scope of land reform regulations; such 'unilateral actions' were related to land conflicts between owners and sharecroppers or squatters. They served as a demonstration of, and as a means to broaden, PKI power as a core part of a radicalized party strategy from 1963, though one which still aimed at working within the existing political system, without adopting the path of armed struggle.[206] PKI research surveys on villages, which were of excellent quality but for the most part made in 1964 and 1965, after the start of the land reform campaign, showed high land concentration in provinces such as Central and East Java and North Sumatra.[207] The Communist Party had to agree to stop their 'unilateral actions' in December 1964, under pressure from President Sukarno, the military leadership, and right-wing groups in the provinces; yet land struggles did not completely cease. More substantial, anyway, was an improvement of sharecropping conditions in accordance with the 1960 Sharecropping Act. Here, the PKI called for a share of the crop for tillers of 50 or 60 percent, while in reality they received only 25 to 50 percent.[208] In 1964–65, the PKI campaigned more broadly against the "seven village devils": Indonesian and foreign landlords, rich farmers, usurers, moneylenders claiming repayment in kind, brokers who purchased agricultural products at the lowest price, and "capitalist bureaucrats," which often meant military officers with administrative functions.[209] In addition, during the famines of 1963–64, the PKI and BTI organized truck shuttles from villages to cities; communist mayors and organizations tried to buy the land and houses of destitute villagers in order to hold and later resell them to their owners, which again brought them into conflict with local elites who wanted to profit from the misery. Communists organized begging, hunger demonstrations, and begging roadblocks where drivers who refused to pay had their cars turned over.[210]

These challenges to the traditional order, as well as the responses to them, found their equivalent in confrontational party politics permeating the countryside.[211] From the revolution of 1945 to the national elections in 1955, politics had become increasingly fragmented into dozens of parties and groups. The years without elections after 1957, the system of Guided Democracy with the disempowerment of parliamentary representation (1959–65), and the regulations on parties of 1959–60 (demanding a total membership of over 150,000 and branches spreading over different regions of the country), resulted not in a decline of party politics, but in parties building stronger organizations with an increased number of branches, improved coordination between them, stronger links to affiliated mass organizations, more rallies and new forms of activities, a younger party leadership, and a drive to win more members as political capital in the quest for influence on national politics. With improved and extended organization, the NU and PNI also tried to respond to the PKI gains in the 1957 regional elections in Java.[212] By mid-1965, Indonesia had nine political parties, three major ones (PNI, NU, and PKI), all with their main bases in Java, and the remaining six with 200,000–400,000 members each.[213] With three million members, the PKI was not even the biggest political party; the PNI claimed four to eight million members, the NU four to six million. Though these numbers were probably exaggerated (some parties did not even require membership fees), they did indicate a growing polarization of local politics.[214] In addition, three parties which had been banned between 1960 and January 1965 had retained some influence: the modernist-Islamic Masyumi (formerly the fourth big force in Indonesian politics, representing the outer islands, and linked to the still legal mass organization Muhammadiyah and the student organization HMI), the Social-Democratic PSI, with some influence among academics, and the nominally Trotskyist Murba Party of Minister Adam Malik, with their main base in West Java.

Not only the PKI, but even the smaller of these parties were affiliated to mass organizations – their own labor unions, and youth and women's associations. For example, the Islamic union Gasbiindo, with relations to Masyumi, claimed three million members, PNI's KBM 1.6 million in 1965 and four million in 1968, and PNI organizations in total more than seven million. Before and after 1965, they were entangled in conflicts not just with the PKI. The PNI and NU had their own peasant organizations as well.[215] All parties reached down to the village level, but in small places there were even party-affiliated boy scouts and, in towns, separate kindergartens, too. In a West Java village there would be PKI-, Masyumi- and PNI-related women's organizations plus two more for the wives of administrators and policemen. In 1963, PKI organizations were present in 62 percent of all Indonesian villages. Depending on the local power distribution, villagers also joined parties for non-ideological reasons, such as to participate in a development project or to place a child in school.[216] A great part of Indonesian adults were thus affiliated in some way to a political party – almost one-third of 52.5 million registered voters to the PKI.[217] Literacy rates of around 60 percent (higher among the younger generation) also show that large parts of the population were in a position to participate in politics.[218] Political fault lines crossed through villages and families. For example, General Parman, the head of military intelligence killed in the 1965 coup, was the brother of the member of the PKI Politbureau, Sakirman, executed without trial in 1966; two other brothers were said to be members of the NU and PNI.[219]

Political organization along these lines was crucial to the low-level violence between Islamic and pro-communist organizations which emerged in 1964–65 as a result of socioeconomic conflict, claiming dozens of lives. Struggles over land were the prevailing starting point of such clashes. The PKI got involved in disputes between, often small, landholders and sharecroppers, in which they sometimes took the side of the former. In any case, the communists alienated the other side.[220] The US Consulate in Surabaya reported "daily" murders, warned against travel in certain regions, and conveyed rumors "that a 'new Madiun Affair' was shaping up," with other observers equally expecting a "genuine confrontation."[221] Aside from the strife over land, the public meetings of the other side were attacked, and diverse Muslim groups, among them Ansor and HMI, attacked communists for allegedly insulting their religion.[222] In East Java, the center of such violence (where later the biggest killings in terms of numbers took place), the Muslim attacks forced the PKI onto the defensive by early 1965, impelling it to change its policy. Violent conflicts also ensued in North Sumatra, Central Java, Bali, and Sulawesi.[223]

These conflicts also resulted in the emergence of two characteristics of the later anti-communist killings, quite typical of extremely violent societies: anti-PKI coalitions and the emergence of militias. Several Muslim political, youth, and student groups teamed up to attack PKI demonstrations in East Java; NU, PSII, Muhammadiyah, and the Gasbiindo union jointly condemned alleged PKI attacks on Islam.[224] The fact that communists often took the side of minorities such as squatters, migrants, or Chinese, facilitated this development. In early 1965, the PKI had revived an earlier proposal to arm millions of Indonesians in a "fifth force" to strengthen territorial defense and deter British–Malaysian attacks on the republic. This was largely opposed by the military, as it would have given the PKI access to armed units and influence in defense matters. Hesitantly, some regional commanders agreed to set up small contingents.[225] Most of them turned the PKI intentions upside down. In North Sumatra, regional commander General Mokoginta planned to draw the vast majority of civilians in the auxiliary force "from non-communist workers and peasant organizations."[226] Similar efforts were made by the territorial Siliwangi division in West Java, whose commander, Adjie, asserted in June 1965 that he could mobilize three million people, arm part of them, organize a military exercise involving one million, and "could crush the PKI organization in West Java" within 72 hours.[227] However, shortly after the coup, in October 1965, Adjie disarmed at least part of the civil guards in order to ease tensions, whereas in Mokoginta's area they were given weapons, encouraging violence. Civilian Defense Corps units had been previously purged of alleged communist sympathizers (73,000 in North Sumatra alone).[228] In December 1965, plans for a Home Defense Guard of no less than twenty divisions were released, of which NU and PNI were to make up 20 percent of the members each and Muhammadiyah, PSI, IPKI, the Catholic Party, and Parkindo 10 percent each.[229] In addition, the army traditionally had three student regiments under arms, based in Solo, Bandung, and Jakarta, whose role in the violence still needs to be explored.[230]

In early 1965, political formations organized as well. In March 1964, Ansor, the NU youth organization, had already established an armed wing. 'Banser' (All-Purpose Units) to counter communist actions, mostly related to land occupations. In 1965, the Muhammadiyah established the Kokam (Vigilance Command of Muhammadiyah Youths) with similar goals, the PNI 'Banra' (in Bali 'Tameng'), and East Javanese Catholics founded the 'Guards of Jesus Brigade.' The military started to train these and other militias.[231] The Ansor leadership boasted that it had two million members and was, compared to the PKI's Pemuda Rakjat, "although quieter, [...] stronger and [it] could if necessary mobilize a much greater number of youth to cope with any threat to Ansor interests," be they "religious" or with "political overtones."[232]

The armed forces were involved in such conflicts because of their ideological differences with the PKI, but also because of growing military economic interests and their building of a web of power and corruption, spurred by martial law powers from 1957 to 1963. For example, by October 1, 1965, every fourth officer from the rank of Colonel up was also employed outside the military, including eighteen cabinet ministers, twelve ambassadors, nine governors, and twenty-five high-ranking government positions – numbers that increased after 1965.[233] Suharto was only one example of the openly practiced and admitted corruption in the officers' corps, which involved several sectors of the economy from foreign trade to mining, and also had to do with to the army's "civic action" program.[234] The PKI stood in the way of armed forces' development strategies of creating a non-Chinese commercial class with heavy military involvement, based on export earnings and capitalist foreign investment.[235] Plantations were a case in point. By 1965, many public estates – namely those formerly in Dutch or British hands – had come under military control. The PKI-affiliated plantation worker union Sarbupri pressed for higher wages and improved working conditions. In particular, transmigrant laborers among the estate workforce, but also among the squatters on unused plantation land, were among the PKI's most ardent supporters.

All this brought the party in conflict with the military. In such ways, the PKI was an obstacle to military economic interests and blocked the intensification of plantation operations.[236] After October 1, 1965, the military resolved this problem by murdering at least 50,000 plantation workers, focusing on Sumatra, with the help of the army-affiliated party IPKI and the pro-army union SOKSI, which had been nurtured by the military in the plantations for several years.[237] Even months before the coup, there had been rumors that the military commander of West Java, Adjie, had had 1,400 pro-communist plantation workers preemptively arrested; 400 were released and 1,000 "buried."[238]

Perhaps the situation in 1965 can best be understood within a framework of conflicting loyalties. Instead of clear-cut divisions between either *alirans* or classes, during this period of profound social transformation rural Indonesians felt they belonged to, or their solidarity was claimed by, groups divided along village community, party, religious, class, and ethnic lines.[239] The point is that not all of these loyalties could coexist, leading to confrontations between groups, with terrible consequences for individuals, depending on which group they felt they belonged to or, more importantly, to which they were seen as belonging. The focal points of the mass killings of 1965 were to be found where rural poverty was worst, the rural proletariat of landless workers, small sharecroppers, and micro-peasants was the most numerous, and where the PKI's unilateral actions had been most intense: in the areas of Klaten, Bojolali, and Solo in Central Java, in Kediri and Banyuwangi in East Java, in Cirebon and Garut (West Java), and in Madura, Bali, Lombok, and near Medan (North Sumatra).[240] Many of these areas also overlapped with the famines and displacements of 1963–65. This does not necessarily mean that the conflicts of the 1960s were based to a lesser degree on *alirans* or party affiliation than on struggles for land.[241] Those were linked. What the critical material conditions triggered was the questioning of identities, traditions, and political roles.

Other victims

Communists and members of PKI-affiliated organizations were not the only people drawn into the maelstrom of violence. The 1966 survey for Suharto included an estimate that of one million victims, every fifth killing had occurred "in error on non-communists."[242] Of these, some were mistaken for leftists; some belonged to minorities trad- itionally assaulted in times of crisis or violence; others still became a target because the atmosphere and practice of violence provided an opportunity for enemies or rivals to get rid of them. By thinking about the heterogeneity of the coalition for violence, this section attempts to contribute to explanations of why persecution against such groups took place, why it was for the most part less intense than against com- munists, why it partially assumed different shapes from the fate of the political left, and why it occurred when it did.

The Chinese minority in Indonesia – about three million people, half of them Indonesian citizens, the others either citizens of the People's Republic of China (PRC), of Taiwan, or without citizen- ship – had traditionally been made victims of violent or official perse- cution. Whether in 1945, 1948, 1959–60, 1963, 1974, or 1996–2000, in times of crisis, the Chinese minority were attacked, their apart- ments, shops, and vehicles ransacked, and members of the community were periodically expelled.[243] Observers noted a coincidence of trou- bles for ethnic Chinese in early 1966 in the Philippines, Burma, South Vietnam, Indonesia, and the secession of Singapore from Malaysia, and a connection to the economic crisis in Southeast Asia, ethno- nationalist policies restricting, closing, or expropriating 'Chinese' commercial property, and Cold War politics.[244]

A considerable part of the Indonesian middle class, includ- ing trade, productive businesses, and free professions, and about 10 percent of the country's urban population, was Chinese. They were envied for their wealth and education, accused of being responsible for the political crisis, and despised for their secluded lives, separate cul- ture and religion, alleged social aloofness, lack of political ideals, and doubtful or merely opportunistic loyalty to Indonesia.[245] The events of 1965–68 added variations and new elements to these themes: through the alleged Chinese masterminding of the September 30, 1965 coup, the Chinese were identified with communism or called traitors finan- cing communist organizations on nationalist impulses. In reality, few members of PKI-affiliated organizations were of Chinese extraction; the Chinese middle class was actually largely unsympathetic to com- munism, and Chinese leftists – and others – organized in the Partindo (Partai Indonesia) or the Chinese self-help association Baperki (Consultative Body for Indonesian Citizenship) rather than joining the PKI. Yet Partindo and Baperki – like other political parties – had moved to the political left in the early 1960s, sometimes echoing PKI policies. In part they did so because of developments in the PRC, but also because the PKI was (aside from Partindo) the only party to take a firm anti-racist stand, to condemn the 1963 anti-Chinese pogroms inspired by Masyumi circles, the army, and police in West Java, and to oppose the 1959 legislation that tried to bar Indonesian Chinese from commercial business in rural areas, driving 136,000 people out of the country in 1960.[246]

Anti-Chinese riots in 1965–66 often took place in conjunction with attacks on Chinese diplomatic buildings in Jakarta, Medan, Makassar, and other cities, from which violence sometimes spread to 'Chinese' civilians spontaneously, though many of these attacks were planned. The army shielded such atrocities, issued demonstration permits, was present during attacks, provided military vehicles, or participated directly.[247] For example, a 10-hour pogrom in Makassar, Sulawesi, on November 10, 1965 that left 2,000 houses, many businesses, and five Chinese schools destroyed, equivalent to 90 percent of Chinese property, with many Chinese lynched, followed a major demonstration by the Muslim youth organizations Ansor and HMI, together with the army-affiliated labor union SOKSI and army troops, led by a Major Sjamsuddin. The Medan pogrom started after a 3-hour meeting of more than 1,000 youths in a stadium.[248]

Contrary to common belief, people of Chinese ancestry did not represent a major proportion of those killed in 1965–66. The numerous Chinese diplomatic notes on anti-Chinese violence – primarily dealing with citizens of the PRC – mentioned only a limited number of deaths. The leading scholar in the field has concluded that up to 2,000 ethnic Chinese were killed.[249] Australian diplomatic sources put the number of Chinese deaths at "hundreds" in Aceh alone, many of them in 1966, and at 200 for the Medan pogrom on December 10, 1965 – a rather conservative figure.[250] As the PRC Embassy stated in a note of April 11, 1966, summing up nationwide assaults: "Many [Chinese] have been murdered in cold blood, or even beheaded, disemboweled, dismembered or burned alive."[251] A large number of further deaths occurred when Chinese were expelled by Dayak tribes, together with the military, from inland parts of West Kalimantan in 1967; between 300 and 3,000 were massacred and a minimum of 1,881 – another estimate is 4,000 – mostly children, died of deprivation in refugee camps afterwards.[252] In addition, in North Sumatra there was a relatively high proportion of ethnic Chinese held in miserable post-coup detention camps in 1966, many of them members of Baperki or Partindo.[253] Many of these camp inmates may have been summarily executed together with leftists. All in all, the number of ethnic Chinese who died as a result of violence from October 1965 to 1968 thus reached at least 3,000 and may have exceeded 10,000, with few of these victims belonging to communist organizations. In addition, over one hundred thousand had to flee their homes, tens of thousands lost a substantial part of their property, thousands left the country, and all Chinese schools, between them teaching over 270,000 pupils, were closed. This means that ethnic Chinese were probably statistically underrepresented among those killed in this wave of violence, but that they were affected more than average Indonesians by forced migration and substantial loss of property.

Attacks on 'Chinese' – mostly without regard to whether they held Indonesian citizenship or not – appear to have served as a sort of starting signal for the breakdown of public order and any moral standards or state of law. They coincided with the takeoff of the worst violence against the PKI in many cities and towns, especially where the army took the lead. Attacks on the buildings of Baperki in Jakarta, including the devastation of Res Publica University, started in mid-October. The West German Embassy dated a first "wave" of anti-Chinese riots across Java around October 20, that is, during the start of the RPKAD killing crusade. In some East Javan towns, attacks on Chinese began on October 14 at the latest.[254] On October 20, three days after the RPKAD had marched into Semarang, Central Java, mobs started to attack 'Chinese' property as well as Baperki and PKI offices, smashing and looting 100 shops. The same happened in the cities of Solo (October 22) and Yogyakarta. A journalist traveling through the region later described most 'Chinese' shops in towns and villages around Semarang as boarded up.[255] Hungarian and Soviet journalists who passed through nine cities from West to East Java between November 2 and 6 noticed Chinese shops destroyed in all of them.[256] Those who led demonstrations against the old order in Bandung in late 1965 were among the same students who had also spearheaded the May 10, 1963 anti-Chinese pogrom, which they had then utilized to confront the Sukarno regime.[257] West German diplomats reported what they called a second "wave" of anti-Chinese violence between November 5 and 14, including mobs attacking Chinese in Ambon (Moluccas), Makassar and Bonthain (South Sulawesi), and Bandjarmasin (South Sumatra). In Sulawesi, this again seems to have coincided with a peak in anti-communist violence.[258] The harassment of Chinese in western and central Bali began in early November 1965 and later grew into violent attacks by hundreds of "hooligans" on the shops and residences of ethnic Chinese, with destruction, looting, and bodily attacks including several murders. This happened in Singaradja from November 29 to December 5, in Denpasar from December 1 to 6, and in Klungkung on December 6 and 7, 1965. In Denpasar, it started with representatives of Chinese businessmen being summoned to army headquarters and asked for financial "sacrifices," or riots would take place, as in Singaradja and Makassar. According to a journalist, the store owners in Singaradja and Denpasar were "liquidated after summary stand-up judgments were issued convicting them of financing the Gestapu,"[259] but such killings are not corroborated by other sources.

Indonesian Chinese saw themselves coerced into demonstrations of loyalty, often including violence against PRC diplomatic installations. In one case, the student organization KAMI sent their members of Chinese ancestry in first in Jakarta. Diplomats regarded it as a "sign of human despair" that 20,000 Chinese demonstrated in front of the Chinese Consulate in Medan under slogans such as "Down with China!," simultaneously beseeching the Indonesian authorities to acknowledge their rights as citizens.[260] Yet most of Baperki's branches were already closed by mid-December 1965, dissolved by their own members under pressure from an "Institute for the Promotion of National Unity."[261] All Chinese organizations of importance ceased to exist. Chinese schools – with over 270,000 pupils, mostly run by Baperki – were confiscated, many destroyed and finally all of them shut down, as well as Res Publica University in Jakarta, meaning that no more institutional instruction in Chinese language or culture was possible.[262]

In April 1966 – at the same time that the murders of leftists petered out – a second wave of anti-Chinese violence began that lasted until late 1968, for the first six months including further mob attacks with more or less input by political and military organizers.[263] Based on the varying political guidelines of regional military commanders, pogroms and boycotts were combined with an official, superficially 'legal' persecution of the Chinese by the authorities, with a particular but not exclusive emphasis on people without Indonesian citizenship. Among other effects, this led to the closing of all Chinese schools by May 1966, the expulsion of almost all ethnic Chinese from Aceh, the concentration of over 10,000 Chinese in camps in the province of North Sumatra (6,000 of them were shipped to China), and the removal of most Chinese merchants from villages and small towns in East Java. This and measures such as the ban on the Chinese language[264] in economic life resembled what happened to Armenian businesses in World War I (see Chapter 3). Though in the end far fewer left the country than in 1959–60, panic among Chinese businessmen, which led them to sell and convert their assets to prepare for departure, was so widespread that it was said to have driven up inflation and the black market rate of the US dollar.[265] Authorities in West Java were reputed to be planning to send 'back' all Chinese who had been members of mass organizations, and restricted the work of "foreign" doctors, dentists, and chemists. Pressure was also high on Chinese nationals in Jakarta.[266] Though this protracted persecution still involved relatively few deaths, unlike the anti-communist violence, there was no relief, with no significant decrease in the harassment of Chinese communities for three years. This went on for that long in order to undermine the economic position of the Chinese compared to non-Chinese/military competitors,[267] to sever relations with the People's Republic of China (which happened in 1967), and to maintain the pressure for the integration and conformity of a group whose strong social and political structures had formerly worked against such integration. In 1967 and 1968, however, the Chinese staged counter-demonstrations that sometimes turned violent, too.[268] In 1968 or 1969, military personnel in Jakarta would still routinely round up a few Chinese shopkeepers and businessmen, hold them in prison for some days and rough them up, until they were finally willing to pay a ransom. Students and other youths extorted "protection money" from the Chinese openly in the streets.[269] Generally, however, conditions improved around 1970, and Chinese people and capital floated back to Indonesia. Suharto had tried to curb the intimidation because he sought the support of 'Chinese' business partners.[270]

Massive physical violence continued even longer in West Kalimantan than elsewhere. There, the anti-communist purge had initially involved relatively few killings, but a small Maoist guerrilla movement, consisting in part of ethnic Chinese, emerged in 1967.

The Indonesian military provoked local Dayak tribes into violent attacks on the Chinese in the inland territories of the province, in which at least 300 people were killed and, co-organized by the military, between 60,000 and 116,000 people were expelled or fled to Pontianak or the coast, including a large number of Chinese farmers. Tens of thousands spent months or even years in camps, where many died due to the bad living conditions. Some 27,000 more were removed in 1970 and 1972.[271] This seems like a peculiar partial implementation of a plan announced in the spring of 1967, according to which the military intended to move 350,000 ethnic Chinese into controlled areas in Kalimantan and deport them to China later. However, the army had initially been unable to carry out a November 1966 rural residence ban.[272]

Indonesian Chinese were persecuted for a diverse mixture of reasons. Different groups had different motives for joining in, which resulted in a relatively broad section of the coalition for violence assaulting them, albeit this varied according to local constellations. The overlapping of ethnic, religious, status- or income level-related, and political differences accounted for how explosive the persecution was in different places.[273] Aggravated by deep-seated contempt, mob violence was often based on rumors linking ethnic Chinese to the PRC and therefore to the '30th September Movement' – or vice versa. Politically more adept figures in politics and especially in the military realized that most of these charges were unfounded, but nonetheless manipulated the mobs, often working somewhat systematically through political youth organizations, in order to directly make some extra money or indirectly impair business competitors.[274] Milking the cow, however, was often preferred to actually slaughtering it; for the sake of such coercion one could live out a strong urge, even lust, for intimidation. Political parties and even some figures in the central government, as well as regional army commanders, adopted anti-Chinese policies, which resulted in sinophobic decrees, orders, and guidelines. Also, for many military officers and politicians, the loyalty of Indonesian Chinese was still in doubt, too, and needed to be assured by coercion. All of this was grounded on racist perceptions about the 'selfish,' secluded Chinese. Except for West Kalimantan, the persecution of 'Chinese' villagers was less intense since they tended to lead a modest, more integrated existence.

In terms of people killed, a more important group of victims than the ethnic Chinese were transmigrants in different parts of the archipelago, especially in rural areas of Sumatra, but even in some regions of Java. By migration, inhabitants of densely populated areas with few jobs tried to escape miserable conditions at home. Sometimes they had also been expelled for some reason from tight-knit village communities in Java or Bali. The background of this cohesion was not merely backward traditionalism, but a reflection of small peasants and already landless villagers desperately clinging on to their spot of land or a place within the community that at least entitled them to some elements (like practices of mutual help), or sometimes only illusions, of security. However, fierce conflicts crystallizing around land use, customs, language, or religion often arose at their new places of settlement, too, with migrants rarely accepted into villages and usually founding their own communities, claiming woodlands or unused estate land.[275] Throughout Indonesia, the BTI and PKI had supported squatters and settlers against local landowners, slash-and-burn agriculturalists, plantation managements, and authorities, which earned the left a strong support base among them. 'Unilateral actions' were also used to help refugees whose land had been destroyed by the 1963 Gunung Agung volcano eruption through sharecropping, as well as on many other occasions.[276] In late 1965, this added to a general suspicion and frequently collective violence against squatters and migrants.

A good deal of the 'unofficial' half of the c.200,000 killings in Sumatra were linked by the British Consul in Medan to "anti-Javanese feeling," spurred by military propaganda against crimes allegedly planned by the "Gestapu."[277] This violence was especially directed against transmigrants in Lampung (South Sumatra),[278] but also resulted in the death of thousands in the northern parts of the island, including plantation workers hit in their camps, for instance in the highlands of Aceh.[279] In Java, too, there lived considerable numbers of migrants who were in no less a danger of becoming a target of local communities or landowners, as near Kediri, Central Java, from where a military officer in civilian clothes set out, according to an eyewitness, "to shoot squatters who had refused to get off his untilled land." So common was this practice that W. F. Wertheim commented that "killing hundreds of thousands of landless people does not solve the problem of landlessness."[280] But it is not possible to identify a general policy by landowner associations or the army to 'solve' this problem by murder, and no party is known to have adopted an anti-migrant platform, but many landowners (sometimes with local military support), village communities, and individuals went so far their in struggles for land resources, and political and cultural dominance, that they killed migrants. Others were intimidated, driven away, or forced off the land.

A third group often mentioned as victims during the 1965–66 mass violence are atheists, animists, Javanists, and other religious dissenters belonging to older forms of beliefs, who lived in substantial numbers in different parts of the country.[281] When interrogated in 1965, those arrested were routinely questioned about their creed and came under suspicion of being atheist, e.g. communist, if they did not belong to one of the monotheistic religions (*agama*) recognized by law.[282] Yet, despite general references to such persecution, there is comparatively little concrete evidence for it.[283] The followers of Mbah Suro, a former village chieftain and reputed black magician who rebelled in the area of Nginggil at the border between Central and East Java in 1966, were apparently bloodily suppressed by the military.[284] Yet while pious individuals and especially local NU members pressed for violence against animists, syncretists, or Hindus, the case of the Pasuruan highlands in East Java would suggest that this had little success, as this unilateral policy lacked support, particularly by the military.[285]

Insofar as analysts have understood the violence of 1965–66 as based on the conflict between purist Muslim *santri* and nominal Muslim Javanese or *abangan* (which, again, also had class and cultural dimensions), they pointed out that the former suspected the latter of engaging in black magic. A similar insinuation affected, for example, mothers who, upon their release from arrest in Bali, were denied the right to get their children back from their patrilinear families: they could represent a political danger to family and children, and influence the minors with their bitterness and by black magic.[286] However, sufficient examples from Java and Bali are documented in which ostensibly strictly Muslim or Hindu murderers – some of them highly educated – narrated that they engaged in magic practices (such as wearing amulets, smearing their own faces with their victims' blood, putting a cat on a victim's stomach, receiving special blessings for weapons so that they could pierce the victim's skin or cut their neck, or beheading and burying the head and torso at different places) to break the alleged magic powers of their enemies as a precondition for being able to kill them.[287] It would appear that the belief in the special spiritual powers of PKI supporters by some of their Ansor, HMI, and PNI persecutors points instead to the latter's own superstition, not necessarily in accordance with Muslim dogma. This tends to undermine the perception that murders can be interpreted simply as a way to enforce strict adherence to the Quran, or that the killers were purist 'santri.' Again, murders rationalized in this way, going beyond the victims being leftists, were not the result of any general policy (even by the NU), but rather of local, even personal, initiatives, which makes them harder to track, but probably also limited their occurrence.

There were other groups victimized, sometimes described as "non-communists and innocent people," as if communists deserved their fate.[288] On November 16, 1965, General Mokoginta warned that "criminals" were using the cover of the anti-communist campaign in Sumatra "as pretext to kill, rape and loot."[289] Often personal grudges constituted the background, or the "paying-off of old scores." The Gayo in Aceh recalled stories where people were denounced for their desire to avoid paying a debt and for rivalries between villages. In Bali, people protesting against the violence, husbands in the way of would-be lovers, and quarrelsome residents all became victims.[290] Others who ended up in prisons or worse included those who were denounced by neighbors for personal reasons, for violating the curfew, for mistaken identity, or who were merely relatives or friends of PKI suspects.[291] Robert Cribb has argued that most such conflicts had some political dimension;[292] yet this would not appear to apply to all these possibilities. Moreover, the events of 1965–66 should not be reduced to 'political' violence even in a broad sense.[293]

However, there was, of course, a strong political dimension. Political parties used the moment for murderous strikes against affiliates of parties other than the PKI in a quest to strengthen their local position. In particular, NU functionaries attacked PNI members in Java (mainly of the left wing of that party). Several local branches of the PNI dissolved under public pressure in October 1965, just like those of the PKI. Later, IPKI activists intimidated or killed PNI members in North Sulawesi. On the other hand, PNI officials in Bali had former members of the banned PSI slaughtered.[294] Several leftist PNI members also died when they came under attack by KAMI students in 1966, leading a KAMI newspaper to state sarcastically: "In Central Java calm and order prevail, except that there is civil war."[295] In the Surabaya area, clashes between armed forces personnel and Madurese apparently claimed 200 lives after an argument about who was allowed to carry weapons, but Madurese were also suspected of killing relatives of the servicemen as communists. Revenge for murdered relatives also led to deadly clashes between soldiers of the Diponegoro division and RPKAD battalions in Central Java, and allegedly to the withdrawal of the RPKAD.[296] Similar situations arose when local leftists and others came under fire in the Gayo highlands of Aceh for having been scouts for the military years before, when it had combated the Darul Islam uprising, or for having helped the armed forces against the Permesta rebellion in Sulawesi and West Sumatra.[297] Ironically, in late 1965, it was the army, manipulated by locals, which shot some of these former allies.

The US Consul in Medan noted about anti-Chinese riots: "Wholesale killing of PKI in recent weeks has created [a] climate of violence here with large g[r]oup of youths living outside normal social restraints for [a] prolonged period."[298] In a similar vein, in Bali a reporter was told, "the killings simply started against the Communists and spread."[299] We have seen that this is not exactly true, including the Balinese example, since it was often anti-Chinese violence that opened the door to tearing down public order and moral standards. Violence did spread against entire social groups (squatters), religious sects, political formations, or economic rivals. People could become a target of religious-conservatives both as modernists (communists) or as overly traditional (animists). Citizens attacked each other in the name of regionalism (migrants as well as former supporters of the government in the 1950s uprisings), or under the pretext of the overwhelming argument of national unity that allegedly justified violence against leftists and the Chinese. Individuals were motivated by personal advantage, including blackmail, looting, sexual gain, and revenge. Aside from the military (by no means a homogenous factor) and other authorities, political parties and organizations, ad hoc groups, ethnic or religious communities, or villages pursued a number of different interests that fanned out, hitting those who were a common enemy harder, and those upon whose persecution few agreed to a lesser degree.

Limits to violence

The balance is shocking enough: 500,000 or maybe a million Indonesians were murdered at a horrific pace during the 1965–66 slaughters, and another 1.8 million arrested at some point over the years. Still, this was far short of the roughly three million members of the PKI and the circa fifteen million members of their mass organizations (only in Bali did the violence seem to have no limits). In other words, there is reason to ask the more unusual questions: Where did the violence stop, and why? Which mechanisms determined whether a person was killed or persecuted – or not? In this section, I shall try to address these questions by returning to the patterns of widespread societal participation in the violence and the motives for it.

The violence in Indonesia 1965–66 derived its thrust and dynamics from the overlapping interests of different social, political, and ethnic groups. As long as they coincided, such motives fueled the complex military–civil web of persecution, preventing violence from declining and determining the extent of killings, arrests, layoffs, and so on. Once either the interests of major forces in the coalition of violence diverged, or a number of such major groups in the coalition shifted interests simultaneously, violence would decrease and finally expire. The end of the bulk of the murders has sometimes been dated to March 1966; this is when Suharto acquired by force an authorization from Sukarno which was immediately interpreted as allowing him to run state business (the so-called 'Supersemar' of March 11). One day later, Suharto used his new powers to dissolve the PKI. It could even be argued that this step, marking as it did victory against the PKI and Sukarno's people, may have dampened the intensity of the persecution; after all, diplomats had noted before that the PKI had been banned in most provinces regionally except for those where the level of violence was at its worst: Bali, East and Central Java, and North Sumatra.[300]

However, it seems to me that a more important political reorientation had already taken place by January 1966: the fight against Sukarno for central political power channeled political efforts back to the capital Jakarta. In fact, it was then, in January, when the most substantial reduction in the number of murders took place.[301]

The parties and the military seem to have decided in late November 1965 to try to bring down Sukarno and the government.

After a conversation with an unnamed private secretary of NU Deputy Chairman Dahlan, US Ambassador Green wired:[302]

> *Political parties now plan to shift offensive from banning of PKI to economic issues. Source said NU no longer interested in official, nation-wide banning of PKI and even sees some disadvantage in this step. Parties now intend create "explosive atmosphere" by exploiting price rises. Although NU leadership approved price hikes, party intended to present different attitude to public as demonstrated by recent editorial in its official organ Duta Masjarakat deploring new gasoline prices. Subchan's Action Group* [the KAP-Gestapu, indicating knowledge of the army; C.G.] *would soon insert anti-inflation theme in public demonstrations. Eventual aim would be to arouse people and "cage up Sukarno in corner".*
>
> *Comment: using price increases as tactic to get Sukarno seems extremely dangerous, particularly since it commonly known that rise in gas and kerosene prices instituted at behest of army. Source was unable to provide satisfactory explanation of how parties plan to direct public "explosion" over inflation toward Sukarno alone.*

This telegram is cited here at length because it laid out with some precision what happened in the following months, especially after more price increases for rice, public transport, etc. and a futile currency reform in December[303] – the only element left out being the role students would play as agents in the public protests. Inflation rose in late November 1965 and reached new heights in January 1966.[304] Some direct adherents of the anti-communist coalition were shielded from these increases, like the armed forces personnel, who received a 500 percent raise.[305] The plan reversed an earlier army policy (namely by Suharto) to increase public support by lowering prices for basic necessities, especially in Jakarta, and to ensure adequate supplies, in order not to give the communists political ammunition.[306] The new manipulative plot, however, which added an economic dimension to pre-existing demands by KAP-Gestapu for a ban on the PKI organizations and a purge of the government, necessarily had repercussions for the tactics of the parties involved, which in a somewhat competitive manner had to prepare for the takeover. Indirectly, it drew energies from the extermination campaign, as the document foretold.

Through a former intelligence officer in South and Southeast Asia, Fujiwara, the Japanese government learned that the Indonesian military planned to take over power, allegedly on December 20, 1965.[307] Malik had already told Green on December 13 that the army planned to unseat Sukarno, but that Suharto and Nasution disagreed about tactics.[308] With reference to inflation and disruptions, the Australian Embassy noted that the "political parties are exploiting this economic discontent systematically, working largely through the Student Front (KAMI)." Their demonstrations would later play a major role in bringing down the government.[309]

By late December 1965, the army had succeeded in bringing the killings in East Java and in Bali under control – which resulted in exactly that: controlled killings, albeit on a much smaller scale.[310] "At the end of December, East Java Military Commander Brigadier General Soemardji issued an order which in effect told the NU to stop the killings of its enemies," which was, according to the US Consul in Surabaya, "gradually enforced" (he added in a footnote: "Army killing of PKI prisoners reportedly is still continuing"). In the district of Banyuwangi, the bulk of the murders stopped on December 25, reportedly after 25,000 had been killed. Local military units and the regional police chief had also repeatedly tried to limit the murders.[311] President Sukarno, who intensified his efforts to curb the violence in December – sending out his Fact Finding Commission, first to Bali on December 27, was part of this attempt – was said to have assured KAP-Gestapu and NU leader Subchan in mid-December that he would outlaw the PKI on December 24 on the condition that Subchan "stop the mass extermination of PKI leaders." Subchan purportedly traveled to Central and East Java to spread the word, which made him locally unpopular, but Sukarno did not keep his promise.[312]

By January, murders in Central Java and North Sumatra were substantially reduced, too. As for North Sumatra, the British Consul in Medan sent a contradictory report in early January 1966, stating that "the Army were arresting, converting, or otherwise disposing of, some 3,000 PKI members a week, mostly rank and file. This rate has fallen sharply," but added that the "rate of killing remains high" with reference to messages from plantations.[313]

Murders did continue unabated or were started after a delay in remote regions, such as some Eastern Islands and in West Sumatra, an "area [that] is at least two months behind events in most of the rest of the country."[314] But overall, foreign observers reported an end to the really large-scale killings by January.[315]

The most obvious, indeed dramatic, sign of a change of political priorities was the relocation of killing units. No single one of these units was more important and strategic than the RPKAD, deployed to Central Java and Bali. RPKAD troops returned from Bali on the last day of 1965, and from Central Java on December 25, to Jakarta, where they held a triumphal parade on January 4, and where commander Sarwo Edhie gave a press conference saying that the PKI's back had been broken.[316] Edhie, together with General Kemal Idris, Nasution, and Ali Murtopo (the head of Suharto's intelligence service), became involved in organizing month-long student unrest in the capital, and RPKAD troops in civilian attire took part in student demonstrations. This was kick-started by an economics seminar at the University of Indonesia in Jakarta, beginning on January 10, where students were addressed by Edhie, Nasution, Kemal Idris, Subchan, and Malik (in addition, a message by the absent Suharto was read to them), and where they heard a series of lectures by PSI-affiliated, US-trained economists from the Army Command Academy SESKOAD, who ridiculed government economic policies and pleaded for capitalist development with strong foreign investment, strong exports, and sharply curbed government spending. In his speech, Edhie again "told a mass rally of students [...] that the back of Gestapu had been broken." The students came up with the Tritura ('Three Demands of the People'), which was presented in a rally to Chaerul Saleh, economic strongman of the Cabinet, and had basically been suggested to them by Sarwo Edhie and other officers. The demands were for the dissolution of the PKI, a government reshuffle purging it of alleged supporters of the September 30 coup, and action to tackle the economic misery of the people.[317] In a sequence of increasingly violent street protests and demonstrations, including the storming of several ministries, first in mid-January and with heightened intensity from mid-February to March 11, the students (organized in the "Action Fronts," KAMI for university students, KAPPI for high-school students, and KASI for university graduates) helped substantially to discredit, weaken, and finally paralyze Sukarno and the government, who did not dare to confront them more than half-heartedly, despite Sukarno's ban on KAMI on February 25. Developing as they did their own political agenda and culture, the students were not just puppets of 'the' military – though they received guidance, money, and logistic support from trucks to radio stations from the army and, after the ban, even protective shelter.[318]

The fact that some of the RPKAD's role in the killings in Central Java and Bali was exposed in the report of Sukarno's Fact Finding Commission on the killings when parts of it were published in an army daily on February 11 and 12, may have served the purpose of adding to its grim reputation and of intimidating opponents.[319] It was RPKAD units who surrounded the President's Palace in Jakarta, prompting Sukarno and Foreign Minister Subandrio to flee by helicopter to the Bogor palace, where they were threatened by RPKAD troops again, which finally coerced Sukarno into issuing his decisive authorization for General Suharto, ostensibly to guarantee public order, on March 11, 1966. And Sarwo Edhie's paratroopers made the first arrests of several government ministers one week later as well.[320]

Not only military units were redeployed. When the Nahdlatul Ulama celebrated its fortieth anniversary on January 31, 1966, it organized a "Grand March" from the President's Palace to the Main Stadium at Senajan in Jakarta. In a message to the Australian Ministry for External Affairs, "some notes made by an Embassy officer who observed the March" were presented:[321]

> The backbone of the march was made up of Ansor Youth
> [...] The Ansor marchers all wore khaki shirts and long
> khaki trousers, black army boots which appeared to be
> new, black webbing belts and black berets. Shoulder
> badges showed the locality from which each platoon came
> and included groups from Tjirebon, Surakarta [Solo],
> Bandung, Semarang, Jogjakarta and Sukabumi. [...] In
> most platoons, every man wore a sheath knife on his left
> hip, with about 10% wearing a second knife on the other
> side. About 15% of the knives were the knuckle-duster
> type. The sheaths for these knives, and possibly the knives
> themselves, were manufactured in Bandung. Undoubtedly
> many of the knives had been active in PKI eliminations
> during the past few months. [...] The marchers moved like
> automatons, apparently thoughtless, feelingless, and ready

to be roused by a word to laughter or holy war. In some
ways [...] it was a depressing reminder of the black shirts
of the Third Reich.

The same scene was also conveyed by East German Vice
Consul Göckeritz:[322]

The Ansor Youth concentrated their communist-
slaughterer battalions [Kommunistenschlächterbataillone]
from all of Java and Madura in Jakarta and staged
a "show of force" on 31 January in the form of a
demonstration by these uniformed and paramilitarily
equipped gangs. Most of these units were not withdrawn
to their places of origin, but have been, as the NU daily
"Duta Masjarakat" reported on 4 February, stationed
in Jakarta indefinitely for the realization of a "special
project" [Sonderprogramms] that has been prepared for
them.

These gangs from West, Central, and possibly East Java were
to add to the manpower, activism, and thus influence of the NU in the
capital during this time of university and high-school student demonstrations against government members and policies. In late 1965,
the Nahdlatul Ulama, for which Jakarta was not a strongpoint, had
already brought in several thousand youngsters from the countryside
and surprised observers by suddenly dominating student demonstrations in the capital.[323]

Of course, the survival of large numbers of Indonesian leftists should not only be credited to their persecutors. One of the pro-
active responses Indonesians chose under the menace of violence was
fleeing. At most, several thousand found a refuge abroad – namely
in China, Eastern or Western Europe. Many more searched for the
limited security in the anonymity of bigger cities such as Surabaya,
Yogyakarta, and especially Jakarta. For example, "substantial numbers" of refugees from the "bloodletting" in Central and East Java
fled to the relative calm of the western part of the island, "adding to
the restless, hungry, unemployed of Djakarta."[324] Particularly in the
early weeks, PKI activists also escaped from cities and towns to the
countryside of, for example, Northern Sumatra.[325] In Central Java,

many teachers, civil servants, and village heads had fled by November. Others left the capital for the Javanese hinterland. Carmel Budiardjo mentions the fate of a man from Jakarta who sought refuge in Central Java during the early wave of arrests but returned to the capital once the violence had risen dramatically in the province.[326] Once released from detention, after the end of the most intense massacres, many former communists left West Sumatra, for example, to start a new life in Java.[327] Flight as a mass survival strategy built on one of the key loopholes in the nets of persecution – lack of knowledge by the authorities. In the longer run, most of these refugees could only survive among the nameless migrants in cities and shanty towns; Ibu Marni narrates how she lived for three years with homeless tramps under a bridge near Magelang, Central Java.[328] In small villages, by contrast, outsiders had to always be much more afraid of being denounced, handed over to the armed forces, or even killed by locals. This also limited their ability to use family support networks, which implied being visible in the neighborhood.

Under tremendous psychological or physical pressure, groups of members of the PKI or affiliated unions, women, youth, and peasant organizations publicly renounced communism in many parts of the country, repented their 'errors,' dissolved their organization's local or regional branches, and pledged support for Indonesia's state ideology Pancasila. During the witch-hunt, confused by events, some functionaries and members felt betrayed by their leadership and became doubtful of communist thinking. Did the overwhelming coalition of enemies not indicate that something had to be wrong with communism, and that it was indeed alien to Indonesia? Was there not perhaps some truth in the charges against the PKI?[329] The abrupt change of the political and moral climate, the hegemony of slander against the PKI that allowed radical violence against its members to appear so natural to many, engulfed and overwhelmed more than a few party members too. The disbanding of party structures started within weeks, especially in West and then in Central Java. In the city of Bandung, West Java, "thousands of people crowded Madjalengka Square to hear nine leading members of the PKI and its affiliates in the city read themselves out of the party and announce the dissolution of party branches in the area" in October 1965. Twenty thousand alleged communists demonstrated against their own party in Kampar Ulu, Riau islands.[330] Lacking any connection with the leadership or policy feedback, people's morale in most sections was extremely low. Soviet diplomats noted with discomfort that predominantly young people demonstratively left communist organizations.[331] In North and West Sumatra, respectively, in accordance with the policies of All-Sumatra Military Commander Mokoginta, no less than 83,000 and 45,361 "repentant members of the PKI" were listed by January 1966 (out of an estimated total of 120,000 PKI members in North Sumatra).[332] Elsewhere, entire sections of other groups such as the leftist organization of ethnic Chinese, Baperki, and the National Federation of University Students also dissolved.[333]

Not infrequently, however, the renunciations were of no avail – in particular in Bali. PNI members murdered the renegades anyway, identifying them by their signatures on the declarations. In Central Java, 'communist' villages which had renounced their affiliation were nonetheless attacked by neighboring communities.[334] In other cases, the retractors were often forced to 'prove' their honesty by denouncing other members of their organization, who in turn could be arrested or murdered. It seems that some even took part in killings themselves.[335] Based on her own experience, Carmel Budiardjo has stressed the role of treason by PKI supporters under the persecution, highlighting the weakness of upper-level functionaries (this also cost the lives of Aidit and other party leaders). No doubt, many families and friends, too, withdrew from alleged or actual communists after October 1965, denying them any help.[336]

Yet if one remembers the many blank spots on the diagrams by the Indonesian armed forces of the communist party functionaries which Budiardjo described seeing (see p. 31), it would seem that networks of solidarity worked within the PKI organizations, and some also beyond this framework. After all, setting up social support for victims of persecution, namely orphans, was one of the key charges of which some Gerwani leaders were convicted in a show trial in 1975.[337] Pro-communist rail workers went on strike in order to obstruct the incoming RPKAD shock troops at Solo and other Central Javanese cities in October 1965; only after being confronted with machine guns by Sarwo Edhie did they resume work. SOBSI representatives abroad maintained that there were more strikes in Sumatra and North Sulawesi.[338] A longer-lasting impact was assured by less spectacular action, such as issuing incorrect non-involvement papers for former PKI activists or their children in the years after 1966, or even the shielding of leftist village heads so that they could hold on to their position.[339] Village communities may also have protected PKI members and sympathizers, saving them from death.[340] In other places, neighborhood associations prevented alleged communists from hiding.[341] Admittedly, there are few reports about the rescue of leftists by citizens of a different persuasion during the height of the killings;[342] but given the lasting popularity of the 1965 murders, not many of these stories are likely to have been passed down even if they happened. More important, though, were apparently leftist comradeship and family ties. In a fascinating account, Ibu Marni has revealed the existence of networks of the former Motor Vehicles Workers Union and sympathizing soldiers near Magelang, Central Java, regularly warning bus passengers without proper identity papers of impending army checkpoints in the late 1960s, when the hunt for communists still continued.[343] It appears that such passive resistance cushioned some of the impact of the persecution.

In the longer run, many former leftists also sought protection and support within religious communities, particularly by joining the Catholic and Protestant Churches. These had already gained considerable numbers of members since the 1950s – in part due to the 1961 regulation that there were only five recognized monotheistic religions, more strictly applied under Suharto – but in the second half of the 1960s their growth rates increased rapidly. They gained 2.8 million members in the six years after 1965 and allegedly 250,000 members within two months.[344] Relief work and mental support for long-term political prisoners earned the Churches special respect.[345] It wasn't communists alone who accounted for this trend – tens of thousands of ethnic Chinese became Catholics and Protestants as well. It is, moreover, safe to assume that many of those who joined Hinduism or Buddhism, especially in Java, or Christian beliefs in West Timor, were former syncretists, animists, or adherents of the polytheistic religions which were not officially recognized.[346] In the strictly Islamic province of Aceh, 2,000 Chinese were said to have been forced to convert to Islam in 1966. The pressure in other regions could be just as large; almost all traditional-syncretist Sasaks in Lombok converted to Islam between 1965 and 1975, and many in the Yogyakarta area.[347] But this sometimes led to an anti-Islamic backlash. Some communists seem to have sought protection by religious communities in the months of the most intense mass murder. Some fled to mosques or temples – often in vain.[348] The bulk of conversions, however, were meant to safeguard

former members of leftist organizations, Chinese, and religious dissenters from ongoing persecution and to help them in case they were
arrested again. Viewed from another angle, this was a more or less
conformist act of social self-integration by either disguising or revok-
ing earlier held ideas or beliefs.

For those who did not want to bow to the enormous strains,
no legal ways were left, so what remained was armed resistance.
However, politically, structurally, and psychologically, the PKI and its
members were ill prepared for fighting. Since 1951, the party had made
every effort to work legally, to become part of the political system and
change it from within, working within a united front strategy but placing much emphasis on elite conflicts. It also turned from a cadre party
into a mass movement with "a loose organization."[349] In areas where
PKI organizations had been banned or restricted in 1960, the building
of a clandestine organization was somewhat less difficult after October
1965.[350] In early October 1965, PKI Chairman Aidit persuaded Central
Javanese party leaders to lie low and abstain from any militant activity. On the initiative of Politbureau member Lukman, soon even PKI
demonstrations ceased. According to the former head of the PKI's
children's organization, Aidit's secret instructions were called "the Tri
Panji formula: find your own escape, say you know nothing, you don't
know each other and have no connection with each other."[351] This was
tantamount to a tacit dissolution of party structures. However, local
party branches in parts of Central and East Java independently set up
systems of defense in October 1965, which could, however, only delay
the start of mass murders, which proved particularly fierce where the
PKI and NU were equally strong and violent conflicts had occurred
before September 1965.[352]

In the initial months – during the peak of the mass murders –
PKI functionaries, while unable even to restore contact with more
than a few regional sections of their party, amazed sympathizing foreign observers by their unrealistic optimism, their downplaying of the
gravity of the situation, and their faith in President Sukarno's will and
ability to save the PKI.[353] Both this and the Aidit line led to passivity.
Those communists who joined the PNI to create a new political platform for the left were disappointed when the Nationalist Party in general and its left wing in particular soon declined.

The culture of reformist mass politics implied that it took
the surviving underground PKI leadership almost a whole year to

make the decision for armed struggle[354] and another year to actually start fighting, which, however, even indirectly involved only a small minority of former members. In 1967, remnants of clandestine fighters, ethnically Chinese, who had fought the Malaysian government during the Confrontation in Sarawak, and PKI members staged an uprising in West Kalimantan that spread to other parts of the island in 1968. In East and especially in Central Java, namely around Blitar and Purwodadi, the bloody suppression of PKI guerrillas in 1968 claimed at least 4,000 lives – many prisoners after capture, unarmed peasants, but also the bigger part of the new Central Committee of the PKI. Armed PKI groups were also reported in parts of Sumatra and the Riau islands.[355] Aside from agrarian revolution, some of the communist fighters were moved by feelings of revenge for the mass murders of 1965–66. Several purportedly responsible NU and PNI activists were killed in the years of 1967–68, though media reports were probably exaggerated.[356] Consequently, the PKI split into three different groups, only one of which supported armed struggle, whilst another condemned it as provoking the "senseless death [of] huge numbers of new comrades."[357] The uprisings wore down, as they proved no viable way to survival or political change as the communists could not overcome their social isolation combined with ruthless state oppression.

International dimensions

As much of the scarce research about the Indonesian killings of 1965–66 has been done by foreign scholars, they have devoted a good deal of attention to the role of their respective countries in the events of 1965–66. Much of this has been state-centered political history focused on the coup and counter-coup. Outside influences on the mass violence itself have only occasionally been explored. Leftist academics and journalists argued that foreign powers – the US government, the CIA, Britain, Australia, Japan, or others – masterminded the coup and possibly the murders, whereas conservatives tried to downplay the role of their governments. In my study, it is important to specify foreign influences not only on the Indonesian government but also on non-state actors to come to a more comprehensive judgment about dynamics in Indonesia.

Several factors restricted foreign involvement. Even if one would agree that external forces had much of an influence on the Indonesian military, which I doubt, the decentralized nature of the process of destruction would have required foreign powers to have made an impact on political and religious groups, and even village communities. There is no evidence for this. Moreover, in order not to compromise the Indonesian military in the eyes of Indonesian public opinion, where nationalism ran high, governments from capitalist countries adopted a "low posture" policy of tacit or confidential support, refraining from giving large, visible economic aid.[358] Due to pressure from the British and Australian governments, plus the attempt to not strengthen Sukarno's government, little foreign material or financial aid was given through March 1966, despite tacit support for the military, with Japan playing the most important role as a creditor.

From foreign sympathy for the military in their campaign against the PKI and Sukarno, one cannot conclude that the murders were always endorsed. Some diplomats of the time tried to make a distinction between these two things, shuddering at the bloodbath. Several politicians, however, expressed far fewer reservations, and this had a longer history. In 1958, the US government had logistically supported the Permesta uprising against President Sukarno's central government; during a 1962 meeting, US President Kennedy and British Prime Minister Harold Macmillan had "agreed to liquidate President Sukarno, depending upon the situation and available opportunities." In July 1965, Secretary of State Dean Rusk mentioned the "potential and hoped for Army-PKI confrontation."[359] In July 1966, Australian Prime Minister Harold Holt would remark in a speech at the River Club in New York, "with 500,000 to 1,000,000 Communist sympathizers knocked off, I think it is safe to assume a reorientation has taken place" in Indonesia, shortly after Dutch Foreign Minister Joseph Luns (later a NATO Secretary General) noted with satisfaction "the blow dealt to the communists (from which they are not likely to recover in the foreseeable future)."[360] The US State Department's Bureau of Intelligence and Research rejoiced that, due to the killing of up to 300,000 communists, and as another estimated 1.6 million Indonesian communists had renounced their membership, leaving only 100,000, the number of communists in non-socialist countries worldwide had dropped by 42 percent within one year.[361]

At a lower level, British Ambassador Andrew Gilchrist reported on October 5, 1965 from Jakarta: "I have never concealed from you my belief that a little shooting in Indonesia would be an essential preliminary to effective change." A US Embassy report called the "destruction of PKI property" a "heart-warming but largely symbolic act," and the impatient West German ambassador complained in early November – amidst rapidly spreading massacres – that the "army continues its anti-communist cleansing campaign step by step with a slowness only comprehensible by Indonesian standards."[362] In the Australian foreign ministry's papers, a secret memo can be found that stated no real improvement of the situation in Indonesia could be reached without the killing of President Sukarno, who was regarded as a leftist.[363] A foreign diplomat was reported to have said in a group discussion about the killings: "I regard myself as a liberal, but I find that my mind, in relief I suppose because the P.K.I. [...] is not now about to take over, is much less shocked than I might expect by what has happened."[364]

This failure, or even positive excitement, was not merely that of some officials, but an issue of broader social responsibility. "No congressman denounced it on the floor of Congress, and no major U.S. relief organization offered help," as Noam Chomsky and Edward Herman have noted. (A notable exception among politicians was Robert Kennedy, and some US academicians and missionaries did help.) A similar response can be observed in Australian political circles and the media community, where the issue of Australia's role was deflected by stories about chaotic violence and the allegedly moderate character of the Suharto regime.[365]

While there is little evidence that capitalist countries specifically contributed to the genesis of the September 30, 1965 coup, they threw their weight behind the Indonesian military shortly afterwards by means of propaganda, along lines developed months earlier. After a few days of assessment of the situation – and at a point on October 5 when Ambassador Green stated he was not sure that the PKI was substantially involved in the "30 September Movement" coup – the US Embassy nonetheless strongly advised the State Department and media such as Voice of America to launch an anti-communist campaign, with daily instructions wired by Ambassador Green on where to put the emphasis ("spread the story of the PKI's guilt, treachery and brutality"). But then, as Green wrote in another telegram on October 5, "it's now or never"; he was not sure of the decisiveness of the army and wished to push them into confronting the PKI. It took the Australian Ministry of External Affairs not even that long; from October 1 on, an official called Radio Australia – widely received in Indonesia – every afternoon with recommendations on how to report the events in Indonesia. "[I]mpressing on Radio Australia that it is a particularly important instrumentality in the present situation," the station was urged to discredit the PKI, implicate China, and to not label the Indonesian military as "right-wing," pro-Western, or as isolated in their effort to crush the PKI. Ambassador Keith Shann in Jakarta regularly sent or was asked for his advice at the Department of External Affairs, sometimes forwarding requests by Indonesian officers ("I can live with most of this, even if we must be a bit dishonest for a while"). According to suggestions by British officers in Singapore on October 5 (a key date, 24 hours after the exhumation of the murdered generals and the start of the army propaganda campaign against the PKI with the forgery about mutilations), British intelligence delivered fabricated material for an anti-communist crusade also denouncing China through covert channels. It seems that the CIA supplied similar material and that this was what its employees regarded as their agency's substantial contribution to triggering the crackdown on the communists.[366] In late October, the British Foreign Office sent Norman Reddaway, an Information Research Department specialist in anti-communist propaganda, to Singapore to supply British and foreign journalists with edited authentic and fabricated material with the purposes of discrediting the PKI (including inventions about alleged communist plans for mass slaughter after a successful coup), implicating the PRC, bringing down Sukarno, supporting the pro-Suharto version of the October 1, 1965 coup, but concealing any news about mass slaughter. The BBC correspondent for Southeast Asia in Singapore, who visited this officer "several times in a week," claims to have been manipulated by him.[367] What the media should report seems also to have been discussed between US, British, and Australian representatives.[368]

All of this led to a synergy between army controlled media inside Indonesia and foreign sources who took up questionable information from each other.[369] This way, the free media of free countries played a part in creating a pogrom atmosphere in Indonesia. Yet it was limited by the small number of radio sets (3.5 million in 1963) and daily newspaper readers; the relatively most effective foreign broadcasting station was Radio Australia, while Indonesians were suspicious of the BBC and Radio Malaysia as enemy stations, and Voice of America was difficult to receive.[370]

Within genocide studies, there are extensive debates about 'intervention.' Many such studies operate from the assumption that indifferent but good-natured 'Western' governments have to be pushed to come to the rescue of threatened people globally.[371] With regard to the Indonesian persecutions in late 1965, capitalist governments did everything in their power to not intervene precisely in order to *not* prevent the bloodbath. Great Britain and Australia were entangled in a low-level military conflict with Indonesia during the "Confrontation" over Malaysia from 1963 to 1966 that tied up the majority of Indonesian troops, mainly on Borneo. Before the Indonesian military launched their full-scale attack on the PKI and its members in mid-October – at the latest by October 8, 1965 – General Nasution (alarmed by the USA announcing the evacuation of their citizens from the country) approached the British and Australian governments through intermediaries in order to make sure that they would not seize the opportunity for a military strike against Indonesia while the army cracked down on domestic communists. The fear of a British–Malaysian attack on Sumatra had initially prompted Suharto to deny General Idris permission to move troops into Medan to hunt down communists. Based on their own deliberations (starting October 6) as well as at the urging of the US government, the British and Australian governments, against some Malaysian resistance, assured the Indonesian armed forces through the same channels that they would not interfere because they wanted the Indonesian military to move against the communists.[372] A US message about the planned British military inactivity was to reach Nasution on October 14, at which his aide told Ambassador Green "that this was just what was needed by way of assurances that we (the army) weren't going to be hit from all angles as we move to straighten things out here." Three days later, RPKAD troops arrived for their murderous campaign in Central Java. In fact, US diplomats had been pondering such a British–Malaysian assurance in the event of a future showdown between the military and PKI as early as nine months prior to the October 1, 1965 coup.[373] In October 1965, ships of the British navy would even escort an Indonesian troop transport under Panama's flag along the Straits of Malacca from North Sumatra to Java – as recalled by a man on board who would become PKI Chairman Aidit's killer in Central Java on November 22, 1965.[374] In this way, barely noticed by scholars to date, capitalist governments deliberately created what the Indonesian army saw as a precondition for their crackdown on the communists. The army raised the question of whether the British and Australians would remain militarily inactive at the same time as they started their anti-communist slander campaign, and waited for the response before starting full-scale slaughter.

A number of US representatives went even further. Through the US Embassy, the CIA passed on lists with names and further particulars of 5,000 communists to the Indonesian army in the fall of 1965. The embassy also provided its own lists, having gathered a card index with details of roughly 2,000 communist functionaries. With the approval of Ambassador Green, the embassy's Political Counselor, Robert J. Martens, handed the lists to an aide of Adam Malik. Malik passed them via another middleman to General Suharto. In return, information about the arrest or killing of members of the PKI and their affiliated organizations was sent back to the embassy, where officials checked names off the lists.[375] As stated earlier, given the fragmentary knowledge of the army about even leading PKI functionaries and those of PKI-affiliated mass organizations, this kind of US support is likely to have contributed to the death of hundreds of people. In addition, managers of US-owned plantations furnished the Indonesian military with the names of troublesome communist union activists who, as a result of their denunciation, were arrested and often killed. An American on a Goodyear rubber estate in Sumatra estimated that on his plantation alone, 290 people had been killed by early January 1966 (in this case, his personal involvement is unclear). In later years, political prisoners would serve as forced workers on some of the same plantations, providing even cheaper labor than before. Prisoner barracks were built right on plantation land.[376]

Just as significant could be the delivery of weapons to the Indonesian military that they could use for the mass slaughter. In 1965, their existing equipment was largely of Soviet origin due to close Indonesian–Soviet relations. In a gruesome twist, many Indonesian communists were in fact shot with Soviet firearms. However, when the Indonesian army developed additional demand for such weaponry, they turned to other foreign suppliers. As a result of the particular circumstances, the circle of potential partners was narrow.[377] Debates here have focused on the role of the USA. Hard evidence for US deliveries of arms is scarce, but it has been corroborated that the CIA allowed and organized the shipment of small arms to Indonesia "to arm Moslem and nationalist youth in Central Java for use against PKI," aimed at the "elimination of the [communist] elements." However, the number of arms supplied was probably limited.[378] In addition, in early December Ambassador Green agreed to the suggestion that through Adam Malik the US provide the KAP-Gestapu, which was "still carrying [the] burden of current repressive efforts targeted against [the] PKI, particularly in central Java," with 50 million rupiahs. Yet by black market value, this amounted only to about US$5,000.[379] Allegedly, the West German foreign secret service (*Bundesnachrichtendienst*) delivered sub-machine guns and radio equipment worth DM300,000 to the Indonesian military.[380]

In fact, of all countries, Swedish arms supplies seem to have been more substantial. According to a report by an Indonesian refugee in Japan, Osman Jusuf Helmi, from early December 1965, Suharto or Nasution had signed "a contract with Sweden for an emergency purchase of $10,000,000 worth of small arms and ammunition to be used for annihilating elements of the Indonesian Communist Party (PKI)."[381] By late January 1966, the Indonesian army had run out of ammunition, and Nasution asked "the Swedes" for more, despite the fact that the army already owed the Swedish company Bofors half a million US dollars for past deliveries. At that point, Bofors not only insisted on due payments, but Swedish sources let the Australian ambassador in Jakarta know that, even after those payments, no more ammunition would be shipped.[382] As we have seen, concerns about the slaughter at the Swedish Embassy did grow some months later, but apparently after the fact.

There are a few documents that suggest that the capitalist powers tried to restrain the violence through the Indonesian military as well. Oddly, it was the East German Consul General who reported that the US, British, Canadian, Australian, and other diplomats had expressed their dissatisfaction with the "brutal way of proceeding by the Army (arrests, torture)" because the army could discredit itself and thereby render its own future leading role in Indonesian politics impossible.[383] Maybe this reflected wishful thinking, based on one of the many rumors circulating in Jakarta at that time, because not much of this can be corroborated by other sources. The French ambassador was said to have made such an intervention, anyway.[384] Probably

there was more to reports that the Japanese and Singaporean governments set an end to the persecution of the Chinese as a precondition
for the intensification or renewal of trade relations, respectively, on the
grounds that much of Indonesia's foreign trade was handled by ethnic Chinese merchants. European and US businessmen had expressed
similar concerns.[385] However, the persecution and harassment of ethnic Chinese did continue after that in 1966, and, in general, there is no
indication that foreign objections to mass violence, if they did exist,
had any impact on Indonesians.

This also applies to protests by socialist countries, although
they were somewhat muted. The government of the People's Republic
of China and the Chinese press had initially been reluctant, but the
Chinese Embassy started on October 18, 1965 to issue a series of fourteen diplomatic protest notes within six months. Those, however, were
dealing mainly with violent attacks on diplomatic institutions and violent attacks on ethnic Chinese – concentrating on those with Chinese
citizenship – in Indonesia. Press reports from China show the same
pattern, giving relatively little prominence to the destruction of the
PKI and the mass murder of its members.[386] If anything, the Chinese
remonstrations, ridiculed in Indonesia after a while because of a lack
of consequences, led only to fiercer anti-Chinese propaganda and
action. Until about April 1966, Chinese foreign policy seems to have
still been based on the hope that Sukarno would stop the political conflict between the two countries, though trade and aid were seemingly
stopped as early as October 1965.[387]

Contrary to some diplomatic and historical narratives, the
Soviet (and other Eastern European) media did report the events, but in
a somewhat defused manner, often in a matter-of-fact way and lacking
details, in order to not undermine diplomatic relations. In hindsight,
the East German Foreign Ministry listed maintaining good economic
and diplomatic relations with Indonesia as having been their priorities
even when Suharto had seized power.[388] There were enough Soviet official or semi-official reactions to fill two volumes with documents.[389]
As far as the Indonesian communists were concerned, despite Soviet
aid efforts for prisoners, there sometimes seemed to be more concern
in the Soviet Union or GDR about the destruction of the PKI as a party
than for the mass murders. By contrast, Polish citizens were reported
to have sent protest petitions en masse, a fact that was explained by
an observer with the supposition that communists there felt much less

secure of their rule than in the USSR and had more personal sympathies for the situation of their Indonesian comrades. Likewise, in October 1965 Hungarian, Rumanian, and Bulgarian diplomats had together called on Indonesian newspapers to protest "bestial" attacks on communists.[390]

Even some hard-boiled anti-communist diplomats and journalists from capitalist countries who left no doubt about their support for the military–rightist bid for power were amazed about the neglect of the Indonesian slaughters in the international media and politics. "If one considers that 86,100 died in Hiroshima, one cannot help but be surprised how little attention the higher number of victims in the Indonesian purge has drawn in worldwide public opinion," commented German Ambassador Werz.[391] A journalist wrote: "Not least disturbing is the outside world's lack of concern for the greatest mass murder since the Nazi genocide in Europe and the communal killings that accompanied the partition of India and Pakistan. The world knew little [...] [and] seemed to care even less, perhaps because the victims were only Communists and Communist sympathizers." "[No one bothered,] so long as they were Communists, that they were being butchered," remembered Howard Federspiel, Indonesia expert in the US State Department.[392] Such indifference from the very outset has helped to virtually wipe out the Indonesian murders of 1965 from international public and private memory.

Governments of capitalist countries provided some aid for the 1965–66 massacres. Yet there were definite limits to the foreign influence and manipulation of Indonesian affairs. The American name lists included only the names of 1 percent or less of the dead in the 1965–66 violence; only a minority of the victims were murdered by shooting, let alone with Swedish or American precision weapons; foreign money and material can hardly have played a major role. Foreigners were partners, not part of the coalition for violence.

On the other hand, Indonesia had challenged the international capitalist order by policies hostile to Britain and the United States, by its leadership of the non-aligned movement, by developing close relations to Maoist China, and even by setting up rival organizations to the United Nations and the International Olympic Committee. So global entanglements regarding the 1965–66 killings cannot be neglected. Indonesia represented one case in a series of right-wing military dictatorships set up in the mid-1960s, be it as a result of direct US military intervention, as in Vietnam, or with more subtle 'Western' support, as in Brazil in 1964, in Argentina, Ghana, or in Greece in 1967. Marshall Green, US ambassador in Jakarta as of late 1965, had been involved in toppling the nationalist–leftist Dominican government by a military US invasion earlier that year.[393]

Less bloody (except in Vietnam), the events in these countries nonetheless resulted in corrupt 'developmental' military dictatorships. They were not simply puppet states, yet favorable to international firms (drawing much of their profits from their control over foreign trade and investment) while, given their lawlessness, creating ambivalent conditions for the rise of domestic capital. The New York based consulting company Business International stated of Indonesia in 1978: "'New Order' policies that consistently favor foreign investment have been possible only because of the post-1965 restructuring that excludes important groups from power and applies a high degree of pressure and coercion against opponents of the regime."[394] The overthrow of the Chilean Allende government in a similar coup in 1973 was foreshadowed by CIA-inspired graffiti, leaflets, and postcards carrying the slogan "Jakarta is approaching" – an attempt to turn the mass killings of 1965–66 into a global menace to the political left.[395]

The Cold War generated an atmosphere of conflict and ideological influences transgressing borders, yet it can be seen as a worldwide confrontation not only between superpowers manipulating non-industrialized countries (that is, in the foreign relations framework), but rather as an international struggle between social groups for economic and political power. The USA, the Netherlands, Eastern European countries, Australia, and others had trained Indonesian university students or military officers for years, trying to promote their models of society, with the US military academies, the Ford Foundation and Berkeley proving quite successful.[396] For the Indonesian military–business mafia that eliminated its rivals in 1965–66, the Cold War provided a national space, an opportunity to proceed with mass violence minimally challenged by any international objections. Global realpolitik from the 1960s to the 1980s meant that Suharto's Indonesia – too important to be offended – was wooed from all sides. Even if, for example, Soviet Prime Minister Kosygin condemned the Indonesian slaughters behind closed doors when meeting Indonesian Foreign Minister Adam Malik in Moscow, this did not change much, not least as both sides were negotiating a rescheduling of Indonesia's

considerable debt.[397] Socialist countries too, were, above all, talking business and pursuing national interests, be it the Soviet Union,
East Germany, or China. Such global opportunism, together with the
robust approval of violence by some capitalist regimes, entailed that a
murderer like Malik could even become President of the UN General
Assembly in 1971–72.[398]

Conclusion

The Indonesian slaughters of 1965–66 rank among the bloodiest anti-
communist purges of the twentieth century such as in the Chinese,
Russian, and Spanish Civil Wars, the German invasion of the USSR,
1941–44, and the Vietnam and Korean Wars. All claimed the lives of
countless civilians, but Indonesia was the most one-sided case of such
violence, even if many other purges were also participatory in character. The Nazi terror against political opponents inside Germany, the
Dirty 'War' of the military against leftists in Argentina 1976–83, or
the Pinochet dictatorship in Chile pale by comparison of numbers.

   Neither state violence controlled and manipulated by the military, nor popular rage, nor the organization imparted by political
party machineries and religious groups alone can explain the power
of the 1965–66 killings; what was crucial was the combination of all
three. In October 1965, there teamed up a coalition with diverse interests which overlapped in their strong will to destroy the PKI and to
murder communists – for reasons that varied by region, persecutor
group, and political and cultural context. What decided a person's
life was not only a matter of an abstract confrontation between the
state apparatus and an individual: it depended – aside from a degree of
chance – on whether somebody had an interest in killing that particular human being, who it was, or how many there were, and how strong
this urge turned out to be. This web of interests created a network of
persecution which could result in a person being repeatedly arrested[399]
or facing death (yet opposing action could equally entail protection
or an opportunity to hide). Where strong motives for persecution in
different contexts overlapped – say in the case of an active communist transmigrant squatter belonging to a religious minority – there
could be almost no escape. Where violence fanned out and was only in
the interest of a few, or murder was not a first choice, the chance for

survival was higher (as for ethnic Chinese or animists). Taking these other persecuted groups into account also enables us to place the violence of 1965–66 within the longer-term background of violence in Indonesia – class conflicts in the transformation of the countryside, the establishing of a non-Chinese domestic elite, migration, clashes between the nation state and regional concerns, between secular modernists, traditional sects, and orthodox Muslims, and between foreign interests and locals.

The coalition for violence also helps explain how pro-violence discourses could become hegemonic even though they were not universally shared. Propaganda, intimidation, and coercion played important roles in that process, which, however, was multi-polar and not simply state-centered. This is about the active adoption of propaganda as much as it is about its distribution. Anti-communist media agitation did not originate only from the military but also from political party press organs. People spread rumors. The new course of persecuting leftists had to be enforced within all political parties (the PNI on a national level was the last, in April 1966), within every ministry, administrations at all levels, and in every town and village. In this process it was important that anti-communist youths increasingly occupied the public space with symbolic acts. With pressure coming from all directions, arguments about communist treachery gained credibility to the point where even many leftists lost faith.

Violence decreased in January 1966, once interests within the coalition diverged and the struggle for power increasingly took priority over murdering communists. In the same year, the coalition began to break apart entirely over differing political agendas, the competition for opening elite positions, Suharto sidelining any personal rivals of stature,[400] and in controversies over precisely the issue of popular political participation. In the end, the political process resulted in the suffocating atmosphere of a numbing military dictatorship. Many portrayed Suharto later as having betrayed them and the common cause, without acknowledging, however, that the goals pursued by different groups and forces inside Indonesia when persecuting the alleged communists had been disparate from the start.

The participatory character of violence, as was obvious in Indonesia, is one of the main characteristics of an extremely violent society. Therefore it is important to note what happened to participatory tendencies in Indonesian politics after 1965. Many of the protagonists of the violence of 1965–66 lost out in the struggle for power precisely because they advocated principles of political participation. The PNI, despite victory for its right wing in an April 1966 party congress, remained deeply divided, without a clear political profile, and also lost influence with the demise of Sukarno.[401] The position of the Nahdlatul Ulama – representing strict adherents of Islam and especially with a rural basis – appeared much more promising, but it was outmaneuvered by Suharto and the moderately Islamic and modernist military elite, starting from Suharto's first Cabinet on March 24, 1966, in which the NU received few seats (NU's "terrible Thursday"). This trend continued with their low representation in the 1966 and 1967 co-optations to parliament (MPRS) and the repeated postponement of general elections, despite the NU consistently calling for them.[402] When elections were finally held in 1971, marred by manipulations favoring the regime's organization Golkar, the NU only managed to repeat their result of 1955 (gaining 18.7 percent of the votes). Much of the NU's political agenda, namely Islamic laws, remained wishful thinking, which turned the party into the principal lawful opposition force. Conflicts between younger and established functionaries and different currents that had already existed before October 1965 added to the problems. Subchan, the former head of the KAP-Gestapu, was elected Vice-Chairman of parliament and managed to climb to the top of his party for some time, but retreated from a leading role in politics in 1972, only forty-one years old, bemoaning the NU's discrimination in the elections.[403]

The KAP-Gestapu had basically attained its goals by March 1966. A month later, Secretary-General Harry Tjan warned in vain that "the most important thing in the 'Post-PKI period' was unity of purpose."[404] With the member organizations growing apart, the Front's activities decreased rapidly, virtually ceasing by mid-1966, though it was not disbanded until 1967.[405] The student action fronts, namely KAMI, proved more resilient, staging forceful demonstrations that still succeeded in bringing down cabinet ministers in 1968. Not infrequently, student protests were about claiming more elite positions, such as in parliament, government, and bureaucracy, and some succeeded in securing these.[406] Under Suharto's rule, the "generation of 1966," as well as succeeding student generations, showed that they were not merely puppets but had their own political goals: they continued to rebel against social crises, inflation, and corruption, and were uneasy about the middle class to which they too belonged.[407] Students would finally help bring down Suharto in 1998. Yet cracks within student Action Fronts, too, began to show by mid-1966 when the high-school students' organization KAPPI split because Muhammadiyah-affiliated groups claimed a leading role. The attempt of KAMI to extend their influence to Central and East Java in 1966 ended in disaster, with violent confrontations with PNI youth, the arrest of a KAMI delegation by the local military and civilian authorities and their military relief by RPKAD.[408]

Military figures were affected by the curbing of political participation as well. The best-known example is the political neutralization of Nasution, Chairman of Parliament (MPRS) from 1966 to 1972, who supported an alternative form of representative system, albeit still with a strong military influence, and who arguably lost the power struggle against Suharto precisely because he did not seek unlimited personal power. It was consistent with this approach that he pursued a career in parliament. Worse, he had actively tackled corruption and was not Javanese.[409] Kemal Idris and others were marginalized, too. Sarwo Edhie – later father-in-law of current Indonesian President Susilo Bambang Yudhoyono, himself a former general who holds Edhie in high esteem – reputedly lost his command of the RPKAD in April 1967 because of his too-populist attitude, especially his continuing proximity to unruly university students. He was sidelined despite a number of his questionable 'achievements' for the regime (oppressing the uprising in West Irian and chairing the army's Military Academy from 1971–77, training a generation of influential regional commanders), and came into conflict with Suharto more than once, before he resigned in protest from parliament in 1988.[410]

Political structures and practice resembled less and less a representative system. The parties protested in vain against the accumulation of power by regional military commanders in their capacity as Pepelrada (Regional Dwikora Authority).[411] The combined daily print run of Indonesia's newspapers dropped from 1.4 million in 1966 to 750,000 in August 1967. Village chiefs, who had been elected up to 1965, were appointed by the authorities under the 'New Order,' and under the principle of the "floating masses" no party was allowed to have a representation below the district level, let alone in villages. Women especially were deprived of representation. Many women's organizations were dissolved and in part replaced by "Women's Duty," a compulsory association for the wives of officials.[412] What remained, however, was an increased role for neighborhood associations, monitoring anything suspicious, plus large civil defense units.[413]

Sukarno had already succeeded in reducing the number of political parties from the more than one hundred parties and political groups contesting the 1955 elections – especially with the regulations on political parties of 1959 that left twelve parties, a number cut back to nine by September 1965.[414] Continuing and radicalizing this policy, the military regime in 1973 coerced all remaining parties into two, the nationalist Unified Development Party (PPP) and the Islam-based Indonesian Democratic Party (PDI) – aside from Golkar which (officially defined as a functional group) was excepted from the restrictions of party politics.[415] One of the most important persecutors, General Mokoginta, the military commander in North Sumatra and for All-Sumatra, threatened in November 1965 that the political parties either had to change or he would abolish all of them.[416] The extermination of communists had been brought about under demands for political co-determination, accompanied by a short blossoming of political participation, only to be later turned into a powerful argument against party politics and disunity by the military–bureaucratic faction which prevailed.[417]

The 1965–66 killings were the foundation of a new "state system"[418] but also of a changed social order in which the poor were silenced once again. The mass murders would have a powerful effect on the interaction among people in many places and between citizens and government representatives for decades. The "alliance" against the PKI was not merely caused by the party's radicalized strategy since 1963, with social change or nation-state building as "merely societal contexts."[419] Instead, the coalition for violence involved a variety of important social groups and varying political visions of the future of Indonesia's society.

3 PARTICIPATING AND PROFITEERING

The destruction of the Armenians, 1915–23

While the previous case study on Indonesia attempted to cover the participatory character of violence within the wide range of dynamics in an extremely violent society, this chapter examines in depth one set of motivations for popular participation in violence. Since I am focusing on the fate of a middlemen minority – a group considered ethnically different and among which is an important part of a country's economic elite – it makes sense to concentrate on economic factors. There was much to gain for people who turned against Ottoman Armenians.[1]

In genocide studies, approaches related to the history of ideas and ideologies dominate. Most studies focus on racial thinking, the formation of nation-states and ethnic identities, and religious hatred. Where the role and actions of the state, interpreted as dictated by certain ideologies, are put in the center, economic contexts remain understudied as a purportedly secondary aspect of mass violence. Thus, some of the reasons for popular participation in extreme violence are understated, and, as a result, the active role of social groups itself.[2]

The importance of robbery and social envy for the expulsion and murder of Ottoman Armenians has been repeatedly emphasized[3] but not as yet comprehensively researched. Probably over half of the Armenians who perished in World War I died from starvation, exhaustion, or dehydration on foot marches or in designated banishment areas. This was because they had been deprived of their livelihood, their homes, and their assets. Plunder and expropriation therefore go to the core of the mass deaths of Armenians. The businesses, jobs,

houses, land, possessions, and valuables of Armenians (9–10 percent of the population) represented a major incentive for expulsion,
deportation, and murder. Their assets were equivalent to two and a
half peacetime state budgets, or more than all foreign investments in
the Ottoman Empire.[4] This chapter explores how the drive for material gain, and competition for the booty, including war financing and
the resettlement of refugees by the government, led to citizens in great
numbers supporting acts of violence against Armenians or actively
engaging in violence themselves.

To be sure, the Armenians were just the worst affected of
several victim groups in the late Ottoman Empire. Hundreds of thousands of Greeks, Kurds, Turks, Assyrians, and Chaldeans perished in
massacres, deportations, expulsions, and starvation, as well as tens of
thousands of Arabs. To cover them all would go beyond the scope of
this chapter, and though some of the same mechanisms used for the
persecution of the Armenians are documented for that of other groups,
the Armenian example also lends itself to examination because of
the relatively well-developed research and the many primary sources
available.

Context

From 1914 to 1918, the Ottoman Empire contained a populace under
enormous stress. Leading a four-front war whilst virtually without a
steel industry, the country was even more than the other parties in the
Great War gripped by ruined state finances, lack of consumer goods,
inflation, a desperate economic situation, and starvation. Like elsewhere, the unprecedented mobilization of soldiers, labor, and material
resources required an expansion of the state apparatus. Four years of
war for self-assertion by the Turkish national movement followed until
1923.

The need to fund the maintenance of the Empire against
foreign pressures and nationalist movements had for a long time
overstretched the state's capabilities, given its outdated taxation system. This had resulted in state bankruptcy in 1877, after which the
Ottoman Public Debt Administration was established – a debt service office run by European powers that, circumventing the government budget, collected 30 to 40 percent of the taxes in the Empire

directly, with its 6,000 employees across the provinces representing the biggest bureaucracy in the country. Sliding into dependency on European powers, the Ottoman state had to grant European citizens privileges such as tax exemptions, separate legal process, their own schools, and religious missions, losing part of its sovereignty over customs and economic policies. This further undermined military spending, contributing to the Empire losing between 1908 and 1913 Bosnia and Herzegovina, Albania, Montenegro, Macedonia, Epirus, western Thrace, Crete, the Dodekanes islands, Libya, and Yemen in wars that exhausted the country financially and militarily. After these disasters, the Ottoman war aims in World War I – a war it could hardly afford – remained largely defensive, except for bigger ambitions in the northeast.[5] It was widely regarded as a war for national independence and survival, while powers such as Russia, Britain, and France attempted to acquire large swathes of Ottoman territory (successfully in the case of Britain and France). In this context, official war aim number one was the abrogation of the 'capitulations' (foreign privileges), and with it the forging of a Muslim commercial elite that officials considered reliable.[6]

Within the Empire, among a population mostly living in rural areas, Muslims held most of the positions in bureaucracy and government, since 1908 mostly led by the partly liberal, secularist, but statist and more and more Ottoman-nationalist Committee for Union and Progress (CUP).[7] Large parts of the economic elites were found among Christian and Jewish minorities (most Christians and Jews lived in utter poverty, too). Given their leading roles in foreign and domestic trade, banking, and rudimentary industries, Armenians and Greeks in particular were increasingly viewed by Muslims as being aligned to foreign interests. The Armenians, once dubbed the faithful *millet* (religious community), came gradually into conflict with the government and other groups. Under intensifying persecution, especially after the 1894–96 and 1909 massacres, in which up to 200,000 were murdered, Armenian politicians called for foreign support in their quest for autonomy and protection, and an autonomy statute for six northeastern provinces was imposed by European powers in 1914. Hence Armenians became collectively portrayed as disloyal and a threat to the territorial integrity and economic sovereignty of the country, and particularly as potential allies of Russia, where there were also many Armenians.

After the general mobilization in August 1914 and the Ottoman Empire's entry in the war in late October, and especially after a disastrously failed offensive against the Russians in January 1915, incorrectly blamed on Armenian 'treachery,' harassment by the authorities against Armenians and violent excesses by Ottoman troops and Turkish and Kurdish irregulars took place more and more frequently. Armenian civil servants were sacked, servicemen put in Labor Battalions, and villagers pillaged, and sometimes massacred. Some Armenian men responded with desertion and acts of armed resistance, triggering fierce government reprisals culminating in uprisings, army sieges of Armenian quarters in Zeitun and Van, Eastern Anatolia, and local deportations in March and April 1915. They coincided with a Russian offensive from Iran into northeastern Anatolia and British landings near the Dardanelles. In this situation, the Ottoman authorities, partially at suggestions from the military, decided, after local deportations, to collectively remove as a security threat all Armenians first from the northeastern provinces and Cilicia roughly from late April/May, then from adjacent provinces (from May/June), and from Thrace, Western and Central Anatolia (from June/August 1915), and northern Syria and Mesopotamia (until fall 1915).[8] After some confusion about their destinations, about one million Armenians[9] were deported to western Mesopotamia and northern Syria; later on, many were brought to southern Syria and some to Lebanon and Palestine.

Deadly marches of undersupplied, progressively ragged, and emaciated Armenians over rough, winding mountain roads took place between May and October 1915. Many perished from deprivation or in attacks by irregulars and armed men en route in the countryside, while assaults or pogroms within cities or towns were rare. Armenian men who were deported or already in the Labor Battalions were often led aside and massacred. In Van and Bitlis provinces and some other districts, most people were killed close to their homes. Mortality was highest among those from northeastern, Eastern, and parts of Central Anatolia, but lower for those driven out of Thrace, the Aegean, Cilicia, parts of southeastern Anatolia, and northern Syria. The worst theaters of death were Harput, Diyarbakir, and Trabzon provinces,[10] and the Taurus mountains. Of those who made it to the designated areas (mostly women and older children), hundreds of thousands more died from starvation, thirst, epidemics and state-organized massacres in the Syrian and Mesopotamian deserts from late 1915 to 1916. Then the persecution eased somewhat. Armenians from some regions of the Empire such as Constantinople and Smyrna/Izmir, in both cities with exceptions, Palestine, and parts of Syria, however, were never deported. The wide variety of treatment regionally, locally, and according to subgroups suggests that there existed no state program to murder all Armenians without exception and no long-term blueprints for deportations, merely activated in May 1915. Yet the Armenians did not just fall victim to government neglect or even to the incapacity of a benign state. A number of different institutions, like the CUP party apparatus, central and regional civil administrations, the army, the gendarmerie, and irregular *çetes*, groups of armed men from neighboring villages, subordinate to various authorities held responsibility, and scores of private citizens took violence into their own hands, shaping the experience of the victims. The number of Armenians killed is intensely contested but may have been around one million.

After the end of the war, many of those surviving in camps, in banishment, in hiding, with Muslim families, or in Russia tried to return home, but often faced mounting hostility as they claimed back their businesses, houses, and farms, or because they lacked sufficient enthusiasm for the emerging Turkish nationalist movement. In a gradual process, most survivors were thus forced to flee to the Soviet Union, Greece, Syria, or Palestine until 1924, and often onward to the USA and several European countries, leaving most of their possessions behind.

Policies

Ottoman government regulations determined that Armenians to be deported were allowed to take with them as many movable possessions as they could carry, as well as animals.[11] The rest was to be left behind. A June 10, 1915 decree provided that property commissions were to be established in every province or district to register Armenian property; under a chairman from the Directorate for the Settlement of Tribes and Immigrants (IAMM), every commission was to include one official from each of the Interior and Finance Ministries.[12] According to the September 26, 1915 provisory law about the liquidation of Armenian property, possessions, proceeds, and real estate were put at the disposal of either the Ministries for Finance or for Religious

Foundations. Theoretically, for every deportee an account was established, and the property commissions calculated credits and debts.[13] In some places, Armenians were allowed to deposit money for debtors with the Imperial Ottoman Bank, if officially approved. They were not allowed to sell landed property, or rent or mortgage it. In Adana, they were forced to give up real estate titles.[14] Generally, agricultural land was to be handed over to Muslim refugees for usufruct.[15]

These regulations emerged gradually in May and June 1915 parallel to the ensuing massive deportations. This does not support the view that a master plan for the removal and extermination policy had been in place;[16] at first, regional authorities lacked clear instructions about what to do with Armenian property.[17] The September 1915 provisory law probably served a number of objectives, among them to reduce the danger of embezzlement, to move toward the liquidation and utilization of assets of the Armenians, and to forestall foreign claims to Armenian property.[18]

Armenian survivor Ephraim Jernazian provided unique insights into the work of a liquidation commission for which he worked as an interpreter in Urfa: as instructed, the group that arrived on December 15, 1915 tried to sell Armenian possessions, to acquit debts of Armenian businessmen, and to collect their bills receivable. They sorted out many forged invoices by Turkish merchants. Yet prices for Armenian goods were set arbitrarily, from ridiculously low to above the real value. Only Muslims could buy them. At night, the chairman of the commission falsified the commission's books, embezzling substantial values. Local functionaries frequently had rugs and valuables removed illegally; people even used secret passages to plunder houses, largely before the commission arrived. In the local branch of the Imperial Ottoman Bank, the commission seized 140,000 gold coins, replacing them by the same sum in paper money (of lesser value in real market terms); the government needed gold coins for military purchases. Swiss missionary Jacob Künzler recalled that a succession of commissions followed each other at Urfa and all enriched themselves.[19] Other commissions in Adana, Bursa, and Trabzon provinces and in Kayseri favored immigrants, local notables, or Muslim merchants, selling or auctioning Armenian property at a fraction of its value.[20]

Publicly organized sell-offs occurred in towns across the Empire. Frequently, heaps of used Armenian clothing and sometimes children's shoes were auctioned.[21] Auctions were conducted by town criers who received half of a 5 percent tax on auctioned goods (the other 2½ percent was transferred to the government).[22] At Aintab, the household implements and merchandise of businesses were sold cheaply to the first interested person.[23]

A number of observers described how collected valuables and money were shipped to Constantinople.[24] Jacob Künzler served as witness at Urfa for the count of valuables (2,000 liras and jewelry) and for the sealing of the bags.[25] The reach of the Ottoman state went further: first, Armenians were sometimes forbidden to withdraw money from their accounts and banks were not allowed to accept additional deposits of money or valuables.[26] Later, the government tried – with partial success – to lay hands on money in Armenian accounts.[27]

In late 1915, the administration also attempted in vain to collect the credits of Armenian policy-holders from foreign insurance companies, arguing that they were virtually all dead and without heirs.[28] Plans for the emigration of surviving Armenians to the USA seem to have failed for financial and organizational reasons – the Ottoman authorities refused to let Armenians take any possessions with them, while the US government did not accept immigrants without financial means.[29]

These were not the only failures. Between regulations and reality yawned a gap. A struggle for the booty ensued between the state, local elites, and the common people. Not everybody, but large parts of the population tried to get their share. Even allowing for the fact that the numerous reports of foreign diplomats and missionaries resembled stereotypes of oriental chaos and corruption, the sources leave no doubt about the scramble for Armenian assets. When, in a 1921 account, Talaat Pasha admitted to mistakes, the most important one was not to have punished sharply enough (unauthorized) misappropriations of Armenian property.[30] Teams from the Interior Ministry, holding investigations from the fall of 1915 to early 1918, found 1,397 persons guilty of graft and corruption and handed them over to martial law courts. But this was only a tiny fraction of the offenders, and the coverage was uneven, with 75 percent coming from Sivas and Mamuret ul-Aziz provinces and Urfa district.[31] The target group was defined by and largely limited to public officials. Relatively few examples of authorities hindering ordinary citizens from looting are known.[32]

Government control over the property left behind was easier in large storage rooms than if the possessions still rested in the thousands of private dwellings which were impossible to guard. Yet even sealed buildings or warehouses were looted, with guards sometimes bribed or participating.[33] If Armenian property ended up unregistered in large warehouses, preventing theft was difficult and any idea of the return or forwarding of proceeds to the owners was "ridiculous."[34] "You could not look out of the window without seeing some one [sic] walking down the street carrying some sort of a load of booty, bought or stolen from Armenian houses," recalled missionary Henry Riggs from Harput, and US Consul Oscar Heizer described a similar scene from Trabzon: "A crowd of Turkish women and children follow the police like a lot of vultures and seize anything they can lay their hands on and when the valuable things are carried out of a house by the police they rush in and take the balance. I see this performance every day with my own eyes."[35]

In a race for houses, businesses, and valuables, governors, mayors, and local officials attempted to secure the best objects for themselves at bargain prices.[36] CUP functionaries, people with good relations to them, and war veterans had the best chances of receiving businesses or of leasing them for small fees, transforming themselves into capitalists.[37] After all, the CUP was a mass party that had claimed 850,000 members by 1909.[38] The case of Mihalıççık, near Eskişehir, was probably typical: the *kaimakan*, court officials, tax and treasury administrators, a title deeds officer, and gendarmes cooperated in a web of corruption whose main beneficiaries were the mayor, some assembly members, and several merchants. Real estate changed hands without charge and movable property "for nothing."[39] In Bursa, Armenians were coerced into signing over their houses and land to Muslims for a ridiculously low sum, which was then taken from them by force after they left the public office; CUP functionaries and notables shared the booty. Similar things happened in Ankara.[40] The governor of Aleppo province reported that he had consciously supported, "according to the intentions of the government," the transformation of Christian businesses into Muslim ones, with the latter up from 20 to 95 percent.[41]

The resources that the government devoted to Armenians on their marches, which lasted up to two months or more, were extremely limited. Very few guards per convoy were deployed – for allegedly extremely dangerous people. These gendarmes were unable to protect the deported even if willing (only some were). The deportees had to spend most of their time outside. If people were transported on the railways, then the authorities paid for part of the tickets, but they provided ox carts for those marching in only a few cases. No compensation was paid nor were land parcels allocated to the exiles, as the regulations had promised;[42] nor, seemingly, were the new houses envisioned by Talaat.[43] Armenians were supposed to get food rations or an allowance – during the marches many didn't. When they arrived in the exile areas the situation seems to have improved slightly, though many still starved to death. Their allotments were often embezzled by corrupt officials. Forbidden from seeking waged employment themselves, Armenians were dependent on the government for food and water, and often had to do hard work for very little money during food price inflation. If food was provided, deaths decreased.[44] Where Armenians or their families actually received a military officer's salary, they faced the same problem as other state servants: it was paid in paper money that had lost most of its value.[45]

Food, fuel, and transportation for the deportees were to be funded by the IAMM.[46] However, out of expenditures of 25 million piasters in 1915, and probably 100 million in 1916 (230,000 and 910,000 liras, respectively),[47] a mere 2.25 million piasters (21,000 liras) were used to support Armenians.[48] Even if completely handed out in 1915, this was less than 10 percent of the Directorate's budget, or just 2¼ piasters per capita, compared to 150 piasters spent per Muslim refugee in 1915–16.[49] In other words, Muslim 'immigrants' suffered from little cash support, yet Armenians received virtually nothing.

In financial terms, the most important objective of the state plunder of the Armenians was the seizure of landed property and the settlement of over one million refugees; first Muslims from the pre-1914 territorial losses.[50] Under normal conditions, the Ottoman state was – as it had shown in the decades before, with lethal consequences – in no position to fund the necessary, tremendously expensive settlement projects, which in 1913–14 also met with stiff local resistance and triggered bloody conflicts.[51] The authorities' inability to care for them led to the refugees living in misery, which made them turn to unrest and petty crime. However, there was a long-established practice of the Ottoman government relocating and settling by force certain minorities for policies of pacification, homogenization, and assimilation. In 1914, there were schemes to send Kurds, Armenians, and Arabs to Central or Western Anatolia, and Bosniaks, Circassians, and other Muslims to Eastern Anatolia. During World War I, these plans were radicalized and carried out in a new dimension.[52] Violence and the redistribution of real estate substituted for insufficient financial resources to facilitate the integration of these refugees, increasing by 862,000 dislocated from the northeastern front until 1918.[53]

With the start of the deportations of the Armenians in spring 1915, efforts for the settlement of pre-1914 refugees took off. Macedonian, Thracian, Bosnian, Albanian, or Bulgarian refugees were settled in Armenian houses and villages in and around Zeitun, Van, Marash, Muş, Diyarbakir, Harput, and Erzurum just days after the Armenians had been driven out (farms and animals could not be left untended for long), yet the Ministry of the Interior demanded more geographic and economic information about the vacancies from the provinces.[54] After some of this had already started, the Ottoman Cabinet determined that the IAMM in the Interior Ministry would organize the deportations of Armenians and administer their property, which could be used for the settlement of Muslim immigrants (who fell in the Directorate's competence, too).[55] This created a direct organizational link between deportations, property, and solving the immigration problem. Balkan refugees were later settled on orchard land in Bandirma on the Marmara coast, in Armenian houses in Samsun and Bursa, were concentrated in Adana even before the Armenian deportations took off, and arrived in the Pasin plain northeast of Erzurum at least shortly afterwards.[56] Even five weeks after the end of the war, the government still continued to settle some refugees on Armenian land and houses.[57]

In addition, the June 1915 regulations about the disposal of Armenian property provided for settling nomads, who would be responsible for the maintenance of buildings and cultivation of the land.[58] In reality, the government had to grapple with overwhelming new streams of refugees, so little actually happened with regard to, for example, the settlement of Bedouin tribes. Meanwhile, Kurds displaced by the Russian advance – or others, such as in Diyarbakir and Harput provinces, supposed to make room for Turkish-speaking refugees from the Russian front – were generally supposed to be shoveled to Central Anatolia for assimilation, and Turkophone Muslims to southeastern Anatolia to foster Turkification.[59] However, settlement offices channeled Kurds increasingly to the southeast as well. Here, many refugees felt neglected, their grievances not addressed, and, being pastoralists, were unable to quickly turn into peasants or townspeople even when given Armenian villages or houses and furniture, so a number of them moved on to Cilicia in 1916–17. In effect, repeated orders indicate that the authorities had difficulties in getting the desired people to the assigned places and keeping undesirables out.[60] Many Kurds were evacuated by force from the front zone, and some found themselves dispersed all over the Empire, lodged in Armenian houses along the Baghdad railway in Mesopotamia or abandoned begging in the streets of Mosul or Aleppo.[61] By October 1916, the IAMM had spent about one million liras (25 million piasters in 1915 and 80 million in 1916) on 702,900 refugees from the northeast – only 150 piasters per person – and had provided thousands with houses free of rent (10,000 in Sivas province alone).[62] As a result, the urge to use Armenian property remained strong. This policy created several waves of settlement; in deserted Armenian villages around Harput, refugees from Bitlis and Van provinces arrived in the autumn of 1915; additional displaced persons from Erzurum province drove out the last remaining Armenians in the spring of 1916. However, local notables had secured the best real estate for themselves.[63]

In some regions, including Thrace and villages in Mamuret ul-Aziz province, a considerable number of Armenian houses remained uninhabited. If not immediately inhabited, chances were that usable parts like doors, windows, and roofs were taken away, often as firewood, which made the walls crumble, leaving places that looked like "Pompeji." That some Armenians were reputed to hide treasures in their house walls provided an additional incentive to tear them down.[64] In 1918, devastated Armenian neighborhoods were reported from Trabzon, Erzincan, and Erzurum.[65] Often, a mixture of occupation, plunder, and destruction may have prevailed, as in Urfa, where the Armenian quarter was pillaged in November 1915, and buildings damaged in the fall uprising were finally gutted. Turks from the city occupied houses near the Turkish quarter, Kurdish refugees from Van and Bitlis areas moved into others, but ripped the rest of the houses apart for building materials.[66]

When Ottoman troops advanced in 1918 against a Russian army that had virtually collapsed, many refugees tried to return to the northeast on their own – a fact suggesting their lack of enthusiasm for state settlement projects and for their treatment. Unable to prevent this, the Ottoman authorities tried to at least control this return, give it an organized form, and support it once again with limited funds, though the planned total of five million liras represented a considerable part of the budget. German experts, asked to do some of the planning work, pushed for larger financial means and commented that, if carried out reasonably, the project – recently reiterated by a law – had the potential to be "of the greatest importance for the development of Eastern Anatolia," including the fact that "a systematic settlement of these currently empty areas with Muslim farmers would be an important step for the final solution of the Armenian question, at least as a domestic political question of Turkey."[67] That the return of surviving Christians was blocked and the northeast Islamized is mainly to be ascribed to political actions below government level, including pogroms. Given desolate finances, the ensuing defeat, and the administrative chaos of the occupation years, the government lacked the capacity to organize these; the systematic modernization of the area that officials still hoped for in 1918 failed.[68] But state policies had succeeded in pitting new Muslim settlers against the former owners: during World War I, some of the former chased away scattered Armenian refugees, and in March 1919, a new, vocal "Immigrant Society" was founded to defend the interests of former Muslim refugees, of which 150,000 had allegedly already been made homeless by Armenians claiming back their homes.[69] In the absence of an effective social policy, the threat of destitution was real. It made small-scale profiteers vehemently block the return of the Armenian survivors.

For the Ottoman state, to take over Armenian possessions – namely landed property – not only substituted for a social policy, but could also help with the overwhelming problem of financing the war. Despite some efforts by the CUP to maintain stronger fiscal discipline and streamline the administration, they were running huge budget deficits and incurred foreign debts from 1908 to 1914 faster than had Sultan Abdul Hamid's administrations before. France was the biggest creditor.[70] After the Balkan Wars, the Ottoman Empire could not afford another war.

Moreover, the economic disruption caused by the August 1914 mobilization triggered a drastic drop in revenue (including proceeds from agricultural tax), allegedly by 80 percent within two years. Even officially, budgets were only half-funded by state income.

The real deficit was much wider.[71] Debt service consumed allegedly more than half of government expenses toward the end of the war.[72] The percentage of military spending rose from 45 percent in 1914 to over 75 percent during the war.[73] Even though the Ottoman government raised taxes and duties, old and new, a new factor caused (as in other countries) even greater financial constraints: war pensions for disabled, widows, and orphans, which required, as early as toward the end of 1916, expenditures of 2 million liras per month, equivalent to no less than 80 percent of peacetime monthly revenues.[74] Given its portrayal of the war as a national cause, the state could not politically afford not to pay for this part of the suffering – and these burdens were there to stay.

As a result of past experiences from the 1850s and 1870s, the financial strongman of the government, Cavid Bey (even though he formally resigned as Minister of Finance in November 1914, only to return in 1917), refused to issue uncovered paper money or certificates. Besides, the Empire lacked a central bank (and even paper usable for bills); the Imperial Ottoman Bank which issued banknotes was a private bank, ironically controlled by British and French capital. It acted uncooperatively.[75] After dogged negotiations, Cavid pushed through a funding method by which Germany and Austria-Hungary financed the issuing of Ottoman paper money by state credits, covered by gold deposited in the central banks at Berlin and Vienna.[76] Starting in the fall of 1915, the Ottoman Empire sent one request for new batches after the other, always rationalized by military expenditures and increasingly also by the necessity of internal political stabilization. Germany and the Habsburg Empire honored them every time, given the invaluable support the Central Powers received from the Ottoman army. As a result of this mutual dependency, the German contribution to Ottoman war financing amounted to 220 million liras (four billion marks), not counting military goods provided. The Ottoman state's debt increased from 170.6 to 465.7 million liras, yet this was later wiped out with the Empire itself.[77]

Despite theoretically maintaining the gold standard, this procedure triggered imported inflation. Confidence in paper money, which had previously been seldom used, was low, especially in the rural parts of Anatolia and Syria. In the countryside, bills lost three-quarters of their value compared to silver and particularly gold coins, and became less and less accepted at all, while gold was hoarded. This often left no means of exchange.[78] Official inflation figures show an increase to 300 in late 1916 and 1,675 by November 1918, over the July 1914 index (100).[79]

Given this desperate financial situation that was undermining the economy and fighting power of the Empire, any substantial relief by way of appropriating Armenian possessions was of extreme importance. One channel through which this materialized was the confiscation of Armenian church property that was to be administered by the Ministry for Religious Foundations; later regulations were based on the assumption that this transfer had actually taken place.[80] German observers assumed that many of the "very substantial funds" of this ministry – most of them land assets – had been transferred to "other government budgets," that is, obviously, for financing the costs of the war.[81] During the second wave of destruction in August 1916, the Ministry tried to gain stricter control of Armenian ecclesiastical assets.[82] Aside from the widespread destruction of churches, Christian religious buildings were converted into mosques, schools, museums, sports complexes, grain bins, farms, and barns.[83]

As described earlier, theoretically all Armenian property was to go through the hands of the Ottoman state, which would then sell (rather than give away free of charge) much of it. Valuables were collected, registered, and the liquidation commissions transferred them to the Imperial Ottoman Bank, where they could be counted toward the state budget and thus help balance it and alleviate inflation. The same went for immovables, even if those were not legally expropriated and formally administered for the interest of the Armenian owner.[84] These were of even greater value than all of the gold and jewelry. In Harput, businesses whose Armenian owner had taken even the slightest credit from the Imperial Ottoman Bank were foreclosed or had large parts of their proceeds collected. There, the liquidation commission simply appropriated all Armenian deposits in this bank.[85]

Personal and institutional links could also suggest factual ties. Not only were the functionaries of the Directorate for the Settlement of Tribes and Immigrants under Şükrü Kaya in charge of both collecting Armenian property and settling refugees. They also fell under the jurisdiction of Talaat Pasha's Ministry of the Interior, who also steered the gendarmerie and, besides, was Minister of the Postal Service, controlling the means of communication (Talaat had once been the director of the Salonika telegraph office). In addition, Talaat was formally

Minister of Finance from November 1914 to February 1917, although Cavid Bey continued to exert a major influence.[86] While there is no proof of a direct link, it is also remarkable that the decision for the deportation of the Armenians fell at a time when the Ottoman government regarded the German–Austro-Hungarian financial support as insecure and conditional (as far as the Habsburg Empire was concerned), and when the transportation of banknotes and assets was endangered due to the lack of a secure land connection. It was only in the fall of 1915 that the Porte considered this means of war financing secure.[87] Under such circumstances, the expropriation of Armenian property could assume a special importance for financing the war effort, although there is no proof that this consideration played a role in deciding upon the deportations.

Popular greed and violence

There is no doubt that most Armenians who perished died from famine conditions, of starvation, exhaustion, dehydration, deficiency diseases (typhus, dysentery, cholera), or froze to death. While certainly true of the deportation marches, this also applies to the second wave of killings from late 1915 to the fall of 1916. For those, Raymond Kévorkian ascribes less than one-third of deaths to direct murder.[88] The shocking and heart-rending images are known from other modern famines: apathetic victims, their hair matted, gradually losing all consideration for others, some abandoning or even selling their children.[89] Most famines do not strike all people equally. They occur if certain population groups lose their means of sustenance, such as land, harvests, income, or assets that allow them access to food, and if state organs are unable or unwilling to provide for their needs.[90] In other words, famines are socially induced events; they originate from interaction between people. By permanently robbing Armenians driven from their homes, land, and jobs, on the march and in inner exile, Ottoman officials, gangs, and individuals therefore on each of these occasions pushed them further to their deaths. And this effect was well known by both the victims, as evidenced by their precautions, and the perpetrators, who didn't care, or worse.

This process started at home. Armenian residences were raided by neighbors or strangers, often after the departure of the convoys, but many did not wait that long. In Efkereh, "soldiers" intruded in Armenian domiciles and demanded jewelry, money, rugs, and valuables from the inhabitants. Turkish men, women, and children carried rugs, lamps, silver, and furniture out of Armenian houses in Konia, leaving a yawning void in the home of Dirouhi Kouymjian even before she left. A crowd of Muslim women broke into an Armenian family's house in Smyrna during the 1922 slaughter and started to grab valuables, linens, silverware, and china. In the August 19, 1915 pogrom, Kurds plundered shops in the Armenian quarter of Urfa, slaughtering everybody in sight; after the end of the fall 1915 uprising triggered by these events, Kurdish men, women, and children again flooded in from neighboring villages to raid the Armenian quarter. Pillaging when the Armenian owners were still present also took place in Erzurum and, by "gypsies" and "riff-raff from the Turkish quarters," in Bandirma. In Harput, "many Muslims considered this the opportunity of a lifetime to get-rich-quick" (according to missionary Henry Riggs), visiting Armenian houses often not only to buy things, but also to scare people into selling things "for a song," or to commit outright robbery.[91] Houses were usually stripped bare, even if the owners returned after just a few days of arrest (this had happened in previous massacres as well).[92] Leon Surmelian did not even find the linoleum floor or any piece of charcoal left in the basement in his Trabzon home.[93] If they waited for the owners' departure, the robbers had little interest in the victims returning; if they struck before, they lessened Armenians' chances of taking money or valuables on the murderous trip.

Knowing how important cash would be for their survival on the marches, Armenians desperately tried to sell their movable property. "Armenian women sat everywhere in front of their houses and offered all their household effects. Everything sold for ridiculously low prices. Peasants and Kurds crowded the Armenian neighborhood and carried away donkey loads of stuff; between them moved heavily laden ox carts," said a report from Erzincan.[94] In some areas, the authorities did not allow them to do so,[95] trying to control the transactions and possibly to get a share. Armenian businesses were among the first objects to be sealed,[96] or officials tried to restrict sales to public auction places for a fee.[97] However, sales went on illegally as Muslims knocked at Armenians' doors.[98] Elsewhere, especially in the countryside, emergency sales were made impossible by the short notice before deportation – 30 minutes in Edirne.[99] Often, wealthy families were driven out first. Where sales were permitted and possible, "universal auction days" took place with "furniture, rugs, horses, dishes, etc." offered at every corner.[100] Prices were extremely low, as Muslim neighbors understood the forlorn situation of the sellers.[101] Nonetheless many – but particularly well-endowed – Armenian families were able to gather considerable sums.[102] Armenians and foreign observers knew how absolutely essential cash was for the survival of the sellers during the deportations, so these opportunistic buyers and officials who prohibited sales were also in a position to know about the deadly consequences of their actions.

On the marches, pillaging became deadly in a more direct way. Countless survivors have described the daily, even hourly, attacks on the marching columns.[103] During these assaults, deportees were sometimes injured and killed, especially men; rapes and abductions occurred more often, but most of the raids were for robbery. Those on Pailadzo Captanian's trek from Samsun became victims of robberies and extortions by gendarmes, the mayors of neighboring towns, cart drivers, "peasants," Kurds, civil servants, and mountain dwellers.[104] Generally, the assailants included çetes, overall many Kurds, but also (often Turkish) gendarmes and sometimes city dwellers.[105] As attacks took place primarily at the head or tail of the columns, the deported attempted to stay in the middle or built circle barricades of wagons if possible, especially at night.[106] Individual strategies consisted of hiding money, or intentionally looking ragged so that assailants would turn elsewhere, or getting food or clothes from still intact Armenian communities in towns which they passed through.[107] The total sum lost per individual could be substantial. Each victim could be robbed seven to ten times.[108] The gendarmes joined in attacks or instead extorted money for the 'protection' of the convoy in order to bribe their assailants; sometimes they did use the money for this purpose, in other cases it served to enrich themselves.[109]

Muslims also charged exorbitant prices for food, carriage, or boat rides.[110] Landlords in Aleppo were notorious for cashing in the advance rent by new Armenian tenants, only to denounce them to the police and look for new victims, or to extort bribes for not reporting them.[111] Observers found it remarkable if they encountered certain convoys that had *not* been robbed. This meant that there had also been few cases of death by exhaustion, the men were still alive, and the survivors in much better shape than usual because they still had money.[112]

The number of deaths rose dramatically once Armenian families had used up their money, or for those who started with little. It is for this reason that when nine-year-old Kerop Bedoukian, attacked by a Kurd, dropped a can containing flour, in which most of the remaining family valuables were hidden, his mother, far from being relieved by his escape, was only concerned with the gold.[113] Through this perpetual string of attacks and extortions, the resources, mental energy, and solidarity of the deported dwindled, and it was this that killed most of them. This process continued in deportation destinations such as Der es-Zor.[114] "What amazed me again and again was the incredible acquisitiveness of these savages [...]," wrote one survivor. "They were only keen of robbing, dreamed of nothing else than hidden gold. Only after they had satisfied their greed they thought of raping the women."[115]

As is to be expected in a famine, this ordeal took its highest toll on infants and small children. Despair about this led thousands of mothers to give away, abandon, sell, or drown their babies or toddlers.[116] While many older children were abducted, the youngest ones perished rapidly. The horrific result of this was that of the first rail transports (at least for the last portion of the trip) with Armenians to arrive in Aleppo from May to July 1915, a mere 16 percent were children; in August 1915, 33 percent.[117] The average survival rate of all, young or adult, during the deportation marches was about 50 percent.[118] Those from Thrace, Western Anatolia, Cilicia, parts of southeastern Anatolia, and northern Syria had a higher chance – having shorter stretches to walk (either because of proximity to their destination or the use of trains) and avoiding large Kurdish areas.

There was a variety of ways through which Armenians managed to remain alive: from some regions they were not deported; in the northeast, many fled to the Russian side; and exceptions were made (but not always) for the families of Protestants, Catholics, artisans, or military personnel. Some in inner exile managed to have money sent to them, either through US diplomatic channels, from relatives abroad, or even by postal order from inside the Empire.[119] For the remainder, the best chance for survival was conversion to Islam and absorption into Muslim households. According to estimates, among those to be deported, 200,000 Armenians survived in Muslim families and another 150,000 to 200,000 otherwise under Ottoman rule.[120] Armenian men were frequently asked to convert to Islam, too (which most refused to do, and even if they did, it did not necessarily save them from deportation and murder[121]), and some were promised that they could keep their property as a Muslim.[122] A systematic conversion policy for children was initiated by Cemal Azmi, the governor of Trabzon province in early July 1915, who simultaneously organized the radical extermination of most Armenian adults in the region. Thousands of girls up to 15 years and boys up to 10 were collected in orphanages and then offered to interested Muslims, resulting in 15,000 Armenians (a quarter to one-third of the original population, with some of the remainder hiding illegally) liberated by the Russians in the region in 1916.[123] State pressure for conversions, for women as well, was also intense in Samsun, Thrace, and Cilicia and allegedly in Mamuret ul-Aziz and Erzurum provinces in 1915,[124] and, with considerable effect, in Syria, Palestine, and Lebanon in 1916–17.[125] By July 1, 1915, even the hesitant Interior Ministry offered state subsidies of 30 piasters per month for needy Islamic families to absorb Armenian children (more than the average subsidy for Muslim resettlers).[126] For leading politicians, conversion was a means of assimilating those Armenians who seemed to embody no danger to the nation.

Islamization took the forms of conversion under duress; Muslim individuals adopting individual Armenians without state interference; officially organized private adoptions; and long-term placements in state orphanages.[127] But by far the highest proportion of Armenians ended up with Muslim families.

Turks, Kurds, Arabs, or Greeks were interested in taking in Armenian women or children as additional workers – in times of a severe labor shortage (especially in agriculture) due to military conscription – and for sex. In Suruc, near Bireçik, deported Armenians became "wives, maids, housekeepers, goatherds, milkers, cheese-makers." Men, especially, also often stated their intention of making a good Muslim out of an 'infidel' child. Some attempted to lay their hand on the property of the adopted child or woman married under duress.[128] They may also have hoped for the aforementioned subsidies. Some Muslims possibly also enjoyed having Armenian servants as a status symbol.[129] Often Muslims (mostly men, sometimes sheikhs) approached convoys or camps to choose Armenian women or children. Near Aintab, Muslim men sent out women to look for "beautiful girls" and female servants.[130] Often, females were openly abducted. However, the experiences afterwards in families or servitude varied hugely between disdainful or brutal treatment and being accepted as a beloved member of the family.[131]

That Armenians were turned into merchandise, mostly for the value of their labor or sexual services, is demonstrated by the open slave markets trading Armenian women and children in Damascus, Beirut, Aleppo, Bireçik, and Konia. Some were sold and resold, others endured sex slavery.[132] Elsewhere, Armenian children were on offer for adoption for free.[133] Some gendarmes sold women and children in Mesopotamia to surrounding communities or to brothels.[134] Near Aintab, Muslim women approached a group of deportees with the shout: "Infidels, have you any children to sell?"[135] Armenians in Tell Abiad offered their daughters of eight to twelve years for sale, for dwindling prices and finally for free, in order to spare them further deportation through the desert. In Der es-Zor and Cilicia, Armenians sold some children cheaply in order to buy some food.[136]

Amidst all this human trafficking, rescue developed into a business, too. The Dersim Kurds north of Harput, who became famous for saving perhaps 10,000 Armenians, often charged them considerable sums, differentiated according to the refugees' wealth.[137] Evidently in an attempt to compete with other financial temptations (like robbery), an Armenian rescue organizer in Russian-occupied Bitlis paid a head price to Kurdish smugglers for every Armenian brought over.[138]

Killings for the prospects of loot were encouraged by officials, but that would have had little consequence if no citizens had been ready to perpetrate them. Muslim refugees residing in Ras ul-Ain were motivated to join the slaughter as volunteers for the promise of getting Armenian houses near Urfa.[139] Some gendarmes sold entire convoys of Armenians for a lump sum to tribal leaders, who tried to recover their investment by searching those they massacred.[140] Sometimes, the clothes of the victims were later sold in the markets.[141]

How destructive the drive for Armenian property became can be seen from the extreme ends to which it drove individuals. In Smyrna, the body of an Armenian notable buried in his garden was dug out and searched for valuables shortly after his death in September 1922 by strangers breaking into his house.[142] After weeks of marching, more-or-less naked women and children from Harput saw themselves at a well confronted with gendarmes charging three lira (30 dollars) per cup of water.[143] Ottoman officials in Konia even demanded bribes for releasing the bodies of executed men for burial by their families.[144] "Turkish women were rummaging in the clothing of the corpses [of Armenians] in hope of some hidden treasure," noted Aaron Aaronsohn about a widespread practice on his journey from Constantinople to Haifa in December 1915.[145] It was widely known that some deportees hid valuables within their bodies, mostly by swallowing them (coins used to re-emerge eight to ten days later).[146] A variety of methods was used to get at these treasures: in the area of Lake Geoljuk and elsewhere in Mamuret ul-Aziz province, Kurds burned the corpses of massacred victims to find devoured gold.[147] According to a Kurdish historian, some Kurdish gangs, aside from pulling their gold teeth, "ripped open the abdomens" of Armenians they had murdered for valuables. This same practice was observed by a US missionary based in Harput and by nine-year-old Kerop Bedoukian, who witnessed it on his march from Sivas southward. Bedoukian also saw Kurdish men and women search with sticks for valuables in the excrement near a camp site where people from an Armenian convoy had relieved themselves – no little mound went unsearched, first by the "owners" themselves. Others turned the earth near Armenian camps over, as some deportees buried their valuables every evening.[148] "A woman still cringed under her labor pains when a gendarme robbed her clothes. He had not left her anything in which she could wrap her newborn that was trembling from cold," as Pailadzo Captanian relates in another scene.[149] In a quarrel among four- or five-year-olds, Ramela Pilibosian was threatened with death by a friend from the Kurdish family where she was hidden because of her refusal to hand over her doll during play. The girl revealed that her father intended to kill the Armenian family anyway.[150] All imaginable ethical barriers were torn down.

Lost in a class society

Ottoman Armenians were victimized not only by a murderous state and by individuals, but also by a specific social system. Within that system, dramatic processes of upward social mobility and mass impoverishment took place, accompanied by attempts at intensified government control over certain economic sectors and the countryside. Every country in the Great War had its war profiteers, but in the Ottoman Empire they stopped at nothing.

Access to Armenian property was not equal for all. The government was unable to confiscate most of the movable possessions of Armenians, which were appropriated instead by local elites, corrupt officials, and scores of neighbors. Control over the redistribution of immovables was also only partly successful as CUP functionaries, civil servants, military officers, and wealthy Muslims grabbed the most attractive goods. The government was in no position to organize this process in terms of finance, apparatus, or skilled personnel. For example, in 1911–12 no more than 2.3 percent of the budget had been spent on education and 1 percent on economic and agricultural administration combined.[151] Without the capacity for state dirigisme, the government favored a somewhat channeled corruption to benefit 'capable' Muslims, especially in regard to Armenians' businesses.[152] The objective – which was, after all, war aim number one – was the nurturing of an Islamic bourgeoisie, less for the immediate economic modernization of society and economy than to strengthen the nation in the long run,[153] as also identified by many contemporary observers.[154] The result of this rather chaotic scramble was the initial accumulation of capital by a new class forged from state officials, wealthy landowners, and merchants. They would in turn finance the Turkish nationalist movement that acted not only against foreign occupants, but also against the return of Armenians and Greeks.[155]

Yet the emergence of a national-Muslim bourgeoisie was about more than appropriating Armenian houses, land, and businesses. For one, it was increasingly about expropriating *Greek* property as well (but rarely Jewish); such an intensified nationalization of the economy also struck foreigners.[156] But in a country with rapidly declining foreign[157] and domestic trade, fortunes could be amassed only in certain sectors of the economy. Perhaps the biggest of all was the food business. Labor shortages and animal requisitions for the military resulted in drastically falling cultivation acreages and yields. Transportation problems, grain requisitions, hoarding, and state mismanagement disrupted food distribution. The Allied naval blockade added to the calamities. Still, great profits could be earned by supplying the military. A number of consecutive administrations oscillated between a free-market approach and stricter state control: a "Food Dictator" (from January 1915), the Food Office (July 1916–August 1917, headed by none other than Talaat Pasha[158]), the General Directorate for Food Affairs (from August 1917), a Supreme Food Commission (from spring 1918), and the Food Ministry (from July 1918, led by, of all people, Kemal Bey, Chairman of the Merchants' Associations).[159] Frequently criticized by German civilian and military observers – some of them working inside Ottoman food authorities – all these administrations essentially neglected the well-being of the consumers, resulting in famines and a major political crisis in 1917, in favor of the enrichment of the food merchants' associations.[160] Corruption was the way to build the new commercial elites. The only groups with access to official rations were civil servants and their families, military personnel, families of officers and the fallen, schools, and orphanages. The rest of the populace was on its own, the poor hit hardest.[161]

There was no government policy to starve or murder Armenians in order to favor others in terms of food; usually Armenians had no rations which could be redistributed to others, and there was little serious elite concern with the nutrition of the Muslim lower classes. The menace of famine did not trigger deportations, but famines rather took place where Armenians happened to live, such as in Constantinople and Smyrna, or in 1916 in Syria and Lebanon (with up to 200,000 victims).[162] Food surpluses were scarce and food was already expensive in the areas through which the Armenians were marched in 1915, and the needs of their marching columns drove prices up further. For other population segments, mostly there were no famine conditions yet. But these did exist in many southeastern areas where the Armenians stayed in 1916–18. They formed just one of several social groups not protected by rationing,[163] yet they particularly struggled with the situation, given aggravated circumstances: lack of residence permits, without any protection by laws, and the reduced capacity of their communities to raise welfare goods (compared, say, to Jewish communities). As a consequence, tens or even hundreds of thousands of Armenians succumbed to hunger and deficiency diseases like typhus, cholera, and dysentery.[164] The situation also worked partially against solidarity among Armenian victims, women included – famines harbored "days of survival of the fittest and the days of 'dog-eat-dog'."[165] Unfortunately, many Armenians died as a result of the policies of the only major politician apparently concerned with the prevention of epidemics in the city that had become a major refuge, Cemal Pasha, who had many deported from Aleppo to Der es-Zor in 1916, where they perished from hunger and massacres.[166] Armenians were reputed to spread epidemics, but the 1914–15 typhus outbreak was caused by another malnourished group – common soldiers.[167] Health care and provisioning in the military formed another complex characterized by steep social hierarchies, blatant corruption, and neglect.[168] If 466,759 Ottoman soldiers succumbed to diseases (and hunger – many more than to injuries), and up to 1.5 million Turkish, Kurdish, and Arab civilians died, mostly of starvation and epidemics,[169] this was not the fault of Armenians, as is sometimes absurdly argued in Turkish historiography, but instead ironically of the same Muslim war profiteers who also created the conditions under which Armenians starved in banishment. It was no coincidence that the takeover of the food trade by the merchants' associations was one of the three charges in the main Ottoman war criminals' trial in 1919.[170] Specifically, the CUP was accused of having established a flour monopoly that earned the party, but not the state, a fortune.[171] The starving Armenians fell victim to intentional neglect by the authorities, as well as to the merciless laws of the market and the reckless self-establishment of a new elite, described by Ottoman contemporaries and historians as the nouveau-riches or "riches of 1916."[172]

Conclusion

"No class of the Mohammedan population, rich or poor, high or low, young or old, men or women kept away from murdering and robbing," wrote Aaron Aaronsohn in 1916.[173] In another view, this persecution was "not the work of friends or neighbors, but rather that of warped-minded intellectual elites, unjust rulers, cruel brigands, deluded and misguided rabble, and corrupt officials."[174] While the former statement rightly recognizes that the diverse groups responsible for the destruction of the Armenians came from the middle of society, and that these definitely included lots of neighbors, it is also overly sweeping. A number of observers held that local Muslim–Armenian relations were good and changed only under the circumstances, or never,[175] and many credible sources testify to local opposition to the persecution and pillaging. A dozen or so district governors and mayors were replaced and many of them murdered for their uncooperative attitude.[176] In some places it was Muslim elites such as wealthy landowners, merchants, mullahs, or Kurdish tribal leaders who opposed the slaughter (though in some cases because of the need for Armenian labor) or refused to take over

Armenian property,[177] whereas in other places these measures were deplored by the common people, and sections of the female population particularly pitied the Armenians.[178] Both participation in and opposition to persecution and robbery occurred in all groups of the population, but whereas the former was public, the latter remained private, marginalized, silenced, or clandestine.

On the other hand, the mass deaths of Armenians at a much higher rate of mortality than among Turkish or Kurdish refugees or even Greek deportees was the easily foreseeable consequence of official policies. And it was foreseen by Armenians and foreign observers who warned of it. Even if one looks just at property issues and ignores the widespread direct murders, the Ottoman state pursued a policy of decimating and disempowering Armenians. Ottoman government action left many Armenians with no livelihood or income and with cash resources running out. They were cut off from the bulk of their property (real estate), usually left with no way to withdraw or wire money, and mostly herded in isolated places with few job opportunities and food rations at starvation levels. The chances for Armenian charities to help the deported were virtually blocked (unlike in the case of the Jews in Palestine), and foreign charities' activities were obstructed by the authorities until late in the war, when many Armenians had already perished. This left Armenians in a situation with hardly any way out – and if there were any, they were usually declared illegal. Add to that little protection from attacks, or even the officials' involvement in them; there was no massive prosecution of robbers, looters, or blackmailers, let alone the return of property worth speaking of. Given all this, Armenians lost their food entitlement, and mass death was the logical outcome.

The destruction of the Armenians was no zero-sum game in which *either* the government *or* large parts of the population were implicated. Both state-organized expropriation and regulations and popular robbery and extortion contributed to the killing of hundreds of thousands of Armenians. More precisely, many deaths resulted from the competition for Armenian assets between the authorities, the elites, and the common man or woman. Consequently, the forms and perpetrators of violence varied. The Armenian persecutions are also a reminder of how little sense it makes to neatly separate deaths by direct killing from those from hunger and deprivation. Not all involved could be designated perpetrators. But the deadly impact of the practices of unequal exchange by private individuals, such as charging exorbitant prices for food, water, services, and rescue, or the forced adoption of children, question the usefulness of the narrow concept of "perpetrator."

Minor as well as leading figures in the destruction of the Armenians piled up fortunes for themselves or allowed their children to ascend into a position in the social elite. These included Enver Pasha, Cemal Pasha, Reşit Bey (all before their early deaths), and Ismail Hakki.[179] On May 31, 1926, the Turkish Republic compensated the families of executed or assassinated former functionaries from the funds of 'abandoned' Armenian property, including the relatives of Talaat, Enver, and Cemal.[180] Important deportation officials later rose to the highest ranks between 1919 and 1923 and then in the Turkish Republic, among them Celal Bayar (from regional CUP functionary in the Aegean to third President of Turkey) and Şükrü Kaya (from IAMM director to Foreign Minister, Interior Minister, and Secretary-General of Atatürk's Republican People's Party).[181]

Not everything worked on economic criteria. Dersim Kurds helped some refugees who had no money at all. An Armenian girl, sold by her grandmother to an Arab couple, was fed by foster parents even if they had to go hungry themselves. Like her, many Armenian children and youths recalled a profoundly ambivalent experience. They had been treated like family in their new foster homes, loved and cared for (though older boys were usually fiercely exploited).[182] This affection is obviously among the reasons why many children wanted to stay with those families, which is possibly true of the majority of cases.[183] Babies and infants were evidently not adopted for immediate material gain, often by childless couples; only much later could returns such as labor, a dowry, or support for the adoptive parents in old age be expected. And people had a variety of motives other than economic interests for persecuting Armenians; for example religious passions amongst many rural dwellers, especially Kurds.[184]

The state organization and the practice of persecution of other groups in the late Ottoman Empire looked largely the same. Greeks, Assyrians, and Kurds were subject to similar policies of forced relocation, dispersal, expropriation, and plunder. The Directorate for the Settlement of Tribes and Immigrants, established in 1913 for settling Muslim refugees and nomad tribes, organized the expulsions and relocations of Greeks in Thrace and in the western Aegean in

1914, substituting them with Muslims displaced in the First Balkan War, before turning against the Armenians.[185] Islamic refugees from Macedonia and Crete pushed for the expulsions of 119,000 Greeks from eastern Thrace in 1913–14, and took over their possessions with the help of Ottoman authorities. Public meetings, boycotts, and the press played major roles in rallying support for this violence. Attacks and wild looting helped to force people into exile, before state-organized forms of property transfer, including land and houses, set in just as in the Smyrna area.[186] Regional CUP functionaries had pushed for a partial removal of Christians and a settlement of Muslim refugees from 1910.[187] In Edirne province, the pillaging of Greeks continued in the fall of 1915; by March 1916, 40,000 Greeks were reportedly expelled, and more Muslim refugees were settled in formerly Greek than Armenian homes.[188] However, protests by the Greek government helped to stop the confiscation of the property by Greeks in Adana province.[189] Many of the Greeks deported from the Pontos in 1916, and from there and Western Anatolia in 1920–22, fell victim to exhaustion and epidemics, the killings of those unable to continue marching, rapes, looting, forced Islamization, partial replacement in their homes by Muslim settlers, and – from 1920 – total expropriation of their property. Thousands of corpses were left lying along the roads.[190] Both Greek and Armenian refugees could end up in the same reception camps in Greece in 1922–23.[191] Notorious çete leader Topal Osman, who first deported and massacred Armenians in 1915, was then dispatched against the Greeks of Samsun province in 1916, later deployed against the Kurdish uprising in Koçkiri, where nearly 10,000 people were killed in 1919–21, and finally against the Armenians of Kars province in 1920–21.[192] Nestorian villages in Van and Mosul provinces were looted by "Kurdish and Turkish soldiers" and many inhabitants killed, as were Armenians.[193] Extortions and blackmail were often followed by the forced Islamization of women and children.[194] Facing a Russian advance, Turks desperately tried to sell their property before fleeing,[195] being confronted with less harsh treatment than the Armenians yet maybe not milder conditions otherwise on their passage. Deported Kurdish women on their march through Harput appeared as destitute, leading some to abandon their babies as Armenian women had done. Half of the Kurds evacuated during World War I may have died.[196] In a twin strategy, the government tried to pacify the unruly Kurds through bribery with Armenian property, and intimidate them by daunting selective repression. Many of the 1915 robbers and murderers were Kurds.

In the years leading up to World War I, in what Taner Akcam calls "mutual ethnic cleansing," hundreds of thousands of Muslims had been expelled from their lands, sometimes killed, where Ottoman rule retreated, which led some Turkish deputies in 1919 to state: "We learned about deportation from our neighbors."[197] None of these bloody evictions was morally justified. While the reason presented for secessions from the Ottoman Empire since the nineteenth century had always been 'Turkish atrocities,' it should be acknowledged that Muslims also became victims of some of the formerly victimized if circumstances changed. The area of Urmia in northwestern Iran experienced a seesaw of mutual plunder between local Muslims and Assyrian Christians, both locals and Ottoman refugees, from an attack by Ottoman Kurds in October 1914 to the return of Russian troops in May 1915 and again in 1916. Militias and irregulars committed most of the atrocities; volunteers usually started the plunder, which was continued and radicalized to expulsion by local Muslims turning against Christian neighbors, or vice versa. Refugees of the religion of the attackers were settled in the empty houses of those driven out.[198] While in eastern Thrace, Islamic refugees from Macedonia, Bosnia, and Epiros were settled in the homes of expelled Greeks in 1914, Christian Greeks appropriated the houses, belongings, and schools of expelled Muslims in western Thrace and Greek Macedonia.[199] After the Ottoman troops retreated from Van in May 1915 before the approaching Russian troops, Armenians ravaged, massacred, and robbed Muslims for three days. During the Russian conquest of the mountains south of Trabzon in April 1916, eleven-year-old refugee Leon Surmelian observed the burning of Turkish houses and took part in plundering some of the furniture, doors, and "anything movable I could find," only to shortly afterwards find his own city home completely emptied.[200]

As mentioned before, other groups were confronted with similar policies and acts as the Armenians were. This, too, was participatory violence, and profiteering was one important driving force among the many motives that led people from different backgrounds to take an active part in these other persecutions. In this sense, we can speak of the Ottoman Empire as an extremely violent society where a variety of people became victims or persecutors in a multi-causal process.

Violence in and around the late Ottoman Empire was multi-polar but not unlimited. Much depended on the distribution of power and state policies. But the authorities were not able to fully control expropriations and with it attacks on Armenians, the worst persecuted victim group. In a highly hierarchical class society, this was connected to a struggle between elites for wealth, positions, and influence. Yet the variety of actions of the less well-to-do allows for no simple manipulation thesis that would declare them tools for murder and robbery in the hands of the state or the rich (although, for example, many Kurdish gangs were probably controlled by feudal landlords). Some wanted escape from misery, homelessness, or famine, others hoped for quick gains or a new career, still others acted upon nationalist or religious feelings, which in turn prompted a few to help the persecuted. Responses differed, but material interests explain a large part of why so many joined in the destruction of the Armenians.

Part II

The crisis of society

4 FROM RIVALRIES BETWEEN ELITES TO A CRISIS OF SOCIETY

Mass violence and famine in Bangladesh (East Pakistan), 1971–77

The second group of case studies in this book will tie the participatory and multi-causal character of the use of force in extremely violent societies to the idea of a crisis of society. It will reconstruct the victimhood and agency of various groups in relation to such a general crisis and make connections to long-term social transformations which involved massive social and geographic mobility as well as legacies of ongoing violence. This requires a very broad contextualization of peak events of destruction.

In a conventional view, matters seem clear for the case of Bangladesh. After the Bengali autonomy movement led by the Awami League won parliamentary elections in late 1970, the military dictatorship refused to hand over power. Instead, it cracked down on the peaceful people of East Pakistan on March 25, 1971 and started to kill Awami League supporters, Bengali intellectuals and troops, and Hindus, as this minority were collectively suspected of being Indian agents. Large parts of the countryside were devastated. The Pakistani army killed three million people, drove ten million out of the country, and raped 200,000 or more women. The East Bengalis started a guerrilla war for self-defense and achieved national independence with the help of an Indian invasion in December 1971. Several thousand people of the non-Bengali Urdu-speaking minority, the so-called Biharis, fell victim to the wrath of Bengalis because they had helped the Pakistani rulers.[1]

Or so goes the mainstream Bengali narrative, adopted by many foreign scholars. The Pakistani version is very different. In defense of

Pakistan's territorial integrity, after all negotiating possibilities were exhausted, the army prevented by military force a virtual takeover in East Pakistan by the Awami League as it had developed since early March 1971. Thereby the military also saved the lives of many non-Bengalis, of whom the Bengalis had killed tens of thousands. Collective reprisals by the military claimed 50,000 or fewer Bengali lives, alienating the Bengalis. Violence was limited by the fact that the government could rely on a mere 12,000 loyal (i.e. non-Bengali) troops in East Pakistan by March 1971. These were actually initially outnumbered by troops of Bengali background.[2] (Foreign diplomats estimated – after reinforcements – some 20,000–25,000 loyal and 20,000 Bengali troops by March 25.[3]) The weak and vulnerable Pakistani troops then bravely reasserted state authority against all odds, albeit with practices that were too heavy-handed.[4] They were reinforced in late March and early April principally by flying in the 9 and 16 Infantry Divisions (the only reserves of the Pakistani military), which added to the 14 Infantry Division already there.[5] In the end, they were defeated – due to incompetent Pakistani political and military leadership – by India's invasion that cut Pakistan in half; India having previously nurtured, armed, and manipulated the insurgents.

Both versions are overly simplified, incomplete, factually questionable in many parts, and take events out of context. Moreover, both of them focus predominantly on government actions. The following account provides a broader contextualization by relating the various forms and directions of violence to their socioeconomic, political, and cultural backgrounds. In order to put events in a longer historical perspective, this chapter will also explore the connections between social change, mass violence, and the 1971–72 and 1974–75 famines in Bangladesh. It explores the repercussions of an elite conflict in wider society.

The emerging conflict

Decolonization combined with partition led to the violent emergence of new elites in East Bengal between 1947 and 1951. The British colonialists and the Hindu economic leadership – Hindus, primarily *zamindari* (big landowners), owned 75 percent of the land – were largely displaced and dispossessed. Hindus also lost many urban homes.[6]

Zamindari estates were expropriated in 1951, to be leased primarily to Muslim refugees from partition.[7] Most vacant and new positions in East Bengal administration and business, including higher management, were taken over by West Pakistanis and *mujahirs*, refugees from India. Jobs as lawyers, teachers, or doctors fell mostly to Bengalis.[8] Soon *mujahirs* controlled over half of Pakistan's industrial assets.[9] As a result of the 'basic democrats' system which had existed under the military dictatorship since 1958, East Pakistani Muslim *jotedars* (medium landowners) could use their position in union councils to consolidate their holdings and power, becoming a "Kulak class."[10] Meanwhile, rural income per capita and real industrial wages declined over much of the 1950s.[11] The main beneficiaries of the Pakistani development policies, expressly designed on the basis of inequality, were Punjabis and *mujahirs*.[12]

At the root of the Pakistan conflict, then, was a "class war between West-Pakistani full-blown capitalists [allied with land-based elites] and the East Bengali petty-middle class." This also resulted in politics diverging between the two halves of the country: sharp class differences and "dictatorial politics" in the west contrasted with more diffused land and business ownership, the "social background for democratic politics" in the east, at least nominally.[13] Some Pakistani analysts, too, have blamed irresponsible elites on both sides for the conflict.[14] In this situation, the Awami League rose to prominence as representative of the demands of the urban middle classes and part of the medium landowners. Even observers who were no leftists called it a "bourgeois" party.[15] Highly educated Bengalis formed its backbone. Most emerged from villages in the 1950s; doubling university and college enrollment between 1959 and 1965, coupled with politicization and graduates getting into new jobs, led to Awami League influence spreading throughout the countryside.[16] This social mobility and Bengali consciousness was not yet incompatible with Pakistani national identity. In 1964, only 29 percent of polled East Bengali college students called themselves Bengalis, and 74 percent Pakistanis. Self-perceptions were fluid, and those of "Bengali" and "Pakistani" could easily coexist.[17]

While the language issue was at the heart of the conflict in the 1950s,[18] in the next decade it evolved around economic issues. Bengali nationalists argued that East Pakistan – home of more than half of Pakistan's population – fell behind due to being systematically disadvantaged by the central governments' designing foreign trade regulations, resource allocation, and taxation according to the wishes of West Pakistani elites. The over-valued currency protected West Pakistani industries, for which the East was a ready market, but hurt East Pakistani exports. East Pakistan earned the majority of the country's hard currency but received little of its imports, external 'aid,' and internal investment, particularly private. This policy asymmetry made the East a supplier of raw materials which indirectly financed industrial accumulation in the West; government, health services, and education were concentrated in the West. Most high-ranking civil servants and military officers were West Pakistanis.[19] Hence Bengalis charged that East Pakistan was exploited by the western part like a colony, as it had been before under the British.

A small increase in public investment in East Pakistan – first for flood control – had begun in the mid-1960s. This trend was substantially increased under Yahya Khan's junta, accompanied by more jobs for Bengalis in state corporations, government administration, and the media. Plans existed for this to go even further.[20] Yet this seemed to only make competition for resources fiercer.

Developments in late 1970 exacerbated the situation in East Pakistan, creating the context for severe crisis, and ultimately civil war. On November 12, 1970, a cyclone causing a giant flood wave struck parts of coastal East Pakistan. Three to four million people lost their houses, animals, and many also their rice crops, and 233,000 died. According to another count, most of the 286,759 dead came from Barisal district, Bhola island, and Noakhali district.[21] Bengali nationalists used the initially procrastinating relief effort for propaganda against the Pakistani government and especially the military, claiming that one million had died.[22] Such numbers appear much inflated.[23] Aside from polarizing public opinion before the national elections, this disaster marked the beginning of dramatic foreign aid inflows; aid agencies established structures that some used during the 1971 conflict and all of them afterwards, soon moving from relief to broader, massive 'development' projects.[24] This influx of capital primarily promoted the rural wealthy, furthering social polarization and helping to transform the countryside of Bangladesh.[25]

In an undemocratic oligarchy, Bengalis were largely excluded from the leading circles and decision-making.[26] Bengali nationalists' demands also posed a threat to the military dictatorship because military spending usually accounted for more than half of government expenses. A more equitable division of resources between East and West would have diminished the resource base of the army, their control of the state,[27] and officers' chances for the generation of private wealth. According to the Awami League's Six Points (1966), advanced by their leader, Sheikh Mujibur Rahman (Mujib), finances for the central government would have depended on the provinces.[28] After the alleged military inactivity following the deadly November 1970 cyclone, Mujib, who intended to greatly curb military spending, charged: "Is this why we have channeled 60 per cent of our budget all these years for defense services?"[29]

After mass protests in both wings of Pakistan brought down Ayub Khan in March 1969, the military junta under his successor Yahya Khan was forced to pave the way for parliamentary elections for a new National Assembly. The Awami League managed in November 1970 to rout all of its rivals, especially the previously influential religious parties, winning 74.9 percent of the votes and 160 of 162 National Assembly seats in East Pakistan, which gave this party an overall majority in the national parliament.[30] But the Pakistan Peoples Party under Ali Bhutto, which had won the elections in much of the western wing, claimed a role in a proposed coalition government.[31] There were differences over the terms upon which the National Assembly should meet. In response, Yahya Khan postponed the constitutional meeting of the National Assembly on March 1, 1971 indefinitely, provoking riots in the East.[32] From March 3 to 25, the Awami League virtually governed East Pakistan, enforcing a strike, controlling economic activity, foreign trade and capital movements, the courts, much of the media, the banks, and the postal service. In negotiations between Yahya and Mujib with their followers, later also with Bhutto, the Awami League insisted on much of its Six Points, which assigned only defense and foreign relations (excluding foreign trade) to the national government and even drew the national currency unity into question. It added demands for the withdrawal of the army, an inquiry into army killings of around 300 Bengalis in March, an end of army reinforcements and a transfer of power to the elected representatives.[33] The junta interpreted this as an attempt to establish a confederation and the breakup of Pakistan, for which leftist students in particular were pushing, and viewed the harassment of army troops as a grave insult.[34] It now seems that the Awami League did indeed want their future government leaders to order the army out of the eastern wing and then pass a resolution for the independence of Bangladesh in the national parliament.[35]

The West Pakistani elites would not relinquish the East willingly. Operation "Blitz," the first scheme for a military crackdown in East Pakistan as a contingency plan in case the Bengalis declared independence, was designed by General Yaqub, Martial Law Administrator for East Pakistan, in December 1970 and approved at a high-level meeting of selected generals with President Yahya on February 22, when Yahya announced he wanted to postpone the National Assembly meeting indefinitely. The day before, Yahya had dismissed the civilian Cabinet that included Bengalis.[36] However, facing a general strike and hostile reactions after troops shot several protestors, and confronted with a popular economic and transportation boycott by Bengalis against the army, Yaqub reported by March 2 that Operation "Blitz" was no longer feasible because a military solution would imply large-scale killings of civilians (and so he resigned soon afterwards). By March 16, Yahya Khan ordered the new Commander in East Pakistan, General 'Tikka' Khan, to design another emergency plan for a crackdown. It was put on hold during Yahya's negotiations with Mujib, but by March 23 was scheduled to be set in motion on March 26.[37]

This new plan, Operation "Searchlight," contained orders to disarm (but not arrest) the East Pakistan Rifles, the East Bengal Regiment, and the police, to secure the cantonments (barracks), the airfields and Chittagong naval base, and the towns, to arrest Bengali political leaders, including certain students, professors, and leftists (how to locate them was left unclear), and to search Hindu houses in old Dacca. Rajer Bagh police station and Dacca University were prominent among the planned and actual targets. While ordering drastic but unspecific "shock action" across the province, the text of the "Searchlight" order did not call explicitly for any killings.[38] Only occasional remarks dropped by Pakistani officers foreshadowed the brutal course later taken, such as the threat by Major-General Khadim Hussain Raja on March 7, should Mujib declare independence, "to kill the traitors and, if necessary, raze Dacca to the ground. There will be no one to rule, there will be nothing to rule."[39] Incited by Yahya, Tikka Khan and his troops went far beyond the written orders on the evening of March 25 and immediately started to kill opposing troops and police, Hindus, students, and some professors. The operation, which started prematurely around 11 p.m., was "neither carried out in the sequence anticipated nor achieved its main objectives."[40] The army seems to have hoped to be able to "sort out" the Bengalis through a bloodbath lasting only 48 or 72 hours, and in Dacca some officers and troops celebrated at that stage, yelling that they had "won the war."[41] An Awami League member called the beginning a "true Indonesian night," referring to the mass murder of Indonesian communists in 1965–66.[42] The military used tanks and fighter planes. In some areas, due to their numerical weakness, army action was initially less severe, and more in line with the actual orders.[43]

The Pakistanis claimed that their crackdown served to pre-empt a Bengali military uprising.[44] Bengali sources leave no doubt that several high-ranking Bengali military officers discussed the possibility of an armed insurgency or pleaded for it before March 25 with Mujib and other Awami League leaders.[45] Bengali troops at some outposts in the Chittagong area began to arrest their West Pakistani colleagues one day before the military crackdown, and a unit under Rafiq ul Islam of the East Pakistan Rifles started an uprising in the city around 8 p.m., several hours before the Pakistanis moved.[46] Moreover, Bengali nationalists had paraded through cities with bamboo spears and iron rods since March 1, blocking army installations, attacking non-Bengalis, looting and burning cars and smashing signs in Urdu and English.[47] At occasions such as Mujib's biggest mass meeting on March 7, 1971, the crowds were incited to take up arms and prepare to destroy the "enemy." Mujib himself called on the crowd to "make a fortress of every home" and "kill them" (the Pakistani soldiers) if any more violence was used: "since we have shed blood, we will shed more, yet we shall free the people of this country."[48] Awami League youths, with the help of paramilitaries, procured weapons by raiding arms shops or theft and trained students as guerrillas.[49] Such training also took place at Iqbal Hall, Dacca University, which became a symbolic place because the Pakistani army stormed it on the night of March 25 and shot dozens of students after facing rifle fire, though no automatic weapons or grenades.[50] These gangs were poorly armed and incapable of offensive action.

For all that, the fact that most Bengali troops remained initially quiet, and the lack of communication among scattered insurrectionists and between them and Bengali political leaders, do not support the thesis of a comprehensive plan for insurgency.[51] Rather, mutual mistrust, fed by incoming news and rumors, created fluid situations that led troops, even within units, to watch each other suspiciously, a situation that could last for days or even a week locally.[52] Bengali troops did then start to take control of many areas of East Pakistan, though still without central coordination,[53] and they were driven away by the Pakistani army. By April 20, the Pakistani army controlled most of the country again after fanning out from the cities and their vicinity to the countryside. Their success was based on the ruthless use of artillery, air power, tanks, spraying civilians with bullets, and torching buildings. The declarations of national independence on March 27 and of a national government of Bangladesh on April 14 could not prevent the Bengali military defeat. A guerrilla war ensued.

It has been claimed that the Pakistani army planned to purify Bengalis of traits that appeared tainted by Hinduism. Pakistani officers denounced Bengalis in general as "unbelievers" and Hindus.[54] Bengalis in armed formations became a target for suspicions of potential military resistance, others because of their possible political ambitions. A Punjabi officer was quoted from the beginning of the conflict as saying: "We are fighting in the name of God and a united Pakistan."[55] Anthony Mascarenhas was repeatedly told in 16 Division headquarters in Comilla: "We are determined to cleanse East Pakistan once and for all of the threat of secession, even if it means killing off two million people and ruling the province as a colony for 30 years."[56] With reference to former military dictator Ayub Khan, Pakistanis were also accused of anti-Bengali racism.[57] Although in South Asia racism is constructed mostly on a cultural basis, even a former press officer of the Pakistani army recalled that "keep the Bingo under control" was a common slogan among military personnel, apparently likening Bengalis to Africans.[58] However, while we can identify specific anti-Hindu policies, the exact impact of anti-Bengali racism in general on the actions of troops is unclear. The army also dehumanized their enemies in a number of ways. Officers used the phrases "for disposal" or to be "disposed of" from the first night for summary executions.[59] Troops also referred to killings with phrases like "sending to Bangla Desh" or "dispatched to Bangladesh," or threatened people by using such language.[60]

Lacking manpower and local knowledge, the Pakistani authorities embraced emerging auxiliary units. After March 25, the Pakistani government dissolved some former auxiliary police (*Ansars*). They were gradually replaced by new, lightly armed *razakars*, consisting of the small mysterious *Al-Badr*, recruited mainly from students connected with religious–conservative parties,[61] to whom the military assigned raids, intelligence, and commando objectives, and the larger *Al-Shams*, who were used mainly for securing objects like bridges.[62] First the *razakars* operated under the Peace Committees, established by older religious–conservative men in April and May 1971. The creation of the *razakars* was officially announced in late August. In early September they were put under army command (in conjunction with the appointment of A. Malik as Governor and an amnesty).[63] Their total number reached 35,000 to 55,000, below the Pakistani plans; by late April there were just 5,000.[64] Together with *mujahirs* and East Pakistan Civilian Armed Forces (EPCAF), their numbers reached 73,000.[65] Bengalis accused non-Bengalis of comprising a large part of the *razakars* and of violent misuse of their positions. Kalyan Chaudhuri even unrealistically claimed that *razakars* and not the army had killed "most" victims.[66] Some Pakistani sources have confirmed that *razakars* plundered, denounced persons (often falsely) as resisters to the Pakistani army, and terrorized Bengalis.[67] However, in reality many *razakars* were Bengalis, particularly in rural areas.[68] This means that the conflicts divided the Bengali communities.

Some scholars describe East Pakistan before 1971 as home of a "homogenous"[69] society and as a peaceful place. Both are utterly wrong. Between 1946 and 1970, at least four million Hindus fled the province and tens of thousands were killed in repeated pogroms (see below). The government organized mass arrests and there were some shootings of leftists, labor unionists, and government opponents.[70] A variety of social conflicts became violently manifest, also in a culture of frequent *hartals* (strikes) and *gheraos* (sieges of persons or objects). Between 1958 and 1966, about 5,000 riots occurred each year, or 15 per day, with increasing frequency! By the early 1970s, they had become even more common.[71] Even mob violence could be fairly organized through community leaders, based on conscious collective decisions.[72] Such collective violence, including the burning of villages triggering streams of refugees, could happen between Muslims and Hindus or Christians, or between Bengalis and non-Bengalis. There were also food riots as in 1956, student demonstrations as in 1962, upheavals connected to the Bengali language movement in 1951, and anti-government and anti-establishment protests like the ones that brought down the Ayub Khan junta in 1968–69, which entailed killings of up to 2000 "evil gentry" or "basic democrats" (elected political representatives) in rural areas, who were "found 'guilty' of 'antipeople crimes' and [...] burnt alive, beheaded, crucified, knifed, drowned, or hacked to death." These atrocities were followed by violence surrounding strikes and lockouts in factories throughout many industries in the first half of 1970.[73] In March 1971, another wave of killings against political representatives and "anti-social elements" claimed 200 more lives before the army crackdown.[74] To some degree, the Awami League's election victory in 1970 was a consequence of its attacks and physical intimidation of rival political parties throughout the year to enforce national unity. Mujib even confided to the US ambassador that on his orders nine communists had been killed by Awami League workers.[75]

Amidst this tradition of militancy in political and economic conflict, politicians used a language of violence. Since late 1970, Mujib repeatedly publicly and internally either predicted an army crackdown and an uncontrollable bloody struggle or asserted that Bengalis were ready to shed blood for their freedom, even to sacrifice "another million," claiming that so many had died in the cyclone.[76] Allegedly, Ali Bhutto also said on March 25 that it would not matter if 100,000 people would die for Pakistan this time.[77]

The scope of the 1971 killings: corrections to a myth

In order to identify the policies, practices, and intentions of violence, one needs to determine its scope and the directions it took. But this is difficult. Due to a lack of detailed or systematic official, judicial, and scholarly inquiries into the 1971 violence in Bangladesh and Pakistan, including the failure to preserve or publish documents,[78] solid statistical evidence is hard to come by. The work of the Bangladesh Inquiry Committee in early 1972 appears to have been tentative, incomplete, and mostly based on oral evidence, which renders figures questionable and apparently overstated. Their total figure of 1,247,000 killed contrasted with just over 80,000 bodies or remains recovered,[79] an unrealistic ratio even given the widespread practice of dumping corpses in rivers.

Since the 1971 conflict, the unsubstantiated, sacrosanct Bangladeshi version has been that three million people were killed.[80] By contrast, more or less official Pakistani sources put the figure ridiculously low at between 26,000 and 50,000.[81] If not relying on much-inflated data in India's press, foreign observers during the conflict mostly estimated 200,000 to 500,000 deaths. A similar estimate was unofficially voiced by some Indian officials years later.[82] Some interesting figures were provided by the Pakistani military during the conflict: Commanding General Niazi claims that he stated in an order on May 13, 1971 that "30,000 rebels had either been killed or made ineffective" so far. Pakistani journalist Anthony Mascarenhas, on his visit to East Pakistan in late April 1971, heard indirectly from officers that 150,000 or more Bengalis had been killed.[83] These figures may have been speculation in part as units often did not seem to count their victims, despite being asked for numbers of enemy losses by their superiors, starting from the first night of the crackdown in Dacca.[84] On the other hand, individual men and officers inside Pakistani units appear to have kept personal killing counts, mocking comrades who had not yet taken a life.[85] One Bengali officer who was summarily shot with others and left for dead on March 30 related that a stream of curious soldiers came in for 2½ hours to take a look at the bodies.[86]

Some scattered data do allow for a partial reconstruction of the magnitude of destruction. Aside from the relatively reliable refugee figures (see below), some evidence lets us probe the thesis that the Pakistani troops aimed at the extermination of the Bengali intelligentsia. The massacres at Dacca University – namely at Jagannath Hall (Hindus), Iqbal Hall (student activists), and Rokeya Hall (female students), and faculty and staff quarters – by companies from three Punjabi and Baluch battalions have become a symbol for this entire 'genocide.'[87] One of the executions was filmed clandestinely by an engineering professor.[88] According to the Bangladesh Ministry of Education, 2,000 teachers from elementary schools to universities lost their lives; a Bangladesh propaganda publication put the number at 989.[89] This would have been 1.2 or 0.6 percent of all teachers, respectively (and 4 percent of all professors, according to the latter source).[90] About 10 percent of university professors, 20 percent of college instructors, and 1.2 percent of other teachers seem to have fled to India.[91] A July 1972 survey at Rajshahi University found that "one in ten students lost at least one member of his family," which points to a mortality rate of far below 10 percent in a (partially) middle-class environment. But no less than 71 percent of these families had left their homes at some point. Some students and several professors were shot after arrest, the students mostly in their legs. Half of the instructors fled but 80 percent were said to be back by October.[92] All this proves that bloody terror, but no systematic extermination of the Bengali intelligentsia, took place.

The West German Embassy estimated that students were killed but noted that the "systematic hunt for students [had been] officially cancelled" on April 18.[93] The military administration then sought support among Bengali intellectuals, with some success.[94] The abduction and murder of up to 280 nationalist intellectuals and civil servants by *Al-Badr* paramilitaries in cooperation with the Pakistani army in December 1971 in Dacca, Khulna, Sylhet, and Brahmanbaria has been blown out of proportion in Bangladeshi historiography as an attempt to exterminate the entire Bengali intelligentsia and therefore prove 'genocide.'[95]

Such relatively low mortality figures find some confirmation in anecdotal evidence that most civil servants loyally stayed in their jobs after the March 1971 military crackdown – and most later continued to serve under the Mujib government. Eight hundred civil servants were imprisoned in Dacca central jail at some point in the conflict. One thousand officials were brought in from West Pakistan within six months to replace Bengalis – amounting probably to less than 1 percent of the province's civil service.[96] Some have argued that "middle-class Muslims" among the Bengalis in general remained "aloof" from the 1971 conflict.[97]

Though losses of the Awami League were higher, they too do not substantiate claims of systematic annihilation. A Bangladesh government board of inquiry announced in April 1972 that 17,000 members of the Awami League had been killed.[98] By mid-June 1971, Pakistani authorities classified League supporters as either "white" (given clearance), "grey" (lost their jobs and could be imprisoned), or "black" (to be killed).[99] The Awami League had the reputation of being a not particularly well organized mass party; aside from between 2,000 and 10,000 paid functionaries,[100] it appears likely that the party had at least 200,000 members (given that it had organizational structures in 80 percent of the 4,000 *unions* and, according to a party leader, members in nearly every one of the 70,000 villages).[101] This would mean that less than 10 percent of Awami League members perished. We can also infer that about 10 percent of the party's leadership died. An Australian diplomat reported in March 1972 that he had heard "that only 15 or 20 members of the 167 [Awami League] members of the National Assembly had failed to reappear," and the same went for Provincial Assembly members.[102] Many prominent party members and even middle ranks had quickly fled to India, so that the party was accused of providing no leadership in the independence struggle. Without help from the Bengali police, the Pakistani army (except in Pabna, where 100 political and intellectual leaders were killed in the first four days) in general lacked the local knowledge to find and arrest even the most prominent members of parliament, despite the marking of some houses. Most escaped.[103] By early July 1971, about two-thirds of the National and Provincial Assembly Members seem to have been abroad, as they took an oath on Bangladeshi victory in India, while only 15 or 16 were reportedly in Dacca.[104] (By comparison, in September 1975, following a coup, famine, and internal political violence, about half of all Awami League members of the National Assembly had been "killed, or [were] in jail or absconding."[105]) While clearly indicative of murderous terror, these death rates do not suggest that the Pakistani military intended to kill all Awami Leaguers or the intelligentsia in broader terms.[106]

The losses among Bengali armed formations in 1971 were much higher. It has been argued that only 3,000 of 6,000 Bengali members of the East Bengal Regiment and 8,000 of 14,000 in the East Pakistan Rifles survived even the initial onslaught. Many were killed during the first night.[107] In January 1972, A. Rahim, Deputy Inspector-General of Police, reported that 12,000 policemen had been wiped out – according to various accounts between 24 and 40 percent of the total.[108] Since the Pakistani army killed many Bengali soldiers and police officers after they were captured, this was in clear violation of the laws of humanity. However, losses among the *Ansar* auxiliary police were apparently much lower; today they are given at 644 officers, men, and staff – probably less than 3 percent – out of a force that numbered tens of thousands.

The Secretary-General of the South-East Asia Buddhist Federation, Dhaumaviriyo, stated that 5,000 Buddhists had been killed (about 1.2 percent of Buddhists in East Pakistan; most lived in the Chittagong Hill Tracts). By May, 100,000 Buddhists from the Chittagong area had reportedly fled to India.[109] More than 20,000 employees of public services such as the postal service, railways, banks, and semi-governmental organizations lost their lives.[110]

If the aforementioned data are reliable, the death toll of the terror against all these groups combined was around 65,000. Without data from the countryside, where 93 to 95 percent of the East Pakistani population lived and most of the killings happened in 1971, it is impossible to establish a reasonably secure total figure for deaths. However, a long-term population survey going on in Matlab *thana* (police district), Comilla district (sample: about 112,000 people) suggests that, compared to the late 1960s, the crude death rate increased by 6/1,000, from 15 to 21, for May 1971 to April 1972.[111] Another study of a sample of 38,366 persons throughout all districts of Bangladesh almost exactly confirmed this 1971–72 death rate increase.[112] Projected onto a population of 75 million, this would suggest an extra 450,000 deaths.[113] Yet, despite army operations in the area, especially after June 1971, in Matlab *thana*, most deaths were probably caused by want and disease: of 868 excess deaths in 1971–72, 571 affected children (60 percent girls), 230 people over 45 years (two-thirds of them men), and there were 44 excess[114] deaths of men between the ages of 15 and 44.[115] Hence relatively few direct army killings must have occurred in Matlab *thana*, for able-bodied men were their prime targets. While this area was therefore not representative of all of Bangladesh, the data do suggest that deprivation and famine killed a major proportion of those who died during the conflict. All in all, the Pakistani army did not organize the total destruction of any group except for captured armed fighters, and it is very unlikely that the fatalities in 1971 exceeded one million people.[116]

Refugees

Indian authorities, scholars, and foreign aid workers and visitors collected a variety of information on the stream of refugees that allows for some deeper insights into what happened inside East Pakistan. Those fleeing from East Pakistan who crossed the border were registered under the 1946 Foreigners Act in India: their stay was considered temporary; they were not permitted to work (many violated this provision) but were provided with food rations if they registered and remained in a refugee camp.[117] According to official Indian figures, the number of refugees reached 9.89 million in mid-December 1971.[118] Most foreign observers (including the CIA) found these data accurate but they had no real means of verifying them.[119] As the Indian authorities lacked the manpower to control the border to East Pakistan in its entirety, the figure of 3.1 million refugees said to be staying with relatives or friends (especially in West Bengal)[120] is to a certain extent questionable; the figures for the refugee camp population appear solid. This was one of the biggest flight movements in history.

By contrast, the Pakistani government officially admitted that there were 2 million refugees, the semi-official history of the conflict 2.8 million.[121] Unofficially, General Rao Farman Ali conceded that there were 6 million refugees, President Yahya Khan less than 4 million, and the pro-Pakistani Jessore district administration 500,000, or 20 percent of that area's population.[122] Much publicity for reception camps for returnees did not help the Pakistani authorities to lure a large number of the refugees back. Pakistan claimed that 200,000 returned (30 percent Hindus); foreign observers estimated far less. Even according to Pakistani figures, 90 percent of the refugees refused to return under their rule.[123]

The available data allow us to further specify who was forced to leave East Pakistan. About 70 to 90 percent of all refugees were Hindus, according to various information.[124] Only initially had a majority been Muslims, and their share of those who crossed into India grew a bit again in the fall of 1971. Their proportion in the Indian state of Tripura, where many Muslim nationalists from Dacca and Comilla areas arrived, stood at 50 percent by August.[125] But overall, this means that a staggering 70 to 90 percent of all Hindu East Pakistanis fled the country, but less than 5 percent of all Muslims. Most in the refugee camps were from families of farmers, landless laborers, rural artisans, fishermen, and petty traders – the last three especially were occupations often held by Hindus. An estimated 1.5 million had an urban background.[126] Most Hindu tea workers from Sylhet district left with their families – amounting to 280,000 people.[127] Yet most Hindu men were not ready to take up arms against the Pakistanis; 80 percent or more of the Mukti Bahini forces set up in India were Muslims, among them many from the urban middle class, primarily students.[128] There were more adult men than women among the refugees, while the low number suggests that many children of these families were left behind with relatives, neighbors, or friends.[129] Some men sent money back across the border to their families.[130]

Most East Pakistanis – coming for the most part from western East Bengal[131] – sought refuge in West Bengal (7.49 million). Here, they were unevenly spread over a few districts: more than half came from northwestern East Pakistan to the districts of West Dinajpur, Cooch Behar, Malda, Darjeeling, and Jaljaipuri. However, another 40 percent stayed in 24-Parganas and Nadia districts (most originated from Khulna, Jessore, Kushtia, Faridpur, and Barisal districts); others moved on to nearby Calcutta. About 1.4 million East Pakistanis fled to Tripura and 700,000 to Meghalaya.[132]

The majority of the refugees (again, predominantly Hindus) were driven out by Pakistani military operations in the countryside from April to June 1971; two-thirds (6.4 million) had left East Pakistan by late June, more than 9 million by late September.[133] In rural areas where local military commanders pursued a less reckless occupation policy or in the coastal areas not reached by the army, far fewer people fled than elsewhere (e.g. from Bogra and Patuakhali districts, 'only' 100,000 and 10,000 people, respectively, fled abroad).[134] The refugees often came in big waves: 300,000 entered Tripura in the third and forth week of April from Comilla, Sylhet, and Noakhali districts. Most of the 1.2 million people who fled to Nadia district, West Bengal, from Kushtia and secondarily Faridpur districts, crossed the border within ten to fifteen days. In late July, another crowd of up to 500,000 refugees reportedly approached the border, coming from Faridpur and Barisal districts.[135] A local study from Chchianobboi Gram describes the decision-making for the collective exodus of 96 villages. Their members formed an eight-mile long column, and their flight routes and halts were highly organized by Hindu leaders in view of repeated attacks on the fringes of the area and the declared inability of Muslim neighbors to offer protection.[136] The escape from the cities proceeded in a much more chaotic way. Fear and danger accompanied the refugees all the way to the border. Treks of refugees or individuals were attacked by Pakistani troops, particularly at river crossings. Four hundred were said to have been killed at Chuadanga, Kushtia district. Observers saw many refugees with gunshot or bayonet wounds in the camps.[137]

In the initial days, most refugees were Muslims.[138] The first arrived in Tripura state by March 26 or 27, apparently from the Comilla area, and in Shillong, Meghalaya. Indian Prime Minister Gandhi announced on March 27 that India would keep her border open for all refugees.[139] However, among the first refugees to India were considerable numbers of non-Bengalis persecuted by Bengalis, and even some non-Bengali Pakistani soldiers.[140]

The number Bangladeshi authorities gave for the internally displaced – 20 million[141] – seems highly exaggerated.[142] No doubt, initially or later on, large numbers of urbanites from Dacca, Chittagong, Jessore, Khulna, and smaller cities fled to the countryside.[143] It is not clear how many rural dwellers did the same. Estimates saw high proportions of refugees from Pabna, Bogra, Rajshahi, Dacca, and Noakhali districts.[144] There were large concentrations of Hindu refugees in the remote southern coastal areas, where the Pakistani army did not operate.[145] Thousands crowded border areas that the Pakistani army had not yet re-occupied.[146] In numbers reaching from a few dozen to the thousands, mostly Hindu refugees took shelter in Christian missions.[147] Little is known about the fate of the large number who stayed with relatives, friends, or even without shelter; these people were vulnerable to diseases, starvation, and assaults.

The Indian authorities did what most foreign observers described as an outstanding job of supplying this flood of refugees with basic necessities,[148] especially with food and medical aid. Sanitation and shelter remained bigger problems. As a result, deaths through starvation were rare, whereas gastro-enteric and respiratory diseases took a higher toll.[149] About 15,000 deaths were reported, mostly among children.[150] A cholera epidemic claimed close to 6,000 refugees' lives (which was, however, in line with the usual number of cholera deaths inside East Pakistan, though in a different season).[151] News about the epidemic slowed down the flow of refugees in early June 1971.[152] In addition, missionaries and journalists spoke of thousands of refugees dying of exhaustion on the march, or small children left by the wayside.[153]

Anticipating that the stream of refugees would lead to a variety of complex social conflicts, the Indian government stated categorically from the beginning that the East Bengalis would have to return home once conditions allowed it.[154] Actual problems caused by the exiles included local food price inflation, envy on the part of local populations because the refugees were said to be better supplied, problems of public finance, competition for jobs and the undercutting of rural wages, hostile reactions by West Bengali Muslims who supported Pakistan or felt their position in India undermined, and anti-Muslim or anti-Bengali propaganda, for example in Assam.[155] In Tripura, some districts of West Bengal, and Meghalaya, the number refugees equaled that of the normal population.[156] For the Indian government, the costs of $1.1 billion were a severe burden, requiring other budget cuts and retarding national economic growth; foreign aid covered only a small portion.[157] Therefore, after the Indian–Bengali victory on December 16, Indian authorities almost immediately exerted pressure on the refugees to return and offered some money, food, and blankets for the journey home (at a cost of over $300 million). This contributed to a tide of returning refugees which overwhelmed the new Bangladeshi administration. By January 6, 1972, one million exiles had already returned, by late January six to eight million, by late February over nine million. The timing was also determined by other considerations than Indian policies. After investigating the state of their property, many peasants hurried back, especially given that the best planting season for the most important rice crop of the year (Aman) ended in January.[158] Many homeless crowded Dacca and other cities, and 2,500 died in a smallpox epidemic in the reception camps, which many avoided anyway.[159] All entered a country that had greatly changed.

Urban areas

The fight for Bangladeshi independence, which so many accounts about the 1971 violence were designed to support, was dominated by parts of the Bengali urban bourgeoisie and petite bourgeoisie. Immediately after the Pakistani defeat, and even in the collections of survivor reports published decades later, most accounts were by urban Muslim men and described the fate of the urban middle class – a small minority of victims. Therefore, and also because I have already described the fate of the urban intelligentsia, I keep this part on violence in urban areas short, although losses in relative terms were higher in urban than in rural areas.

As in Dacca on March 26 and 27, the Pakistani army assaulted Hindu quarters, market areas, and Hindu and Muslim slum dwellers alleged to be ardent Awami League supporters. The military shot people, looted stores, and burned houses or entire blocks. This made town centers such as Kushtia look like "the morning after a nuclear attack."[160] Afterwards, official signs were even posted: "The government is cleaning out the slum areas and will replace them with modern markets."[161] Such brutality, often exerted right after the army had taken back control of a town, as in Rajshahi and Comilla,[162] triggered streams of refugees. Thus, many urban settlements had lost more than half of their population by mid-1971.[163]

While some who had panicked returned, killings continued in many places as part of the Pakistani army's campaign of terror. People arrested in towns or brought there after apprehension in nearby villages by the military, often with the help of local paramilitaries, were brought to improvised places of detainment, interrogation and torture, rape, and murder. River port areas especially turned into killing grounds, where groups of men were stabbed or shot, and then thrown in the water, often after having been tied with ropes to each other in groups so that they could not survive.[164] Other victims were brought in trucks or buses to army facilities or public building compounds such as post offices, telephone exchanges, radio or power stations, or schools, and slaughtered there.[165] Killing sites apparently used for months were also found in many remote places outside town.[166]

The countryside

Around 93 percent of the East Pakistani population lived in rural areas. It was there where most of the violence took place, which ultimately made many people turn secessionist.[167] Yet due to the lack of official data collection and scholarship, most of what we have is anecdotal evidence. From that it emerges that the Pakistani military pursued policies of driving out and selectively killing Hindus, intimidating the population with shocking brutality, and destroying settlements near important lines of communication and, less systematically, close to the border.

Anti-guerrilla warfare often evolves in year-long processes (see Chapter 5). In the short nine months of this conflict, Pakistani military strategies remained fairly unsophisticated. They used brute force. Military presence in the countryside was very limited due to the small number of troops, many of whom were concentrated in Dacca, a few other cities, and the border areas. In between, the army operated sporadically, basically through small units conducting raids.[168] By December 1971, there were about 50,000 regular troops and 45,000 auxiliaries under arms; by April, there seem to have been 34,000 regulars (giving a fighting strength of 23,000).[169]

These troops lashed out against a rural population that was mostly taking no action against Pakistani rule, though many had voted for the Awami League.[170] In fact, the mainly urban-based Awami League and insurgents were criticized for not mobilizing rural dwellers.[171]

Nobody seems to have crafted the army's strategies in the countryside more than Lieutenant-General Niazi, who became Commander, Eastern Command on April 11, 1971 (Governor and Martial Law Administrator Tikka Khan has overshadowed his infamy in a historiography focusing on urban oppression, not violence in the countryside; Niazi himself also gladly put the blame on Tikka Khan[172]). Upon arrival, Niazi designed a risky and rapid shock attack strategy, "without caring for flanks and rear, shoot out with multiple columns for the borders and seal the routes of reinforcement and withdrawal" for the independence fighters (which was carried out by late April). Then he planned in phase two to open essential river, road, and rail communications (which he achieved by late April or early May); in phase three to clear all towns; and in phase four to finally comb the countryside.[173] With that, Niazi responded to the task of securing control "especially of the lines of communications and in the larger towns, and helping the civil administration in dealing with the insurgent activities in the interior of the country" in order to "sort out the complex, intricate and 'messed up' situation in East Pakistan".[174]

This strategy explains the dramatic swelling of the streams of refugees from late April 1971 (with the independence fighters forced to switch to guerrilla tactics). Niazi's troops could not take the 1,700 km border under control, but they created panic among the peasants. What happened can be concluded from the pattern of destruction of buildings observed later. For one thing, buildings and villages along major roads were systematically burned, as many observers noted, especially up until May. This tactic had already seemed to be prophylactically applied in late March or early April by a brigade under Brigadier Arbab, allegedly on Tikka Khan's orders, according to Major-General Mitha. Arbab is also said to have told a battalion commander to "destroy all houses in [the town of] Jodevpur," an order largely carried out.[175] Second, where a guerrilla attack occurred (often at roads or bridges), the army usually assaulted surrounding villages in reprisal.[176] Martial Law Order 148 of April 27, 1971 even stated publicly: "Inhabitants of the surrounding area of all or any such affected place or places [destroyed traffic or communication lines] will render themselves liable to punitive action collectively."[177] The same could happen along rivers or near towns during re-conquest.[178] Third, due to frequent fighting and preemptive violence by Pakistani troops, many houses and settlements in proximity to the border were devastated. Based on air reconnaissance, staff of the UN Relief Operation in Dacca (UNROD) – noting that Bangladeshi authorities' figures of 10 million destroyed homes were much inflated – estimated that 30 percent of all houses in a fifteen-kilometer strip along the borders were destroyed (1.16 million), 20 percent along rivers, railroads, and main roads (350,000), but relatively few in the rest of the country (1 percent, or 50,000).[179] Destruction was fiercest west of the Jamuna river from Dinajpur to Khulna.[180]

Survivors and observers often perceived this destruction as random.[181] Though indiscipline played a major role, West Pakistani soldiers inside East Pakistan had proven their capacity to maintain discipline for some time through much of March 1971, although lacking most supplies while being virtually under siege.[182] Orders, tactics, and circumstances explain much of the army brutality in the countryside, together with chauvinist attitudes. Soldiers had "orders for firing blindly into occupied houses, burn down entire villages and slaughter the occupants as they fled" in order to break resistance.[183] These were called "kill-and-burn" operations inside the army.[184] With its minimal manpower, the Pakistani military moved along major roads, rarely in between; without helicopters, they usually came overland, and were therefore detected early by villagers; also, given their small forces, they mostly lacked the capacity to surround settlements. This is why most inhabitants could usually flee, as villagers reported. Often the troops then gathered the remaining people, tried to identify male Hindus and supporters of the insurgents, and killed these. Such operations took place from April to the end of the conflict, as is acknowledged even in Pakistani sources.[185] For instance, in the week following May 14, 1971, the military and local auxiliaries destroyed 26 mostly Hindu villages forty kilometers north of Dacca, searched for Mukti Bahini, shot at fleeing civilians, abducted girls, and burned homes, triggering a major refugee wave. In Baira, 49 people died, 174 homes were totally and 86 partially destroyed, and 500 tons of rice stolen or burned. In July and

August, Christian villages, too, were put to the torch.[186] At times the killing went further, as in Demra near Dacca, where all men between 12 and 35 or 40 years old were said to be killed and all women raped. Sometimes, all men were shot. There was no uniform pattern; sometimes orders changed during an operation.[187]

The persecution of Hindus

As the number of refugees makes clear, the ten to eleven million Hindus of the country were especially hard hit by violence in the East Pakistan conflict.[188] This victimization was not without precedents. Communal riots between Muslims and Hindus in Bengal seem to have started in 1918. Though violence during partition in Bengal was less severe than in the Punjab and Kashmir, repeated massacres between 1946 and 1950 and the abolition of the *zamindari* system in 1947–51 resulted in the emigration of two million Hindus to India, including much of the upper class and civil servants. The first massacre of Hindus in East Bengal outside the cities occurred in 1950. Another wave of anti-Hindu violence followed in 1964, and mass arrests and expropriations during the India–Pakistan war of 1965. Between 1947 and the 1960s, about four million Hindus left.[189] West Bengal alone received 248,158 Hindus from East Pakistan in 1970.[190] The remaining Hindu communities mostly consisted of artisans, fishermen, and small peasants. Compared to other villagers, Hindus tended to be better educated, self-employed or employers, in middle-income ranges.[191] Hostile feelings against Hindus were widespread even among Bengali urban leftists.[192] In 1971, the persecution of Hindus in East Pakistan was transformed, but mass violence against Hindus had happened before, and their repression did not end in that year either.

During the conflict, some Pakistani officers tried to "eliminate all suspected Indian collaborators, especially Hindus." Anthony Mascarenhas quotes Major Rathore, a staff officer with the 9 Infantry Division in Comilla in April 1971, saying of Hindus who had allegedly collectively done harm to Pakistan: "Now under the cover of fighting we have an excellent opportunity of finishing them off. [...] Of course [...], we are only killing the Hindu men. We are soldiers, not cowards like the rebels." Colonel Naim of the same division argued that Hindus had "undermined the Muslim masses" and "bled the province white" through smuggling money and goods to India. Bengali culture had largely become Hindu culture: "We have to sort them out to restore the land to the people."[193] Hindus were also alleged to have corrupted the Awami League. In the Jessore area, rumors that Hindus had killed non-Bengalis drew the ire of non-Bengalis but also of religious Bengalis.[194] Pakistani soldiers more than once boasted to US Consul Archer Blood that they had come "to kill Hindus."[195] To drive out Hindus seemed a useful multi-purpose measure to weaken Bengali culture, diminish Indian influence, strip the residues of Hindu elites of their status, recruit collaborators by sharing the booty, and win back the support of conservative Muslims. However, as a means of defeating Bengali nationalism and guaranteeing Pakistani unity, persecuting Hindus turned out an ineffective tool.

It has been maintained that the Pakistani army wanted to systematically drive out Hindus in order to reduce East Pakistan to parity in population with West Pakistan.[196] While corroboration for such a long-term goal is lacking, there is evidence that the military intended to expel most Hindus through a policy of terror, as the fate of many refugees suggests.[197] US Embassy staff in Islamabad in April and May also observed this shift and the increase in official anti-Hindu propaganda, even though they were otherwise reluctant to admit wrongdoing by the Pakistani government.[198] That Niazi, by his sudden anti-insurgency attack with army columns toward the borders and the following combing of the country in April and May, intended to drive Hindus out, can be inferred from his own writings; he wanted to spread "panic" and asserts that he later suggested to the army Chief of Staff to attack India, again also to "create panic among the civilians" in Calcutta through air raids, blowing up bridges, and sinking ships.[199] Murders during the expulsion of Hindus were apparently welcomed by army leaders. According to a Pakistani inquiry, Niazi, visiting troops in the Thakargaon and Bogra areas, inquired how many Hindus a unit had killed. In May, Brigadier Abdullah Malik of 23 Brigade issued a written order to kill Hindus.[200] In Sathkira, between Barisal and Khulna, a witness heard an officer shouting at his men during the re-conquest of the town by April 8: "Why you have killed muslims [sic]. We ordered you to kill only Hindus."[201] By May 14, the US Consulate in Dacca reported that army units entering villages, inquiring where Hindus lived, and killing male Hindus was a "common pattern," while they murdered few if any women and children. For the rapid expeditionary operations, population registers, if they existed, were of little value. Bengali *razakars* or Peace Committee members helped to find Hindus, in Faridpur by painting a big "H" on houses owned by Hindus (for protecting themselves, Muslims inscribed "Muslim house" on theirs). Often Hindu men were also identified because they were not circumcised.[202] Sometimes the military also massacred Hindu women.[203] Areas where no Hindus were killed appeared exceptional.[204]

The systematic murder of Hindu men in cities had started in the first 24 hours of the crackdown, often with non-Bengalis identifying Hindu quarters for the troops.[205] For example, hospitals were periodically searched. Massacres occurred up to December 1971.[206] But other sources suggest there was no clear pattern, but a variety of treatments, ranging from beatings, robbery, forced conversion, forced labor, and denial of work permits or food rations, to shootings.[207]

Under these conditions, unsurprisingly, virtually all Hindus left from many areas. Thereby most of them succeeded in escaping death or a life that had been made unbearable for them. For example, the Bangladesh Inquiry Committee stated in 1972 that "nearly 20,000" fishermen – a common Hindu occupation – had been killed (as compared to 46,000 inland fishermen in the 1970 cyclone), while one million people from fishermen's families were directly or indirectly affected by the destruction of property (suggesting that most fishers survived). One million weavers were out of employment by 1972, "mainly Hindus."[208]

Within the villages, Hindus lived either in other *paras* (settlements) than Muslims, or were segregated within the same *para* so that they could easily be found or identified. The loss of social integration between Muslims and Hindus can also be seen by the fact that very few intimate relationships seem to have existed, few mutual invitations as wedding guests, or even friendships.[209]

An indicator of the active involvement of local Muslims in the persecution of Hindus are forced conversions to Islam during the 1971 conflict, as had been widespread during the 1950 pogroms.[210] In 1971, of the allegedly millions of conversions to Islam, some took place in reaction to Pakistani army attacks, others involved an ultimatum by local Muslim leaders, or beatings and robberies by *razakars*. Most Hindus de-converted after the war.[211] Elsewhere, Hindu men grew long beards in order to be able to travel.[212] Hindus also turned to Christianity for protection, but some US missionaries denied swift conversions, finding "wonderful opportunities to explain that a person doesn't become a Christian by signing a paper or a membership roll, or even by baptism or church membership; that real Christianity involves an act of faith whereby the person admits he is unable to save himself and accepts God's gift of salvation. Some listened; others were in too much of a hurry to get that precious piece of paper in their hands."[213] The haste was understandable, as this brotherly instruction probably claimed some lives of Hindus, despite missionaries' relief efforts for Hindus.

The reception of the Hindu refugees returning in early 1972 has been described as a "red carpet welcome."[214] If so, it did not last long. Many Hindus left the country in the following years and decades because a hostile climate quickly evolved again and their material losses of 1971 were insufficiently compensated,[215] though after 1971 crossing the border became more difficult with the erection of a barbed-wire fence and closer border controls between Bangladesh and India. By early 1975, about 500 visas were granted per day to Hindus and most applicants were expected to stay in India.[216] By the late 1970s, forced conversions of Hindus or abduction of girls who rejected Islam again became a frequent occurrence.[217]

By contrast, the Christian minority of about 200,000 in East Pakistan did not experience uniform persecution in 1971. In some regions, local Christians enjoyed relative immunity, though this may have been overstated by missionary chroniclers constructing narratives convenient for the spread of their faith. In other areas Christians were killed.[218] Around Dacca, the army destroyed Christian villages and killed hundreds, sometimes apparently because their settlements were located close to a railway line; near Faridpur, Christian families stayed in hiding during May 1971; occasionally, isolated Christian families fell victim to army violence in various parts of the country.[219] After the conflict, many Baptists were either displaced or dead – numerous letters for bible correspondence courses were returned with notes, "Addressee missing."[220] Apparently there was no repetition of the 1964 events when (alongside the persecution of Hindus) Garo tribals from the Mymensingh area – 20,000 Catholics and 15,000 Baptists – were forced to flee to Assam, shot at during their flight by Bengali troops and paramilitaries, or threatened by looting and the women by abduction.[221] But one-third of all Christians from the Ballabpur area near Nadia, Dinajpur district, amounting to "several thousand," fled to India in April 1971 after army troops had raped or killed many women.[222]

Violence by and against non-Bengalis

An examination of the fate of the non-Bengali minorities makes clear that physical attacks in East Pakistan 1971 had a lot to do with a struggle between elites. This section will basically discuss two: West Pakistanis staying in East Bengal as military officers and rank and file, civilian officials, or businessmen, each with their families; and so-called Biharis, Urdu-speaking Muslim émigrés from India who had migrated to East Pakistan during or after partition in 1947 (often from Bihar), mostly living in separate settlements in urban areas and holding jobs in the bureaucracy, in business, and forming much of the industrial workforce.[223] 'Biharis' tended to harbor prejudices against Bengalis as backward and rustic, while some Bengalis viewed 'Biharis' as "parasites" and allies or protégés of the central government in the West.[224]

According to many Bengali narratives, civilian non-Bengalis made up a large part of the pro-Pakistani auxiliary militias, took over many administrative posts, and, even in unofficial capacities, denounced Bengalis to the military, practiced torture and killings directly in small groups or through mob violence, and seized Bengali possessions.[225] Although these stories may have been exaggerated, many could be corroborated by independent observers.

However, many scholars have used these events to understate, marginalize, or even justify the violence against non-Bengalis, or to suppress the memory of atrocities against them reported earlier. The magnitude of these attacks is, of course, contested (as is the number of Biharis in general[226]). Pakistani authorities claimed that 100,000 non-Bengalis were killed, though the August 1971 Pakistani "White Paper" specified killings of 'only' about 64,000, and 20,000 bodies had been found by April.[227] In June, Bihari representatives claimed that there were 500,000 victims dead, and later a Pakistani journalist claimed even more than one million.[228] Bengali sources privately or publicly admitted the death of "a few thousand" to 30,000 or 40,000 non-Bengalis.[229] International analysts and observers have given estimates of between 20,000 and 200,000; the US Consul estimated up to 66,000.[230]

The exact timing when these killings occurred is telling about the motivations. A large part of this violence did not take place prior to March 25 – contrary to Pakistani claims that served to justify the military clampdown.[231] After March 1, arson and looting against "Biharis" in cities were quite widespread. However, for that time period the Pakistani White Paper actually reported that non-Bengali deaths were 'only' in the hundreds, depicting the riots in Chittagong on March 3 to 4 – namely in Ferozeshah and Wireless colonies, two 'Bihari' neighborhoods – as the worst, probably leaving several hundred dead, while 57 were killed in Khulna on March 5.[232] Chittagong demonstrates that part of this violence was mutual, committed by mobs and gangs from both sides; Bengalis aggressively marched into 'Bihari' quarters to make them comply with the general strike, were attacked, and then torched many buildings; then West Pakistani soldiers set Bengalis' houses ablaze.[233] Pakistani authorities also alleged that hundreds were killed in an anti-Bihari pogrom in Rangpur on March 3. Former General Rao Farman Ali stated that 800 non-Bengalis, including women and children, had been killed in Saidpur up to March 25.[234] Foreigners also observed such incidents.[235] Mujib and popular leftist Maulana Bhashani issued appeals to stop the attacks on non-Bengalis – Mujib first on March 1 and then in an appeal on March 3 to protect the lives and property of all inhabitants of East Pakistan regardless of ethnic background and religion.[236] Yet, after a lull, and immediately before the military assault, serious Bengali assaults on non-Bengalis began in Saidpur, Dacca, and Chittagong, where the army seems to have temporarily prevented a counter-attack by non-Bengalis. Mujib condemned riots against non-Bengalis in Rangpur, Saidpur, Jodevpur, and Chittagong, arguing that "non-locals [...] are our people."[237]

Such attacks by large enraged mobs or small organized gangs – both occurred equally, with fluent transitions[238] – grew significantly after the army crackdown and through much of April, wherever and as long as the military could not take control. 'Bihari' men especially were either shot or stabbed on the spot or abducted in groups and taken to killing places, while young women were sometimes held captive for longer and some killed as well. The Pakistani White Paper asserted 15,000 non-Bengalis were killed in Santahar, Bogra district (here Bengali informers spoke of 6,000 victims), 10,000–12,000 in Chittagong in late March, almost 5,000 in Jessore on March 29 and 30, 5,000 in Dinajpur town between March 28 and April 1, and 5,000 in Mymensingh from April 17 to 20 (here US Consul Blood put the figure at 500 to 2,000).[239] In Khulna, Lalmonirhat, Kushtia, and Chittagong, riots involving attacks by both sides seem to have occurred in late March or April.[240] Railway facilities and colonies (railway worker quarters) especially, as well as factories, became battlegrounds. Communal riots had already occurred at such places in the 1950s and 1960s, and labor unrest in the first half of 1970 had increased tensions. Now the conflicts became charged up, groups barricaded themselves in, and negotiations failed, leading to mutual massacres, to which Bihari managers also fell victim. The Pakistani military later committed retaliatory killings.[241] This is one reason why Bangladeshi union and government officials later reported that an exceptionally high proportion of workers had been killed.[242]

Observers emphasized the vehemence of the violence, also against non-Bengali women and children, although there was no clear pattern – in some cases all males were killed, in others also women and children, in still others little killing took place.[243] Evincing the murderous sentiment, the Superintendent of Police in Jhenida, who pointed to the semi-colonial exploitation of Bengalis, said in a statement to the press in April: "These bastard Punjabis and these bastard Biharis – we've got a lot to kill!" In May, Bengali Major Osman Choudhury told a journalist: "If we get a Bihari, we kill him. We are raiding the houses and killing them [...] because they are spies and have sided with West Pakistan."[244] The role of the Awami League in such atrocities was ambivalent, with some functionaries working for moderation or protection while others organized killings.[245] Christian missionaries took non-Bengali families under their protection. In early April, foreign journalists also witnessed the massacres of non-Bengalis.[246] When non-Bengali survivors of the Mymensingh massacres led a mob attack on Bengalis in Mirpur neighborhood in Dacca, killing fifty, and 'Biharis' tried to march into the city center, they were prevented from doing so by the Pakistani army who shot several of them dead.[247]

Even before March 25, when numerous businesspeople and families of West Pakistani military personnel left the province, they were sometimes being robbed at Awami League checkpoints on their way to Dacca airport. Refugees crowded the Dacca cantonment.[248] In April, the wave of atrocities prompted more non-Bengalis to flee from the provinces to Dacca and some further to West Pakistan, or directly to India. A flight steward reported seeing "maimed and wounded" Bihari women and children, often deeply disturbed by their horrific experiences.[249]

Pakistani troops of non-Bengali background also fell victim to the wrath of Bengali fighters or civilians, often being hacked to death or torn into pieces after they tried to shoot their way out. Few if any prisoners were taken. From the army detachments in Pabna (300 men) and Kushtia (150), there were few survivors.[250] At the orders of insurgent leader and later President Ziaur Rahman, the 8 Bengal Battalion killed their West-Pakistani prisoners as revenge for the killings of Bengali troops by Pakistani troops in Chittagong in late March. A non-Bengali captain who wanted to join the insurgents was rejected by Ziaur before being killed: "You're not being judged as a soldier but as a member of a hostile race, a treacherous nation. I'm really sorry!"[251] Ziaur possibly even ordered the murder of the wives and children of Pakistani soldiers; according to an informer for Mascarenhas, he told his troops about the women: "You can do what you want with them," and his speeches then included passages like the following: "Those who speak Urdu are also our enemies because they support the Pakistani army. We will crush them."[252] Mobs killed families of military personnel in Kaptai and Bengali troops under different command did the same in Jodevpur, Mymensingh, Hilli, and Sylhet.[253] Later on, there were more incidents of Bengali civilians slaughtering wounded or captured Pakistani troops.[254] In addition, between May and November, 3,000 to 5,000 Peace Committee members, *razakars*, or their relatives were also killed or injured.[255] All of this testifies to the severity of the onslaught against different kinds of non-Bengalis, as well as to the diversity of those carrying it out.

Another wave of violence in revenge against non-Bengali civilians as alleged collaborators of the Pakistanis, together with Bengalis suspected of being paramilitaries or Peace Committee members, followed during and immediately after the December 1971 war. Governor Malik warned the Pakistani government of "thousands of pro-Pakistan elm [elements] being butchered."[256] The Indian government assumed responsibility for the safeguarding of Pakistani military and paramilitary forces and non-Bengali civilians,[257] but didn't have full control of the situation. Pakistani officials maintained that thousands of non-Bengalis were killed.[258] A UN report from Mymensingh district suggests even higher victim numbers, stating that 25 percent of the so far more than 187,000 Bengali returnees "receive 100 per cent of the last harvest because it was kept by collaborators who, consequently, have been killed."[259]

Journalists reported that a 165-strong Mukti Bahini unit in Jessore claimed to have slain 500 to 600 *razakars* and Pakistanis (two fighters alone claimed 37 and 25, respectively). "Many" entire families in the town and its outskirts were murdered in a "frenzied violence" that, according to analyst Partha Mukherji, made for a "heartening" welcome for returning Hindu refugees. Between Chittagong and Malumghat, 28 "Bihari businessmen" and tribals were killed.[260] Participants of revenge killings recalled such action in Shibchar, Faridpur district, and other places.[261] A ghastly mass slaughter of many hundred non-Bengalis (men and boys, but also a number of women, killed under shouts of "We'll finish your race!") took place in Chittagong right before the arrival of Indian troops, who rescued the survivors.[262] About 300 men described as "Bihari soldiers" – possibly auxiliaries – were massacred by an unknown force at Golando dock near Faridpur and thrown into the river.[263] There are reports of entire families being killed, disappearances, and shooting squads in action.[264] The killings in Dacca started the night after the fall of the city when gangs of young armed Bengali men began to raid houses in non-Bengali neighborhoods, looting and abducting young women. For days, these gangs shot non-Bengalis on the spot or strangled them, beat them to death, or stabbed them at a killing site near a river in Ati.[265] Mukti Bahini arrested people on their own authority, some never to be heard of again; among people officially arrested were many professors, doctors, businessmen, or former officials. Some took refuge with their families in Dacca military compound and were protected by the Indian army, which refused to hand them over to Bangladeshis.[266] In the capital, four men were even stabbed to death as the climax of a public meeting in a stadium under guerrilla leader Kader Siddiqui. This scene and others were shown on British and West German television. Similar things happened in Khulna.[267]

At a lower intensity, persecution dragged on for years. In late January 1972, dozens of non-Bengalis and Bangladeshi forces were killed when the latter stormed Mirpur and Mohammedpur, non-Bengali neighborhoods in Dacca. Several hundred were reported killed in Khulna in March and Dacca in May.[268] Lacking food and water supplies, shelter, and sanitation in refugee camps created a desperate situation.[269] In 1979, Oxfam had credible information that 8,000 children had died "unnecessarily" in the refugee camps; similar claims had been made in 1975–76.[270] East German flight crews transporting 6,978 'Biharis' from Bangladesh to Pakistan in 1973 reported that these were in "extremely bad physical condition," including cases of open tuberculosis, dysentery, smallpox, and leprosy. Some had to be carried aboard.[271] About half a million 'Biharis' assumed Bangladeshi citizenship. Of the rest, from 126,941 to 193,590 would emigrate to Pakistan between 1973 and 2002, while by 1992 no less than 238,093 were still stranded in 66 camps. Most lived in the Dacca and Saidpur areas. Despite some improvement between 1975 and 1977, when many Biharis were allowed back into jobs under the conservative government, in 1997 close to half still had doubts about whether they could integrate into Bangladeshi society.[272]

While many non-Bengali men played an instrumental role in the Pakistani terror, and some carried out killings on their own in local militias, 'Biharis' were also victims of mass violence. Hundreds of them were killed between March 1 and 22, 1971, tens of thousands in late March and April (maybe as many as Bengalis by the Pakistani army in that period), thousands in December, and hundreds in early 1972. The big massacres against 'Biharis' occurred after the Pakistani army crackdown, but before the Pakistani military built auxiliary forces in great numbers. This sequence means that neither could the military clampdown be justified by Bengali pogroms against non-Bengalis, as was claimed in Pakistan, nor could the biggest anti-Bihari pogroms be justified by the action of 'Bihari' *razakars*, as many Bangladeshis have argued. In any case, aside from the confrontation between the central government and East Pakistanis, a conflict between social groups within the province of East Pakistan was exacerbated with the parties increasingly viewed in ethnic terms. However, it was interwoven with class issues as well, and Bengali and Bihari elites competed for leadership. In terms of mortality, non-Bengalis belonged to the hardest hit groups in East Pakistan/Bangladesh, and many survivors lost for ever their socially advantageous position, which they had tried to strengthen with help of the army. Violence against and by non-Bengalis contributed to the fact that urban areas became battlefields with especially high mortality rates during the 1971 conflict.

Rape

The Bangladesh independence conflict is also notorious for the rapes committed by Pakistani troops. In fact, while much sexual abuse occurred in all cases covered in this book, the level in East Pakistan does appear exceptional. Any inquiry into rape is hampered by especially grave source problems, and mine cannot claim to be comprehensive because important material is only available in Bengali. What this section aims to do is to put mass rapes in Bangladesh in a broader context in order to show that female victimization also had a lot to do with broader attitudes and practices in Pakistani and Bengali society.

As usual, the number of rapes is extremely difficult to determine. On an individual basis, victims of sexual abuse and their families are extremely reluctant to report it; but alleged mass rape is also an important topic of atrocity propaganda. Rape is therefore often both underreported and overstated. Even where official registration of victims happens, it has little claim to precision; in Bangladesh it was at best fragmentary. There is no way to verify the official Bangladeshi number that 200,000 women were sexually abused during the independence conflict, or figures of up to 400,000.[273] Officials at the time found 200,000 plausible because it meant that less than four women would have been raped in each of the countries' 62,000 villages.[274] Reports of the 1972 inquiry from the districts added up to close to 80,000 cases of "women ravished," with almost a quarter concentrated in Dacca and Comilla districts combined. Another source saw the northwestern districts of Dinajpur and Bogra most severely affected.[275]

Often gang rapes happened in public. Sometimes this involved the murder of male relatives, or of small children who disturbed the soldiers during their deed.[276] Complaints to the Martial Law Authorities could lead to more rape and destruction.[277] Women of all ages and social backgrounds, urban and rural, were affected, but it is unclear in which proportions. The claim that 80 percent were Muslim[278] has no clear basis. After the war, Hindu activists accused the Bangladesh government of not helping Hindus to find their abducted and forcibly converted women.[279]

Rape started on the very first night of the crackdown with the attack on Rokeya Hall at Dacca University, and continued to the last days of the war. Early incidents were large enough to find mention in a restraining order by Niazi on April 15, four days after he took over the

Eastern Command, who warned this "may well boomerang involving your own women-folk."[280] (Though acknowledging his orders for restraint, the Hamoodur Commission stated that "at the same time there is some evidence to suggest that the words and personal actions of Lt.Gen. Niazi were calculated to encourage the killings and rape."[281])

In many cases, women were held captive as sex slaves for months, mostly in military cantonments or camps.[282] In July, stories circulated that a doctor had declined to perform abortions on some of the 500 women held at an army base in Dacca.[283] In a March 1972 interview, Niazi put this number at 'only' 50, denying a figure of 250.[284] Obviously, these women could not be held without the knowledge and therefore the support of commanders.[285] The same goes for their group transports on army trucks.[286] Other victims were captives of soldiers or *razakars* in factory buildings, camps, or brothels.[287] Indian troop Commander General Aurora said his troops liberated about 100 women from army compounds. By December 25, 1971, 4,000 women were reported to have been "recovered" – in Dacca alone 300 within one week, another 300 in Chittagong. Most were between fourteen and thirty years old.[288]

In the debate about the motives for the mass rapes, some have argued that Pakistani troops tried to impregnate Bengali women to bring the country back under firm Pakistani control. Allegedly, Tikka Khan gave orders to this effect.[289] A Pakistani officer confirmed the existence of such considerations with the story of an unspecified officer who thought "a masculine image would convince others of the 'potency' of his command," based on his "pet theory concerning the need to change the genetic make-up of the Bengali[s], substituting subservience for 'treachery'. He proposed these 'views' freely, without reservation" and seems to have found some followers, who were allegedly restrained by responsible officers.[290] A Pakistani soldier leaving the Dacca cantonment after defeat in December 1971 was quoted as having shouted: "We are going. But we are leaving our seed behind."[291] However, some events suggest that not all rape served this purpose: according to the Pakistani army, Hindus should be excluded from the East Pakistani social fabric, and yet soldiers and other men raped Hindu women. The frequent rapes following which the victim was murdered or during which she was severely injured or mutilated did not substantiate the impregnation theory either.[292] A high-ranking Pakistani officer told the Hamoodur Commission: "The troops used to say that when the Commander (Lt.Gen. Niazi) was himself a raper [sic], how could they be stopped."[293] If this statement on official Pakistani record is damning, it also points to general misogyny, racism, and tolerance of violence, rather than an organized impregnation policy.

Rape could also serve as a means of terror in order to expedite the expulsion of religious or cultural minorities, in the post-1971 period[294] or before. It obviously could also help to humiliate men unable to protect female family members; as in other cases of mass violence, Bengali men were in turn 'feminized' in the view of West Pakistanis who, referring to the *lungi* customary in Bengal, had a saying: "In the East [...], the men wear the skirts and the women the pants. In the West, things are as they should be."[295] Others have cited desperate action by Pakistani soldiers isolated in the countryside, who "turned into looters and gangsters."[296] The example of East Pakistan shows that monocausal explanations fail to account for the causes of rape.

Susan Brownmiller has rejected the impregnation and rape-as-terror theses, suggesting that worldwide male oppression of females was at the root of the problem and this outbreak resembled other war situations.[297] However hegemonic patriarchy may be, one cannot understand its specific articulations without the specific context – the particularly rigid restrictions and low social status under which women in Bangladesh were forced to live in a patrilinear society. Young girls are viewed as a burden because their own families have to pay a dowry for them and they are worth little investment as they will leave the family after marriage. In their husbands' family, they are often treated like maids (especially by their mothers-in-law who see their own relationship to their son loosening, with the consequent loss of prestige) until they give birth to a son.[298] Rules of inheritance that grossly discriminate against women reinforce this effect.[299] Bangladesh is one of the few countries in the world where women have a lower life expectancy than men (except in famines).[300]

These restrictions made many families after the war refuse to take back their female members perceived as 'dishonored' by sexual abuse, either because of their own attitudes or for fear of the family's reputation in the village community.[301] This rejection had already started in the refugee camps in India, where about 500 rape victims had to be housed separately; in 1992, three female witnesses in a tribunal against Gholam Azam who made statements about being abused in 1971 were still humiliated upon their return.[302] A 1972 government recovery program and sympathy drive labeling the rape victims as *biranganas* (war heroines) was of little avail. The official "marry them off" campaign failed due to a lack of male candidates and the far-reaching demands of volunteers, ranging "from the latest model of Japanese car, painted red, to the publication of unpublished poems."[303] A number of raped women and girls were killed by their own relatives, especially husbands.[304] Others fled to Pakistan or committed suicide.[305]

In this atmosphere of fear, humiliation, despair, and repression, thousands of pregnant rape victims had their children aborted. Estimates of between 25,000 and 150,000 abortions have been suggested; the latter is probably inflated. Often, newborns were killed, some by nurses throwing them into dustbins.[306] But the secondary policy of the rehabilitation centers (if no abortion seemed possible) was to take the babies away from the mothers, by force when necessary, and have them adopted abroad. Mujib encouraged this practice: "I do not want those polluted blood [sic] in this country."[307]

Not only was his remark racist, it also missed the point that the problem had not just been rapes by Pakistani occupation soldiers. The fact that many rapes in 1971 had been committed by Bengalis, as victims and Bengali witnesses confirmed, remained a taboo for decades and became a matter of debate in Bangladesh only in the 1990s. These rapes included the well-known sexual abuse of Bengali women by *razakar* auxiliaries,[308] but also by many Bengali men without sympathy for the Pakistani regime.[309] Given such unwelcome memories, it is easier to understand why the depositions by more than 5,000 "war repressed women" were destroyed after Mujib's 1975 assassination and the takeover by the conservative regime under Ziaur Rahman.[310] Moreover, Mukti Bahini independence fighters, especially in Dacca just after victory, raped non-Bengali women.[311] Armed men also "abducted women and forced them into 'sten-gun weddings'."[312] Earlier, in the weeks after the army crackdown of March, gang rapes of non-Bengali females by Bengali men seem to have been frequent and sometimes public, often followed by their murder.[313] Collective rape had already been a frequent occurrence in riots against Hindus from 1946 to 1964.[314] After 1971, violence against females became generally more common. Its most dramatic expression were frequent acid attacks against women in the 1980s and 1990s, usually against unmarried females for their refusal of marriage, love, or sexual relationship, but there were also assaults with acids or pesticides within families against brides, or violence against women in police custody.[315] Some activists assert that "violence against women cuts across the boundaries of age, education, class, caste, and religion" and that domestic violence is "almost routine" in Bangladesh.[316] Today, it is estimated that 15,000 Bangladeshi minors, mostly girls, are annually being kidnapped or sold to India or lured there under some pretext where they are adopted or exploited as workers or prostitutes.[317]

Without doubt there was much sexual violence by Pakistani troops in 1971. It can be attributed to ideas about changing the genetic make-up of East Bengal or forcing out Hindus, but mostly to lust, colonial racism against Bengalis in general, the desire to humiliate Bengali men and women, and sadism. Military involvement reveals some degree of organization but not much of a clear purpose. Mass rapes in Bangladesh in 1971 were not based simply on state policy or intent, but were the product of an extremely violent society, including a much longer history of open violence against women in East Bengal with undercurrents from two cultures of contempt and depreciation of women (West and East Pakistani). The 1971 societal crisis led to the breakdown of norms, ethics, and general social control; the protection of women afforded by families, communities, and police diminished radically, as did the guardianship of men due to their flight, expulsion, or arrest, which separated them from the women. All of this rendered females of different backgrounds unsafe and vulnerable to attacks by a variety of men. No account has demonstrated this more shockingly than that by Ferdousi Priyobashinee, who – after her fiancé and relatives had left Khulna – became fair game for a colleague, then a factory manager, then a businessman (mostly non-Bengalis), and finally for various Pakistani army officers and junior officers. She had to become the lover of an officer to escape greater harm.[318]

In this extremely violent society, many women were left defenseless not only at the time of rape, but also afterwards.[319] A mockery of reestablishing 'ethical' values, by which relatives accepted the norms of the perpetrators, happened at their cost; their exclusion from solidarity added to the injustice, often ending in murder, suicide, or starvation. Facing rapid social change, men tried to reinforce their predominance. From the 1970s, social exclusion and impoverishment forced more women to seek wage labor and other jobs which had not previously been open to them, a process that would help to challenge gender roles.[320]

Redistribution and violence

The deep crisis in which East Bengali society was plunged cannot be fully appreciated without a brief account of the social mobility, accumulation, and redistribution processes at work in the early 1970s. This was an inherently participatory development, in which state regulations also played a role. The Enemy Property Act of 1965 allowed for the arbitrary expropriation of the property of Hindus whose relatives had fled to India, and prevented Hindus from selling their property and even from withdrawing money from their accounts.[321] After late March 1971, these edicts were applied with new force. In July, Hindu property was reported by foreign journalists to be listed as "alien" or "enemy property" and occasionally auctioned to Pakistan supporters. Indian officials even alleged that the Pakistani administration was destroying title deeds for land owned by Hindus to perpetuate their emigration.[322] Anthony Mascarenhas summed up this Pakistani policy which aimed to reestablish political stability and was pursued with the "utmost blatancy": "When the Hindus have been eliminated by death and flight, their property will be used as a golden carrot to win over the underprivileged Muslim middleclass."[323] Many houses and shops owned by Hindus were not destroyed but redistributed among government supporters, among them many non-Bengalis in the cities and members of conservative Muslim parties in the countryside.[324] As Shahabuddin Ahmad, bank manager of the Dacca Urban Development Bank, recalled, in 1971 numerous circulars – some secret – ordered the freezing of accounts of Awami League members and alleged supporters.[325] Citizens just as often took matters into their own hands, such as the "Fund of Five" around Maulana Sayeedi in Pirojpur, who had the property of independence fighters and Hindus looted and ran a business selling it on.[326] "Most peace committee members were fortune hunters whose only aim was to share the plunder and loot," one historian stated.[327] Meanwhile, West Pakistani entrepreneurs continued to sell off their property, while some Bengalis still boycotted non-Bengali consumer goods.[328]

There was plenty of room for private initiative where public order broke down. Looting by Bengalis had started even before March 25.[329] In late March and April, Bengali mobs and retreating Bengali troops engaged in pillaging.[330] Marauding by non-Bengalis was admitted even by Pakistani propagandists. Others set up a "lucrative protection racket."[331] Yet Bengalis also blamed 'Biharis,' while actually themselves plundering the property of Hindus.[332] The problem reached to the very top of the Pakistani army: General Niazi removed Brigadier Arbab on charges of "looting and theft" and condemned the practice of commanders tolerating widespread pillaging and troops sending loot to West Pakistan,[333] including "cars, refrigerators and air conditioners" as well as up to 233,000 rupees in cash per person.[334] In the streets of Dacca, Pakistani soldiers sold plundered wristwatches, TV sets, and radios – and this means there were also buyers.[335] All of this seems to have originated from high-level orders in late March 1971 to live off the land, take goods without proper receipts, and treat East Bengal as "enemy territory."[336]

Armed auxiliaries of the Pakistani government were especially "openly pillaging and terrorizing villagers without apparent restraint by the Army."[337] Maoist guerrillas robbed the wealthy, killing some landholders and moneylenders, while criminal gangs – sometimes posing as liberation fighters – mugged the general population, especially in regions outside the control of the Pakistani military. Houses were looted in broad daylight.[338] Villagers set up armed patrols against bandit attacks.[339] Thirty minutes after a napalm attack on Narsingdi bazaar, east of Dacca, on March 31, witnesses "saw people were coming down the road in rickshaws loaded with bales of cloth. Merchants? No, looters!"[340]

All of this happened in an environment of general violence, where different guerrilla groups also fought against each other.[341] And it happened against the backdrop of greatly reduced industrial production, commerce, traffic, and port activity, the closure of schools, uncollected taxes, and the temporary ceasing of bank operations in cities and their permanent closure in the countryside. The income of much of East Pakistan's non-farming population was severely affected and the country divided into isolated mini-economies.[342]

Usually, houses vacated by refugees were plundered after they had left. But some observers noted that it was greed that led Bengali Muslims to take part in terrorizing Hindus in the first place.[343] In the

Malumghat area in May, Muslim neighbors, some of whom had earlier protected Hindus, not only looted possessions and livestock left behind by the latter, but also tracked them to their hiding places in the jungle for blackmail, robbery, and rape.[344] In mid-June, the missionary Goedert wrote in bewilderment from Baira that of twenty-six villages devastated in the area, "the Army destroyed only five of these; the others were looted or destroyed by their Muslim neighbors. Good Muslims who try to stop these Judasses find themselves in trouble." Catholic priests reported similar events from the Bondbari region, Rajshahi district, a mixed area where no anti-Hindu riots had happened for twenty-five years.[345] In a village in the Lalganj area, Hindus were forced to flee after being "left at the mercy of Muslim bandits and looters." Though Muslim neighbors stored their possessions for them, their livestock, tin roofs, bamboo groves, and even doors, beams, or house walls were plundered – obviously by other neighbors. In several villages in Bogra and Rangpur districts, Hindus fled under threat from both the army and local Muslims; upon their return, they found their fruit trees cut and sold, wells polluted, looms stolen, or houses "looted clean" or burned.[346] Hindus in Jessore district noticed that there were sympathetic or helpful Muslims. "However, the evacuees, without exception, were at a complete loss to explain the behaviour of many Muslim Bengali neighbours, with whom their relations had always been cordial, indulging in indiscriminate loot of whatever they could lay hands on, from cattle to cooking utensils to metal crockery. [...] This appeared to have been a universal phenomenon."[347]

The refugees continued to be robbed on their way to the border. Muslim gangs living near the escape routes mugged groups or individuals on the road or when they came through villages from the southwest to the northeast and southeast of the country. In Baghachera, the Peace Committee collected a toll from the refugees of one rupee per person, five per bike and ten per bullock cart.[348] Pakistani troops instead resorted to extortion through threats of violence, including rape, or through collecting ransom for men or children they held (in the same way prisoners were at times able to bribe their way out of jails).[349]

Those who returned tried to recover their property. Usually they were quickly able to find out where it was. In a rural environment, the return of plundered movable assets worked mostly through appealing to local Mukti Bahini or Muslim leaders, who then asked the profiteers to hand these goods back. Sometimes the looters returned the stolen goods to these community leaders of their own accord, and sometimes the Mukti Bahini pressured the beneficiaries to return the property. However, the return of goods dropped to low levels once the government stripped former guerrillas of their power.[350]

For all that, many possessions were lost and many houses destroyed (1.56 million according to UN estimates). What remained was often just the land owned by a family. The worst situation arose for those without land, because they had nothing to mortgage or sell to buy necessities.[351] Officials estimated that 200,000 artisans, weavers, and fishermen needed new equipment, as did another 200,000 (mostly small) traders.[352] Following the practice established during periods of political tensions, during the conflict Hindu farmers either sold their land in order to emigrate (and had difficulties in recovering it if a land title was absent, while others were "able to accumulate land at a very low price"); or Muslim neighbors occupied Hindu land and utilized it for a few harvests to gain additional income.[353] Rural poverty and land hunger were powerful incentives for land occupation; only one day after India's attack on East Pakistan, the East Pakistani authorities announced that they would distribute 250,000 acres of "state land" to the landless.[354] In other cases, much of the land just lay fallow.[355] In the case of Muslim refugees, it was customary for the land occupant to share the harvest with the returning owner, yet this was not so clear in the case of Hindus, and there was nothing to share where the land had lain idle because entire village communities had left. With even the mud houses destroyed and little food to be obtained from neighboring villages, families were in dire need.[356]

In many cases, the land ownership of refugees was uncontested once they returned.[357] *Jotedars* (medium landowners) had grabbed land, but in certain areas were stripped of it and even their own in "land reforms" staged by leftist guerrilla groups; the *jotedars* later had it restored with help of Bangladeshi authorities, collecting sums of 50 rupees per acre for crops harvested by the temporary cultivators.[358] The land grabbing of tribals' lands by Muslim Bengalis in 1971 was also reported from the Chittagong Hill Tracts, yet these were not returned. Eighty percent of villages there were reportedly looted.[359]

Enforced redistribution did not stop at the end of the war. In 1974, the state modified the existing expropriation laws and their

coverage was in some ways extended, allowing the Bangladeshi government to seize the businesses of persons residing outside the country
or with foreign citizenship as enemy property and facilitating the dis-
possession of their assets and land. During 1974, a year of hunger and
frantic speculation, seizures affected the property of non-Bengalis who
had recently been resettled to Pakistan, and were still being applied to
Hindus.[360] In 1972, the government had already announced the distribution of 468,000 acres of land to landless and poor persons, while
it auctioned off "abandoned shops and commercial establishments"
(probably those of non-Bengalis), instead of nationalizing it, thereby
putting the emerging bourgeoisie at an advantage.[361] The basis for this
consisted of two 1972 public orders which permitted the confiscation
of the assets of people not present in Bangladesh, not living in or managing their property, and all citizens of a state "which was at war
with or engaged in military operations against" Bangladesh – as all
Pakistanis were. As a result, Bengalis (namely Awami League leaders
and military officers) even took over the property of non-Bengalis who
had voted for the Awami League in 1970, resulting in "chaos, corruption and plunder."[362]

The "house grabbing [of Biharis] was another profitable
action" by independence fighters in the early days of victory in Dacca
in December 1971, acting without orders. Biharis were forced at gun-
point to hand over or sign over houses (especially in Dacca's best neighborhoods), factories, or businesses.[363] Bengalis reportedly appropriated
60,000 houses belonging to non-Bengalis. By 1977, many Biharis
still had difficulties getting such "properties abandoned" back.[364] In
addition, the Bangladesh Collaborators (Special Tribunals) Order of
January 24, 1972 enabled the government to seize all property of a
"collaborator," apparently even without trial.[365]

Land and houses became important tools for amassing wealth
in the 1970s, while in addition to the strong public sector already in
existence prior to 1971, banks, foreign trade, major industries (mainly
in the possession of West Pakistanis), and much of transportation were
nationalized in 1972. Until 1973 there was also a limit on foreign investment. All of this gave the government a central role in the economy for
some years. The Bangladeshi bourgeoisie seemed to approve of the
state bearing financial losses in industry in a transitional period (much
as in West Pakistan after 1971). Much of the struggle for ascendancy,
power, and influence took place as a result not of direct plunder, but in

the form of competition for senior positions in the civil service and in the management of nationalized companies and foreign trade.[366]

Famines

Mass violence in 1971 resulted for many in displacement, the loss of property, livelihood, family, and other social networks, and it was connected with the corrupt accumulation of wealth. In a multi-year process, this caused mass impoverishment and famines which killed more people than fell victim to murders directly. This section describes this process and attempts to illustrate the relationship between famines and mass violence, both of which had to do with the massive redistribution of property. Many of those worst affected in the famines had been refugees in 1971.

At first, it seemed that, despite the November 1970 cyclone and the upheaval, famine was averted for most of 1971 through a number of fortunate circumstances: the excellent harvest of the Boro rice crop in April and May was as unaffected as had been the planting of the Aus crop in March and April; the most important rice crop, Aman, of 1970 could be moved to deficit districts where necessary before the upheaval; considerable food imports were arriving; and the mass emigration reduced demand.[367] Food prices seem to have dropped at first and steep rises by May seem to have been temporary; by August prices were up 20 percent, usual for the season. They even sank substantially by January 1972.[368] Hoarding was reported in June and September 1971 but seems to have been limited.[369] Rice production – earlier anticipated to be down 30–35 percent or two million tons – declined by only 10–20 percent.[370] Foodgrain stocks were reported at 778,000 tonnes for March 1, only 451,000 tonnes at June 1, but at November 1 they were again at the relatively comfortable level of 650,000 tonnes.[371] Some have attributed many of the deaths in 1971 to starvation, but the new government of Bangladesh optimistically estimated that only about 8,000 perished from hunger between June and October. News about food scarcity came particularly from Faridpur, Barisal, and Jessore districts.[372] In December 1971, politicians such as Prime Minister Tajuddin and Relief and Rehabilitation Minister Kamruzzaman denied that the threat of a famine existed.[373] They were wrong, as were UN representatives who stated that a famine had been prevented.[374]

As mentioned above, data from Matlab *thana* as well as selective data from across Bangladesh suggest a countrywide excess mortality in the range of 500,000, especially among young children and elderly men.[375] Yet it is unclear when this peak took place. According to UNROD, famine "never materialized" in 1971 but seemed to build up in early 1972.[376] The monthly distribution of mortality figures in the Matlab area seems to have been based on projections (they indicated August 1971 to January 1972 was the worst period).[377] Other sources point instead to early 1972 as the peak. By early April, the government stated that the "peak of the food crisis" was over.[378] But in May 1972, international experts noted a dramatic level of drastically underweight children; the rate returned to almost normal levels by October.[379] By June, public criticism of the government for food problems and shortages mounted and in September there were hunger marches and demonstrations.[380]

Unfortunately, the statistical data from Matlab and elsewhere included no details on a person's social background. But those who suffered most in the 1972 famine were reported as being landless laborers, and displaced and returned refugees who often had no homes left: "Most of the destitute people gradually had to sell off all their belongings, including the hundred-rupee housing grant received from the Government, just to buy the food to keep them alive."[381] Child malnutrition was obvious, "especially in the families of weavers, fishermen, the landless and the small landholders."[382] Geographically, the northwest was most seriously affected by the 1972 famine, especially Dinajpur (annual mortality at 30.2 per 1,000, March 1971 to May 1972) and Faridpur (29.6), but also Rangpur and Sylhet districts (23.6), whereas Dacca, Comilla, and the southwest fared a little better.[383] Weavers and fishermen were predominantly Hindu professions, and Dinajpur and Sylhet had seen the biggest flight movements in absolute figures (Dinajpur by far in relative terms) and, like Faridpur, had high percentages of Hindu populations; proportionally, many people had also fled from Faridpur and Rangpur districts.[384] Apparently the famine affected the returned refugees from northern Bangladesh most severely, especially Hindus and the rural poor. Since the refugees had appeared relatively well nourished when in India, the reasons for their demise – and particularly that of their children and elderly people – have to be found in the time after their return with few or no resources left.

Even before, large parts of the East Bengali population had experienced long-term impoverishment, but 1971–72 brought additional burdens, 1973 continued stress, and 1974–75 an even deeper crisis. Per-capita income in East Pakistan had been stagnant between 1949 and 1969. From 1948 to 1969–70, food availability had dropped from 15.84 to 13.63 ounces per day.[385] Between 1963–64 and 1973–74 (the worst was still to come), by ILO standards, the proportion of people in East Bengal consuming less than 1,935 calories per day ("absolute poverty") rose from 40.2 to 78.5 percent; even more significantly, the proportion of those consuming less than 1,720 calories ("extreme poverty") increased from 5.2 to 42.1 percent. In 1984–86, daily calorie intake (1,800) was still below the 1965 level (1,964).[386] The background to this was increasing poverty. Since 1965, average real wages had remained below the 1949 level, sinking to between 80 and 95 percent of that figure during 1966–70, then to a mere 60 to 68 percent of the 1949 standard from 1972 to 1975.[387] Price increases for essential products, particularly rice – first slowly, and then steeply from early 1974 to early 1975 – plunged the poor even deeper into misery.[388]

Meanwhile, others tried to amass wealth. A "sea of corruption" was in part made possible by $2 billion in foreign 'aid,' whether cash or kind, flowing into Bangladesh within a few years, exceeding the estimated $1.2 billion worth of damage in 1971. It was appropriated by corrupt elites, used for their "primitive accumulation" and contributed much to inflation. Hindus failed to obtain preference in the relief because others misappropriated aid funds.[389] This process was very soon observed by the Communist Party of Bangladesh as happening in the "entire country."[390] In order to tap these resources, one needed good connections to a new set of elites: Awami League officials, influential former independence fighters, or government people in Dacca. They pushed aside the older generation of local leaders, in particular religious conservatives.[391] By June 1972, Le Monde called the Awami League simply an "association of pillagers."[392] After 1975, the military became another machine facilitating economic ascendancy, conservative elites were gradually co-opted and entered more equally into a struggle for hegemony. Periodic anti-corruption and anti-smuggling operations after 1972 were soon terminated because army officers were using them to eliminate rivals and because too many Awami League functionaries were involved in shady business.[393] Manipulations of foreign trade or trade licenses and smuggling to India, often involving officials, were other lucrative activities.[394] Others simply occupied "businesses and property abandoned by West Pakistani owners" or "land or shops belonging to luckless refugees or to anyone who can be accused of being a 'Bihari'" after independence.[395] Corruption "ate deeply and irreversibly into the social fabric and everywhere there was a palpable undercurrent of violence."[396] As Sheikh Mujib had pointed out earlier, Pakistan's taxation system was already "one of the most regressive in the world," with direct taxes realizing only 2 percent of the gross national product, as opposed to 6 percent in other non-industrialized countries.[397] Transparency International listed Bangladesh in 2003 as the most corrupt among 133 countries.[398]

This social crisis culminated in the 1974–75 famine that is estimated to have caused the death of one million people by February 1975 and another 500,000 by mid-1976.[399] Infamously, the famine happened even though the preceding harvests were much improved over previous years, especially in the affected districts.[400] It hit special groups of people, those deprived of their livelihood by flooding or by lack of access to income in the ensuing food price inflation caused by speculation. "The food supply was there; it just didn't get to the right people," as a US official in Dacca said.[401] In July and August, monsoon floods affected especially Mymensingh, Sylhet, Dacca, Comilla, and Faridpur districts in terms of area flooded, rice crops damaged, and population displaced. The damage to the jute crop took away the income opportunities of rural laborers.[402] Public procurement failed. By July 1, national grain reserves had sunk to a dangerously low level.[403] News about the event was exaggerated and hoarding began. Rice prices, already displaying a stronger upward trend since the second quarter, rose to extreme levels until the spring of 1975.[404] Traders increased their profits; spans between wholesale and retail prices for rice that had been almost down to 1970 levels (ca. 6 percent) in 1973–74, rose again to 1971–73 ranges of 8 to 10 percent in the second half of 1974, and 19 percent in November, when a new harvest reduced prices slightly.[405] But they were up again by April and May 1975; villagers in the Lalganj area commented: "The merchants drink our blood."[406] In the villages, where, in a long-term "bitter struggle for survival," even brothers forced brothers to sell mortgaged land, families of notables seized control of the relief goods, as they otherwise did with fertilizer and other agricultural inputs, in part by manipulating cooperatives.[407] By contrast, the smuggling of rice to India was probably of much smaller proportions than General Ziaur Rahman and some observers asserted, having little impact on the food situation.[408] Anti-smuggling campaigns were traditionally, and now again, used as a means of whipping up anti-Hindu sentiments as Hindus were suspected of running contraband to their families across the border in India.[409]

A food aid embargo by the USA in the worst period between July and October 1974, intended to coerce Bangladesh into terminating jute deliveries and economic relations with Cuba, generally restricted imports amidst high world market prices during the world food crisis and added significantly to speculation and hoarding. In September and October, food grain imports dropped to very low levels. In October 1974, Bangladesh was forced to agree to the formation of an Aid Consortium by capitalist industrial nations and to open the country to more foreign investment.[410] Agricultural wages and land prices dropped.[411] Intensifying a trend from the two previous years, the famine became a time of extreme redistribution, with long lines even at night not only in front of rice kitchens, but also in front of land registry offices – lines made up of desperate sellers and profiteers buying at bargain prices.[412] In famine areas, a "flourishing secondary market for used utensils" such as pots, plates, and spoons emerged.[413]

This crisis, and government corruption and inaction, made Mujib's popularity plunge dramatically. He tried to counterbalance this by imposing a virtual dictatorship, but this ultimately led to his assassination and overthrow.[414] In August 1974, Mujib had confided to a UN representative that the "Country is fighting for survival. I am fighting for survival."[415] Leftist groups such as the JSD campaigned against the government; others assaulted police stations and broke into government grain warehouses, distributing food to the hungry.[416] However, Bangladesh's leaders did seem to be able to exert some leadership against hoarding and black-marketeering in 1971 and 1972, in combination with threats by both Mukti Bahini and the Pakistani army, as well as fear of looting.[417]

Food rationing primarily shielded the military and public servants with their families, secondarily urban dwellers (to a reduced extent in early 1974 and again early 1975), but hardly anybody in the countryside. In the public relief effort, relatively small amounts were channeled to the countryside. Public relief kitchens were phased out in late 1974.[418] The Rangpur (less affected by the 1974 flood) and

Mymensingh districts were among the worst affected. People started to flee their home areas. Some parents deserted, some sold their children, and buying children became frighteningly cheap. Observers sent reports about horrific scenes from the town of Rowmari – a border area that the Pakistani army had been unable to control in 1971.[419] Sylhet, Dacca, and Noakhali districts were also battered.[420] In Rangpur, the number of unclaimed bodies reached 50 per day in August 1974, in Dacca 700 per month, only declining substantially in October 1975. In January 1975, the government deported up to 200,000 slum dwellers to the Demra area and put at least 50,000 of them behind barbed wire, guarded by *Rakki Bahini* paramilitaries; the *Guardian* called it "Mujib's man-made disaster area."[421] Children and adults between 45 and 64 years (again, girls and adult men in particular) seem to have been hit hardest by excess deaths.[422] Usually, deaths from hunger decreased by the end of the year, but not this time.[423]

Death rates were highest among the families of rural laborers, other workers, mini landowners, petty traders, boatmen, fishermen, and certain craftsmen.[424] Common to those who were swept into public relief kitchens was the possession of next to no land (three-quarters seem to have had less than 0.04 hectares) and virtually no other assets either; half of them also lacked a plow or cattle.[425] In an area near Matlab *thana*, the crude death rate in landless families was three times higher than in families with more than 1.2 hectares of land. Social status, also correlated to housing conditions and education, determined mortality more than gender differences.[426] Rangpur and Mymensingh districts in mid-1972 had had the highest incidence of inadequate housing,[427] obviously as a result of war-time flight and destruction. Placed at the low end of political priorities, the 'Biharis' still living in camps were nearly helpless and children were starving. In 'Bihari' camps in the Saidpur area, the famine led to suicides.[428] It was the rural poor, especially in the north of the country, and discriminated-against groups like the Hindus and 'Biharis' who suffered most, in part as a consequence of long-term or repeated distress.[429]

A "legacy of blood"

The 1971 conflict did not only leave hundreds of thousands of guns in the country, but, in the words of Anthony Mascarenhas, a complex "legacy of blood"[430] characterized by corruption, poverty, criminality, dictatorships, and militarization, with struggles becoming manifest along party, class, religious, and ethnic lines. For many years, this resulted in much structural but also direct physical violence. Similar things can, of course, be said about Pakistan.[431] In recent years, conflicts in Bangladesh have crystallized around the struggle between moderate secularists and conservative Muslims or Islamicists, as symbolized by the fight between the family members of Mujib and Ziaur Rahman, Sheikh Hasina for the Awami League, and Khaledda Zia for the BNP (Bangladesh Nationalist Party).

Despite considerable army and police forces and about 190,000 *Ansars* (auxiliary police) in 1973, widespread violence by armed gangs persisted for several years, with activities ranging from extorting food from weekly markets to "robbery of banks and post offices; break-ins of homes; the killing and beheading of influentials in the rural areas; attacking on power plants, telephone installations, and industrial plants; armed robbery of trains, river barges, and country boats; highway holdings; rape; and armed theft of cars and trucks; looting of government arsenals, police stations and army posts; and throwing of grenades into government offices." Between May 1972 and November 1973, 7,700 murders were reported.[432] Transitions between common criminality and political violence were fluid.

Among the most aggressive men involved were a number of the former independence fighters who had not secured any lucrative post, university admission, aid, pension, or place in the (underpaid) military. Especially in the time of the coups d'état in 1975, soldiers and officers ran protection rackets.[433] In 1989, Bangladesh's Home Minister admitted that "we are living in a virtually lawless society" as rural policemen received part of their income from local dignitaries in whose favor they worked.[434] From 1972, murders of members of various political groups, but of Awami League functionaries in particular (sometimes by rivals in their own party), mounted, often due to "resentment resulting from the apparent privilege and influence"; by 1974, their number reached 3,000 or 4,000.[435] The establishment of a virtual dictatorship and of another paramilitary youth force by Mujib did not solve these problems.[436] Generally, an "upsurge of violence was in direct proportion to the increase in corruption, market-manipulation, smuggling and political oppression by the cohorts of the Awami League."[437] Armed clashes of rival political student groups also killed academic debate.[438] Riots between transmigrants from Noakhali and locals in the Adamjee Jute Mills in Narayanganj were said to have claimed 300 lives.[439] Local collaborators of foreign aid organizations were killed or terrorized: "This is the result of having so much money around, and [of] jealousy over not getting jobs and/or relief, as well as personal grudges."[440] Crowds tried to get a share of relief work through *gheraos* (sieges) of corrupt officials.[441]

A military without a function became a factor in political insecurity, leading to "20 or so coup attempts and mutinies" from 1975 to 1981, despite or possibly because of the enlargement of the police and militia forces, including a Village Defense Force of no less than 900,000.[442] Soldiers' committees in the November 1975 mutiny called for a classless society and started to kill their officers.[443] General Ziaur Rahman staged a coup and crushed the leftist JSD party. Even earlier, 10,000 JSD members were imprisoned; by 1976, Oxfam reported there were 60,000 "political suspects" in jail.[444] The use of torture against opponents has since become endemic.[445] In the troop rebellion of September and October 1977, between 230 and 1,000 men were killed by the regime and 600 later executed after mass trials.[446] The initial ban on communalism and religious discrimination in the 1972 constitution of Bangladesh[447] (according to the Awami League policy to hold down the conservative Muslim political groups) gave little protection to Hindus or tribals. Once these laws had been changed again, former 1971 supporters of the Pakistani army started their ascent into a variety of leadership positions.[448]

By 1976, aside from ruling the country, the army acquired a new raison d'être with the Chittagong Hill Tracts insurgency, the most visible bloody conflict in post-independence Bangladesh. This area was populated by a wide variety of tribes, most neither Muslim nor Bengali. Hilly, more sparsely settled than the rest of the country and not dominated by wet-rice growing, this region appeared as Bangladesh's frontier. After the British had restricted outside settlement in the area, the military takeover in 1958 had accelerated the opening up of the territory.[449] In the absence of large domestic energy resources, the Kaptai hydroelectric project built from 1959 to 1963, sponsored by the US Agency of International Development, seemed crucial to foster industrial development as it was to provide electricity for much of East Pakistan. As a result, 40 percent of the arable land of the district was submerged and 100,000 people (one-quarter of the population) driven out, chiefly Chakmas. Following suppressed riots, 40,000 fled to India.[450] Only 11,000 of about 18,000 displaced families received some, though insufficient, new land, which they used in part for what was initially fairly successful fruit cultivation.[451] For President Ziaur Rahman, under whose government the most aggressive settlement policy in the Chittagong Hill Tracts was carried out, Bangladesh's motto was "develop or perish," but in the region those two options were unevenly spread.[452] The natural resources of the region, from fisheries to forestry to electricity, were largely exploited by Bengalis for Bengalis, which triggered economic growth but changed the entire livelihood, lifestyle, and ecology of the region and undermined the traditional shifting cultivation (*jhum*). Locals increasingly had to turn to cash crops, sharecropping, and wage labor, but were often declared unfit for the last and not hired by employers. By 1979, most felt pushed around, robbed, and economically insecure.[453] Most shops and businesses had been in non-tribal hands by 1951. By 1964, Pakistan's National Assembly took the region off the list of Excluded Areas.[454] Through conflict, compensation, and education, Chakma elites were the first in the region to be politicized.[455]

In the 1971 conflict, most Chittagong Hill Tracts tribal people remained neutral, with some (including a number of the Mizo refugees from India) supporting the Pakistani government and a minority the Bengali independence struggle.[456] Once the Pakistani military took control in April, they shot pro-Awami League or Hindu civilians over a stretch of five days, but few or no tribal people.[457] From December 1971 to early 1972, hundreds of locals were killed in revenge actions by Mukti Bahini fighters who also seem to have searched for Pakistani troop holdouts and *razakars*. They evicted tribals (except Hindu Tripuras) from the Feni and Chengri valleys. Hundreds of houses were burned and looted. Locals were also endangered by a wave of common crime.[458] The evictions cleared the way for 30,000 to 50,000 Bengalis to occupy land in the Ramgarh subdivision, displacing Marma, Tippera, and Chakma locals and doubling the number of Bengalis in the region. For some of these settlers, this was designed as rehabilitation after they had been forced to flee from the Pakistanis to India and lost their homes.[459]

Repeatedly, tribal delegations or elected members of parliament demanded autonomy for their region from Bangladesh's leaders. The government rejected such demands in the name of 'national integration' and 'development'; Mujib more than once responded by calling on them to give up their identity and become Bengalis.[460] The 1972 constitution removed any restrictions left after the 1964 status changes, which meant that outside settlers could move freely to the Chittagong Hill Tracts.[461] Tribal leader M. N. Larma then founded the People's Solidarity Association (JSS) and a little later their armed wing, the Shanti Bahini (Peace Fighters). Despite some economic incentives for the region and monthly allowances to win over local leaders in 1975–76,[462] an insurgency began in January 1976 with attacks on Bengali settlers, following which the military established a massive presence in the area.

Between 1979 and 1984 (especially 1980–82), a secret transmigration program brought in about 400,000 Bengali settlers,[463] co-funded by USAID, the Asian Development Bank, the WHO, and UNICEF.[464] The number of settlers resembles an alleged threat by Mujib in 1972 to "send in five lakhs Muslims" to the Chittagong Hill Tracts if they did not assimilate (one lakh is 100,000).[465] This surge was accompanied by a reign of terror by the military and settler paramilitaries, blanket arrests, disappearances, massacres of villagers, rape, eviction, and resettlement into clustered villages. Estimates of locals killed range between 15,000 and 20,000 (3–4 percent of the local population), with most families displaced.[466] By 1994, 532,260 tribals and 423,972 Bengalis were registered as residents.[467] The Bengali settlers were to receive about 4.5 hectares of land from the government (paddy, mixed, and hilly plots), but as it was often not available, they instead displaced tribespeople who often held no formal land titles.[468]

Yet the insurgency was not defeated. In the late 1970s, the diverse tribals had reinvented themselves as "Jumma" people[469] and wielded increasing international pressure on the Bangladesh government. Up to 130,000 tribals from the area fled to India at some point, including 40,000 in 1963–64, at least 40,000 in 1979, 50,000 around 1986, and 20,000 more in 1988/89. By the early 1990s, these refugees came under severe pressure from state governments in Tripura and Arunachal Pradesh, being cut off from employment, trade, food rations and deliveries, and schooling. Nonetheless, returns in the 1990s were few because only some returnee families received land, as Bengali settlers were not to be displaced.[470] On this basis, neither a secure existence for many returned Jumma nor full reconciliation were possible. The December 1997 peace agreement – resulting from a process started under President Ershad in 1983 – rested on the basis of the continued and legalized presence of the Bengali settlers. Few troops or army camps were withdrawn.[471]

To a considerable extent, Bengali settlers exerted the violence in the Chittagong Hill Tracts.[472] On the other hand, the Shanti Bahini frequently attacked, threatened, and expelled settlers and killed a number of them.[473] There was also bloody infighting between insurgent groups in 1983.[474] Even after the peace accord, riots continued.[475]

The story of this area is part of a (mostly illegal) settlement movement of millions of East Bengalis into India's northeast and Burma that intersects with regional insurgencies and a militarization by Bangladeshi, Indian, and Burmese troops.[476] The Chittagong Hill Tracts were crucial to the 'development' plans of the Pakistani bourgeoisie and international 'development' organizations for all of East Pakistan/Bangladesh, as well as for the appropriation of key resources by the Bangladeshi middle class. Again, we can see the state, elites, and commons active in this process. The army organized the oppression of the locals and facilitated the full incorporation of the territory, which intensified over several steps, with the events of 1971 as one catalyst, but especially after Bangladeshi nation-building and military rule coincided. Corruption by military personnel notwithstanding, most of the benefits were reaped by others – Bengali businesspeople and settlers trying to escape the grip of land poverty, even if this meant committing or suffering from violence.

Conclusions

An escalating conflict between post-colonial elites in East Pakistan triggered a landslide of multi-polar popular violent struggles, in which many participated, one way or another, for protection, survival, or gain. Most parties embraced violence and committed atrocities.[477] These widespread phenomena by far exceeded state repression. To be sure, the Pakistani army did use bloody terror against Bengali intellectuals, political activists, and armed forces, driving many of them abroad or underground. But it also coerced even more local elites into an uneasy submission.

The violence of 1971 consisted of different interwoven threads. Much of it was not new. Massacres and the mass flight of Hindus had occurred in East Bengal for a quarter of a century. Non-Bengalis and Bengalis had repeatedly been entangled locally in deadly clashes, particularly staged at industrial sites. The persecution of Christians was not new, nor were violent protests against the army junta or their suppression, or abductions of women and collective rape. Several of these things had often coincided, always including non-state actors; the innovation of 1971 was the massive role of state violence. Still, the 1971 events – especially the many modalities of non-state violence – can only be understood as part of longer-term processes.

The year of 1971, and the early 1970s generally, also saw massive social mobility. Expulsion, flight, plunder, and destruction, families divided, return, coerced sales or borrowing, and lack of government help all intensified this. Even villages marginally affected by the fighting, the civil war of 1971, and the 1974–75 famine experienced a myriad of downward and upward social family trajectories, which increasingly linked the new rich to urban politics.[478] Not all residents experienced social decline, but insecurity was great in this volatile situation. Both direct violence and the 1972 and 1974–75 famines were redistributive events; and many of those displaced or dispossessed in 1971 fell victim to the ensuing starvation, exhausted from a series of blows of fate, above all Hindus, the rural poor, and non-Bengalis.

All rules seemed to be in doubt in 1971. This is what led Sakeema Begum, a Bihari woman, to recall this as "the year of anarchy and end of humanity in Bangladesh."[479] Amidst this social crisis, there was a desire to restore some kind of order, and group allegiances strengthened for the protection of the individual, alongside the building of armed forces, militias, or gangs. "I had never thought of people as Hindus or non-Bengalis or whatever, but all that had changed suddenly" on the night of March 25 to 26, 1971, recalled Rumi Mosharraf, then a young Bengali housewife in Chittagong.[480] People defined their own and other collectivities more sharply, their mistrust of others grew. In many ways, the conflict between West Pakistanis, Bengalis, and 'Biharis' for elite positions seems to have contributed to the solidifying of ethnic identities.

Far from all responses to the surrounding threats were violent. One major reaction was evasion – accommodation where possible, but in millions of cases flight within or out of the country. In the countryside, it was often organized by community leaders as menacing signs mounted – soldiers operating close to the village, some houses burned, shots, mutilations, abductions or rape, and hostility on the part of Bengalis.[481] In fact, the mass flight kept the numbers of those directly killed down (and those actively fighting for independence, too.) The Pakistani army with their ruthless behavior and contempt for Bengalis deserves no credit for this. Where they struck rapidly and mass escape was impossible, especially close to the main lines of communication, it often ended in a massacre. However, in the absence of the troops, the violence was by no means over.

5 SUSTAINABLE VIOLENCE
Strategic resettlement, militias, and 'development' in anti-guerrilla warfare

This chapter pursues the connection between societies in crisis and violence by examining certain forms of anti-partisan warfare. The emergence of guerrilla movements in the affected marginal rural areas resulted from social tensions which were in turn radically intensified by government repression. The fact that many people were drawn into the use of force – by now a familiar trait of extremely violent societies – prolonged the conflict immensely.

My Lai, Chatyn, Wiriamu, Pingdingshan, San Francisco (Nentón), Nyazonia, Lari, Philippeville. Symbols for military brutality, many such sites of massacres during anti-guerrilla wars in the twentieth century were located in areas designated 'free-fire,' 'no-go,' or 'dead' zones from which all people were to be removed: expelled, resettled, or killed.

When fighting protracted, brutal wars against uprisings in the countryside, a variety of regimes developed distinct concepts of counter-insurgency. In order to limit the political success of guerrilla movements among the rural population, to cut off their supplies and recruitment, and to destroy any shelter for them, armies hit out against civilians rather more than against the partisan forces. Militaries combined bloody sweeps and the destruction of buildings in marginal areas with the mass removal of the survivors and their resettlement in model villages in areas easier to control and closer to roads. Movements of people and distribution of food were radically restricted. In government-controlled areas, however, rural dwellers were promised economic advancement and some of the men recruited for armed militias, formations that turned out to be surprisingly loyal. Responding to political–military movements that profoundly challenged the existing socioeconomic order, governments were essentially trying to compete with the guerrilla movements in offering rural dwellers social improvements and modernization. Many of the insurgencies combated along these lines were based on Mao Tse-tung's ideas, but others followed different communist paths, somewhat leftist–nationalist, or anti-colonial, non-leftist concepts.[1]

In addition to the far-reaching social consequences of the dislocation per se, the special practices during these campaigns (euphemistically called a 'hearts and minds' approach) have actively involved substantial population groups in committing violence and induced or aggravated deep conflicts within societies, transforming them profoundly. Despite some variations, the measures described above were part of one comprehensive concept and can therefore be considered as a distinct phenomenon, whether settlements were dubbed New Villages (Malaya), *Wehrdörfer* (Belarus), *centres de regroupement* (Algeria), or strategic hamlets (South Vietnam), *aldeamentos* (Angola), *aldeos modelo* (Guatemala), or *koykent* in Eastern Anatolia, and militias *patrullas de autodefensa civil* (Guatemala), *rondas campesinas* (Peru), Home Guard (Malaya), *korucu* (Turkish Kurdistan), or *groupes d'autodéfense* (Algeria).

Some figures can illustrate the impact of this phenomenon. Listed below are cases in which over thirty million civilians were displaced and at least four million people killed. Some nine million South Vietnamese and millions from the North lost their homes, more than three million Algerians, probably five million Chinese, and four million Turkish Kurds, over a million each of Malayans, Kenyans, Mozambiquans, Angolans, and Guatemalans, and three-quarters of a million Greeks and Zimbabweans. Ten percent of all Greeks, Malayans, Kenyans, Angolans, Mozambiquans, and Portuguese-Guineans, one in three El Salvadorans, 40 percent of Algerians, and half or more South Vietnamese and East Timorese were removed. Every fifth Kurd in Turkey, one-third ethnic of the Chinese and half of the Indians in British Malaya were relocated, as well as half of all Africans in northern Mozambique, more than half of all people in eighteen Algerian *arrondissements* and more than 75 percent in eight of them (see Table 5.1).[2] In southeastern Turkey, about 77 percent of all existing settlements were evacuated.

Agriculture and animal husbandry came to a standstill, as a high official admitted. In the Mizoram area of India, 74 percent of the population was resettled.[3]

In scholarly discussions about mass violence in the twentieth century, anti-partisan warfare has played a marginal role, even though it accounted for a great proportion of the victims.[4] Most cases discussed here have not concerned genocide scholars very much (except for East Timor, Guatemala, and, in the early years of genocide studies, Vietnam). This is perhaps because not enough blood has seemed to have been shed, whereas death through starvation may not have appeared sufficiently 'intentional' and government-driven; or the focus of genocide scholars on ethnic backgrounds (that seemed to be absent) forestalled their interest. Most of them did not notice the ethnic aspects of anti-guerrilla warfare. The same goes for analysts of forced population movements and 'ethnic cleansing.'

There are two main interpretative currents among those who have paid more attention to guerrilla wars. Leftist critics of anti-guerrilla warfare have analyzed depopulation with strategic resettlement as a one-sided oppressive action. Counter-insurgency experts are interested in outcomes of the power struggles between rulers and insurgents. With perceiving the civilian population either as an object of government atrocities or as a problem for government control, both have only selectively addressed the fate of unarmed civilians and have tended to understate conflicts arising among them.

Employing the extremely violent societies approach, this chapter pays more attention to mass participation, multi-polar violence, the victimization of civilians, and the emergence of elites. It contributes to a social history of this neglected, interconnected set of practices in anti-guerrilla warfare that have already been briefly mentioned in Chapter 4 when touching upon the Chittagong Hill Tracts. It tries to show the links between setting up armed formations of rural citizens, mass resettlements, enforced social change, and longer-term transformation and conflicts. Many civilians became victims, but others perpetrators of violence.[5] How were civil wars with multiple participants induced or promoted, based on older conflicts? What role did 'loyalists' – under-researched groups that warrant a more precise term – taking the side of the regime play? Why and how did they appropriate ideas of modernization? What were the social contexts and consequences of mass resettlements in the longer run? Where were the limits to the

Table 5.1 *Resettlement and militias in anti-guerrilla warfare**

Country	Colonial/ imperial power involved	Dates	People resettled in model villages (in parentheses: additionally regrouped)	Numbers of persons additionally displaced: domestic/abroad	Militia membership (in parentheses: total auxiliaries)	Deaths
China	Japan	1932–45	>3,500,000		(200,000)	>2,300,000
Belarus	Germany	1943–44	20,000	>110,000	(100,000)	345,000
Greece	(British, US advisors)	1945–49		830,000/100,000	<50,000	>100,000
Malaya	Britain	1948–60	570,000 (650,000)	30,000	300,000	>20,000
Vietnam	France	(1946–) 1949–54	3,000,000	?		?
Cambodia	(French advisors)	1951–54	500,000 to 1,000,000	?		?
Kenya	Britain	1952–56	1,100,000	100,000	25,000 (50,000)	>100,000
Algeria	France	1954–62	2,350,000	1,000,000/300,000	60,000 (200,000)	500,000
South Vietnam	(US and British advisors)	1959–65 (–1975)	8,700,000 (relocated 2,000,000)	7,000,000	up to 3,000,000	1,000,000
Angola	Portugal	1962–74	>1,000,000	500,000	35,000	>52,000

Country	Foreign involvement	Period				
Indonesia (Kalimantan)		1967–68	>60,000			3,000
India (Mizoram)		1967–70	236,000			>10,000
Mozambique	Portugal	1968–74	1,300,000		230,000(?)	
Guinea Bissau	Portugal	1968–73	60,000			10,000 (18,000)
Thailand	(US advisors)	1968–73			170,000	
Rhodesia		1973–79	>750,000	400,000/228,000	20,000	>30,000
East Timor	Indonesia	1975–99	>300,000	400,000/300,000	50,000(?)	100,000
Bangladesh		1976–97	130,000			>15,000
Guatemala		1982–96	>60,000	1,000,000/200,000	900,000	150,000
El Salvador	(US advisors)	1981–93		750,000/1,000,000	11,000	75,000
Ethiopia		(1979–) 1984–90	700,000			>50,000
Turkey (Kurdistan)		1984–		4,000,000	70,000	>23,000
Peru		1989–93	>56,000	600,000	400,000	>25,000

* See note to Table 5.1 on page 455

authorities' abilities to transform marginal rural areas? And to what extent were anti-guerrilla strategies locally developed or internationally inspired?

The list in Table 5.1 has no claim to completeness. Some cases are not mentioned for reasons of scale (as with the displacement of indigenous people in northern Nicaragua in the 1980s) or lack of information (Nagaland in northeast India in the late 1950s).[6] Others are not included because they do not match all of the criteria, for instance if no militias were established.[7]

Enforced resettlement and population concentration during the combating of small-scale armed resistance are not historically new. These had been an old colonial practice, for instance against the indigenous population in the North American West. However, then there was not even a promise of economic development and social betterment, and/or locals were not armed in militias[8] (or offered political participation). Both of these consequently limited the emergence of local elites, social differentiation, tensions within groups affected by relocation, and their loyalty to the rule by the resettling power.

A traditional champion of mass removal and resettlement for pacification was the Ottoman Empire, where for centuries armed men with their families were shifted from one corner of the Empire to the other for defense purposes. Yet there was hardly any element of economic 'development' planning to this or to the forced resettlement or dispersal of Kurds (especially notables) in Turkey in the 1920s and 1930s. Capitalist penetration of the countryside, typical for other cases, remained weak.[9] Around the turn of the twentieth century, mass resettlement in small-scale warfare was practiced in a number of countries: by the Spanish in Cuba from 1895 to 1898, during which far more than 100,000 out of about 400,000 relocated people perished in the "reconcentration" areas;[10] by the British during the Boer War in South Africa, 1899–1902, when they put between 120,000 and 150,000 Boers into concentration camps (with Boer "Town Guards") in which more than 20,000 whites and an equal number of Africans died; and by US troops after they occupied the Philippines (1899–1906). But only the last case included substantial offers of social improvements for those resettled or expelled, and so an attempt to win over their sympathies, indeed their participation, for the evolving colonial system. Locals for the Philippine constabulary and village militias were recruited from the non-Tagalog-speaking groups especially. Medical services, sanitation, schooling, limited food supplies, and public works projects were provided in resettlement areas, after the US military had forced locals to move with all their possessions out of forbidden areas. Nonetheless, some 250,000 to 750,000 Filipinos died of deprivation.[11]

Mass resettlement and mass death

Destruction and 'development', the emptying of some areas and the stabilization, improved control over, and exploitation of others, were two sides of the same coin in anti-guerrilla warfare. Violence, whether through killing or deportation, was hence collective, often disregarding what a local individual had done. Usually, anti-guerrilla forces developed a zonal approach, identifying no-go areas where all unauthorized persons were systematically shot on sight and buildings destroyed, and sectors where the population, economy, and infrastructure were to be maintained and violence used rather selectively. Zones could be large-scale (as in Algeria[12]) or localized, with fertile, productive, or important areas for communication lines kept largely intact, but inaccessible, economically peripheral mountainous, wooded, or border regions devastated.[13]

This "spatial dichotomization" between "villages" and "wilderness" (as an enemy space) was supposed to reestablish the military's capability for action.[14] In several countries, three zones were designated, to include intermediate regions in which only some settlements were collectively assailed. In the German-occupied Soviet Union, they were marked "bandit-infested," "threatened by bandits," and "pacified," in Guatemala "red," "pink" (or "yellow"), and "white,"[15] in the British colonial tradition, with equally telling symbolism, "black," "grey," and "white" (also applied to camp internees in Kenya at different stages in a so-called "screening" and 'pipeline' of re-education).[16] However, British advisor Robert Thompson suggested to South Vietnamese President Diem "yellow" (government-controlled), "blue" (disputed), and "red" (insurgent) areas.[17] The French differentiated between "rotten," "very heavily contaminated," "contaminated," and other areas in Algeria; according to another account, between *"zones normales," "zones de contrôle renforcé," "zones d'isolement,"* and *"zones interdites."*[18] Other places, other symbolisms: in East Timor, the Indonesians called areas not controlled "white zones"; in eastern China during World War II, territories under Japanese, Chinese nationalist, and communist control, and neutral territories were distinguished.[19]

As a result, there is not necessarily a contradiction between large-scale sweeping operations and clear-and-hold strategies allegedly aiming at the welfare of the population as construed by some counter-insurgency specialists. Such sweeps led to enormous civilian losses (most victims were unarmed): up to 13,000 died in one operation in German-occupied Belarus; "Jumelles" in Algeria led to the deaths of 11,000 humans in early 1958 – the French troops also systematically killed donkeys, mules, and horses. "Speedy Express" in South Vietnam left 10,883 people dead with 267 US fatalities and only 751 weapons captured from December 1968 to July 1969; a Japanese operation in China caused 13,000 deaths; "Gordian Knot" in northern Mozambique in 1970, "Terminus" in Greece in 1947, or "Hurricane" in Rhodesia are similar examples where thousands were killed.[20] Those who could afford it resorted to air power rather than ground massacres. Large civilian casualties are inherent in any aerial bombings, but systematic "saturation bombings" of entire no-go areas claimed especially large numbers of civilian lives, not only in Vietnam and East Timor.[21] The high number of victims also reflected the fact that many villagers were unwilling to leave their homes and fields for an uncertain and dangerous fate as refugees, some were unfit to travel, and others did not know that their homes were included in a forbidden zone: the boundaries of zones often shifted, and government attacks tried to use the element of surprise.[22]

European or other colonial settlers were among those calling for the use of harsh terror in order to uphold the racist order, from Algeria to Angola, from Kenya to Rhodesia, from Malaya to Manchuria to Mozambique. Settler representatives in Kenya called early in the insurgency for the murder of 50,000 Africans.[23] In a similar vein, many Turks started to call for a "Dersim solution" in Kurdistan (that is, a 1938-style mega-massacre) around 1990, and anti-Kurd "demonstrations or mob attacks" in cities were almost "commonplace" in the years thereafter.[24]

Colonial so-called emergencies led to special regulations of (in)justice and executive measures respecting virtually no boundaries. Not calling these events a war enabled those in power to criminalize opponents and deny their political goals legitimacy.[25] But outright executions of alleged insurgents after a – more or less – legal process only generated a small proportion of the total population losses. Still, in the Greek Civil War, according to government figures, more than 1,500 persons were executed up to May 1948.[26] British authorities hanged no fewer than 1,015 Kenyans between 1952 and April 1956, two-thirds of them for lesser offenses than murder, including taking anti-European oaths. Hence portable gallows came in handy.[27] Hundreds in Kenya and Rhodesia were reported shot "after trying to escape" or as curfew breakers. Nationalists in Algeria estimated that 4,000 to 5,000 prisoners disappeared. In one prison near Constantine alone, more than 108,000 people were taken into custody.[28] Numbers of mass arrests were much higher: between 1947 and 1950, the number of Greek left-wing prisoners and detained military suspects of left-wing persuasion oscillated between roughly 19,000 and 27,000; prior to this, 50,000 had been arrested in 1945 alone and 75,000 during twelve months in 1945–46.[29] By late 1957, South Vietnam's regime had arrested 65,000 alleged communists and killed hundreds.[30] In British Malaya, 35,000 people were arrested under emergency regulations and 24,000 deported, 90 percent of them ethnic Chinese.[31] Within twenty-five days of an "emergency" being declared in Kenya on October 20, 1952, 8,000 people were arrested. At some point, almost all adult Kikuyu men in Kenya were in detention camps, with a total of between 150,000 and 320,000 inmates at different points in time. In these camps, torture was widespread and mortality substantial.[32] The situation in French Algeria was similar, where from 1959 to 1961 the number held in detention facilities fluctuated between 16,000 and 25,000.[33]

Military technologies used as part of zonal 'solutions' to guerrilla warfare included airplanes, the helicopter, chemical defoliants, and napalm. Helicopters and aircraft monitored no-go territories and brought troops swiftly into remote combat areas; aerial bombings and napalm served both to drive people out and wipe out suspects in prohibited areas (insurgents or refugees); napalm along with herbicides was used to destroy vegetation – not only crops that guerrilla forces could use but also woods they used for hiding in. Napalm was invented in 1943 and seemingly first employed against guerrillas during the Greek civil war in 1948 under the covert direction of Royal Air Force advisors. Later the US air force used it in South Vietnam from 1962, the Portuguese in Guinea Bissau in 1967 and Angola in 1968, the Thai military in the same year, and the Indonesians in East Timor.[34]

Incendiaries like napalm were also used to kill groups of people by fire in zones of destruction in East Timor.[35] Two-thirds to three-quarters of Algerian forests were destroyed by napalm,[36] a figure equivalent to the woods in Belarus burned by German forces (without napalm) between 1941 and 1944. Incendiary devices and chemicals supplied by the USA reduced much of northern Greece and the Thessaly coastline "to sort of a lunar desert."[37]

The British turned from the slow and expensive ground spraying of chemicals (developed in cooperation with the multinational firm Imperial Chemical Industries) to British and Australian air forces dropping defoliants and napalm on the Malayan jungle. In the end, British-led forces sometimes destroyed crops in remote regions of Malaya and Kenya by uprooting them manually.[38] The infamous dropping of defoliants such as agent orange in agricultural areas in South Vietnam, ultimately designed to weed out not only vegetation but peasants with it (and which resulted in widespread diseases and birth defects in newborns) found early proponents among British military advisors.[39] Herbicides were also used for destroying plants in devastation areas of Portuguese Angola and Mozambique, in Guatemala, and Indonesian East Timor.[40] In Rhodesia, pesticides also served as a means of killing people.[41]

In many countries, more deaths resulted from starvation, diseases, and exhaustion than direct killings (except for the massacres during the Japanese counter-guerrilla war in China, the German campaign in the Soviet Union, possibly Guatemala, plus the massive US aerial bombings in South Vietnam). Generally, for traditional communities, resettlement under any circumstances is a traumatic process because of dramatic shifts in agricultural production or the enforced move into new economic sectors, along with new types of housing, disrupted social relations, and a crisis of meaning and cultural identity.[42] Rural dwellers forced into resettlement areas during anti-guerrilla warfare in addition suffered nearly everywhere from neglect and confinement. Conditions in New Villages in Malaya in general have not been thoroughly scrutinized, but among the 50,000 Orang Asli (indigenous people), some 8,000 died – a mortality of about 16 percent – before they were released or fled from the resettlement camps in 1952.[43] Of the more than one million people (virtually all Kikuyu) in 854 strategic villages in Kenya during the uprising of the traditionalist–nationalist Land and Freedom Army, tens of thousands died of starvation and many were tortured or murdered, but again conditions have hardly been examined. A guerrilla leader estimated that 150,000 perished in these "unsanitary villages."[44] The FLN calculated that this much of a death toll in the Algerian resettlement areas occurred *annually*; 60 percent of all inmates were children. This was more or less confirmed by some French sources. French finance inspector Michel Rocard, later a Prime Minister of his country, estimated a mortality rate in early 1959 (after a major extension of the regroupment centers) that – calculated on a basis of 800,000 inmates in regroupment centers – was equivalent to 400 children's deaths per day or 144,000 per year. This was about the same as the total death toll from the French organized direct killings. There were also signs of massive hunger among the refugees in Tunisia, 60 percent of whom suffered from tuberculosis.[45] Loyalist chief Mutoko stated of the Rhodesian counter-insurgency war: "More of us are dying inside the villages than outside," that is, in armed fighting.[46] The death rate among regrouped Mizos in northeast India was also considerable.[47] Such conditions turned places of resettlement – contrary to the intentions of their initiators – into pools of support for the resistance in countries such as Rhodesia, Algeria, and East Timor.[48]

Ruthless relocation by the socialist Ethiopian government of already weakened Tigrayans and Wollo during the 1984–85 famine and civil war, and gross neglect during the resettlement process, led to thousands of additional deaths.[49] There is similar, though sketchy, evidence about the refugees from counter-insurgency in Guatemala and El Salvador in the 1980s, who were hunted and besieged in inhospitable jungle and mountain areas for long stretches of time by their state's military, who destroyed their food stocks and animals and kept the trade in food, fertilizers, and agricultural tools under tight control.[50] It seems that in East Timor during the Indonesian occupation, about 80 percent of excess mortality was caused by hunger, exhaustion, and disease. Mass deaths were worst among refugees in the mountains and bush land when they came under military siege in 1977–79, and then through starvation in the resettlement sites until 1981. Staggering numbers of people in the resettlement villages were reported ill. By 1977, two-thirds of the population still lived outside the power of the Indonesians, who controlled only the centers and main lines of communication.[51] One way or another, "food control" took a terrible toll. In a 1958 publication by the Sections Administratives Spécialisées in French Algeria, the objective was formulated to "starve the rebel to death and bring progress to the village."[52] All grain was confiscated from Algerian peasants and their annual ration was fixed at just 80 kilograms of grain – less than that granted by Nazi Germany to Soviet civilians in World War II.[53] This is not to say that there were not also outright massacres in Guatemala, East Timor, and Algeria.

What did such removal campaigns look like? From 1933 to 1939, combating nationalist and later communist rebels, Japan evicted from remote rural areas, or herded into at least 10,000 strategic villages, between 3.5 million and 5.5 million people in Manchuria, plus an undetermined number elsewhere in Northern China. Kept behind palisades, mud walls, and barbed wire, with any homes outside the fortifications destroyed, all inhabitants were registered and many provided with limited health services, credits, and famine relief by the Japanese authorities.[54] Resistance remained strong in North China, even though 9,000 places with 11 million inhabitants were additionally declared "Communication Protection Villages" by 1942, under the supervision of the North China Railway Company. All these measures were combined with brutal killings. Still, this case could also be considered a precursor to later campaigns, since the Japanese hesitancy to arm Chinese people meant that – aside from a more symbolic army of 25,000, 63,000 policemen, and 72,000 in the Internal Security Police – Chinese militias (often linked to Mutual Aid Societies, that is, cooperatives) played only a small role in the Japanese security patchwork, and there was not yet a comprehensive system integrating resettlement, social policy, and militias, as in all earlier cases.[55]

That is also true for the civil war between communist insurgents and the nationalist government in Greece, when more than 700,000 dwellers from the northern, northwestern, and central mountain areas had to take refuge in improvised shanty towns close to the cities where they lived in dire need. The army relocated most by force between 1947 and 1949; few went voluntarily. In more secure areas, militias were set up. Tens of thousands emigrated after the victory of the right.[56] Compulsory resettlement and collective punishment had been part of the emergency regulations in Malaya in the face of a Maoist uprising from 1948, but it took until 1951–52 for the planned mass removal to take shape. More than 570,000 people from the jungle fringes – largely ethnic Chinese, half of them squatters, the other half peasants, mostly in the states of Perak, Johore, and Selangor, who were suspected of supporting the guerrillas after having suffered many hardships since World War II – were resettled into 480 "new villages." Another 650,000 workers on rubber estates and tin mines were "regrouped" on the company grounds in what is considered one of the most successful anti-guerrilla operations.[57] Anthony Short, author of an officially commissioned history of the so-called Malayan Emergency, called this "the largest development project in modern South-East Asia" and "the largest and perhaps the most important social engineering project in South-east Asia [sic] since the war."[58] As in other countries, the free movement of people was extremely limited by decree and military practice, and food trade and transport were kept under tight control to deny insurgents provisions. In northern Vietnam, under General Francois Gonzales Linares, the French colonial administration forced about three million people, mainly in the Red River delta under the buzzwords "pacification through prosperity," into "protected villages," later *agrovilles*, and encouraged them to form militias between 1952 and 1954. In Cambodia, the French resettled half a million or more scattered border peasants into fortified settlements.[59] All this could not prevent a Viet Minh victory. The South Vietnamese government tried a number of resettlement and militia projects in South Vietnam from 1957 on, until they adopted, in early 1962, the plan to systematically force most of the twelve million rural dwellers into 16,000 strategic hamlets within just one year. By late 1963, the actual official number had reached 8.7 million in 8,500 hamlets.[60] Without economic aid and population control, the guerrillas rapidly gained support within these settlements. After the fall of the Diem regime in November 1963, the program was modified and all but 3,000 strategic hamlets dissolved by 1965. However, this did not mean the end of the practices discussed in this chapter. US bombing campaigns displaced millions in later years, and militia enlistment reached its peak of three million around 1969.[61]

In French Algeria, resettlement started with 300,000 from the Aurès and the eastern border areas being brought into 250 new settlements or simply displaced, beginning less than three weeks after the nationalist–leftist insurgency of November 1, 1954. Further, similarly improvised displacement of over two million Algerians, and the resulting misery and chaos forced the colonial government to adopt a scheme for 1,000 "new villages" to be erected, but the majority of the people who had lost their homes were kept in provisional camps.[62] The terrible conditions generated considerable support for the National Liberation Front. In the midst of an intensifying campaign of village burnings and massacres in response to small operations by several guerrilla organizations, the Guatemalan military under General turned President Ríos Montt declared a 'guns and beans' program. This included an amnesty for refugees and invitations to return to the northwestern highlands, some to new clustered villages, though only after the army had set up militias under army control everywhere. Within months, this led to the return of about 700,000 refugees.[63]

For assessing how many people were displaced, it is important to note that not all of those who became inhabitants of strategic villages lost their homes. In Malaya, 32 percent of New Villages were on new isolated sites, 16 percent were 'new suburbs,' 24 percent were built around existing villages, and 28 percent were unclassified.[64] Possibly a quarter of the 8.7 million people herded into strategic hamlets in South Vietnam in 1961–63 were moved to a new location, particularly in the Mekong delta and *montagnard* areas. The actual figures of resettlers may have been higher, given that chief political advisor Nhu complained that there were too many resettlements. Whereas in northern Vietnam strategic villages had been organized by the French, where nucleated settlements were common, in the Mekong delta, people used to live in scattered houses.[65] However, displacement as a result of massive US bombing campaigns and ground raids, as well as renewed systematic mass removal from 1967, took on even larger dimensions, bringing the number of those displaced in South Vietnam to about nine million, or close to half of the population. Despite huge sums poured in by the USA, relief efforts remained patchy.[66] The German military, SS, police, and civilian administration established about 100 *Wehrdörfer* in Belarus in existing villages, but additionally transplanted at least 50,000 Russians, Cossacks, and Caucasians into the region. In Guatemala and East Timor, all of the people in model or resettlement villages were evacuees or refugees. Some resettlements in Algeria – especially outside the evacuated border areas – took place within 5 or 10 kilometers, but the distance could be as much as 120 kilometers.[67] But an enforced move over even 5 or 10 kilometers made tending crops on their own fields difficult for agriculturalists, especially in mountainous or otherwise inaccessible areas, even in cases where leaving the immediate area of the village was not prohibited.[68] Hence not all those designated for resettlement went into strategic villages or stayed there. In three "Tribal Trust Lands" in Rhodesia, 60 percent of the population ended up in "Protected Villages," the rest fled to Salisbury (Harare), other reserves, or to the bush.[69] As previously mentioned, even if armed rebel operations diminished, opposition against rulers was reignited by their brutality and their inability to provide a livelihood for those whose movement they restricted, and communal resentment continued among the inmates of strategic villages. Though some groups who did profit showed their support, the "hearts and minds" of the people were often not won, for example in Malaya in the 1950s and 1960s, and in South Vietnam, Algeria, Kenya, and eastern Angola.[70] Where resettlement seemingly succeeded, as in Malaya and Guatemala, it usually did so not because of any economic benefits it generated for a majority, but through sheer force.

Ethnic and religious factors

Where colonial governments or foreign occupants tried to prevent nationalist movements from succeeding, the former played on existing ethnic and cultural differences. By highlighting ethnic and religious differences, they attempted to determine the political discourse and distract the populace from social questions, land distribution, and the illegitimacy of colonial rule. Resettlement and other oppressive measures in British Kenya targeted Kikuyu (and their Meru and Embu cousins), and in British Malaya Chinese people, but also ethnic Indians and indigenous people, while ethnic Malays were favored. Here the segregated New Villages meant the "artificial creation of the mono-ethnic" in country settlements.[71] The Portuguese tried to side with the Fula in Guinea Bissau, the Yao in Mozambique (mostly against the Makonde), and the Ovimbundu in Angola.

On the other hand, cramming people into resettlement areas or forcing them to escape to cities could also level tribal and cultural differences, thereby unwillingly forging a common Algerian, Vietnamese, or Angolan national identity.[72]

Post-colonial states, on the other hand, ascribed cultural identities to populations suspected of supporting an insurgency and labeled them as traitors of the nation, insisting on unconditional unity. In Thailand, communist insurgents were portrayed as belonging to the Chinese, Lao, or Hmong minorities, in Kalimantan, Indonesia, as Chinese, while in Turkey the discrimination against the Kurds was obvious, and three-quarters of the acts of violence in Guatemala affected Mayas. The percentage of indigenas targeted was even higher in Peru. In Laos, on the other hand, the US military and the CIA tried to employ Hmong people against the communist Pathet Lao movement. Even during the Greek civil war, forced evacuations primarily affected Macedonians dubbed as Slavs or Bulgarians, in areas acquired by Greece only in 1912.[73] However, more recently Turkish authorities have reframed their Kurdish problem as a 'social question,' in denial of Kurdish ethnicity.

Insurgent groups primarily based on one ethnic group tried to reach out to others while colonialists tried to confine them by means of propaganda and by offering material benefits to and arming other ethnic groups. British colonial authorities in particular, by emphasizing ethnic affiliations when trying to maintain their empire, helped invigorate or create ethnic identities, heterogeneity, and 'communalism' while denying that there was a common identity of Kenyans, Malayans, Cypreans, etc.[74] In Kenya, colonial authorities depicted the deportation of half of Nairobi's Kikuyu as an economic opportunity for other ethnicities (mainly Nyanza and Kamba), cultivating the rise of non-Kikuyu politicians and trade unionists.[75] The resulting tensions could have severe consequences for such post-colonial countries, even though, as we will see, there was usually an additional attempt by outside rulers to further divide the discriminated ethnicities themselves.[76]

The authorities also tried to maintain their power by exploiting religious divisions. In the colonial tradition, they worked through Christian communities. In Guatemala, Protestant groups were privileged with permissions to resettle the devastated northwestern highlands and were among the first to set up militias, especially under the 'newborn Christian' President Ríos Montt. Missionaries preached intensely among Kenyan detention camp inmates and some used physical force to persuade them to revoke 'Mau Mau' membership, though the Protestant church also lobbied against abuses. The French tried to mobilize various religious groups, but Catholics and Cao Dai in particular, against the Viet Minh.[77] The Diem regime in South Vietnam relied heavily on Catholics.

However, it is striking how much Islam was used as a tool against leftist guerrillas. Catholic-authoritarian Portugal preferentially armed members of the Muslim Fula in Guinea Bissau and Muslims in

Mozambique and sought their support – even by providing free airline tickets for Fula leaders to Mecca. The government of Bangladesh pitted Muslims against Buddhists when encouraging Bengali settlers to move into the Chittagong Hill Tracts after 1972 and supporting or organizing them militarily. The Germans tried to settle Muslims from the Caucasus in Belarus in 1944, and in French Algeria there were at least plans to use the Muslim religious brotherhood for maintaining colonial rule.[78] In contrast, the Greek government hardly lobbied in the civil war for Macedonian Muslims; caught between the lines, 18,000 of them escaped to Turkey.[79]

There also was a deeper layer of religion in anti-guerrilla warfare. Forced mass resettlement, by destroying the customs and faith that bound people to their inherited land, ancestral graves, collective relationships, and ties to animals and nature, shattered the localized beliefs of rural dwellers. Uprooted spiritually, as well as physically, resettlers' religious creeds in effect became more modernized and more uniform. The relative loss of influence of the elderly on younger, more action-oriented men reinforced this process.

"Loyalists," militias, and political outcomes

When fighting guerrillas, regimes usually (to use a German proverb) shoot with cannons at sparrows. Not only does one hit very few sparrows (guerrillas) in this way, much else gets destroyed instead. Government forces were usually vastly superior in weapons technology and financial resources, but also in troops.[80] In British Malaya, government forces started out with 21,000 men against 5,000 insurgents, in 1951 reaching a 25:1 and then a 50:1 ratio (300,000 vs. 6,000 men).[81] The figures for Kenya were 56,000 to 12,000, Algeria 400,000 to 8,000 (1956), South Vietnam 4:1 in 1964 and 8.75:1 in 1968, and Portuguese Africa 149,000 to 27,000 in 1974 (here excluding militias). Counter-insurgency strategists consider a 10:1 advantage necessary to defeat an insurgency.[82]

Mass participation in violence is a key feature of extremely violent societies. From there originates a special interest in the involvement of locals in the violence, but also in their chances of political participation that are created during anti-guerrilla wars and, in a broader view, an interest in the emergence of new elites.

Regimes gained much of their vast superiority in manpower by recruiting locals.[83] This was to limit the number of troops used from the metropole (or main social base of the government); 'Vietnamization,' 'Africanization,' etc. only followed after many US, Portuguese, French, etc. troops had been recruited, an unpopular draft had been set up at home, and political and financial costs endangered the government, that is, after the percentage of Vietnamese, African, Algerian, etc. armed forces had initially dropped.[84] In Malaya, Kenya, and Indochina, Britain and France also fielded many troops from their empires outside the so-called motherland, but most men under arms usually came from the colony itself (except for South Vietnam 1964–1969 and Algeria). For instance, in Malaya, of twenty-three regular infantry battalions in 1953, seven were Malay, six British, and ten from elsewhere; 40,000 Commonwealth forces, 70,000 armed Malay police, and 300,000 Home Guards were employed.[85] By building local forces, regimes also responded to the perceived need to gain local political support.[86]

As a result, the number of locals under arms on the government side was usually considerably larger than the number of guerrillas. In Portuguese Africa, the former outnumbered the latter by three to one, in Algeria by six to one.[87] What's more, guerrilla violence usually targeted and killed many more local functionaries, including auxiliaries, than regular soldiers. The partisans suffered higher casualties. Many of them were inflicted by the auxiliaries, and the same goes for a great portion of the sacrifices by civilians (which generally exceeded all other losses combined).[88] Militias carried divisions into every village. What resulted amounted to civil war. In such multi-polar conflicts, the fronts even cut through families, such as that of Nobel Peace Prize winner Wangari Maathai in Kenya.[89]

In Kenya, the King's African Rifles, Kenya Police and Police Reserve, Kenya Regiment Territorials, and Home Guards took the brunt of "Mau Mau" attacks; they were also responsible for many of the killings of insurgent fighters and civilians, and much of the torture, rapes, and general terror when running the internment camps and strategic villages under European supervision.[90] The incident for which the British started the war in Kenya was the assassination of the Christian, pro-British chief Wariuhia on October 7, 1952. Only two weeks later the first European was killed. In the biggest massacre during the war, which claimed about 400 civilian lives, the Home

Guard committed many of the murders in Lari, in retaliation for the selective massacre by insurgents of over 100 (Kikuyu) chiefs, ex-chiefs, headmen, councilors, and prominent Home Guard members or their relatives (and potential heirs, as the initial attack was, like many intra-Kikuyu struggles, intertwined with a land conflict).[91] Even in the early stages, the Algerian FLN killed hundreds of so-called traitors such as *caids* and tax collectors. From 1958, four times as many Muslims were killed in FLN attacks than were Europeans.[92] By 1973, Frelimo was said to have killed 900 traditional leaders (among them 100 chiefs) in Mozambique. Some scholars also point to a civil war among Africans during the Zimbabwean war of independence and to inter-communal killings between members of different village communities in Ayacucho, Peru.[93]

The motives of pro-regime auxiliaries are grossly under-researched. The term 'loyalists' is somewhat misleading because, though supporting the authorities in power, they mostly did not take arms out of sympathies for the rulers.[94] Instead they seem to have fought for traditional social structures, customs, or values (often on religious grounds) while often viciously rejecting change and related ideas – particularly communism and any leadership by youths.[95] In some case, historians argue that militias served locals to construct "society, identity and autonomy."[96] For Kenya, Bethwell Ogot distinguished between wealthy constitutionalist, traditionalist, and Christian opponents of the uprising.[97] However, not all of those joined militias; for example, moderate nationalist Jomo Kenyatta, who disapproved of the violent insurgency but was imprisoned by the British, was a wealthy land-owner who had married the daughters of two chiefs.[98]

A mix of poverty and coercion has also been cited as driving the local auxiliary rank and file. In Turkey, arrests and the burning and looting of property exerted massive pressure on men to become village guards.[99] Generally, men who desperately tried to feed their families are said to have joined militias or the military as a survival strategy when threatened by the military, insurgents, and hunger.[100] However, members of Self-Defense Groups in Algerian villages or the Home Guard in Kenya were not paid for their services, though the latter received food rations, tax breaks, clothes, and school fees for their children.[101] It was rather the misuse of newly acquired power by militia leaders and men that facilitated personal gain, a "primitive accumulation"[102] through extortion, robbery, and exploitation.[103]

In Peru, cooperation between militia members, coca cultivators, and drug dealers emerged in the context of world market slumps for other export products, while in southeastern Turkey, a 12 percent crime rate among village guards was officially reported, including charges of drug and arms trafficking, organized crime, bribery, and kidnapping.[104] Tendencies toward accumulating real power were minimized in Rhodesia by recruiting poor urban Africans, who volunteered for high wages. Later this was supplemented by plans for a guard force made up of black military veterans.[105] Home Guards forced villagers in Kenya to do communal work on their farms or those of chiefs and headmen instead of building roads or schools.[106] Household effects, crops, animals, and livestock became the booty of the Home Guards; Guatemalan Civil Patrols also took away land.[107] In general, Kikuyu villages considered loyal received extra amenities, special sugar allocations, medical supplies, and vitamins for children, as did strategic villages under the Germans in Belarus.[108] In Peru, charges of the appropriation of government funds by leaders, nepotism, the misuse of communal work, and the manipulation of irrigation committees by militia leaders were frequent, whereas in Turkish Kurdistan, part of the government pay of the village guards was pocketed by the *aghas* (feudal landlords).[109] In Ethiopia, militia members were randomly recruited from young men among the resettlers, but they started to enjoy immediate privileges, such as extra housing and food, for themselves and for their families.[110]

The structures within which locals were armed differed even within the same theater. By the end of the war in Guinea Bissau, there were 3,000 locals in the army, 8,000 in the civil militia, and 7,000 "'self-defense' village soldiers." Among the auxiliaries in French Algeria were the Self-Defense Groups, the *harki* (supplemental combat troops; the term was also used in a generic sense for all auxiliaries in Algeria), Mobile Security Groups (police), the *maghzen* (armed auxiliaries of the militarized "Special Administrative Sections"), and several smaller formations.[111] In South Vietnam during the 1960s, British military advisor Robert Thompson counted "approximately" eight military or paramilitary organizations: Armed Forces (ARVN), Civil Guard (rural constabulary), Self-Defense Corps (paid home guard), Gendarmerie, National Police, Special Force, Republican Youth (central for the strategic hamlets), Hamlet Militia, and "Madame Nhu's Women's Solidarity Movement."[112]

The size of militias depended on a number of factors among which racism was prominent. Fueled especially by European settler racism, militias in sub-Saharan Africa remained small in size, whether in Kenya, Angola, or Rhodesia. Northern Mozambique remained an exception.[113] In Algeria, militia-type structures were built under the centralized control of the French military or administration and thus had to be accepted by the settlers, who themselves held 110,000 men – every third adult European male – in militias by 1960.[114]

The lack of trust in the auxiliaries was reflected in their initially small scale and the limited numbers of weapons handed out: Malay Kampung Guards (established in 1949 and armed only with shotguns) and the Auxiliary Police Force (made up of Malays) in Malaya were followed by the foundation of a Chinese Home Guard in September 1950, in 1951 all three being merged and brought to close to 300,000 men, one-third of them Chinese.[115] By 1954, some 250,000 Malayan Home Guards were equipped with 89,000 weapons; in every Chinese village the handing out of weapons was a lengthy process. In the People's Self-Defense Forces in South Vietnam, three million members shared 400,000 firearms.[116] The official arming of the *rondas campesinas* started on a small scale under Peruvian President Garcia in 1990, before being enlarged and put on a legal basis under Fujimori in 1992. Many bought their weapons personally or as a collective.[117]

In post-colonial states, the size of the military was one factor that determined in turn the size of the militia. In Turkey and Greece, armies relatively strong in numbers felt less of a need for large militias. In 1949, of 232,500 armed forces in Greece, only 50,000 belonged to the *Ethnophrourà* (National Defense Corps), the military being initially hesitant to employ them.[118] By contrast, the Guatemalan military numbered only 30,000 to 35,000 men, whilst the Civil Self-Defense Patrols, officially decreed in September 1981, had 25,000 members in early 1982, 700,000 in late 1983, 900,000 in early 1984, and still about 500,000 in early 1990s before being dissolved in 1996. For some time, all men in the highlands between sixteen and sixty years of age were forced into the militia.[119] Even a bigger army such as Peru's organized massive peasant militias.

Militias were not set up simply for the sake of boosting man-power or firepower but also for sowing divisions. As a French military officer put it, General Challe "launched this policy of self-defense villages not so much for military reasons, but because he saw in it the only way to bring the mass of Moslems to our side once and for all." It exacerbated guerrilla moves and a rapprochement between insurgents and civilians.[120] Militias also served to provide local knowledge to the regime and to protect village officials, which made them a precondition for socioeconomic programs such as those in Peru and South Vietnam.[121] In Guatemala, the Civil Patrols helped bring villages and their administration under strict military control; an army pamphlet called this the "People's Response to a Socio-Economic Political Integration Process in Guatemala."[122] Under the surface, however, cleavages were intensified, despite hopes to create a spirit of national anti-communist solidarity among farmers collectively defending their property, thereby overcoming atomized rural lifestyles.[123]

Mobilizing the local opponents of guerrillas under arms with the claim of representing a better socio-political formation did, of course, raise the question of granting political participation, at least to the loyalists. However, political expression was by no means becoming free; what the authorities and strategists envisioned instead were regime-controlled political movements with the ability to disqualify any representatives (even if elected) and restrict their room for decision-making.[124] Nonetheless, these processes in independent countries led to a partial transfer of power and in colonies, despite the vehement and often violent protests of racist European settlers,[125] ultimately to formal independence, even where the colonialists claimed to have won the war.[126]

British tactics were characterized by "splitting the nationalist movement; constructing a moderate alternative political focus; isolating radical nationalists through the encouragement of ethnic organizations."[127] The authorities in Malaya expected from local politics and from the political parties, the United Nationalist Malay Organization and the Malayan Chinese Association, a "political education" that would immunize the populace against communism.[128] From 1952, an increasing number of Malayan villages had elected councils[129] (a development also witnessed in Algeria[130]), and the Chinese portion of the electorate in regional elections was enlarged, yet general elections, as demanded by Chinese politicians, were delayed for a long time.[131] When organizing botched elections in Kenya in 1957–58, the British provided unequal voter registration and representation for loyalist areas in order to reward loyalist African elites.[132] Manipulated local elections and administrative reforms could also lead to the decline of old elites such as the *caids* in Algeria, where a mix of old and new elites (village officials, merchants, ex-soldiers, militia members, "and other potential leaders") were trained in administration and budget management or civic affairs.[133] Contrary to his assumption that the population in Algerian regroupment centers would be "totally destroyed, homogenized, levelled, and reduced to the lowest stage of misery," Pierre Bourdieu found in a household consumption study that there were "all the differentiations that one expects in a normal population."[134] In a more integrationist approach, Portugal granted citizenship to her African colonial subjects in 1961, abolished compulsory labor in 1962, ended racial segregation in public facilities in 1971, and declared Angola and Mozambique "states" within the Portuguese "nation" in 1972. Africans began to be promoted to high administrative posts.[135]

The Diem regime in South Vietnam, while calling for mass mobilization at the village level, had replaced traditional elections by the appointment of officials before turning to elections at the hamlet and village council levels. The fact that improved communications, special newspapers, and radio programs were part of the strategic hamlet program indicates the amount of pro-government indoctrination. Whereas the insurgents offered a say and a role for the locals in politics, the government only held village elections between 1967 and 1969.[136] Political power sharing and the rise of black militias seemed the only way out for the Smith regime in Rhodesia where militias came under the control of Bishop Muzorewa's party, a proponent of moderate changes.[137] India's government made similar attempts in Mizoram, above all through the Mizo People's Conference.[138] Japan created dependent states with formal governments in Manchuria (Manchukuo) and China to bolster a cooperative attitude, and Germany at least allowed a Central Rada (parliament) to convene in Belarus in 1944.

Results in post-colonial states varied greatly. While in Guatemala a peace process in which civil society organizations played a major role took place, civil society in Peru (which returned to civil–democratic rule in 1980 at the onset of the uprising) had broken down by the early 1990s and the insurgency petered out in a total government victory. Unlike in Guatemala, ethnic civil organizations of indigenous people remained unimportant and an ideology of bourgeois national integration prevailed (*peruanidad*), which resulted in low election turnouts in the highlands.[139]

In one regard, the difference in political outcomes was striking. Basically, in all the post-colonial nation-states mentioned here, the government prevailed in maintaining the socioeconomic system (and mostly the political system), with the single exception of Ethiopia. The insurgencies in Greece, the Philippines, India, Thailand, Guatemala, El Salvador, eastern Turkey, Peru, and Bangladesh were all denied success. By contrast, most old and new empires (Germany, Japan, France, USA, Portugal, Rhodesia, Indonesia) ultimately failed to quell guerrilla movements.[140] Britain seemingly succeeded yet could not prevent independence for Malaya and Kenya.[141] Despite usually being economically weak, post-colonial government could mobilize more power, and at times more domestic support, in order to avoid defeat.[142]

The transformation of society

Pitting some population groups against others was not enough to regain control of rural areas under the influence of an insurgence movement. Beyond political rights, and tied into brutal repression, the authorities needed to offer loyal subjects chances for upward social mobility and improved life conditions. "Development" aims became a standard ingredient of anti-guerrilla campaigns that would stabilize society within a capitalist framework.[143] Governments thus promised new amenities and services such as running water, electric light (often restricted merely to the perimeter fence), schools, health clinics, stores, markets, and improved agricultural techniques.[144] But this would require clustered settlements, that were incidentally also easier to control militarily and politically.[145] Military operations and civic action were sometimes merged, as in the Guatemalan Civil Affairs and Local Development (S-5) units or Inter-Institutional Coordinators.[146] Signs advertised the *aldeamentos* in Mozambique with the slogan "*agua para todos*" (water for everybody); Portuguese military governor Spinola ran his campaign in Guinea Bissau in 1968 under the headline "*Um Guiné Melhor*" (For a better Guinea); and the US Information Service provided resettlers in Vietnam's strategic hamlets with the pamphlet, "Towards the Good Life." The El Salvadoran 1983 regional government program based on that model was dubbed "*Bienestar para San Vincente*."[147]

The authorities thereby tried to induce or accelerate social change. The enforced modernization that followed alongside the resettlement programs spelled restructuring the countryside. In an economic sense, the planned strategic villages meant land consolidation, clearing out marginal agriculture and eliminating dispersed settlements; it amounted to standardized small farms, villages, social services, and often housing facilities. Less egalitarian consequences included upward social mobility for those emerging elites who took up opportunities in administration or the militias, or who were successful in commerce.

This was to lead to profound social change as most of the affected areas were remote regions, characterized by marginal agriculture, low market integration, weak infrastructure, and often by illiteracy.[148] Resettlement, which was a tool for military success, therefore also became one of the aims of the reconfiguring of society. As Robert Thompson, a British counter-insurgency specialist active in Malaya and advisor to the South Vietnamese government from 1961 to 1964, put it, strategic villages were to put traditionalist, individual, isolated farmers in contact with the world: "This attitude is no longer in keeping with the times nor with the general aspiration for progress and advancement." Shifting agriculture and the cultivation of hillsides and river banks were to be eliminated.[149] With reference to Walt Rostow's "Stages of Economic Growth," the South Vietnamese President's brother and chief political advisor Ngo Dinh Nhu told regime cadres that strategic hamlets would serve to discard "traditional society" and to facilitate the economic "takeoff."[150] Likewise, in Bangladesh's Chittagong Hill Tracts' clustered settlements, tribals were forced to abandon shifting cultivation by growing fruit or entering wage labor.[151] Lieutenant Colonel Rebocho Vaz, former governor of Angola's Uíge district, had already said in 1963 that Portugal could win this war "only with a radical transformation of the social environment that still exists today."[152] In Peru, military officers who felt that economic development was being neglected in combating the Shining Path were sidelined; only around 1990 did admissions such as that of General Adrián Huamán ("there definitely is structural violence," "people [...] protest against injustice and immorality") gain ground.[153] The Guatemalan army's National Plan for Security and Development of 1982, when they formed their S-5 Civic Affairs division, called the causes for "subversion heterogeneous, based on social injustice, political rivalry, unequal development, and the dramas of hunger, unemployment, and poverty." Yet such attitudes usually went hand in hand with nationalist and often racist views that branded localized perspectives as stubbornly backward, held by people who had to be forced through a modernizing development process.[154]

A chief planner of Guatemalan counter-insurgency, General Hector Gramajo, thought that "subversion could be deterred through agricultural modernization based on market oriented production and consolidation of private landownership in Mayan communities," according to analysts. Gramajo himself characterized the strategy as "nationalist, egalitarian, developmentalist and reformist."[155] This required a move against subsistence agriculture. A colonel and former zone commander in northern Guatemala recalled that "it was critical to push the peasants off the land – to show them who was in charge, to show them that the guerrilla could not protect them, to break the cycle of agricultural production which fed both peasants and guerrilla. 'Two seasons at least'."[156] Better national integration could also mean damaging existing regional market networks, which in Guatemala were run by indigenas for whom it served to foster their autonomy.[157] According to an Algerian scholar, single or repeated resettlements that a person had to experience served the French authorities in that country as "social surgery" that would, along with the new habitat, change social perceptions, interactions, and thinking, loosening kinship ties and splitting larger families into nuclear units – an application of the theories of Claude Lévi-Strauss.[158] President Kennedy's Deputy National Security Advisor Walt Rostow – a major proponent of modernization theory and author of the "non-communist manifesto" "The Stages of Economic Growth" – held in 1961 that the inevitable modernization process was disturbing for many in the Third World; communists tried to exploit this, and their opponents had to respond with "programs of village development, communications and indoctrination," as well as violence.[159]

In fact, even before the start of the guerrilla wars, the speed of socioeconomic change was often stunning, and with it the spread of inequality, which spurred on the insurgency in the first place. Remote mountain, jungle, or marshy areas were often affected[160] as the very traditional living styles of sedentary farming, swidden agriculture, and nomadic herding were undermined by the rapid penetration of elements of capitalist production, displacing many from the land. At the start of the decolonization war in Algeria in 1954, two-thirds of adults of labor age were unemployed (one million) or underemployed (two million mostly doing less than 100 days of wage labor annually). Social differentiation had advanced radically, with European settlers on top of the hierarchy, but with also just 4 percent of Muslim agricultural producers accounting for one-third of the Muslim output.[161] Symbols of the emergence of the new lifestyles, caused by capital penetration, included paved roads, transistor radios, cash, and mineral fertilizers. Often this was accompanied by tensions. Hmong people in northern Thailand later remembered that they had lived in perfect harmony with the Karen "until the introduction of roads to the village."[162] In rural areas of the Mekong delta, people noticed new clothing styles, music, and urban-influenced behavior in the 1960s. Among the insignia of this new time were plastic bags, motorbikes, and sewing machines. In the 1960s and 1970s, encouraged by the national cooperative movement, people started to travel further outside their local area in the Guatemalan highlands, including some indigenas who acquired higher education; medical services, streets, piped water provision, and fertilizer appeared, radios were everywhere, and money became widely used.[163] In Niassa district in northern Mozambique, it was "only in the late 1960s that a Portuguese presence was felt and that cash began to be used for transactions in trade and barter,"[164] at about the time that the guerrilla war started. "Meanwhile transistor radios, bicycles, sugar, additional clothes and more find – often by way of installment payments – their way into the kraal."[165] Traditional education, marriage contracts, and religious rites were eroded in Kenya's Central Highlands before the 1952 uprising. In Turkish Kurdistan, hundreds of thousands began to leave the land for Diyarbakir, Istanbul, Ankara, or Adana, cities in Kurdish areas or in Western Anatolia, from the 1950s, when feudalism collapsed. Some press organs called for efforts in education and the economy leading to cultural Turkization and the destruction of tribal systems around 1970, before the guerrilla war.[166] So Turkish President Özal argued, when talking to US Ambassador Abramowitz in March 1993, that "half of the people of the southeast had already left, primarily for economic reasons" (a picture much too idyllic); as the people lived in misery, it was necessary to "install incentives to get the remaining population of the southeast to move out."[167] These incentives were truly brutal. In Rhodesia, 113,000 Africans had been removed from tribal lands even in the years before unilaterally declared independence in 1965 to make room for white settlers.[168] Life in the Peruvian Andes changed in the 1980s and 1990s, during the war, when people started to listen to the radio, wear tennis shoes, and drink Nescafé. But some processes, such as migration, had been initialized earlier there too.[169] In the course of such shifts, living standards and per-capita calorie intake among the lower classes dropped dramatically in countries such as Peru and El Salvador, although the regimes reported infant mortality rates dropping during the conflict.[170]

In many cases, the commodity boom in the colonies in World War II precipitated new land being put under cultivation by Europeans, capital invested into the mechanization of agriculture, and increasing colonial restrictions on African or Asian economic activities to the benefit of white settlers. In Kenya, Africans saw their credit facilities limited, coffee growing prohibited, and grazing rights restricted, and were also disadvantaged by the low official corn procurement prices of the marketing board and by being pushed off the land. European farmers systematically tried to turn squatters into wage laborers. District officers observed the simultaneous "tendency to create a [African] land-lord class" or a "Kulak" gentry. By 1948, one in four Kikuyus already lived as wage laborers or "squatters" outside the designated reserves. Their lives were made miserable by inflation triggered by the boom.[171] With coffee cultivation prohibited and education prospects for their children vanishing, many rural poor joined the insurgency.[172]

Such changes accelerated in the anti-guerrilla wars, during which the regimes wanted to get modernization right. From 1948 to 1963, the number of white settlers in Kenya almost doubled from 29,700 to 53,000 (with plans to double that figure once more), and the number of "Indians" from 98,000 to 177,000. "Paradoxically, this most rapid period of growth in white immigration over the entire history of the colony precisely coincided with the height of the fighting in the emergency," as David Anderson states.[173] Therein lay not much of a paradox if it was precisely the white hunger for land that increased the tensions leading to the uprising – and to infighting between Africans. Settler influx, land accumulation, and inflation created a very particular social differentiation and therefore led to an uprising earlier than in neighboring countries.[174]

Similarly, the number of Europeans in Angola and Mozambique almost quadrupled between 1940 and 1960 and, after the start of the insurgency in 1961, doubled in Angola again from 1960 to 1970 while increasing by over 50 percent in Mozambique: from 44,100 to 172,500 and 350,000 in Angola and from 27,400 to 97,200 and

150,000 in Mozambique.[175] Though most of them settled outside
the combat areas, Angola and Mozambique became theaters of massive economic expansion during the wars of decolonization, with an
average growth rate of 11 and 9 percent per annum, respectively.
Resettlement in Central Angola was to free land for white settlers.
Attracted by the Portuguese authorities, industrial investment in
Mozambique greatly increased, primarily foreign (above all British)
investment in export-oriented projects. By 1975, Mozambique also
'exported' about 100,000 workers to South Africa and Rhodesia.[176]
During the insurgencies, construction led to a doubling of the length
of the road system in Angola, whereas the increase in Mozambique
was one-third and in Guinea Bissau one-sixth (not counting quality
improvements).[177] The Zamco consortium building the Cabora Bassa
dam in Mozambique's Tete province was led by French, West German,
and South African capital and also included companies from Portugal,
Italy, and Switzerland. In a similar vein, the Turkish Ilisu dam project depends on foreign private and public capital, which has not been
secured at this point.[178] However, unlike in Kenya, white immigration
in northern Mozambique (as well as in Rhodesia) prevented the emergence of a black middle class of farmers and others, "leveling the vast
majority to a state of extreme poverty" through squeezing Africans
out of cotton, corn, and beef production and therefore limiting the
emergence of loyalists during the wars of independence.[179]

Dam projects often became strategic engines of change in
insurgency areas – usually also involving foreign capital and 'development' experts. Dams were to facilitate industrialization by providing
electricity, giving incentives for construction industries, and making
intensive agriculture possible by way of large-scale irrigation. This
usually also entailed the partial substitution of the local population
and would submerge the most fertile land. In southeastern Turkey,
twelve of twenty-two planned big dams were completed around
2003, dislocating 350,000 locals, mostly Kurds, but attracting ethnic Turks as well as some of those displaced with new jobs. For the
Ilisu dam alone, 184 villages had to be destroyed, of which 85 were
already "supposedly empty" anyway as a result of counter-insurgency
measures.[180] If one accepts the figure of four million Kurds who were
forced from their homes during the oppression of the insurgency from
the 1980s, 9 percent of these had to go for dam projects. In the Tete
province of Mozambique, the 325-meter-high Cabora Bassa dam was

supposed to allow for the implanting of one million new white settlers, while 25,000 Africans had to leave their homes. Around the Cunene dam project in southern Angola, another 1970s project, half a million Portuguese were to settle. In both cases, African pastoralists and peasants had already been resettled into strategic villages in order to have them available as a labor reserve.[181] Plans for huge hydroelectric projects also emerged in the envisioned northern transversal 'development' strip of Guatemala, between 1972 and 1974 – in the very area that became soon embattled; independent groups say that some of the later massacres near the Pueblo Viejo dam in the northwest of the country were to get off their land those peasants who refused to leave it.[182] In East Pakistan, the erection of the Kaptai dam, between 1959 and 1963, fell at the beginning of the Chittagong Hill Tracts conflict, causing mass displacement and the perception of the locals that they were to be deprived of their land, livelihood, and culture.[183] Generally, dam construction sites became military and political battlegrounds over different visions of the future of society.

Access to resources channeled into resettlement areas or earmarked for those evacuated was not equal. In Greece, individuals, groups, and associations tried to outdo each other in anti-communist rhetoric in order to tap relief funds. The most promising patronage networks that emerged involved deputies, administration officials, army and gendarmerie officers, veterans, and leaders of local militias.[184] The close connection of regimes to the interests of large landowners put limits on equality. For example, the land question in Guatemala remained unresolved, and in South Vietnam, land reform remained slow and limited and served in part to redistribute land back to former owners who had been earlier dispossessed by the Viet Minh. The reestablishment of government control there meant "the return of the landlords and the collection of back rents."[185] British land reform plans in Kenya, hammered out in the Swynnerton Plan of 1954, were to work through land consolidation, land titles, and cash-cropping to supply part of the Kikuyu with viable farms, while others would provide labor for European and African farms. This plan – "stabilize a conservative middle class, based on the loyalists," as its purpose was summed up by M. P. K. Sorrenson – worked only as a result of large-scale displacement, intimidation, and coerced labor. However, job generation through this land accumulation scheme remained low, land distribution more limited than planned, and the displaced forcefully demanded their share.[186] In El Salvador, large holdings over 100 hectares were excluded from redistribution, smallholders but not the landless became the beneficiaries of land reform, and if land pressure was somewhat reduced by 1990, it may have been more because one-sixth of the population had fled the country.[187] Land reform would have challenged the very foundations of colonies such as Algeria, so settler racism and latifundists' interests largely prevented it, and job generation remained low.[188] Modest "freehold titles" for up to one acre of land in Rhodesian "Protected Villages" were prevented by the traditional allies of the white government, the African chiefs, who wanted to maintain control over internal land distribution among blacks.[189]

In the processes of social differentiation sketched out here were forged local elites that to varying degrees consisted of the traditionally and the newly privileged. This contributed to the genesis of guerrilla wars, and it fueled them further once they were under way. Militia members, administrators, and shopkeepers formed a new "class of profiteers."[190] The arrest of many Kikuyu political leaders in British Kenya allowed for younger Kikuyu leaders and for elites from other ethnicities to rise.[191] On the other hand, militias were often set up or controlled by old elites: in Kenya by chiefs, headmen, and church leaders (who were given opportunities but also came under pressure from the dispossessed in the aggravating conflicts during increased capitalist penetration); in Malaya by shopkeepers, wealthier members of the community, and Guomintang members; in southeastern Anatolia by clan leaders opposing Kurdish nationalism and communism (whereas other *aghas* supported the PKK); in the Guatemalan highlands by *ladinos*, Evangelical and Catholic church leaders.[192] A local study from Guatemala suggests that important figures in the local power structure, such as moneylenders, shop and bar owners, and mayors, assumed positions as military commissioners or patrol leaders. Most patrol leaders were former soldiers. This corresponds with the observation that by 1986 Civil Patrol actions had turned away from wholesale massacres to selective killings of rival "upcoming community leaders," returned refugees, objectors against patrol duty, and local human rights activists. Former Civil Patrol commanders kept considerable power even after the patrols were disbanded, and *ladinos* were grateful to them for having been able to retain their lifestyle.[193] Despite the aspirations of the Diem regime in South Vietnam to get rid of old conservative French-trained 'unpatriotic' elites and create a newly stratified society – three classes to consist of combatants and their families, hamlet leaders and elected officials, and poor peasants and workers – it was the old power holders who continued to dominate the villages.[194] The persistence of old elites went so far that in socialist post-colonial Mozambique, villagization led to social stratifications along lineage lines, contrary to intentions.[195] Apparently, the peasant patrols in Peru were set up by Indian communities collectively; many of their leaders had previously held ranks with the Shining Path insurgents, indicating their drive for upward social mobility regardless of the prevailing ideology. This can be linked to a process of social differentiation after the late 1960s land reform, and the introduction or strengthening of private landownership had created lots of small farms.[196] It has been argued that peasant participation among Rhodesian guerrillas was also driven, beyond white oppression and exploitation, by inequalities among Africans, such as unequal access to education, labor opportunities, and land distribution. During the struggle, insurgent youths sought social advantages.[197] Likewise, the radicalization of the oaths in colonial Kenya that led to the Land and Freedom Army insurgency ("Mau Mau") came from landless youths, who were often expelled as squatters.[198] Meanwhile, social differences were leveled in the "Protected Villages" due to the loss of houses, tobacco and farming land, and the stressing of communal labor bonds. Militias challenged the authorities of elders.[199]

With this rise of aggressive young men generally came generational conflict and the erosion of traditional ethical values, norms, and forms of the communal construction of justice. The Civil Patrol system in Guatemala undercut community conflict-resolving mechanisms, but also replaced parts of the old judicial system "as an institution for resolving local conflicts and disputes."[200] The loss of elders and ancestors and the breakup of families also implied that traditional customs, values, mutual respect, and obedience disappeared; this process had begun earlier due to labor migration.[201] In Peru, peasant militia leaders assumed a varied influence on the organization of communal life, but were largely excluded from foreign co-sponsored economic 'development' efforts in the 1990s, and patrols were later relatively easily dissolved.[202]

Pierre Bourdieu has attempted to describe the consequences of enforced mass resettlement during anti-guerrilla warfare in his study of Algerian society.[203] The French military preferred to clear those secluded areas of the country that had so far been least affected by the colonial enterprise. Border and mountain regions lost population that fled abroad, to France, to the cities, or were transferred to resettlement areas, designed to also "assure the emancipation of the Moslem masses." Adult men often became separated from their families, and women were drawn into the workplace and the public and political sphere. The displacement – this is the central point of Bourdieu's analysis – led to a breakup of old forms of behavior and customs, of extended families, clans, and village communities. The 200,000 nomads of the country underwent the most radical transformation by being forced into settlements behind barbed wire with the daily rhythm governed by a curfew. Through the separation from their own land, peasants were morally broken and lost their urge to work, undergoing "deruralization" and "*bidonvillisation*," the conversion into shanty-town dwellers and clients of social welfare institutions. According to Bourdieu, agriculturalists were transformed into "a sub-proletariat who had lost all memory of their former ideals of honor and dignity and who wavered between attitudes of meek resignation and ineffectual revolt," nurturing resentment against the colonialists.[204] Others spoke of "[u]rban patterns of life spreading[ing] rapidly among [...] 'urbanites without cities'" and a "brutal proletarianization or lumpenproletarianization of a large number of peasants."[205] In Rhodesia, too, "resettlement into these villages entailed a move from a rural to an urban community, with a concurrent increase in prostitution, delinquency, vagrancy and malnutrition" caused by the abrupt, involuntary change.[206] This traumatic crisis of cultural identity[207] has been called a "proletarianisation of the peasants" in the sense that they were separated from their means of production (agricultural production having collapsed), while often not becoming wage earners.[208] In terms of space, domestic displacement could become the first step toward moving to bigger cities and then mostly urban environments abroad, as was the case in Algeria, Greece, and El Salvador.[209]

Without the benefit of hindsight, Bourdieu, who did notice that some Algerians jumped at the opportunity that modernization offered them, and also that there was the "appearance of a class of profiteers, who were often supported by the army by reason of their 'loyalty', who held a majority of administrative responsibilities,"[210] may have underestimated both the processes of social differentiation and the resilience of the old social structures, customs, and values among the locals while overstating demoralization and passivity. The overthrow of the political order in Algeria allowed many to return to their land (though far from all did), but swept away the new elites of the civil war who had sided with the French. Nonetheless, the abrupt changes proved traumatic.[211] With villages destroyed, families torn apart, land changing hands, and urban centers growing, resettlement during anti-guerrilla warfare changed social structures even where people made strong efforts to rebuild their old homesteads and communities, such as in Guatemala. Lifestyle changes were particularly hard on pastoralists and shifting cultivators.[212]

Social differentiation was also intensified through the transformation of dislocated agriculturalists into a labor pool for industry or plantations. Therefore, government offensives against guerrillas often started with large-scale clampdowns on the urban labor movements as in Malaya in 1948, Kenya in 1952 and 1954, and Guatemala up to 1981. These included the outlawing of labor organizations, mass arrests, killings, and disappearances.[213] Enforced concentration in resettlement areas provided for coffee estate workers in Northern and Central Angola, for construction workers and servants near the Cabora Bassa dam project in Mozambique, and for farm and industrial laborers for white businesses in Rhodesia. The shanty towns around the towns and cities of Greece provided hundreds of thousands of workers, further undermining wages in a country gripped by inflation and economic crisis and generating labor migrants for Western Europe.[214] Traditional economic patterns were dismantled; normal means of subsistence ceased to exist: grain production collapsed in Macedonia and Thrace in 1947 just as wheat, barley, and cattle production did in Algeria from 1954 to 1960, herds in East Timor (especially the water buffalos needed for trampling the fields before sowing), and manioc and rice production plus the cattle trade in Moxico, Angola, in 1969.[215]

In Malaya, the measures during the "Emergency" of 1948 can be said to have directly served capitalist business interests: at the outset, plantation owners and tin miners had complained about a lack of casual labor and assaulted the rights of organized labor (however, most laborers were ethnic Chinese or Indian). Literally in the week before the declaration of the "emergency," leftist unions were de facto prohibited, thereby robbing the ethnic Chinese workers of their labor representation.[216] Not only did the resettlements and "relocations" create one of Asia's most urbanized societies,[217] three-quarters of the resettlers ended up in New Villages of over 1,000 inhabitants. More specifically, undesirable squatters were removed from plantation land in order to replant it, and better control of the workers was facilitated by the concentration of their settlements on estates and near mines. Many of both the squatters and the farmers (each represented about half of the close to 600,000 resettled) were converted from agriculturalists selling rice and vegetables into workers in mines and on plantations – very profitably so, given the rubber and tin booms during the Korean War.[218] As in most cases discussed in this chapter, the resettlers were given hardly any land. Within only two years, from 1950 to 1952, the percentage of agriculturalists in these settlements dropped from 60 to 27, while the number of wage earners increased accordingly, mostly in the rubber industry (52 percent). Others remained unemployed. With so much labor readily available, the real wages of rubber field toilers, that in 1950–51 had finally almost caught up with those of 1939, dropped again significantly, offsetting a decrease in labor productivity. However, relocations favored bigger enterprises in European hands, whereas many smaller, mostly Asian- (namely Chinese-) owned, mines and estates saw themselves disadvantaged as it was hard to obtain credit, and their workers were resettled to other sites.[219] The very name of the Malayan "Emergency" was selected because of capital interests – if it had been dubbed a war, the insurance contracts of British estates would not have applied and many plantations would have been given up by their owners.[220] Prime targets of the Min Yuen guerrillas thus were rubber estates and tin mines, symbols and carriers of the capitalist order and of the violent socioeconomic changes taking place.[221]

Similar practices could be observed earlier: US forced resettlements in the Philippines around 1900 helped create a labor pool for the plantations of US corporations, and the depopulation of entire areas in North China and the resettlements of five million or so in "Manchukuo" served to a large degree to provide cheap labor for the Japanese industrialization of Manchuria.[222] Similar developments took place in French Algeria. However, overall labor demand was lower; 25 percent of the resettlers worked on their own farms or as agricultural laborers, 44 percent remained unemployed, the rest owned some kind of small business. In 1960, about one-third of Algerians of working age worked for less than 100 days per year. A similar effect was observed for El Salvador and South Vietnam.[223] In the "emergency" in Kenya, recorded employment of men increased, while chiefs appointed by the colonialists provided labor and the authorities tried to attract more European settlers with cheap land and labor.[224] In East Timor, the Indonesian army promoted cash-crop cultivation from 1981, helped by the US-based Catholic Relief Service. Much of this benefited the military monopolies, namely coffee estates.[225] The population in East Timor was used to a dispersed settlement structure. Forced population concentration started in September 1976 and was essentially complete after two large campaigns in 1977–79 and 1981–82. In the late 1970s, 318,921 East Timorese rural dwellers had been crammed into just fifteen resettlement centers, to be transferred to nucleated villages after 1984. By 1991, the total number of settlements in East Timor had decreased from 1,717 in 1975 to 442.[226]

Not only through organized resettlement, but also through forced evacuation, expulsion, and refugees, anti-guerrilla warfare contributed more generally to urbanization and housing shortages as a result. For example, Guatemala City doubled in size from 1976 to 1987. The East Timorese capital of Dili grew from 28,000 to 80,000 people between 1974 and 1985, Diyarbakir (Turkey) from 140,000 in 1970 to 400,000 in 1990 and 1.5 million by the late 1990s, Van from 151,000 to 500,000, Urfa from 226,000 to 700,000, Algiers by 203,000 from 1954 to 1960. The areas of Algiers, Constantine, and Oran (Algeria) gained 67.5, 63, and 48 percent, respectively, in population within the six years after the 1954 insurrection. South Vietnam's urban population grew from 15 to 20 percent at the onset of the 1960s to 40 percent in 1968, Saigon from 2.3 to 3.3 million (1960–70). From 1981 to 1993, the proportion of the urban population in Huanta province in Peru increased from 18 to 39 percent of the total. Many Africans from Central Angola escaped from strategic villages to the cities in the 1970s.[227] Samuel Huntington dubbed the refugee movements caused by US bombings and attacks in South Vietnam "forced-draft urbanization" that, as he hoped, undermined the "rural revolutionary movement."[228]

The case of Kenya embodies a brutal but far-reaching social restructuring, based on sophisticated plans. Building on observations of the trends of differentiation during the previous two decades, British colonial officers developed a scheme (the Swynnerton plan) for the emergence of a capitalist society in Kikuyu lands and for the social groups that would defend it: a land-based middle class that would offer impoverished Kenyans employment, "the anchor of the tribe, the solid yeoman farmer, the land owner who knows that he has too much to lose if he flirts, however lightly, with the passions of his nationalistic friends."[229] The already fierce struggle taking place between the smaller and medium landholders in the African reserves came to a head after 100,000 Kikuyu squatters were evicted from European farms in 1952. This "was bound to escalate the already chaotic conflict. Murders over land were a common occurrence, as were all sorts of physical deprivation and abuse."[230] About 100,000 coffee and pyrethrum grow-ing licenses were given to Kikuyu supporters of British rule from the mid-1950s; they were also allowed to take loans on their land, and so they reaped the profits of the coffee boom and accumulated wealth.[231] In contrast, only a small portion of former detainees received lands (which they had to buy) in settlement programs in Kenya, and no spe-cial jobs or pensions were offered to them, so some went back into the bush after independence.[232] Still, with holdings of 0.25–3 acres, not much surplus production nor employment was generated.[233] The result has – like Malaysia and Greece – been characterized as a neo-colony, extremely welcoming to foreign capital, and with some of the most blatant contrasts between rich and poor in Africa.[234]

Limits to engineering social change

The power of rulers to manipulate the rural population through mod-ernizing the countryside in a way compatible with the capitalist system was, however, far from total. Organized resettlement is expensive. For example, the colonial authorities in Kenya had to make do with Kenya's financial and human resources to defeat the Mau Mau uprising, which cost UK£55 million.[235] The El Salvadoran government's *Unidos para Reconstruir* plan and the establishment of one thousand villages for 500,000 displaced failed in 1986 due to an earthquake and the switch to a foreign-imposed austerity program.[236] The services provided to resettlers often concentrated on quite traditional functions of nine-teenth-century style penetration of the countryside, namely medical and educational facilities. "Winning the population" was attempted through "minor social benefits which can easily and fairly inexpen-sively be provided, such as improved health measures and clinics [...]; new schools [...]; and improved livelihood and standard of living" such as improved seeds, livestock, and advice to produce cash crops.[237] But, as in most other affected countries, resettlers in Malaya had to build their new homesteads with their own hands. And, in reality, with little per-capita spending for resettlers or refugees, often even the most basic amenities such as land, water, and schools were not provided; there were health clinics but no medicine; children were forced to work.[238] In Mizoram (India), the government allocated a mere 130 rupees to each resettler over ten years. In the South Vietnamese *agrovilles* program, the government spent a mere US$5 per capita. Due to the high costs of "Protected Villages" with their fences and lighting, the Rhodesian government turned in 1975 to another type, "consolidated villages," which required much less investment. Resettlement in Rhodesia (as in Kenya) appeared as rather punitive action to observers. The annual costs of the planned resettlement of 1.5 million people would have required the entire Ethiopian government revenue.[239]

The United Kingdom's shaky state finances after World War II and the desire to build a welfare state in Britain required capital flows by the "second colonial occupation," provoking social differentiation among the locals and thus the insurrections in Malaya and Kenya.[240] Then the Korean War boom facilitated financing the suppression of the Malayan communist resurrection. Even before, Malaya was the British Empire's prime dollar earner (contributing three times as many dollars as all other colonies combined in 1946); between 1946 and 1950 (largely before Korea), the USA imported US$700 million worth of rubber from Malaya. According to one official at the time, "without Malaya the sterling currency system as we know it would not exist." The British Government directly provided £520 million of the c.£700 million that the war cost, but this was financed through export-related state revenues, that is, indirectly from international sources.[241] By comparison, the total means provided for the resettlement of about 573,000 Malayans accounted for about Malayan $100 million (£12.5 million). In Kenya, funds pledged for social and economic development, namely agricultural programs, were also only a fraction of military costs.[242] Much of the profits from the Korean War boom actually ended up in the pockets of the predominantly European business community in Malaya, an incentive for British managers to stay on the rubber plantations despite the aggravated threat through guerrilla attacks. Part of the boom money indirectly helped the insurgents, since some mine and plantation workers were awash with cash but did not know how to spend it, sometimes instead donating it to the communists.[243]

The practice of settlement tended to reflect a racist hierarchy: to settle a single white family in Portugal's African colonies required $8,000–20,000.[244] Only a small fraction of this sum was provided for black involuntary resettlers. In Malaya, the British authorities financed the relocation of circa 573,000 mainly Chinese rural dwellers in "new villages" with around Malayan $100 million (about M$180 per person), and allocated just M$810,000 for the relocation of the indigenous Orang Asli people in 1949 to 1951 (M$16 per person, the bulk of which was spent on the salaries of administrators, propaganda material, office furniture, and books). Under these circumstances, the consequent mass deaths of the aborigines come as even less of a surprise.[245]

While providing large populations with the means for settling at a new location is a luxury many states cannot or do not want to afford, militias are comparatively cheap. The territorial forces in the villages of South Vietnam received only 2 to 4 percent of the war budget, but they sustained 30 percent of the fatalities of communist and government forces combined, so that a Vietnamese analyst called them "the most cost-efficient military forces employed on the allied side." A similar effect was recorded for the Philippine Constabulary in the insurgency in the early 1900s.[246]

Conversely, employing great numbers of troops or keeping them in overseas territories tended to overstretch the financial capabilities of rulers. The case of US troops in the Vietnam War is obvious, but for the Portuguese to have more than 50,000 soldiers in Angola or for the French to have 400,000 in Algeria financially exhausted these countries and led to soldiers being conscripted for two years or more. Before the Algerian War, France had already kept 52 percent of its regular army in Indochina in 1953. The Algerian War cost France UK£250 million in 1960 alone.[247] The Portuguese spent UK£1,461 million from 1961 to 1974 for anti-guerrilla wars (or US$523 million in 1974 alone), equivalent to about 28 percent of the government budget, including the contributions of the colonies. This led to a net capital outflow from the mainland and perceptions such as that "90 per cent of gross domestic product left for the colonies."[248] The costs of counter-insurgency as a proportion of government expenditure in Rhodesia rose from 6.5 percent in 1967 to 25 percent in 1976 and 47 percent in 1979. When rubber and tin prices fell due to the end of the Korean War in 1953 and British Malaya faced a deficit, the Special Constabulary was cut down by more than 10,000 men to reduce costs.[249] Turkey deployed 140,000 to 150,000 regular troops to the southeast, in addition to 50,000 gendarmes and 40,000 police. Around 1997, total costs had already reached US$40 billion.[250] Attempts by the Guatemalan military to finance the war against the guerrillas, as well as welfare measures to pacify the highland population, by raising taxes resulted in repeated major conflicts with the business elites in the 1980s. A similar development took place in Kenya.[251]

Anti-communist governments or colonial regimes financed part of their costs from foreign sources, for the most part from the USA. Between 1951 and 1954, Washington provided the regime of their former colony, the Philippines, with US$95 million of non-military aid, in part to fund social improvements during the Huk rebellion. In Greece, the US government spent US$10,000 to "eliminate one guerrilla."[252] Most of the US aid to Greece from 1947 was channeled to the military, and a large part of a downsized reconstruction budget was used for airport and road construction. Essentially, American financial support served to cover budget and balance of payment deficits.[253] According to the commander of the Greek counter-insurgency forces, "thanks to American aid the size of the Army was notably enlarged" in 1948; the same applied to local militias.[254] The Indochina War cost France US$1 billion per year, which was in part recovered by means of the Marshall Plan. In addition, the US government bore one-third of French costs by 1950 and poured US$1 billion annually into this proxy war in 1953–54.[255] In South Vietnam, the US Civil Organization and Revolutionary Development Support (CORDS), financed largely through USAID, had 7,600 personnel and a budget of US$891 million by 1968.[256] From 1980 to 1988, Guatemala received US$575 million in military and economic aid. El Salvador was granted about ten times that sum, but, as in South Vietnam, this was not enough to stabilize anti-communist rule after causing a giant refugee crisis. In 1983–84, the USA spent $135,000 per enemy guerrilla fighter in that country.[257] Little of such money actually reached the population; instead, much was wasted on oversize 'development' projects or appropriated by way of corruption, such as with most of the US 'development aid' for South Vietnam.[258] Ironically, one reason for the survival of chronically underemployed El Salvadorans was the remittances sent by hundreds of thousands of illegal immigrants to the USA to their families at home – another way of outsourcing indirect counter-insurgency war finance.[259]

Another part of the costs of the 'development' projects initiated by the Guatemalan military to cover the basic needs of the population was financed by UN agencies and international non-governmental organizations and administered by military officers. While similar plans in Rhodesia were thwarted by the Finance Minister, international development agencies funded economic projects at "strategic sites" in East Timor and for relocated Hmong people in northern Thailand, including an effort to dissuade them from cultivating poppy seeds and turning them to alternative cash crops. Earlier, a representative of the US Agency for International Development stated before the US Congress that three-quarters of USAID money was devoted to "counterinsurgency activities," including Thai police forces.[260]

The case of Guatemala illustrates the limits to social engineering. The argument has been made that plans for a capitalist penetration of the north–central development belt in the 1970s, including oil drilling, estates, cattle ranches, and hydroelectric and highway projects, in part owned by military figures, caused the military's drive for control of the highlands.[261] Others have stressed that estates hardly expanded in the 1970s; rather, successive waves of settlers came into conflict in the western highlands, taking new land serving as substitute for land reform. Then social differentiation set in between valley communities and poor mountain peasants in villages that had only been founded in the 1960s and 1970s.[262] Corruption during the reconstruction after the devastating 1976 earthquake which had made one million homeless further deepened social differentiation and resentments, and the Committee for National Reconstruction set up to deal with this would later also become the vehicle for reconstruction after military devastation from 1983.[263] The effects of counter-insurgency were mixed: they reduced the numbers of seasonal migrations from the Maya highlands to the coastal plantation areas in the south because highland dwellers tried to avoid the trip due to insecurity, traffic disruption, and increased travel costs. Simultaneously, as a result of depressed world market prices, labor demand for the coffee, cotton, and sugar estates dropped, while less labor-intensive products such as soybeans, sorghum, and beef were expanded, though in other regions of the country. The nation's industry slumped and Guatemala City especially, though still growing, lost its capacity to absorb labor. Some military commissioners, mayors, or chiefs of Civil Patrols in the highlands were also contractors or financers of the recruitment of workers for the coffee and cotton plantations, linking local violence and the labor supply of other regions.[264] Some of the former seasonal migrants tried to settle permanently near the estates.[265] All this caused new waves of immigration to the northwestern highlands, where returning refugees would find their fields settled by other indigenas who had been given the land by the army, which triggered (as in El Salvador) protracted conflicts between *antiguos* and *nuevos*.[266] In Chimaltenango and the Ixil area, the situation of the population was desperate, with access to land drastically restricted (and conflicts about those portions that were not off limits), real wages down below subsistence levels, rising corn prices, and non-agricultural production like construction, small crafts, and commerce decimated.[267] This situation put limits on the ability of the military to dictate the terms of social reconstruction. Their lack of legitimacy forced them into the 1996 peace agreement.[268]

Great schemes for a capitalist modernization of the countryside often failed due to a lack of resources, in conjunction with the priority being placed on purely military operations and objections by the old elites against the massive redistribution of property. This is most obvious (aside from Guatemala, where budget restraints prevented the establishing of many model villages called 'development poles') in the Portuguese colonies – especially in eastern Angola, a semi-arid area with about two inhabitants per square kilometer, which Portugal was unable to develop or administer, and where the Portuguese mostly could not afford electric installations or doctors for strategic villages.[269] Guatemala and other post-colonial countries showed similar tendencies, and in South Vietnam, 8,000 strategic hamlets were hastily established in 1961–63, but villagers hardly received any financial support or services. Despite the infusion of huge resources through USAID, social change in South Vietnam was beyond the control of the South Vietnamese regime or the communist National Liberation Front, as David Elliott has argued. The result of resettlement, expulsions, terror, and insecurity was an opportunity for upward mobility leading to the establishment of a middle class of peasants that also prevented the effective collectivization of agriculture in socialist South Vietnam after 1975.[270] What happened instead of the planned transition was a transformation through the emergence of new elites, who ascended in a chaotic struggle through functions in the militias or administrations, establishing businesses and accumulating land.

Long-term fall-out

On December 2, 1989, newspapers reported that the East German parliament had deleted the leading role of the Party of Socialist Unity (SED) from the constitution of the German Democratic Republic. It was only that same day that the chairman of the Malaysian Communist Party, Chin Peng, signed a peace agreement with the government of Malaysia. In all, 1,188 registered guerrillas surrendered, forty-one years after the start of the Malayan "Emergency."[271] Malaysia is considered a relatively peaceful society, but the Malay–Chinese tensions, heightened in the insurgency, contributed to the split into Malaysia and Singapore in 1965, to race riots in both countries in the late 1960s, and to the New Economic Policy favoring 'indigenous' (e.g. Malay) citizens in Malaysia's public service that was adopted in 1969 and is still in effect. Many observers have dubbed Malaysia, where more than half of all economic capital has remained in foreign hands, as a neo-colony which communalism has served to maintain.[272]

In many countries the long-term consequences of strategic resettlement and civil involvement in anti-guerrilla warfare are even more obvious. Again, this fall-out demonstrates the deep roots of the social conflicts created or widened by large-scale counter-guerrilla warfare, which impeded the transition from an extremely violent society after the end of military conflict.

The most obvious outcome was the retaliatory and often long-term repression of former 'loyalists' of the succumbing regimes through informal killings, imprisonment and re-education, trials and executions, economic disadvantages, and exile – from Vietnam to Algeria, from East Timor[273] to former Portuguese colonies in Africa. Aside from one million Europeans who left Algeria, estimates of Muslims killed in 1962 because of their former support of French rule range between 10,000 and 150,000 (some French historians think 70,000 is a realistic figure). According to information gathered by French authorities, violence was widespread, with thirty to fifty former members of pro-French armed formations and higher functionaries killed per village. In June 1963, Algerian Prime Minister Ben Bella announced that 130,000 former *harkis* had been pardoned, 6,000 to 7,000 remained imprisoned, while others were sentenced to forced labor.[274]

Many former 'loyalists' felt compelled to emigrate, including hundreds of thousands of supporters of the capitalist South Vietnamese and Cambodian regimes (leaving for the USA), among them over 100,000 Hmong from Laos and Vietnam, who became scattered all over the world,[275] tens of thousands of former *harkis* from Algeria,[276] and several thousand Belorussian peasants from "armed villages" or local police who left their country with the Germans in 1944.

Elsewhere, former opponents to the resistance movement were held in re-education camps for years, as in Vietnam, or civil wars followed, some of which lasted for decades, such as in Cambodia and Angola, and in Mozambique, where up to one million people died. Recent scholarship on Mozambique has stressed the domestic origins of conflict between the government and the notorious Renamo. Where the anti-communist guerrillas took control, supported by the white governments of Rhodesia and South Africa and commanded by a former auxiliary of the Portuguese army, Afonso Dhlakama, they re-installed petty chiefs and tax collectors, policemen, village elders, and animist priests, as those had existed under the Portuguese, and enjoyed support among those who had lost property in the new socialist communal villages.[277]

Insurgencies along class, religious, or ethnic lines have periodically flared up in the Philippines, armed fighting in East Timor (for example, in 2002, 2006, and 2007), and Kurdish resistance as well as its oppression is still going on. Bloody riots in Kenya, pitting different political parties against each other, Kikuyu against other ethnicities, poor against rich, often evolving around landholding issues, erupted in early 2008; 1,500 were killed, 350,000 fled.[278] Algeria was shaken by a bloody civil war in the 1990s, with massacres committed by Islamist insurgents as well as government forces. In Greece, the military dictatorship from 1967 to 1974 drew from policies of the civil war 1945 to 1949; applicants for a position in public service needed a police certificate, approved by a board of the prefecture, about their "healthy beliefs" for a quarter of a century after the defeat of the communist insurgency; and only 10,000 out of 28,000 children evacuated abroad by the guerrillas in 1948–49 had returned to their home country by the 1970s.[279] Many never did. Zimbabwe likewise demonstrates the ramifications of the anti-guerrilla war of the 1970s. These can be seen in conflicts between Africans and Europeans resulting in the exodus of most of the latter, in protracted land occupations by people trying to return to land taken from them between 1946 and the 1970s, and conflicts over grazing rights, in continuous *Landflucht* (migration into cities), resulting in poverty and conflicts between squatters and the authorities, in a persecution of the Ndebele minority in the 1980s some even call "genocide," and in fierce conflicts between political parties. According to the Catholic bishops of the country, the Mugabe government has never revoked any of the security laws adopted by the white minority regime.[280]

A culture of violence, abrupt migration, urbanization, and the disappearance of older social bonds and values, combined with the impoverishment of large groups, all caused by long counter-guerrilla wars, often also result in a surge of ordinary "banditry." Ongoing political violence and intimidation in Guatemala after the peace accord, as well as criminal lawlessness, accounted for 6,229 fatalities in the first eleven months of 1997, while 1,231 people were kidnapped or disappeared. In 2009, there were 6,461 murder victims, and the fact that 98 percent of these crimes went unpunished also resembled a war situation.[281] Violence had become a "way of life," primarily in the central highlands, but it was also intrinsic in the nation's capital, where South Americans passing through on their way from the airport to Mexico and further to the USA were frequently assaulted.[282] In El Salvador, there were 8,000 to 9,000 violent deaths each year from 1994 to 1996 – more than during an average civil war year. In 2006, close to 4,000 people were still being murdered.[283] By the late 1980s, a large proportion of the violent attacks during the Mozambican civil war originated not from Renamo insurgents nor from government troops, but from criminal gangs; a US diplomat estimated that "freelancers" accounted for one-third of violent attacks.[284] Violent common crime, indicating deteriorating living standards, sometimes also preceded some of the civil wars described here. These were not just the fabrications of reactionary propagandists. In British Kenya, crime rates had risen from the end of World War II; in Nairobi, the insurgents of the 1950s were suspected of having close links to criminal gangs. Similar developments were observed in Manchuria before and after the Japanese occupation (possibly half of the initial resistance movement – up to 140,000 people – were supposed to come "from a [ordinary, C.G.] bandit background"), in Algiers, in southeastern Turkey (Kurdistan), and in British Malaya, where inter-ethnic violence caused hundreds of additional deaths.[285] Many partisan movements were confronted, as ELAS in Greece, with the problem of restoring a minimum of social discipline and acting against "professional cattle thieves, killers and other fugitive criminals" who exploited villagers to feed their own clan.[286]

Long-term changes also affected the role of women in society. In most cases discussed here, far more men than women were killed by direct violence,[287] but women faced different hardships. Rapes and beatings by militias in Kenya, Rhodesia, and Guatemala and by soldiers in Angola were common,[288] threatening the cohesion of families. Violence against both men and women served to humiliate men and undermined their role as protectors. Male dominance was sometimes later restored through beatings, rape, and abduction.[289] As Caroline Elkins has argued, British colonial agents in Kenya targeted as symbols of the manhood of Kikuyus their women, their children, their land, and their bodies.[290] Most Malayans removed as squatters from 1949 to 1952[291] and most inmates of the resettlement villages in Angola and Kenya were women and children. The same goes for the relocation centers in Algeria, where the women were forced to stay inside the standardized shacks of French design even if they adopted the headscarf, spending their time on concrete floors unsuitable for their style of living.[292] Even where there were women members in militias, the leadership remained in male hands,[293] cementing traditional gender roles, ascribing to women backwardness and the role of the bearers of tradition. Patrol practice and indoctrination worsened machismo to a point that male violence, lack of perspective, and alcoholism prevented some Guatemalan women from remarrying.[294] On the other hand, families were broken up during resettlement, either because men were arrested, forced into plantation labor, went underground, or were killed. This forced women to earn money, come into contact with public authorities, travel, and widen their radius of activity. In the case of a longer military occupation, such as in East Timor, some were forced to enter relationships with a soldier. So women bore special burdens, unprotected in the resettlement areas, responsible for the survival of children and elderly family members under extreme conditions, and suffering distinct trauma.[295]

Violence dragged on in countries affected by strategic resettlement along with the new settlement patterns created through anti-guerrilla war. Scholars have documented that resettlement villages persisted long after the end of an insurgency. Less than 2 percent of the New Villages in Malaya had been abandoned by the early 1960s, with population losses under 20 percent, and the population increased by 78 percent by 1970, resulting in the highest degree of urbanization in Asia. Inhabitants cited high costs, security pressures and concerns, and the desire to maintain new friends and basic amenities for their decision to stay. This said, the New Villages suffered from gross government neglect from the start, and this continued up to the 1980s (as in Algeria), and many unemployed turned back to 'illegal' cultivation. By contrast, virtually all people had left the regroupment areas on the estates and mines under pressure from their owners.[296] In Mozambique, two-thirds of the former Portuguese-enforced *aldeamentos* in Tete province still existed in 1982, seven years after the end of the war of decolonization, despite the fact that people there had been used to dispersed settlements or nomadism before 1968, not life in villages. More than half of the 'new' communal villages under the socialist government in the northern provinces of Tete, Niassa, and Cabo Delgado around 1980 came out of *aldeamentos*, though many such settlements had been abandoned at first.[297]

In Algeria, the colonial authorities actually gave some support for and encouragement to "dégroupement" after the cease-fire in 1961–62, but only a minority of inhabitants of the much-hated regroupment villages and centers returned to their former places of living, perhaps 250,000. By 1966, more than half of the regroupment places still existed with over 60 percent of the former population. Largely, it was the small regroupment places that had disappeared. Surveys with smaller samples suggested that up to 90 percent of regroupment settlements and their 1961 population levels were still in place even up to 1973. With this, "depeasantisation" proved a lasting legacy.[298] However, this hides a dynamic situation in which high numbers of people moved in and out of former regroupment places or new villages, and from one to the next.[299] Again, new amenities such as housing, schools, water, electricity, roads, stores, mosques, and clinics – or the expectation that these would come sooner in the new than in the old settlement – explained part of this development; in 1977, only 21 percent of rural houses were connected to piped water, 13 to 15 percent to a sewage system, and 25 percent to electricity; in former "new villages" these figures were probably higher.[300]

Elsewhere, the picture was more mixed. In Kenya's western highlands, the British authorities were very reluctant to admit Kikuyus back to their land in the late 1950s, but when they did, the landless and poor (though fewer in numbers than in Algeria) tended to stay on. British plans to merge the Emergency villages into bigger, more centralized ones at new sites materialized only to some degree.[301] In 1996, only one-third of the displaced from the Peruvian countryside had returned and one-sixth commuted between a city and their home region.[302] By contrast, 87 percent of displaced Kurdish villagers in Turkey indicated in 2000 that they wanted to return.[303] The Indian army had to burn down one Mizo village in the late 1960s nineteen times and another one seven times before the villagers apparently gave up on a return.[304] Once villagers were allowed to return officially in the 1970s, they still received smaller financial government support than those in regrouped villages, and yet about one-third returned.[305] In the Greek civil war, virtually no model settlements were created, yet many damaged or destroyed mountain villages regained only part of their population afterwards. Lack of government support resulted in slow returns, particularly to Macedonia, Thrace, Thessaly, and Evia, and many of those who did go back to their old villages would later leave again due to starvation, poverty, and loosened social cohesion, adding to the new urbanites and to labor emigration from Greece in the 1950s.[306] Likewise, there was little government-organized resettlement in El Salvador, but we know that the existence of health care and schools was more important than security to the displaced for choosing a new place to live.[307] The Greek and also the Algerian example hint at another factor: resettled families feared the financial and social costs that *dégroupement* would cause to them again, a misery which would make return another dramatic and traumatic change in their lives, instead of simply going home.[308] We lack data about the durability of model settlements in many other countries. Information about long-term social change and stratification in former resettlement villages seems especially scant. Future research in this direction could deepen our understanding of ongoing or decreasing tensions and conflicts in such settlements.

The spread of knowledge

Of course, repression against guerrilla movements did not take place in isolated national spaces. The proliferation of the strategies portrayed

here was boosted by new technologies, but "helicopters, weed killers, and rapid-fire rifles merely added a new dimension of speed and
bloodiness [...]."[309] Likewise, terminology seems to have been imi-
tated: communist guerrillas were called "bandits" in the German-
occupied Soviet Union, in Greece, and in Portuguese Guinea, as well
as by the Guomintang in the Chinese Civil War and by the British
colonial authorities in Malaya. Then the British considered this reference to China counter-productive because there the 'bandits' had
won, so that term was replaced in Malaya by "Communist Terrorists"
(CTs) in May 1952.[310] In local Chinese parlance (the New Villages
were called "concentration camps"), British actions "recalled Japanese
tactics in Manchuria in the 1930s," and this was not to be.[311] Above
all, however, it is the international dissemination of experiences of tangible counter-insurgency techniques that is at first glance baffling.

Great Britain's involvement in the Greek Civil War has been
called a "significant shift in high-level British thinking about anti-
guerrilla warfare."[312] Clear-and-hold operations combined with large-
scale population relocations, planned by the Greek Army, were approved
by the over 1,000-strong British Military Mission in Greece (BMM(G))
and the British Chiefs of Staff in 1947. Some analysts claim that with this
the British military learned from the *mistakes* of German anti-partisan
warfare in Greece between 1942 and 1944 (which in turn took up strategies from German-occupied Yugoslavia and Belarus).[313] However,
the BMM(G) was apparently unaware that British troops themselves
had elsewhere practiced similar mass relocations before.[314] While there
was some British criticism (with limited impact) of the huge encircle-
ment operations by the Greek National Army, the fact remains that the
BMM(G) recommended that the Greeks drive out tens of thousands of
people just like the Germans had done. Sometimes this affected literally
the same persons, since British-approved forced evacuations largely took
place in the same mountain areas of northern and northwestern Greece
as under the Germans (at a time when Britain still gave some support
to the leftist ELAS partisans). The British had concentrated their own
troops just there by late 1946.[315] Plans for further no-man's-lands were
drafted and militias set up in February 1948 in cooperation with the US
Military Mission in Greece. However, even after the Joint US Military
Advisory and Planning Group had taken the lead in August 1947, US
Army officers continued to approach and involve British officers for
operational proposals of the Greek Army.[316]

Such experiences were then taken further through the British Empire. High-ranking officers during the Malayan insurgency included General Officer, Commanding, Charles H. Boucher, who had served in the Greek Civil War, High Commissioner Henry Gurney, former Chief Secretary in Palestine (from which he drew to formulate part of the Malayan Emergency regulations), and Harold Briggs, commander of the 5th Indian Division in the Burma campaign in World War II and active during the Tharrawaddy revolt in 1931. In addition, the chief of staff of Britain's Far East Land Forces, Brigadier John Kirkman, had served in Greece and drawn "useful conclusions" from the Greek and Chinese anti-guerrilla fighting. Both Boucher and Gurney were accompanied by hundreds of troops and policemen, respectively, who had been deployed in the same theaters.[317] Later on, units such as the Devonshire Regiment were transferred from Malaya to Kenya, as were companies of the King's African Rifles Battalion.[318] The lessons from Malaya were disseminated to other British colonial troops in 1950 and 1952.[319]

British experts were also sent to countries beyond the Empire. When resettling Mizo villages in Assam from 1967, Indian Major-General Sagat Singh carried with him Robert Thompson's book on counter-insurgency in Malaya.[320] Developing the strategic hamlet model in Vietnam and several militias has been credited to US military and CIA advisors, but even more to the British Advisory Mission in Vietnam (BRIAM) under Robert Thompson, a former Defense Secretary of the Malayan Federation.[321] South Vietnamese President Diem, who showed interest in the Malayan experience, also brought in as advisors Edward Lansdale (a US officer called with some exaggeration the "Clausewitz of Counterinsurgency") and the Colonel of the Filipino Army, Napoleon Valeriano, who had both participated in the abatement of the Hukbalahap rebellion.[322] Roger Hilsman, an important advisor on counter-insurgency to President Kennedy, had fought in Burma during World War II.[323] The US government tried to learn from the perceived British success in the Malayan insurgency; the State Department commissioned the Rand Corporation to prepare a six-volume study about Malaya, British officers were invited for lectures, and US officers attended the British jungle-warfare school in Johore, Malaya.[324] Earlier, the US military commissioned a number of scholarly studies based on captured German and Japanese records "from which conclusions may be derived for consideration in planning

US Army counterguerrilla action." For example, the German Federal Archive holds among its records returned by the USA an original copy of the anti-partisan instructions of the Plenipotentiary of the Reichsführer-SS for Anti-Bandit Operations of February 1943, with a Pentagon stamp on it.[325] With regard to the insurgency in northern Thailand, numerous US anthropologists and other researchers cooperating with US military authorities and the CIA between 1964 and 1973 came up with suggestions such as for village militias (in various formats) and food control policies that were subsequently implemented, partially financed by the US Agency for International Development.[326] Thai officers were also influenced by the British experience in neighboring Malaya.[327] Rhodesian officers made a conscious choice between British methods borrowed from Malaya and the Portuguese model.[328]

A number of researchers have pointed to the influence of US manuals, advisors, and instructors of the US-led and USAID-financed military school in Panama (where, for example, Turkish officers were also educated) on counter-insurgency in Guatemala and Peru, especially in the 1960s and 1970s. Among others, General Ríos Montt later received training in the USA.[329] However, the architect of the murderous sweeps through the Guatemalan Highlands of 1981–82, Benedicto Lucas Garcia, Army Chief of Staff and brother of the President, was trained in the French Army and had fought in Algeria.[330] In fact, Algeria was another focal point of the emergence of counter-insurgency. There existed the "Center for Training and Preparation in Counter-Guerrilla Warfare" in Arzew, where about 10,000 officers were trained, including foreigners, though only in the final years with some emphasis on socioeconomic planning. French training and theory had an impact on Portuguese and Peruvian anti-guerrilla strategies, including civil–military cooperation.[331] During the war in Algeria, there were frequent field visits by foreign military attachés and officers, some of them from Latin America.[332] Several high-ranking Peruvian military officers received training in Britain, and British counter-insurgency specialists visited Peru in the 1990s.[333] Influences were often diverse: South Vietnamese chief presidential advisor Nhu and CIA post chief William Colby discussed lessons from the anti-guerrilla wars in French Indochina, Malaya, and Algeria, and looked into the model of the Israeli kibbutzim.[334] One architect of the Guatemalan model village program, Colonel Eduardo Wohlers, said that it emulated Israeli kibbutzim, Taiwanese farms, and Korean communes.[335] However, in the 1980s, the Guatemalan military developed an increasing sense of independence from the USA and pride in their own structural policy of counter-insurgency, leading a colonel to declare in May 1987, "in this we are being original, we are not copying models."[336]

As within the British and French Empires, there were attempts to disseminate concepts within the Portuguese colonial sphere. When Portuguese General Spinola arrived as commander in Guinea Bissau in 1968, he brought with him experiences from Angola, just as his predecessor Schultz had done, but he also tried to learn by studying works by his opponent Amilcar Cabral, borrowing methods from the PAIGC insurgents, and encouraging African political and economic participation. There, in turn, officials stressed the need to take into account Portuguese as well as international experiences with strategic resettlements against insurgencies.[337] Dictator Salazar was said to have closely followed the examples of the British experiences in Palestine, Malaya, Borneo, Kenya, and Cyprus, as well as those of the French in Algeria.[338]

It goes without saying that insurgents themselves tried to apply earlier international lessons. Mao Tse-tung's writings were obviously very influential. The Algerian FLN drew experiences from Tito's partisans in Yugoslavia during World War II. Some FLN officers had even themselves fought on the French side in Indochina.[339] Some observers had similar first-hand knowledge, too. Before Basil Davidson started a six-week walk with MPLA guerrillas into Angola in 1970, he had fought or worked as an advisor with the partisans in Yugoslavia, in Italy during World War II, and had visited the guerrilla war theatres of Guinea Bissau in 1967 and Mozambique in 1968.[340] Indonesia's army, having emerged from an anti-colonial liberation force itself, later transplanted certain tactics of population involvement in anti-guerrilla war from province to province, such as the fence-of-legs method from West Kalimantan to East Timor.[341]

Yet the transplanting of such concepts had limits as the genesis of mass resettlement and militia building shows. French Algeria is the only case from which complaints among officers are known about *too many* generalizations being applied from the Indochina War. In Algeria, resettlements were "very popular in military circles, particularly among the readers of Mao Tse-tung and the veterans of the war in Indochina."[342] But when, for example, John Harding, former Commander-in-Chief of the British Far Eastern Land Forces and then Chief of Imperial General Staff, toured Kenya in February 1953, "he found that virtually none of the lessons of Malaya were being applied" in practice, although they were known. That happened, to a degree, later in that year and 1954, when villagization was applied systematic-ally in four districts.[313]

More generally, despite a number of booklets, manuals, and instructions from the 1920s, up to the 1950s there existed no com-prehensive statement of British policies in counter-insurgency. A comprehensive manual was only put together by the late 1950s and counter-insurgency has been taught at Sandhurst since 1961, at which point most British anti-guerrilla warfare was over. The flow of know-ledge in practice worked rather accidentally and unsystematically, often through unofficial book publications by officers, including ideas about socioeconomic development opportunities for the population and political measures.[344] This is not actually surprising. Due to adverse geographic conditions, and bad communication and infrastructure, local commanders in anti-guerrilla warfare are generally given a free hand in their choice of methods.[345]

As a result, with regard to strategic resettlement and mil-itia building, the wheel has been reinvented time and again since the 1940s. The evidence comes from the ways in which such concepts have concretely emerged and been realized in affected countries. Usually, instead of being thought out by a general staff or a centralized facil-ity, based on theoretical studies of international military experiences, and then imposed from above, such measures were developed through trial and error by local or regional commanders, military, and some-times civilian authorities, or from private initiatives. It mostly took years to get them accepted by the military and political leadership and make them a general, systematic, and widespread practice in a country or colony. The existence of hundreds of thousands of evac-uees and refugees, such as in Guatemala, Algeria, and Mozambique, or the floating back of the relocated to their territories as in Malaya, triggered the search for orderly settlement and strategic village pro-grams. As a chief planner of Guatemalan counter-insurgency, General Hector Gramajo, expressed it, refugees became "a new actor in the Guatemalan scenario" that had to be reckoned with.[346] Where this was not the case, the housing and poverty of refugees drew much criticism in the media (as in Greece[347]), or they were more or less left to their own means and survival skills (as in South Vietnam after 1964, or the Kurds in Turkey).

Algeria reflects a common pattern: the first mass displacements were carried out on the basis of local decisions from November 1954, weeks after the start of the insurgency, based on considerations about which areas were declared forbidden zones. But most people were simply expelled. Until 1955, officers "seemed to have taken expedient, intuitive measures without recourse to past experiences," ignoring the fact that there had been repeated earlier efforts in Algeria at replacing isolated settlements by nucleated villages for European interests since the nineteenth century. Only since mid-1957 was the erection of no-go areas transformed into a systematic resettlement policy. Yet even afterwards, a parliamentary inquiry in 1959 found that some of the so-called "regroupment centers" had been established "illegally," that is, by local commanders or authorities without authorization by the government.[348] After 1959, civil authorities tried to replace temporary military regroupment centers by socially bearable and economically viable "new villages," as well as to replace "la politique anarchique des commandants du secteur, de quartier, et de sous-quartier." These policy shifts resulted in the acceleration of displacements in 1958 and 1960. There were considerable conflicts between the military and the civilian administrations over resettlement. Earlier on in Indochina, French forces had likewise needed years to develop various forms of strategic resettlements and militias, ignoring older writings by French military officers.[349] The British authorities in Malaya had a more comprehensive approach to resettlement from the beginning of the insurgency in 1948–49, recommended by a Government Squatter Committee member and then by Director of Operations Briggs. Yet, until 1951 the resources earmarked for this limited both the size of projects and their success (among other things, through the bad quality of land), resettlement initiatives were left to individual states and remained local, and the laws at that time still allowed that people "drifted back" to their home areas.[350] By March 1950, less than 7,000 people in Malaya had been resettled or "regrouped."[351] In Rhodesia, district commissioners in 1976 and 1977 repeatedly called in vain for the resettlement of people from Tribal Trust Lands or Purchase Areas.[352]

Although the South Vietnamese strategic hamlets have often been credited to US or British advisors, it was actually a home-grown program derived from national forerunners such as Land Development Centers (mostly in the central highlands, after 1957), Agglomeration Centers (for families suspected of support for the communist underground), so-called regulated hamlets for loyal families prone to insurgent attacks, and, from 1959, *agrovilles*, of which, however, only twenty-three, with some 40,000 inhabitants (instead of the envisioned half a million), were ever inaugurated. All of these projects by the South Vietnamese authorities had, beneath the official development rhetoric, military purposes; some, on the other hand, were somewhat inspired by earlier French tactics.[353] Studies based on Vietnamese language sources point to the Vietnamese origins of strategic hamlets, emerging from model villages in three provinces in 1961 and established as a national policy in January 1962, and to the futility of British and American criticisms.[354] Earlier, in French Indochina, local military officers had decided whether to set up militias and of what ethnic or religious group they should be made up.[355] After most of the strategic hamlet program had collapsed by the summer of 1965, certain units of the US Marines started the Combined Action Platoon Program that used marine squads to regain and hold control of villages according to an oil spot strategy, but despite some modest success the program never gained the full support of the US military command in South Vietnam.[356] Counter-insurgency in El Salvador depended heavily on US training, money, strategies, officers, and civilian experts, but El Salvadoran officers rejected some aspects, such as the "National Plan," as a "gringo plan," which partially explains why little came of these.[357] South Vietnam and El Salvador are the two cases where US influence was strongest, relatively speaking, but for the most part, US displacement-related strategies in anti-guerrilla warfare have not been internationally regarded as very impressive or successful, and the impact of US-led knowledge dissemination is questionable.[358]

In Uíge district in northern Portuguese Angola, 150 concentrated resettlement villages with various amenities such as schools, clinics, and cooperative stores were erected under the label of *reordenamento rural* in order to lure back some 500,000 refugees of the Kongo ethnic group from Congo in 1961–63 that were needed as workers on coffee plantations. Only in 1967 were such tactics, now dubbed *aldeamentos*, also applied in eastern Angola, and from 1968 in the central districts of that colony, after the former Governor of Uíge district had become General Governor.[359] In Portuguese Mozambique, ideas for mass resettlements into nucleated villages for easier control, tax collection, labor recruitment, and better amenities had emerged during World War II, at first being considered to be unacceptable to Africans, before being put into practice through the *aldeamentos* from the late 1960s. In neighboring British Southern Rhodesia, villages had likewise been regrouped in the 1940s and 1950s before the radicalized revival of such ideas in 1972.[360]

The same goes for militias. The *rondas campesinas* (village patrols, a name preferred by the military from the early 1980s) emerged from local, self-organized Civil Autodefense Committees in the north of Peru that were to provide protection against thieves and resolve internal conflicts. In the central highlands, too, peasants formed a number of these on their own before they were put under military control and finally expanded and systematically armed in the early 1990s. Even then, those in the north were less hierarchical, had fewer links with the army, and fewer weapons.[361] Developments in Guatemala were similar, volunteer civic patrols emerged from the 1960s to combat violence by drunks and the stealing of land; the first Civil Autodefense Patrol was inaugurated in Alta Verapaz in 1976, before their expansion started in 1981, initially promoted by local *ladinos* or Mayas backing the anti-communist MLN party in the western highlands. The militias were systematized and extended in the following years.[362] African guards established from 1951 by chiefs, headmen, and church priests who felt threatened by the Kenya Land and Freedom Army first evolved into local militias, from which the British-organized Home Guard emerged in late 1952.[363] In Malaya, the Perak Chinese Mining Association began to set up Home Guards in 1948, *kampung* guards were first established in Malay villages in 1949, while in the New Villages, Home Guards became compulsory in July 1951.[364]

From a global perspective, the gradual emergence of strategic resettlement and militias refutes the idea that there was a central power imposing them, some omnipotent string-pullers in a reactionary Internationale pushing all the buttons. Resettlements and militia building followed no blind application of abstract theories. Despite the international flow of ideas, the localized development of anti-guerrilla strategies confirms that the violence implied in these strategies was above all embedded in these societies themselves (and those from which their imperial rulers came), while amazing similarities in concepts stemmed from parallel social developments on national levels that were rather loosely interconnected.

Conclusions

Since the 1930s many governments, imperial and post-colonial, have depopulated large areas of the countryside, chased rural dwellers away, and resettled a large number of them in strategic villages, and established or encouraged the founding of local militias. Power-holders thus triggered or deepened civil wars that took a long time to subside. Usually, economic development was an element crucial to such strategies to gain political support during the struggle in the countryside. To extend government control and the reach of a state administration to such areas was in turn to facilitate or deepen the capitalist penetration that had already begun. However, the social changes that did take place were often not in accordance with the existing more- or less-sophisticated plans. Traditional modes of life in remote areas gave way to social differentiation, migration, and a state of insecurity. These social processes were a result of the actions of the government authorities but went beyond their control.

Evidently, in many incidents the social conflicts revolving around these anti-guerrilla wars had been set in motion by world historical events such as the upheavals and mobilization of rural resources and the workforce during World War II (Belarus, China, the Philippines, Greece, Malaya, French Indochina, Kenya) or in the world economic crisis of the early 1980s (El Salvador, Guatemala, Peru, Turkish Kurdistan).

What was in effect the violent opening up of marginal regions (or of their labor) spelled death or suffering for thousands of civilians. The reference to the so-called principle of "minimum force" (sometimes claimed for British anti-guerrilla warfare[365]) appears absurd where millions were herded into extremely frugal settlements, deprived of sufficient access to land, exposed to systematic harassment and often torture, and where no-go zones were comprehensively bombed or defoliated. It was precisely the soft means that usually caused most victims through hunger, diseases, and exhaustion. Only the gross neglect of these topics has made the denial of substantial population losses possible. More research is especially necessary on the conditions and strategies of survival in resettlement villages or the hiding places of refugees.

In order to understand the suffering and multi-polar violence during open military fighting and the long-term impact of the social conflicts involved, it is also important to examine the processes of social differentiation triggered through mass dislocation and militia building. All of the cases discussed here involving an imperial power ultimately resulted in the colonial or occupation forces leaving, and hence in the formation of new elites. Racism limited investment. In effect, there was no way to uphold an overtly racist order if a backward country was to be comprehensively penetrated with capital, so the colonial order tumbled. Post-colonial regimes were usually successful in oppressing guerrilla movements, but in the process new elements were co-opted into elite ranks. In the former case, massive and extended reprisals against former loyalists occurred. Many of those expelled or resettled never returned, cementing social change and especially a turn away from subsistence agriculture. The rise of ordinary violent crime and continuing civil strife reflected insecurity during a social transformation and uprooting that at times also carried unrest into the cities. Finally, the mobilization of ethnic groups during the (anti-)guerrilla wars led to the crystallization of ethnic identities and the hardening of future confrontations. The reconstruction of society after such wars needs to take these processes into account.

6 WHAT CONNECTS THE FATE OF DIFFERENT VICTIM GROUPS?

The German occupation and Greek society in crisis

The fact that there are a variety of victimized groups in one country – which is a key trait of an extremely violent society – suggests that there are complex interlocking processes at work. While Chapter 4 on East Pakistan/Bangladesh arguably dealt with violence within one country and Chapter 5 on anti-guerrilla warfare placed less emphasis on the diversity of victims, this chapter is a brief study of the impact of imperialist violence on various groups. It examines the influence of foreign aggression on a society already ridden by political, ethnic, and social conflicts. It exemplifies relationships between the persecutions of multiple victims by glancing at one of the countries most thoroughly devastated by German policies and actions in World War II – Greece.[1] On one level, this revolves around the German treatment of various collectivities; however, Axis violence and the extraction of resources aggravated conflicts among the local population which led to infighting during famine and finally to civil war, aside from armed resistance against the invaders from Bulgaria, Italy, and, from 1942, also from Germany. This crisis of Greek society in the early 1940s can be related to upheavals stretching from the Balkan Wars of 1912–13 to the end of the military dictatorship in 1974. I try to point to these long-term processes and conflicts in the final section, but begin with some general observations on the multitude of victims of German policies.

The multiple victims of German imperialism

In Nazi German concentration camps, badges were used to distin-
guish groups of inmates: red triangles for political prisoners, pink for
homosexuals, green for common criminals, green with the base down
for prisoners in "security confinement," black for so-called asocials
or for forced foreign workers who had fled from their jobs, brown
for Sinti and Roma ("gypsies"), violet for Jehovah's Witnesses, blue
for emigrants, and an additional yellow triangle for Jews, forming a
star of David combined with any other mark. In December 1944, the
registry-book of Buchenwald concentration camp listed separately
prisoner numbers for twelve categories of inmates originating from
twenty-seven countries.[2] In some respects, the camp personnel tried to
treat them differently, in other ways they suffered from the same terrible conditions, and additionally, the guards tried to play groups off
against each other.

True, concentration camps may have been overemphasized as
symbols of Nazi rule and society.[3] Still, this example shows that there
were – inside and outside of these camps – different, interconnected,
though not identical, logics of violence against a variety of those persecuted. It is not possible to fully explain the functioning of such a
camp and the horrific results by inquiring into just one victim group.
And yet, in the historiography of the concentration camps – and of
Nazi Germany in general – a group-by-group approach is routinely
taken.

The prevalent focus of research on the destruction of the Jews
has overshadowed the fate of other groups. However, of the twelve
to fourteen million non-combatants who perished as a result of
German actions, six to eight million were not Jewish. Three million
Soviet POWs were destroyed, one million people died in the course
of anti-guerrilla warfare in the countryside, especially in the USSR,
Yugoslavia, and Greece, close to one million Soviet, Polish, Greek, and
Dutch civilians starved to death, hundreds of thousands of non-Jewish
Polish and Soviet citizens fell victim to German terror, as did 250,000
mentally disabled people, a similar number of forced civilian workers, and many others.[4] Within the concentration camps, Jews actually
formed small minorities among prisoners, except for two times (in late
1938 and from the summer of 1944). The first to be systematically
murdered by gas were disabled people. The first to be made wear a

mark in public in Nazi Germany were Polish forced workers. The first to be gassed in Auschwitz, and the first to get their prisoner number tattooed there, were (for the most part) Soviet prisoners of war. Other prisoners, including Jews, noticed that these POWs received considerably less food even than themselves, and in vain tried to help them.[5]

Multiple categories of Germans and foreigners were persecuted during the Nazi regime, but the vast majority of those who suffered came from abroad. Ninety-six percent of the Jews killed during World War II were neither Germans nor Austrians.[6] Similarly, taking all non-combatants who lost their lives combined, only about 4 percent were Germans, 96 percent were not.[7] Out of approximately 250 million Europeans and Africans who came under German occupation, between 5 and 6 percent perished; by contrast, of 70 million Germans, 0.7 percent fell victim to violence organized by their own state.[8] If Germans predominantly killed foreigners, and at a much higher rate than compatriots, this suggests that it makes sense to place this violence in the context of imperialism. We also ought to think anew about the relationship between German-organized human destruction and the context of World War II, because it was during the war that not only were all these non-Germans murdered, but also by far most Germans fell victim to Nazi rule.

Contrary to popular perception, the practice of Nazi German imperialism – except for some annexed areas – was not significantly about implanting German settlers[9] (though Germans made their presence felt as soldiers and functionaries). Instead, German representatives and businesspeople tried to control territories, make use of their resources, and attack perceived enemies in a situation of menacing scarcity. Military expansion opened up new labor resources in occupied countries but also necessitated that these be mobilized and exploited. What we frequently observe throughout World War II is an interplay between German policies to forcibly mobilize various large population segments for labor and other purposes, a form of violent substitution, one factor that linked the fate of different groups. But whoever came to be so used did not need merely to be brought into a place, he or she also needed, at a minimum, to be fed, housed, clothed, kept in place, controlled, and given motivation to work productively, and their close relatives were to be taken care of. This implied that all sorts of resources needed to be channeled to some and withdrawn from others.

What Götz Aly has called a "giant mobilization" mid-way through the war thus extended much further than just financial considerations. A promise of social security for Germans, Aly argues, required a racist "master's position" abroad.[10] For many groups of Europeans under German rule, whose fates became entangled in the process, this mobilization of resources, although it lacked efficiency as is the nature of forced labor, meant ever harsher conditions of life, internal competition and conflicts, and that there was increasingly nowhere to hide, as ever-larger areas, also in the countryside, were affected by the war economy. It is such a process that I explore in the rest of this chapter in Greece.

Greece in the Second World War

Attacked by Italy in October 1940, Greece defended itself successfully before it was defeated by incoming German troops in April 1941 and divided into Italian, German, and Bulgarian occupation zones. Within three-and-a-half years, about 300,000 Greeks out of a population of seven million perished and roughly one million were displaced. Ruthless exploitation of the resources of this country that depended highly on grain imports caused rampant inflation and a famine that may have killed 100,000, mostly between December 1941 and April 1942, though in some regions dragging on into 1943. Beginning in March 1943, most Greek Jews were deported to Auschwitz and Treblinka and murdered – only about 15 percent out of 77,000 survived. German operations in a guerrilla conflict that escalated in the middle of the war claimed another estimated 100,000 lives, mostly in 1943–44, and caused hundreds of thousands of internal refugees; finally, also during the German occupation, conflicts descended into civil war. About 35,000 Greeks were taken voluntarily or by force to work in Germany, and over 200,000 had to toil for the German military inside Greece. Some 100,000 fled from the Bulgarian to the Italian and German zones.[11] What did these events during World War II have to do with each other?

Italian troops had invaded Greece as part their government's effort to extend her colonial empire beyond Albania, Libya, Abyssinia, and the Dodecanese islands in the Aegean in a move that also included attacks on British forces in Egypt and British Somaliland in 1940–41.

For Germany, Greece was strategically important against British dominance in the eastern Mediterranean and the Near East, to secure the Balkan flank before the attack on the USSR, to secure Italian and Bulgarian loyalty, and for Greek mineral resources. As a result, German functionaries needed Greek labor primarily inside that country for mining, road construction, and fortification works. Given widespread unemployment[12] and a predominantly rural economy regarded as inefficient, no labor shortages were envisioned, a point confirmed by the fact that Hitler promptly had all Greek POWs released in explicit recognition of their brave fighting.

In fact, in 1941 and 1942 Hitler and German functionaries in Greece tended to express officially and internally their high esteem for the Greeks, pointed to the Hellenic heritage and concluded that the Greeks were of a noble 'racial' background. It was more or less from 1943 on that it became fashionable to call Greeks perfidious scum, uncivilized, or miserable hawkers and to point to their allegedly Slavic heritage.[13] The invention of German anti-Greek racism thus coincided with the stiffening of Greek political resistance that led to the occupiers' economic projects running into difficulties. This shift in German perception may also have been linked to the pictures of misery, destitution, and moral decline they saw but there has not been enough research about this. In September 1943, German General Karl von LeSuire called Greece "the land of slackers, grafters and corruptors."[14] The racist mindset of imperialism made Germans treat Greeks – with some variations – increasingly as a mass without rights. They shoveled around batches of people, they substituted one population segment for another in workplaces or living quarters, devastated some regions, and also tried to mobilize some locals against others.

From the beginning, German and Italian troops enriched themselves but were also bound to rely on purchases, black market business, plunder, outright robberies, and later even gang criminality, initially due to insufficient supplies of their own.[15] This way they stripped Greece of food and various consumer goods so thoroughly that shortages and inflation set in immediately. Foreign trade was strictly reduced; under this enforced tributary near-autarchy, a downturn in industrial production set in due to the lack of raw materials, fuel, and transportation, and due to regional market imbalances, rationing systems, and black markets for all sorts of goods. In economic terms, the Germans (as was often the case in the eastern half of Europe) destroyed more than they extracted. The fact that Italian and German authorities set the value of the Greek drachma against their currencies artificially low, and imposed huge tributes to cover occupation costs on Greece, contributed greatly to this process.[16] All of these factors contributed to a famine.[17] Above all, wheat, olive oil, and sugar were lacking. In fear of confiscation and looting, farmers hid their grain and avoided markets. The Greek government had worried about the situation long before the German invasion, due to what was called the British navy's "starvation blockade" in the eastern Mediterranean, and had already lowered food rations to disastrously low levels in early May 1941.[18] By July 1941, a British Foreign Office bureaucrat considered it possible that Greece's population would be reduced by 2.5 million or one-third due to starvation.[19] But Britain retained the blockade, delayed emergency grain deliveries supervised by the International Red Cross until the fall of 1942, and the US government stuck by their principle not to ship food to occupied countries.[20] The economy was disrupted and many urban dwellers lost their income as a result of the breakdown of sea traffic, which also occurred to and between the Greek islands. Other transportation was in part reserved for use by the occupiers and limited by fuel shortages, the partial disconnection between urban and rural spheres and the division of the country severed intra-regional economic links, and the movement of goods was restricted even within the occupied zones.[21] "Greece was disintegrating into a patchwork of isolated economic units," as Mark Mazower summed it up.[22] Consumer goods industries shrank; it was in such trades that Greek Jews held a large share.[23] In conjunction with inflation, even those who retained a job suffered a substantial decline in real income, which forced almost everybody onto the black market.

As far as the locals were concerned, the "dissolution of the national market in many small enclaves […] threw the majority of small peasants back into a subsistence economy."[24] Yet even specialized peasants such as those who grew fruit or olives could usually cope with the situation by barter (some of it outlawed). Many, especially bigger landholders, could even gain wealth as food inflation surpassed general price rises.[25] But for those owning poor and isolated mountain or island lots, as well as shepherds and fishermen, food supplies became precarious.[26] Among urbanites, how the upper classes fared depended on their ability to employ their capital resources either in black market speculation or in deliveries to the occupation forces. Some were gradually forced to sell off their assets, while others amassed fortunes and founded new trading or one of 6,500 new industrial companies, these "new rich" drawing much public criticism.[27] Those who suffered most were the urban poor, including workers and the unemployed with their families, widows, and orphans, and many military veterans, the soon forgotten heroes of 1940 begging in the streets of Athens where the famine was worst. Infants, small children, adult men, and the elderly made up most of the deaths.[28] Most who starved survived, further impoverished and often politically radicalized, sided with the left and thus transformed this into a mass movement, hateful of the occupiers, and embittered against those whom they viewed as collaborators, profiteers at their expense, or indifferent elites.[29] Thus the famine set the stage for more conflict. In the short run, the famine had slowed down guerrilla activity as people focused on physical survival, but resentment against the occupiers, namely the Germans, grew. Activists soon tried to threaten hoarding shopkeepers into selling food at reasonable prices and reserve some for families with children. In 1943, EAM, the strongest partisan group, turned to looting food from stores and immediately distributing it among the population.[30]

The economic crisis did not only cause want, it led German functionaries to turn to more violence to extract a larger part of the waning resources. Violence became an (inefficient) means of penetrating economies, first in the cities, then in the countryside. For the occupiers, the Germans in particular, inflation and famine spelled grave problems for mobilizing and financing labor. Workers tended to leave underpaid jobs and replacements were hard to recruit. The deteriorating health, notably of men, undermined productivity, and the need for them to enter the black market, even when employed, increased absences. Some 12,000 Greeks, chiefly urban dwellers, agreed to work in Germany in 1942 with the promise of escaping starvation, but most Greeks rejected the idea. Once in the Reich, Greek workers became notorious for low qualifications and performance, ragged outfits, black marketeering, and openly showing anti-German sentiments.[31] After International Red Cross relief deliveries started to arrive from the fall of 1942 (as well as negative reports about living conditions for the Greeks in the Reich, taken up in resistance propaganda), the incentive to work in Germany diminished even further.[32]

This development became intertwined with the fate of the 55,000 Jews from Salonika, where three out of every four Greek

Jews lived, leading to their deportation to the death camps in the spring of 1943.

In July 1942, the German military turned to forcibly recruit about 3,500 Jews from Salonika for work in the mines, and on road and airfield construction in Thessaly and Macedonia.[33] It seems that the Greek Inspector-General for Macedonia had complained about Greek non-Jews being coerced to work on such projects, or that he was "in agreement" with the German Military Commander Salonika-Aegean.[34] Strictly guarded, fewer of the Jewish forced workers ran away than the non-Jewish workforce, but the hard labor and harsh treatment caused many to fall ill or even die and many of those who did escape joined the partisans, playing into German stereotypes about Jews being a security threat.[35] A Jewish committee in Salonika attempted to get out individual Jewish forced workers who could pay a per-capita sum of one million drachmas, raising a total of 700 million, and tried to replace others as well. What had started as a relief effort led, in October 1942, to a proposal by Dr. Merten, head of the German military administration branch, for a collective buyout for 3.5 billion drachmas. Of this, 1.5 billion was waived in return for giving up property rights to the 55 hectare traditional Jewish cemetery.[36] A part of this sum was enough for the military administration to hire in the countryside as many new non-Jewish construction and mining workers as there had been Jews and to pay them improved wages. It was precisely the fear that non-Jews could be hired for these unpopular jobs with this money that left local Greeks disgruntled. (Though Jewish workers had been less productive, some hundred Jewish men from Salonika had to continue construction work for the German Organisation Todt before being deported to Auschwitz in August 1943.)[37]

Meanwhile, in October 1942, coordinated German–Italian efforts to stabilize the Greek currency and mobilize civilian labor were introduced, including restrictions on military purchases and the cash supply of individual German soldiers, a freeze on financial occupation tributes, raising food imports to Greece and stopping exports from it, getting International Red Cross food aid in, indirect taxes on Greek joint stock companies to be paid to the Greek state, and the introduction of a mandatory labor service. Historians have linked these measures to the effects of the military situation in North Africa. Victory there would, for Germans and Italians, have necessitated the improvement of the infrastructure in Greece to support further attacks toward the Near East; defeat would have required more fortifications in Greece.[38] All measures were to limit inflation and bring order into labor deployment. In fact, inflation, and especially food prices, were brought down as hoarders panicked in early November 1942, selling their stocks because of the arrival of international food aid, the British victory at El Alamein in October, and, it has to be added, the November 8, 1942 Allied invasion in Morocco and Algeria, in conjunction with the German–Italian measures.[39] However, mass protests against compulsory labor recruitment (also for work in Germany) culminated in the storming of the labor administration in Athens, where demonstrators destroyed the labor records on March 5, 1943.[40] But in these violent demonstrations and riots, protests against the deportation of Jews did not, apparently, play a role.[41]

As using force against non-Jews met too much resistance, compulsory recruitment to Germany was slowed down and, within Greece, economic incentives were offered to workers: improved wages and partial payments in kind, namely food and clothing. What provided the financial means for all of this was the deportation and murder of the Jews of Salonika (and of the smaller communities in northern Greece), organized in cooperation with the German military by a Gestapo team sent by Eichmann, between March and June 1943, after several months of planning. Their mobile property, the equivalent of twelve tons of gold, was confiscated, given to the Greek state and used to support the drachma, which helped to hold down inflation until August 1943.[42] This had a greater effect on employment than putting all able-bodied Jews to work could have had, as proposed by the Jewish elder of Salonika, Koretz.[43] (Similar methods were used during the expropriation of 22,000 political exiles in the late 1940s and early 1950s, including collective punishment when the homes of the exiles' families were confiscated. In Greek Macedonia they were replaced by Greek-speaking colonists.[44])

While this is not meant as a sufficient or indeed the only explanation for the murder of most Greek Jews in 1943, it may allow for a better understanding of their destruction amidst a profound general social crisis, which the occupation had triggered and which in turn endangered German occupation objectives. Briefly put, the Head Office of Reich Security (RSHA) wanted to extend their extermination program against Europe's Jews to another country in early 1943 (organizing deportations from the German and Bulgarian zone of Greece to the death camps simultaneously), and German military authorities cited security concerns and the cooperation of Jews with guerrillas, in addition to the complex economic considerations sketched out above that also motivated Germany's top envoy in the Balkans, Hermann Neubacher. To be sure, in their first proposal for the deportation of Jews from Greece in July 1942, the RSHA had themselves emphasized that removing Jews could improve security and help combat the black market.[45] For the Bulgarian authorities, deporting Jews was to provide housing, jobs, and funding for the settlement of Bulgarians in Macedonia, and particularly in Thrace, in an aggressive incorporation policy.

Non-Jewish Greeks' reactions to the persecution of Jews in a polarized society varied widely. In an extraordinary move, leaders of academic, religious, professional, and economic organizations called on Prime Minister Konstantinos Logothetopoulos to protest against the deportations; this pressure may have contributed to his fall.[46] Solidarity was preached in some churches and taught in some schools in Salonika.[47] By contrast, others in the same city seem to have petitioned for the deportations. According to the Italian Consul General, most Salonikans opposed the deportations, except for merchants who would be relieved from business competition.[48] And, as late as three days after the Anglo-American invasion in Normandy in June 1944, the prefect and police chief of Corfu celebrated the local deportations with a proclamation issued on that same day: "Now trade will be in our hands! Now we ourselves will reap the fruit of our labour! Now the food supply and economic situation will change to our benefit!" The deportations enjoyed the support of many locals.[49] Thousands benefited directly from Jewish property. The possessions of the Jews of Salonika, like those of other deported Jews, were sold by the Greek authorities under the Governor-General of Macedonia to other citizens. Just weeks after their deportation, the clothes of Salonikan Jews were on sale in the Peloponnese. Much of the Jewish furniture and business stocks were looted in break-ins. The Greek gendarmerie shot at least four young Greek looters in the former ghetto.[50] Greek refugees from the Bulgarian zone were accommodated in Jewish homes. Other formerly Jewish neighborhoods in Salonika were leveled by contractors. The events are reminiscent of the persecution of the Armenians during World War I. Just as Turks in Van or Trabzon twenty-eight years earlier, people searched for valuables hidden in the walls, not entirely without reason.[51] The Jewish cemetery, which the Greek authorities had attempted to move since 1925, was destroyed in December 1942 to make room for the university that is located there today. The grave-stones were used as building materials.[52]

Similar procedures in the Bulgarian zone resulted first in Jews receiving a worse exchange rate than non-Jews in the enforced exchange of drachmas for leva in mid-1941, a special tax in 1942, and, in conjunction with their murder in Treblinka in March 1943, in the confiscation of the assets of the more than 11,000 Macedonian and Thrakian Jews. These goods were in part embezzled by Bulgarian officials and otherwise sold or auctioned off, adding 36 million leva (worth US$445,000) to state revenue. Greek refugees, too, were expro-priated in the Bulgarian occupation zone (just as the Rallis govern-ment of Greece robbed exiles of their assets in 1943). Bulgarian settlers moved into their homes, as well as those formerly belonging to Jews.[53] The death rate of Jews from the Bulgarian zone was at least 96 per-cent, even higher than in the German zone, let alone in the former Italian-occupied zone.[54]

Such economic incentives that got fellow non-Jewish citizens involved did not end with the war, nor did the difficulties for surviving Jewish Greeks. When they returned in 1944–45 and tried to get back their apartments, houses, and businesses, many compatriots who had replaced them "did not want to know anything about the previous owners." Tenants or holders of formerly Jewish properties founded an association to defend their rights (like Turks in 1919 regarding Armenian property, see Chapter 3), demanding that they be allowed to pay off any claims in drachmas unadjusted for inflation, and the government, feeling an obligation to these potential voters, in 1948 (amidst the civil war, when army measures had displaced 700,000, see Chapter 5) declared the eviction of squatters illegal. Just a tiny frac-tion of Jewish houses and businesses were returned. Compensations for Jews, paid out of reparations, amounted to the value of 1 percent of their family's movable and 15 percent of their immovable property. Most returnees were not able to go back to their own places of living, heightening their sense of uprootedness.[55]

But back to 1943: if the Germans enjoyed only partial suc-cess with economic stabilization in the first half of 1943, it was to some degree because of the partisans' efforts. In the second quarter, the *andartes* brought many mines to a standstill, and this forced the occupiers to concentrate production on the few most productive and easiest-to-defend mines. At the same time, resistance by industrial workers stiffened; in chrome mining, the number of laborers dropped by about 40 percent.[56] The guerrillas created their own economic and administrative zones, thereby denying Germans and Italians access to the resources of these areas, instead organizing and distributing them on their own. They revived schools, local courts, and utilities, established factories and assemblies, and started land reform.[57] The *andartes* fed on the German violence, recruiting young urbanites by warning of the dangers of labor deportations to Germany, or Jews of the threat of an even worse kind of deportation.[58]

But the Germans struck back. In large anti-guerrilla operations, they depopulated sizeable areas of Epiros, Macedonia, and Central Greece in 1943–44, razing more than one thousand villages, killing tens of thousands, making one million Greeks homeless by creating 'dead zones' as in Belarus, destroying the areas they could not control, and tightening their grip on those they could. The most infamous of the many massacres of villagers took place in Kalavryta and Distomo. Now people in some mountain regions were starving.[59] Designing anti-guerrilla operations as raids for winning forced labor, occasionally practiced in Greece before, was made compulsory in June 1944. Raids in poor workers' districts in Salonika and elsewhere resulted in the arrest of the unemployed.[60] Through such systematic brutality, the Germans succeeded in driving up "all index figures" of the Greek economy they exploited, including labor recruitment within Greece and for Germany.[61] However, continued exploitation, and a crisis papered over in part with financial tricks, led to a fall into hyperinflation by June 1944.[62]

For Hagen Fleischer, a Greek historian with German roots, the most striking fact about wartime Greek society was its disunity. The inner conflicts grew with the duration of the occupation.[63] After 1943, with the Communist Party gaining dominance in the partisan movement through the EAM guerrilla force, the Greek political right organized itself out of fear of revolution. Mass radicalization worked both ways. The fight for hegemony, for the future social order in Greece, started under the Germans. The Greek right, with their Security Battalions and death squads, tried to instrumentalize the Germans as much as vice versa.[64] In many localities, this led to a civil war within the occupation, in which atrocities, also by leftists, resulting from guerrillas and Security Battalions competing for local control, were usually based on a mixture of political motives and personal grudges.[65] Arbitrary arrests at road blocks, neighborhood raids, and assassinations by rightists increasingly endangered the lives of Athenians.[66]

The remaining Jews could either find refuge with the partisans (there were 650 Jewish fighters, and many other youths serving as nurses), or in the anonymity of Athens; but given the socio-political crisis, they were endangered by starvation and could be caught in the nets woven by raids or by mutual suspicion, particularly in areas where they were not well integrated with the locals. EAM/ELAS provided hideouts and protection for Jews in exchange for eight million drachmas. In a divided society, Jews could find help and refuge as well as hostility.[67] Only about 2,000 returned from German camps, 8,000 survived inside Greece (many in Athens and the rest of the former Italian-occupied zone) – only 1,500 of the survivors were under 16 years old and 240 over 65 years.[68] On Greek islands such as in Corfu and Rhodes in June and August 1944, Gestapo efforts to lay their hands on Jews in the last corner of Europe could succeed only with the help of local military authorities because of the lack of police manpower. Local military officers were divided on the subject. Military support was finally granted for quite different considerations than the Gestapo's: security concerns (when facing the threat of British naval invasion), food crises, and attempts by the military to finance their supplies on isolated outposts by seizing Jewish property.[69]

Not only had the lives of a number of different Greek population groups become threatened during the occupation, but the war had also caused major population movements, first out of the cities to the countryside, from the Bulgarian zone west and south, and from contested areas into the mountains and then into the towns and cities. The occupation also entailed major property flows, from urban to rural, from poor to existing or emerging elites, from Jewish to non-Jewish. The Greek famine undermined solidarity and was extremely divisive. Nothing was more participatory than the fight for survival and enrichment: "People of all classes and ages, men, women, children, clean and dirty, tricksters and fools, old men with worn hands and women wearing gloves and shabby blouses, young 'Don Juan' spivs with slicked-back hair – all of them make up the black market […]."[70] This struggle itself represented structural violence and became intimately linked to political polarization and open, manifest violence not only by the invaders, but increasingly among Greeks as well.

Greece was not unique in World War II: not for its famine (there were many famines in countries under German occupation, but also in those under Japanese rule, in colonies of the European powers, and in countries under Allied occupation or independent states from 1941 to 1947); not for expulsions, refugees, or the deportation of forced workers; not for the German-organized murder of Jews; and not for its civil war (several civil wars went on under the Germans, as in Yugoslavia and western Ukraine, all with ethnic, religious, and class aspects, or elsewhere as in China). Foreign armies induced violence in societies that were often ridden with ethnic, religious, and class conflicts anyway. With this they set in motion or accelerated redistributive processes, the emergence of new elites, migration, social change, and new tensions.

Greece, 1912 to 1974: Sketch of an extremely violent society

Greece is the one country that figures in three of the five case studies of this book. It is an unlikely candidate and by no means the 'worst case' of all extremely violent societies, but it does exemplify some of the general points of this volume.

The foreign occupation during World War II plunged Greek society into a profound and bloody crisis. But many of the conflicts that surfaced were neither entirely new, nor did they end with the Allied victory over Germany. Instead, previous political and social tensions were aggravated or revived in the war, and they simmered on or boiled over later as well.

Between 1912 and 1974, Greece underwent a number of experiences of violence in the course of which Greek society changed profoundly: from the 1912–13 Balkan Wars, the expansion and expulsions of Muslims toward the Ottoman Empire (and 80,000 Macedonians toward Bulgaria), to the 1914–16 flight of Christian Orthodox Greek speakers in the opposite direction, through the casualties of World War I (which Greece entered under massive foreign pressure), the attempted annexation of Western Anatolia 1919–22, involving brutalities against Muslims, especially in 1922, to defeat and the reception of 1.4 million Christian immigrants through flight or population exchange in

1922–23, whereas 356,000 Muslims had to leave Greece.[71] This was followed by the 1936–41 Metaxas dictatorship, during which thousands were exiled and tens of thousands arrested,[72] then the 1940–41 defensive war against Italy and Germany, the occupation by these two countries and Bulgaria, the mass flight of 100,000 from the Bulgarian zone, the 1941–42 famine, the destruction of most Jews, and the mass murders and devastation in the course of anti-guerrilla warfare. Next came the 1943–49 civil war, leading to the flight of more than 100,000 communists, Bulgarians, Macedonians, and other Muslim minorities, then two decades of oppression of the political left and the women's movement, and the 1967–74 military dictatorship that in 1974 also overthrew the Makarios government in Cyprus, reviving inter-community violence there and provoking the division of the island by a Turkish military invasion.[73] On the other hand, a stream of Christian Orthodox refugees continued to come into the country from Turkey after 1923, swelling in the mid-1920s, 1942–44, 1955, and in the early 1970s due to Turkish government policies of discrimination combined with occasional riots.[74]

From 1912 to 1974, mass violence was practiced by Greeks against Greeks (including minorities), and Greeks became victims of foreign violence, but they were also assaulting foreign civilians during their own territorial expansion, especially against the Ottoman Empire, Turkey, and Bulgaria. Greek Orthodox immigrants, or politicians acting on their behalf, played an important role in the bloodshed and in new expulsions. The mass arrival of refugees between 1914 and 1923 played out as a blessing from the perspective of the Grecification of Thessaly and Macedonia that had been annexed shortly before. Yet the framework of nation-state building or 'borderland' conflicts accounts for only parts of this suffering – these aspects were intertwined with issues of class and clashing visions of the future social order in Greece.

Two long-term developments within this period are striking: first, religious minorities were shrinking. In large expulsions, most of the Muslim community were forced off the territory of today's Greece in the first half of the twentieth century, from the Balkan Wars to the civil war. About 100,000 Muslims remained. The number of Jews declined from about 110,000 in 1904 to about 5,000 by 1959.[75] The Jewish communities had suffered under Greek nationalism and state claims for loyalty and assimilation since the nineteenth century.

The 1912–13 Greek annexation of Thessaly and parts of Macedonia and Thrace and the waves of incoming refugees over the next decade (and in 1941–43) changed the economic, cultural, and political character of what became northern Greece.[76] The immigrants strengthened economic competition for Jewish-owned businesses in cities and towns, the latter being discriminated against by the authorities who otherwise had little to offer to the new arrivals. Growing anti-Jewish resentment culminated first during the world economic crisis in the 1931 Campbell riots in Salonika. New borders severed connections between Jewish communities in Greece, Bulgaria, and the emerging Yugoslavia.[77] By 1940, the Greek Jewry had declined to less than 80,000 through emigration to the USA, the Ottoman Empire, Palestine, Italy, France, and other countries. Only 10,000 survived the German extermination in 1943–44, most with help of neighbors or leftist partisans. Yet the latter made them support the left, or at least rendered them suspicious to the nationalist right in the civil war. By 1959, further emigration had left only about 5,000 Jews in the country. Greek Jews got caught up in the conflicts that had to do with the rise of the Greek nation-state and its border conflicts, as well as class struggles; cultural and economic policies discriminated against them, and they did not represent a numerous enough minority to have an impact on mass politics and elections. Jews lived in towns and cities; they disappeared from an urbanizing society.

The second long-term factor was the partial depopulation of poor and remote mountain areas in northern, northwestern, and central Greece.[78] Anti-guerrilla strategies by Germans and the Greek right in the civil war included the systematic expulsion, evacuation, or slaughter of villagers, particularly in the north and northwest of the country in 1943–44 and 1947–49. Both times, 700,000 or more people were driven out, often fleeing to the towns and cities. In part, those displaced were on both occasions the same people. Lack of government support made many who tried to return to their destroyed homes give up in the 1950s and join the industrial labor reserve, either settling in urban shanty towns or becoming labor émigrés (some of them, ironically, moved to West Germany). More left over the years to escape poverty.[79] Political affiliations – namely the leftist insurgency first against the Italians and Germans and then against the right – interfered with religious orientation and ethnic ascriptions as the insurgents were labeled Macedonians, 'Bulgarian wolves,' etc.; yet it has been argued that the political orientation in the civil war often determined whether Greek Macedonians sided with the nationalists (if more assimilated) or with the communists (if favoring more autonomy).[80]

Again, the participatory aspect of the violence is obvious – not only during the famine or civil war (whether under German occupation or after). This is highlighted by the so-called "parastate" in Greece between 1949 and 1967, with its "paraconstitution" characterized by emergency regulations that remained in place despite contradicting the written constitution. Much of the "white terror" in the late 1940s and beyond was committed by unofficial death squads, tolerated by the government. Camps for political prisoners like Makronissos and Trikeri continued to exist, although laws and leading politicians after 1950 said the contrary (in fact, Makronissos had been illegal until October 1949, too). If political prisoners wanted to recant, they were forced to denounce, persuade, and beat up other camp inmates.[81]

Mass violence in Greece between 1912 and 1974 was intimately linked to massive processes of social change, class conflicts, regional imbalances, and migration that included the expulsion of Muslim, Bulgarian, Macedonian, and Albanian minorities, as well as leftists, numbering over 500,000, and in turn the reception of over 1.5 million refugees. In addition, non-Greek-speaking commercial elites (Jewish and Muslim) became marginalized and were often violently removed, especially in the north, replaced by a Greek merchant class that was gaining strength. Among further features of social mobility was the co-option of new circles into the Greek industrial bourgeoisie that emerged during the occupation and famine and who consolidated their position in the civil war and shortly afterwards, remaining weak, but still strong enough to cause widespread urban impoverishment in the 1940s. Industrialization and urbanization after 1948 were highly dependent on foreign capital, international influences, and imported economic models, while marginal regions were left impoverished and partially abandoned.[82] Only structural policies following Greece's accession to the European Community in 1981 helped to cushion further conflicts.

As Steven Bowman has remarked, "To date no researcher has integrated the Jewish story into any aspect of the general Greek experience during the [Second World] war."[83] Much less does an analysis of

Greece as an extremely violent society exist that tries to account for these violent acts over six decades in relation to each other or as a single process.[84] Naturally, this brief exploration, if anything, can only illustrate the potential of such an approach rather than exhaustively reconstruct the social and political developments involved. For Greece, as well as for other societies, such histories remain to be written.

Part III

General observations

7 THE ETHNIZATION OF HISTORY

The historiography of mass violence and national identity construction

Scholarship along the lines of the concept of genocide (and more recently ethnic cleansing) has been intertwined with narratives intended to create national identities. This connection is so common and has led to so many limitations, simplifications, and distortions in research on mass violence that it appears worthwhile to discuss it in detail and to devote a section of this book to it. The example of Bangladesh, to which I shall refer throughout this chapter, is symptomatic of these politics but in no way exceptional. Occasionally I will also point to interpretations of other cases of mass violence, including some that have been dealt with in previous chapters as well as some others.

According to the standard version in genocide studies, the Pakistani military clamped down on the peaceful East Bengali autonomy movement that had won general parliamentary elections. The West Pakistani junta attempted to kill off the Bengali intelligentsia (including Awami League supporters, professors, and university students) and the Hindus, an attempt that was overcome – after claiming three million lives, driving ten million into exile, and devastating the country – by the general resistance of Bengalis. Pakistani soldiers raped 200,000 Bengali women. Some thousand 'Biharis' also fell victim to the understandable wrath of the Bengalis, given that they had aided the Pakistani hordes (see Chapter 4).

This story is skewed in several respects. The available data do not support the view that the Pakistani army wanted to exterminate the Bengali intelligentsia. Their pattern of action suggests that they intended to drive the Hindu minority out of East Pakistan by the brutal killing of large numbers of men in particular. The overall number of deaths has been inflated. Violence was not one-sided but multi-polar. Many Muslim neighbors joined in the plunder and expulsion of Hindus. The Bangladesh movement was not peaceful, though the Awami League did win the 1970 elections, and violence by Bengali mobs and gangs against non-Bengalis peaked in late March to late April 1971, before the Pakistani army had started to make large-scale use of local auxiliaries. The Bengalis were not united in their struggle against the Pakistanis, especially in the countryside, but this is also the case with the urban middle class and the Hindus. Material destruction was exaggerated by the Bangladeshi authorities, though it was grave in border areas, settlements along the lines of communication, and urban slums and market areas (see Chapter 4).

The standard version tells a Manichean story. Its overarching objective is not to explain 'genocide' but to justify why the nation of Bangladesh had to come about and what its virtues are. The story underscores the ruthless, wanton, and irresponsible brutality of the 'Pakistanis' and exaggerates victim numbers so as to rationalize why Pakistan could not stay together as a country and to explain through contrasting levels of morality and identity the difference between 'Bangladeshis' and 'Pakistanis.' The Bangladeshi people were united in equal suffering, a semi-sacral experience that builds the foundation of a nation that has emancipated itself from a country exclusively founded on religious grounds (Islam). As this nation is pure, it had no part in the unjustified mass killings of 'Biharis' or rape. The alleged Pakistani attempt to annihilate their intellectuals serves to prove that Bengali culture as such was endangered; it was rescued by a national liberation struggle.

Without empirical research, the validity of these stories cannot be checked. Numbers are telling in this respect. From a human point of view, it seems almost a moot point how many people suffered when mass slaughter approaches abstract magnitudes. But in order to understand what happened and why, it is important to know how many people from which groups became victims, where, when, and in which ways. It is essential to avoid falling into the trap posed by atrocity propaganda. In the case of East Pakistan, instead of three million, it is likely that about half a million were killed, many of whom fell victim to famine; the death toll is very unlikely to have exceeded one million. By inflating the numbers of those suffering, nationalists try to prove the legitimacy of their cause. When it comes to international comparison, they enter a 'my-genocide-is-bigger-than-yours' game, a competition in gravity in order to underline the uniqueness of their nation's (or group's) experience on which, after all, the identity of the group rests to no small degree. "Many people in Bangladesh believe that the world has not witnessed a genocide as horrifying in its intent and as wide in its scope since the extermination of six million Jews by Nazi Germany,"[1] or "The Bangladeshi genocide was, undoubtedly, the most brutal genocide in the annals of history."[2] Some genocide scholars have been all too receptive to this line of argument, calling Bangladesh "the most lethal of the contemporary genocides."[3]

Genocide scholars and human rights activists tend to present high-end estimates for victim numbers to underline the seriousness of their topic, exaggerating the proportion of direct killings while understating the deadly share of hunger, exhaustion, and disease. For many years, they maintained that the Indonesian army killed 200,000 East Timorese; only recently an independent, systematic calculation found that about 100,000 died, more than 75 percent of them from starvation and deprivation (still a horrible proportion in a country of 800,000).[4] About 100,000 instead of the often-claimed 250,000 people lost their lives in the Bosnian civil war, two-thirds of them Muslims, and 58 percent of those killed were military or paramilitaries.[5] Though six million Jews were indeed murdered in the 1939–45 persecution, the long-cited figure of four million Jews killed in Auschwitz was actually inflated by a factor of four (hyperbolizing the centralized character of the extermination). The epitome of qualitative arguments derived from quantitative data far removed from actual empirical work are the sensationalist publications by Rudolph Rummel; based on secondary sources themselves, his greatly inflated numbers have unfortunately repeatedly been lent credence by reputable scholars, and so the process is perpetuated.[6]

While the number of Armenians killed between 1915 and 1923 is still controversial, the figure of 1.5 million deaths put forward by Armenian representatives appears to many scholars just as overstated as the Turkish nationalist number of 300,000 to 600,000 seems underplayed (and there were not merely victims of hunger and disease; see Chapter 3). Similarly, a death toll of 500,000 in East Pakistan in 1971 would deflate the number canonized by Bangladeshis, but exceed at least ten times what Pakistani historians, military, or politicians have conceded. Research about mass violence usually starts on the basis of competing national histories, as a brief glance at Internet websites under the search term 'Armenian genocide' can illustrate. In a way, these two versions embody a continuation of the conflict between two or more elites that are often involved in the acts of mass violence themselves; elites write, finance, or facilitate the writing of history and its scholarship. For example, there is still not one unified history of the destruction of the European Jews – it is divided into a variety of national histories that do not ask the same questions and do not tell the same story. German histories of the destruction of European Jews diverge substantially from Israeli ones, and Jewish non-Zionist, Russian, Polish, French, etc. mainstream accounts are different still. All of these narratives have served the purpose of establishing a narrative of a nation's history. For a long time, these stories, with some anti-Jewish undertones, involved much downplaying and the repression of memory. Now that the wind has changed, bizarre things happen, such as an aggressive rivalry between the Polish and Russian authorities as to who may claim the victimhood of Jews from Eastern Galicia, Volyn, or western Belarus on commemorating plates in Auschwitz.[7] The earlier Soviet history version counting all victims of the German occupation as 'peaceful Soviet citizens' without further specification was just another form of national narrative, emphasizing the unity and equal suffering of the Soviet peoples.

The preponderant mission of these national or group histories is to construct national or ethnic identities, not to explain mass violence.[8] Therefore they tend to portray the perpetrators in terms of "absolute evil." This demonization of those responsible for violence – often even their dehumanization as 'beasts,' 'inhuman,' etc.[9] – obscures any real understanding and removes the perpetrators from the human community, thereby belittling mass violence as a problem distant from one's own group, society, or polity. On the basis of a claim to the uniqueness of the crime, such demonization goes hand in hand with "constructing little corrals of appropriation" that reserve explanatory power over the murder of Jews to Jews, for Armenians to Armenians, for Roma to Roma, and so on.[10] This may include the right to give destruction a name (Holocaust, Shoah, Porrajmos, Holodomor), with a capital letter, as it is supposedly unique.[11] The demonization of the perpetrators and the thesis of uniqueness or incomparability are linked to the claim that the deed was irrational, so that by tendency it cannot be explained or perhaps even told, existing beyond the limits of representation, or falling out of history.[12]

As already mentioned in passing, nationalist claims also build arguments around the intentionality of violence. The supposed intention for violence reinforces the notion of absolute evil and connects to the view of the destruction having been centrally planned and strictly organized. Claims that famines constituted 'genocide,' an expression of the destructive and repressive rule by an outside power, have been a core rationale for national independence from the Irish famine of 1845–47 to the so-called 'Ukrainian' famine of 1932–33 (starvation actually also affected large parts of southern and central Russia), and the Great Bengal famine of 1943.

On the other hand, where these forces do not exist, where no creation of positive group or national identity nourishes historical work on mass violence, we see some value in the impulses for research by nationalist or cultural movements. In the case of the 1965–66 killings in Indonesia, after which the victim group was demonized and their memory long repressed, there was simply very little in the way of a history of the victims for thirty years or more.

Links between nationalist narratives and genocide studies

What accounts for the similarities between nationalist narratives and the picture drawn in comparative genocide studies? First of all, this academic field was established by social scientists who were model-oriented rather than prone to meticulous empirical research. In their mostly broadly designed studies, they could hardly question the factual framework provided by more specialized scholarly works, which in turn rested on nationalist narratives. For example, Donald Beachler's recent study of why the case of Bangladesh has been neglected by Europeans and North Americans has its merits, yet it amounts to an appeal to accept in full the Bangladeshi nationalist narrative.[13] This acceptance is also reflected in the assertion that Bangladesh represented "the only case in which the victims of genocide have won out over the perpetrator,"[14] an interpretation which exaggerates the contribution of the Mukti Bahini independence fighters to defeating the Pakistani forces, which were actually largely crushed by the Indian army. The very label "Bangladesh" put on the 1971 events in East

Pakistan in genocide studies confirms how close to the Bangladeshi nationalist view foreign scholars are.

The lack of empirical verification may be not accidental, as there are intrinsic congruences between national narratives and basic assumptions of genocide studies. A major criticism of genocide studies is the primordial interpretation of ethnicity which prevails within it, instead of an understanding of race, ethnicity, and nation as a dynamic process of definition as to what characterizes it and who is a member.[15] Thereby is "set *a priori* as a given" what would need to be examined.[16] That is even stranger, given that much of recent scholarship on nationalism has emphasized that nations are not natural units, but usually invented or "imagined" under the leadership of certain middle-class elites.[17] This is not to say that the lower classes have no part in the complex processes of constructing nationhood; I do not think simple manipulation or mobilization theories apply, according to which poor people just follow nationalist leaders blindly. But in general, there has been criticism of such "arguments which treat genocidal victim groups as fixed entities as in some Linnean system of plant and animal classification."[18] If scholars view ethnicity as immutable and rank it as a cause of violence by itself, they rarely discuss just why and how ethnic ascriptions may become so strong and irreconcilable. Researchers may thus immortalize persecutor ascriptions, though for reasons very different from those of the persecutors themselves. For example, many European "Jews" in the 1930s did not consider themselves as part of a Jewish community of an ethnic sort (though others did). The process of how part of the former changed their attitude under persecution has – for instance, in Israel – relatively scarcely been scrutinized, apparently because this would lead to the recognition that other Jews – including survivors – continued to reject the notion of ethnic belonging and question the founding myth of Zionism: the existence of a Jewish nation.[19] And since the claim to 'genocide' is supposed to prove the existence of a nation, it is not only important for nation-building domestically but also has strategic importance for nationalists in order to gain international support.

Such a primordial interpretation of ethnicity is reinforced by the UN Genocide Convention, where 'genocide' is reserved for the destruction of national, ethnic, racial, and religious communities precisely because they were considered "stable and permanent groups," in contrast to others.[20] In the chapter where he laid out the concept of genocide, Lemkin had already lauded nations as "essential elements of the world community" and called them "natural groups."[21]

This ethnization in a wider sense is specific to European and North American thinking. "Race, ethnicity, nation and religion are favored categories in modern discourse," writes Alex Hinton, who notes the "reification of concepts such as race and ethnicity" is "not surprising, given the historical privileging of perceived biological difference in much Western discourse."[22] Quite ironically, the objects of this view are often located outside the 'West' – Vinay Lal argues that particularly conflicts outside the so-called West are "all too easily" seen as primordial.[23] In a way this 'Western' urge also applies to the "desire to demonstrate a racial dimension to Soviet communist policies," which has been ascribed to an overdose of the "Holocaust paradigm."[24] In contrast, certain types of imperialist violence have been marginalized in genocide studies, which again suggests a close relationship between that field and nationalism: the Vietnam war seems to have been defined away from the realm of 'genocide' in a field dominated by North American scholars.[25] One can only maintain that as a result of the "1846–48 Mexican–American War," "Mexico was truncated without genocide occurring,"[26] if one ignores the mass destruction of indigenous peoples inside the territories annexed by the USA from Mexico in the following years and decades. Such marginalization – though not everybody in the industrialized North subscribed to it – was apparently undertaken quite consciously, as Helen Fein's remark would suggest: "If both the US and France [...] are in the same class (of perpetrators) as Nazi Germany and the USSR, we have a construct good for nothing."[27]

It has to be added that the ethnization of history has been strengthened by the ostensible triumph of Western European and North American capitalism and its values after the breakdown of European socialism around 1990. In the period since then, we have experienced something like a takeoff phase for genocide studies as a field in academia and in the public sphere, the rise of so-called humanitarian interventionism, as well as the birth of "ethnic" cleansing as a conceptual category. And socialist ideals in Eastern Europe itself had already been replaced in the 1980s by a surge of nationalism.

The genocide framework has in turn had numerous influences on nationalist arguments. During the Bangladesh conflict, the insurgents used the term "genocide" to whip up support for the independence struggle at home – including in their proclamation of independence[28] – and abroad,[29] calling it senseless destruction, but simultaneously saying it targeted the political leadership, intelligentsia, administration, industries, and public amenities.[30] In Europe, representatives of the Bangladeshi independence movement sometimes preferred to instrumentalize the term "holocaust" for the ongoing violence.[31] Within days of the Pakistani military crackdown in East Bengal, the Indian government had denounced it as "genocide."[32] In fact, even before the crackdown began, charges of "genocide" had been made by Bangladesh nationalist leader Mujibur Rahman, published in the Indian press, and forwarded to the UN.[33] However, the "genocide" claim was only pursued in as much as it was relevant for nation-building. No systematic government effort materialized to collect and preserve documents pertaining to the independence struggle,[34] and a systematic collection of statistical data was aborted, possibly because the tentative data did not substantiate the claim that three million had died and at least 200,000 women had been raped. Consequently, not much was done in terms of analysis.

Ultimately, 'genocide' is paradoxically held to prove the existence of a nation. As Kalyan Chaudhuri wrote: "To destroy a people – to remove or destroy what makes them a people – that is genocide." Accordingly, he saw the murder of Bengali intellectuals at the core of 'genocide.'[35] John Bowen has put it more prosaically: "Ethnic groups come into existence legally, then, when someone is trying to wipe them out."[36]

Sidelining religion

Ethnization has led to marginalizing other factors in the genesis of mass violence, among them even one dignified in the UN Genocide Convention: religion. Very roughly, ethnicity, race, and particularly nationalism have represented the values of the bourgeoisie and petite bourgeoisie, religion those of rural elites – at least up to the 1970s. Not surprisingly, recent research has stressed how small a role religious affiliations have played in twentieth-century 'genocides.'[37] Yet the religious factor may be understated by European, North American, and Australian scholars of middle-class background declaring or reinterpreting nearly every cleavage in recent history as ethnic, or with ethnic and religious identities being "fully intermingled."[38] In fact, there is a school of thought that has argued that "forms of identity based on social realities as different as religion, language, and national origin all have something in common, such that a new term is coined to refer to all of them – 'ethnicity'." This is based on the notion that the importance of religions declined "as specific foci of attachment and concern," while during conflicts people increasingly emphasized their ethnic group affiliation and used it to gain access to power, money, and education – against the expectations of 1970s social scientists.[39] Survivor communities who fostered research by their stories and funding often did so while undergoing their own secularization process, understanding themselves as less and less religious than as ethnic communities; heroic or tragic narratives of the past served precisely to establish such a cultural–ethnic group, while the trauma of violence had undermined the faith of many survivors.[40] This ethnization also corresponds with historians' possible over-emphasis on urban actors and the state. Rural agents, almost like their victims, have often been not very articulate and their voices have not been heard much by scholars, so their role and motives are therefore often overlooked. Many lacked literacy, financial means, and often access to political institutions, or they were primarily concerned with their everyday struggle for survival.[41] Yet, as mentioned throughout this volume, there are clear indications that religious ideas were one driving force for the many non-state persecutors of various groups in rural areas in the late Ottoman Empire, in East Pakistan, especially in Indonesia, and also in parts of German-occupied Eastern Europe, although the Nazi leadership had certainly made the step from religious to racist anti-Judaism (see Chapters 2, 3, and 4).[42]

While it is too early for categorical statements, the partial decline or stagnation of the nation-state under the impact of supranational forces in the last three decades[43] seems to have led to the resurgence of religious identities also among urbanites in some parts of the world. During the same time period, secularization theory, which predicts an automatic decline of the significance of religion in 'modern' societies, has been challenged by many scholars. This trend has yet to arrive in genocide studies, and perhaps it will relativize what I call "ethnization." In the future, researchers may be confronted much more with the task of tracing religious influences, including pro-Islamic and, more importantly, anti-Islamic violence.

Toward a global history of mass violence

Much needs to be done in order to arrive at a "distinctive social science approach to genocide studies, i.e. to achieve genuine independence for the researcher," which Jacques Sémelin has demanded.[44] In historiographical terms, this means that one needs to write global history – ideally a history not dictated by national interests or concepts but one that attempts to overcome restrictions in questions asked and perspectives taken and that compares experiences from different world regions or cultures and analyzes links between them.

Such an attempt will necessarily conflict with national narratives on several levels. Not only will interpretations, questions, and perspectives collide, but global history may also necessitate working with other sources (much as this volume works with, among others, diplomatic records). Their use will draw criticism. The work of scholars who have not devoted a lifetime to studying a particular society may appear as an intrusive or even as an imperialist practice. On the other hand, with specialized works on Rwanda, East Timor, and so on mounting, and more on India and Pakistan, China, etc. to come, the effects of globalization on historical consciousness will also work toward overcoming Eurocentric models such as state crimes based on "totalitarianism." Of course, this path will be paved by conflict.

Among the risks when one produces global history are overgeneralization and the possible exaggeration of international links. History serves to create identity, and global history seems to promote a fairly affirmative view of global interconnectedness, attributing positive values to the flow of ideas and technology and to the movement of people, goods, and culture. Global history seems to replace narratives of progress in national histories by a new demi-god: globalization. While national history created national communities by constructing a common past, most of global history seems designed to talk us into a world community that may not actually exist: hence the hazard of overemphasizing global interconnectedness and neglecting contradictions. The inevitable tendency toward superficiality if one cannot specialize on each particular country reinforces this danger.

Applying the strictest possible empirical standards may help to overcome some of these challenges. The work of scholars without a personal heritage from a nation or group involved in a certain case of mass violence, like Christopher Browning's studies on the destruction of the European Jews and Hilmar Kaiser's on the persecution of late Ottoman Armenians, has opened up new perspectives for research. It is no accident that both have worked on a highly empirical level. Discussions between scholars primarily concerned with their own nation and foreign researchers will help to clarify national peculiarities, provided that they can take place on an equal footing.

8 CONCLUSIONS

This book has explored the phenomenon of extremely violent societies in which, in simple terms, the occurrence and the thrust of physical violence depend on a broad and diverse range of support. This participatory character is based on a variety of motives and agendas of people from multiple backgrounds. This variety causes the violence to spread in different directions, against different groups, in varying intensities and forms. Written by a historian, my account serves to establish historical patterns, not a watertight model. The extremely violent societies approach does not lend itself to monocausal or all-encompassing explanations or miracle remedies. This chapter presents some core findings, based on common or widespread occurrences across decades and continents, yet without claiming that they account for all mass violence in history. And of course, if one uses the extremely violent societies approach, other points of emphasis than those applied here are quite possible.

Extremely violent societies are societies in a temporary state of crisis. Rather than searching for simple causal relationships – either a crisis caused by mass violence, or violence caused by crisis[1] – I suggest that the *process character* of both social crisis and mass violence should be acknowledged. These processes mutually influence each other. Such a crisis – observed by many genocide scholars but described in rather general terms – is characterized by conflicts between elites and processes of accumulation of capital and power. Large population groups get involved in such processes, acting to protect or improve their livelihood, which results in killings, but also the massive forced geographic and social mobility of various groups, reaching far beyond the circles of elites or armed men. The bulk of the violence has hit non-industrialized and industrializing societies and regions.

Social mobility

It is correct to say that poverty by itself does not necessarily generate violence and that the poor mostly do not respond to their situation by means of physical violence. Millions in many different societies have lived in misery without turning to direct mass violence.[2] This study suggests that violence is rather linked to a wide range of aspects of social mobility: drastic drops in living standards, or perceived threats to the livelihood of people who may even be living a comfortable life, or opportunities for individuals to enrich themselves, tend to generate destructive action – and then there are the interrelationships between all of these.[3] We must therefore pay attention to large and sudden redistributive processes such as war, famine, inflation, and revolution.

All the societies discussed in this volume witnessed struggles between elites and the emergence of a new economic and political leadership. Whether in Nazi Germany, Indonesia, or Bangladesh, in the Ottoman Empire, Kenya, Malaya, East Timor, Mozambique, or Guatemala, or in the beginnings of colonization,[4] new groups ascended into elite status, or further improved their social standing, rose into new jobs, and amassed wealth, as part of processes that included direct mass violence as well as impoverishment and starvation for others. In such processes, violence was rarely one-sided, but, as far as those responsible for the greatest destruction were concerned: if they kept political control, emerging groups were usually co-opted into existing elites; if people linked to main victim groups gained the upper hand, they often initiated severe violence against civilians themselves, and elite change was more profound (as in Algeria, Bangladesh, or Rwanda). In this sense, revolutions as processes involving elite change and other abrupt upward and downward mobility warrant further study in relation to mass violence.[5]

The rise of new elites in conjunction with mass violence had several implications. One was the transformation of the countryside. In all countries dealt with regarding anti-guerrilla warfare from Guatemala to East Timor, in Bangladesh, Indonesia, Cambodia, or, say, the Soviet Union after 1929, the newly accumulated power was used to (further) change the face of the rural sphere, to penetrate it with capital, and in the process to accumulate even more, which spelled years of misery, famine, or loss of home and property for large segments of the population. Among the results were land changing hands and often profoundly shifting settlement patterns. Transitions from this rural change to direct murder were fluid,[6] and while the Nazis, the Ittihadists, or the political elites in Cambodia or Rwanda (we may add the Chinese Cultural Revolution) idealized the countryside,[7] these elites were precisely among those who wanted to violently transform it and have it generate surpluses, an agenda which their populist propaganda served. In fact, many of these developments also led to higher productivity and were accompanied by the diffusion of new consumer goods and government services, including education or road construction.

East Pakistan/Bangladesh is the example in this volume that demonstrates most clearly the effects of elite competition. With Pakistan's independence in 1947, the British colonial elites left Bengal, the overwhelmingly Hindu *zamindari* (big landowner) estates were expropriated, and many Hindus were expelled or fled. In government, the military, and business they were largely replaced by West Pakistanis and 'Bihari' refugees from India (the latter also represented much of the industrial workforce); in the professions, culture, and education, Bengalis ascended. The Bengali autonomy movement went through its cultural emphasis phase in the 1950s and its economic phase in the 1960s, threatening the dominance of West Pakistani economic elites as well as military rule. In 1971, the latter two groups tried to violently coerce the rising Bengali elites into submission, destroying the remnants of Hindu influence and affluence. Yet the Muslim Bengali middle class won out with Indian help and took over all positions of influence that Pakistanis, Biharis, and gradually also Hindus lost. Among Bangladeshi Muslims, a struggle for elite status between generations manifested itself in the conflict between secularism and Islam. Beyond elite concerns, this struggle left countless ordinary urbanites, Hindus, Biharis, rural dwellers, and finally Jummas in the Chittagong Hill Tracts dead, displaced, or without a livelihood – above all, many of the rural poor. Women were pushed back into submission. Significantly, redistributive elite struggles resulted from structures created by colonialism. Similar conflicts have also been cited as a root cause of other cases of mass violence at that time, such as Biafra/Nigeria in 1966 to 1970 and Burundi in 1972.[8]

A second implication of the emergence of new elites was the forced decline of middlemen minorities. This is what we call leading commercial or cultural groups primarily based in towns and cities, belonging to a larger collectivity and viewed by others (and often by themselves) as different in religion, culture, or language, and increasingly portrayed as alien. In part they simply came under pressure from new economic competition, but this process was usually accelerated by state policies favoring the newly emerging commercial elites of the dominant ethnicity or religion, who were perceived as more loyal to the government and nation, especially during international conflict. The very accumulation or 'modernization' process that facilitated the rise of many such minorities before the outbreaks of violence also brought about the emergence of competition for them, as well as the impoverishment of other groups. Here, too, the transition from economic rivalry amongst elites to the open persecution of more or less the entire minority could be fluid, and this could make the latter some of the worst affected in a wider circle of multi-target violence, be it Jews in Nazi-occupied Europe, Armenians and Greeks in the late Ottoman Empire, Hindus and Biharis in Bangladesh, South Asians in Uganda, aristocrats and Kulaks in the Soviet Union, or Chinese in Cambodia and Vietnam. All of them were accused of being linked to foreign interests at a time when upward-pushing elites argued that the nation-state needed to be strengthened. The Chinese in Indonesia were less affected than the national average by killings, but lost much property and influence in 1965–66. (Not all middlemen minorities became targets; Jews in the late Ottoman Empire and Indians in 1960s Indonesia seem to have been perceived as less of an economic competition, less disloyal to the nation, or less culturally provocative.) Jews, Armenians, Hindus, and Chinese had experienced a long history of persecution with repeated outbreaks of pogroms against them, which regularly happened in the context of wider religious conflicts or social emergencies.[9]

Despite this experience, all of these groups were surprised by the sudden magnitude of violence they faced in the context of a deeper, comprehensive modern societal crisis involving the destruction or expulsion of a wide array of groups. They were equally horrified when the cruellest violence against them went far beyond elites with attractive property or jobs, and beyond an urban setting – for the majority of Jews, Armenians, Chinese, Biharis, etc. were poor or lived very modestly.[10] This persecution did not seem to make sense. If these minorities lived in separate quarters or neighborhoods (as many did), such assaults on the collective became even easier. In times of crisis, such minorities in their entirety were all too readily construed and accepted as a threat, often with the help of government propaganda (but not always, as the fate of the 'Biharis' in East Pakistan up to April 1971 shows). However, attempts to explain the degree of violence against such groups by finding causes within the middlemen minorities themselves generate sparse results[11] – only by a more comprehensive analysis of socioeconomic processes can one find out more.

Common to virtually all incidents, and intimately related to the rise of new elites, were the phenomena of corruption and nepotism, core tools for individual social advancement. Such developments are striking in the Ottoman and Bangladeshi cases, as well as for the Indonesian military or the militias arising during anti-guerrilla warfare. Rampant corruption in Nazi Germany highlights the self-establishment of new elites amassing fortunes there, too. Many of them did so in occupied countries, helped by the total disenfranchisement of the locals and the lack of German bureaucratic control of functionaries.[12] By mingling private and public interests, these groups facilitated or solidified their ascent. This involved manipulating state institutions in order to acquire assets and to put 'undesirables' away, silencing or removing them. Just like militias, corruption lies at the junction between state and society. Although one speaks of 'corrupt regimes,' corruption affects society in a broader sense. And it brings individuals into partial conflict with the state and the law, which creates problems of justification for the perpetrators – and sometimes entails more illegal acts.

However, my emphasis on elites is not to advance manipulation theories that would assign to ordinary people a role merely as puppets in the hands of more powerful string-pullers.[13] Such an understanding would neglect the active role of ordinary people who only seem to lack influence. On the other hand, an understanding of mass violence as based on an uprising of the poor would be misleading or at best simplistic. Rather, it appears that the redistributive processes that trigger violence and/or are exacerbated by it also affect underprivileged members of society, prompting them to struggle for survival, for a new home, job, or piece of land, or to seek their own advantage on a smaller scale, all of which could lead to mass participation in violence. This effect has been described in the chapters about the destruction of the Armenians, Greece in World War II, and anti-guerrilla warfare. The looting, robbery, extortion, private use of forced labor, and black marketeering by German soldiers, police, and administrators in occupied countries in many ways belong in the same category.[14]

It is these redistributive processes involving not only spatial but also social mobility (often in conjunction) that link different forms and directions of violence and make any separation of direct mass violence and famines or issues such as forced labor appear artificial. For both had to do with the same processes of the accumulation of wealth, resources, land, goods, or power. In a broader sense, direct violence and structural violence[15] were thus closely linked and it is pointless to try to explain them separately. What is important is to locate at exactly which points structural turns into direct violence.

Famines are not simply natural events, but result from human interaction, as the research of the past thirty years has established.[16] Even if they stem from an overall lack of food in a society – which is far from always the case – different population segments are usually affected to very unequal degrees by a famine. Certain groups lose their access to food through their own production or loss of income, having to sell their land and possessions and then being displaced as beggars, while others remain unaffected and some accrue land or make profits through thriving speculation. Famines, therefore, are market-related, redistributive, selective, and hierarchical phenomena. And, as often seen in this volume, mass hunger and mass violence are frequently interwoven with another massively redistributive process – inflation.

At the same time, famines also involve (shifting) relations of power and mostly also government policies. Yet the complex struggles for survival or enrichment in a famine cannot be fully grasped by examining government policies. We do know about policies of starvation, but governments do not and cannot fully control famines. Famines and the question of who suffers most in them are not just about the allocation of resources by a government. There are similarities between the processes in famines and mass violence; in fact, they overlap to no small degree. Both lead to large-scale displacement and often split up families; in both cases, the displaced become more vulnerable through the loss of social support networks and social capital.

Famines and mass violence can each make the afflicted more prone to the other, as has been shown for Central Java and Bali, where previous mass hunger had increased tensions and poverty by 1965, and in Bangladesh where mass violence led to famines among the impoverished in 1972 and 1974–75. Many who perished in what genocide scholars count as acts of violence in fact died of hunger and related diseases: hundreds of thousands of European Jews, the majority of the three million Soviet POWs who fell victim to German captivity, at least half of those who succumbed during the Pol Pot regime in Cambodia, many in the Soviet Union under Stalin, three-quarters of East Timorese who lost their lives under Indonesian rule, and numberless victims of colonial expansion. The same goes for most victims of the Algerian war of independence, for many Armenians, Greeks, and Kurds in the Ottoman Empire in and around World War I, and those who succumbed to brutal oppression among the Herero and Nama in German Southwest Africa in 1904–07, in the Philippines during US colonial rule between 1899 and about 1910, in British Kenya during the 1950s Land and Freedom Army uprising, or in Guatemala in the 1980s.

Conversely, many of those who starved in famines have been claimed as victims of mass violence: in the Irish famine of 1845–47, in the Soviet famine of 1932–33, in the Great Bengal famine of 1943–44. The realization that both famine or "scarcity" and mass violence are complex processes not based merely on the relations between a state and its citizens, or between a state and foreign subjects, may help overcome schematic and simplistic chicken-and-egg categorizations and interpretations about one simply causing the other.[17] As the case of the Armenians in this book has shown, a flurry of private assaults for a multitude of reasons created in part the web of persecution that killed at least half of those who perished.

The Armenian example, the cases of resettlement discussed under anti-guerrilla warfare, and the suffering of many refugees before and after they returned to Bangladesh in early 1972, highlight the connections between famine and forced migration. Often death is the consequence of removal or flight, of the loss of local support, local knowledge, or family, or of the loss of belongings during one's absence from home. For survivors, displacement may result in downward social mobility and long-term loss of socioeconomic status. During displacement, being confined by state-organized measures to a certain area with restricted movement (whether a neighborhood, village, or camp[18]) under adverse conditions and with no livelihood provided leads to life chances further shrinking. Little wonder that 'resettlement' became a *chiffre* for direct mass murder in Nazi Germany – even for many of the people who were actually 'only' forcibly removed this spelled death anyway.

Conflict and crisis

Mass violence is about conflict, or a perceived conflict.[19] Victim groups are almost invariably portrayed as a threat by their persecutors. In fact, some within the victim groups may have turned to armed violence before (like the Armenian gangs, political groups, or militias) or may have exerted structural violence; even if the victim groups had not used violence before, the assault on them will lead mostly to armed acts of defense or resistance.[20] The retrospective dehumanization of the *perpetrators* as beasts, inhuman, etc. – serving one's psychologically understandable distancing from them, but not helpful for analytical purposes[21] – just confirms the existence of a conflict. Yet, among the persecuted groups, only a few do act violently or respond with counter-aggression. By definition, we are concerned with violence against unarmed persons and thus with collective attacks turned against those who remained peaceful or who had surrendered. Nonetheless, this should not lead scholars to unlink mass violence from the context of conflict and declare it "one-sided";[22] rather our objective should be precisely to explain the paradox of how violence spreads from an altercation between fighters or activists to engulf the defenseless, who are presented and perceived as a threat. If entire victim groups are simply portrayed as helpless, the victims tend to become thought of, inaccurately, as merely passive, though they may seek protection, allies, and sometimes even armed resistance.

The crises of society analyzed in this book happened mostly when countries were at war (Nazi Germany and those who it attacked, the Ottoman Empire, or Japan), or when civil wars or uprisings against colonial powers raged (in Bangladesh, anti-guerrilla warfare, or Rwanda). Wars, too, cause processes of mass destruction, massive redistribution of property, and displacement. Other historical cases of mass violence, however, were farther removed from a wartime context.[23] Of those covered here, Indonesia was involved in only a low-level military confrontation with Britain, Australia, and Malaysia but the inner conflict emerged in a Cold War context; at the same time, the country was shaken by landlessness, inflation, and political tensions at both local and national levels. Elsewhere, the problem went beyond military fighting too: hunger, devastation, and loss of home were a reality for many, whether in the Ottoman Empire, German- or Japanese-occupied areas, Bangladesh, or theaters of guerrilla wars. But even Cold Wars or international ideological conflict contribute to sharpening domestic political mobilization and polarization, which may then feed into mass violence.

Temporary coalitions for violence may emerge between social groups who have few other interests in common and who participate in violence for a variety of reasons. The case of Indonesia sketched in this volume is just one example. In the late Ottoman Empire, most politicians, higher-level bureaucrats, large landowners, military officers, medical doctors, refugees from the Balkans and from the northeast, and Kurdish leaders as well as Turkish and Kurdish commons turned against the Armenians. The Jumma people in the Chittagong Hill Tracts of Bangladesh are another example of people facing temporary coalitions between the central government, the army, Bengali settlers, foreign commercial companies, and 'development helpers.' How much the interests of various groups of persecutors overlap may – as in the case of Indonesia – help to explain how intense mass violence is, what form it takes against different victim groups, and at which point direct violence ends or decreases. Looking at it from the other perspective, groups become victimized as they become isolated within society, losing allies and protection, which finally results in dwindling chances to hide and endure. They fight for survival by seeking allies and reintegration, if possible.

The context: violent transformation of non-industrialized regions

The extremely violent societies approach can be used to examine the society from which violence arises or the society that it engulfs.[24] Whether internal or imperialist, violence in striking proportions and intensity, dwarfing all other atrocities, has taken place in the past 500 years in *non-industrialized* countries or regions in the process of capitalist penetration, transforming them into more productive or surplus-generating areas. This resulted in land concentration and the shrinking of a majority of farms to below-subsistence levels, undermining the livelihood, lifestyle, and social order of vast populations, as shown for Indonesia's inner islands and Bangladesh.[25] (People could also be affected by being transplanted from such a country or area to an industrial nation and discriminated against, such as forced labor brought into Germany and Japan – just one example of the migratory processes such developmental violence entailed.) It is difficult to understand the destruction without this transformation. With this, I set a different emphasis than approaches that – while placing 'genocide' in the context of the emerging capitalist world system – see the problem above all in a system of fiercely competing nation-states.[26] Industrialization is nearly everywhere financed through the extraction of capital from peasants whose labor is systematically undervalued – a structurally violent process that involves hunger, misery, and migration and can be organized by political-bureaucratic means or market relations (for which governments set rules and sometimes prices). In historical phases of overt violence, the countryside was usually to be abruptly 'developed', penetrated with capital and new administrations, often based on rival concepts of rural change. Such major socioeconomic changes were more or less intended by state and non-state actors.

Settlement programs served to pacify rural dwellers or refugees, often supported by violent official resettlement programs (as in anti-guerrilla warfare or in the Ottoman Empire during World War I). These were also intended to create viable and surplus-producing farms, individual or collective, that could deliver goods to an invader such as Nazi Germany, to a colonial power, or to emerging domestic industrial zones and growing urban areas as in the Soviet Union, China, Greece in the late 1940s, or even Ethiopia in the 1980s. It is such strategies for restructuring society, and not merely the existence of a dictatorship, which connect proto-capitalist, capitalist, and socialist systems here,[27] although an authoritarian government was often necessary to enforce rural change. But again, this was not merely a state affair: while many rural dwellers resisted, others among them embraced the induced change on the way to perceived 'progress.'

Above all, this book's chapter on anti-guerrilla warfare has portrayed policies and practice regarding this rural transformation, while all case studies have depicted elements of the socioeconomic change involved. For decades the research on Soviet mass violence has focused on the persecution of urban elites, including those within the Communist Party and in the military, while more recently it has emerged that rural dwellers, displaced 'anti-social elements,' and people from 'backward ethnicities' suffered in much larger numbers. Roughly 90 percent of the victims of Nazi German violence – Jewish or non-Jewish – originated from sparsely industrialized Eastern and Southeastern Europe (the same goes for Japanese atrocities or the victims of US imperialism). Even during World War II, the Soviet Union was still industrializing, the regime fiercely instilling discipline among the workforce, exploiting the agricultural sector and especially women. In this context, the USSR, including the countryside, suffered from major famines in 1942–43 and 1947. Settler colonialism from the late eighteenth century, working with a whole set of direct violence, microbes, alcohol, and other means, introduced capitalist relations to the land, destroyed its traditional use, and dislocated traditional livelihoods, socioeconomic structures, and lifestyles as well as, finally, the indigenous people themselves. "The progress of civilization across the face of the earth," commented Eric Wolf on this development, "is also a process of primary accumulation, of robbery in the name of reason."[28] Because of such dramatic and socially costly change, Vinay Lal has called Western-style "'development' [...] indubitably the clearest example of the genocidal violence perpetrated by modern knowledge systems on the integrity of human communities."[29]

The consequences of spatial and social dislocation during mass violence have been especially severe for rural smallholders. Many observers have pointed to the extreme losses that hunters, gatherers, pastoralists, or slash-and-burn cultivators have suffered in such cases (in this volume the Jumma people of the Chittagong Hill Tracts, East Timorese swidden farmers, and the herders in Algeria). However, twentieth-century peasants, sharecroppers, and the landless workers of the land have turned out to be very vulnerable, too, because they seem to have few resources in economic, social, and psychological terms once their village communities and clans disintegrate, and also few skills useful in a new environment. It is this often deadly effect that actually blurs the line between direct mass violence and dislocation per se, making abrupt mass displacement itself an act of potential destruction.

While historians and other scholars have often privileged 'civilized' urbanites (and especially comparatively small groups of the urban intelligentsia, as in the case of Soviet mass violence), the 'lesser' rural and often illiterate victims resulting from elite struggles remained neglected, consigned to the shadows of history.[30] Few sources have become accessible about them; few activists found them worthy of protection; few scholars overcame cultural barriers to tell the tale of the 'victims without history.'

In the urban sphere of such a non-industrialized country, we have observed processes of capital accumulation and social stratification linked with massive outflows or inflows of populations, often reinforced by measures of extreme force.[31] This indicates that rural and urban developments are of course linked. Nazi-occupied Warsaw or Minsk, Constantinople and Izmir during World War I, shrank, while Jakarta and Manila under Japanese rule grew, as did Luanda in the 1970s, Dili in the 1970s and 1980s, and Guatemala City in the 1980s, and Soviet cities in the 1930s. Dacca first shrank in 1971, only to rapidly expand soon afterwards. Often, refugees formed a major labor reserve for industrial development. Middlemen groups lost their influence, were substituted, expelled, or even murdered.

Destruction has hit people in industrial societies less often and quite differently, as embodied by the more selective violence against Northern and Western Europeans compared to that of Eastern Europeans by Nazi Germany. These policies were not determined by racial thinking alone, as the less brutal treatment of Czechs shows. In general, if victimized, people in industrial nations became the targets of mass violence by an enemy power in the context of major wars. From World Wars I and II, forced labor, expulsion or deportation, naval blockade, and aerial bombings seem to be the most prevalent forms, whereas ground massacres against foreign subjects occurred on a smaller scale, except for the murder of over 400,000 Central and Western European Jews by Germans.[32] During the Nazi period, the German government organized the killing of about half a million of their own citizens.[33] The expulsions and slaughter in Bosnia during the civil war from 1992 to 1995, to which about 100,000 people fell victim, happened in an industrial nation too. Even hunger strikes industrial societies in other ways: it usually torments city dwellers, especially those with little connection to the countryside, by contrast to non-industrial countries where it is largely a scourge for the rural poor (some of whom are swept into cities where many spend their last days). Germany, Austria, and Japan experienced famines under foreign occupation after the end of World War II, and the former two also during World War I, without being occupied.

Internal vs. imperialist violence

Still, unlike in the eyes of many genocide scholars, in some respects a major distinction also has to be made between imperialist and internal violence.[34] In the latter case, despite pressure from the international system (through military conflict, threatening alliances, financial or economic measures, ideologies, or propaganda), persecutors and victims for the most part originated from the same society, as in the Ottoman Empire, Indonesia, Guatemala, or the Soviet Union, Rwanda, and Yugoslavia. In the former case, persecutors and victims may have come from two (or more) different societies, such as for Nazi Germany, Japan, nineteenth-century colonialism, or twentieth-century struggles of decolonization (as in Algeria, Kenya, or East Timor), which raises important questions about the motivations and social processes involved.[35] Massive imperialist violence may occur in different contexts, during sudden colonial conquest and enforced social restructuring, but also when the rule of the imperial power is threatened.[36] In the beginning, such a crisis is often limited to the colonial territory itself, but it tends to get aggravated during political problems within the imperial homeland.

In cases of imperialist violence, the society occupied or colonized was likewise being profoundly transformed. Under the surface of seemingly overwhelming foreign rule and exploitation, new indigenous elites emerged, capital was accumulated, and conflicts over local dominance, influence, possessions, or positions ensued.[37] This was accompanied by open hostility between different local factions, as is shown not only by Chapter 5, insofar as it deals with wars of decolonization, but also by any example of colonization, though presumably with a lower level of popular participation. Such fighting would determine who could hold power after the occupier had left, such as in the civil wars in German-occupied Yugoslavia, Greece, and western Ukraine in 1943–44. As demonstrated in Chapter 5 on anti-guerrilla warfare, studies primarily concerned with political rule and state action tend to overlook or downplay such home-grown (albeit foreign-induced) violence.

At the same time, in imperialist violence, two societies – not merely two states – are in confrontation, with the bulk of the violence of course exerted by the occupiers against the occupied. This created plenty of opportunities to invent otherness, with groups treated differently according to their value in the use of the acquired territory. Unfortunately, the reasons for the mass support of imperialism and imperialist violence at home in the empire-building country – which clearly go beyond immediate personal gain, however important that may have been – are generally scarcely researched.[38] Yet clearly, mechanisms of exclusion, the legal aspects, and also the memory of such events differ greatly between cases of imperialist and internal violence.[39]

Nazi Germany has been cited as exceptional, but sometimes for the wrong reasons. Other highly industrialized countries, too, have committed mass violence in an imperialist context, even in the twentieth century (Japan in East and Southeast Asia, the USA in the Philippines and Vietnam, France in Algeria, or Britain in Kenya). What makes the German case extraordinary, except for the sheer amount of violence and brutality, is the fact that an industrial nation turned to mass murder against groups *within* it, as well as to its particularly radical internal racism.[40] This has led to a certain, though implicit, fascination with the fate of German victims, which resulted in the relative neglect of the imperialist aspect of German violence that caused 96 percent of all deaths. An indicator of this misperception are enumerations of non-Jewish victims of Nazism that include the disabled, 'gypsies,' homosexuals, political enemies, Jehovah's Witnesses, or 'asocials' and 'professional criminals' (that is, mostly Germans[41]), but less frequently much larger victim groups like Soviet prisoners of war, peasants affected by anti-partisan warfare, or forced labor.

The roles of state and society

In all societies discussed in this volume, organization by state authorities was crucial for mass violence to come about: during anti-guerrilla warfare, in Indonesia, in East Pakistan/Bangladesh, in the Ottoman Empire, and in the countries under German rule in World War II.

Governments and bureaucracies organized violence, set frameworks, defined policies. As the twentieth-century state claimed to express the will of its citizens, gaining legitimacy through their backing, it generated new and unprecedented power that in some cases resulted in massive violence.

Yet in these as well as in other cases, no state monopoly for violence in a Weberian sense existed. Part of the violence in some forms and against some groups was not state-organized, or was performed by non-state actors; and often 'the state' was not a monolithic entity since there were also physical conflicts between different factions of officials. Hence, violence cannot be simply and solely explained by looking at 'the state.' Government or administrative decisions are being made for the murder, expulsion, or enslavement of people,[42] yet these policies have to be seen in relation to a myriad of choices and decisions by individuals inside and outside of the state machinery.

For one thing, the state is part of society. State institutions are staffed with citizens with their own judgment of situations and interpretations of laws, regulations, orders, instructions, and policies, and with their own visions and interests. Initiatives or mini-policies for violence by middle- or lower-level functionaries have been widely documented for Nazi Germany and to some degree also for the Soviet Union and Cambodia.[43] Individual initiatives for violence can thus be channeled through the state. Such practice is surely not independent of government policies, but it allows for certain deviations and variations, or for policies not to materialize as officially planned. In this vein, Martin Shaw explains the particularly destructive character of war which has (as Clausewitz argued) "no logical limit," or war's immanent "genocidal tendency" (as Shaw calls it), through the involvement of the people whose input on war, according to Clausewitz, consists of raw violence.[44]

Popular involvement in mass violence cannot be fully grasped through a state-centered approach. The idea that a government organized "social projects that mobilized people" and that people only "operated within a structure of action defined by regime goals" that merely left it to perpetrators to create "rituals of their own" falls short of a full analysis.[45] In all the cases of anti-guerrilla warfare dealt with in Chapter 5, there were policies of social engineering, but they all failed – social change got out of control. Social engineering never works completely as planned. Social change and violence were appropriated by people. The violence that did materialize was not always organized by or in the interest of the state. This applies even to supposedly strong, even supposedly 'totalitarian' states in Europe, the "small number of historiographically dominant European paradigms" on which many theories about the "violent state" are built.[46] German POWs in Soviet hands often fell victim to hate crimes near the front, and mass rapes by Soviet soldiers against women in Central Europe did not follow government policy. In the case of Nazi Germany, ethnic German militias played a significant role in the killings in 1939 in Poland and in 1941–43 in Bukovina, Bessarabia, and Transnistria; and tens of thousands of Soviet POWs in German hands died due to brutal actions by their guards, an action that delayed the realization of the German government's policy switch toward a better treatment of prisoners fit for work in late 1941. Denunciations from the Soviet populace against fellow citizens in the 1930s and 1940s and by German citizens especially against foreign forced labor were rampant.[47] Such private initiatives, however, often functioned in interaction with state organs or frameworks set by the authorities. While weak states may be prone to feeling threatened by certain minorities in a war situation or insurgency,[48] a weak state is not a precondition for an extremely violent society.

There was certainly no state monopoly of violence in the eighteenth- and nineteenth-century settler societies that in some ways resemble early modern European states. A similar observation has been made about the partition violence in India and Pakistan in 1947 and about the expulsion of a large number of Palestinians in the same year.[49] Rwanda, Darfur, or Congo would be comparable examples. For the forms of anti-guerrilla warfare discussed in this volume, the active involvement of colonial or post-colonial subjects in violence through militias, paramilitaries, or by other forms was constitutional. Such strategies were also pursued by powerful states such as the USA, Great Britain, France, Germany, and Japan – precisely because even their leaders felt their states otherwise possessed insufficient means to win the conflict. The Pakistani military was less successful in a somewhat similar effort. Likewise, the Indonesian military depended on the help of citizens inside and outside militias for their policies of destruction against leftists. In the Yugoslav succession wars, militias played a major role in the violence.[50] And there are numerous indications that the infamous Teskilat-i Mahsusa (Special Organization), supposedly a parallel to the German SS as an instrument of the Ottoman state for destroying the Armenians, can rather be viewed as loosely organized tribal militias.[51] In short, militias seem to be crucial for mass violence as formations that link military and state with citizens on a local basis, that help citizens assume authority and exert power, and as formations for which fewer rules of warfare apply; they deserve much more attention in future research.

In extremely violent societies, several groups become the targets of violence. Some of them may be victimized in the absence of any official policy of persecution. Violence may be circumventing the state; it can still be very intense, but tends to be more localized. Transmigrants slaughtered in parts of Sumatra in 1965–66 were not the target of military policies. Up to May 1971, there was no formulated policy to kill non-Bengalis in East Pakistan; rather there is some evidence that many functionaries of the Awami League, who de facto ran the country in March, tried to prevent the mass killings of 'Biharis.' The examples of anti-guerrilla warfare and Indonesia 1965–66 show how many individuals or groups settled private scores under the guise of general violence, a practice that the authorities were unable to prevent. Ethnic Chinese were assaulted in late 1965 by military personnel, who acted, however, for private gain through extortion and robbery and not in any official capacity.

The military has played an important role in many incidents of mass violence, as shown in this volume for Indonesia, East Pakistan, and Nazi Germany. A concentration on the wartime context of mass violence against civilians may actually result in too much of a focus on the state,[52] obscuring the fact that mass violence may be merely semi-organized and not fully state-controlled. Yet far from being cohesive blocs, militaries are often instead divided into factions. In an extremely violent society, these may come into conflict with each other, in which case some military personnel may victimize comrades, or the military and paramilitaries may clash. This happened in Indonesia in 1965–66, in East Pakistan in 1971, in the USSR during the 1930s, and in China during the Cultural Revolution.[53] Part of the military also refused to participate in official violence against unarmed people (in the USSR there was little indication of that). Nor were civilian apparatuses monolithic. In all of these incidents, struggles in the military occurred within the context of broader conflicts between elites that also pertained to government or administration, pitting high state or party officials against each other, most glaringly in the show trials against political leaders in the Soviet Union and in Indonesia in 1966, when President Sukarno and many government ministers opposed the mass slaughter. In such a view, "ideology [would appear] not so much as a causative factor in its own right but as an element in the political struggle within the state apparatus between different groups and factions, whose interests ride on the promotion or termination of violence."[54] Note also that political differences in all four cases cited involved disputes about future social relations in and with the countryside.

In the context of German mass exterminations, many of my colleagues were bemused that I could both emphasize the crucial role of local initiatives for the vehemence of violence and yet argue that Hitler took a decision in principle to murder all European Jews in December 1941.[55] But this is no contradiction. Impersonal structures as well as collective and individual actors are important. Since mass violence originates from state policies as well as social relations, and from the interaction of state and society, it has to be thought both "from above" as well as "from below."[56]

Socio-psychological implications

Mass violence – like famine, inflation, and war – is a *social* event. They all materialize through the participation of the many. They are forms of a crisis of society. They are events with winners and losers, and hence divisive. All of them involve panic. For those affected, they become traumatic.

Conflict and violence in such a troubled situation are multipolar but neither universal nor wanton. Yet apparently there is no arbitrary fight of all against all. Still, in such a crisis, social cohesion is being eroded and normal levels of morality are lowered. We can observe a loosening of solidarity. Social and family bonds disintegrate step by step, leaving "fear [and] confusion." Then "material misery hits the individual profoundly, because it accelerates the breakdown of the value system that was the basis for the identification of an individual with the entire group and protected him from discovering his loneliness. The group can no longer fulfill its role as regulating agent, because it is no longer sure of its norms and values, which are weakened by the situation and by damage to its permanent structures."[57]

Thus ethical norms and values are devalidated not only among persecutors or profiteers, but also among the vulnerable groups. This leads to atomization, betrayal, corruption, opportunism, ignorance, and cruelty.[58] Even abstract ideas about solidarity may be shunned as violating group or state interests. For Daniel Feierstein, the very purpose of many modern "genocides" lies in the "reorganization" of social relations and the substitution of principles like solidarity, cooperation, reciprocity, autonomy, and equality by other concepts more suitable for the exercising of power.[59] But these may actually be concomitants of larger social processes that can only partially be controlled by any government. The ultimate experience of shattered solidarity is famine – such a familiar companion of violence in our case studies – when people lose their social networks, their home, any livelihood, and then family ties dissolve with men deserting women and children abandoned, killed, sold by their mothers, or even eaten by them.[60] True, this last is exceptional; families may stick together even in a famine or unite against the outside world in an adverse situation. Still, starvation is the ultimate threat not only to humans, but also to humanity.

The crisis of society described here creates insecurity and fear. Among the immediate social consequences of fear can be listed inhibited communication, impeded organization, lack of confidence in the community, and the questioning of values.[61] People scared in times of dramatic social shifts, including the dissolution of traditional bonds – especially in the countryside – feel frustrated and threatened by difficult life conditions and seek security in stable, seemingly natural communities based on religious, ethnic, or class identities. Kinship and ethnicity have provided for a long time a "structure for social exchanges within and without" and served to establish control of political and economic resources. In the process, these identities, now serving new purposes, are reformulated, a development that involves the polarization of people with conflicting interests and the vehement exclusion of others, resentment, and revenge, often expressed in performative acts.[62] An important aspect is the desire that some order is restored, which, although allegedly traditional, is a new order. Militias and paramilitaries seem to offer one way of bringing such order to a local level. To various degrees, political movements may offer renewal, a better world or nation to overcome existential fear and chaos, and may present some social groups as obstacles to this goal.[63] Agents of change such as middlemen minorities or political leftists and their sympathizers may be among the victims.[64] However, different groups of persecutors may pursue different ideas of a new order (as it was explicitly called in Indonesia after 1965 and in the Soviet territories under German rule in the 1940s) and the way society should function, based on varying values.

Such processes often involve promises of the renewal of older forms of order and of purification, a theme which adds a dimension of "religion or secular sacredness"[65] – but this is not unique to mass violence or 'genocide.' Religious salvatory movements, anti-colonial movements, and leftist revolutionaries have all used notions such as purification, and it is standard rhetoric in any military coup to save the nation from immorality and corruption and, for the most part, the common man from neglect. This is an indicator that not only abstract ethical values are concerned, but also an occurrence emphasized above for extremely violent societies: the accumulation of wealth by an elite, which through a *putsch* is replaced or complemented by a new leading group that can soon in turn also be accused of corruption. Entire countries have been named after such purification efforts (Pakistan, the 'land of the spiritually pure,' and Burkina Faso, the 'land of the incorruptible men').

Unlike in many coups d'état or religious movements, authority is established not only by force but also by shocking public violence.[66] Every state rule is based on force internally and externally. A new social order and a new distribution of power are often established through violence and intimidation. Visible cruelty serves to "magnify the terror." Atrocities are to instill trauma in onlookers, divide groups for the future, and make reconciliation impossible.[67] What's more, in extremely violent societies, cruelty serves as a symbolic act to overcome a position of weakness, to seize and concentrate power,[68] to impose a new order, and even in a way to establish legitimacy.[69] Violence then helps to constitute and signal a new moral hegemony, against which victims may become ethically defenseless.[70] However, such violence tends to be regarded as acceptable only for the duration of an emergency-like situation, laying the foundations of a new moral order that is later not necessarily characterized by ongoing atrocities.

In this context, the horrific occurrence of sexual abuse, including public rape, may become clearer. There is not a single cause for collective rape, just as there is not one reason accounting for mass murder. *Machismo* and male opportunism, the general devaluation of moral values, the desire to humiliate women, but also the men who are unable to protect them, the vulnerability of women separated from their families, the intention to undermine a group's social fabric, and sometimes the will to force women into a relationship or marriage all contribute to mass rape in extremely violent societies. Rape is ordered or controlled by governments less than other forms of violence.[71] Sexual abuse is also an important tool for mass expulsion. But in addition, rape can be meant – in a transitional phase – as proof of a new moral order and as a demonstration of the power of those who create that order, highlighting the powerlessness of the victims.[72] And, in a situation where traditional rules seem undermined, rape that occurs more or less in public can also be read as confirming female subjugation under men, especially in an environment where (allegedly) traditional values such as nationalism, religion, or tribal hierarchies become dominant. Both aspects mentioned in the previous two sentences have been encountered in mid-1960s Indonesia, in East Pakistan in 1971, in the Ottoman Empire, and in Guatemala and Kenya during counter-insurgency. If women are forced back into traditional roles at the end of a social crisis,[73] this may finally happen through pressures below the level of sexual abuse.

It is consistent with an intention to force women back into subjugation that in most cases they become less subject to murder than men. However, even the vilest violence cannot prevent the role of women changing in societies that are in transition from rural to urban and industrial. And that is especially so for victimized women who have to take care of children on their own: in Indonesia, many females who had lost their husbands and were barred from public service after 1965 started successful businesses, ironically laying part of the foundations for the economic upswing in Suharto's Indonesia. Women in Bangladesh who were ostracized by their families or had lost them, or Algerian women deprived of their husbands and older sons, saw themselves forced to enter the public sphere, the labor market, or the business world to support themselves and their families, challenging Muslim role models assigned to women.

An important aspect of the erosion of social bonds and the devaluation of values, or the shift in ethical values, is the struggle between generations as described for anti-guerrilla warfare, in Bangladesh and Indonesia, where the infamous "generation of 1966" was raging. In Cambodia, thirty- to forty-year-olds – men in particular – seem to have been the worst affected cohorts with a death rate of about 40 percent, while many persecutors were male teenagers.[74] In Rwanda and Bosnia, too, many murderers were very young (much younger than those from Nazi Germany, many of whom were between thirty and forty); in Rwanda, elderly people holding more land than the average peasant were at least regionally overrepresented among the victims.[75] Usually, collective physical violence is committed by young men whose careers are blocked due to a socioeconomic crisis but who may be able to rise in social status and economic position through violence, like numerous militia members during anti-guerrilla warfare. However, these youngsters were often used or manipulated by older, conservative elites, and in other cases young men ascended through other ways than directly perpetrating violent acts, such as with the Bengali middle class in 1971–72. The implications of a generational rupture are more profound: they undermine traditional authority in families, clans, villages, religious communities, or urban neighborhoods, and with them traditional principles of order, systems of ethics and conflict resolution, and gender relationships.

And yet (as in a famine) usually far from everybody is affected by mass violence. Both hit certain population groups only: it is minorities who ultimately fall victim, while many may be struggling – and others not at all. On the subject of mass violence, one of the biggest mysteries is what is going on in the regions, the neighborhoods, the families not directly involved by either participation or victimhood. How can we explain that they just seem to go on with their business? How can one reconcile the existence of everyday life and mass murder? Mass violence does engulf all of society, but only in a limited sense – certain ethical values lose their universal validity, and the existence of a potential threat through the example of those persecuted may urge otherwise unaffected people to conform or seek protection within social networks. In this sense, this study has found the concept of the "bystander" questionable.[76] If unaffected people continue to live their everyday lives and try to keep a distance from the suffering of others, or even deny it, this may also be a psychological defense strategy against entering the dangerous realm of violence and disorder (just as persecutors and persecuted – as far as possible – carry on with a private life). In brief, bystanders are actors. Still, the relationships between mass violence and the everyday warrant far deeper research.

Prospects for prevention

Given what has been said previously, I concur that "the evidence suggests that genocide [or mass violence], far from being a freak occurrence, is a psychologically intelligible and, to that extent 'normal' response to a particular kind of social and political crisis. And if that is so, we can expect genocide to prove a recurring phenomenon unless and until we can devise strategies for neutralizing the conditions which provoke it."[77] Only I wonder who exactly that "we" might include.

The complex roots, the participatory character and the context of mass violence have several implications for the chances for prevention, intervention, and reconstruction. Given that destruction in an extremely violent society may not be fully controlled by a rogue regime, or any government, chances are that it will not be stopped by the removal of that regime by international force, or by political pressure put on the leadership of a country.[78] The introduction of a new political system may not be a guarantee for halting the violence either. If various social groups are involved, and if not only deeply entrenched attitudes come into play (that could perhaps be addressed by some re-education) but also deep-rooted inner-societal conflict based on contradicting interests, the problem appears much more complex than 'genocide prevention.' It requires reducing the potential for social conflict and far-reaching economic steps. Instead of politically spectacular measures with a great symbolic effect for domestic public opinion (especially starting a war of intervention), international circles may be able to help only through an arduous, long-drawn-out effort and major financial support, and that only if it is well targeted, promotes equality, education, inter-communal cooperation, and contributes to curb sentiments of insecurity. However, 'development aid' has usually not met these criteria (aside from the fact that public opinion often does not allow industrial or other nations to mobilize the necessary resources). The current practice of foreign intervention in countries such as Afghanistan, Bosnia, or Iraq, which is of an imperialist character, would appear instead to foster special group interests, rapid social mobility – upward and downward – and therefore polarization in these countries.

This book argues, among other things, that the bulk of modern mass violence occurs in the context of socioeconomic change that transforms a traditional countryside into a surplus-generating sphere

of a national, imperial, or world economy, which serves industrial capital accumulation and thereby also affects the urban sphere. Vinay Lal
has put this succinctly in saying that if the "developing world" were
only to follow the European model, then "the future of the tribal or
peasant" is "genocide."[79] A core question is then how can profound
social change be brought about without massive violence or forced
migration? It is hard to see how this could happen in a capitalist world
of inequality, imbalances, and exploitation. While less unequal, socialist accumulation has also shown a high incidence of mass violence
and misery. Sadly, the modernization aficionado's argument that mass
violence is historically a transitional problem that will go away after
industrialization – if only at the price of considerable suffering – has
little validity.[80] Many countries suffer from a blocked industrialization
accompanied by the decay of old social structures, a sort of capitalism without industrialization, for instance in sub-Saharan Africa.
For the capitalist world system is based on inequality within nations
but also internationally, with industrial powers (and societies) using
non-industrial regions for their selective business interests. Some of the
massive violence brought about in this process has been described in
previous chapters. Part of it in the twentieth century was also directly
inflicted by industrial nations, whether bourgeois democracies or not –
during the expansion of new empires such as Germany, Japan, and the
USA, and wars of emancipation from Algeria to Kenya.[81] As has been
argued, even "national democracy can be compatible with war and
genocide," while only "global democracy creates different standards."[82]
Unfortunately, there is no such thing as global democracy.

NOTES

1 Introduction

1 The use of the term "mass violence" as an alternative to more normative concepts has become quite common in recent years. Cf. the Online Encyclopedia of Mass Violence, www.massviolence.org/ and the Center for the Study of Genocide and Mass Violence, www.genocidecentre.dept.shef.ac.uk/ (both accessed August 25, 2009).

2 However, in my definition, cases where there is "only" widespread structural violence (discrimination, exploitation, poverty, etc.) do not qualify as extremely violent societies. But, links between physical and structural violence are subject to my analyses.

3 Martin Shaw, *War and Genocide* (Cambridge: Polity, 2003), p. 36, has a similar view.

4 With this I do not suggest "lumping together" different kinds of violence or conflict, but I do propose not to ignore possible common contexts and causal links between these occurrences. For the charge of "lumping together," see Frank Chalk and Kurt Jonassohn, "Introduction," in Chalk and Jonassohn (eds.), *The History and Sociology of Genocide* (New Haven and London: Yale University Press, 1990), p. 15; for an argument against this author see Jürgen Zimmerer, "Seminar am 8.2.2008," www.iz3w.org/iz3w/kolonialismustexte/seminar.html (accessed January 12, 2009).

5 Mark Levene, "The changing face of mass murder: massacre, genocide, and post-genocide," in George Andreopoulos (ed.), *Genocide* (Philadelphia: University of Pennsylvania Press, 1994), p. 446, with reference to atrocities in the late Ottoman Empire; cf. Eric Weitz, *A Century of Genocide: Utopias of Race and Nation* (Princeton: Princeton University Press, 2003), pp. 6, 15, 73.

6 Shaw, *War*, pp. 2, 6, 20 (first quote), 26 (second quote), 66–74, 93.

7 Michael Mann, *The Dark Side of Democracy: Explaining Ethnic Cleansing* (Cambridge: Cambridge University Press, 2005), pp. 1–33.

8 Shaw, *War*, p. 74, who presents contradictory thoughts about this point.

9 Birthe Kundrus, "Entscheidung für den Völkermord? Einleitende Überlegungen zu einem historiographischen Problem," *Mittelweg 36* 15(6), 2006, p. 10; Eric Weitz, "The modernity of genocides: war, race and revolution in the twentieth century," and Edward Kissi, "Genocide in Cambodia and Ethiopia," in Robert Gellately and Ben Kiernan (eds.), *The Spectre of Genocide* (Cambridge: Cambridge University Press, 2003), pp. 56, 316; Jacques Semelin, *Purify and Destroy: The Political Uses of Massacre and Genocide* (New York: Columbia University Press, 2007), pp. 207–9; Leo Kuper, *Genocide: Its Political Uses in the Twentieth Century* (New Haven and London: Yale University Press, 1981), p. 93.

10 This corresponds to the idea that different meanings can be assigned to violence over time, as long as these meanings are not imagined as the same for all social actors. See Birgitta Nedelmann, "Gewaltsoziologie am Scheideweg," *Kölner Zeitschrift für Soziologie und Sozialpsychologie*, Sonderheft 37, 1997, pp. 78–9.

11 This is in accordance with the approach that views violence as social interaction as suggested in Nedelmann, "Gewaltsoziologie," pp. 66–7, 73. For the concept of the bystander, see Raul Hilberg, *Perpetrators, Victims, Bystanders: The Jewish Catastrophe, 1933–1945* (New York: Aaron Asher, 1992).

12 Other approaches that I do not subscribe to revolve around the terms "ethnic cleansing," "war crimes," "massacre," or the "camp." In a similar vein, "crimes against humanity" is a generic term for juridical purposes which is of little scholarly value. Due to its unspecific

character, it has played no significant role in the social sciences and is hardly useful as a tool of analysis. Therefore, I do not think that it can replace the extremely violent societies approach, unlike Anthony Court, "Do we need an alternative to the concept of genocide?", *Development Dialogue* 50, December 2008, pp. 125–52, esp. 146–8.

13 A "state or state-regime crisis," according to Mark Levene, *Genocide in the Age of the Nation-State, vol. 1: The Meaning of Genocide* (London: I. B. Tauris, 2005), p. 86, cf. pp. 76, 179–80.

14 Helen Fein, *Genocide: A Sociological Perspective* (London: Sage, 1993), p. 36; Chalk and Jonassohn, "Introduction," p. 28.

15 Typologies – a very popular exercise in genocide studies – are based on the idea that there is a prime cause of each "genocide"; "the important thing in classifying genocides is to recognize the primary goal of the killing," says Peter du Preez, *Genocide: The Psychology of Mass Murder* (London and New York: Marion Boyars, 1994), p. 67. For genocide typologies, see Chalk and Jonassohn, "Introduction," pp. 17, 29–31; Fein, *Genocide*, pp. 28–9; Daniel Feierstein, *El genocidio como práctica social* (Buenos Aires: Fondo de Cultura Económica, 2007), pp. 99–100; Israel Charny, "Toward a generic definition of genocide," in Andreopoulos, *Genocide*, pp. 76–7.

16 Mark Levene, *Genocide in the Age of the Nation-State, vol. 2: The Rise of the West and the Coming of Genocide* (London: I. B. Tauris, 2005); Dirk Moses, "Conceptual blockages and definitional dilemmas in the 'racial century': genocides of indigenous peoples and the Holocaust," *Patterns of Prejudice*, 36(4), 2002, pp. 19–36.

17 Mann, *Dark Side*.

18 "Convention on the Prevention and Punishment of the Crime of Genocide," December 9, 1948, in Chalk and Jonassohn, *History*, p. 44.

19 Chalk and Jonassohn, "Introduction," pp. 12–22.

20 Michael Wildt, "Biopolitik, ethnische Säuberungen und Volkssouveränität," *Mittelweg 36* 15(6), 2006, p. 105.

21 Weitz, *Century*, p. 9; Chalk and Jonassohn, "Introduction," pp. 26, 42. However, perpetrators need not have "awareness" of their own "intent" and "motive," according to these latter authors (p. 43).

22 For Lemkin, see Dirk Moses, "Genocide and settler society in Australian history," in Moses (ed.), *Genocide and Settler Society* (New York and Oxford: Berghahn, 2004), p. 24.

23 As criticized by Tony Barta, "Relations of genocide: land and lives in the colonization of Australia," in Isidor Wallimann and Michael Dobkowski (eds.), *Genocide and the Modern Age* (New York: Greenwood, 1987), p. 238.

24 See for example Fein, *Genocide*, pp. 12, 27, 37–8; Chalk and Jonassohn, "Introduction," p. 26; Frank Chalk, "Redefining genocide," in Andreopoulos, *Genocide*, pp. 57–9.

25 Chalk, "Redefining," p. 60.

26 Three scholars have recently particularly stressed that there is no direct way from ideas about violence to action, and that governments usually first pursue other, less risky options than mass destruction – incidentally, none of them used the genocide framework: Mann, *Dark Side*, pp. 7–8; Benjamin Valentino, *Final Solutions: Mass Killing and Genocide in the 20th Century* (Ithaca and London: Cornell University Press, 2004), pp. 66–90; Jacques Sémelin, "Elemente einer Grammatik des Massakers," *Mittelweg 36* 15(6), 2006, p. 26.

27 Roger W. Smith, "Pluralismus und Humanismus in der Genozidforschung," in Mihran Dabag and Kristin Platt (eds.), *Genozid und Moderne, vol. 1: Strukturen kollektiver Gewalt im 20. Jahrhundert* (Opladen: Leske + Budrich, 1999), p. 312.

28 Michael Dobkowski and Isidor Wallimann, "Introduction," in Dobkowski and Wallimann (eds.), *The Coming Age of Scarcity: Preventing Mass Death and Genocide in the Twenty-first Century* (Syracuse: Syracuse University Press, 1998), p. 2.

29 Barta, "Relations of genocide," pp. 237–51.

30 Feierstein, *Genocidio*, esp. pp. 13, 26, 34–5, 70, 83, 98–100, 104–7, 127–8, 139, 202–3; Daniel Feierstein, *Seis estudios sobre genocidio* (Buenos Aires: EUDEBA, 2000).

31 A similar tendency shows in Alexander Laban Hinton, "Zündstoffe: Die Roten Khmer in Kambodscha," *Mittelweg 36* 15(6), 2006, pp. 74–5.

32 Mark Levene, "Creating a modern 'zone of genocide': the impact of nation- and state-formation on Eastern Anatolia, 1878–1923," *HGS* 12(3), 1998, pp. 393–433.

33 Frank Bajohr, *Parvenüs und Profiteure: Korruption in der NS-Zeit* (Frankfurt a.M.: Fischer, 2001), p. 195; see also Frank Bajohr and Dieter Pohl, *Der Holocaust als offenes Geheimnis: Die Deutschen, die deutsche Führung und die Alliierten* (München: C. H. Beck, 2006), p. 10; similar state-fixation in Feierstein, *Genocidio*, esp. pp. 13, 104.

34 Frank Bajohr, "Vom antijüdischen Konsens zum schlechten Gewissen: Die deutsche Gesellschaft und die Judenverfolgung," in Bajohr and Pohl, *Holocaust*, pp. 17–79.

35 Kuper, *Genocide*, pp. 57–83.

36 Guenter Lewy, *The Armenian Massacres in Ottoman Turkey: A Disputed Genocide* (Salt Lake City: University of Utah Press, 2005), pp. 132–3; Khatchig Mouradian, "On the freedom of access to the Ottoman archives: an interview with Hilmar Kaiser," in *Aztag* (Beirut), September 24, 2005 (my thanks to Hilmar Kaiser for a copy); a slightly different text is available at www.aztagdaily.com/interviews/kaiser.htm (accessed August 24, 2007).

37 The first fully integrated study in terms of Ottoman and international sources is Ugur Ü. Üngör, "'A Reign of Terror': CUP rule in Diyarbekir Province, 1913–1918" (MA thesis, University of Amsterdam, 2005), http://home.uva.nl/uu.ungor/thesis.pdf (accessed August 24, 2007). David Gaunt, *Massacres, Resisters, Protectors: Muslim–Christian Relations in Eastern Anatolia during World War I* (New Jersey: Gorgias, 2006), also includes Russian, Iranian, and Arabic (published) sources.

38 Carol Warren, *Adat and Dinas: Balinese Communities in the Indonesian State* (Kuala Lumpur: Oxford University Press, 1993), p. 130, n. 24; Budiawan, "Tortured body, betrayed heart: state violence in an Indonesian novel by an ex-political prisoner of the '1965 Affair'," in Charles Coppel (ed.), *Violent Conflicts in Indonesia* (London and New York: Routledge, 2006), pp. 244 and 257, nn. 6 and 14; Anna-Greta Nilsson Hoadley, "Political violence in Indonesian literature: the legacy of 1965," in Ingrid Wessel and Georgia Wimhöfer (eds.), *Violence in Indonesia* (Hamburg: Abera, 2001), p. 260. For example,

the former leader of the PKI's national children's organization claimed to have known very little about politics: Ibu Marni, "I am a leaf in the storm," *Indonesia* 47, April 1989, p. 55.

39 A notable exception is the usage of British documents by Audrey Kahin, *Rebellion to Integration: West Sumatra and the Indonesian Polity 1926–1998* (Amsterdam: Amsterdam University Press, 1999), pp. 238–49. By contrast, diplomatic records have been frequently employed to discuss the role of foreign governments in the 1965–66 events or Indonesia's foreign relations.

40 For Indonesia, the analysis of British, Dutch, Malaysian, Chinese, and Japanese documentation would also appear promising. I was not able to get access to Singaporean diplomatic records. For East Pakistan, Indian, British, and Chinese archives could illuminate events further; for the Ottoman Empire the archives of Spain and other neutral countries.

41 Staff: telegram State Department to US Embassy Jakarta, October 12, 1965, NARA, RG 84, 631/14/50/2–3, Jakarta Embassy, Box 114, EP-6; Frederick Bunnell, "American 'low posture' policy toward Indonesia in the months leading up to the 1965 'Coup'," *Indonesia* 50, 1990, p. 50. Censorship: John Hughes, *Indonesian Upheaval* (New York: David McKay, 1967), p. 262; interview with Ulrich Makosch (a former GDR television journalist), November 7, 2005.

42 Hinton, "Zündstoffe," pp. 71, 74; Alexander Laban Hinton, "The dark side of modernity: toward an anthropology of genocide," in Hinton (ed.), *Annihilating Difference: The Anthropology of Genocide* (Berkeley: University of California Press, 2002), p. 29; Barbara Harff, "The etiology of genocide," in Wallimann and Dobkowski, *Genocide*, pp. 43, 48, 57; Jacques Semelin, "Toward a vocabulary of massacre and genocide," *JGR* 5(2), 2003, p. 201; Weitz, *Genocide*, pp. 205, 251; Mark Levene, "Why is the twentieth century the century of genocide?," *Journal of World History* 11(2), 2000, p. 322; Chalk and Jonassohn, "Introduction," p. 19; George Andreopoulos, "Introduction," in Andreopoulos (ed.), *Genocide*, p. 4; see also Michael A. McDonnell and Dirk Moses, "Raphael Lemkin as historian of genocide in the Americas," *JGR* 7(4), 2005, p. 504.

43 Hansjörg Siegenthaler, *Regelvertrauen, Prosperität und Krisen* (Tübingen: J. C. B. Mohr, 1993), esp. p. 16.

44 This does not mean, however, to deny grave deficiencies in the specific set-up of socialist systems themselves.

2 A coalition for violence

1 See Loren Ryter, "Youth gangs and the state in Indonesia," Ph.D. thesis, University of Washington, 2002, pp. 68–9.

2 Achmad Yani, "The doctrine of revolutionary war," address, Command and Staff College, Quetta, Pakistan, March 3, 1965, in Herbert Feith and Lance Castles (eds.), *Indonesian Political Thinking 1945–1965* (Ithaca and London: Cornell University Press, 1970), p. 464; Freek Colombijn and Thomas Lindblat, "Introduction," in their edited volume *Roots of Violence in Indonesia* (Leiden and Singapore: KITLV, 2002), p. 1. For various strings of political and gang violence in Bali 1945 to 1965, see Geoffrey Robinson, *The Dark Side of Paradise: Political Violence in Bali* (Ithaca and London: Cornell University Press, 1995), pp. 3, 181, 190, 225, 270.

3 Secret telegram Green, October 1, 1965, NARA, RG 84, 631/14/50/2–3, Box 118, POL 23–9, Oct 1–3, 1965; CIA Research Study, *Indonesia – 1965: The Coup That Backfired* (n.p.: CIA, 1968), p. 290. Australian diplomats wrote that the existence of a Council of Generals was "no secret": ANA, 3034/2/1/8, part 4, pp. 61, 279 (quote).

4 Benedict Anderson and Ruth McVey, *A Preliminary Analysis of the October 1, 1965, Coup in Indonesia* (Ithaca: Cornell University Southeast Asia Program, 1971); CIA, *Indonesia*; W. F. Wertheim, "Whose Plot? New Light on the 1965 Events," *Journal of Contemporary Asia* 9(2), 1979, pp. 197–215; Coen Holtzappel, "The 30 September Movement: A Political Movement of the Armed Forces or an Intelligence Operation?," *Journal of Contemporary Asia* 9(2), 1979, pp. 216–40; R. E. Elson, *Suharto* (Cambridge: Cambridge University Press, 2001), pp. 110–18.

5 GDR Foreign Ministry, 2. AEA, Sektion Indonesien, "Zusammenfassung zu den erhaltenen Informationen zu den Ereignissen in Indonesien," November 11, 1965, PA AA, MfAA, A16166, p. 117; David Mozingo, *Chinese Policy toward Indonesia, 1949–1967* (Ithaca and London: Cornell University Press, 1976), pp. 252–4; fragment

of telegram Green, November 30, 1965, about a conversation with the First Secretary of the Polish Embassy, Gradziuk, NARA, RG 59, Jakarta Embassy Files, 250/7/2, Box 2379, POL INDON-USSR; Harold Crouch, *The Army and Politics in Indonesia* (Ithaca and London: Cornell University Press, 1978), pp. 109–18.

6 Memorandum of Conversation Mary Vance Trent with Suharto, September 25, 1965, NARA, RG 59, 250/7/2, Box 2307, POL 2 INDON 7/1/65; GDR Consulate General, January 11, 1966, PA AA MfAA, A16175, pp. 70–1 (with reference to SOKSI journal *Ampera*).

7 The coup has been blamed on the PKI, the CIA, the British secret service, Sukarno, Suharto, the Indonesian Air Force, and the Chinese government, in turn. There is a vast, often speculative, literature on this topic which has once again grown considerably in the past ten years.

8 Except for some places in Central Java.

9 Cf. Mary Zurbuchen, "History, memory and the '1965 incident' in Indonesia," *Asian Survey* 42(4), 2002, pp. 564–81; Colombijn and Lindblat, "Introduction," p. 15.

10 Helen Fein, "Revolutionary and antirevolutionary genocides: A comparison of state murders in Democratic Kampuchea, 1975 to 1979, and Indonesia, 1965 to 1966," *Comparative Studies in Society and History* 35(4), 1993, p. 802.

11 Philippe Gavi [that is, Jean Contenay], *Konterrevolution in Indonesien* (Frankfurt a.M.: Europäische Verlaganstalt, 1969), pp. 11–12; Ryter, "Youth," pp. 65–6; Pipit Rochijat, "Am I PKI or non-PKI," *Indonesia* 40, 1985, p. 45; see Robert Hefner, *Civil Islam: Muslims and Democratization in Indonesia* (Princeton and Oxford: Princeton University Press, 2000), p. 244, n. 12.

12 Robert Cribb, "Introduction," in Cribb (ed.), *The Indonesian Killings, 1965–66* (Victoria: Monash University, Center of Southeast Asian Studies, 1990), p. 17.

13 Rex Mortimer, *Indonesian Communism Under Sukarno: Ideology and Politics 1959–1965* (Ithaca and London: Cornell University Press, 1974), pp. 293–4, 307, 366, and general (reformism); for the mass organizations, Justus van der Kroef, *The Communist Party of*

Indonesia (Vancouver: University of British Columbia, 1965), pp. 197–212; Françoise Cayrac-Blanchard, *Le Parti Communiste Indonésien* (Paris: A. Colin, 1973), pp. 80–4.

14 Quote: Ruth McVey, "Teaching modernity: The PKI as an educational institution," *Indonesia* 50, 1990, p. 26; PKI self-criticism of September 1966, in Feith and Castles, *Indonesian Political Thinking*, p. 271; "Die Entwicklung der PKI," n.d., BA, DY 30 IVA2/20/668; Mortimer, *Communism*, pp. 153, 293–4, 307.

15 Cayrac-Blanchard, *Parti Communiste*, pp. 76–8.

16 Robert Cribb and Colin Brown, *Modern Indonesia: A History Since 1945* (London and New York: Longman, 1995), p. 103.

17 Steven Farram, "Revolution, religion and magic: The PKI in West Timor, 1924–1966," *Bijdragen tot de Taal-, Land- en Volkenkunde* 158(1), 2002, p. 36.

18 See Robert Cribb, "How many deaths? Problems in the statistics of massacre in Indonesia (1965–1966) and East Timor (1975–1980)," in Ingrid Wessel and Georgia Wimhöfer (eds.), *Violence in Indonesia* (Hamburg: Abera, 2001), pp. 82–98; Cribb, "Introduction," pp. 7–14. The PKI, while in no position to give a proper estimate, assumed 500,000 had been killed.

19 Australian Embassy Jakarta, Savingram No. 66, January 7, 1966, ANA, 752/2, part 17, p. 128; see GDR Consul General, "Zur Lage in den indonesischen Streitkräften," March 4, 1966, PA AA, MfAA, A 16175, p. 90.

20 Cribb, "Introduction," p. 8.

21 Australian Embassy Jakarta, Savingram No. 52 (secret), October 15, 1965, ANA, 3107/40/106, part 13, p. 48 ("We will never know"); Savingram No. 28, June 10, 1966, ANA, 3034/2/2/2, part 15, p. 69 ("would never be known," referring to Attorney General Sugiharto); undated summary of killings, no author, ANA, 3034/2/1/8, part 15, p. 35 ("unlikely that the full story will ever be known," referring to numbers); Rusk to President Johnson, enclosure, August 1, 1966, Foreign Relations of the United States [FRUS], 1964–1968, vol. 26, p. 450 ("will never be known"); CIA, *Indonesia*, pp. 70–1 ("there never was – and never will be – a reliable figure"); Seth King, "The great purge in Indonesia," *New York Times*, May 8, 1966, p. 26 ("may never be known").

22 British Consul in Medan, quoted after Audrey Kahin, *Rebellion to Integration: West Sumatra and the Indonesian Polity 1926–1998* (Amsterdam: Amsterdam University Press, 1999), p. 244; East Java: Tarzie Vittachi, *The Fall of Sukarno* (New York and Washington: Andre Deutsch, 1967), p. 144, and Gunnar Myrdal, *Asian Drama: An Inquiry into the Poverty of Nations* (New York: Pantheon, 1968), p. 378, n. 1 (400,000 in Malang district alone); account of the over-crowded orphanage in Purwodadi, Central Java: William L. Williams *et al.*, *Javanese Lives: Women and Men in Modern Indonesian Society* (New Brunswick and London: Rutgers University Press, 1991), p. 192; see Kenneth Young, "Local and national influences in the violence of 1965," in Cribb, *Indonesian Killings*, p. 81. "If the commonly cited figures for the provinces are to be believed, the total would reach one million persons": US Embassy Jakarta, April 15, 1966, NARA, RG 59, 250/7/2, Box 2308, POL 2 INDON 1/1/66.

23 Horace Sutton, "Indonesia's night of terror," *Saturday Review*, February 4, 1967, p. 26; Hermawan Sulistyo, "The Forgotten Years: The Missing History of Indonesia's Mass Slaughter (Jombang-Kediri 1965–1966)," Ph.D. thesis, University of Arizona, 1997, pp. 52–4, 106.

24 Central Intelligence Bulletin, November 29, 1965, NARA, CIA database.

25 Australian Embassy Washington, April 19, 1966, ANA, 3034/2/1/8, part 13, p. 124; Roland Challis, *Shadow of a Revolution: Indonesia and the Generals* (Phoenix Mill: Sutton, 2001), p. 106 (quotes a February 23, 1966 letter by British Ambassador Gilchrist); US Embassy Jakarta, telegram February 21, 1966, NARA, RG 59, 250/7/2, Box 2319, POL 23–9 INDON 2/1/66. Cf. H. W. Brands, "The limits of manipulation: How the United States didn't topple Sukarno," *Journal of American History* 76, 1989, p. 786, n. 1 (Stockwell); Record of Conversation by T. Warren with Major-General Ibrahim Adjie, Commander Kodam VI/Siliwangi, June 20–22, 1966, ANA, 3034/1/1, part 2, p. 199; Vittachi, *Fall*, p. 145. Edhie: Saskia Wieringa, *Sexual Politics in Indonesia* (Basingstoke and New York: Palgrave Macmillan, 2002), p. 344; Benedict Anderson, "Petrus Dadi Ratu," *New Left Review* 3, May–June 2000, p. 12.

26 John Bresnan, *Managing Indonesia: The Modern Political Economy* (New York: Columbia University Press, 1993), p. 23.

27 Telegram FRG Embassy Jakarta, "Allgemeine Wahlen," July 16, 1970, PA AA, IB5, 81, vol. 208 (1,730,779 were to be denied voting, most for alleged involvement in the 30 September affair; in West Java, the number was revised downward by 40 percent after a "careful check": Antara, September 3, 1970, PA AA, IB5, 81, vol. 208); Iwan Gartono Sudjatmiko, "The Destruction of the Indonesian Communist Party (PKI) (a comparative analysis of East Java and Bali)," Ph.D. thesis, Harvard University, 1992, p. 5, n. 10; Cribb, "How many," p. 91 (both 1.8 million). Cf. Amnesty International, *Indonesia* (London: Amnesty International, 1977), pp. 13, 15, 41–2.

28 In reality, not only was this a crude invention, but civilians from PKI-affiliated organizations in general were not involved in the killing of the generals nor in military action in the coup in Jakarta except for a late attempt to occupy buildings near Merdeka Square. CIA, *Indonesia*, p. 20; Carmel Budiardjo, "Indonesia: Mass extermination and the consolidation of authoritarian power," in Alexander George (ed.), *Western State Terrorism* (Cambridge, MA and Oxford: Blackwell, 1991), p. 189.

29 Autopsy report in Ben Anderson, "How did the generals die?," *Indonesia* 43, 1987, pp. 109–34; Geoffrey Simons, *Indonesia: The Long Oppression* (New York: Palgrave Macmillan, 2000), pp. 173–4, for the forensic team. Cf. Anderson and McVey, *Preliminary Analysis*, p. 55; Elson, *Suharto*, pp. 108–9; Indonesian account of first days of October 1965, PA AA, IB5, 84, vol. 204. Sukarno's later disclaimers of the mutilations, based on the autopsy, were reported by some Indonesian media but marginalized by army propaganda. Australian Embassy Jakarta, Economic Savingram No. 65, December 23, 1965, ANA, 3034/2/1, part 48, p. 193; Anderson and McVey, *Preliminary Analysis*, p. 71, n. 46.

30 Gabriel Kolko, *Confronting the Third World: United States Foreign Policy, 1945–1980* (New York: Pantheon, 1988), p. 180, citing a CIA document of October 8, 1965.

31 Day-by-day report by Ulrich Makosch to Frei starting October 6, 1965, PA AA, MfAA, A 16166, pp. 1–5; Anderson and McVey, *Preliminary Analysis*, p. 58. Gestapu: Budiardjo, "Indonesia," p. 190. The term "Gestapu" is ascribed to General Sugandhi, director of the army daily *Angkatan Bersendjata*: Arnold Brackman, *The Communist Collapse in Indonesia* (New York: Norton, 1969), p. 229, n. 1.

32 C. Penders and Ulf Sundhaussen, *Abdul Haris Nasution* (St. Lucia: University of Queensland Press, 1985), p. 187 (October 1, 1965); Australian Embassy Jakarta, cablegram October 23, 1965, ANA, 3034/2/1, part 48, p. 52.

33 See John Hughes, *Indonesian Upheaval* (New York: D. McKay, 1967), pp. 149–50. Press statements: I Gusti Agung Ayu Ratih, "Soeharto's New Order State: Imposed Illusions and Invented Legitimations," M.A. thesis, University of Wisconsin, Madison, 1997, p. 52, n. 78 (November 18, 1965), mkb.kerjabudaya.org/mkb-arsip/ayratih/ayu. finale.pdf (accessed July 6, 2006); Anderson and McVey, *Preliminary Analysis*, p. 77, n. 97 (November 26, 1965). Quote and propaganda units: Gavi, *Konterrevolution*, p. 31. Further, Karen Strassler, "Material witness: Photographs and the making of reformasi memory," in Mary Zurbuchen (ed.), *Beginning to Remember: The Past in the Indonesian Present* (Singapore and Seattle: Singapore University Press, 2005), pp. 294–6, 308, n. 18, 19. For foreign reporters, see n. 61, 92.

34 "Report from East Java," *Indonesia* 41 (1986), p. 137 (by a military intelligence officer, late November 1965).

35 FRG Embassy Jakarta, "Kommunistischer Staatstreichversuch in Indonesien," November 15, 1965, PA AA, IB5, 84, vol. 204; "Record of Conversation with Dr. Hatta," November 15, 1965, ANA, 3034/2/1/8, part 7, p. 249 (alleged that PKI wanted to kill two million people); Paul Gardner, *Shared Hopes, Separate Fears: Fifty Years of US–Indonesian Relations* (Boulder and Oxford: Westview, 1997), p. 229; Brackman, *Collapse*, p. 232, n. 18.

36 See Anderson and McVey, *Preliminary Analysis*, p. 84, n. 172; Madiun: Soerastro Sastrosoewignjo, "You have stabbed us in the back again," *Mertjusuar* (Muhammadiyah newspaper), October 15, 1965, in *Indonesia* 1, April 1966, quote p. 374.

37 Andreas Kabus, "Information über eine Unterredung mit dem Antara-Korrespondenten Singhi," November 3, 1965, BA, DY 30 IV A2/20/670; Mozingo, *Chinese Policy*, p. 242, n. 4.

38 US Embassy Jakarta, telegram September 23, 1966, NARA, RG 59, 250/7/2, Box 2312, POL 12–6 INDON 1/1/64.

39 Anderson and McVey, *Preliminary Analysis*, pp. 59, 61, 85, n. 180; see PKI statements between October 2 and 8, 1965, *Indonesia* 1, April 1966, pp. 184–90; Hughes, *Indonesian Upheaval*, p. 121.

40 Summary of Nasution speech to Central Action Unit of Indonesian Students at Armed Forces Headquarters of November 12 from Berita Yudha, November 15, 1965, *Indonesia* 1, April 1966, pp. 182–3; Australian Embassy Jakarta, Political Savingram No. 58, November 19, 1965 (speeches of November 12 and 15), ANA, 3034/2/1, part 48, p. 152; Brackman, *Collapse*, pp. 118–19. These activities of Nasution do not surface in Penders and Sundhaussen, *Nasution*, pp. 187–93. For Suharto see Elson, *Suharto*, p. 125.

41 Telegram US Embassy Jakarta (Jones), March 19, 1964, FRUS, 1964–1968, vol. 26, p. 81.

42 Hughes, *Indonesian Upheaval*, p. 194.

43 "Bericht über den Inhalt der Februar-Nummer von 'Tanah Air', der Zeitschrift für Indonesier im Ausland," cover letter by Press- and Information Office of FRG Federal Government, April 15, 1966, PA AA, IB5, 37, vol. 255.

44 Telegram Green 191A, October 5, 1965, containing the text of a telegram of the French Ambassador, NARA, RG 84, 631/14/50/2–3, Box 118, POL 23–9, October 4–6, 1965. For the concept of propaganda as a part of terror, see Babette Quinkert, "Die nationalsozialistische Propaganda gegenüber der Zivilbevölkerung der besetzten sowjetischen Gebiete 1941–1944 am Beispiel des Generalkommissariats Weißruthenien," Ph.D. thesis, Technical University Berlin, 2006.

45 Telegram Green 373A, October 8, 1965, NARA, RG 84, 631/14/50/2–3, Box 118, POL 23–9, October 4–6, 1965 ("several thousand"); Hsinhua report, October 19, 1965, ANA, 3107/40/106, part 13, p. 208 (3,000 at October 17); telegram FRG Embassy Moscow, October 13, 1965 (in telegram of October 15), referring to Soviet reports citing Reuters (3,500 arrests), PA AA, IB5, 81, vol. 198; Elson, *Suharto*, p. 124 (1,334 in Jakarta by October 16); information report by ADN correspondent Jakarta, November 4, 1965, BA, DY 30 IVA2/20/671.

46 *Kampungs*: telegrams Green 420A of October 9 and 490A of October 11, NARA, RG 84, 631/14/50/2–3, Box 118, POL 23–9, October 7–14, 1965; FRG military attaché, October 25, 1965, PA AA, IB5, 37, vol. 169A. Last quote: FRG Embassy Jakarta, "Verluste der indonesischen Bevölkerung seit 1. Oktober d.J.," December 14, 1965, PA AA, IB5, 37, vol. 169A. Earlier quotes: telegram Green, October 21,

1965, NARA, RG 84, 631/14/50/2–3, Box 118, POL 23–9, October 4–6, 1965. Prisons: Information report by ADN correspondent Jakarta, October 21, 1965, BA, DY 30 IVA2/20/671; CIA, *Indonesia*, p. 92, n.

47 Telegram Green 372A, October 9, 1965, NARA, RG 84, 631/14/50/2–3, Box 118, POL 23–9, October 7–14, 1965.

48 FRG Embassy Jakarta, "Verluste der indonesischen Bevölkerung seit 1. Oktober d.J.," December 14, 1965, PA AA, IB5, 37, vol. 169A.

49 US Embassy Jakarta (Masters), "Indonesian Sociologist Views Conditions in East Java," January 19, 1965, NARA, RG 84, 631/14/50/2–3, Box 118, POL 18; telegram Green, October 28, 1965, NARA, RG 84, 631/14/50/2–3, Box 118, POL 23–9, October 26–31, 1965; Ulf Sundhaussen, *The Road to Power: Indonesian Military Politics 1945–1967* (Kuala Lumpur: Oxford University Press, 1982), p. 175.

50 Telegram Green, October 21, 1965, NARA, RG 84, 631/14/50/2–3, Box 118, POL 23–9, October 4–6, 1965 (Jakarta–Bogor area); Sundhaussen, *Road*, pp. 216–17; Cribb, "Introduction," p. 26.

51 Crouch, *Army*, p. 142, n. 13, cites figures of 3,000 to 10,000 victims.

52 Kahin, *Rebellion*, p. 243; Hughes, *Indonesian Upheaval*, pp. 141–2.

53 FRG Embassy Jakarta, "Verluste der indonesischen Bevölkerung seit 1. Oktober d.J.," December 14, 1965, PA AA, IB5, 37, vol. 169A; Kahin, *Rebellion*, p. 243; Vittachi, *Fall*, p. 143.

54 Telegrams Green, November 6 and 8, 1965, NARA, RG 84, 631/14/50/2–3, Box 118, POL 23–9, October 26–31, 1965; telegram US Consul Medan, November 27, 1965, NARA, RG 84, 631/14/50/2–3, Box 118, POL 23–9, November 20–30, 1965; Budiardjo, "Indonesia," p. 191.

55 Kahin, *Rebellion*, p. 244; Ann Laura Stoler, *Capitalism and Confrontation in Sumatra's Plantation Belt, 1870–1979* (Ann Arbor: University of Michigan Press, 1995 [second edition]), pp. 157–66. From 1965 to 1966, the number of men on these plantations decreased by about 44,500, the number of female employees plus non-working women dropped by close to 6,000. Philippe Gavi estimated that 20

percent of Sumatran plantation workers were killed (*Konterrevolution*, p. 38).

56 Sudjatmiko, "Destruction," pp. 113–14, 200–1.

57 Kahin, *Rebellion*, pp. 242, 245–8; see also Erwiza Erman, "Generalized violence: A case study of the Ombilin coal mine, 1882–1996," in Colombijn and Lindblat, *Roots*, p. 128. Cf. speech of Caretaker Commander of the 72th Military Resort (Yogyakarta–Surakarta), Col. Widjojo, published October 8, 1965, *Indonesia* 1, April 1966, p. 181.

58 Ken Conboy, *Kopassus: Inside Indonesia's Special Forces* (Jakarta and Singapore: Equinox, 2003), pp. 117, 119, 127–44 (a neither scholarly nor critical study). Cf. Julie Southwood and Patrick Flanagan, *Indonesia: Law, Propaganda and Terror* (London: Zed, 1983), p. 77 (assignment in Jakarta); Arnold Brackman, *Indonesia: The Gestapu Affair* (no place: American–Asian Educational Exchange, 1969), p. 31.

59 "Crushing the G30S/PKI in Central Java," in Cribb, *Indonesian Killings*, p. 163; Conboy, *Kopassus*, pp. 146–8, with meagre remarks about killings; "Kurzzusammenfassung eines Naszabadsag-Korrespondenten über seine Reise nach Zentral- und Ostjava," November 10, 1965, PA AA, MfAA, A 16166, pp. 112–13; Hughes, *Indonesian Upheaval*, pp. 149–54; Crouch, *Army*, pp. 148–9. Edhie's initiative: Crouch, *Army*, pp. 149–51; Elson, *Suharto*, p. 125.

60 In mid-November, Suharto traveled to Central Java: R. E. Elson, "In fear of the people: Suharto and the justification of state-sponsored violence under the New Order," in Colombijn and Lindblat, *Roots*, pp. 180–1; photo of Suharto at the parade: CIA, *Indonesia*, pp. 81ff. Nasution: secret telegram Green, November 1965, NARA, RG 84, 631/15/50/2–3, Box 116, POL – Polit. Aff. & Rel. I/M/P, June 1-, 1965.

61 J. R. Burgess, "Record of Conversation with Mr. Tiwari of the 'Indian Express' on 16th November 1965," ANA, 3034/2/2/2, part 16, p. 228; Kenneth Orr, "Schooling and village politics in Central Java in the time of the turbulence," in Cribb, *Indonesian Killings*, pp. 184–5; Australian Embassy Jakarta, Political Savingram No. 58, November 19, 1965, ANA, 3034/2/1, part 48, p. 150; Hughes, *Indonesian*

Upheaval, pp. 150, 154; Gavi, *Konterrevolution*, p. 13; Robinson, *Dark Side*, p. 298.

62 Southwood and Flanagan, *Indonesia*, p. 78; Hughes, *Indonesian Upheaval*, p. 180.

63 Political Action Group [a group of Dutch intellectuals], Open letter [July 1967], ANA, 3034/2/2/2, part 16, p. 81; Ratih, "Soeharto's New Order," p. 23, n. 24.

64 Mark Curtis, "Democratic genocide," *Ecologist* 26(5), September–October 1996, pp. 202–4; Robert Goodfellow, "Forgetting what it was to remember the Indonesian killings of 1965–6," in Kenneth Christie and Robert Cribb (eds.), *Historical Injustice and Democratic Transition in Eastern Asia and Northern Europe: Ghosts at the Table of Democracy* (London and New York: RoutledgeCurzon, 2002), pp. 53–4, n. 20 (airfield near Klaten, Central Java, October 1965).

65 Hans Thoolen (ed.), *Indonesia and the Rule of Law: Twenty Years of "New Order" Government* (London: F. Pinter, 1987), p. 67 (quote); Amnesty International, *Indonesia*, p. 76; Southwood and Flanagan, *Indonesia*, p. 104; Liem Soei Liong, "It's the military, stupid!," in Colombijn and Lindblat, *Roots*, p. 199; regionally: US Consulate Medan, December 6, 1965, NARA, RG 59, 250/7/2, Box 2310, POL 12 INDON, 10/1/65.

66 Such orders were given on November 15, 1965: Elson, *Suharto*, pp. 123, 126; GDR Consulate General, January 11, 1966, PA AA, MfAA, vol. 16175, p. 73.

67 Sudjatmiko, "Destruction," pp. 188–9.

68 Australian Embassy Jakarta, January 11 [1966], ANA, 3034/2/2/4, part 2, p. 230; GDR Embassy Bucharest, "Vermerk über ein Gespräch mit dem Rat in der indonesischen Botschaft, Herrn Paul, am 21.1.1966," February 2, 1966, BA, DY 30 IVA2/20/670; Cayrac-Blanchard, *Parti Communiste*, p. 73; Koentjaraningrat, "The village in Indonesia today," in Koentjaraningrat (ed.), *Villages in Indonesia* (Ithaca: Cornell University Press, 1967), p. 386.

69 Jakarta: Australian Embassy Jakarta, Political Savingram No. 64, December 23, 1965, ANA, 3034/2/1/8, part 8, p. 197. Yogyakarta: Goodfellow, "Forgetting," p. 44. According to Gavi, *Konterrevolution*,

p. 33, officials said 3,000 people were killed in Yogyakarta but he estimated 15,000 dead.

70 Amnesty International, *Indonesia*, pp. 71–81 (US$0.17 per day in 1977); "Political Killings in Indonesia," July 1966, ANA, 3034/2/1/8, part 15A, pp. 84–5; Harold Munthe-Kaas, "Indonesia: Gestapu in jail," *Bulletin*, November 25, 1967, ANA, 3034/2/2/2, part 16, p. 239; Anne Pohlman, "A fragment of a story: Gerwani and Tapol experiences," *Intersections* 10, August 2004, p. 9, www.sshe.murdoch.edu.au/intersections/issue10/pohlman.html (accessed December 16, 2005); Ananta Pramoedha Toer, *The Mute's Soliloquy* (New York: Hyperion, 1999), pp. xx, 24–7, 35–9, 44.

71 Southwood and Flanagan, *Indonesia*, p. 111; Carmel Budiardjo, *Surviving Indonesia's Gulag* (London and New York: Cassell, 1996), p. 51 (cf. p. 169 about a facility in Lampung); Toer, *Mute's Soliloquy*, p. 59; Gavi, *Konterrevolution*, p. 35.

72 Budiardjo, *Surviving*, p. 113. Buru: Toer, *Mute's Soliloquy*, pp. 65, 348–63; see Amnesty International, *Indonesia*, pp. 90–101.

73 Stanley Karnow, "Suharto's worry: How to heal the wounds of the anti-Red holocaust?," *Straits Times* (Singapore), February 19, 1970 (copy), BA, DY 30 IV A2/20/668.

74 Southwood and Flanagan, *Indonesia*, pp. 106–9; English version of the defense speech of PKI Politbureau member Sudisman, 1967, BA, DY 30 IVA2/20/1051, p. 44 of the document; Budiardjo, *Surviving*, pp. 40, 78–83, 169, 176, 178; Toer, *Mute's Soliloquy*, pp. 4–5.

75 J. M. Starey, "Notes on anti-PKI measures in Nusa Tenggara", February 25, 1966, ANA, 3034/2/1/8, part 11, p. 68.

76 Wieringa, *Sexual Politics*, pp. 9–15, 295–301; Pohlman, "Fragment," pp. 5–11; Leslie Dwyer, "The intimacy of terror: Gender and the violence of 1965–66 in Bali," *Intersections*, 10, 2004, www.sshe.murdoch.edu.au/intersections/issue10/dwyer.html (accessed December 16, 2005), pp. 5–9.

77 Questionable 'confessions' by Untung and a few others had been published earlier (see PA AA, IB5, 84, vol. 204).

78 Trials, sentences, media, and executions: Southwood and Flanagan, *Indonesia*, pp. 48, 88, 134, n. 1, 153 (sample of 598 trials),

155–6, 238–40. Gerwani: Pohlman, "Fragment," pp. 3–5; Amnesty International, *Indonesia*, p. 103.

79 Einar Schlereth and B. D. Bintang, *Indonesien: Analyse eines Massakers* (Frankfurt a.M.: März, 1970), p. 196; Stephen Sloan, *A Study in Political Violence: The Indonesian Experience* (Chicago: Rand McNally, 1971), p. 37, n. 27; Sundhaussen, *Road*, p. 167; "The Indonesian army and the future of Indonesia," January 7, 1966, RG59 150/69/32/03, entry 5222, Gen. Records Lot Files Box 2, POL 2; *Frankfurter Allgemeine Zeitung*, October 15, 1968; generally: Conboy, *Kopassus*.

80 Anderson and McVey, *Preliminary Analysis*, p. 66, n. 13; Hughes, *Indonesian Upheaval*, pp. 25–6.

81 Hughes, *Indonesian Upheaval*, p. 159.

82 See details for his abduction in Anderson and McVey, *Preliminary Analysis*, pp. 13–14; CIA, *Indonesia*, Preface; cf. Hughes, *Indonesian Upheaval*, pp. 16, 37, 104; Howard Jones, *Indonesia: The Possible Dream* (New York: Harcourt Brace Jovanovich, 1971), p. 374.

83 Report Green, August 10, 1966, quoted in editors' note, *Foreign Relations of the United States, 1964–1968*, vol. XXVI (Washington, 2001), p. 387.

84 Data given vary: FRG Embassy Jakarta, "Kommunistische Untergrund- und Guerillatätigkeit," October 31, 1967, PA AA, IB5, 81, vol. 208 (ca. 30 of 83/quote); Christian Roll, "Fragezeichen über Indonesien," *Industriekurier*, December 19 [1967], BA, DY 30 IVA2/20/672 (35 of 83); *Sydney Morning Herald*, November 6, 1966, and report of August 1966, ANA, 3034/2/2/2, part 15, pp. 135, 219; telegram Green, August 10, 1966, NARA, RG 59, 250/7/2, Box 2312, POL 12 5-1-66 (31 of 68); CIA, Office of Current Intelligence, Intelligence Memorandum, "Indonesian Communist Party," April 29, 1966, NARA, CIA database (22 of 50).

85 See Information report by ADN correspondent Jakarta, October 1968, copy, BA, DY 30 IVA2/20/672; Report of PKI Exile Committee at the 50th PKI anniversary (German translation), May 23, 1970, BA, DY 30 IVA2/20/672, vol. 1052 (p. 24 of the report); Arnold Brackman, "Foreign help for the reds in Indonesia" (German translation), *Straits Times* (Singapore), July 17, 1972, BA, DY 30/

IVB2/20/282 (83 percent of PKI Central Committee dead, detained or in exile).

86 Budiardjo, *Surviving*, p. 129.

87 Telegram US Embassy Jakarta, June 18, 1966, NARA, RG 59, 250/7/2, Box 124, POL 29 1966; cf. FRG military attaché, February 25, 1969, PA AA, IB5, 84, vol. 204 (page 24 of report); Justus van der Kroef, "Indonesian communism since the 1965 coup," *Pacific Affairs* 43(1), 1970, p. 34

88 Hefner, *Civil Islam*, p. 48; Gavi, *Konterrevolution*, pp. 19, 34, 36; Schlereth and Bintang, *Indonesien*, p. 176; Ralph Gehee, "The Indonesian massacres and the CIA," *Covert Action Quarterly*, fall 1990, www.thirdworldtraveller.com/CIA/McGehee_CIA_Indo.html (accessed May 22, 2006). Exceptions: police in Kupang, West Timor: Goodfellow, "Forgetting," p. 53, n. 11; Sudjatmiko, "Destruction," p. 202 (Malang; but see pp. 225–7 for Bali); Challis, *Shadow*, p. 108 (case in Bali).

89 UPI report, November 9, 1965, ANA, 3034/2/1/8, part 5, p. 178 (Madura); Australian Embassy Jakarta, "Post-Gestapu developments," June 10, 1966, ANA, 3034/2/2/2, part 15, p. 69; Rochijat, "Am I PKI," p. 44; Kahin, *Rebellion*, p. 248; US Consulate Surabaya, telegram November 27, 1965, NARA, RG 59, 250/7/2, Box 2316, POL 23–8 INDON 9/1/65.

90 Sundhaussen, *Road*, pp. 190–2; David Jenkins, "The evolution of Indonesian army doctrinal thinking: The concept of dwifungsi," *Southeast Asian Journal of Social Science* 11(2), 1983, pp. 15–30.

91 Speech by Suharto to the central and regional leaders of the National Front, October 15, 1965, *Indonesia* 1(1), April 1966, p. 161, with n. 2.

92 J. R. Burgess, "Record of Conversation with Mr. Tiwari of the 'Indian Express' on 16th November 1965," ANA, 3034/2/2/2, part 16, p. 228 (my emphasis). For Australian journalists visiting the RPKAD: US Embassy London, November 8, 1965, NARA, RG 59, 250/7/2, Box 2306, POL INDON 1/1/64; "A.B.C. News 12:30 PM," November 10, 1965, ANA, 3034/2/1/8, part 5, p. 216.

93 H. E. Stannard (UPI), report of November 24, 1965, ANA, 3034/2/1/8, part 6, p. 117.

94 Hughes, *Indonesian Upheaval*, p. 151; cf. p. 156. Edhie had first asked Suharto for more troops and then turned, with his superior's consent, to civilians. See Crouch, *Army*, pp. 149–51; Sundhaussen, *Road*, p. 215; "Crushing the G30S/PKI," p. 166. Edhie also made use of Catholic youth.

95 Gavi, *Konterrevolution*, pp. 16, 31–35.

96 Robert Shaplen, *Time out of Hand: Revolution and Reaction in Southeast Asia* (New York: Harper & Row, n.d.[1969]), pp. 123, 158.

97 For the official narrative, Amnesty International, *Indonesia*, p. 41; Suharto speech at the PNI Congress, April 24, 1966, *Indonesia* 1(1), April 1966, p. 146.

98 Benedict Anderson, "Introduction," in Anderson (ed.), *Violence and the State in Suharto's Indonesia* (Ithaca: Southeast Asia Program, Cornell University, 2001), p. 13; see Colombijn and Lindblat, "Introduction," esp. p. 23.

99 "Kami Bandung promise sincerely to struggle for the peace and justice," n.d., PA AA, IB5, 37, vol. 255; last quote: Roger Paget, "The military in Indonesian Politics: The burden of power," *Pacific Affairs* 40, 1967, p. 301.

100 Telegram Green, October 14, 1965, NARA, RG 84, 631/14/50/2–3, Box 118, POL 23–9, Oct 7–14, 1965; telegram Heimsoeth, October 9, 1965, PA AA, IB5, 37, vol. 169A; similar Werz's report of October 18, 1965, IB5, 84, vol. 204.

101 "Kurzzusammenfassung eines Naszabadsag-Korrespondenten über seine Reise nach Zentral- und Ostjava," November 10, 1965, PA AA, MfAA, A 16166, pp. 112–13 (based on a trip November 2 to 6, 1965).

102 Stanley Karnow, "500,000 Perish in Orgy of Vengeance" (April 1966), ANA, 3034/2/1/8, part 13, p. 120; "Bericht des Auslandskomitees der KPI zum 50. Jahrestag der Gründung der KPI," May 23, 1970, BA, DY 30 IVA2/20/1052, p. 24 of document.

103 Descriptions in Hughes, *Indonesian Upheaval*, pp. 155, 160, 179; Vittachi, *Fall*, p. 141; Theodore Friend, *Indonesian Destinies* (Cambridge, MA and London: Belknap, 2003), p. 109; "Die Lage nach den Ereignissen des 30. September" (ca. April 1966), PA AA, MfAA, A16075, p. 3.

104 Clifford Geertz, *After the Fact: Two Centuries, Four Decades, One Anthropologist* (Cambridge, MA: Harvard University Press, 1995), p. 9.

105 Quote: US Consulate Medan, "The IPKI Party Rides High in North Sumatra," January 25, 1966, NARA, RG 59, 250/7/2, Box 2311, POL 12 INDON 1/1/66; Loren Ryter, "Pemuda Pancasila: The last loyalist free men of Suharto's order?," in Anderson, *Violence*, p. 135; Note of the Chinese Embassy in Jakarta, December 20, 1965, PA AA, IB5, 81, vol. 198; Crouch, *Army*, p. 65, n. 40.

106 Other popular *chiffres* for killing (in East Java) were "sent to school" and "sent to like the earth." Sulistyo, "Years," pp. 175–6, 186.

107 Ryter, "Youth," pp. 62–6.

108 Telegram US Consulate Medan, November 16, 1965, FRUS, 1964–1968, vol. 26, pp. 366–7.

109 André Feillard, *Islam et Armée dans l'Indonésie contemporaine: Les pionniers de la tradition* (Paris: L'Harmattan Archipel, 1995), p. 64 (but with little information about killings by NU members, pp. 64–9); Young, "Local," pp. 80–3; contradictory UPI reports, October 10, 1965, ANA, 3034/2/1/8, part 1, pp. 421, 423; quote: Donald Hindley, "Alirans and the fall of the old order," *Indonesia* 9, April 1970, p. 41; W. F. Wertheim, "Indonesia before and after the Untung coup," *Pacific Affairs* 39(1–2), spring–summer 1966, p. 122; Gardner, *Shared Hopes*, p. 231; Southwood and Flanagan, *Indonesia*, p. 78; Hughes, *Indonesian Upheaval*, p. 159; Williams *et al.*, *Javanese Lives*, pp. 26–7.

110 "President wants 1965 killings investigated," *Tapol* 157, April 2000, with reference to Mike Carey's documentary film, "Indonesia's Killing Fields." Hasjim was the father-in-law of post-Suharto Indonesian President Abdulrahman Wahid. For Islamic schools, Wertheim, "Indonesia," p. 121.

111 Feillard, *Islam*, p. 64; GDR Consulate General, "Information zu Fragen der Entwicklung der Muhammdiyah und der SOKSI," February 9, 1966, PA AA, MfAA, A16166, p. 202; FRG Embassy Jakarta, "Indonesisches Parteiwesen," December 13, 1965, PA AA,

IB5, 81, vol. 208. Jakarta: Australian Embassy Jakarta, Savingram No. 53, October 22, 1965, ANA, 3034/2/1, part 48, p. 61.

112 FRG Embassy Kuala Lumpur, telegram October 8, 1965, PA AA, IB5, 84, vol. 204 (under reference to Radio Malaysia); FRG Embassy Kuala Lumpur, telegram October 27, 1965, PA AA, IB5, 37, 169A; FRG Embassy Kuala Lumpur, report of December 14, 1965, PA AA, IB5, 37, 169A; report by dpa correspondent in Jakarta in telegram October 27, 1965, PA AA, IB5, 37, 169A; UPI reports October 11, 1965, ANA, 3034/2/1/8, part 2, 4, and 9; telegram Green, December 27, 1965, RG 84, 631/14/50/2–3, Box 118, POL 23–9, December 1–31, 1965; Australian Embassy Jakarta, Political Savingram No. 55, November 5, 1965, ANA, 3034/2/1, part 48, p. 117; "Report from East Java," pp. 139–40.

113 Anderson, "Introduction," p. 18; John Bowen, *Sumatran Politics and Poetics: Gayo History, 1900–1989* (New Haven and London: Yale University Press, 1991), pp. 118–21; quote: Simons, *Indonesia*, p. 176.

114 Hughes, *Indonesian Upheaval*, p. 179; cf. Robinson, *Dark Side*, p. 273, n. 2.

115 Marshall Green, *Indonesia: Crisis and Transformation 1965–1968* (Washington DC: Compass, 1990), p. 57; Ibu Marni, "I am a leaf in the storm," *Indonesia* 47, April 1989, p. 56 (Semarang); Southwood and Flanagan, *Indonesia*, p. 78.

116 US Embassy Jakarta, "Report on trip to Jogjakarta" (Masters), September 17, 1965, RG 84, 631/14/50/2–3, Box 118, POL 17.

117 US Embassy Jakarta, telegram October 21, 1965, POL 23–9, October 20–25, 1965; US Embassy Jakarta, telegram November 20, 1965, POL 23–9, November 20–30, 1965.

118 Robert Cribb, *Historical Atlas of Indonesia* (Honolulu: University of Hawaii Press, 2000), p. 170; Wertheim, "Indonesia," p. 123; Hilmar Farid, "Indonesia's original sin: Mass killings and capitalist expansion, 1965–66," *Inter-Asia Cultural Studies* 6(1), 2005, p. 15, n. 7.

119 Williams *et al.*, *Javanese Lives*, p. 26; Conboy, *Kopassus*, pp. 149–50.

120 The quotes are from Cribb and Brown, *Modern Indonesia*, pp. 106–7. Hindley, "Alirans," p. 42, called this an "alliance" of officers corps, modernist and traditionalist *santris*, Christians, and the "PSI-type group."

121 Schlereth and Bintang, *Indonesien*, pp. 244, 246; Elson, *Suharto*, p. 123; Brian May, *The Indonesian Tragedy* (London et al.: Routledge, 1978), p. 132; Hindley, "Alirans," pp. 40–1; Sundhaussen, *Road*, pp. 210–11. Meeting with Nasution: Bresnan, *Managing*, pp. 36–7.

122 Feillard, *Islam*, pp. 67, 70; Memorandum of conversation, July 5, 1964, NARA, RG 59, 250/7/2, Box 2311, POL 12 7/1/64; "bright": G. Miller to Secretary, Australian Dept. of External Affairs, December 1, 1965, ANA, 3034/2/1, part 48, pp. 170–2; Wieringa, *Sexual Politics*, p. 302; Hindley, "Alirans," pp. 40–1, n. 32; Hefner, *Civil Islam*, p. 90; US Embassy Jakarta, January 29, 1965, NARA, RG59 250/7/2, Box 2312, POL 13.

123 Anderson and McVey, *Preliminary Analysis*, p. 83, n. 163; Sloan, *Study*, pp. 67–8, cf. p. 59, n. 11; Feillard, *Islam*, pp. 67–71; Statement by KAP-Gestapu, October 4, 1965, *Indonesia* 1, April 1966, pp. 203–4; Chronology of the Coup and Counter Coup (secret), n.d., ANA, 3034/2/1/8, part 2, p. 84; telegram Heimsoeth, October 8, 1965, PA AA, IB5, 84, vol. 204; Djuhartono: telegram Green, 372A, October 9, 1965, NARA, RG 84, 631/14/50/2–3, Jakarta Embassy, Box 118, POL 23–9, October 7–14, 1965; Hindley, "Alirans," p. 41; Sudjatmiko, "Destruction," p. 192. The first member parties were NU, IPKI, the Catholic Party, and the Muslim PSII. "Crescendo": US Embassy Jakarta, secret telegram, October 4, 1965, NARA, RG 59, 250/7/2, Box 2317, POL 23–9 INDON 10–1–65.

124 Telegram Green, November 9, 1965, NARA, RG 59, 250/7/2, Box 2311, POL 12 INDON 10/1/65; fragment of US Embassy telegram, November 3, 1965, Box 2312, POL 12–6 INDON 1/1/64.

125 Telegram Green, December 2, 1965, FRUS, 1964–68, vol. 26, p. 379; FRG Embassy, October 18, 1965, PA AA, IB5, 84, vol. 204; for Bali see Robinson, *Dark Side*, p. 298; see also Friend, *Indonesian Destinies*, pp. 118–19. For Central Java, see also Schlereth and Bintang, *Indonesien*, p. 271; for Catholic leaders Tjan and the Dutch Father Beek, Wieringa, *Sexual Politics*, pp. 302, 332, n. 55.

126 US Embassy Jakarta, 26 October 1965, NARA, RG59, 250/7/2, Box 2318, POL 23–9 INDON, Oct. 16, 1965; Australian Embassy Jakarta, Political Savingram No. 58, November 19, 1965, ANA 3034/2/1, part 48, p. 151.

127 There were at least seven more "Action Fronts" – for graduates, teachers, labor, women, private businessmen, and "for Cheap Food and Clothing": Australian Embassy Jakarta, Political Savingram No. 14, March 25, 1966, ANA, 3034/2/1/8, part 12, p. 75. Cf. François Raillon, *Les étudiants indonésiens et l'Ordre Nouveau: Politique et idéologie du Mahasiswa Indonesia (1966–1974)* (Paris: Edition de la Maison des sciences de l'homme, 1984), pp. 19–21.

128 Southwood and Flanagan, *Indonesia*, p. 179; Hughes, *Indonesian Upheaval*, pp. 218–19; Bresnan, *Managing*, pp. 37–8; Ratih, "Soeharto's New Order," pp. 35–7; FRG Embassy, "Studentenunruhen in Indonesien," March 3, 1966, PA AA, IB5, 37, vol. 255.

129 "Report from East Java," pp. 136–7.

130 North Sumatra: Southwood and Flanagan, *Indonesia*, p. 134; Budiardjo, "Indonesia," p. 191. Mokoginta: telegram US Embassy Jakarta, November 18, 1965, NARA, RG 59, 250/7/2, Box 2318, POL 23–9 INDON, 11/1/65. West Sumatra: Kahin, *Rebellion*, pp. 245–7.

131 Center for Village Studies, Gadjah Mada University, "Rural violence in Klaten and Banyuwangi," pp. 153–4; Sudjatmiko, "Destruction," pp. 198–9; Jacob Walkin, "The Moslem–Communist confrontation in East Java, 1964–1965," *Orbis* 13(3), 1969/70, p. 831. Cf. US Embassy Jakarta, "Conditions in the Kudus area of Central Java," January 7, 1966, NARA, RG59, 250/7/2, Box 2318, POL 23–9 INDON, 1/1/66; Geoffrey Robinson, "The post-coup massacre in Bali," in Daniel Lev and Ruth McVey (eds.), *Making Indonesia* (Ithaca: Southeast Asia Program, Cornell University, 1996), p. 132, n. 57, with reference to the journal *Suara Denpasar*, November 21, 1965.

132 Anderson and McVey, *Preliminary Analysis*, p. 84, n. 166; Acting Governor of Central Java, Policy Guidelines, October 16, 1965, *Indonesia* 1, April 1966, pp. 190–1. For the National Front UPI reports October 26, 1965 and Australian Embassy Jakarta, cablegram, October 24, ANA, 3034/2/1/8, part 3, pp. 333, 361–2; UPI reports, December 9 and 13, 1965, part 7, pp. 146, 168; but see UPI report, November 9, 1965, ANA, 3034/2/1/8, part 5, p. 118.

133 "Information zu den Ereignissen in Indonesien (Stand: 21.10.1965)," November 13, 1965, PA AA, MfAA, A 16166, p. 123; telegrams US Embassy Jakarta, July 22 and August 10, 1966, NARA, RG 59, 250/7/2, Box 2312, POL 12 INDON, 5–1-66; UPI reports, December 13, 1965, ANA, 3034/2/1/8, part 6, pp. 208–9.

134 Hughes, *Indonesian Upheaval*, p. 128 (on Cabinet meeting of October 6, 1965); Weeka no. 3 and 4, January 25 and 29, 1966, and telegrams Green February 11 and 18, 1966, NARA, RG 59, 250/7/2, Box 2309, POL 2–1 Joint Weekas INDON and POL 2–1 INDON 1966, respectively; Crouch, *Army*, pp. 137–40, 156–7, 167–73.

135 Hughes, *Indonesian Upheaval*, pp. 175, 180; Jones, *Indonesia*, p. 386; Geertz, *After the Fact*, p. 8; FRG Embassy Jakarta, telegram October 29, 1965 and report December 14, 1965, PA AA IB5, 37, vol. 169A.

136 Information report by ADN correspondent in Jakarta, September 21,1966, PA AA, MfAA, A16075, p. 131; UPI report, December 13, 1965, ANA, 3034/2/1/8, part 7, p. 204; Sloan, *Study*, p. 72, n. 33; Vittachi, *Fall*, p. 143; Adrian Vickers, *Bali: A Paradise Created* (Berkeley and Jakarta: Periplus and Java, 1990), pp. 170–1; Geertz, *After the Fact*, p. 8.

137 Sulistyo, "Years," pp. 214, 217.

138 Information report of ADN correspondent in Jakarta, December 21, 1965, PA AA, MfAA, A16166, p. 154; Jean Contenay, "Another bloodbath?," German translation from *Far Eastern Economic Review*, November 23, 1967, pp. 357–67, BA, DY 30 IV A2/20/668; Budiardjo, *Surviving*, p. 92 (talked to survivor from Central Java); Simons, *Indonesia*, p. 176 (even servants were murdered in Aceh); I Nyoman Darma Putra, "Reflections on literature and politics in Bali: The development of LEKRA, 1950–66," in Thomas Reuter (ed.), *Inequality, Crisis and Social Change in Indonesia: The Muted Worlds of Bali* (London and New York: Routledge, 2003), p. 68 (immediate family members of LEKRA artists in Bali).

139 Bali: Dennis Warner, "'Bloody liquidation' of Indonesia's P.K.I.," *Sydney Morning Herald*, June 15, 1966, ANA, 3034/2/1/8, part 14, p. 316; Shaplen, *Time*, p. 125; Vickers, *Bali*, pp. 170–1 (by the military because the village had resisted); Jones, *Indonesia*, p. 386; Hughes,

Indonesian Upheaval, p. 175. Central Java: Hughes, *Indonesian Upheaval*, p. 155 ("except the youngest children"); cf. Shaplen, *Time*, p. 122. Aceh: Bowen, *Sumatran Politics*, p. 120.

140 "Reign of terror in Java," *Times*, April 13, 1966 (no place specified); undated secret summary, ANA, 3034/2/1/8, part 15, p. 35.

141 Australian Embassy Jakarta, Political Savingram No. 10, February 25, 1966, ANA, 3034/2/1/8, part 10, p. 299, and J. M. Starey, "Notes on anti-PKI Measures in Nusa Tenggara," February 25, 1966, ANA, 3034/2/1/8, part 11, p. 67; for Bali: Stanley Karnow, "Mazz frenzy of killing," *New York Times*, April 18, 1966, ANA, 3034/2/1/8, part 13, p. 121.

142 Goodfellow, "Forgetting," p. 53, n. 11; Budiardjo, *Surviving*, pp. 158, 174–9, 190.

143 Die Verfechter des Kommandos des Präsidenten [The Advocates of the Commands of the President], "Stellt Gerechtigkeit und Wahrheit wieder her!," early December 1965, BA, DY 30 IV A2/20/671. Nasution: UPI report, January 18, 1966, 3034/2/1/8, part 9, p. 173. Quote: Danny Sunanja to Bob Haldeman, NARA, Nixon papers, WHCF SF CO Box 37 [GEN] CO 67 INDO 1969–70; similar thoughts in reference to economic success: Contenay, "Heritage of blood," German translation from *Far Eastern Economic Review*, December 14, 1967, BA, DY 30 IV A2/20/668. Himmler's Posen speech, October 4, 1943, *The Trial of the Major War Criminals before the International Military Tribunal*, vol. 29 (Nuremberg, 1948), pp. 145–6.

144 Robert Cribb, "Genocide in Indonesia, 1965–1966," *Journal of Genocide Research* 3(2), 2001, pp. 236–7.

145 Sudjatmiko, "Destruction," pp. 180, 186, 198–211; "Additional data on counter-revolutionary cruelty in Indonesia, especially in East Java," in Cribb, *Indonesian Killings*, pp. 169–76; different emphasis in "Report from East Java," pp. 136–49. See Hughes, *Indonesian Upheaval*, pp. 154, 158–61; Robert Hefner, *The Political Economy of Mountain Java* (Berkeley *et al.*: University of California Press, 1990), p. 210; Contenay, "Another bloodbath?." Fishers: "By the banks of River Brantas," in Samuel Totten, William S. Parsons and Israel W. Charny (eds.), *Century of Genocide: Eyewitness Accounts and Critical Views* (New York and London: Routledge, 1997), pp. 249–52;

interview with Ulrich Makosch, then correspondent of GDR television, November 7, 2005.

146 Sulistyo, "Years," pp. 188, 199–204, 210; supported by telegram US Consul Surabaya, December 28, 1965, NARA 250/7/2, Box 2316, POL 23–8, INDON 9/1/65.

147 Rochijat, "Am I PKI," p. 43; Cribb, "Introduction," p. 10; Hughes, *Indonesian Upheaval*, pp. 157–9.

148 Vittachi, *Fall*, p. 143.

149 Regional PKI leader Ktut Kandel claimed 100,000 members in PKI mass organizations on the island, 75,000 in the BTI and 30,000 within the party itself: US Embassy Jakarta (Vance Trent), June 30, 1965, NARA, RG59, 250/7/2, POL 18 INDON, 1/1/64. The People's Youth had 21,000–23,000 members: US Embassy Jakarta (Whittington), April 24, 1964, NARA, RG 59, 250/7/2, Box 2311, POL 12 INDON 1/1/64.

150 Robinson, *Dark Side*, pp. 286–90.

151 The RPKAD is blamed by Robinson, *Dark Side*, pp. 273–303; Robert Cribb, Soe Hok Gie *et al.*, "The mass killings in Bali," in Cribb, *Indonesian Killings*, p. 247. For the older view, which was based on the wrong assumption that the RPKAD only arrived in mid- or late December 1965: Hughes, *Indonesian Upheaval*, pp. 175–80; Vittachi, *Fall*, p. 143; Shaplen, *Time*, pp. 124–5; comments by Robinson, *Dark Side*, pp. 296–7. Uncritical Conboy, *Kopassus*, p. 149.

152 UPI report, November 7, 1965, ANA, 3034/2/1/8, part 5, p. 48 (Suharto speech to Association of Indonesian Journalists); Elson, "In Fear," pp. 180–1 (Suharto during tour to Central Java in mid-November); Sudjatmiko, "Destruction," p. 223, n. 90; for Edhie, Sundhaussen, *Road*, p. 218 (November 27); Crouch, *Army*, pp. 153–4. However, doubts remain about the intentions of such statements; on November 18, 1965, Edhie denied in the Catholic newspaper *Kompas* the obvious fact that the RPKAD conducted killing operations in Central Java (Ratih, "Soeharto's New Order," p. 52, n. 78). The military commander of the Kediri–Madiun area publically ordered an end to violence but privately said the contrary: US Embassy Jakarta, telegram December 6, 1965, NARA, RG 59, 250/7/2, Box 2317, POL 23–9, 12–1–65.

153 According to Gavi, *Konterrevolution*, p. 40, a paratrooper asserted that 5,000–7,000 people had been killed in Negara before the RPKAD arrived. Cf. FRG Embassy Jakarta, "Verluste der indonesischen Bevölkerung seit 1. Oktober d.J.," December 14, 1965, PA AA, IB5, 37, vol. 169A.

154 FRG Embassy Jakarta, "Verluste der indonesischen Bevölkerung seit 1. Oktober d.J.," December 14, 1965, PA AA, IB5, 37, vol. 169A (RPKAD arrived December 1; also noting a "first wave of riots" with numerous houses burned in mid-November); US Embassy Jakarta, November 24, 1965, NARA, RG59 250/7/2, Box 2318, POL 23–9 INDON, 11/1/65 ("extensive anti-PKI violence in Bali [...] House burning have become nightly entertainment"); US Embassy Jakarta, November 30, 1965, Box 2316, POL 18; US Consulate Surabaya, November 30, 1965, NARA, RG59 250/7/2, Box 2317, POL 23–8; Sloan, *Study*, p. 72, n. 33 (was in Bali in November 1965, where "village burnings and wholesale slaughter" were taking place); Geertz, *After the Fact*, p. 8 (a number of villages destroyed in early November); Sudjatmiko, "Destruction," pp. 217–18; Harry Thürk and Diethelm Weidemann, *Indonesien '65* (Berlin [East]: Militärverlag der DDR, 1975), p. 282. This speaks against the – contradictory – chronology established by Robinson, *Dark Side*, pp. 290–2, 303. Different interpretation in Cribb, Soe *et al.*, "Mass killings," p. 241. Arrival of RPKAD: Robinson, *Dark Side*, p. 295 (December 7–8); Conboy, *Kopassus*, p. 149.

155 Conboy, *Kopassus*, pp. 149–50; Information Nr. 6/66 for the Members and Candidates of the SED Politbureau "zur Lage der Kommunistischen Partei Indonesiens," January 19, 1966, based on a report by GDR Consulate General, January 12, BA, DY 30 IVA2/20/668; US Embassy Jakarta, telegram January 5, 1966, NARA, RG59, 250/7/2, Box 2318, POL 23–9 INDON, 1/1/66.

156 Vickers, *Bali*, pp. 171–2; see also Vittachi, *Fall*, p. 143, Seth King, "Indonesian reds still are slain despite the ouster of Nasution," *New York Times*, March 5, 1966, p. 3; US Embassy Jakarta, Masters, "Killings continue in Bali," February 25, 1966, NARA, RG 84, 631/14/50/2–3, Box 122, file without label.

157 Robert Cribb, "From Petrus to Ninja: Death squads in Indonesia," in Bruce Campbell and Arthur Brenner (eds.), *Death Squads in Global*

Perspective (New York *et al.*: Palgrave Macmillan, 2000), p. 184, with a different emphasis.

158 Goodfellow, "Forgetting," p. 54, n. 21; Amnesty International, *Indonesia*, p. 24.

159 "Rural violence in Klaten," pp. 121–57. Sudjatmiko, "Destruction," p. 4, n. 4, a fierce anti-communist, has dryly given the number of victims of leftist violence with "below 500" killed.

160 Wertheim, "Indonesia," p. 123; see Contenay, "Another bloodbath?" (Madura).

161 Southwood and Flanagan, *Indonesia*, p. 115; Mary Somers Heidhues, "Kalimantan Barat 1967–1999: Violence on the periphery," in Wessel and Wimhöfer, *Violence*, pp. 142–6; Stanley Karnow, "Suharto's worry: How to heal the wounds of the anti-Red holocaust?," *Straits Times* (Singapore), February 19, 1970 (copy), BA, DY IVA2/20/668.

162 Nancy Lee Peluso, "Passing the red bowl: Creating community identity through violence in West Kalimantan, 1967–1997," in Charles A. Coppel (ed.), *Violent Conflicts in Indonesia* (London and New York: Routledge, 2006), pp. 112, 117.

163 Wertheim, "Indonesia," p. 124; Farid, "Indonesia's original sin," p. 10. For the limited magnitude of Indonesia's land reform until 2000, see Roy Prosterman and Robert Mitchell, "Concept for land reform on Java," May 2002, www.rdiland.org/PDF/RDI_LandReformOnJava.pdf (accessed July 6, 2009), pp. 2–3; Dianto Badriadi, "Land for the landless: Why are the democrats in Jakarta not interested in land reform?," *Inside Indonesia*, October–December 2000, www.serve.com/inside/edit64/diant01.htm (accessed August 11, 2006).

164 Budiardjo, *Surviving*, p. 36; Stanley Karnow, "Mazz Frenzy of Killing," *New York Times*, April 18, 1966, ANA, 3034/2/1/8, part 13, p. 121.

165 Material in Sudjatmiko, "Destruction," pp. 241–4; Friend, *Indonesian Destinies*, p. 110; Hughes, *Indonesian Upheaval*, p. 161; Hefner, *Political Economy*, p. 210; Hefner, *Civil Islam*, p. 108; quotes: "Moslem-Flugblatt verteilt in Djakarta am 8. Oktober 1965," PA AA, IB5, 84, vol. 204.

166 Wertheim, "Indonesia," p. 123; Gardner, *Shared Hopes*, p. 203; Hindley, "Alirans," p. 32, n. 16; Sulistyo, "Years," pp. 158–60; Mortimer, *Communism*, pp. 317–19.

167 Robinson, *Dark Side*, p. 299; Vickers, *Bali*, p. 169; Gardner, *Shared Hopes*, p. 230; Hughes, *Indonesian Upheaval*, p. 177; Sudjatmiko, "Destruction," pp. 176–8.

168 Hefner, *Political Economy*, p. 210.

169 "Reign of Terror in Java," *The Times*, April 13, 1966; Cribb, "How many," p. 91; Farram, "Revolution," p. 44.

170 Dennis Warner, "'Bloody Liquidation' of Indonesia's PKI," *Sydney Morning Herald*, June 15, 1966, ANA, 3034/2/1/8, part 14, p. 316; J. M. Starey, "Notes on anti-PKI Measures in Nusa Tengarra," February 25, 1966, ANA, 3034/2/1/8, part 11, p. 68; US Consul Surabaya, April 27, 1966, NARA, RG59, 250/7/2, Box 2317, POL 23–8 INDON, 3/1/66; Ki Tristuti Rachmadi, "My life as a shadow master under Suharto," in Zurbuchen, *Beginning*, p. 42.

171 US Consulate Surabaya, telegram November 27, 1965, NARA, RG 59, 250/7/2, Box 2316, POL 23–8 INDON, 9/1/65 (from interview with a female missionary); Contenay, "Heritage of blood"; Sidney Jones, *Injustice, Persecution, Eviction: A Human Rights Update on Indonesia and East Timor* (New York and Washington: Asia Watch, 1990), p. 94.

172 Hughes, *Indonesian Upheaval*, p. 188; for different data, see Shaplen, *Time*, p. 151; Olle Törnquist, *Dilemmas of Third World Communism: The Destruction of the PKI in Indonesia* (London: Zed, 1984), p. 234; Cribb, "How many," p. 91. Cf. Goodfellow, "Forgetting," p. 53, n. 11; Orr, "Schooling," p. 183 (locally 90 percent arrested); Bowen, *Sumatran Politics*, p. 120; Farram, "Revolution," pp. 42–3 (West Timor).

173 "Reign of terror in Java", *The Times*, April 13, 1966, ANA, 752/2, part 17, p. 265.

174 Airgram, "Problems in Forming a New Indonesian Political Regime," April 23, 1966, NARA, RG 59, 250/7/2, Box 2312, POL 15 INDON.

175 Putra, "Reflections," esp. pp. 67, 74–5; Friend, *Indonesian Destinies*, p. 111; Rochijat, "Am I PKI," pp. 43–4, 50; Gavi, *Konterrevolution*, p. 13; Wieringa, *Sexual Politics*, p. 306.

176 Ryter, "Youth," pp. 60–2, 98 (quote), 124–6; CIA, *Indonesia*, photos pp. 95ff.; Cribb and Brown, *Modern Indonesia*, p. 92. Gambling: Jones, *Indonesia*, p. 402.

177 May, *Indonesian Tragedy*, p. 132.

178 Examples: Bowen, *Sumatran Politics*, p. 120; Amnesty International, *Indonesia*, p. 24. For assessments, see Dwyer, "Intimacy," pp. 5–9; Jean-Louis Margolin, "Indonésie 1965: Un massacre oublié," *Revue Internationale de Politique Comparée*, 8(1), 2001, p. 83.

179 Kahin, *Rebellion*, p. 244; Amnesty International, *Indonesia*, pp. 35–6, 103 (2,000 of 15,000–30,000).

180 See Wieringa, *Sexual Politics*, pp. 301–17.

181 Clifford Geertz, *The Religion of Java* (Glencoe, IL: Free Press, 1960), esp. pp. 5–6; Geertz, *Agricultural Involution: The Process of Ecological Change in Indonesia* (Berkeley: University of California Press, 1963). It is controversial whether these distinctions were valid in cultural–religious terms and in how far Javanese themselves regarded the *prijaji* as a separate group: Eka Darmaputera, *Pancasila and the Search for Identity and Modernity in Indonesian Society* (Leiden: E. J. Brill, 1988), pp. 74–83, and Ernst Utrecht, "Class struggle and politics in Java," *Journal of Contemporary Asia* 2(3), 1972, p. 282, n. 18; cf. Törnquist, *Dilemmas*, pp. 134–6.

182 Koentjaraningrat, "Village," p. 393 (the manuscript was completed in June 1964); see Sartono Kartodirdjo, *Modern Indonesia: Tradition and Transformation* (Yogyakarta: Gadjah Mada University Press, 1984), pp. 60–2.

183 Van der Kroef, *Communist Party*, pp. 192, 327–8, n. 39; Kartodirdjo, *Indonesia*, p. 60.

184 Ingela Gerdin, *The Unknown Balinese: Land, Labour and Inequality in Lombok* (Gothenburg: Acta Universitatis Gothoburgensis, 1982), pp. 85, 96; van der Kroef, *Communist Party*, p. 194; Lance Brennan, Les Heathcote and Anton Lucas, "The causation of famine: A comparative analysis of Lombok and Bengal 1891–1974," *South*

Asia 7, 1984, p. 16; Margo Lyon, *Bases of Conflict in Rural Indonesia* (Berkeley: University of California Press, 1976 [first edition 1971]), pp. 17, 25, 27.

185 Kolko, *Confronting*, p. 185; Schlereth and Bintang, *Indonesien*, p. 200; Farid, "Indonesia's original sin," p. 11.

186 Bresnan, *Managing*, pp. 56, 66.

187 Ina Slamet, "Youth and village development" (from her 1963 book *Principles of Village Development*), in Feith and Castles, *Indonesian Political Thinking*, pp. 405–6.

188 Shaplen, *Time*, pp. 150, 158 (observations near Bandung and in Solo); Marni, "I am a leaf," pp. 56–7.

189 Utrecht, "Class struggle," pp. 279–80.

190 Clark Cunningham, "Soba: An Atoni village of West Timor," and Koentjaraningrat, "Tjelapur: A village in South Central Java," in Koentjaraningrat, *Villages*, pp. 80, 265; Carol Warren, *Adat and Dinas: Balinese Communities in the Indonesian State* (Kuala Lumpur *et al.*: Oxford University Press, 1993), pp. 42–6.

191 Bresnan, *Managing*, p. 19; van der Kroef, *Communist Party*, p. 207.

192 Van der Kroef, *Communist Party*, p. 207. East Java: "Informationsbericht unseres Korrespondenten in Djakarta: Bedrohliche Wirtschaftslage in Indonesien" (no date, late 1964), BA, DY 30 IV A2/20/671, and George Benson, "Conversation with Major Sutedjo [...]," May 27–30, 1964, NARA, RG 59, 250/7/2, Box 2311, POL 12 INDON, 1/1/64.

193 Maslyn Williams, *Five Journeys from Jakarta: Inside Sukarno's Indonesia* (New York: W. Morrow, 1965), p. 127; Vickers, *Bali*, p. 169; Robinson, *Dark Side*, pp. 239–40; Jones, *Indonesia*, p. 385; Graeme MacRae, "The value of land in Bali: Land tenure, landreform and commodification," in Reuter, *Inequality*, p. 145; even higher figures are given by Sudjatmiko, "Destruction," pp. 143–4 (148,000 "menaced by hunger"). For West Timor 1964–65, Farram, "Revolution," pp. 38–9.

194 Brennan *et al.*, "Causation," pp. 15–18; Schlereth and Bintang, *Indonesien*, p. 200; US Embassy Jakarta, Joint Weeka no. 38,

September 22, 1966, NARA, RG 59, 250/7/2, Box 2309, POL 2–1, INDON 1966; FRG Embassy Jakarta, "Neue Naturkatastrophen in Indonesien," September 29, 1966, PA AA, IB5, 37, vol. 255 (quote).

195 Williams, *Five Journeys*, pp. 291–4; cf. Mortimer, *Communism*, p. 300; Robinson, *Dark Side*, p. 241.

196 Biweekly Economic Review, July 11–24, 1966, NARA, RG59 250/6/4, SNF Box 722, E 2–2 1/1/66.

197 For the latter, R. A. F. Paul Webb, "The sickle and the cross: Christians and communists in Bali, Flores, Sumba and Timor, 1965–67," *Journal of Southeast Asian Studies* 17(1), 1986, pp. 99–100.

198 Sloan, *Study*, p. 84; fundamental: J. A. C. Mackie, *Problems of the Indonesian Inflation* (Ithaca: Southeast Asia Program, Cornell University, 1967), for redistributive effects pp. 51–63.

199 Bresnan, *Managing*, pp. 55–9; FRG Embassy Jakarta, "Innenpolitische Situation in Indonesien," September 27, 1965, PA AA, IB5, 37, vol. 169A; various reports in ANA, 752/2/2, part 5, pp. 13, 27, 37, 53–4, 98–99, in 3107/40/106, part 13, pp. 227–8, and NARA, RG 84, 631/14/50/2–3, Box 115, E 2–2, 1965; Williams *et al.*, *Javanese Lives*, pp. 17, 27, 50, 148.

200 Gardner, *Shared Hopes*, p. 211. For regional variations, see Information report by ADN correspondent Jakarta, September 21, 1966, PA AA, MfAA, vol. 16075, p. 130, and ANA, 752/2/2, part 4.

201 See Slamet, "Youth," based on a case study of the Klaten area where violence would later be excessive.

202 See Wieringa, *Sexual Politics*, pp. 288, 301, stressing the first of the two arguments.

203 Wieringa, *Sexual Politics*, pp. 1–9; Marianne Klute, "Women against violence: A spectator's view on political change within and initiated by the Indonesian Women's Movement," in Wessel and Wimhöfer, *Violence*, pp. 212–3.

204 Mortimer, *Communism*, pp. 284–91; van der Kroef, *Communist Party*, p. 202; Warren, *Adat*, pp. 292–3.

205 Utrecht, "Class struggle," p. 277; MacRae, "Value," pp. 154–5; Mortimer, *Communism*, p. 290; Robinson, *Dark Side*, pp. 268–9. Limited reach: Bresnan, *Managing*, p. 17.

206 Mortimer, *Communism*, pp. 277, 296–303, 309–22; Warren, *Adat*, p. 275; Lyon, *Bases*, pp. 52–3.

207 McVey, "Teaching Modernity," pp. 5, 25–6; van der Kroef, *Communist Party*, pp. 147, 201; see also Törnquist, *Dilemmas*, p. 208, Mortimer, *Communism*, pp. 304–8.

208 Mortimer, *Communism*, pp. 282–4; Clifford Geertz, "Thingan: A Balinese village," in Koentjaraningrat, *Villages*, pp. 136–7.

209 Utrecht, "Class struggle," p. 274.

210 Williams, *Five Journeys*, pp. 292, 294; Farram, "Revolution," pp. 38–9.

211 Some analysts hold that there was already a longer tradition of political competition and radical social movements in the countryside: Bresnan, *Managing*, pp. 20–1.

212 J. Eliseo Rocamora, "Political participation and the party system: The PNI example," in William Liddle (ed.), *Political Participation in Modern Indonesia* (New Haven: Yale University Southeast Asia Studies, 1973), pp. 143–76; indicating a similar trend more reluctantly: US Embassy Jakarta, Airgram, September 16, 1964, NARA, RG 59, 250/7/2, Box 2311, POL 12 INDON, 7/1/64.

213 These included the Catholic Party, Parkindo (Party of Indonesian Christians [Protestant]), the PSII (Islamic Association Party), IPKI, Perti (a leftist Islamic party), and Partindo (Indonesian Party, the party of Indonesian Chinese).

214 See PA AA, IB5, 81, vol. 208, particularly FRG Embassy Jakarta, July 26, 1965; "Political Parties," March 11, 1961, ANA, 3034/2/2/4, pp. 162–3 (noted 565,987 registered NU members and 1,750,000 PNI members "checked by the authorities"); Rocamora, "Political participation," pp. 154, 174, n. 7; Mortimer, *Communism*, p. 314, n. 84 (PNI peasant organization Petani claimed three million members).

215 Telegram Lüdde-Neurath, November 10, 1966, PA AA, IB5, 37, vol. 255; GDR Consulate General, April 1, 1965, PA AA, MfAA, vol. 16186, p. 37; US Embassy Jakarta, Airgram, August 9, 1965, NARA, RG 59, 250/7/2, Box 2311, POL 12 INDON, 7/1/65. For labor unions cf. BA, DY 34, vol. 11466 (Sarbumusi linked to NU, KBM linked to PNI, SOBSI to IPKI, SOBRI to Murba, GOBSI to PSII, etc.), and DY 30/IV A 2/20/670; Rocamora, "Political participation," p. 166.

216 Utrecht, "Class struggle," p. 278, citing Clifford Geertz; Andrea Wilcox Palmer, "Situradja: A village in Highland Java," and Harsja Bachtiar, "'Negeri' Taran: A Minangkabau village community," in Koentjaraningrat, *Villages*, pp. 323–4, 384; Cayrac-Blanchard, *Parti Communiste*, p. 75. The dissenting view that political parties represented urban politics isolated from the village (Sloan, *Study*, pp. 25, 29–30, 42) appears much exaggerated.

217 Guy Pauker, "Communist prospects in Indonesia," prepared for the US Air Force/Rand Corporation, November 1964, p. 20.

218 US Foreign Service Dispatch, "Illiteracy in Indonesia," September 8, 1960, ANA, 3034/1/1, part 2, p. 112; Heads of Mission Meeting, Bangkok, December 1965, ANA, 3034/2/1, part 48, p. 179.

219 CIA, *Indonesia*, p. 145, n., and Hughes, *Indonesian Upheaval*, pp. 37–8. For members of a royal family in Bali killed as communists see Gardner, *Shared Hopes*, p. 230.

220 Sudjatmiko, "Destruction," pp. 241–4; "Rural violence in Klaten," pp. 123–6; Sulistyo, "Years," pp. 140–1, 148–54, 160–8; Lyon, *Bases*, pp. 48–59, 65. Emphasis on PKI supporting sharecroppers in US Embassy Jakarta, "Some Observations By Professor Ruth McVey on the PKI and Political Currents in East and Central Java," February 23, 1965, NARA, RG 59, 250/7/2, Box 2311, POL 12, 1/1/65; Center for Village Studies, Gadjah Mada University, "Rural violence in Bali," in Cribb, *Indonesian Killings*, pp. 249–51.

221 "Report on Land Reform Strife," March 10, 1965, NARA, RG 84, 631/14/50/2–3, Box 115, E12; and Fred Coffey, Voice of America, Washington, to Green, "Surabaya – Impressions and Recommendations," August 19, 1965, NARA, RG 84, 631/14/50/2–3, Box 116, Political Affairs and Religion, Pol Affs: Countries A–Z.

222 See ANA, 3034/2/1, part 45, pp. 86, 241; FRG Embassy telegram March 9 and reports of March 15 and 29, 1965, PA AA, IB5, 37, vol. 169A; US Embassy Jakarta reports February 23, March 22 and 30, 1965 and US Consulate Surabaya, May 18, 1965, NARA, RG 59, 250/7/2, Box 2311, POL 12, 1/1/65; Sudjatmiko, "Destruction," pp. 171–4.

223 Walkin, "Moslem–Communist confrontation," pp. 822–47; Sudjatmiko, "Destruction," pp. 148, 241–6; Brackman, *Collapse*, pp. 45, 222, n. 3; Robinson, *Dark Side*, p. 270.

224 Hefner, *Civil Islam*, p. 54; FRG Embassy Jakarta, March 15 and 29, 1965, PA AA, IB5, 37, vol. 169A.

225 Mortimer, *Communism*, pp. 381–5, 116–17; Crouch, *Army*, pp. 87–94.

226 Telegram Jones, March 16, 1965, NARA, RG 84, 631/14/50/2–3 Jakarta Embassy, Box 116, DEF 1–8; see Kahin, *Rebellion*, p. 239.

227 British Embassy Jakarta, "Visit to Major General I. Adjie," NARA, RG 59, 250/7/2, Box 2311, POL 12 INDON, 1/1/65; similar remarks to the CSSR Ambassador are mentioned in a report by the GDR Consul General, June 3, 1965, PA AA, MfAA, A16073, 63 (Adjie threatened to "kill Aidit with his own hands" if the PKI deviated from state policies).

228 Telegram Green 635A, October 14, 1965, NARA, RG 84, 631/14/50/2–3 Jakarta Embassy, Box 118, POL 23–9, Oct 7–14, 1965; Telegram Green, December 1, 1965, NARA, RG 84, 631/14/50/2–3 Jakarta Embassy, Box 118, POL 23–9, Dec 1–31, 1965 (20,000); Australian Embassy Jakarta, Savingram No. 22, May 16, 1966, ANA, 3034/2/2/8, part 14, p. 40 (56,000); Schlereth and Bintang, *Indonesien*, p. 242 (73,000 by 1969).

229 UPI report, December 11, 1965, ANA, 3034/2/1/8, part 7, p. 162.

230 See Schlereth and Bintang, *Indonesien*, p. 187; GDR Consulate General to FDJ Central Council, February 8, 1966, PA AA, MfAA, A16184, p. 45.

231 Kees van Dijk, "The privatization of the public order: Relying on the Satgas," in Wessel and Wimhöfer, *Violence*, p. 158; Hefner, *Civil Islam*, pp. 54–5; "Rural violence in Klaten," p. 133; Sudjatmiko, "Destruction," p. 170. For earlier village defense bodies in Bali Robinson, *Dark Side*, pp. 228–9.

232 Memorandum of Conversation, "NU Youth Group," July 14, 1964, NARA, RG 59, 250/7/2, Box 2311, POL 12, 7/1/64. The Ansor leaders implicitly asked the US Embassy for financial support.

233 Australian Embassy Jakarta, Political Savingram No. 54, October 28, 1965, ANA, 3034/2/1, part 48, p. 64; see Charles Coppel, *Indonesian Chinese in Crisis* (Kuala Lumpur: Oxford University Press, 1983), pp. 31–4; Törnquist, *Dilemmas*, pp. 102–4; Crouch, *Army*, pp. 47, 244.

234 Hamish McDonald, *Suharto's Indonesia* (Honolulu: University of Hawaii Press, 1980), pp. 29–32; Elson, *Suharto*, pp. 60–5, 71–2, 76–8, 88; Bresnan, *Managing*, p. 46; Bryan Evans III, "The influence of the United States Army on the development of the Indonesian Army (1956–1964)," *Indonesia* 47, April 1989, pp. 34–7. With emphasis on post-1965, when this became "normal business practice," Crouch, *Army*, pp. 277–9, 282, 285–99.

235 Farid, "Indonesia's original sin," p. 4; Crouch, *Army*, pp. 302–3.

236 Cf. Stoler, *Capitalism*, pp. 157–61; Utrecht, "Class struggle," p. 279; LR Dr. Hallier, "Politische Lagebeurteilung für Nordsumatra," February 26, 1965, PA AA, IB5, 37, vol. 169A.

237 Stoler, *Capitalism*, pp. 163–6; Kahin, *Rebellion*, pp. 243–5.

238 FRG military attaché, report of January 8, 1965, PA AA, IB5, 37, vol. 169A.

239 Fein, "Revolutionary," p. 805, refers to this in terms of "cleavages."

240 Schlereth and Bintang, *Indonesien*, 177; Robinson, *Dark Side*, p. 272. In Lombok, local memory records 50,000 victims with Muslim Sasaks targeting communists, Balinese, and Chinese elites: Cribb, "Introduction," p. 25.

241 Utrecht, "Class struggle," pp. 278, 280.

242 Challis, *Shadow*, p. 107.

243 For 1959 to 1974, see J. A. C. Mackie, "Anti-Chinese outbreaks in Indonesia, 1959–1968," in Mackie (ed.), *The Chinese in Indonesia* (Honolulu: University of Hawaii Press, 1976), pp. 77–138.

244 Seymour Topping, "Violence and bias buffet the Chinese alien in Southeast Asia," *New York Times*, April 24, 1966, p. 9.

245 Coppel, *Indonesian Chinese*, esp. pp. 5, 31–41; Mackie, "Outbreaks," pp. 129–31; and the files PA AA, IB5, 81, vol. 198, and PA AA, MfAA, A 16165.

246 Coppel, *Indonesian Chinese*, pp. 43–51; Mackie, "Outbreaks," pp. 82–110; Schlereth and Bintang, *Indonesien*, p. 109; US Consulate Medan, "Fearful Mind of the Chinese in Java Pushes Them

Leftwards," early September 1965, NARA, RG 59, 250/7/2, Box 2311, POL 12 INDON 7/1/65.

247 Note of the Chinese Embassy in Indonesia, April 11, 1966, I Isinhua version (copy), PA AA, IB5, 81, vol. 198, Note of the Chinese Embassy in Indonesia, November 4, 1965, PA AA, IB5, 37, vol. 255. Part of the following rests on a series of such protest notes by the Chinese Embassy in Jakarta which appear as detailed and well-informed sources.

248 "Thursday – 25.11.1965," note about a broadcast by Radio Peking of November 24, citing from the diplomatic note of the Chinese Embassy in Indonesia, PA AA, IB5, 81, vol. 198; US Embassy, Joint Weeka no. 43, November 30, 1965, NARA, RG 59, 250/7/2, Box 2309, POL 2–1 INDON; US Embassy, telegram December 20, 1965, NARA, RG 59, 250/7/2, Box 2317, POL 23–9 INDON, 12/1/65. For Medan, Note by Chinese Embassy Jakarta, December 18, 1965, PA AA, IB5, 37, vol. 255.

249 Coppel, *Indonesian Chinese*, p. 58.

250 "Further Notes on the Problem of the Indonesian Chinese," October 28, 1966, ANA, 3034/2/5/1, part 3, p. 122; Coppel, *Indonesian Chinese*, pp. 60–1; for Aceh, see also Anderson, "Introduction," p. 18; "Political Killings in Indonesia," July 1966, ANA, 3034/2/1/8, part 15A, pp. 84–5; Mackie, "Outbreaks," p. 117.

251 Note of the Chinese Embassy in Indonesia, April 11, 1966 (copy), PA AA, IB5, 81, vol. 198.

252 Jamie Davidson and Douglas Kammen, "Indonesia's unknown war and the lineages of violence in West Kalimantan," *Indonesia* 73, April 2002, pp. 68, 72–3; "A visit to West Kalimantan 14th–20th November 1968," ANA 3034/2/6/5, p. 159 (by October 1968, at least 20,000 people were still living in camps, 14,000 had left the province).

253 Australian Embassy Jakarta, Savingram No. 28, June 10, 1966, ANA 3034/2/2/2, part 15, p. 69 (based on a conversation with the Attorney General, Major-General Sugiharto); Kahin, *Rebellion*, p. 244 (refers to observations by Oei Tjoe Tat, leader of Baperki and member of Sukarno's Fact Finding Commission).

254 Telegram FRG Embassy Jakarta, October 18, 1965, and report Werz, December 6, 1965, PA AA, IB5, 81, vol. 198; telegram Green,

October 14, 1965, NARA, RG 84, 631/14/50/2–3 Jakarta Embassy, Box 118, POL 23–9, October 7–14, 1965 (smaller cities in East Java). Crouch, *Army*, p. 146, states that anti-Chinese demonstrations started around October 7.

255 Arthur J. Dommen, "The attempted coup in Indonesia," *Chinese Quarterly* 25, January–March 1966, p. 151; Anderson and McVey, *Preliminary Analysis*, p. 61; Shaplen, *Time*, p. 150; Note by Chinese Embassy Jakarta, November 27, 1965, PA AA IB5, 37, vol. 255.

256 "Kurzzusammenfassung eines Naszabadsag-Korrespondenten über seine Reise nach Zentral- und Ostjava," PA AA, MfAA, A 16166, p. 114. Towns and cities mentioned were Bandung, Bandjar, Purwokarto, Solo, Bojolali, Klaten, Yogyakarta, Semarang, and Surabaya.

257 Interview with Rahman Tolleng, former student activist, December 1980, in Raillon, *Etudiants*, p. 306.

258 Report Werz, December 6, 1965, PA AA, IB5, 81, vol. 198; cf. telegram Green, November 12, 1965, NARA, RG 84, 631/14/50/2–3, POL 23–9, November 10–19, 1965; for more cases: Note by Chinese Embassy, December 9, 1965, PA AA, IB5, 37, vol. 255.

259 Note of Chinese Embassy in Indonesia, December 20, 1965, PA AA, IB5, 81, vol. 198; second quote: Vittachi, *Fall*, p. 143; cf. Vickers, *Bali*, pp. 171–2.

260 Report Heimsoeth, "Indonesisch-chinesische Beziehungen," April 14, 1966, PA AA, IB5, 81, vol. 198; his telegrams April 15 and 18, 1966, PA AA, 37, IB5, vol. 255; Coppel, *Indonesian Chinese*, pp. 66–7.

261 Australian Embassy Jakarta, Savingram No. 62, December 17, 1965, ANA, 3034/2/1, part 48, p. 189; cf. telegram Werz, November 10, 1965, PA AA, IB5, 37, Nr. 169A.

262 Telegram Heimsoeth April 15, 1966, PA AA, 37, IB5, vol. 255; Report Heimsoeth, "Indonesisch-chinesische Beziehungen," April 14, 1966, PA AA, IB5, 81, vol. 198; Charles Coppel, "Patterns of Chinese political activity in Indonesia," in Mackie, *Chinese*, p. 64.

263 Sheldon W. Simon, *The Broken Triangle: Peking, Djakarta and the PKI* (Baltimore: Johns Hopkins Press, 1969), p. 142; US Embassy Jakarta, Joint Weeka no. 17, April 29, 1966, NARA, RG 59, 250/7/2,

Box 2309, POL 2–1, 1966 INDON; in general Mackie, "Outbreaks," pp. 115–28.

264 Extensive material in ANA, 3034/2/5/1, Part 3, and PA AA, IB5, 81, vol. 198; Coppel, *Indonesian Chinese*, pp. 66–9, 92–3, 100–1, 159–60; Mackie, "Outbreaks," pp. 116, 120, 233, n. 79.

265 US Embassy Jakarta, Joint Weeka No. 17, April 29, 1966, NARA, RG 59, 250/7/2, Box 2309, POL 2–1 INDON 1966; US Embassy Jakarta, Biweekly Economic Review, November 30, 1965, RG 84, 631/14/50/2–3, Box 115, E 2–2 1965.

266 US Consulate Medan, "Political Notes – September 1966," NARA, RG 59, 250/7/2, Box 2308, POL 2 INDON, 1/1/66; "Einschätzung der illegalen Partindo," ca. August 1966, PA AA, MfAA, A 16075, p. 124; Simon, *Broken Triangle*, p. 161; Hughes, *Indonesian Upheaval*, pp. 200–1; Inward Savingram no. 17, April 14, 1967, ANA, 3034/2/5/1, part 3, p. 222.

267 See US Embassy Jakarta, Airgram April 27, 1966, NARA, RG 59, 250/7/2, Box 2313, POL 15 INDON; Mackie, "Outbreaks," p. 131.

268 Several reports in ANA, 3034/2/5/1, part 3; Coppel, *Indonesian Chinese*, pp. 102–3, 117–19.

269 Budiardjo, *Surviving*, p. 125; Ryter, "Youth," p. 127; cf. Coppel, *Indonesian Chinese*, p. 58; "Position of the Chinese," excerpt, January 1967, ANA, 3034/2/5/1, part 3, p. 177.

270 FRG Embassy Jakarta, March 2, 1971, PA AA, IB5, 81, vol. 198.

271 FRG Embassy Jakarta, "Unruhen in West-Kalimantan," November 21, 1967, PA AA, IB5, 81, Nr. 208; "A Visit to West Kalimantan 14th–20th November 1968," ANA 3034/2/6/5, p. 159; Davidson and Kammen, "Indonesia's unknown war," pp. 56–87; Justus van der Kroef, "The Sarawak–Indonesian border insurgency," *Modern Asian Studies* 2(3), 1968, pp. 245–65; Somers Heidhues, "Kalimantan Barat," pp. 241–6; Coppel, *Indonesian Chinese*, pp. 145–9.

272 [Sydney Morning] *Herald*, April 24, 1967, ANA, 3034/2/5/1, part 3, p. 242; van der Kroef, "Border insurgency," p. 255; Mackie, "Outbreaks," pp. 96, 234, n. 90.

273 See also the thoughts by Mackie, "Outbreaks," p. 129.

274 A Partai Katolik members gave a list of 200 Baperki members in Kudus for arrest to the military that "constituted a 'Who's Who' of the Kudus business community." All were interrogated. US Embassy Jakarta, Martens, December 10, 1965, NARA, RG 59, 250/7/2, Box 2312, POL 12 INDON, 10/1/65.

275 Kampto Utomo, "Villages of unplanned resettlers in the Subdistrict Kaliredjo, Central Lampung," in Koentjaraningrat, *Villages*, pp. 282, 297. In North Sumatra (except Aceh), for example, 2.5 million out of a population of 4.5 million were Javanese, compared to only two million Bataks and others of regional origin: LR Dr. Hallier, "Politische Lagebeurteilung für Nordsumatra," February 26, 1965, PA AA, IB5, 37, vol. 169A.

276 Cf. Budi Agustono, "Violence on North Sumatra's plantations," in Colombijn and Lindblat, *Roots*, esp. p. 134; Utomo, "Villages," pp. 282, 297; Wertheim, "Indonesia," p. 124.

277 Kahin, *Rebellion*, p. 244, cf. p. 249.

278 See Elizabeth Fuller Collins, "Indonesia: A violent culture?," *Asian Survey* 42(4), 2002, p. 600; Cribb, *Historical Atlas*, p. 170 ("many thousands" killed).

279 Bowen, *Sumatran Politics*, pp. 120–1.

280 Wertheim, "Indonesia," pp. 123, 125.

281 For example, 400,000–500,000 in North Sumatra, according to note by Hallier (see note 275); 747,000 of a population of 1.9 million in West Kalimantan: "A visit to West Kalimantan, 14th–20th November 1968," ANA, 3034/2/6/5, p. 163.

282 Webb, "Sickle," p. 97. These five 'monotheistic' religions included Islam, Buddhism, Protestantism, Catholicism and, oddly, Hinduism.

283 For Bali: Challis, *Shadow*, p. 108; Leslie Dwyers and Degung Santikarma, "'When the World Turned to Chaos': 1965 and Its Aftermath in Bali, Indonesia," in Robert Gellately and Ben Kiernan (eds.), *The Spectre of Genocide* (Cambridge: Cambridge University Press, 2003), p. 302. Cf. Cribb, "Introduction," pp. 24–5. See Farram, "Revolution," pp. 35–6.

284 Van der Kroef, "Indonesian communism," p. 40; Conboy, *Kopassus*, p. 170.

285 Hefner, *Political Economy*, esp. pp. 210–1. By contrast, Margolin, "Indonésie," p. 82, points to the persecution of Hindus in East Java yet without presenting evidence.

286 Cribb, "Genocide," p. 227; Dwyer, "Intimacy," pp. 6–8.

287 Gavi, *Konterrevolution*, pp. 12–13; J. M. Starey, "Notes on anti-PKI Measures in Nusa Tengarra," February 25, 1966, ANA, 3034/2/1/8, part 11, p. 67; Vickers, *Bali*, p. 171.

288 Hughes, *Indonesian Upheaval*, p. 186, with reference to Adam Malik; CIA, Office of National Estimates, Memo, "The Outlook for Indonesia," March 2, 1966, NARA, CIA database.

289 US Consulate Medan, November 18, 1965, NARA, RG 84, 630/14/50/2–3, POL 23–9, November 10–19.

290 British Consul in Medan, March 30, 1966, quoted in Kahin, *Rebellion*, p. 244; Australian Embassy Jakarta, Political Savingram No. 52, October 22, 1965, ANA, 3107/40/106, part 13, p. 131; Bowen, *Sumatran Politics*, p. 121; Dwyer, "Intimacy," pp. 4–5; eyewitness report "By the banks of River Brantas," in Totten *et al.*, *Century*, p. 252; "*The Age*," Melbourne, September 13, 1966, ANA, 3034/2/2/2, part 15, p. 135.

291 Southwood and Flanagan, *Indonesia*, p. 103; Budiardjo, *Surviving*, pp. 73–4, 78; Robert Cribb, "The Indonesian massacres," in Totten *et al.*, *Century*, p. 241.

292 Robert Cribb, "Unresolved problems in the Indonesian killings of 1965–66," *Asian Survey* 42(4), 2002, pp. 554–5 (Cribb errs if he asserts an "absence of even anecdotal evidence of such revenge seeking").

293 In this sense, political violence would include religious, ethnic, and economic motivations.

294 Die Verfechter des Kommandos des Präsidenten, "Stellt Gerechtigkeit und Wahrheit wieder her!" (pro-Sukarno leaflet, early December 1965), BA, DY 30 IVA2/20/671; interview with Ulrich Makosch, November 7, 2005; Rocamora, "Political participation," p. 143; US Embassy Jakarta, July 13, 1966, NARA, RG59, 250/7/2, Box 2316, POL23. PSI: Sudjatmiko, "Destruction," pp. 228–30.

295 Quoted after information report by ADN correspondent in Jakarta, July 20, 1966, PA AA, MfAA, A 16075, pp. 110–11.

296 US Consulate Surabaya, November 30, 1965, NARA, RG 59, 250/7/2, Box 2317, POL 23–8; US Embassy Jakarta, telegram, January 6, 1966, NARA, RG 84, 631/14/50/2–3, Box 124, POL 18 Central & East Java.

297 Bowen, *Sumatran Politics*, pp. 118, 120–1; Kahin, *Rebellion*, p. 245.

298 US Consulate Medan, December 12, 1965, NARA, RG 59, 250/7/2, Box 2317, POL 23–9, 12–1–65.

299 Quoted after Warner, "Bloody liquidation."

300 Australian Embassy Jakarta, Savingram No. 64, December 23, 1965, ANA, 3034/2/1, part 48, p. 222; cf. the thoughts by Hefner, *Civil Islam*, pp. 64, 244, n. 13.

301 The further phases of mass violence cannot be discussed in detail here. On a lower level, murders continued until mid-1966, open killings wore down in 1969 when guerrilla fighting ceased. The transfer of prisoners to Buru island marked the "tail end" of this period (Budiardjo, *Surviving*, p. 133). The release of most prisoners from Buru by 1979 – under pressure by Amnesty International and some foreign journalists – terminated the phase of mass detention, during which hundreds still died from the miserable conditions in prisons and camps. By then, both economic conditions and the Suharto regime had stabilized.

302 Confidential telegram Green, November 27, 1965, NARA, RG 59, 250/7/2, Box 2318, POL 23–9 INDON, 11/1/65. Petrol and transportation prices had been raised on November 22: Sundhaussen, *Road*, p. 229.

303 FRG Embassy Jakarta, telegram January 11 and reports of January 13 and May 12, 1966, PA AA, IB5, 37, vol. 255

304 Various reports in ANA, 752/2/2, part 5, pp. 13, 27, 37, 53–4, 98–9, in 3107/40/106, part 13, pp. 227–8, and NARA, RG 84, 631/14/50/2–3, Box 115, E 2–2, 1965.

305 Hughes, *Indonesian Upheaval*, p. 203.

306 Ratih, "Soeharto's New Order," pp. 22, 32; Information report by ADN correspondent in Jakarta, October 21, 1965, BA, DY 30 IV A2/20/671.

307 Masashi Nishihara, *The Japanese and Sukarno's Indonesia: Tokyo–Jakarta Relations 1951–1966* (Honolulu: University of Hawaii Press, 1976), p. 201 (cf. pp. 195–6).

308 Quoted in secret cablegram by Australian Embassy Jakarta, January 4, 1966, ANA, 3034/2/1/8, part 8, p. 243.

309 Weekly Political Savingram No. 2, January 14, 1966, ANA 3034/2/1, part 48, pp. 245–6; Elson, *Suharto*, pp. 130–4.

310 For Bali, a local history states that after January 1, 1966 "mass actions" against communists ceased and the military brought "order to the methods used": quoted after Robinson, *Dark Side*, p. 297.

311 US Consulate Surabaya, "The NU Star Declines," March 21, 1966, NARA, RG 59, 250/7/2, Box 2311, POL 12 INDON, 1/1/66; US Consulate Surabaya, telegrams November 30, December 10 and 28, 1965, Box 2316, POL 23–8 INDON, 9/1/65; "Additional Data," in Cribb, *Indonesian Killings*, pp. 174, 176. For a local sequence of uncontrolled violence brought under control, Hefner, *Political Economy*, p. 210, who also argued the "greatest portion" of killings was over by late December (Hefner, *Civil Islam*, p. 64). Stanley Karnow argued that such calls were "largely ignored" and killings continued to February: "Mazz frenzy," p. 121. An Ansor spokesman said that the killings lasted "from October to January": Hughes, *Indonesian Upheaval*, p. 159. For Bali, J.M. Starey, "Notes on anti-PKI Measures in Nusa Tengarra," February 15, 1966, ANA, 3034/2/1/8, part 11, p. 68.

312 US Embassy Jakarta (Masters), "Sukarno lies to Subchan," January 21, 1966, RG 59, 250/7/2, Box 2312, POL 15–1 INDON, 1/1/66 (based on a meeting with "second echelon Masjumi leader" H. Susidy). Cf. Australian Embassy Jakarta, Political Savingram, January 7, 1966, ANA, 3034/2/1/8, part 9, p. 16. Possibly, Second NU Chairman Sjaichu had been sent on a similar mission to East Java but rather called to "liquidate all communists" earlier: telegrams US Consulate Surabaya, November 30 and December 6, 1965, NARA, RG 59, 250/7/2, POL 23–9 INDON, 12–1-65.

313 Report of January 3, 1966 quoted after Kahin, *Rebellion*, p. 243; Cribb, "Introduction," p. 27.

314 US Consulate, "Medan Bi-Weekly Roundup of Events," January 19 to February 1, February 2, 1966, NARA, RG 59, 250/7/2, Box 2308;

Australian Embassy Jakarta, Political Savingram No. 10, February 25, 1966, ANA, 3034/2/1/8, part 10, p. 299.

315 Copy of an undated, secret document of the Australian Ministry of External Affairs without title summarizing the violence, ANA 3034/2/1/8, part 15, p. 35 ("The period of greatest violence seems to have been between November [1965] and January [1966], but killings on a lesser scale seem to have been continued until quite recently"); Information report by ADN correspondent in Jakarta, February 10, 1966, PA AA, MfAA, A 16166, p. 204 ("the wave of murders und the hunt on communists have finished"); Michael van Langenberg, "Gestapu and state power in Indonesia," in Cribb, *Indonesian Killings*, p. 51, n. 12.

316 Conboy, *Kopassus*, pp. 149–50; *Canberra Times*, January 5, 1966, ANA, 3034/2/1/8, part 8, p. 266; Central Java: "Crushing the G30S/ PKI," p. 166. Cf. for a retreat in late January from Bojolali, Gavi, *Konterrevolution*, p. 14.

317 Australian Embassy Jakarta, "KAMI Economic Seminar," February 10, 1966, ANA 752/2, Part 17, pp. 176–85; Australian Embassy Jakarta, Weekly Political Savingram No. 2, January 14, 1966, ANA 3034/2/1, part 48, pp. 245–6; CIA, *Indonesia*, p. 95, n.; Elson, *Suharto*, pp. 130, 134; May, *Indonesian Tragedy*, p. 133; Sundhaussen, *Road*, p. 230; Penders and Sundhaussen, *Nasution*, p. 195; Southwood and Flanagan, *Indonesia*, p. 179.

318 FRG Embassy, Reports of January 11 and March 3 (twice), PA AA, 37, IB5, vol. 255; Sundhaussen, *Road*, pp. 230–4.

319 Excerpts of the report were published in *Angkatan Bersendjata* which was, according to an East German diplomat, controlled by General Nasution, while the report was said to have been launched by General Sukendro. A fierce opponent of Sukarno's, Sukendro hardly meant to damage the reputation of RPKAD at all. GDR Consulate General, "Zur Lage in den indonesischen Streitkräften," March 4, 1966, PA AA, MfAA, Nr. 16175 ("The report discredited Soeharto's cutthroats of the RPKAD units who had acted in an SS manner in Central Java and Bali").

320 Conboy, *Kopassus*, pp. 150–3; Hughes, *Indonesian Upheaval*, pp. 233–4, 245–6; Southwood and Flanagan, *Indonesia*, p. 127.

321 Inward Savingram No. 6, February 4, 1966, ANA 3034/2/2/5, part 1, p. 77.

322 Göckeritz to Central Council of FDJ, Department of International Relations, February 8, 1966, PA AA, MfAA, Nr. 16184, p. 44.

323 Telegram Green, October 28, 1965, NARA, RG 59, 250/7/2, Box 2311, POL 12 INDON, 10/1/65.

324 Report Masters, "Djakarta conversation," February 25, 1966, NARA, RG 59, 250/7/2, Box 122, unmarked file [Pol Aff & Rel INDO 1966]; Shaplen, *Time*, p. 150; Thürk and Weidemann, *Indonesien '65*, p. 283; US Consulate Surabaya, December 8 and 16, 1965, NARA, RG 84, 631/14/50/2–3, Box 118, POL 23–9, December 1–31.

325 Kahin, *Rebellion*, p. 242; CIA, *Indonesia*, p. 63.

326 Memorandum of conversation Martens with Robert Hewitt, journalist, November 15, 1965, NARA, RG 84, 631/14/50/2–3, Box 118, POL 23–9, November 20–30; Marni, "I am a leaf," p. 56; Budiardjo, *Surviving*, p. viii.

327 Kahin, *Rebellion*, p. 248.

328 Marni, "I am a leaf," pp. 56–7.

329 For the sense of betrayal by lower-ranking PKI members in Cirebon, West Java: Australian Embassy Jakarta, Political Savingram No. 52, October 15, 1965, 3034/2/1, part 48, p. 41.

330 Australian Embassy Jakarta, Savingram, October 15, 1965, ANA 3034/2/1, part 48, p. 23 (Savingrams No. 62, December 17, 1965, p. 192, mentioning Malang, East Java, and East Kalimantan, and No. 59, November 25, p. 168); UPI reports October 21 and 22, 1965, ANA, 3034/2/1/8, part 3, pp. 195, 205; telegram Werz, 22 and twice on October 27, 1965, PA AA, IB5, 37, vol. 169A (mentioned North Sulawesi as well); GDR Consulate General, "Zu den Ereignissen im Zusammenhang mit der Bewegung des 30. September," October 30, 1965 [the document is from November 3 at the earliest], PA AA, MfAA, A 16166, p. 64. Quote: Brackman, *Indonesia*, p. 30; see Sundhaussen, *Road*, pp. 216–17.

331 Bayerlacher to Central Committee of SED, November 1, 1965, BA, DY 30 IVA2/20/668; Mortimer, *Communism*, p. 391.

332 Kahin, *Rebellion*, p. 244, based on records by the British Consulate in Medan.

333 FRG Embassy (Werz), Report of December 6, 1965, "Chinesen in Indonesien; Probleme einer Minderheit," PA AA, IB5, 81, vol. 207; Australian Embassy Jakarta, Political Savingram No. 66, January 7, 1966, ANA 752/2, part 17, p. 127.

334 Hughes, *Indonesian Upheaval*, p. 179; Farid, "Indonesia's original sin," pp. 8–9; "ABC News 12:30 PM", November 11, 1965, ANA, 3034/2/1/8, part 5, p. 216.

335 Dewa, "The mass killings in Bali," in Cribb, *Indonesian Killings*, p. 260; Simon, *Broken Triangle*, p. 153; Brackman, *Collapse*, p. 130.

336 Budiardjo, *Surviving*, pp. 40–1, 78, 82, 87, 139; cf. Wieringa, *Sexual Politics*, pp. 9–15; Mortimer, *Communism*, p. 391.

337 "Indonesien 'begeht auf seine Art' das Internationale Jahr der Frau," BA, DY 34, Nr. 11466; Pohlman, "Fragment," p. 4. The Indonesian Institute for the Study of the 1965–66 Massacre Sulami founded with others at the end of the Suharto era also included social support for thousands of survivors.

338 Telegram Werz, October 29, 1965, PA AA, 37, IB5, vol. 169A; Australian Embassy Jakarta, Political Savingram No. 58, November 19, 1965, 3034/2/1, part 48, p. 150; "An appeal by the SOBSI," Prague, December 24, 1965, BA, DY 34, vol. 11466.

339 Warren, *Adat*, pp. 110–11.

340 But there is little concrete evidence: John T. Sidel, "Riots, church burnings, conspiracies: The moral economy of the Indonesian crowd in the late twentieth century," in Wessel and Wimhöfer, *Violence*, p. 52.

341 Sulistyo, "Years," p. 212.

342 Marni, "I am a leaf," p. 55 (Jakarta police took leftists into custody to protect them from mob attacks); Feillard, *Islam*, p. 66 (an imam forbade killing of communists who converted to Islam); Agustono, "Violence," p. 135 (a local PNI official in North Sumatra helped leftists for money). Former Masyumi chairman Nasrir tried to stop the carnage with messages out of prison: Brackman, *Collapse*, p. 118.

343 Marni, "I am a leaf," pp. 56–7.

344 Cribb "Indonesian massacres," p. 245; FRG Embassy Jakarta, "Aufbrechen religiöser Gegensätze in Indonesien," PA AA, IB5, 81, Nr. 208; "Spannungen zwischen Christen und Moslems Indonesiens," Deutsche Industrie-Zeitung, 5.6.1968, BA, DY 30 1VA2/20/672. Hinduism was declared a monotheistic religion in Indonesia.

345 "Survival: Bu Yeti's story," in Cribb, *Indonesian Killings*, pp. 227–39, is instructive in this regard. Forty percent of the prisoners on Buru island were said to have become Christians: May, *Indonesian Tragedy*, p. 33.

346 Coppel, *Indonesian Chinese*, pp. 108–9; Darmaputera, *Pancasila*, p. 84; Farram, "Revolution," p. 45.

347 Fragment "The Chinese," n.d. (after December 29, 1966), ANA 3034/2/5/1, part 3, p. 169; Gerdin, *Unknown Balinese*, pp. 40–1. For Yogyakarta, where an additional 7,000 became Hindus: Robert Hefner, "Hindu reform in an Islamizing Java: Pluralism and peril," in Martin Ramstedt (ed.), *Hinduism in Modern Indonesia* (London and New York: RoutledgeCurzon, 2004), p. 99.

348 Feillard, *Islam*, p. 66; Young, "Local," p. 83; Shaplen, *Time*, p. 124 (for Hindu temples).

349 PKI self-criticism of September 1966, in Feith and Castles, *Indonesian Political Thinking*, p. 279; Mortimer, *Communism*, pp. 152–64.

350 Schlereth and Bintang, *Indonesien*, p. 96.

351 Marni, "I am a leaf," p. 56; cf. Wertheim, "Whose Plot?," p. 202; Crouch, *Army*, p. 145.

352 Sudjatmiko, "Destruction," pp. 43, 180.

353 Action Committee for the Support of PKI, "Der Herausforderung mit den 5 Prinzipien der Revolution begegnen," November 20, 1965, BA, DY 30/IVA2/20/1051; Njoto interview, *Asashi Evening News*, December 2, 1965, ANA, 3034/2/1/8, part 7, p. 75; telegram Green, November 20, 1965, NARA, RG 59, 250/7/2, Box 2311, POL 12 INDON, 10-1-65; telegram Bayerlacher (copy), January 4, 1966, about a meeting with PKI Central Committee member Amir on December 28, BA, DY 30/IVA2/20/668; Information report by ADN correspondent in Jakarta, May 3, 1966, PA AA, MfAA, A 16075, pp. 46–8.

354 Information report by ADN correspondent in Jakarta, July 20, 1966, PA AA, MfAA, A 16075, p. 113; Mozingo, *Chinese Policy*, p. 255 (for the PKI's Beijing group); van der Kroef, "Indonesian communism."

355 Schlereth and Bintang, *Indonesien*, pp. 237–51; May, *Indonesian Tragedy*, pp. 203–5; van der Kroef, "Border insurgency"; van der Kroef, "Indonesian communism," pp. 51–4; Maskun Iskandar, "Purwodadi: Area of death," in Cribb, *Indonesian Killings*, pp. 203–11; Conboy, *Kopassus*, pp. 172–4; "Probleme der inneren Sicherheit Indonesiens," *Neue Zürcher Zeitung*, September 8, 1968, BA, DY 30 IVA2/20/672; Information report by ADN correspondent in Jakarta, October 1968, BA, DY 30 IVA2/20/672.

356 Van der Kroef, "Indonesian communism," pp. 36, 42; Brackman, *Collapse*, p. 168.

357 SED Central Committee, Department for International Relations, March 11, 1970, BA, DY 30 IVA2/20/1052. Quote: "To the Central Committees of Communist and Workers Parties" (signed: Djowirio and Suiono), May 1971, BA, DY 30 IVA2/20/1052.

358 See Frederick Bunnell, "American 'low posture' policy toward Indonesia in the months leading up to the 1965 'Coup'," *Indonesia* 50 (1990), pp. 29–60; ample evidence in FRUS, 1964–1968, vol. XXVI.

359 1962: CIA memo of June 1962, cited in William Blum, *The CIA: A Forgotten History* (London and New Jersey: Zed, 1986), p. 219. The CIA officer added: "It is not clear to me whether murder or overthrow is intended by the word liquidate." 1965: confidential telegram Rusk to US Embassies Jakarta and Kuala Lumpur, July 24, 1965, NARA, RG 84, 631/14/50/2–3 Jakarta Embassy, Box 116, DEF 19–8 1965.

360 Holt as quoted by the *New York Times*, July 6, 1966, cited in Noam Chomsky and Edward Herman, *The Washington Connection and Third World Fascism* (Boston: South End Press, 1979), p. 217; Luns to Rusk, April 6, 1966, NARA, RG 59, 250/7/2, Box 2312, POL 13, INDON, 1/1/64.

361 "US says few reds remain in Indonesia," *New York Times*, June 5, 1966, p. 5.

362 Gilchrist, quoted after Curtis, "Democratic genocide"; Weekas no. 42 for October 20 to 27, November 6, 1965, NARA, RG 59, 250/7/2.

Box 2309, POL 2–1 Joint Weekas INDON; telegram Werz, November 5, 1965, PA AA, 37, IB5, vol. 169A.

363 "Indonesia: Possible Future Developments," n.d., ANA, 3034/2/2/8, part 2, pp. 190–2.

364 Quoted after Dennis Warner, "'Bloody liquidation' of Indonesia's PKI," *Sydney Morning Herald*, June 15, 1966, ANA, 3034/2/1/8, part 14, p. 316.

365 Chomsky and Herman, *Washington Connection*, p. 215. For Kennedy, cf. Bunnell, "American 'low posture'," p. 60; for Australia, see Scott Burchill, "Absolving the dictator," *Journal of Contemporary Analysis* 73(3), 2001, http://scottburchill.net/absolving.html (accessed December 16, 2005).

366 For Britain: Curtis, "Democratic genocide." For Australia, R. A. Woolcott, "Indonesian situation – Radio Australia," October 12, 1965; "Quatripartite [sic] discussions on Indonesia; Brief for Australian delegation" (n.d., mid-November 1965); Jockel to Shann, October 15, 1965, all in ANA, 3034/2/1/8, part 2, pp. 61, 244, 286–7; ANA, 3034/2/1/8, part 1, pp. 261, 357 (October 6 and 10); part 3, pp. 150–4, 161, 320, esp. D. Hay, "For Minister," pp. 46–7 (quote); part 4, p. 110; cablegram November 5, 1965, part 5, p. 141 (Shann quote). For Green, cf. telegram no. 120A, October 3, 1965, NARA, RG 84, 631/14/50/2–3, Jakarta Embassy, Box 118, POL 23–9, October 1–3, 1965; telegram no. 178A and 179A of October 5, 10:25 and 10:45, same box, POL 23–9, October 4–6 (Green quote also FRUS, 1964–1968, vol. 26, p. 307); Robinson, *Dark Side*, p. 283, n. 23; quote after Kolko, *Confronting*, p. 180; Brands, "Limits," p. 802. Green had tried to influence Voice of America reporting on Indonesia since August 1965 at the latest: Bunnell, "American 'low posture'," p. 53. Months: Memo for National Security Council, February 23, 1965, FRUS, 1964–1968, vol. 26, pp. 234–7. For the CIA, Gehee (a former CIA officer), "Indonesian massacres"; Budiardjo, "Indonesia," p. 190; Southwood and Flanagan, *Indonesia*, p. 14; Peter Dale Scott, "The United States and the overthrow of Sukarno, 1965–1967," *Pacific Affairs* 58(2), 1985, pp. 257–61. For an evaluation similar to this author's, Cribb, "Genocide," pp. 238–9, n. 26. In CIA, *Indonesia*, the role of the CIA is not discussed.

367 Challis, *Shadow*, pp. 94–5, 99–103.

368 "Quatripartite [sic] discussions on Indonesia; Brief for Australian delegation" (n.d., mid-November 1965), ANA 3034/2/1/8, part 2, pp. 286–303.

369 David Easter, "'Keep the Indonesian pot boiling': Western covert intervention in Indonesia, October 1965–March 1966," *Cold War History* 5(1), 2005, pp. 63–4.

370 *Ibid.*, p. 68.

371 Samantha Power, *A Problem from Hell: America and the Age of Genocide* (New York: HarperPerennial, 2003).

372 Top secret correspondence October 8 to 19, 1965 in ANA, TS 383/6/1, part 8, pp. 114–23; cf. 3034/2/1/8, part 4, 137A, pp. 270–5, 307; Curtis, "Democratic genocide"; Challis, *Shadow*, p. 107; secret telegram State Dept. to US Embassy Jakarta, November 11, 1965, NARA, RG 59, 250/7/2, Box 2326, Pol.- Political Affairs and religion INDON-UK, 1/1/64. For Idris, see Hughes, *Indonesian Upheaval*, pp. 141–2.

373 Secret telegram Green to State Dept., October 14, 1965, FRUS, 1964–1968, vol. 26, p. 321. Cf. telegram Bell, US Embassy Kuala Lumpur, October 25, 1965, NARA, RG59, 250/7/2, Box 2325, POL 32–1 INDON Malaysia, 5/1/65. For January 1965, see Bunnell, "American 'low posture'," pp. 34–6.

374 Challis, *Shadow*, p. 113, n. 23.

375 Kathy Kadane, "Ex agents say CIA compiled death lists for Indonesians," *San Francisco Examiner*, May 20, 1990, www.namebase. org/kadane.html (accessed January 26, 2006); editors' note in FRUS, 1964–1968, vol. 26, pp. 386–7; secret airgram Green, August 10, 1966 (CIA-sanitized copy), NARA, RG 59, 250/7/2, Box 2312, POL 12 INDON, 5–1–66. Card index: Richard Cabot Howland, "Lessons of the September 30 affair," *Studies in Intelligence* 14(2), 1970, p. 17, NARA, CIA database.

376 Kahin, *Rebellion*, p. 243; Wieringa, *Sexual Politics*, p. 300, quotes an Indonesian woman whose American husband – a plantation manager near Madiun, Central Java – was a member of a screening team that dispatched 300 people to their death; Gavi, *Konterrevolution*, p. 39. See telegrams US Embassy Jakarta, October 30 and November 1, 1965: NARA, RG 84, 631/14/50/2–3, POL 23–9, Box 117, October

15–19, 1965 and Box 118, November 1–9, respectively; US Consulate Medan, November 27, 1965, same box, November 20–30.

377 Socialist countries stopped their military cooperation due to the anti-communist persecution, and opponents in the Confrontation such as Great Britain and Australia were out of the question, too.

378 Bunnell, "American 'low posture'," pp. 59–60, citing a US Embassy telegram of November 5, 1965 (first quote) and referring to an interview with General Sukendro. See also Kolko, *Confronting*, p. 181 (second quote); and Gardner, *Shared Hopes*, p. 227.

379 Telegram Green to State Dept., December 2, 1965, in FRUS, 1964–68, vol. 26, p. 379; cf. Friend, *Indonesian Destinies*, pp. 118–19.

380 Scott, "United States," p. 244, n. 27.

381 "Part II: Later developments in Indonesian situation," December 5, 1965, referring to a subordinate of Nasution, with cover letter by Friedrich Hayek of July 17, 1966, PA AA, 37, IB5, vol. 255. Helmi had left Indonesia by December 1, 1965.

382 Australian Embassy Jakarta, Political Savingram, January 28, 1966, ANA 3034/2/1/8, part 10, p. 125.

383 Bayerlacher to GDR Foreign Ministry, November 5, 1965, PA AA, MfAA, A 16166, p. 103.

384 Documented are misgivings – but no intervention – by the West German Ambassador about the future social reintegration of 150,000 to 200,000 arrested PKI suspects and people who had lost their jobs, namely union members, and the political repercussions for the army: FRG Embassy Jakarta, "Ungelöste Probleme Indonesiens und die politische Zukunft der Armee," November 22, 1965, PA AA, IB5, 37, vol. 169A.

385 Information report by ADN correspondent in Jakarta, July 13, 1966 (copy), BA, DY 30/IVA 2/20/671; US Embassy Jakarta December 19, 1965, NARA, RG 59, 250/7/2, Box 2308, POL 2 INDON, 1/1/66.

386 Simon, *Broken Triangle*, pp. 126–8.

387 *Ibid.*, pp. 118, 125–40; Mozingo, *Chinese Policy*, pp. 234, 248. Diplomatic relations were finally cut off in 1967.

388 See German translation of a *Pravda* article of December 26, 1965, as well as report about the February issue of "Tanah Air" for Indonesians abroad, April 1966, PA AA, 37, IB5, vol. 255; interview with Ulrich Makosch, then correspondent of GDR-TV in Jakarta, November 7, 2005; GDR Foreign Ministry, Dept. for South and Southeast Asia, "Beziehungen DDR-Indonesien," January 31, 1967, PA AA, MfAA, C774/70, pp. 45–6; 2. AEA, Sektion Indonesien, "Die Lage in Indonesien und die Haltung der DDR," November 4, 1965, MfAA A 16073, pp. 69–71 ("strengthen relations normally").

389 Ragna Boden, "The 'Gestapu' events of 1965 in Indonesia: New evidence from Russian and German archives," *Bijdragen tot de Taal-, Land- en Volkenkunde* 163(4), 2007, p. 514.

390 Arnold Brackman, "Foreign help for the Reds in Indonesia" (German translation), *Straits Times* (Singapore), July 17, 1972, BA, DY 30/IVB2/20/282; telegram Green September 13, 1966, NARA, RG 59, 250/7/2, Box 2312, POL 12 INDON, 5–1-66, about 200,000–300,000 letters received by Polish authorities and newspapers, according to the Polish Ambassador in Jakarta; telegram Green October 15, 1965, NARA, RG 84, 631/14/50/2–3 Jakarta Embassy, Box 118, INDON 23–9, October 15–19, 1965.

391 FRG Embassy Jakarta, "Flaute in Indonesien," February 10, 1966, PA AA, 37, IB5, vol. 255. Similar "Division heads meeting," Australian Foreign Ministry, June 1, 1966, ANA 3034/2/1/8, part 14, p. 158.

392 Robert Elegant, "Indonesia comeback," *Bulletin/Australian Financial Times*, August 6, 1966, BA, DY 30 IVA2/20/671; Federspiel, quoted after Simons, *Indonesia*, p. 180.

393 Green's name has also been brought into a connection with a failed coup in South Korea in 1961, but his role therein is controversial: Gardner, *Shared Hopes*, p. 209.

394 Quoted after Southwood and Flanagan, *Indonesia*, p. 16.

395 Chomsky and Herman, *Washington Connection*, p. 403, n. 5; Scott, "United States," p. 259.

396 Evans, "Influence," pp. 25–48; David Ransom, "Ford country: Building an elite for Indonesia," in Steve Weissman *et al.* (eds.), *The Trojan Horse: A Radical View at Foreign Aid* (Palo Alto: Ramparts, 1975), pp. 93–116.

397 GDR Embassy Moscow, Political Dept., "Information über den Besuch des indonesischen Außenministers Malik in der Sowjetunion," October 26, 1966, BA, DY30/IVA2/20/671. The USSR was Indonesia's biggest creditor with about US$1 billion, equivalent to 40 percent of Indonesia's external financial obligations.

398 Malik (1917–1984), who left the Murba Party in 1966, was Indonesia's Foreign Minister from 1966 to 1977 and Vice President from 1977 to 1983. Another example of UN indifference is that in Soemardjan, *Indonesia: A Socio-Economic Profile*, a publication financed by UNESCO in 1988 and appearing in a series sponsored by UNESCO, the 1965–66 murders went entirely unmentioned.

399 Examples mentioned in Budiardjo, *Surviving*, pp. 28–32; Information report by ADN correspondent Jakarta, November 4, 1965, BA, DY 30 IVA2/20/671.

400 For Suharto's moves within the military, see Crouch, *Army*, pp. 229–32.

401 GDR Consulate General, report of May 4, 1966, PA AA, MfAA, A 16075, pp. 57–9; several reports from 1967 in BA, DY 30 IVA2/20/672.

402 US Embassy Jakarta, Airgram of November 5, 1966 and Record of Conversation between New Zealand Counselor and Subchan, April 6, 1966, NARA, RG 59, 250/7/2, Box 2311, POL 12 INDON, 1/1/66.

403 Feillard, *Islam*, pp. 71–4, 79–9; Hefner, *Civil Islam*, pp. 91–2; Hindley, "Alirans," p. 52; May, *Indonesian Tragedy*, pp. 261, 283. More generally, see Crouch, *Army*, pp. 245–72.

404 M. Clapham, "Record of Conversation with Mr. Harry Tjan, S.N.," April 11, 1966, ANA, 3034/2/1/8, part 13, p. 15.

405 Hindley, "Alirans," pp. 45, 57.

406 Australian Embassy Jakarta, Savingram No. 23, May 19, 1966, ANA, 3034/2/1/8, Part 14, pp. 54–5; FRG Embassy Jakarta, Report of November 14, 1967, PA AA, IB5, 81, Nr. 208; Information report by ADN correspondents Jakarta, July 13, 1967, ADN report, January 1968, and *Frankfurter Rundschau*, July 15, 1968, all in BA, DY 30 IVA2/20/672; Ryter, "Youth," pp. 70, 74, 118. Other view: Paget, "Military," pp. 310–12.

407 Ann Willner, *Public Protest in Indonesia* (Athens, OH: Ohio University, Center for International Studies, 1968), pp. 5–8; Southwood and Flanagan, *Indonesia*, pp. 178–90; Georgia Wimhöfer, "Indonesian students in 1998: Civil society and the effects of violence," in Wessel and Wimhöfer, *Violence*, pp. 171, 175; Sloan, *Study*, p. 79.

408 Record of Conversation M. H. Clapham and Abdul Gafur, KAMI President, April 27, 1966, ANA 3034/2/2/8, p. 187; Australian Embassy Jakarta, Political Savingram No. 20, [May 5, 1966], ANA, 3034/2/1/8, part 13, pp. 250–3; Schlereth and Bintang, *Indonesien*, pp. 228–9.

409 See arguments made by Penders and Sundhaussen, *Nasution*, pp. 182–4, 207–29.

410 Conboy, *Kopassus*, pp. 167–8; telegram Green, May 6, 1966, NARA, RG 59, 250/7/2, Box 2312, POL 12 INDON, 5-1-66 ("prohibited from public speech without Suharto's permission"); Ingo Wandelt, "Die Kinder Suhartos übernehmen die Macht: Der schleichende Generationenwechsel im Militär Indonesiens," *Indonesien-Information* 1, 2004, http://home.snafu.de/watchin/II_1_04/macht. htm (accessed December 16, 2005); Jun Honna, "Military ideology in response to democratic pressure during the late Suharto era: Political and institutional contexts," in Anderson, *Violence*, p. 61, n. 24.

411 May, *Indonesian Tragedy*, pp. 235–88; US Embassy Jakarta, Airgram, November 30, 1966, NARA, RG 59, 250/7/2, Box 2311, POL 12 INDON, 1/1/66.

412 Schlereth and Bintang, *Indonesien*, pp. 197–8; Soemardjan, *Indonesia*, pp. 88, 155; Klute, "Women," p. 211.

413 Schlereth and Bintang, *Indonesien*, p. 240; van Dijk, "Privatization of the public order."

414 Soemardjan, *Indonesia*, p. 152; excerpt of Savingram No. 47, March 25, 1961, ANA 3034/2/2, part I, especially p. 187.

415 Soemardjan, *Indonesia*, p. 90.

416 US Embassy Jakarta, November 18, 1965, NARA, RG 59, 250/7/2, Box 2318, POL 23–9 INDON, 11/1/65.

417 The latter half of the argument is made by Cribb, "Indonesian massacres," pp. 243–4.

418 Langenberg, "Gestapu," p. 61.

419 These are views by Sudjatmiko, "Destruction," pp. 8, 40–1.

3 Participating and profiteering

1 This chapter draws from my more extensively documented contribution "Nationsbildung im Krieg: Wirtschaftliche Faktoren bei der Vernichtung der Armenier und beim Mord an den ungarischen Juden," in Hans-Lukas Kieser and Dominik Schaller (eds.), *The Armenian Genocide and the Shoah* (Zurich: Chronos, 2002), pp. 347–422.

2 That said, one could investigate instead how religious fanaticism fed into violence by non-state actors against Armenians, though this approach has not been at the center of existing research.

3 Vahakn N. Dadrian, *The History of the Armenian Genocide: Ethnic Conflicts from the Balkans to Anatolia* (Providence and New York: Berghahn, 1995), pp. 222–5; Taner Akçam, *A Shameful Act: The Armenian Genocide and the Question of Turkish Responsibility* (New York: Metropolitan Books, 2006), pp. 190–1; Wolfgang Gust, *Der Völkermord an den Armeniern* (Munich: Carl Hanser, 1993), pp. 249–54; Raymond Kévorkian, *Le Génocide des Arméniens* (Paris: Odile Jacob, 2006), p. 253.

4 Armenian representatives at the Paris Peace Conference estimated Armenian property losses at about 1.8 billion French francs (in 1914 francs) or about 80 million liras: Dickran Kouymjian, "La confiscation des biens et la destruction des monuments historiques comme manifestations du processus génocidaire," in Comité de défense de la cause arménienne (ed.), *L'actualité du génocide des arméniens* (Paris: Edipol, 1999), pp. 221–2; memo by Aharonian and Boghos Nubar in Kevork K. Baghdjian, *La confiscation, par le gouvernement turc, des biens arméniens … dits "abandonnés"* (Montreal: K. K. Baghdjian, 1987), pp. 261–9; cf. file "Die Finanz-Verhandlungen mit Djavid Bey," NARA T 136, R 477, pp. 827 ff., esp. F. Köbner, "Bemerkungen zu der Denkschrift vom 10. Mai 1917, betreffend 'die Liquidation feindlicher Unternehmungen in der Türkei'," May 14, 1917, p. 837; Memo "Liquidation des feindlichen Eigentums in der Türkei" (May 13 or June 21, 1918), NARA T 136, R 49 (AA Türkei 134, vol. 40).

5 In Thrace and the Suez, territorial aims were quite limited. Ulrich Trumpener, *Germany and the Ottoman Empire 1914–1918* (Princeton: Princeton University Press, 1968), pp. 28–9; see Christopher J. Walker, *Armenia: The Survival of a Nation* (New York: St. Martin's, 1980 [revised second edition]), p. 198; for troop deployments 1914–15, focusing on the West, see Edward J. Erickson, *Ordered to Die: A History of the Ottoman Army in the First World War* (Westport and London: Greenwood, 2001), pp. 42–7.

6 There is a wide scholarship on this issue; see Fatma Müge Göçek, *Rise of the Bourgeoisie, Demise of Empire: Ottoman Westernization and Social Change* (New York and Oxford: Oxford University Press, 1996); Gerlach, "Nationsbildung," pp. 359–65.

7 The CUP governed with a brief interruption throughout the dissolution phase of the Ottoman Empire, 1908–18.

8 Donald Bloxham, *The Great Game of Genocide: Imperialism, Nationalism, and the Destruction of Ottoman Armenians* (Oxford: Oxford University Press, 2005), pp. 72–89; Johannes Lepsius, "Einleitung," in Lepsius (ed.), *Deutschland und Armenien: Sammlung diplomatischer Aktenstücke* (Potsdam: Tempelverlag, 1919), p. xxv; for a Turkish version, Kamuran Gürün, *The Armenian File: The Myth of Innocence Exposed* (London: K. Rustem and Weidenfeld & Nicolson, 1985), pp. 199–212.

9 According to Talaat Pasha's notebook, 924,158 Armenians were deported, excluding Van province: David Gaunt, *Massacres, Resistance, Protectors: Muslim–Christian Relations in Eastern Anatolia during World War I* (New Jersey: Gorgias, 2006), p. 68.

10 For the highly organized character of many massacres, see Hilmar Kaiser, "'A scene from the inferno': The Armenians of Erzurum and the genocide, 1915–1916," in Kieser and Schaller, *Armenian Genocide*, p. 164.

11 Sublime Porte, Ministry for the Interior, Department for Settlement of Tribes and Immigrants, Regulation related to settlement and board and lodging and other affairs of Armenians relocated to other places because of war conditions and emerging political requirements, May 30, 1915, article 2, in *Documents on Ottoman Armenians, vol. II* (Ankara: Prime Ministry, Directorate General of Press and Information, 1983), pp. 91–3.

12 Yusuf Halaçoglu, *Facts on the Relocation of Armenians (1914–1918)* (Ankara: Turkish Historical Society, 2002), p. 75; Hilmar Kaiser, "Armenian property, Ottoman law and nationality policies during the Armenian genocide, 1915–1916," in Olaf Farshid *et al.* (eds.), *The First World War as Remembered in the Countries of the Eastern Mediterranean* (Beirut and Würzburg: Ergon, 2006), p. 62, n. 42, lists 33 commissions in provincial capitals and some provincial towns (but not Van).

13 Loi provisoire concernant des liens, les dettes et les créances des personnes transportées ailleurs, 13 (26) September 1915, in Arthur Beylerian (ed.), *Les grandes puissances, l'empire ottoman et les Arméniens dans les archives françaises (1914–1918)* (Paris: Université Paris I – Panthéon-Sorbonne, 1983), pp. 112–14; Gürün, *Armenian File*, p. 209.

14 Talaat's telegram, July 20, 1915, in Salahi Sonyel (ed.), *Displacement of the Armenians: Documents* (Ankara: Turkish Historical Society, 1978), p. 3; Henry H. Riggs, *Days of Tragedy in Armenia: Personal Experiences in Harpoot 1915–1917* (Ann Arbor: Gomidas Institute, 1997) p. 89; regional: Official Proclamation, June 28, 1915 (Trabzon), in Ara Sarafian (ed.), *United States Official Documents on the Armenian Genocide*, vol. II (Watertown: Armenian Review, 1994), p. 16; Adana: Peter Balakian, *The Burning Tigris: The Armenian Genocide and America's Response* (New York: HarperCollins, 2003), p. 271.

15 Gürün, *Armenian File*, p. 208, referring to the May 30, 1915 Cabinet decision.

16 Kaiser, "Scene," p. 172.

17 Hamit Bozarslan, "L'extermination des Arméniens et des juifs: Quelques éléments de comparaison," in Kieser and Schaller, *Armenian Genocide*, p. 342, n. 86; Kaiser, "Scene," p. 153.

18 Excerpt from the annual report at the CUP general assembly, September 28, 1916, in Beylerian, *Puissances*, pp. 246–9; Kaiser, "Armenian property," pp. 58–9; Kaiser, "Scene," pp. 152–4. For other prohibitions to sell to foreigners, see Talaat's telegram, July 20, 1915, Sonyel, *Displacement*, p. 2.

19 Ephraim K. Jernazian, *Judgment unto Truth: Witnessing the Armenian Genocide* (New Brunswick and London: Transaction, 1990), p. 94; in addition, see Dominik Schaller, "Der Völkermord

an den Armeniern im Osmanischen Reich, 1915–1917: Ereignis, Historiographie und Vergleich," in Schaller *et al.* (eds.), *Enteignet – Vertrieben – Ermordet: Beiträge zur Genozidforschung* (Zurich: Chronos, 2004), p. 242; Jacob Künzler, *Im Lande des Blutes und der Tränen: Erlebnisse in Mesopotamien während des Weltkrieges (1914–1918)* (Zurich: Chronos, 1999), p. 92. Similar situation: US Consulate Mersin, Nathan, October 30, 1915, in Sarafian, *Documents*, vol. II, p. 96.

20 Kaiser, "Armenian property," p. 59. The Interior Ministry then instructed the commissions to choose a favorable moment for auctioning: Kaiser, "Armenian property," p. 61. Cf. Kaiser, "Die deutsche Diplomatie und der armenische Völkermord," in Fikret Adanir and Bernd Bonwetsch (eds.), *Osmanismus, Nationalismus und der Kaukasus* (Wiesbaden: Reichert, 2005), p. 232.

21 Rouben Paul Adalian, "American diplomatic correspondence in the age of mass murder: The Armenian genocide in the US archives," in Jay Winter (ed.), *America and the Armenian Genocide in the US Archives* (Cambridge: Cambridge University Press, 2003), p. 177; Guenter Lewy, *The Armenian Massacres in Ottoman Turkey: A Disputed Genocide* (Salt Lake City: University of Utah Press, 2005), p. 173; Faiz El-Ghusein, *Martyred Armenia* (New York: G. H. Doran, 1918), p. 20 (Diyarbakir); Johannes Lepsius, *Der Todesgang des armenischen Volkes* (Potsdam: Tempelverlag, 1919 [second edition]), p. 131 (Dewank near Kayseri).

22 Riggs, *Days*, pp. 88–9.

23 US Consulate Aleppo, August 21, 1915, *Armenian Review* 37(1), 1984, pp. 114–16.

24 By Governor Resid Bey: El-Ghusein, *Martyred*, p. 20 (Diyarbakir); by deportation organizer Seki Bey: Gust, *Völkermord*, p. 50; for movable goods, Arthur C. Ryan, "Statement on the misuse of Turkey and her cruel treatment of non-Muslim subjects," March 28, 1918, in James L. Barton (ed.), *"Turkish Atrocities": Statements of American Missionaries on the Destruction of the Christian Communities in Ottoman Turkey, 1915–1917* (Ann Arbor: Gomidas Institute, 1998), pp. 181–5 (Bardizag).

25 Künzler, *Im Lande*, p. 92.

26 William S. Dodd, "Report of the cruelness witnessed in the Armenian deportations in Knoya, Turkey," December 21, 1917, in Barton, *Turkish Atrocities*, p. 148; Austro-Hungarian Consulate Brussa, August 20, 1915, in Artem Ohandjanian (ed.), *The Armenian Genocide: Documentation*, vol. 2 (Munich: Institut für armenische Fragen, 1988), p. 216.

27 Hans-Lukas Kieser, *Der verpaßte Friede: Mission, Ethnie und Staat in den Ostprovinzen der Türkei 1839–1938* (Zurich: Chronos, 2000), p. 427 (Harput); Jernazian, *Judgment*, p. 30 (Urfa); Dadrian, *History*, pp. 232–3, n. 30; report by Elizabeth Webb, June 1, 1918, in Barton, *Turkish Atrocities*, p. 169 (Adana); US Consulate Trabzon, Heizer, September 25, 1915, in Sarafian, *Documents*, vol. II, pp. 44–5 (Erzurum).

28 Baghdjian, *Confiscation*, p. 71; cf. Henry Morgenthau, *Ambassador Morgenthau's Story* (Garden City: Doubleday, 1918), p. 339.

29 Austro-Hungarian chargé d'affaires Constantinople, Trautmanndorff, to Burian, October 13, 1915, in Ohandjanian, *Armenian Genocide*, vol. 2, pp. 247–8.

30 "Posthumous Memoirs of Talaat Pasha," *Current History*, November 1921, in Richard Kloian (ed.), *The Armenian Genocide: News Accounts from the Armenian Press, 1915–1922* (n.p.: ACC, 1985), p. 361.

31 Gürün, *Armenian File*, p. 213, listing cases from eight provinces and seven autonomous districts, with no cases from Erzurum, Van, and Trabzon provinces. See Lewy, *Armenian Massacres*, pp. 110–15; Akcam, *Shameful Act*, p. 264. Examples surface in Riggs, *Days*, pp. 101–2 (Harput county mayor); Khoren K. Davidson, *Odyssey of Armenian from Zeitoun* (New York: Vantage, 1985), pp. 137, 142 (Roumkale mayor, denounced by "some distinguished Turks"; the investigators heard the Armenian author as a witness).

32 Harry Yessaian, *Out of Turkey: The Life Story of Dinik "Haji Bey" Yessaian* (Dearborn: Wayne State University Press, 1994), pp. 184–5 (Smyrna, 1922).

33 Künzler, *Im Lande*, p. 92 (Urfa); Maria Jacobsen, *Diaries of a Danish Missionary, Harpoot, 1907–1919* (Princeton and London: Taderon, 2001), p. 79 (Harput); Donald Miller and Lorna Touryan Miller,

Survivors: An Oral History of the Armenian Genocide (Berkeley: University of California Press, 1999), p. 69; Baghdjian, ~~Confiscation,~~ p. 66 (Eskişehir, Izmit); Kouymjian, "Confiscation," p. 223.

34 US Consulate Trabzon, Heizer, July 28, 1915, *Armenian Review* 37(1), 1984, p. 106; see also verdict by Trabzon court martial, May 22, 1919, in Taner Akçam, *Armenien und der Völkermord: Die Istanbuler Prozesse und die türkische Nationalbewegung* (Hamburg: Hamburger Edition, 1996), p. 180.

35 Riggs, *Days*, p. 88; Heizer, July 28, 1915, in Sarafian, *Documents*, vol. II, p. 27; cf. US Consulate Aleppo, Jackson, August 19, 1915, in Sarafian (ed.), *United States Official Documents on the Armenian Genocide*, vol. I (Watertown: Armenian Review, 1993), p. 53 (Aintab).

36 Kieser, *Friede*, p. 426, and Jacobsen, *Diaries*, p. 80 (Harput); Jernazian, *Judgment*, p. 93 (Urfa); Rafael de Nogales, *Four Years Beneath the Crescent* (New York and London: Charles Scribner's Sons, 1926), p. 169 (Adana); German Consulate Trabzon, Bergfeld, to Reichskanzler, August 27, 1915, in Gust, *Völkermord*, p. 270.

37 Stephen H. Astourian, "Genocidal process: The Armeno–Turkish polarization," in Richard Hovannisian (ed.), *The Armenian Genocide* (New York: Palgrave Macmillan, 1992), pp. 71–2; Levon Marashlian, "Finishing the genocide: Cleansing Turkey of Armenian survivors, 1920–1923,", in Richard Hovannisian (ed.), *Remembrance and Denial: The Case of the Armenian Genocide* (Detroit: Wayne State University Press, 1998), p. 115; Austro-Hungarian Consular Agency Brussa, August 19, 1915, in Ohandjanian, *Armenian Genocide*, vol. 2, pp. 214–15.

38 Kévorkian, *Génocide*, p. 79.

39 Documents from a January 1916 investigation, in Ahmet Tetik (ed.), *Armenian Activities in the Archive Documents 1914–1918*, vol. II (Ankara: Genelkurmay ATASE ve Genelkurmay Denetleme Başkanlığı Yayınları, 2006), pp. 141–3.

40 Austro-Hungarian Consular Agency Brussa, August 23, 1915, in Ohandjanian, *Armenian Genocide*, vol. 2, p. 217; Dadrian, *History*, p. 232, n. 26; Kévorkian, *Génocide*, p. 259; Gust, *Völkermord*, p. 47.

41 Annual report by the Aleppo governor for 1916, quoted in "Konfidenten-Bericht" (for the Austro-Hungarian Embassy in Constantinople), February 27, 1917, in Ohandjanian, *Armenian Genocide*, vol. 2, p. 374.

42 Akçam, *Shameful Act*, p. 189; see also Ara Sarafian, "Introduction to volume I," in Sarafian, *Documents*, vol. I, p. xx.

43 For houses to be built, farmland, implements, seeds, and business credits to be provided, according to Talaat's May 23 and 27, 1915 messages and the May 30, 1915 Cabinet decision, see Halaçoglu, *Facts*, pp. 70, 72–3, 88. The placement of Armenian exiles under Cemal Pasha needs to be scrutinized in this regard, cf. Raymond H. Kévorkian, "Ahmed Djemal pacha et le sort des déportés arméniens de Syrie-Palestine," in Kieser and Schaller, *Armenian Genocide*, p. 200.

44 Aaron Aaronsohn, "Pro Armenia," November 16, 1916, in Yair Auron, *The Banality of Indifference: Zionism and the Armenian Genocide* (New Brunswick and London: Transaction, 2002), p. 378; Abraham H. Hartunian, *Neither To Laugh nor To Weep* (Boston: Beacon, 1968), p. 77; cf. Governor of Hüdavendigar province, 8 Ramazan [July 20] 1915, in Sonyel, *Displacement*, p. 6. See also US Consular Agent Damascus, Young, September 20, 1915, 83; former US Consul in Aleppo, Jackson, "Armenian atrocities," March 4, 1918, *Armenian Review* 37(1), 1984, pp. 135, 139. More references in Gerlach, "Nationsbildung," p. 418, n. 280.

45 James Kay Sutherland, *The Adventures of an Armenian Boy* (Ann Arbor: Ann Arbor Press, 1964), pp. 125, 149; see Fritz Grobba, *Die Getreidewirtschaft Syriens und Palästinas seit Beginn des Weltkrieges* (Hanover: Orient-Buchhandlung Heinz Lafaire, 1923), pp. 38–40. For a case of women and children drafted to the army for construction works for over one year, but at least fed and protected there, see Dirouhi Kouymjian Highgas, *Refugee Girl* (Watertown: Baikar, 1985), pp. 87–91.

46 Council of Ministers decision, May 31 [30?], 1915 and Regulations for the settlement and ration allowance [...] June 10, 1915, in Ahmed Tetik (ed.), *Armenian Activities in the Archive Documents 1914–1918*, vol. I (Ankara: Genelkurmay ATASE ve Genelkurmay Denetleme Başkanlığı Yayınları, 2005), pp. 134–6; Telegram Interior Ministry, Ali Fevzi, August 30, 1915, and letters by the Secretariat of Hüdavendigar

province, respectively, August 28, 1915, in Sonyel, *Displacement*, pp. 3, 9–10.

47 To the Office of the Prime Minister [December 4, 1916], in Sarafian, *Documents*, vol. I, p. 168. For 1916, the document states that 80 million kurush (piasters) had been spent by the end of October, but the budget allowed for 20 million more until the end of the year. Halaçoglu, *Facts*, p. 92, cites 78 million piasters in 1915 and 200 million in 1916 (0.7 and 1.8 million liras, respectively).

48 Halaçoglu, *Facts*, p. 92. With these figures, Halaçoglu meant to demonstrate the generosity of the Ottoman authorities.

49 Based on the assumption that one million Armenians were deported.

50 Bloxham, *Game*, p. 63 (minimum 400,000); Walker, *Armenia*, p. 203 (750,000); Rouben Paul Adalian, "Comparative policy and differential practice in the treatment of minorities in wartime: The United States archival evidence on the Armenians and Greeks in the Ottoman Empire," *JGR* 3(1), 2001, p. 39 (261,000 from Salonika region alone). From 1878 to 1904, 850,000 refugees had been settled primarily in regions also inhabited by Armenians: Akçam, *Shameful Act*, p. 86.

51 Gerlach, "Nationsbildung," pp. 371–2; see also Tessa Hofmann, "Mit einer Stimme sprechen – gegen Völkermord," in Hofmann (ed.), *Verfolgung, Vertreibung und Vernichtung der Christen im Osmanischen Reich 1912–1922* (Münster: LIT, 2004), pp. 26–7. Hilmi Pasha estimated in 1913 that the settlement of the refugees would cost 250 to 300 million francs: Kévorkian, *Génocide*, p. 179.

52 See Hilmar Kaiser, "The Ottoman government and the end of the Ottoman social formation, 1915–1917," www.hist.net/kieser/aghet/Essays/EssayKaiser.html (accessed June 16, 2008); Gaunt, *Massacres*, pp. 65–6.

53 Ahmed Emin, *Turkey in the World War* (New Haven and London: Yale University Press, 1930), p. 248. By October 1916, the authorities had taken care of 702,900 Muslims dislocated from the northeast. These figures confirm the estimate by Kamal Madhar Ahmad, *Kurdistan During the First World War* (London: Saqi, 1994), p. 141, n. 49, that less than the sometimes assumed 700,000 Ottoman Kurds were deported or evacuated.

54 Akçam, *Shameful Act*, p. 182; Ugur Ü. Üngör, "'A Reign of Terror': CUP Rule in Diyarbekir Province, 1913–1918," (MA thesis, University of Amsterdam, 2005), pp. 91–3, http://home.uva.nl/uu.ungor/thesis. pdf (accessed August 24, 2007); Bloxham, *Game*, p. 254, n. 182; US Consul Aleppo, Jackson, May 12 and June 26, 1915, in Sarafian, *Documents*, vol. I, pp. 14, 24. For a local initiative to replace Armenians by "nomadic Turks" by the district governor of Maras on March 30, 1915, see Halaçoglu, *Facts*, p. 59.

55 Kaiser, "Armenian property," pp. 55–7.

56 Bandirma: Elise Hagopian Taft, *Rebirth* (Plandome, NY: New Age, 1981), p. 78. Samsun: Kaiser, "Armenian property," p. 65, n. 52. Bursa: Yves Ternon, *Tabu Armenien: Geschichte eines Völkermords* (Frankfurt a.M. and Berlin: Ullstein, 1988), p. 192. Adana: Kouymjian Highgas, *Refugee Girl*, p. 45; Fikret Adanir and Hilmar Kaiser, "Migration, deportation, and nation-building: The case of the Ottoman Empire," in René Leboutte (ed.), *Migrations et migrants dans une perspective historique: Permanences et innovations* (Brussels: Peter Lang, 2000), p. 292, n. 64; US Consulate Mersin, Nathan, October 30, 1915, Sarafian, *Documents*, vol. II, p. 96; Rolf Hosfeld, *Operation Nemesis: Die Türkei, Deutschland und der Völkermord an den Armeniern* (Cologne: Kiepenheuer & Witsch, 2005), p. 190.

57 Akçam, *Shameful Act*, p. 257.

58 Regulations of June 9, 1915, in Bilal Simsir (ed.), *Documents* (Ankara: Prime Ministry, Directorate General of Press and Information, 1982), pp. 76–80.

59 Adanir and Kaiser, "Migration," p. 283; Üngör, "Reign," pp. 84–6, 90–1; David McDowall, *A Modern History of the Kurds* (London and New York: I. B. Taurus, 1996), p. 106.

60 Kieser, *Friede*, pp. 398, 426, 432; Leslie A. Davis, US Consul in Harput, Report of 1919, in Ara Sarafian (ed.), *United States Official Documents on the Armenian Genocide*, vol. III (Watertown: Armenian Review, 1995), p. 121; about a local settlement commission settling Kurds in a formerly Armenian village: Riggs, *Days*, pp. 179–81 (for furniture provided to Islamic refugees in 1916, p. 135); Kerop Bedoukian, *Some of Us Survived* (New York: Farrar Straus & Giroux, 1979), p. 126 (Bireçik); see also "To the Office of the Prime

Minister," December 4, 1916, in Simsir, *Documents*, pp. 118–24. For the last point, cf. Üngör, "Reign," p. 92.

61 Madhar Ahmad, *Kurdistan*, p. 131; McDowall, *History*, pp. 105–6; Mark Levene, "Creating a modern 'zone of genocide': The impact of nation- and state formation on Eastern Anatolia, 1878–1923," *HGS* 12(3), 1998, pp. 393–433; railroad: Mae M. Derdarian, *Vergeen: A Survivor of the Armenian Genocide. Based on a Memoir by Virgina Meghrouni* (Los Angeles: Atmus Press, 1996), p. 149.

62 "To the Office of the Prime Minister," December 4, 1916, in Simsir, *Documents*, pp. 118–24.

63 Jacobsen, *Diaries*, pp. 80, 108, 132; Kieser, *Friede*, p. 426.

64 Ryan, "Statement," p. 183; Balakian, *Burning Tigris*, p. 242; Riggs, *Days*, p. 135; de Nogales, *Years*, p. 67 (Van); Leon Z. Surmelian, *I Ask You, Ladies and Gentlemen* (New York: E. P. Dutton & Co., 1945), p. 152 (Trabzon).

65 Report by German journalist Paul Weitz, June 20, 1918, in Gust, *Völkermord*, pp. 569, 572–3, 575.

66 Künzler, *Im Lande*, p. 136; see also Jernazian, *Judgment*, p. 96.

67 Bernstorff to Reichskanzler Graf von Hertling, July 6, 1918, NARA T 136, R 67 (AA Türkei 134, vol. 40).

68 This seems true despite the legislation by the nationalist Ankara government. After initial decrees of the Istanbul government for the restoration of Armenian property in late 1918 and January 1920 (Akçam, *Shameful Act*, p. 177), the tide changed. The September 1915 expropriation laws were revived by the Ankara government in September 1922. In 1919, the Kemalists had already declared that Armenians needed their permission to return to the eastern vilayets (Akçam, *Shameful Act*, p. 254; Balakian, *Burning Tigris*, p. 323). The Turkish government made the expropriations of Armenians permanent in 1927 (Kouymjian, "Confiscation," p. 224). For popular pressure not to continue with the reconstitution of Armenian property, see Akçam, *Shameful Act*, pp. 279–80 (fall 1919) and p. 337 (killings of Armenians, especially landholders, spring 1919).

69 Üngör, "Reign," p. 93, and Akçam, *Shameful Act*, p. 276. Government regulations of fall 1918 about the return of Armenian

property had remained unclear about how to balance the interests of returnees and immigrants living in their dwellings: Governor of Hüdavendigar province, 28 Zilka'de [September 5] 1918, in Sonyel, *Displacement*, p. 13; Halaçoglu, *Facts*, 111–13 (Interior Minister Mustafa Pasha to Prime Minister, January 4, 1919).

70 Emin, *Turkey*, pp. 93–4; Donald C. Blaisdell, *European Financial Control in the Ottoman Empire* (New York: Columbia University Press, 1929), p. 179; Charles Issawi, *The Economic History of Turkey 1800–1914* (Chicago and London: University of Chicago Press, 1980), pp. 321, 324, 361–2; Madhar Ahmad, *Kurdistan*, pp. 40, 52.

71 German Foreign Office to Reichskanzler Bethmann Hollweg, October 28, 1916 (according to Cavid Bey), unsigned note of October 30, 1916 and letter by Kühlmann, December 15, 1916, NARA T 136, R 47 (AA Türkei 110, vols. 88 and 89); cf. Issawi, *Economic History*, pp. 7, 366; Emin, *Turkey*, p. 160.

72 "Die Wirtschaftslage der Türkei" (no date, 1917), NARA T 139, R 477, p. 891; Emin, *Turkey*, p. 92.

73 Madhar Ahmad, *Kurdistan*, p. 52.

74 German Foreign Office to Bethmann Hollweg, October 28, 1916, NARA T 136, R 48 (AA Türkei 110, vol. 88); for taxes see "Erhöhung von Alkohol- und Tabaksteuern [...]," May 16, 1915, NARA T 136, R 47 (AA Türkei 110, vol. 79); Emin, *Turkey*, p. 158.

75 For Cavid see NARA T 136, R 46 (AA Türkei, vol. 73); for the IOB, NARA T 136, R 46 (AA Türkei, vol. 73) and Blaisdell, *Financial Control*, pp. 27–9, 68–73, 218–21; Trumpener, *Germany*, pp. 273, 275.

76 German–Ottoman agreement of April 20, 1915, NARA T 136, R 47 (AA Türkei 110, vol. 76) and two protocols of March 20, 1915, NARA T 136, R 47 (AA Türkei 110, vol. 76); cf. Trumpener, *Germany*, pp. 272–83, and Blaisdell, *Financial Control*, pp. 185–9.

77 Emin, *Turkey*, pp. 162–4; Issawi, *Economic History*, p. 366; Jehuda L. Wallach, *Anatomie einer Militärhilfe: Die preussisch-deutschen Militärmissionen in der Türkei 1835–1919* (Düsseldorf: Droste, 1976), p. 238.

78 Emin, *Turkey*, pp. 144–6, 161–2; Issawi, *Economic History*, p. 328; Neurath to Bethmann Hollweg, November 21, 1915 and Reichsschatzamt memorandum, March 25, 1916, NARA T 136, R 48 (AA Türkei 110, vol. 84); copy of an unsigned telegram, December 24, 1916, NARA T 136, R 49 (vol. 89; see vol. 92 in same series).

79 Emin, *Turkey*, pp. 144–6.

80 Loi provisoire, September 26, 1915, in Beylerian, *Puissances*, pp. 112–14; Loi sur les biens, dettes et créances laissés par les personnes transportées dans d'autres localités, April 15, 1923, in *Confiscation des Biens des Réfugiés Arméniens par le Gouvernement Turc* (Paris: Imprimerie Massis, 1929), p. 87; cf. particularly Baghdjian, *Confiscation*, p. 130. An incomplete list of lost Armenian church property can be found in Baghdjian, *Confiscation*, pp. 270–83. Thanks to Hilmar Kaiser for helping me clarify the competences of this ministry.

81 Paper by Renner with corrections, September 4, 1916, NA T 136, R 49 (AA Türkei 110, vol. 88).

82 Journal Officiel, August 10, 1916, Le Statut du Patriarchat arménien, in Beylerian, *Puissances*, pp. 329–37, esp. p. 334.

83 Kouymjian, "Confiscation," pp. 224–6.

84 For example, houses of Armenians to be deported from Adana underwent an official appraisal: Hilmar Kaiser (ed.), *Eberhard Count Wolffskeel Von Reichenberg, Zeitoun, Mousa Dagh, Ourfa: Letters on the Armenian Genocide* (Princeton: Talderon, 2001), p. 44 (April 24, 1915).

85 Riggs, *Days*, pp. 89, 93; Leslie Davis, US Consul Harput, Report of 1919, in Sarafian, *Documents*, vol. III, p. 59.

86 Trumpener, *Germany*, p. 380; for the Post Ministry, cf. Üngör, "Reign," p. 10, n. 17.

87 For detailed documentation, see Gerlach, "Nationsbildung," p. 380.

88 195,000 out of 630,000 estimated deaths: Kévorkian, "Ahmed Djemal," pp. 206–7.

89 See Mike Davis, *Late Victorian Holocausts: El Nino Famines and the Making of the Third World* (London and New York: Verso, 2001).

90 Amartya Sen, *Poverty and Famines* (Oxford: Clarendon Press, 1981).

91 Yessaian, *Out of Turkey*, pp. 143, 184–5; Kouymjian Highgas, *Refugee Girl*, pp. 47–8; Vice Consul Samuel Edelman, "Armenian massacre at Ourfa," August 26, 1915, in Sarafian, *Documents*, vol. I, p. 73; Lewy, *Armenian Massacres*, p. 202; Kaiser, "Scene," p. 136. Quote about Bandirma: Hagopian Taft, *Rebirth*, p. 36; quote about Harput: Riggs, *Days*, p. 85.

92 Riggs, *Days*, p. 173; cf. Hartunian, *Neither*, p. 20, about 1895.

93 Surmelian, *I Ask You*, pp. 47–8.

94 Report by a German doctor in Erzincan, June 1915, in Wolfgang Gust (ed.), *Der Völkermord an den Armeniern 1915/16* (Springe: zu Klampen, 2005), p. 179.

95 Official Proclamation, Trabzon, June 28, 1915 and US Consulate Trabzon, Heizer, July 28, 1915, in Sarafian, *Documents*, vol. II, pp. 15, 25. It is unclear whether the prohibition was later lifted: Kevork Yeghia Suakjian, "Genocide in Trebizond" (Ph.D. thesis, University of Nebraska, Lincoln, 1981), p. 230; report Stange (German Military Mission), August 23, 1915, in Gust (ed.), *Völkermord*, p. 268. Further "Die Ausrottung eines Volkes," *Baseler Neueste Nachrichten*, September 16, 1915, in Institut für armenische Fragen (ed.), *The Armenian Genocide*, vol. I (Munich: Institut für armenische Fragen, 1987), pp. 401–2; Miller and Touryan Miller, *Survivors*, p. 69, and Derdarian, *Vergeen*, p. 38 (Kayseri); "Reports of an eyewitness, Miss Alma Johansson (German Missionary)," no date, cover letter by Morgenthau, November 9, 1915, *Armenian Review* 37(1), 1984, p. 122.

96 Austro-Hungarian Consular Agency Brussa, August 16, 1915, in Ohandjanian, *Armenian Genocide*, vol. 2, p. 211; Bedoukian, *Some*, p. 12 (Sivas).

97 Riggs, *Days*, pp. 85, 88.

98 John Minassian, *Many Hills Yet To Climb* (Santa Barbara: Jim Cook, 1986), p. 48.

99 Kaiser, "Armenian property," p. 67; Kaiser, "Scene," p. 135 (Pasin plain, two hours); US Consulate Aleppo, Jackson, May 12, 1915, in Sarafian, *Documents*, vol. I, p. 14 (Zeitun).

100 Sutherland, *Adventures*, p. 113 (quote, Killis); US Consulate Trabzon, Heizer, September 25, 1915, in Sarafian, *Documents*, vol. II, p. 44 (Erzurum, 15 days); US Consular Agency Damascus, Young, September 20, 1915, in Sarafian, *Documents*, vol. I, p. 85; Riggs, *Days*, pp. 84–5; Kouymjian Highgas, *Refugee Girl*, p. 45 (Konia, one week); Davidson, *Odyssey*, p. 77; Bedoukian, *Some*, p. 15 (Sivas).

101 US Consulate Harput, Davis, June 30, 1915, in Sarafian, *Documents*, vol. III, pp. 5–6; reports by Isabelle Harley and Elizabeth Webb, April 15 and June 1, 1918, in Barton, *Turkish Atrocities*, pp. 67, 169 (Harput and Adana); Lepsius, *Todesgang*, pp. 44, 59 (Erzincan and Merziwan).

102 Riggs, *Days*, p. 89; Derdarian, *Vergeen*, pp. 39–40.

103 Mary Graffam, Director of the missionary girls' high school in Sivas, took notes when she accompanied a deportation transport from Sivas in early August 1915 for some days: letter Graffam, *Boston Herald*, December 1915, in Institut für armenische Fragen, *Armenian Genocide*, vol. I, pp. 444–7; cf. Susan Billington Harper, "Mary Louise Graffam: Witness to Genocide," in Winter, *America*, pp. 228–33. Further examples: Miller and Touryan Miller, *Survivors*; Kouymjian Highgas, *Refugee Girl*, pp. 51–2; letter by F. H. Leslie, Urfa (copy), August 6, 1915, in Sarafian, *Documents*, vol. I, p. 49; Kaiser, "Scene," p. 141; "Armenian Exodus from Harpoot" (October 1915), in Sarafian, *Documents*, vol. I, pp. 106–8; Peter Balakian, *Black Dog of Fate: A Memoir* (New York: Basic Books, 1997), pp. 202, 219.

104 Pailadzo Captanian, *1915: Der Völkermord an den Armeniern* (Leipzig: Gustav Kiepenheuer, 1993 [first edition 1919]), pp. 29, 35–44, 47, 73–4, 88.

105 For the last point, see Üngör, "Reign," p. 52 (Diyarbakir).

106 Bedoukian, *Some*, pp. 17–21; Graffam letter, in Institut für armenische Fragen, *Armenian Genocide*, vol. I, pp. 444–7; Billington Harper, "Mary Louise Graffam," pp. 228–33; Derdarian, *Vergeen*, pp. 43–4.

107 Hagopian Taft, *Rebirth*, p. 49; for Armenian charity works, Minassian, *Hills*, pp. 79, 97 (Aintab and Aleppo); Auron, *Banality*, p. 68 (Haifa); US Consulate Baghdad, August 29, 1915, in Sarafian, *Documents*, vol. I, p. 62 (Mosul, on government orders); US Consulate

Aleppo, Jackson, "Armenian Atrocities," March 4, 1918, in Sarafian, *Documents*, vol. I, pp. 150–2 (Aleppo and Urfa); Lewy, *Armenian Massacres*, pp. 194–6 (Aleppo); Isabel Kaprielan-Churchill, "The Armenian genocide and the survival of children," in Alexandre Kimenyi and Otis L. Scott (eds.), *State-Sponsored Mass-Killings in the Twentieth Century* (Lewiston: Edwin Mellen Press, 2001), p. 228 (Aleppo).

108 400 liras (of total losses claimed of 3,900 liras) according to Nafina Hagop Chilinguirian, Application for the Support of Claims against Foreign Governments, May 15, 1919, printed in Balakian, *Black Dog*, p. 198. Cf. Kaiser, "Scene," p. 161.

109 Hartunian, *Neither*, pp. 90–5; Minassian, *Hills*, pp. 64–6. A different view is held by Kaiser, "Scene," p. 171, but it remains to be proven that such money was deposited with state coffers. Selecting possessions on different piles according to their nature could point to such official looting: Derdarian, *Vergeen*, p. 78.

110 US Consulate Mersin, Nathan, September 27, 1915, and Memorandum by Walter M. Geddes (November 1915), in Sarafian, *Documents*, vol. II, pp. 93–4, 123; Bedoukian, *Some*, p. 51 (boatmen killed Armenian women who could not make the extorted payment for their forced passage across the Euphrates).

111 Sutherland, *Adventures*, p. 122; Minassian, *Hills*, p. 88.

112 Leslie Davis, Report of 1919, in Sarafian, *Documents*, vol. III, pp. 80–1.

113 Derdarian, *Vergeen*, p. 71; Captanian, *1915*, p. 30; cf. Bedoukian, *Some*, pp. 36–7.

114 A similar point is made by Lewy, *Armenian Massacres*, p. 222, who, however, puts most blame on the Kurds; for Der es-Zor, Lewy, *Armenian Massacres*, p. 213.

115 Captanian, *1915*, p. 86.

116 Mortality: Katherine Derderian, "Common fate, different experience: Gender-specific aspects of the Armenian genocide, 1915–1917," *HGS* 19(1), 2005, p. 9; Kaprielan-Churchill, "Armenian genocide," p. 251; Minassian, *Hills*, p. 92; Captanian, *1915*, p. 80. Abandoned etc.: Riggs, *Days*, p. 143; US Consulate Harput, Davis, December 30, 1915,

in Sarafian, *Documents*, vol. III, p. 32; US Consulate Mersin, Nathan, September 22, 1915, in Sarafian, *Documents*, vol. II, p. 91; Ramela Martin, *Out of Darkness* (Cambridge, MA: Zoryan Institute, 1989), p. 8; Miller and Touryan Miller, *Survivors*, pp. 97–100; Suakjian, "Genocide," p. 122; Lewy, *Armenian Massacres*, pp. 185, 187.

117 "Movement by railway to Aleppo," enclosure to US Consulate Aleppo, Jackson, September 29, 1915, in Sarafian, *Documents*, vol. I, pp. 97–8. The lists by transport comprised seemingly only poorer deportees who did not pay fares; it was estimated that one was to add 25 percent of the total who had bought tickets.

118 Cf. Raymond H. Kévorkian, "Le sort des déportés dans les camps de concentration de Syrie et de Mesopotamie," in Kévorkian (ed.), *L'extermination des déportés dans les camps de concentration de Syrie-Mésopotamie (1915–1916): La deuxième phase du génocide* (Paris: Revue d'histoire arménienne contemporaine, tome 1, 1998), esp. pp. 60–1; Gerlach, "Nationsbildung," pp. 392–3.

119 Through diplomats: Leslie Davis, ex-US Consul Harput, Report of 1919, in Sarafian, *Documents*, vol. III, pp. 55–6, 61–2, 97–8; US Consulate Trabzon, Heizer, August 8, 1915, in Sarafian, *Documents*, vol. II, p. 32; by postal order: Captanian, *1915*, pp. 121, 126 (Der es-Zor); Davidson, *Odyssey*, pp. 122, 148 (Bireçik and Roumkale); Riggs, *Days*, pp. 89–90. But Talaat tried to stop this practice for some time: see his telegram to Army headquarters, March 25, 1916, in Tetik, *Armenian Activities*, vol. II, pp. 9–10 but then his telegram to the Supreme Military Command, October 18, 1916, in Tetik, *Armenian Activities*, vol. VII (Ankara: Genelkurmay Askerî Tarih ve stratejik Etüt Başkanlığı Yayınları, 2007), p. 318. Halaçoglu, *Facts*, p. 95, asserts that liquidation commissions did send money to deported persons. No evidence is known for the announced reimbursement of Armenians for their immovables (for the announcement, Gürün, *Armenian File*, p. 209). Proceeds could only be claimed after the end of the "present situation" (Kaiser, "Armenian property," p. 60, cf. p. 62).

120 Akçam, *Shameful Act*, p. 183 (200,000 in "Kurdish families") and p. 277; Kaprielan-Churchill, "Armenian genocide," pp. 247–8 (200,000 children); Madhar Ahmad, *Kurdistan* (E. V. Tarle estimated 250,000 converts). Sarafian's estimate that 5 to 10 percent of the Armenians were taken into Muslim households may be too low: Ara Sarafian,

"The absorption of Armenian women and children into Muslim households as a structural component of the Armenian genocide," in Omer Bartov and Phyllis Mack (eds.), *In God's Name: Genocide and Religion in the Twentieth Century* (New York and Oxford: Berghahn, 2001), p. 211. Kévorkian, "Ahmed Djemal," pp. 206–7, indicates that only a fraction of an estimated 240,000 survivors stayed with Muslim families, appearing to neglect the adoption issue.

121 Riggs, *Days*, p. 97; Üngör, "Reign," pp. 61, 65; for an order by the Ministry of the Interior of July 1, 1915 to also deport the converts, see Gürün, *Armenian File*, p. 212.

122 Auron, *Banality*, pp. 380–1 (Constantinople); Kaprielan-Churchill, "Armenian genocide," p. 227 (Harput); Halaçoglu, *Facts*, p. 89 (government instruction, Sivas, March 9, 1916). On November 23, 1916, Şükrü Bey (IAMM) ordered the provincial authorities in Diyarbakir to liquidate the property of Armenians not deported: Kaiser, "Armenian property," p. 70.

123 US Consulate Trabzon, Heizer, July 7, 1915 and Heizer's report of April 11, 1919 in Sarafian, *Documents*, vol. I, pp. 12–13, 38; Suakjian, "Genocide," pp. 132–3, 138, 213, 231. From a victim perspective: Surmelian, *I Ask You*. Vahakn N. Dadrian, "Children as victims of genocide: the Armenian case," *JGR* 5(3), 2003, pp. 421–37, takes Trabzon as a case study without elaborating on the adoptions.

124 Akçam, *Shameful Act*, p. 175; Riggs, *Days*, p. 98; US Consular Service Samsun, Peter, July 10, 1915 in Sarafian, *Documents*, vol. I, pp. 56–7; US Consulate Mersin, Nathan, September 27, 1915, in Sarafian, *Documents*, vol. I, p. 94. In 1916, forced conversions of Armenians in Thrace were allowed to be revoked: US Consular Agency Adrianople, Allen, March 18, 1916, in Sarafian, *Documents*, vol. I, pp. 71–2.

125 Kévorkian, "Ahmed Djemal," p. 202; Erik Jan Zürcher, "Ottoman Labour Battalions in World War I," in Kieser and Schaller, *Armenian Genocide*, p. 194; Hartunian, *Neither*, p. 115; Lewy, *Armenian Massacres*, p. 219; Auron, *Banality*, p. 339.

126 Gürün, *Armenian File*, pp. 211–12; for another version, Halaçoglu, *Facts*, pp. 88–9.

127 See Sarafian, "Absorption," p. 210.

128 Derderian, "Common fate," p. 11; Riggs, *Days*, pp. 92, 99 (Harput). The value of such property could be substantial as these children inherited the possessions of their original family: telegram by Talaat Pasha, July 29/30, 1915, in Sonyel, *Displacement*, p. 2. Quote: Bedoukian, *Some*, pp. 54–5.

129 Madhar Ahmad, *Kurdistan*, pp. 154, 178, n. 36 (Diyarbakir).

130 Auron, *Banality*, p. 183; Hartunian, *Neither*, p. 102.

131 Cf. Surmelian, *I Ask You*, pp. 115–22, 140, 169–70; Riggs, *Days*, pp. 98–9, 149.

132 Auron, *Banality*, pp. 191, 379–80; Kouymjian Highgas, *Refugee Girl*, p. 74; Derderian, "Common fate," pp. 6–7, 11–12; Kaiser, "Scene," pp. 171, 177, n. 55; Dadrian, "Children," pp. 425–8.

133 Surmelian, *I Ask You*, pp. 111–14 (Jevizlik, Trabzon province); report by German nurses von Wedel-Jarlsberg and Elvers, June 28, 1915, in Gust, *Völkermord*, p. 260 (Kemagh).

134 Derderian, "Common fate," pp. 11–12; Lewy, *Armenian Massacres*, p. 210 (Ras ul-Ain); Derdarian, *Vergeen*, pp. 79–93; report by E. Neuner (early 1918), in Gust, *Völkermord*, p. 562.

135 Hartunian, *Neither*, pp. 102–3.

136 German Consulate Aleppo (Rössler) to Reichskanzler, July 27 and 30, 1915, in Gust, *Völkermord*, pp. 214, 221; Report Monsignore Dolci, August 19, 1915, in Gust, *Völkermord*, p. 249.

137 Ara Sarafian, "Editor's Introduction," in Riggs, *Days*, p. viii; Riggs, *Days*, pp. 98, 108–17; Gerayer Koutcharian, "Der Völkermord an den Armeniern (1915–1917)," in Hofmann, *Verfolgung*, p. 69; Report Davis (1919), in Sarafian, *Documents*, vol. III, pp. 102, 112. According to Davis, province Governor Sabit Bey, himself a Kurd, allowed these groups to help Armenians get through the Russian lines: Sarafian, *Documents*, vol. III, pp. 45–6, 115.

138 Madhar Ahmad, *Kurdistan*, p. 155.

139 Report by W. Spieker, July 27, 1915, in Gust, *Völkermord*, p. 218.

140 US Consulate Harput, Davis, December 30, 1915, and his 1919 report in Sarafian, *Documents*, vol. III, pp. 28, 86; Madhar Ahmad,

Kurdistan, p. 155; Gaunt, *Massacres*, p. 154; a survivor is Captanian, *1915*, p. 86.

141 Anonymous report, August 1915, in Gust, *Völkermord*, p. 257.

142 Yessaian, *Out of Turkey*, p. 187.

143 "Armenian exodus from Harpoot" with cover letter by US Consul Jackson (Aleppo), October 16, 1915, *Armenian Review* 37(1), 1984, p. 118.

144 Kouymjian Highgas, *Refugee Girl*, p. 47.

145 Aaronsohn, "Pro Armenia," p. 376; similar report of survivor Georgian Garabeth, June 23, 1915, in Gust, *Völkermord*, p. 229.

146 Kaiser, "Scene," p. 158; Captanian, *1915*, pp. 60, 71.

147 Leslie Davis, ex-US Consul in Harput, Report of 1919, in Sarafian, *Documents*, vol. III, p. 84.

148 Madhar Ahmad, *Kurdistan*, p. 155; Riggs, *Days*, p. 142; Bedoukian, *Some*, pp. 38, 40; Captanian, *1915*, p. 74; Gaunt, *Massacres*, p. 154 (Mardin).

149 Captanian, *1915*, p. 79.

150 Martin, *Out of Darkness*, p. 14.

151 Emin, *Turkey*, p. 94.

152 See Kaiser, "Armenian property," pp. 63–4, 67; Regulations of June 9, 1915, article 16, in Sarafian, *Documents*, vol. I, p. 174. Officially the government did try to outlaw appropriations by civil servants: telegram Talaat, August 22, 1915, in Sonyel, *Displacement*, p. 4. Talaat also urged the authorities to give individual Muslim businesses and citizens a chance to appropriate Armenian business property against the improvised corporations: Kévorkian, *Génocide*, pp. 256–7.

153 Cf. Caglar Keyder, *State and Class in Turkey: A Study in Capitalist Development* (London and New York: Verso, 1987), pp. 49–69; Feroz Ahmad, "Vanguard of a nascent bourgeoisie: The social and economic policy of the Young Turks 1908–1918," in Osman Okyar and Halil Inalcik (eds.), *Türkiye'min Sosyal ve Ekonomik Tariki, 1071–1920* (Ankara: Meteksan, 1980), pp. 29–50. Somewhat in contrast, Levene, "Creating," pp. 419–20, summarizes: "Modern genocide, in conclusion, is developmental."

154 Pallavicini to Burian, August 31, 1915 and Konfidenten-Bericht Nr. 300, Constantinople, August 19, 1915, in Ohandjanian, *Armenian Genocide*, vol. 2, pp. 212–14, 228–29; Morgenthau, *Ambassador*, p. 337 (Talaat's comments); Strauss, "Volkswirtschaftliche Studien in der Türkei," July 6, 1916, NARA T 136, R 66 (AA Türkei 134, vol. 35); see Akçam, *Shameful Act*, p. 91 (Cavid).

155 Taner Akçam, *From Empire to Republic: Turkish Nationalism and the Armenian Genocide* (London and New York: Zed, 2004), pp. 238–40. For this, short-term losses in taxes and retarded development of the general economy were accepted: Gérard Chaliand and Yves Ternon, *The Armenians: From Genocide to Resistance* (London: Zed, 1983), pp. 79, 82; Morgenthau, *Ambassador*, pp. 338 (apparently refers to Talaat calculating reduced annual tax revenues of 5 million liras), 348.

156 Gerlach, "Nationsbildung," pp. 381–2.

157 From 1913 to 1918 imports dropped by 89 percent and exports by 74 percent: Madhar Ahmad, *Kurdistan*, p. 132.

158 Hugo Meyer to German Embassy Constantinople, July 11, 1917, NARA T 136, R 48 (AA Türkei 134, vol. 38) and more material in vols. 37 and 38; Emin, *Turkey*, p. 128.

159 Grobba, *Getreidewirtschaft*, pp. 21–3, 31, 54, 58, also for laws; Gerlach, "Nationsbildung," pp. 385–8.

160 Gerlach, "Nationsbildung," pp. 385–8; Grobba, *Getreidewirtschaft*, pp. 19, 22, 96.

161 Grobba, *Getreidewirtschaft*, p. 60.

162 L. Schatkowski Schilcher, "The famine of 1915–1918 in Greater Syria," in John P. Spagnolo (ed.), *Problems of the Modern Middle East in Historical Perspective: Essays in Honor of Albert Hourani* (Reading: Ithaca Press, 1992), pp. 229–58; Hassan Kayali, *Arabs and Young Turks* (Berkeley: University of California Press, 1997), pp. 188–91, 199; Grobba, *Getreidewirtschaft*; Gerlach, "Nationsbildung," p. 389; Lewy, *Armenian Massacres*, pp. 55–6.

163 For Greater Syria, Grobba, *Getreidewirtschaft*, esp. pp. 35–6, 60, 83 (in March 1918 there were 100 deaths per day in Aleppo, primarily Armenians); for Aleppo Lewy, *Armenian Massacres*, pp. 191–3,

and Minassian, *Hills*, p. 106; for Aintab 1916–18 Hartunian, *Neither*, pp. 111–12; Bireçik 1916–17: Kouymjian Highgas, *Refugee Girl*, p. 95.

164 Ellen Marie Lust-Okar, "Failure in collaboration: Armenian refugees in Syria," *Middle Eastern Studies* 32(1), 1996, pp. 53–68 (Mesopotamia and Syria, typhus 1916–17); Kévorkian, "Ahmed Djemal," p. 201 (typhus in Hauran, early 1916). Syriacs and Chaldeans deported to Mosul province were also forced to subsist on the welfare services of their churches: Gaunt, *Massacres*, p. 298.

165 Sutherland, *Adventures*, pp. 130–3 (quote p. 133) about Aleppo in early 1916; Bedoukian, *Some*, pp. 81–90 (Bireçik); on the marches: Riggs, *Days*, pp. 147–8; Bedoukian, *Some*, pp. 21–4; Minassian, *Hills*, p. 78.

166 Prevention: Sutherland (later a physician), *Adventures*, pp. 115, 152; evictions: Hilmar Kaiser, *At the Crossroads of Der Zor: Death, Survival and Humanitarian Resistance in Aleppo, 1915–1917* (Princeton: Gomidas Institute, 2001), pp. 24–8, 58; J. B. Jackson, "Armenian atrocities, March 4, 1918," *Armenian Review* 37(1), 1984, pp. 132–3; Kieser, *Friede*, p. 357; Bedoukian, *Some*, p. 56. Many victims were then thrown into rivers – hardly an act serving epidemics prevention: German Consulate Aleppo, Rössler, April 27, 1916 in Gust (ed.), *Völkermord*, p. 465.

167 Armenians: Üngör, "Reign," p. 77; Hofmann, "Mit einer Stimme," p. 42; de Nogales, *Years*, p. 266. Soldiers: Clarence D. Ussher with Grace H. Knapp, *An American Physician in Turkey* (Boston and New York: Houghton Mifflin, 1917); de Nogales, *Years*, pp. 272–3; Kaiser, "Scene," p. 131, and Davis's report about Harput (1919), in Sarafian, *Documents*, vol. III, p. 50. Kurdish refugees spreading cholera: Riggs, *Days*, p. 181.

168 Ussher, *Physician* (although he exaggerates his own role); Riggs, *Days*, pp. 8–19, 38–44; Lewy, *Armenian Massacres*, pp. 58–60.

169 Lewy, *Armenian Massacres*, pp. 60–1; for the military see de Nogales, *Years*. The figures are controversial.

170 Akçam, *Armenien*, p. 359 (cf. pp. 149, 347). The other counts were the Armenian massacres and the entry in the war.

171 Kévorkian, *Génocide*, p. 256.

172 Quote: Erik Jan Zürcher, *Turkey: A Modern History* (London and New York: I. B. Tauris, 1993), p. 131.

173 Auron, *Banality*, p. 379.

174 Dennis R. Papazian, "Introduction," in Yessaian, *Out of Turkey*, p. xxii.

175 Riggs, *Days*, pp. 45–6, 60 (Harput); Hagopian Taft, *Rebirth*, p. 2 (Bandirma); Minassian, *Hills*, p. 36 (Gurun).

176 Koutcharian, "Völkermord," p. 65; Akçam, *Empire*, pp. 171–4; Üngör, "Reign," pp. 53–6.

177 Riggs, *Days*, p. 85; Taner Akcam, "Anatomy of a crime: The Turkish Historical Society's manipulation of archival documents," *JGR* 7(2), 2005, p. 276, n. 35; Kaiser, "Scene," p. 163.

178 Riggs, *Days*, p. 96; for general popular disapproval, see Martin Niepage, *The Horrors of Aleppo* (London: T. F. Unwin, n.y. [1917]), p. 7; Akçam, *Shameful Act*, pp. 179–80.

179 De Nogales, *Years*, pp. 25–6, 166, 170, 273, 275; Üngör, "Reign," p. 112, n. 708; Lewy, *Armenian Massacres*, p. 210.

180 Akçam, *Shameful Act*, p. 353.

181 Akçam, *Shameful Act*, pp. 106, 362–4.

182 Derdarian, *Vergeen*, p. 126; Miller and Touryan Miller, *Survivors*, pp. 97–102; Kaprielan-Churchill, "Armenian genocide," pp. 232–3, 247; Riggs, *Days*, pp. 166–7.

183 Derdarian, "Common fate," p. 10; Kaprielan-Churchill, "Armenian genocide," p. 250. Derdarian, *Vergeen*, pp. 142–3, relates the story of children in 1919 'rescued' from Kurdish families against their will.

184 See Madhar Ahmad, *Kurdistan*, pp. 156–7; McDowall, *History*, p. 104.

185 Akçam, *Shameful Act*, p. 89; Üngör, "Reign," pp. 19, 21.

186 Adalian, "Policy," pp. 33–7, 39–42; Matthias Bjoernlund, "The 1914 cleansing of Aegean Greeks as a case of violent Turkification," *JGR* 10(1), 2008, pp. 41–57; Akçam, *Empire*, pp. 146–8; Hofmann, "Mit einer Stimme," pp. 13–14; Harry Tsirkinidis, "Der Völkermord

an den Griechen Kleinasiens (1914–1923)," in Hofmann, *Verfolgung* pp. 139, 145–6.

187 Kévorkian, *Génocide*, p. 155.

188 US Consular Agency Adrianople, Allen, October 23, 1915 and March 5, 1916, in Sarafian, *Documents*, vol. II, pp. 66, 69–70; Balakian, *Burning Tigris*, p. 269.

189 Kaiser, "Armenian property," p. 69.

190 Tsirkinidis, "Völkermord," pp. 142, 157–8, 163, 167, 171; Konstantinos Fotiadis, "Der Völkermord an den Griechen des Pontos," in Hofmann, *Verfolgung*, pp. 189–90, 197–9.

191 Martin, *Out of Darkness*, p. 73.

192 Hofmann, "Mit einer Stimme," p. 38.

193 US Consulate Baghdad, August 29, 1915, in Sarafian, *Documents*, vol. I, p. 63; Gaunt, *Massacres*, p. 128.

194 Martin Tamcke, "Der Genozid an den Assyrern/Nestorianern (Ostsyrische Christen)," in Hofmann, *Verfolgung*, p. 100.

195 Riggs, *Days*, p. 181.

196 Madhar Ahmad, *Kurdistan*, pp. 130–1; McDowall, *History*, p. 109; Üngör, "Reign," pp. 87–8; Riggs, *Days*, pp. 177–9, 183–4. The particular convoy that Riggs observed was allowed to turn back in reaction to threats by Kurdish tribal leaders against the authorities.

197 Akçam, *Shameful Act*, pp. 322, 108, cf. pp. 328–9 for the time after World War I; Akçam, *Empire*, pp. 92–100; Bloxham, *Game*, pp. 42, 63; Lewy, *Armenian Massacres*, pp. 116–20 for during World War I.

198 See W. A. Shedd, Urmia, to Caldwell, US Minister, Teheran, June 23, 1915, and E. T. Allen, "Outline of events in the District of Urmia [...]," June 1918, in Sarafian, *Documents*, vol. II, pp. 135–7, 144–5; Gaunt, *Massacres*, pp. 95, 99, 104, 110–17, 120.

199 Konstantinos A. Vakalopoulos, "Vertreibung und Genozid an den Griechen Ost-Thrakiens (1908–1922)," in Hofmann, *Verfolgung*, pp. 129–31.

200 Ussher, *Physician*, pp. 283–5; Surmelian, *I Ask You*, pp. 141–2, 147–8.

4 From rivalries between elites to a crisis of society

1 See Rounaq Jahan, "Genocide in Bangladesh," in Samuel Totten *et al.*, (eds.), *Genocide in the Twentieth Century* (New York and London: Garland, 1995), pp. 371–402; Wardatul Akmam, "Atrocities against humanity during the liberation war in Bangladesh: a case of genocide," *JGR* 4(4), 2002, pp. 543–59; Shahriar Kabir, "Introduction," in Kabir (ed.), *Tormenting Seventy One: An Account of Pakistan Army's Atrocities during Bangladesh Liberation War of 1971* (Dhaka: Nirmul Committee, 1999), www.mukto-mona.com/Special_Event_126_ march/shariar_kabir/Tormenting71_1.pdf (accessed March 9, 2007), p. 2. Early accounts along these lines: Simon Dring, "Tanks crush revolt in East Pakistan," *Daily Telegraph*, March 30, 1971; US Consulate Dacca, telegram, March 28, 1971, "Selective genocide," in Sajit Gandhi (ed.), *The Tilt: The US and the South Asian Crisis of 1971*, National Security Archive Electronic Briefing Book 79, December 16, 2002, www.gwu.edu/~nsarchive/NSAEBB/NSAEBB79 (accessed March 9, 2007); Anthony Mascarenhas, *The Rape of Bangla Desh* (Delhi: Vikas, n.y. [1971]), pp. 116–17.

2 Hakeem Arshad Qureshi, *The 1971 Indo-Pak War: A Soldier's Narrative* (Oxford *et al.*: Oxford University Press, 2002), pp. 20, 35; Faizal Muqeem Khan, *Pakistan's Crisis in Leadership* (Islamabad *et al.*: National Book Foundation, 1973), p. 67; A. A. K. Niazi, *The Betrayal of East Pakistan* (Karachi *et al.*: Oxford University Press, 1998), p. 45.

3 Situation report, FRG Consulate General Dacca, October 28, 1971, PA AA B37/629; see also Archer K. Blood, *The Cruel Birth of Bangladesh: Memoirs of an American Diplomat* (Dhaka: University Press Limited, 2002), pp. 67–8. (Pro-)Bengali sources put the number of early reinforcements, mainly through Pakistani International Airlines, higher than Pakistani authors: statement Prime Minister Tajuddin, April 18, 1971, in I. N. Tewary (ed.), *War of Independence in Bangla Desh* (New Delhi: Navachetna Prakashan, 1971), p. 162 (one division); Mascarenhas, *Rape*, pp. 87, 103–4 (12,000); Kalyan Chaudhuri, *Genocide in Bangladesh* (Bombay *et al.*: Orient Longman, 1972), pp. 14–15; Blood, *Cruel*, p. 179. Siddiq Salik, *Witness to Surrender* (New Delhi: Lancer, 1998 [first ed. 1977]), pp. 40, 52, 62, and former Pakistani Chief of Staff Gul Hassan Khan, *Memoirs*

(Karachi *et al*.: Oxford University Press, 1993), pp. 260–1, 285, speak of two battalions.

4 Qureshi, *Indo-Pak War*, pp. 32–84.

5 Anthony Mascarenhas, "Genocide," *Sunday Times*, June 13, 1971, in Fazlul Quader Quaderi (ed.), *Bangla Desh Genocide and World Press* (Dacca: Begum Dilafroz Quaderi, 1972 [second, revised edition]), pp. 132, 137, Muqeem Khan, *Pakistan's Crisis*, p. 82; Chaudhuri, *Genocide*, p. 37.

6 Muhammad Ghulam Kabir, *Minority Politics in Bangladesh* (New Delhi: Vikas, 1980), pp. 5–38.

7 Bertil Lintner, "The plights of ethnic and religious minorities and the rise of Islamic extremism in Bangladesh," in K. V. Paliwal (ed.), *Islamism and Genocide of Minorities in Bangladesh* (New Delhi: Hindu Writers' Forum, 2005), p. 3.

8 Ghulam Kabir, *Minority Politics*, p. 41; Ramkrishna Mukherji, "Social background of Bangladesh," *EPW* 7(5/7), February 1972, p. 270; Angus Hone, "Bangladesh: Political economy of reconstruction," *EPW* 8(10), March 10, 1973, p. 312; Sumit Sen, "Stateless refugees and the right to return: The Bihari refugees of South Asia," part 1, *International Journal of Refugee Law* 11(4), 1999, p. 628.

9 Omar Noman, *Pakistan: A Political and Economic History Since 1947* (London and New York: Kegan Paul International, 1988), p. 20.

10 Ghulam Kabir, *Minority Politics*, pp. 70–1. The "basic democrats" system meant that there were popular elections of local representatives, who then went on to elect representatives on a larger local (*thana*) level; these elected district, and those in turn provincial, representatives. As a result, local elites gained virtually all the important seats and strengthened their position.

11 Noman, *Pakistan*, pp. 19–20.

12 Noman, *Pakistan*, pp. 36, 40.

13 Kabir Uddin Ahmad, *Breakup of Pakistan: Background and Prospects of Bangladesh* (London: Social Science Publishers, 1972), pp. 1, 59.

14 Kalim Siddiqui, *Conflict, Crisis and War in East Pakistan* (New York and Washington: Macmillan, 1972).

15 *Frontier* article, December 19, 1970, April 24, and May 8, 1971, in Muntassir Mamoon (ed.), *Media and the Liberation War of Bangladesh, vol. 2: Selections from the* Frontier (Dhaka: Centre for Bangladesh Studies, 2002), pp. 30, 100, 112; Australian High Commission, London, Inward Cablegram, September 8, 1972, ANA 855/2, part 1, p. 238 ("true status as a largely bourgeois nationalist party which had not really enjoyed majority support is again emerging").

16 Mukherji, "Bangladesh," p. 270; Rounaq Jahan, "Members of Parliament in Bangladesh," *Legislative Studies Quarterly* 1(3), 1976, esp. pp. 358–60; Richard Pilkington, "A 'Time when Principles Make best Politics?': The United States' Response to the Genocide in East Pakistan," (M.A. thesis, Concordia University, 2006), p. 17.

17 Howard Schuman, "A note on the rapid rise of mass Bengali nationalism in East Pakistan," *American Journal of Sociology* 78(2), 1972, pp. 290–8.

18 Bengali was not made an official language, although more than half of all Pakistanis spoke it, whereas Urdu, which was spoken only by a small minority, became Pakistan's official language.

19 Uddin Ahmad, *Breakup*, pp. 26–51; Md. Abdul Wadeed Bhuiyan, *Emergence of Bangladesh and Role of Awami League* (Delhi: Vikas, 1982), pp. 77–96; Mohammad Ayoob and K. Subrahmanyam, *The Liberation War* (New Delhi: S. Chand, 1972), pp. 31–48; Paul Dreyfus, *Du Pakistan au Bangladesh* (Paris: Arthaud, 1972), pp. 96–8; Pradbodh Chandra, *Bloodbath in Bangla Desh* (Delhi: Adarsh, n.y. [1971]), pp. 85–6; Tanweer Akram, "The Bangladesh genocide of 1971," Working Paper, Allied Social Sciences Association Chicago, revised November 13, 2006, http://papers.ssrn.com/s013/papers.cf?abstract_id=984686#PaperDownload (accessed December 15, 2007), p. 14. Cf. Suman Sarkar, "Pakistan: Patterns of exploitation," *Frontier*, August 28, 1971, in Mamoon, *Media*, pp. 56–9; for the West Pakistani view, L. F. Rushbrook Williams, *The East Pakistan Tragedy* (New York: Drake, 1972), p. 108.

20 G. W. Choudhury, *The Last Days of United Pakistan* (Bloomington: Indiana University Press, 1974), pp. 63–4; Mascarenhas, *Rape*, p. 51;

US Embassy Rawalpindi, telegram, March 5, 1970, NARA RG59, Gen. Rec., Economic, Box 484, AID 9 PAK 1/1/70.

21 Dom Moraes, *The Tempest Within: An Account of East Pakistan* (New York: Barnes and Noble, 1971), pp. 54–78; Blood, *Cruel*, pp. 73–121; Dreyfus, *Du Pakistan*, pp. 113–21, esp. p. 117; François Massa, *Bengale: histoire d'un conflit* (Paris: Editions Alain Moreau, 1972), p. 141; James and Marti Hefley, *Christ in Bangladesh* (New York *et al.*: Harper & Row, 1973, pp. 19–31.

22 Mascarenhas, *Rape*, pp. 56, 59; Muqeem Khan, *Pakistan's Crisis*, p. 44; Niazi, *Betrayal*, pp. 37–8; Christian Gerlach, "Der Versuch zur globalen entwicklungspolitischen Steuerung auf der World Food Conference von 1974," *WerkstattGeschichte* 11(31), 2002, pp. 83–4.

23 Blood, *Cruel*, pp. 307–8 (a US team extrapolated 230,000 deaths).

24 Oxfam Archive, Asia Field Committee, February 1970–October 1976, esp. reports by Richard Taylor, December 16, 1970, p. 4, and G. W. Acworth, March 11, 1974, 2, 7.

25 Sheena Grosset, Tour Report – Bangladesh, November 15–29, 1978, Oxfam Archive, Overseas Division Field Reports, Bangladesh Tour Reports 1972–1987; Gerlach, "Versuch," pp. 79–86.

26 See Choudhury, *Last Days*, pp. xii, 18.

27 Onwar Marwah, "India's military intervention in East Pakistan, 1971–1972," *Modern Asian Studies* 13(4), 1979, p. 559; Siddiqui, *Conflict*, pp. 94–5; Noman, *Pakistan*, pp. 19, 60; Bhuiyan, *Emergence*, p. 81; Ayoob and Subrahmanyam, *Liberation*, p. 45.

28 Mascarenhas, *Rape*, pp. 64, 86.

29 Quoted in Bhuiyan, *Emergence*, p. 148.

30 Choudhury, *Last Days*, p. 129; Ayoob and Subrahmanyam, *Liberation*, p. 117.

31 Perhaps the ambitious Bhutto even steered toward a national breakup if he could only secure leadership in a restructured western wing: Ayoob and Subrahmanyam, *Liberation*, p. 99.

32 Richard Sisson and Leo E. Rose, *War and Secession: Pakistan, India, and the Creation of Bangladesh* (Berkeley *et al.*: University of California Press, 1990), pp. 82–96.

33 Sisson and Rose, *War*, pp. 112–30; Blood, *Cruel*, p. 173. Army killings: "E Pakistan claim of 300 shot dead," *The Times*, March 5, 1971; Salik, *Witness*, pp. 56–7.

34 Government of Pakistan, White Paper on the Crisis in East Pakistan, n.p. [Rawalpindi], August 5, 1971, pp. 15–27.

35 Sukharanjan Dasgupta, *Midnight Massacre in Dacca* (New Delhi et al.: Vikas, 1978), pp. 52–3; Lawrence Lifschultz, *Bangladesh: The Unfinished Revolution* (London: Zed, 1979), pp. 28–9.

36 Niazi, *Betrayal*, pp. 38, 40; Muqeem Khan, *Pakistan's Crisis*, pp. 53–4; Sisson and Rose, *War*, pp. 81–90; Robert Payne, *Massacre* (New York: Macmillan, 1973), p. 13; Salik, *Witness*, pp. 39–40.

37 Muqeem Khan, *Pakistan's Crisis*, pp. 59–60, 66–70; Sisson and Rose, *War*, pp. 95, 112, 132–3; again with some slightly different dates: Salik, *Witness*, pp. 62–6, 68.

38 Text in Salik, *Witness*, pp. 228–34. See Muqeem Khan, *Pakistan's Crisis*, p. 71; Niazi, *Betrayal*, pp. 44, 46; for an intercepted order to Dinajpur ("Disarm Bengalis"), see Chaudhuri, *Genocide*, p. 60.

39 Quoted in Salik, *Witness*, p. 53. Cf. Jim McKinley, *Death to Life: Bangladesh as Experienced by a Missionary Family* (Louisville: The Highview Baptist Church, 1978), p. 8.

40 Niazi, *Betrayal*, pp. 46–7; Salik, *Witness*, pp. 73–5; quote: Sisson and Rose, *War*, p. 158. See Chaudhuri, *Genocide*, pp. 25–56.

41 GDR Consulate Calcutta, "Vermerk über ein Gespräch mit Oberstleutnant B. P. Rikhye," May 4, 1971, PA AA MfAA C1052/77 25; from personal observations, Salik, *Witness*, pp. 66, 78; quote: Simon Dring, "Tanks crush revolt in Pakistan," *Daily Telegraph*, March 30, 1971; cf. Payne, *Massacre*, p. 44.

42 Amir Tahari, "Five views of a tragedy," *Kayhan International*, July 28, 1971, in Quaderi, *Bangla Desh*, p. 195.

43 Chaudhuri, *Genocide*, pp. 59–60 (Dinajpur, Rangpur, Hilli, Bogra).

44 In fact, the "Searchlight" plan corresponded to most of the alleged targets of the Bengali uprising, except for the border stations. White Paper, p. 40; Muqeem Khan, *Pakistan's Crisis*, p. 45.

45 Account by then Brigadier M. R. Majumdar, in Kabir, *Tormenting*; Rafiq ul Islam, *A Tale of Millions* (Dacca: Bangladesh Books International, 1981), pp. 55–67; A. M. H. Muhith, *Bangladesh: Emergence of a Nation* (Dacca: Bangladesh Books International, 1978), p. 210; Talukder Maniruzzaman, *The Bangladesh Revolution and Its Aftermath* (Dacca: Bangladesh Books International, 1980), pp. 84–5.

46 Islam, *Tale*, pp. 3–6, 72–88, esp. p. 79.

47 Jahanara Imam, *Of Blood and Fire* (New Delhi: Sterling, 1989), pp. 8–9; Blood, *Cruel*, pp. 156, 158, 163; David Loshak, *Pakistan Crisis* (New York: McGraw Hill, 1971), p. 74; "Wave of protests sweeps across East Pakistan," *The Times*, March 3, 1971.

48 Blood, *Cruel*, p. 173 (first quote); Islam, *Tale*, pp. 49–50.

49 Account by then *Ansar* Btl. Commander Mosharraf Hossain, in Kabir, *Tormenting* (Pabna); accounts by Waliul Islam (Chittagong), A. K. M. Jahangir (Rajshahi), and Arief Razzaque (Ishurdi), in Ishrat Firdousi (ed.), *The Year That Was* (Dhaka: Bastu Prakashan, 1996), pp. 15–24, 115; "Pakistan: Death of an ideal," *Newsweek*, April 12, 1971, in Quaderi, *Bangla Desh*, p. 55; Muhith, *Bangladesh*, p. 210; Blood, *Cruel*, p. 186.

50 Accounts by Syed Mushtaque and Afsan Chowdhury, in Firdousi, *Year*, pp. 30, 337; Peter Hazelhurst, "Bengalis out for independence by any means," *The Times*, March 25, 1971; Sarmila Bose, "Anatomy of violence: Analysis of civil war in East Pakistan in 1971," *EPW*, October 8, 2005, www.epw.org.in/showArticles.php?root=2005&leaf=10&filename=9223&filetype=html (accessed March 9, 2007); Muhith, *Bangladesh*, p. 222; partial transcript of Pakistani army wire traffic, night of March 25, 1971, recorded by Dr. M. M. Husain, Atomic Energy Center, Dacca, www.bd71.com/docs/LWM/tape.html to www.bd71.com/docs/LWM/tape4.htm (accessed December 14, 2007); other excerpts in Jag Mohan (ed.), *The Black Book of Genocide in Bangla Desh* (New Delhi: Geeta Book Centre, 1971), pp. 25–9. Cf. Imam, *Blood*, pp. 26–7 (March 16, 1971); Sisson and Rose, *War*, p. 123.

51 Muhith, *Bangladesh*, pp. 230, 287.

52 Maniruzzaman, *Bangladesh*, pp. 85–95; Amita Malik, *The Year of the Vulture* (New Delhi: Orient Longmans, 1972), p. 24.

53 Muhith, *Bangaldesh*, p. 287; Maniruzzaman, *Bangladesh*, pp. 99–100. Bengali control: Maniruzzaman, *Bangladesh*, pp. 85–95.

54 Akmam, "Atrocities," p. 551; Mascarenhas, *Rape*, pp. 18, 117 (9 Division headquarters).

55 Simon Dring, "Tanks crush revolt in Pakistan," *Daily Telegraph*, March 30, 1971.

56 Mascarenhas, "Genocide."

57 Noman, *Pakistan*, p. 30; for the 1967 book perceived as racist, Ayub had a ghost writer: see Dasgupta, *Midnight*, p. 28.

58 Salik, *Witness*, p. 94. For general information on South Asian racism I am indebted to Clemens Six.

59 Partial transcript of Pakistani army wire traffic, night of March 25, 1971 (see note 50); Mascarenhas, "Genocide," and Mascarenhas, *Rape*, p. 119 (Comilla, April 1971).

60 Statements by Lt. Col. Mansirul Haq and Mohammed Ashraf, Additional Deputy Commissioner Dacca, in Hamoodur Commission report, part V, chapter II, §15 and 16; Malik, *Year*, pp. 72, 115, citing a Dacca taxi driver and a tea estate manager. This is a remarkable parallel to the "sending to China" in Indonesia, 1965.

61 In a poll among Pakistani students in 1968, only 8 percent in the East and 17 percent in the West "took pride in Islam and Islamic nationalism." Herbert Feldman, *The End and the Beginning: Pakistan 1969–1971* (London *et al.*: Oxford University Press, 1975), p. 47.

62 Niazi, *Betrayal*, pp. 78–9; Sisson and Rose, *War*, p. 165.

63 Niazi, *Betrayal*, p. 78; "Razakar," Banglapedia, http://banglapedia.search.com.bd/HT/R_0159.htm (accessed March 5, 2007). For the Peace Committees, see Bhuiyan, *Emergence*, p. 219; Ahmed Sharif *et al.* (eds.), *Genocide '71: An Account of the Killers and Collaborators* (Dhaka: Muktijuddha Chetona Bikash Kendra, 1988), pp. 39–46, 50, 52, 58–9, 92, 100, 123–5; Imam, *Blood*, p. 62 (April 14, 1971); *Pakistan Observer*, April 26 and May 11, 1971; Second Report on the Findings of the People's Inquiry Commission (1995), Moulana A. K. M. Yousuf; Salik, *Witness*, p. 105.

64 Niazi, *Betrayal*, p. 79, and Robert Jackson, *South Asian Crisis: India, Pakistan, and Bangla Desh, a Political and Historical Analysis of the 1971 War* (New York: Praeger, 1975), p. 132 (35,000 or 70 percent); Salik, *Witness*, p. 105 (50,000 or 50 percent); 5,000: Mascarenhas, "Genocide"; Sharif *et al.*, *Genocide '71*, p. 125.

65 Muqeem Khan, *Pakistan's Crisis*, p. 276; cf. Sisson and Rose, *War*, pp. 164–5. There were 25,000 (initially 11,000) EPCAF forces: Jackson, *South Asian Crisis*, p. 132; Niazi, *Betrayal*, p. 52.

66 Chaudhuri, *Genocide*, p. 23; FRG General Consulate Dacca, Situation report, October 15, 1971, PA B37/629; for the example of students from Sharshnia madrassah, Barisal district, accused of having killed thousands of locals: Sharif *et al.*, *Genocide '71*, p. 112.

67 Memo Williams, November 5, 1971, FRUS 1969–76, vol. E-7, doc. 152 (General Farman); Muqeem Khan, *Pakistan's Crisis*, pp. 100–1; Sharif *et al.*, *Genocide '71*, p. 68.

68 Niazi, *Betrayal*, p. 79; International Commission of Jurists, Events, IIb, "Razakars"; Chaudhuri, *Genocide*, p. 193; Report on the Findings of the People's Inquiry Commission (1994); cf. Imam, *Blood*, pp. 206–7 (October 23, 1971).

69 Jahan, "Genocide," p. 384.

70 "In Pakistan: Schwere Massenrepressalien gegen die demokratischen Kräfte," BA DY/30/IVA2/20, Nr. 615; Ghulam Kabir, *Minority Politics*, p. 66.

71 Noman, *Pakistan*, p. 32. Circa 1,000 riots per year were registered in West Pakistan. In Bangladesh, 11,890 riots were registered in 1972, 7,323 in 1973, and 8,458 in 1974: Mohiuddin Alamgir, *Famine in South Asia* (Cambridge, MA: Oelgeschlager, Gunn & Hain, 1980), p. 139.

72 Beth Roy, *Some Trouble with Cows: Making Sense of Social Conflict* (Berkeley *et al.*: California University Press, 1994), on an incident in Panipur, Faridpur district, in 1954. Unfortunately, the kind of restraint shown there in the actual violence, resulting only in wounds not deaths, did not apply everywhere.

73 Marian N. Olsen, *Bangladesh: Tears and Laughter* (Willmar: Willmar Assembly of God, 2002), pp. 104–6; Sisson and Rose, *War*,

p. 13; Moraes, *Tempest*, pp. 31, 34, 38; Siddiqui, *Conflict*, pp. 121–31; McKinley, *Death*, p. 38; Ayoob and Subrahmanyam, *Liberation*, p. 79; Salik, *Witness*, p. 21. Second quote: Loshak, *Pakistan*, pp. 32–3. 2000: Peter Heß, *Bangladesch: Tragödie einer Staatsgründung* (Frauenfeld and Stuttgart: Huber, 1972), p. 43.

74 Maniruzzaman, *Bangladesh*, p. 65.

75 Blood, *Cruel*, p. 151; Massa, *Bengale*, pp. 140–1; Qureshi, *Indo-Pak War*, p. 12; Salik, *Witness*, pp. 5, 15; White Paper, pp. 6–8. For the 1973 elections: Anthony Mascarenhas, *Bangladesh: A Legacy of Blood* (London et al.: Arnold Overseas, 1986), pp. 33–4.

76 Mujib speech, *Hindustan Standard*, March 11, 1971, in Tewary, *War*, p. 119; Mujib speech, *Morning News*, November 27, 1970, in Ministry of External Affairs, India (ed.), *Bangla Desh Documents* (Madras: B. N. K. Press, n.y. [1971]), pp. 123–4; Blood, *Cruel*, pp. 117, 131, 136; Sisson and Rose, *War*, p. 293, n. 2; Noman, *Pakistan*, p. 53, n. 70; Maniruzzaman, *Bangladesh*, pp. 76–7. Before his March 7 speech, Mujib warned of bloodshed in an internal meeting of Awami League leaders: Ayoob and Subrahmanyam, *Liberation*, pp. 118–19.

77 Muntassir Mamoon (ed.), *The Vanquished Generals and the Liberation War of Bangladesh* (Dhaka: Somoy Prokashan, 2000), p. 26, www.bd71.com/docs/71generals.pdf (accessed December 15, 2007).

78 Kabir, "Introduction," p. 1; Mamoon, *Media*, vol. 2, p. 3; Akram, "Bangladesh," pp. 30, 32. Foreign studies: Jahan, "Genocide," p. 386; Donald Beachler, "The politics of genocide scholarship: The case of Bangladesh," *Patterns of Prejudice* 41(5), 2007, pp. 467–92.

79 See Chaudhuri, *Genocide*, esp. pp. 3, 22, 199–202. No data from the Chittagong Hill Tracts are included.

80 This version seems to have been adopted right after Mujib's return to Bangladesh in January 1972. Some government ministers cited 1.5 million deaths. Dreyfus, *Du Pakistan*, p. 171; critical comments by Qureshi, *Indo-Pak War*, pp. 278–9. Purportedly, the number of three million was first mentioned by Soviet daily *Pravda* on January 3, 1972: Chaudhuri, *Genocide*, p. 22.

81 Hamoodur Commission Report, supplementary report, late 1974, www.bangla2000.com/bangladesh/Independence-War/Report-Hamoodur-Rahman/default.shtm (accessed March 12, 2007), part V, ch. 2, para 33 (26,000 according to Pakistani Army Headquarters); interview with General Rao Farman Ali, in Mamoon, *Vanquished*, p. 154; Chaudhuri, *Genocide*, p. 5.

82 Chaudhuri, *Genocide*, p. 71 (Emergency Mission report to IRC, June 1971, 200,000); FRG, General Consulate, Dacca, October 28, 1971, PA AA B37/629 (300,000 to 500,000); "Pakistan: Polishing a tarnished image," *Time*, May 24, 1971, in Quaderi, *Bangla Desh*, p. 89 (over 200,000); Sisson and Rose, *War*, p. 306, n. 24 (300,000–500,000). See Loshak, *Pakistan*, pp. 100–2, about Indian atrocity propaganda.

83 Niazi, *Betrayal*, p. 61; Mascarenhas, "Genocide," p. 118 (a figure of 250,000 violent deaths was given, up to 100,000 of which were supposed to be non-Bengali victims of mob violence).

84 Malcolm Browne, "Bengalis depict how a priest died," *New York Times*, May 9, 1971; Massa, *Bengale*, p. 187; Hamoodur Commission Report, part V, ch. II, para 17 (General Gul Hassan, Chief of General Staff, on visit "used to ask soldiers 'how many Bengalis have you shot'"); partial transcript of tape recording of Pakistani Army radio traffic, March 25–26, 1971, www.bd71.com/docs/LWM/tape.html (accessed December 14, 2007).

85 Mascarenhas, "Genocide," pp. 120–5 (Comilla, April 1971).

86 Sydney Schanberg, "Hours of terror for a trapped Bengali officer," *New York Times*, April 17, 1971.

87 Partial transcript of Pakistani army wire traffic, night of March 25, 1971, recorded by Dr. M. M. Husain, Atomic Energy Center, Dacca, www.bd71.com/docs/LWM/tape.html to …tape4.html; Bose, "Anatomy"; US Consulate Dacca, telegram, "Killings at university," March 30, 1971, *The Tilt*, doc. 4; FRG Consulate General Dacca, October 28, 1971, PA AA B37/629; accounts by Abul Fazal and Syed Mushtaque Ali, in Kabir, *Tormenting*; account by Rabiul Husain, in Firdousi, *Year*, pp. 309, 313–14; account by Kali Ranjansheel, in Jahan, "Genocide," pp. 390–3. Muqeem Khan, *Pakistan's Crisis*, gives the official number of civilians killed at Dacca University at 150. For the units: Salik, *Witness*, pp. 72–3. For Rajshahi University: Malik, *Year*, pp. 27–8.

88 Malik, *Year*, pp. 79–83; footage in NBC News, January 7, 1972, www.youtube.com/watch?v=sMg9Ly9nKog&feature=related (accessed December 15, 2007).

89 Chaudhuri, *Genocide*, p. 152; detailed, tentative data in Nurul Islam Patwari, "Onslaught on intellect and intelligentsia," in Bangladesh Ministry of Information and Broadcasting, *Bangladesh* (n.p. [Dacca], 1972), p. 87.

90 GDR Embassy in Dacca, "Zur Einschätzung des Klassenkräfteverhältnisses [...]," December 12, 1972, PA AA, MfAA C1052/77, 128 (166,640 teachers at all levels by 1969–70). If one trusts the lower death figures, 21 of 890 university professors were killed, 59 of 4,200 college teachers, 270 of 45,550 secondary school teachers, and 639 of 116,000 elementary school teachers (same document and Patwari, "Onslaught," p. 87).

91 94, 839, and 1,900 according to a Calcutta University count: International Rescue Committee Emergency Mission to India for Pakistani refugees, Angier Biddle Duke [June 1971], in *Bangla Desh Documents*, p. 466. It was estimated that 10,000 teaching staff (6 percent) had emigrated.

92 Maniruzzaman, *Bangladesh*, pp. 235, 106, n. 40; Malik, *Year*, pp. 27–8; Sukumar Biswas, "Killing fields in Rajshahi," in Kabir, *Tormenting*; FRG General Consulate Dacca, October 28, 1971, PA AA B37/629.

93 FRG General Consulate Dacca, October 28, 1971, PA AA B37/629.

94 Salik, *Witness*, p. 93, emphasizing his success was limited; but see Sharif *et al.*, *Genocide'71*, pp. 190–216.

95 Chaudhuri, *Genocide*, pp. 190–7; Bhuiyan, *Emergence*, pp. 251–2; account by survivor Md. Delwar Hossain in Sharif *et al.*, *Genocide '71*, pp. 78–84, cf. pp. 130–89; Hamoodur Commission report, part V, ch. II, §25–26 (plans for arrests of 2,000–3,000 nationalists were allegedly cancelled).

96 Mascarenhas, *Bangladesh*, pp. 15–16; Imam, *Blood*, pp. 194, 206–7 (September 13, October 23, 1971); Chaudhuri, *Genocide*, pp. 35, 105; Sharif *et al.*, *Genocide '71*, pp. 216–21. Earlier, there were 300,000

civilians employed by the central government and 350,000 by local and regional authorities in all of Pakistan: Henry Frank Goodnow, *The Civil Service of Pakistan: Bureaucracy in a New Nation* (New Haven and London: Yale University Press, 1964), p. 40.

97 Dasgupta, *Midnight*, p. 48; Amir Taheri, "The decline and fall of Sheikh Mujib," *Kayhan*, August 1, 1971, in Quaderi, *Bangla Desh*, p. 205. For the part of Bengali intellectuals, Sharif *et al.*, *Genocide '71*, pp. 190–216.

98 Payne, *Massacre*, p. 58.

99 "Pogrom in Pakistan," *The Sunday Times*, June 20, 1971, in Quaderi, *Bangla Desh*, p. 143; Payne, *Massacre*, p. 58, dates this step to April. In fact, Tikka Khan had first tried to win over Awami League members in a speech on April 18: Blood, *Cruel*, p. 82.

100 M. Rashiduzzaman, "The Awami League in the political development of Pakistan," *Asian Survey*, 10(7), 1970, pp. 578–81; "Die Awami-Liga" [ca. 1973], PA AA, MfAA C1046/77, p. 83; Blood, *Cruel*, p. 58; Dasgupta, *Midnight*, p. 28.

101 Two rival student leagues currently or formerly affiliated with the Awami League had a total of 700,000 members in 1973: GDR Embassy in Dacca, "Information über die Lage in den Jugend- und Studentenorganisationen Bangladeschs," PA AA, MfAA C1053/77, pp. 145–51.

102 P. G. F. Henderson, Visit to Dacca – 29 February/4 March 1972, March 9, 1972, ANA 855/2, part 1, pp. 139, 145. This is supported by reports about few Awami Leaguers cooperating with the Pakistani military authorities while most went into exile: "The Mukti Fouj is still fighting," *Economist*, July 10, 1971, in Quaderi, *Bangla Desh*, p. 166. Cf. Heß, *Bangladesch*, p. 100.

103 See Choudhury, *Last Days*, p. 184; Sisson and Rose, *War*, p. 158; Blood, *Cruel*, p. 207; Pabna: Second Report on the Findings of the People's Inquiry Commission (1995), "Moulana Abdus Sobhan."

104 Amir Taheri, "The reluctant president," *Kayhan* (International), July 27, 1971, in Quaderi, *Bangla Desh*, p. 187; Bhuiyan, *Emergence*, p. 193; two articles in *Frontier*, Calcutta, April 24 and May 1, 1971, in Mamoon, *Media*, pp. 101, 105; Sisson and Rose, *War*, p. 159; Jackson,

South Asian Crisis, p. 76; US Embassy Pakistan, telegram August 20, 1971, FRUS 1969–1976, vol. XI, p. 355; Muhith, *Bangladesh*, p. 230. Lack of intelligence: Qureshi, *Indo-Pak War*, p. 100; Muqeem Khan, *Pakistan's Crisis*, p. 73.

105 Dasgupta, *Midnight*, pp. 76–7.

106 In a US Senate Judiciary Committee hearing on June 29, 1971, Archer Blood, the former US Consul in Dacca critical of the Pakistani government, denied that the army had "concentrated on eliminating intellectual elements from East Pakistan": Blood, *Cruel*, p. 329.

107 Ayoob and Subrahmanyam, *Liberation*, pp. 152, 155; Lifschultz, *Bangladesh*, p. 31; Chaudhuri, *Genocide*, pp. 176–7; Biswas, "Killing fields in Chittagong," in Kabir, *Tormenting*; survivor account of 8 Bengal: Mohammed Naum Miah, in Firdousi, *Year*, p. 52; US Consulate Dacca, telegram, March 29, 1971, FRUS, 1969–1976, vol. E-7: Documents on South Asia 1969–1972 (Washington, 2005), www. state.gov/r/pa/ho/frus/nixon/e7/ (accessed December 13, 2007), doc. 126. For the killing of 932 Bengali troops in Comilla: Hamoodur Commission, part V, para 15. Abdul Malek of the East Pakistan Rifles from Dacca stated that when he was shot and left for dead in August, over 500 out of 1,500 troops from his unit had been killed in smaller actions: Chaudhuri, *Genocide*, p. 178. Islam, *Tale*, p. 81, claims 1,000 East Pakistan Rifles troops were killed in Chittagong in the first night.

108 Chaudhuri, *Genocide*, pp. 103–5, 108–12; eyewitness account from Rajar Bagh police station in Dacca by Rabeya Khatun (February 18, 1974), in Kabir, *Tormenting*; Chaudhuri, *Genocide*, p. 57 (Kushtia). A FRG Consulate General Dacca situation report of October 28, 1971 stated there were initially 30,000 police: PA AA B37/629. 11,500 Bengali policemen continued service under the Pakistani troops: Niazi, *Betrayal*, p. 77. For the *Ansars*, see "Ansar and Village Defense Party" in Banglapedia, www.banglapedia.org/httpdocs/HT/A_0256.HTM (accessed May 3, 2010).

109 Malik, *Year*, p. 152. Chaudhuri, *Genocide*, pp. 173–4, reports the same statement putting the figure killed at 500, but gives examples that add up to 730 violent deaths alone. For the total number of Buddhists, see D. Bhattacharjya *et al.*, "What is happening in the once secular Bangladesh," in Paliwal, *Islamism*, p. 47; Dreyfus, *Du Pakistan*, p. 107; Ghulam Kabir, *Minority Politics*, p. 6; Roland Breton, *La*

population du Bangladesh (Paris: La documentation française, 1972), pp. 37, 53. Refugees: Mohan, *Black Book*, pp. 41–2.

110 Chaudhuri, *Genocide*, p. 108.

111 George T. Curlin *et al.*, "Demographic crisis: The impact of the Bangladesh civil war (1971) on births and deaths in a rural area of Bangladesh," *Population Studies* 30(1), 1976, pp. 91–2; see also A. K. M. Alauddin Chowdhury and Lincoln C. Chen, "The interaction of nutrition, inflation and mortality during recent food crisis in Bangladesh," *Food Research Institute Studies* 16(2), 1977, p. 49; Tim Dyson, "On the demography of South Asian famines, Part II," *Population Studies* 45(2), 1991, p. 286.

112 James B. Sprague and Stanley O. Foster/Government of Bangladesh and UN Relief Operation in Dacca, "Second Bangladesh National Nutritional Assessment," Information Paper No. 21, October 1972, Archiv für Zeitgeschichte Zurich (AfZ), Nachlass Umbricht, Bangladesh UNROD/UNROB, Information Papers I. Paper No. 21, table 5, gives a projected annual death rate of 20.9 for March 1971 to May 1972, compared to 14.9 between May and October 1972.

113 Curlin *et al.*, "Demographic crisis," p. 103, put this figure at "nearly 500,000" but include 1972–73. Various sources suggest population figures of 70 to 75 million for East Pakistan in 1971.

114 "Excess" here means that 44 more men between 15 and 44 died than one would have expected on a long-term statistical basis.

115 Curlin *et al.*, "Demographic crisis," pp. 89, 98.

116 "Random checks at the local level" by Marcus Franda in 1972 also showed "invariably" that Awami League functionaries had inflated victim numbers between three and ten times: Marcus Franda, *Bangladesh: The First Decade* (New Delhi: South Asia Publishers, 1982), p. 28.

117 K. C. Saha, "The genocide of 1971 and the refugee influx in the east," in Ranabir Samaddar (ed.), *Refugees and the State: Practices of Asylum and Care in India, 1947–2000* (New Delhi *et al.*: Sage, 2003), pp. 212, 230; Jackson, *South Asian Crisis*, p. 46. Franda, *Bangladesh*, p. 111, writes that those who stayed with relatives or friends were registered and received food rations as well.

118 Chaudhuri, *Genocide*, p. 94. Another 50,000 people from East Pakistan fled to Burma: Chaudhuri, *Genocide*, p. 77.

119 CIA: Minutes of Senior Review Group Meeting, July 23, 1971, FRUS, 1969–1976, vol. XI: South Asia Crisis (Washington, 2005), p. 31, www.state.gov/documents/organization/4587.pdf (accessed December 13, 2007). Dissenting view: Dreyfus, *Du Pakistan*, p. 179.

120 P. N. Luthra, "Problem of refugees from East Bengal," *Economic and Political Weekly* 6(50), December 11, 1971, p. 2471 (Luthra headed the Indian refugee relief effort); Partha N. Mukherji, "The great exodus of 1971: I – Exodus," *EPW* 9(9), March 2, 1974, p. 365.

121 Saha, "Genocide," p. 235; Muqeem Khan, *Pakistan's Crisis*, p. 88.

122 Memorandum Maurice Williams for State Department, November 5, 1971, FRUS, 1969–1976, vol. E-7, doc. 152; "A war waiting to happen," *Newsweek*, November 8, 1971, in Quaderi, *Bangla Desh*, p. 385; Field Report by Hendrik Van der Hejden, June 23, 1971 in *Thousand My Lais: World Bank Study on Bangla Desh* (n.p., n.y. [1971]), p. 3.

123 FRG Consulate General Dacca, "Lage der Hindus in Ostpakistan," July 30, 1971, PA AA B37/628; [Williams], Mission to Pakistan to Review Relief, Refugee and Related Issues, September 3, 1971, FRUS, 1969–1976, vol. E-7, doc. 143; Mamoon, *Media*, p. 122; Saha, "Genocide," pp. 237–8.

124 Ghulam Kabir, *Minority Politics*, p. 84; Muqeem Khan, *Pakistan's Crisis*, p. 88; Sisson and Rose, *War*, p. 296, n. 23; Saha, "Genocide," p. 214 (refugees from Khulna district to 24-Parganas district); Malik, *Year*, p. 32. Contradictory figures in Chaudhuri, *Genocide*, pp. 6, 88–9, 171. Over 90 percent (6.971 of 7.556 million) according to "Refugees from Bangladesh," *Bangla Desh Documents*, p. 446; cf. Breton, *Population*, p. 26.

125 Sydney H. Schanberg, "The only way to describe it is 'Hell'," *New York Times*, June 20, 1971; "Humanitäre Hilfe für ostpakistanische Flüchtlinge in Indien," June 18, 1971, PA AA B37/629: Chaudhuri, *Genocide*, p. 89 (Tripura).

126 Chaudhuri, *Genocide*, pp. 6, 77, also mentions 5.7 million peasants and 2.5 million landless workers, citing an UNROD report (it is

unclear who collected such data, which only Indian authorities could do); cf. local data in Malik, *Year*, pp. 17, 33; Mukherji, "Great exodus," I, p. 366; F. Cochet, UNHCR, Appraisal of the situation in the area Comilla-Feni-Cox's Bazar, January 10, 1972, AfZ, Nachlass Umbricht, Bangladesh UNROD/UNROB, Information Papers I, Information Paper No. 1.

127 Chaudhuri, *Genocide*, pp. 133, 144.

128 Sisson and Rose, *War*, pp. 300–1, n. 10; A. K. M. Aminul Islam, *Victorious Victims: Political Transformation in a Traditional Society* (Cambridge, MA: Schenkman, 1978), p. 99; cf. Maniruzzaman, *Bangladesh*, p. 113; D. K. Palit, *The Lightning Campaign* (Salisbury: Compton, 1972), p. 57. Islam, *Tale*, pp. 199–200, states that less than 1 percent of Mukti Bahini came "from the refugee camps," implying Hindus.

129 Of 9.733 million refugees by November 30, only 2.319 million were children under eight years, compared to 3,301 million older females (Chaudhuri, *Genocide*, p. 96); see also Partha N. Mukherji, "The great exodus of 1971: II – Reception," *EPW* 9(10), March 9, 1974, p. 401.

130 Account by M. R. Chowdhury, in Firdousi, *Year*, p. 463.

131 The June 1971 IBRD mission report called this "the area of greatest population loss": *Thousand My Lais*, p. 21.

132 Luthra, "Problem," pp. 2467, 2471; Dreyfus, *Du Pakistan*, p. 179; Chaudhuri, *Genocide*, pp. 95, 141. 2.6 million refugees came from Dinajpur (1.5 million alone), Rangpur, and Rajshahi districts, from Sylhet 800,000, Mymensingh 600,000, Jessore 590,000, Faridpur 583,000, Khulna and Comilla 500,000 each, Dacca 442,000, Barisal 386,000: reports by UNROD or UNICEF observers, January 1972, AfZ, Nachlass Umbricht, Bangladesh UNROD/UNROB, Information Papers I, Information Paper No. 1. These data given by Bangladeshi authorities were from Indian sources. With slightly different data William Greenough III and Richard Cash, "Post-civil war in Bangladesh: Health problems and programs," in Lincoln C. Chen (ed.), *Disaster in Bangladesh: Health Crises in a Developing Nation* (New York *et al.*: Oxford University Press, 1973), p. 243.

133 Chaudhuri, *Genocide*, p. 95.

134 See sources in notes 132 and 141; for Bogra, Muqeem Khan, *Pakistan's Crisis*, p. 76.

135 Chaudhuri, *Genocide*, pp. 88–9 (Tripura and July); Saha, "Genocide," pp. 216–17.

136 Mukherji, "Great exodus," I, pp. 367–9.

137 Chaudhuri, *Genocide*, pp. 39–41, 87, 93; Chandra, *Bloodbath*, p. 5; Malik, *Year*, pp. 65–6; "The Bengali refugees: A surfeit of woe," *Time*, June 21, 1971, in Quaderi, *Bangla Desh*, p. 151; Bose, "Anatomy."

138 Conversation Nixon, Kissinger, Keating (US Ambassador to India), June 15, 1971, FRUS, 1969–1976, vol. E-7, doc. 137.

139 Telegram US Embassy New Delhi, March 27, 1971, FRUS, 1969–1976, vol. XI, 31; Saha, "Genocide," p. 222; Gandhi: *Pakistan Observer*, May 25, 1971, www.docstrangelove.com/2007/12/23/bangladesh-genocide-archive-pakistani-reports-pakistan-observer-march-26-december16-1971/ (accessed January 4, 2008).

140 Rushbrook Williams, *East Pakistan*, p. 11; Muqeem Khan, *Pakistan's Crisis*, p. 88, puts the figure at 400,000 non-Bengali civilians; cf. Bhuiyan, *Emergence*, p. 192; Sisson and Rose, *War*, pp. 146, 160.

141 GDR Consulate Calcutta, Note about the December 18 conversation with Bangladesh's Minister for Interior and Rehabilitation, A. K. M. Kamruzzaman, December 18, 1971, PA AA MfAA C1052/77, p. 100; UNROD, Information Paper No. 17, S. K. Dey, Bangladesh: A survey of damages and repairs, AfZ, Bangladesh UNROD/UNROB, Information Papers I, Information Paper No. 1, p. vii. According to Lincoln Chen and Jon Rohde, "Civil war in Bangladesh: Famine averted?," in Chen, *Disaster*, p. 198, n. 11, another UNROD paper included an estimate of 16.6 million internally displaced.

142 Jahan, "Genocide," p. 379, even writes that "approximately thirty million people from the cities took refuge in the villages." The total urban population of East Pakistan stood at five to six million.

143 *Thousand My Lais*, pp. 2, 3, 8, 11, 17. For the fate of a middle-class family from Mymensingh, see Taslima Nasreen, *My Girlhood*, pp. 4–21, http://taslima-nasreen.com/MY%20GIRLHOOD.pdf (accessed July 21, 2008).

144 Greenough and Cash, "Post-civil war," p. 243.

145 Chaudhuri, *Genocide*, p. 129 (Patuakhali district); account by Iqbal Mahmood, Firdousi, *Year*, p. 81 (Manpura); "The Mukti Fouj is still fighting," *Economist*, July 10, 1971, in Quaderi, *Bangla Desh*, p. 167 (Barisal area). No army: McKinley, *Death*, p. 51 (Noakhali district); Niazi, *Betrayal*, pp. 60, 62. A UN Report on Patuakhali District, January 30, 1972, AfZ, Bangladesh UNROD/UNROB, Information Papers I, Information Paper No. 1, states that half of the district's 1.5 million people were displaced but only 10,000 fled to India. See also report on the area of Galachipa, Barisal, January 10, 1972, same file.

146 Imam, *Blood*, p. 86 (Saidpur area, May 11).

147 Hefley, *Christ*, pp. 46–52.

148 "Statement on East Bengal refugee situation in India," Oxfam, Field Committee for Asia, "Field Secretary's Report," and G. W. Acworth, "India–Pakistan–Bangladesh," September 20, October 6, 1971 and January 8, 1972, Oxfam Archive, Asia Field Committee, 1970–1976; Tony Hagen, UNROD Information Paper No. 3, 3–4, February 18, 1972, AfZ, Nachlass Umbricht, Bangladesh UNROD/ UNROB, Information Papers I, Information Paper No. 3. The Indian government provided Rs. 1,000 per refugee, more than India's per capita income (Rs. 589): Alo Kar, "Refugee relief", October 23, 1971, in Mamoon, *Media*, p. 238. Child malnutrition in the camps was at half the rate compared to India's population: Luthra, "Problem," p. 2472.

149 Chaudhuri, *Genocide*, pp. 73, 77, 86; Betsy Hartmann and James Boyce, *A Quiet Violence: View from a Bangladesh Village*, pp. 171–2.

150 Chaudhuri, *Genocide*, p. 98; a similar number can be calculated from the figures given by Indian district officials: Saha, "Genocide,", pp. 217–22. Higher figures, including starvation: Jon Rohde *et al.*, "Refugees in India: Health priorities," in Chen, *Disaster*, pp. 156–8 (mortalities of 23/1000 and up); "East Pakistan: Even the skies weep," *Time*, October 25, 1971, www.timecom/time/printout/0,8816,877316,00. html (accessed December 14, 2007) (a British doctor with Save the Children Fund estimated 150,000 children had died); Malik, *Year*, p. 62 (citing a nurse from the same charity); Chaudhuri, *Genocide*,

pp. 73, 93. 20 percent of the nearly 50,000 refugees to Burma appear to have died: Chaudhuri, *Genocide*, p. 77.

151 Saha, "Genocide," p. 228; Sisson and Rose, *War*, p. 153. Again, foreign observers and some refugees suggested higher death figures: Chaudhuri, *Genocide*, pp. 79, 91; account by Muhammed Nazrul Islam, in Firdousi, *Year*, p. 172. In a normal year, 100,000 East Pakistanis died of cholera: William McCormick and George Curlin, "Infectious diseases: Their spread and control," in Chen, *Disaster*, p. 70.

152 Jackson, *South Asian Crisis*, p. 75; Imam, *Blood*, p. 102 (June 12, 1971); India appealed for international help against the outbreak on May 31: Lester Sobel (ed.), *The World Food Crisis* (New York: Facts on File, 1975), p. 19.

153 Saha, "Genocide," p. 238; Hefley, *Christ*, p. 56; Jeannie Lockerbie, *On Duty in Bangladesh* (Grand Rapids: Zondervan, 1973), p. 48.

154 Sisson and Rose, *War*, pp. 295–6, n. 22, think this was based on an informal decision in April 1971.

155 "East Bengal and Assam," June 9, 1971, Ashim Mukhopadhyay, "The refugees," May 8, 1971, both in *Frontier*, in Mamoon, *Media*, pp. 45, 198–200; "The Bengal pressure builds on Mrs. Gandhi," *Weekly Economist*, July 17, 1971, in Quaderi, *Bangla Desh*, p. 174; Sisson and Rose, *War*, p. 181; Franda, *Bangladesh*, p. 112.

156 Luthra, "Problem," p. 2471; Saha, "Genocide," p. 220.

157 Chaudhuri, *Genocide*, pp. 81–5; Saha, "Genocide," p. 241.

158 Mukherji, "The great exodus of 1971 – III Return," *EPW* 9(11), March 16, 1974, p. 449; somewhat contradictory data: Saha, "Genocide," pp. 216, 233.

159 Chaudhuri, *Genocide*, p. 137; cf. reports by the UNROD/UNHCR observers, January 1972 (see note 132).

160 Undated manuscript starting "Pakistan does not exist," PA AA B 37/583; report Van der Heijden and official World Bank group report, *Thousand My Lais* p. 11 (quote) and p. 15; International Commission of Jurists, II(b), Indictment, under "Attacks on Biharis."

161 McKinley, *Death*, p. 51.

162 Imam, *Blood*, p. 117; D. Chakrabarti, "Rajshahi: A post-mortem," *Frontier*, May 1, 1971, in Mamoon, *Media*, p. 105; "Horrid tale of Pakistani army bestiality," *Bangladesh Observer*, February 4, 1972; Chaudhuri, *Genocide*, pp. 37–8.

163 *Thousand My Lais*, pp. 2, 8–9, 11, 21.

164 Payne, *Massacre*, pp. 55–6; Lewis Simons, "The killings at Harikarpara," *Washington Post*, January 10, 1972; Gawanga Nandi, "Killing fields in Khulna," in Kabir, *Tormenting*; Malik, *Year*, p. 47.

165 Biswas, "Killing fields in Rajshahi" and "Killing fields in Chittagong"; Lockerbie, *Duty*, p. 174; "Many mass graves found in Pabna," *Bangladesh Observer*, February 7, 1972; "75,000 killed in Dinajpur", *Bangladesh Observer*, February 11, 1972.

166 Chaudhuri, *Genocide*, pp. 185–8; "Pak Army killed one lakh men in Ctg.," *Bangladesh Observer*, January 31, 1972; Nandi, "Killing fields in Khulna," and Biswas, "Killing fields in Chittagong," in Kabir, *Tormenting*.

167 See also Choudhury, *Last Days*, pp. 182, 188, 190.

168 For example, "70 anti-state elements killed in Mymensingh," *Pakistan Observer*, August 10, 1971 (here the raids with killings in four villages were performed by *razakars*).

169 Qureshi, *Indo-Pak War*, p. 3 (assuming 5,000 dead and missing); Niazi, *Betrayal*, p. 52. 14 Division controlled the center and northeast, 16 Division the northwest, 9 Division the southeast, and a separate brigade Chittagong area and the Chittagong Hill Tracts: Niazi, *Betrayal*, pp. 61–2.

170 Mamoon, *Media*, pp. 77, 101 (*Frontier* articles, April 10 and 17, 1971); "Bangla Desh struggle," *The Age* (New Delhi), September 26, 1971, in Quaderi, *Bangla Desh*, p. 304; "Ostpakistan – kurze Information zur Lage," April 29, 1971, PA AA MfAA C1052/77, p. 19. Elections: Blood, *Cruel*, p. 279; Shyamali Ghosh, *The Awami League 1949–1971* (Dhaka: Academic Publishers, 1990), p. 277; contrary view for the 1960s in Frank Hughes, Relief after Disaster, book manuscript, II-5, AfZ, Nachlass Umbricht, Bangladesh General I, file General II.

171 Defense speech by former insurgent Abu Taher, July 1976, in Lifschultz, *Bangladesh*, pp. 81–6; few peasants among the guerrillas:

Maniruzzaman, *Bangladesh*, p. 113; peasants' "enthusiasm for the Bangla Desh cause appeared about as limited as their enthusiasm for a united Pakistan": Peter Gill, "Still no end to Bengal fight," *Sunday Telegraph*, July 25, 1971, in *Bangla Desh Documents*, p. 484.

172 Niazi, *Betrayal*, pp. 46–9; Hamoodur Commission Report, Part V, ch. II, para 10.

173 Niazi, *Betrayal*, pp. 58–61; Muqeem Khan, *Pakistan's Crisis*, pp. 86–7. According to Mascarenhas, "Genocide," p. 133, the "comb-out-operation" started in the third week of May.

174 Manuscript of a report by General Abdul Hamid Khan, April 1972 (former Chief of Staff, Pakistani army), in Niazi, *Betrayal*, pp. 280–1.

175 Bose, "Anatomy"; Hamoodur Commission Report, part V, ch. 2, para 18. See also McKinley, *Death*, pp. 43–4, 54, 97, 103 (roads Feni–Comilla–Dacca, Dacca–Faridpur, Dacca–Pabna, April 16 and May); International Commission of Jurists, Events, IIb, "The refugees" (roads around Faridpur); Salik, *Witness*, p. 88 (Karatea on road Dacca–Tangail, April 1); Chaudhuri, *Genocide*, p. 55 (Jessore–Benapole, early April); Mascarenhas, "Genocide," p. 127 (near Chandpur, April 17).

176 Secretariat of the International Commission of Jurists, The Events in East Pakistan (Geneva, 1972), part IIb, Indictment, http://nsm1.nsm.iup.edu/sanwar/Bangladesh%20Genocide.htm (accessed January 8, 2008); Blood, *Cruel*, p. 299 (view of the British High Commissioner); Salik, *Witness*, p. 102.

177 Quote: Chaudhuri, *Genocide*, pp. 115–16; see Mascarenhas, "Genocide," p. 127.

178 Karaniganj near Dacca: Salik, *Witness*, pp. 94–5; near Jessore and Rajshahi: Chaudhuri, *Genocide*, pp. 55–6; plan to lay down forests between Sarankhola and Mongla river ports: Chaudhuri, *Genocide*, p. 134; operation along the Brahmaputra river in November 1971: Muqeem Khan, *Pakistan's Crisis*, p. 128.

179 See reports in AfZ, Nachlass Umbricht, Bangladesh UNROD/UNROB, Information Papers I, Information Paper No. 1, especially Toni Hagen, Destruction of Houses and Requirements for building materials, February 1, 1972 and reports on Dacca–Sylhet and Patuakhali areas; see also UNROD, Information Paper No. 21,

October 1972, table 8, same record location, Information Paper No. 21; summary of the former in Chaudhuri, *Genocide*, pp. 147–8.

180 World Bank report in *Thousand My Lais*, p. 21; in October 1972, Khulna and Dinajpur were still most severely affected by housing damage: UNROD, Information Paper No. 21, table 8.

181 For example Payne, *Massacre*, pp. 82–4, who calls the phase from late April to June the "second massacre," characterized by "aimless destruction [that] is in itself an aim," as "troops fanned across the country."

182 Mascarenhas, *Rape*, p. 105.

183 Chandra, *Bloodbath*, p. 159, citing David Loshak, *Daily Telegraph*, April 15, 1971; see also Barbara Joiner, *Gloria! A Biography of Gloria Thurman, Missionary to Bangladesh* (Birmingham, AL: WMU, SBC, 1993), pp. 56–7 (Manikganj, May 26, 1971).

184 Mascarenhas, "Genocide"; FRG Consulate-General Dacca, "Lage der Hindus in Ostpakistan," July 30, 1971, PA AA B37/628.

185 The *Pakistan News Digest* 19(22), December 1, 1971, p. xli, reported that 204 "Indian agents" were killed by troops and *razakars* within six days in early November (ANA 189/10/7, part 1). For late phase destruction, see also Hefley, *Christ*, pp. 71–2; Williams Memo for State Department, November 5, 1971, FRUS 1969–1976, E-7, doc. 152; Malik, *Year*, p. 105 (Sonamura, near Dacca, November 25–27).

186 Hefley, *Christ*, pp. 46–51; Clare Hollingworth, "Pakistan Army on Christian community," *Sunday Telegraph*, August 1, 1971, in *Bangla Desh Documents*, pp. 425–6.

187 Payne, *Massacre*, pp. 47–8 and "The sub-continent: A losing battle," *Newsweek*, November 15, 1971, in Quaderi, *Bangla Desh*, p. 392. Other cases of all men killed: Blood, *Cruel*, p. 221 (Bondbari mission, May 3); Afsan Chowdhury, "The Bewas village," http:drishtipat.org/activists/Afsan/bewas.htm (accessed December 14, 2007); Biswas, "Killing fields in Rajshahi" and "Killing fields in Chittagong" (128 people machine-gunned in Pakuria and about 150 in Shakpura, Boalkhali *thana*, August 28 and April 20, 1971); Bose, "Anatomy."

188 There is no empirical proof for the assertion by Jahan, "Genocide," p. 380, that the "majority of the victims were Bengali Muslims."

Chaudhuri, *Genocide*, p. 171, with the more likely version that the "majority of the dead" were Hindus.

189 Ghulam Kabir, *Minority Politics*, esp. pp. 5–15; A. Roy, *Genocide of Hindus and Buddhists in East Pakistan–Bangladesh* (Delhi: Kranti Prakashan, 1981), p. 3, claims 9 million left 1947–70. Cf. Roy, *Trouble*, pp. 14–15, 66, 115; Chandra, *Bloodbath*, p. 28; Samuyendra Nath Tagore, "Persecution of minorities in Pakistan," in Roy, *Genocide*, pp. 31–50; "In Pakistan: Schwere Massenrepressalien gegen die demokratischen Kräfte" (1967), BA DY/30/IVA2/20, Nr. 615.

190 Franda, *Bangladesh*, p. 103. In 1964, 667,125 East Pakistanis fled to West Bengal.

191 A. F. Imam Ali, *Hindu–Muslim Community in Bangladesh* (Delhi: Kanisha, 1992), pp. 61, 64, 115–35, 207.

192 Schuman, "Note," p. 295 (in a poll taken December 1963–April 1964, 30 percent of respondents said Hindus did mostly harm); Moraes, *Tempest*, pp. 25, 45–6. But see a statement by the Pakistan Muslim League (Qayyum), ca. March 1971, about positive steps toward the scheduled castes, in Tewary, *War*, p. 100.

193 Qureshi, *Indo-Pak War*, p. 89; Mascarenhas, "Genocide," pp. 117, 122; cf. Viggo Olsen with Jeannette Lockerbie, *Daktar/Diplomat in Bangladesh* (Chicago: Moody Press, 1973), p. 277.

194 Mukherji, "Great exodus," I, p. 367.

195 Blood, *Cruel*, p. 218.

196 Ghulam Kabir, *Minority Politics*, p. 84; International Commission of Jurists, Events, IIb, Indictment.

197 Mukherji, "Great exodus," I, p. 369: "the policy of the martial law government was to uproot the Hindus, not to eliminate or exterminate them, and in this they seemed to have succeeded admirably."

198 Blood, *Cruel*, p. 218; telegram US Embassy Islamabad, May 14, 1971, FRUS, 1969–1976, vol. XI, p. 120.

199 Niazi, *Betrayal*, pp. 59, 65–6.

200 Hamoodur Commission Report, part V, ch. II, para 18, citing Lieutenant-Colonel Aziz Ahmed Khan, Commanding Officer, 86 Mujahid Battalion.

201 Account by Capt. (ret.) Syed Suzauddin Ahmad, in Kabir, *Tormenting*.

202 Blood, *Cruel*, p. 217; FRG Consulate-General Dacca, "Lage der Hindus in Ostpakistan," July 30, 1971, PA AA B37/628; account by Arief Razzaque, in Firdousi, *Year*, p. 334; Michael Hornsby, "Villagers still pay with lives for being Hindu in Pakistan," *The Times*, July 1, 1971; Sydney Schanberg, "East Pakistan: An 'alien' army imposes its will," *New York Times*, July 4, 1971; Malik, *Year*, p. 58; press reports in Quaderi, *Bangla Desh*, pp. 58, 120, 163–4; Chaudhuri, *Genocide*, pp. 141, 172. "H": Sydney Schanberg, "Hindus are targets of army terror in East Pakistani town," *New York Times*, July 4, 1971, in *Bangla Desh Documents*, pp. 578–9.

203 People's Inquiry Commission Report, Abdul Alim (Koroikadipur, Joypurhat area); Blood, *Cruel*, pp. 219–21 (Nagari, northwest Dacca, women victims of shelling and machine-gun fire); Sydney Schanberg, "Hindus are targets of army terror in an East Pakistan town," [*New York Times*, July 4, 1971], in *Bangla Desh Documents*, pp. 578–9 (story told by a 70-year-old Faridpur lady shot through the neck).

204 Olsen, *Daktar*, pp. 281, 286 (from Cheringa to Ramu).

205 Hefley, *Christ*, p. 23; FRG Consulate-General, "Lage in Ostpakistan," April 17, 1971, PA AA B37/630 (Jessore, Khulna); accounts by Mustafa Kamal and Ambia Begum (Khulna, Dacca, both first day), in Firdousi, *Year*, pp. 489, 508; telegram US Consulate Dacca, March 29, 1971, FRUS 1969–1976, vol. E-7, doc. 126; Imam, *Blood*, p. 52 (March 30).

206 Account by Durgadas Mukerjee, in Kabir, *Tormenting*; Lockerbie, *Duty*, p. 176 (Chittagong); perpetrator account by Yaqub Zainuddin (Firdousi, *Year*, p. 516), a *razakar* who took part in the stabbing of six or seven Hindu women and children in Dacca in November.

207 R. W. Timm, Catholic Relief Services, October 8, 1971, PA AA, B37/629; FRG Consulate-General Dacca, "Lage der Hindus in Ostpakistan," July 30, 1971, B37/628 (Chittagong; Manpura); account by Rumi Mosharraf, in Firdousi, *Year*, pp. 40–1 (Chittagong).

208 Chaudhuri, *Genocide*, p. 137; Alamgir, *Famine*, p. 113.

209 Imam Ali, *Hindu–Muslim Community*, pp. 87–8, 198, 204–5.

210 Ghulam Kabir, *Minority Politics*, pp. 114–17, 132, 138.

211 Roy, *Genocide*, p. 188; account by Rumi Mosharraf, in Firdousi, *Year*, p. 41; R. W. Timm, Catholic Relief Services, October 8, 1971, PA AA, B37/629; Jay Walsh with Patricia Oviatt, *Ripe Mangoes: Miracle Missionary Stories from Bangladesh* (Schaumburg: Regular Baptist Press, 1978), p. 82.

212 McKinley, *Death*, p. 109.

213 Lockerbie, *Duty*, pp. 134–7 (quote pp. 136–7), cf. pp. 97, 149, pointing to an Indian businessman denied baptism though he was once arrested and his house was searched nine times by pro-Pakistan Bengalis searching for his young daughters. Similarly Olsen, *Daktar*, pp. 278 ("And their myriad gods and goddesses were powerless to assist them"), 288, 298.

214 Mukherji, "Great exodus," III, p. 449.

215 See Roy, *Genocide*, esp. pp. 4–5, 188; Report on the Findings of the People's Inquiry Commission on the Activities of the War Criminals and the Collaborator[s], March 26, 1994, www.secularvoiceofbangladesh. org/Report%20on%20the%20war%20criminals.htm (accessed January 16, 2008); Jahan, "Genocide," p. 385.

216 Meenakshie Verma, *Aftermath: An Oral History of Violence* (New Delhi: Penguin, 2004), p. 114; G. Mazumdar, [Indian] Border Security Force, situation report, March 12, 1975, in Dasgupta, *Midnight*, p. 111. This would imply about 150,000 visas per year.

217 Roy, *Genocide*, pp. 10–12, 62–3, 71.

218 Lockerbie, *Duty*, pp. 114 ("perhaps God wanted to show the world that He really does care for His own in a special way"), 190; Olsen, *Daktar*, p. 262; but see Hefley, *Christ*, p. 72.

219 Hefley, *Christ*, pp. 50, 54, 73; McKinley, *Death*, p. 55; Chaudhuri, *Genocide*, p. 173. Three of about 320 foreign missionaries were killed: Olsen, *Daktar*, p. 280, and Hefley, *Christ*, pp. 21, 44, 70–1.

220 Olsen, *Bangladesh*, p. 200.

221 Nath Tagore, "Persecution," pp. 52–7.

222 Malik, *Year*, pp. 67, 152.

223 Qureshi, *Indo-Pak War*, p. 9; Ben Whitaker *et al.*, *The Biharis in Bangladesh* (London: Minority Rights Group, n.y. [1977]), p. 8; Zaglul Haider, "Repatriation of the Biharis stranded in Bangladesh: Diplomacy and development," *Asian Profile*, 31(6), 2003, p. 530. This section does not cover tribals in the southeast and northeast of Bangladesh.

224 Haider, "Repatriation," pp. 528–9. In West Pakistan, too, refugees from partition dominated the entrepreneur class· Noman, *Pakistan*, p. 20.

225 FRG Consulate-General Dacca, "Lage in Ostpakistan," April 17, 1971, PA AA B37/630; Imam, *Blood*, pp. 67, 72 (April 22 and 29); accounts by Reza Haque and Golam Sarwar, in Firdousi, *Year*, pp. 47, 389–90; Hefley, *Christ*, pp. 18–19; Heß, *Bangladesch*, p. 99; account by former Bihari persecutor Yaqub Zainuddin, in Firdousi, *Year*, pp. 512–17.

226 See Breton, *Population*, pp. 47–51 (about 300,000); Haider, "Repatriation," pp. 526–7 (500,000 to 1 million).

227 White Paper, pp. 41, 64–9; Mascarenhas, "Genocide," p. 120; see also Sen, "Stateless," p. 631, n. 22.

228 Heß, *Bangladesch*, p. 145; Qutubuddin Aziz, *Blood and Tears* (Karachi: United Press of Pakistan, 1974), whose own estimates, however, rather add up to about 350,000 non-Bengali deaths, spread over 110 localities but heaviest in Dinajpur district, Chittagong, and Khulna. In 1971, Aziz, an experienced journalist, worked as a public relations man for the Pakistani government. He claims to have put together his book in a mere twelve weeks after publishing a call for survivor stories in February 1974 (pp. 12–14). In his propagandistic account, Aziz omits or denies violence against Bengalis, inflates Bihari victim numbers, and makes unproven inferences about Awami League, Hindu, or Indian participation in the killings. Many of the accounts he cites claim automatic weapons' fire when Bengalis could hardly possess those, describe the culprits as "rebels" before March 25, and/or tend to date pogroms early. Nonetheless, the accounts cited by him appear credible in many regards and can be cross-checked with other evidence.

229 Akram, "Bangladesh," p. 29 (quote); Haider, "Repatriation," p. 531, n. 40; Dreyfus, *Du Pakistan*, p. 153.

230 Chaudhuri, *Genocide*, p. 69 (20,000); "Pakistan: Polishing a tarnished image," *Time*, May 24, 1971, in Quaderi, *Bangla Desh*, p. 90 ("perhaps 20,000"); Heß, *Bangladesch*, p. 73 ("gegen 100,000," ["'almost 100,000' or 'about 100,000'"]); Rushbrook Williams, *East Pakistan*, p. 11 (120,000 or more); Lisa Sharlach, "Rape as genocide: Bangladesh, the former Yugoslavia and Rwanda," *New Political Science*, 22(1), 2000, p. 94 (150,000); Massa, *Bengale*, p. 181 (150,000–200,000); cf. Blood, *Cruel*, p. 250, citing his own telegram.

231 Niazi, *Betrayal*, p. 42; Sami Mustafa, "Who is conducting a genocide?," *Pakistan Forum* 3(4), 1973, p. 15; Muqeem Khan, *Pakistan's Crisis*, p. 88; Siddiqui, *Conflict*, pp. 150–2. Yet Siddiqui himself stated that seven of his relatives were killed in Sylhet, among them two women and four children.

232 White Paper, pp. 29–39; cf. Mascarenhas, *Rape*, pp. 91–3; Rushbrook Williams, *East Pakistan*, pp. 53, 64. Salik, *Witness*, p. 51, speaks of 102 non-Bengalis killed in Pahartali neighborhood alone, but cites an official press handout claiming 78 had been killed and 205 injured in Chittagong on both sides (pp. 56–7). Chaudhuri, *Genocide*, p. 69, brings forth the much exaggerated claim of 20,000 non-Bengali deaths before March 25.

233 International Commission of Jurists, Events, IIa; accounts by Mohammed Ishaque, Qayum Reza Chowdhury, and Fazlur Rehman, in Firdousi, *Year*, pp. 25–8, 296, 345–6; account by former Brigadier M. R. Majumdar, brought in on March 4 to stop the killings, in Kabir, *Tormenting* (maintains most victims he saw in hospitals were Bengalis). For Mirpur, Parbatipur, and Saidpur: Imam, *Blood*, p. 33 (March 21, 1971).

234 "Charges against 16 more MNAs," *Pakistan Times*, August 18, 1971, PA AA B 37/629; Mamoon, *Vanquished*, pp. 154–5.

235 Telegram from Dacca, March 6, 1971, PA AA, B37/630; Lockerbie, *Duty*, pp. 24 (Barisal), 78.

236 Ayoob and Subrahmanyam, *Liberation*, p. 114; Mascarenhas, *Rape*, pp. 91–3; interview with Rao Farman Ali, in Mamoon, *Vanquished*, p. 155.

237 Account by Yaqub Zainuddin in Firdousi, *Year*, p. 514; Waliul Islam in Firdousi, *Year*, pp. 15–24, describes the storming of the Kabuli

building in Chittagong on the morning of March 25, during which he himself shot three men and a woman was gang-raped; cf. Sisson and Rose, *War*, p. 91. Mujib: *Dawn*, March 26, 1971, in *Bangla Desh Documents*, pp. 273–4. Aziz, *Blood*, claims that large-scale pogroms against non-Bengalis started before 11 p.m. on March 25 in Dacca, Chittagong, Khulna, Sathkira, Dinajpur, Parbatipur, Laksham, Kushtia, Chuadanga, Ishurdi, Noakhali, Maulvi Bazar, Bheramera, Saidpur, Rangpur, Jessore, Noapera, Barisal, Comilla, Naogaon, and Santahar.

238 See Aziz, *Blood*.

239 White Paper, pp. 41–3, 64–9; Aziz, *Blood*, pp. 48–78, 97–113, 160–8, 182–97, 213–18; see Blood, *Cruel*, pp. 276–8; Michael Hornsby, "Pakistan Army intervention sets off events which led to vengeance killings in East Bengal," *The Times*, July 12, 1971; Muhith, *Bangladesh*, pp. 226–7, 230, 235. The International Commission of Jurists, Events, IIb, mentions eight places; see account by Arief Razzaque in Firdousi, *Year*, p. 330 (Ishurdi).

240 Account by Ferdousi Priyobhashinee, in Kabir, *Tormenting*; Sufiya Huq, Golam Sarwar, M. R. Chowdhury, and Mustafa Kamal, in Firdousi, *Year*, pp. 66, 389–90, 463, 489; at the port of Chittagong, non-Bengalis and Bengalis got into a conflict about unloading weapons: letter by A. Majid, *International Herald Tribune*, August 9, 1971, in Quaderi, *Bangla Desh*, p. 247. Over 5,000 non-Bengalis were allegedly killed in Khulna and at least 1,000 in Kushtia: White Paper, p. 66.

241 Aziz, *Blood*, pp. 27–8, 39, 51, 61, 81, 84, 88–9, 130, 137, 172, 175–6, 208; Imam, *Blood*, pp. 114–15 (July 1, 1971); Bose, "Anatomy" (Crescent Jute Mills, Khulna); Salik, *Witness*, p. 81; Muqeem Khan, *Pakistan's Crisis*, p. 79; Chaudhuri, *Genocide*, p. 34; "Fresh evidence of mass killings in Khulna," *Bangladesh Observer*, January 31, 1972; Feldman, *End*, p. 42, n. 16; Sen, "Stateless," p. 631. Earlier: Sen, "Stateless," p. 628, n. 12; Sisson and Rose, *War*, p. 13; Salik, *Witness*, p. 21. Later: Biswas, "Killing fields in Chittagong."

242 Chaudhuri, *Genocide*, pp. 135, 137. The data given (every third victim was a worker; one-third of all workers died) require further scrutiny, as does the definition of 'worker' used. The number of refugees was considerable. For Bengali workers killed en masse, see "Minister

gives accounts of Pakistani atrocities" and "Khulna's days of terror," *Bangladesh Observer*, February 4, 1972.

243 Aziz, *Blood*; Mascarenhas, *Rape*, p. 118; Blood, *Cruel*, p. 275; International Commission of Jurists, Events, IIb (observations by a US engineer at Kaptai); Maniruzzaman, *Bangladesh*, p. 93 (near Jessore).

244 Colin Smith, "The fading dream of Bangla Desh," *Observer*, April 18, 1971, in Quaderi, *Bangla Desh*, p. 63; Peter Hazelhurst, "Officer admits that Bengalis are murdering Biharis," *The Times*, May 17, 1971. For Jhenida: Aziz, *Blood*, p. 173.

245 Maniruzzaman, *Bangladesh*, p. 87, calls the late March 1971 perpetrators of the killing spree in Chittagong "Awami League volunteers." Aziz, *Blood*, generally charges Awami League functionaries but also mentions communal moderation or rescue efforts (pp. 58, 79, 164, 187, 201, 216).

246 Lockerbie, *Duty*, p. 78; Olsen, *Daktar*, pp. 11, 261, 269; Rushbrook Williams, *East Pakistan*, p. 74; Muqeem Khan, *Pakistan's Crisis*, p. 74; Nicholas Tomalin, "Mass slaughter of Punjabis in East Bengal," *The Times*, April 2, 1971.

247 FRG Consulate-General telegrams, April 27 and 30, 1971, PA AA B37/627; Imam, *Blood*, pp. 68, 70 (April 23 and 25).

248 Imam, *Blood*, p. 26 (March 13); Lockerbie, *Duty*, p. 27; Statement by Taijuddin, April 18, 1971, in Tewary, *War*, p. 162; Salik, *Witness*, pp. 44, 49.

249 FRG Consulate-General Dacca, "Lage in Ostpakistan," April 17, 1971, PA AA B37/630 (Jessore); account by Masoudul Hossain Khan, in Kabir, *Tormenting*; Salik, *Witness*, p. 64; Amir Taheri, "Five views of a tragedy," *Kayhan* (International) [Tehran], July 28, 1971, in Quaderi, *Bangla Desh*, p. 201; for India, see note 140.

250 Qureshi, *Indo-Pak War*, p. 33; Dan Coggins, "Pakistan: The battle of Kushtia," *Time*, April 19, 1971, in Quaderi, *Bangla Desh*, p. 74; account by Sufiya Huq, in Firdousi, *Year*, p. 65; cf. Masudur Rahman in Firdousi, *Year*, p. 453; McKinley, *Death*, pp. 12–13, about a civilian attack on the West Pakistanis in the Feni military post; Mamoon, *Media*, p. 76, and "Pakistan: Death of an ideal," *Newsweek*, April 12, 1971, in Quaderi, *Bangla Desh*, p. 50 (Jessore).

251 Account by Mohammed Naum Miah, then an 8 Bengal soldier, in Firdousi, *Year*, p. 53; Muhammed Nazrul Islam (in Firdousi, *Year*, p. 167) describes how Bengalis arrested a Captain whose mother was Bengali and whose father was West Pakistani.

252 Mascarenhas, *Bangladesh*, pp. 118–19, 122; Muqeem Khan, *Pakistan's Crisis*, p. 79. See also account by Nasseem Rahman in Firdousi, *Year*, pp. 465–6, for the killing of a non-Bengalis officer's family and several civilian families in Chittagong.

253 International Commission of Jurists, Events, IIb; Muqeem Khan, *Pakistan's Crisis*, pp. 79–80; Bose, "Anatomy"; Maniruzzaman, *Bangladesh*, p. 93 (Chuadanga); Aziz, *Blood*, p. 182.

254 Account by Mohammed Abdul Karim, Firdousi, *Year*, p. 403 (Kalabagan, September 1971).

255 Muqeem Khan, *Pakistan's Crisis*, p. 119; M. Rashiduzzaman, "Leadership, organization, strategies and tactics of the Bangla Desh Movement," *Asian Survey* 12(3), 1972, p. 195.

256 Quoted in Qureshi, *Indo-Pak War*, Appendix I (December 7, 1971); further telegrams in Hamoodur Commission Report, part V. ch. IV, paras 13, 19, 21.

257 Text of Instrument of Surrender, December 16, 1971, in Salik, *Witness*, p. 235; FRUS 1969–1976, vol. XI, 732, n. 2.

258 Salik, *Witness*, p. 212. Heß, *Bangladesch*, p. 146, estimated that 10,000–15,000 Biharis were killed between December 1971 and May 1972.

259 Report on Mymensingh, January 20, 1972, AfZ, Nachlass Umbricht, Bangladesh UNROD/UNROB, Information Papers I, Information Paper No. 1.

260 Dreyfus, *Du Pakistan*, pp. 232–3; Mukherji, "Great exodus," I, p. 367, and III, p. 449; Lockerbie, *Duty*, pp. 157–8; account by S. A. H. Saeed, in Firdousi, *Year*, pp. 261–2. Cf. Nicholas Tomalin, "Bengal's elite dead in a ditch," in Quaderi, *Bangla Desh*, p. 423.

261 Accounts by Kabiruddin Miah and Belal Chaudhuri, in Firdousi, *Year*, pp. 102, 111.

262 Account by Mohammad Jafar Ali Khan in Firdousi, *Year*, pp. 520–5. This witness – then ten years old – was stabbed in the chest.

263 Walsh, *Mangoes*, pp. 60–1. The victims were probably local forces since 700 relatives asked US missionary Tom Thurman for protection.

264 Sen, "Stateless," p. 633. Aziz, *Blood*, does not concentrate on the December 1971 events and suggests that often only men were killed (pp. 35–43, 158, 196, 217).

265 Account by Humayun Kabir, in Firdousi, *Year*, pp. 377–8; cf. Afsan Chowdhury and Muneer-u-Zaman in Firdousi, *Year*, pp. 343, 440; Olsen, *Bangladesh*, pp. 207–8; Julian Kerr, "Mukti Bahini settling old scores in Dacca," *The Times*, December 18, 1971; Sydney Schanberg, "In Dacca, killings amid the revelry," *New York Times*, December 18, 1971.

266 NBC News, December 31, 1971, Ron Nessen, "Stranded Pakistanis," www.youtube.com/watch?v=twxww9vT4_8&NR=1 (accessed December 15, 2007).

267 Photos in Aziz, *Blood*, pp. ix–xii; Heß, *Bangladesch*, after p. 144. Cf. Brian May, "Indian Army arrests 'Tiger of Tangail' after Dacca bayonettings," *The Times*, December 21, 1971; accounts by Reza Haque, Ibrahim Sabir, and Zakiuddin Ahmed in Firdousi, *Year*, pp. 50, 95, 284–7. Anwar Hossain, a Bengali student, was forced to hand over his film after photographing a similar event at a Dainik Bangla river crossing near Dacca: in Firdousi, *Year*, p. 133.

268 Telegram from New Delhi, February 4, 1972, PA AA B37/692; Bernard Ullmann, "Biharis bury dead after clashes," *The Times*, February 2, 1972; Peter Hazelhurst, "Hundreds of non-Bengalis slaughtered in Bangladesh," *The Times*, May 8, 1972; Whitaker *et al.*, *Biharis*, pp. 9, 14, 16.

269 William S. Ellis, "Bangladesh: Hope nourishes a new nation," *National Geographic* 142(2), September 1972, pp. 320–1, 331–2; Whitaker *et al.*, *Biharis*, pp. 28–9; downplayed in Malik, *Year*, pp. 120–5.

270 Guy Stringer, "A passage through Bangladesh and India: Visit to Bangladesh, 5–10 December 1979," Oxfam Archive, Tour Reports

India, Sri Lanka, Bangladesh, Pakistan, file "Bangladesh Tour Reports, 1972–1987"; see also Oxfam Archive, Project Files, Box 1012, BD55A and BD55C; Report on Concern Survey [...], January 1976, AfZ, Nachlass Umbricht, Bangladesh Aid Group/World Bank, Various, file Bangladesh Aid Group, World Bank.

271 "Bericht über die Durchführung des Befehls des Genossen Minister vom 1. November 1973 zur Aktion Austausch," January 1, 1974, PA AA MfAA C1047/77.

272 Haider, "Repatriation," pp. 527, 534, n. 50, 539–40.

273 Susan Brownmiller, *Against Our Will: Men, Women and Rape* (New York: Simon and Schuster, 1975), p. 80.

274 Malik, *Year*, p. 142, citing the (male) Director of the Bangladesh Organization of Rehabilitation of Women. Pakistani officials rejected the figure as inflated: Hamoodur Commission Report, part V, paras 10, 11, 32, 34.

275 Chaudhuri, *Genocide*, pp. 163, 199–202.

276 Brownmiller, *Against*, p. 79; Malik, *Year*, pp. 97, 100. Rokeya Hall, the female student hall of Dacca University, was haunted by mass rape twice: Chandra, *Bloodbath*, pp. 133–5 (March 26, 1971, many students killed); Chaudhuri, *Genocide*, p. 160 (the October 7, 1971 mass rape by soldiers under Major Aslam was even criticized by the Pakistani newspaper *Dawn*).

277 Malik, *Year*, p. 60

278 Brownmiller, *Against*, p. 80. According to some accounts, girls were spared from rape if they could recite Muslim prayers: Sharlach, "Rape," p. 94.

279 "A report on Hindus in Bangladesh," in Roy, *Genocide*, p. 188.

280 Niazi's confidential order, April 15, 1971, in Niazi, *Betrayal*, pp. 282–3.

281 Hamoodur Commission report, part V, para 36.

282 Brownmiller, *Against*, pp. 79 (Jessore district), 82, 83 (Mohammedpur); account by M. Akhtaurazzaman Mondol, in Jahan, "Genocide," p. 398.

283 McKinley, *Death*, p. 47.

284 Chaudhuri, *Genocide*, p. 160, n.

285 Chaudhuri, *Genocide*, p. 163.

286 Malik, *Year*, p. 99.

287 Sridham Chandra Das, "Killing fields in Laksam," in Kabir, *Tormenting*; account by Humayun Kabir, in Firdousi, *Year*, p. 375 (Manikganj); "Pogrom in Pakistan," *Sunday Times*, June 20, 1971, in Quaderi, *Bangla Desh*, p. 146 (Agrabad).

288 Malik, *Year*, p. 155; Chaudhuri, *Genocide*, pp. 160–1.

289 Interview with Dr. Geoffrey Davis by Bina D'Costa, June 1, 2002, http://drishtipat.org/1971/docs/interview2davis_bina.pdf (accessed December 15, 2007), p. 3.

290 Qureshi, *Indo-Pak War*, p. 103.

291 Malik, *Year*, p. 154.

292 Killed or injured: Harjee Malik, "The war heroines of Bangladesh," *Holiday*, June 4, 1972, PA AA B37/693; account by Rabeya Khatun, in Kabir, *Tormenting* (Dacca); account by Samoondari, in Firdousi, *Year*, pp. 153–4; Chaudhuri, *Genocide*, p. 56 (Basabaria in mid-April). Hindus: Hefley, *Christ*, pp. 52–3 (Mymensingh area); account by Farooque Ahmed, in Firdousi, *Year*, p. 395 (Raghunathpur).

293 Lt-Col. Aziz Ahmad Khan, quoted in Hamoodur Commission report, chapter 1, para 16, adding that Niazi "enjoyed the same reputation at Sialkot and Lahore" (where he was Martial Law Administrator, para 15). Niazi is also quoted upon arrival in Dacca in April 1971 having said to Major-General Khadim: "When are you going to hand over your concubines to me?" Salik, *Witness*, p. 92. President Yahya Khan was also known as a great womanizer: Blood, *Cruel*, p. 42; Salik, *Witness*, p. 107.

294 A serious argument brought up in a rather propagandistic source: Bhattacharjya *et al.*, "What," pp. 62–3.

295 "Pakistan: The ravaging of golden Bengal," *Time*, August 2, 1971, in Quaderi, Bangla Desh, p. 229.

296 Chaudhuri, *Genocide*, p. 159.

297 Brownmiller, *Against*, esp. pp. 85–6.

298 Gudrun Martius-von Harder, *Die Frau im ländlichen Bangladesch* (Saarbrücken: Breitenfeld, 1978), esp. p. 90.

299 Habiba Zaman, "Violence against Women in Bangladesh: Issues and responses," *Women Studies International Forum* 22(1), 1999, pp. 38–40.

300 Jane Menken and James F. Phillips, "Population change in a rural area of Bangladesh, 1967–1987," *Annals of the American Society of Political and Social Science* 510, July 1990, p. 92.

301 Santi Rozario, "'Disasters' and Bangladeshi Women," in Ronit Lentin (ed.), *Gender and Catastrophe* (London and New York: Zed, 1997), pp. 264–5; Harjee Malik, "The war heroines of Bangladesh," *Holiday*, June 4, 1972, PA AA B 37/693; Kabir, "Introduction," p. 4; Malik, *Year*, pp. 94, 96, 138–41.

302 Saha, "Genocide," pp. 216–17; "Who is my neighbour?," *Far Eastern Economic Review* 73(35), August 28, 1971, p. 80; Gholam Azam: account by Ferdousi Priyobhashinee, in Kabir, *Tormenting*.

303 Brownmiller, *Against*, p. 83.

304 Interview with Dr. Geoffrey Davis, see note 289, pp. 2, 5.

305 Rozario, "Disasters," p. 265; "U.N. asked to aid Bengali abortions," *Washington Post*, March 22, 1972 (authorities spoke of 300 suicides per month).

306 Brownmiller, *Against*, p. 85; Bina D'Costa, "War babies: The question of national honour," http://drishtipat.org/1971/docs/warbabies_bina.pdf, pp. 4–5; interview with Respondent A (January 2000), http://drishtipat.org/1971/docs/interview1_bina.pdf (both accessed December 15, 2007); interview with Dr. Geoffrey Davis (an abortion specialist then working in Bangladesh), see note 289, p. 5.

307 D'Costa, "War babies," pp. 4–5 (quote), and interview with respondent A, see previous note. Jack Adams of the Christian Holt Adoption Program was able to find less than 100 rape babies: Hefley, *Christ*, p. 89.

308 Brownmiller, "Against," p. 81, calls them the "most enthusiastic rapists"; Malik, *Year*, pp. 19–20; Qureshi, *Indo-Pak War*, p. 69; 2nd Report on the findings of the People's Inquiry Commission on

the activities of the War Criminals and the Collaborators, March 26, 1995, entry for Ali Ahsan Muhammad Mujahid, www.secularvoi ceofbangladesh.org/Report%20on%20the%20war%20criminals.htm (accessed January 16, 2008).

309 Rozario, "Disasters," p. 264; interview with Respondent A, see note 306; Mukherji, "Great exodus," I, p. 368.

310 Kabir, "Introduction," p. 3.

311 Accounts by Afsan Chowdhury and Hummayun Kabir Muneer-u-Zaman, in Firdousi, *Year*, pp. 343, 377, 440; Yasmin Saikia, "Beyond the archive of silence: Narratives of violence in the 1971 liberation war of Bangladesh," *History Workshop Journal*, 58, 2004, pp. 275–87, esp. pp. 278, 285.

312 Zaman, "Violence," p. 39.

313 Account by Waliul Islam, in Firdousi, *Year*, p. 24 (Chittagong March 25, 1971); "Charges against 16 more MNAs," *Pakistan Times*, August 18, 1971, PA AA B37/629 (Thakurgaon, Bogra, Santahar, Jessore, Khulna).

314 Ghulam Kabir, *Minority Politics*, pp. 108–12, 132, 149; Roy, *Genocide*, pp. 10, 33.

315 Mriduh Bandyopadhyay and Mahmuda Rahman Khan, "Loss of face: Violence against women in Southeast Asia," in Lenore Manderson and Linda Rae Bennett (eds.), *Violence Against Women in Asian Societies* (London and New York: Routledge, 2003), pp. 67–73; Roksana Nazneen, "Violence in Bangladesh," in Stanley G. French *et al.* (eds.), *Violence Against Women* (Ithaca and London: Cornell University Press, 1998), pp. 77–91; Lutz Oette (Redress), Torture in Bangladesh 1971–2004 (August 2004), www.redress.org/publications/ Bangladesh.pdf (accessed December 15, 2007), pp. 11–12. Similarly: Farida Shaheed, "The experience in Pakistan," in Miranda Davis (ed.), *Women and Violence* (London and New Jersey: Zed, 1994), p. 214.

316 Zaman, "Violence," pp. 37, 43.

317 Willem van Schendel, "Neue Aspekte der Arbeitsgeschichts-schreibung: Anregungen aus Südasien," *Sozial.Geschichte* 22(1), 2007, p. 61.

318 In Kabir, *Tormenting*.

319 The observation is from Jahan, "Genocide," p. 381.

320 Jahan, "Genocide," p. 385.

321 Roy, *Genocide*, p. 16; Sydney Schanberg, "Hindus are targets of army terror in an East Pakistan town," *New York Times*, July 4, 1971. This responded to wealthier Hindu families leaving an older member behind to manage the remaining property, sending the proceeds to India (Ghulam Kabir, *Minority Politics*, pp. 5–11).

322 Chaudhuri, *Genocide*, p. 171; Peter Kann, "A nation divided," *Wall Street Journal*, July 23, 1971, in *Bangla Desh Documents*, p. 423; "India," *Time*, July 12, 1971, in Quaderi, *Bangla Desh*, p. 169. Auction: Murray Sayle, "A regime of thugs and bigots," *Sunday Times*, July 11, 1971.

323 Mascarenhas, "Genocide," p. 138.

324 Chaudhuri, *Genocide*, p. 49; "Pogrom in Pakistan," *Sunday Times*, June 20, 1971, in Quaderi, *Bangla Desh*, pp. 147–8; Sydney Schanberg, "East Pakistan: An 'alien army' imposes its will," *New York Times*, July 4, 1971; for demands for Hindu property by Peace Committees: Sharif *et al.*, *Genocide '71*, pp. 48, 55.

325 Malik, *Year*, p. 57. Hindu bank accounts were frozen: Sydney Schanberg, "Hindus are targets of army terror in an East Pakistan town," *New York Times*, July 4, 1971, p. 579.

326 People's Inquiry Commission Report, Sayeedi.

327 Maniruzzaman, *Bangladesh*, p. 120.

328 FRG Consulate-General Dacca, situation report, April 29, 1971, PA AA B37/627; Blood, *Cruel*, p. 293 (cites own May 25, 1971 telegram); cf. Imam, *Blood*, p. 7 (March 1).

329 Account by S. A. H. Saeed, in Firdousi, *Year*, p. 256.

330 Blood, *Cruel*, pp. 277–8 (Mymensingh); International Commission of Jurists, Events, IIb (Kaptai).

331 Salik, *Witness*, p. 69 (Dinajpur); account by Ataur Rahman, in Firdousi, *Year*, p. 425 (Dacca); Blood, *Cruel*, p. 278 (Mymensingh).

332 As in the family of Taslima Nasreen in Mymensingh: Nasreen, *Girlhood*, p. 281.

333 Niazi, *Betrayal*, pp. 50, 282–3, here quoting his confidential order of April 15, 1971.

334 Hamoodur Commission report, part V, ch. II, paras 10–11 (quote) and ch. I, para 13 (also "typewriters, watches, gold"); Chaudhuri, *Genocide*, pp. 154–5.

335 "Pogrom in Pakistan," *Sunday Times*, June 20, 1971 in Quaderi, *Bangla Desh*, p. 149.

336 Hamoodur Commission report, part V, ch. I, paras 11–12.

337 Memo Williams for State Department, November 5, 1971, FRUS 1969–1976, vol. E-7, doc. 152 (from a conversation with General Farman).

338 FRG Consulate-General, "Kriegshysterie in Ostpakistan," October 15, 1971, PA AA B 37/629 (Noakhali district); Blood, *Cruel*, p. 293, with text of his May 25, 1971 telegram; Lockerbie, *Duty*, p. 25 (Barisal); Paresh Saha, "Move to uproot Chakmas from their homes," *Amrita Baxar Patrika*, April 20, 1980, in Roy, *Genocide*, p. 135 (Chittagong Hill Tracts, late 1971/early 1972).

339 Accounts by S. A. H. Saeed and Premankur Roy, in Firdousi, *Year*, pp. 258–9, 379; Maniruzzaman, *Bangladesh*, pp. 144–5; Willem van Schendel, *Peasant Mobility: The Odds of Life in Rural Bangladesh* (New Delhi: Manohar, 1982), p. 145.

340 Account by Obeid Jagirdar, in Firdousi, *Year*, p. 139.

341 Bhuiyan, *Emergence*, pp. 247–53; account by S. A. H. Saeed, in Firdousi, *Year*, p. 262.

342 World Bank reports in *Thousand My Lais*, esp. pp. 17–19; Chaudhuri, *Genocide*, pp. 134–5; Qureshi, *Indo-Pak War*, p. 101.

343 International Commission of Jurists, Events, IIb.

344 Olsen, *Daktar*, pp. 277, 284–5.

345 Blood, *Cruel*, p. 221; quote: Hefley, *Christ*, pp. 47–8.

346 Hartmann and Boyce, *Quiet Violence*, pp. 68, 171; van Schendel, *Peasant Mobility*, pp. 94–5, 155, 179; cf. Chaudhuri, *Genocide*, p. 101;

Joiner, *Gloria*, p. 64; Malik, *Year*, p. 33; Kasturi Rangan, "Hindu refugee returns, finds ruins in East Pakistan," *New York Times*, December 29, 1971.

347 Mukherji, "Great exodus," I, p. 368.

348 Mukherji, "Great exodus," I, p. 368; Bose, "Anatomy"; Chowdhury, "Bewas village."

349 Chaudhuri, *Genocide*, p. 93; Malik, *Year*, p. 43; "The Bengali refugees: A surfeit of woe," *Time*, June 21, 1971, in Quaderi, *Bangla Desh*, p. 151; "Senator Edward Kennedy on the Hindu genocide in East Bengal '71," www.hinduhumanrights.org/Bangladesh/kennedy. htm (accessed December 14, 2007); Payne, *Massacre*, p. 57.

350 Mukherji, "Great exodus," III, pp. 449–50.

351 Hartmann and Boyce, *Quiet Violence*, p. 172; van Schendel, *Peasant Mobility*, pp. 94–5.

352 Chaudhuri, *Genocide*, p. 102.

353 Anjan Kumar Datta, *Land and Labour Relations in South-West Bangladesh: Resources, Power and Conflict* (Basingstoke and New York: St. Martin's, 1998), pp. 46–7 (about a village south of Khulna); Ron Ochwell, Report on Field Visit to Sylhet and Comilla Districts, January 24, 1972, AfZ, Nachlass Umbricht, Bangladesh UNROD/ UNROB, Information Papers I, file Information Paper No. 1; van Schendel, *Peasant Mobility*, pp. 94–5; for 1964 see also Nath Tagore, "Persecution," pp. 53–4.

354 *Pakistan News Digest* 19(24), December 15, 1971, XCIII (November 24), ANA 189/10/7, part 1.

355 Hendrik van der Heijden, Field Report, June 23, 1971, in *Thousand My Lais*, p. 9; "Senator Edward Kennedy on the Hindu genocide in East Bengal '71," see note 349.

356 Ambassador Erna Sailer's Report, March–April 1972, I, 5, AfZ, Nachlass Umbricht, Bangladesh, UNROD/UNROB Reports, file List of UNROD Papers/Ambassador Sailer's Report; Report on Field Visit to Sylhet and Comilla Districts, January 24, 1972 (see note 353).

357 Mukherji, "Great exodus," III, p. 449.

358 "Toaha on B.D. situation," *Pakistan Forum* 2(7/8), 1972, p. 21.

359 "Chittagong tribals up in arms," *Statesman*, May 3, 1980, in Roy, *Genocide*, p. 121; Chaudhuri, *Genocide*, p. 174.

360 Prakash Singh, "Foreword," in Paliwal, *Islamism*, p. ix, referring to the 1974 Enemy Property (continuance of) Emergency Provisions (Repeal) Act and the Vested and Non-Resident Property (Administration) Act of 1974. Cf. Roy, *Genocide*, p. 191.

361 Australian High Commissioner Dacca, Savingram 6/72, August 14, 1972, ANA 855/2, part 1, pp. 225–6.

362 Sen, "Stateless," pp. 636–9, citing the Acting President's Order I and the Bangladesh Abandoned Property (Control, Management and Disposal) Order 1972.

363 Account by Humayun Kabir, in Firdousi, *Year*, pp. 377–8; Sen, "Stateless," pp. 635, 639; Dasgupta, *Midnight*, p. 48.

364 Maniruzzaman, *Bangladesh*, p. 159; Ian Guest, "The context of Bangladesh in 1977," in Whitaker *et al.*, *Biharis*, p. 28.

365 Ziauddin Ahmed, "The case of Bangladesh: Bringing to trial the perpetrators of the 1971 genocide," in Albert Jongman (ed.), *Contemporary Genocides* (Leiden: PIOOM, 1996), p. 102.

366 Talukder Maniruzzaman, "Bangladesh in 1974: Economic crisis and political polarization," *Asian Survey* 15(2), 1975, pp. 118–20; Lifschultz, *Bangladesh*, pp. 42–3, 133; "Die Entwicklung der VR Bangladesch seit der Erringung der Unabhängigkeit," July 25, 1972, PA AA MfAA C1052/77, pp. 114–15. For pre-March 1971 demands for nationalization from leftist students, the Awami League, and the religious Jama'at-i-Islami party, see Tewary, *War*, pp. 37, 46; Awami League Manifesto, *Dawn*, June 15, 1970, in *Bangla Desh Documents*, pp. 70–1; Blood, *Cruel*, p. 125. Cf. Noman, *Pakistan*, pp. 75–7.

367 Swadesh R. Bose, "Foodgrain availability and possibilities of famine in Bangla Desh," *EPW* 7(5/7), February 1972, pp. 293–306.

368 Imam, *Blood*, p. 57 (April 4); account by Samoondari, in Firdousi, *Year*, p. 154; FRG Consulate-General, "Lage in Ostpakistan, hier: Ernährungslage," May 21, 1971, PA AA B37/627; "Pakistan: The ravaging of golden Bengal," *Time*, August 2, 1971, in Quaderi, *Bangla Desh*, p. 225; Bose, "Foodgrain," p. 303; UNHCR, UNROD, and UNICEF reports on Comilla-Feni-Cox's Bazar [including Dacca and

Chittagong data], Faridpur, and Comilla, January 10 and 14–15 and February 5, 1972, AfZ, Nachlass Umbricht, Bangladesh UNROD/ UNROB, Information Papers I, Information Paper No 1.

369 Mascarenhas, "Genocide," p. 134 (allegedly hoarding was tolerated by the authorities to bring Bengalis, through starvation, "to their senses"); Mascarenhas, *Rape*, p. 131; Chen and Rohde, "Famine," p. 200; and see note 415.

370 World Bank report in *Thousand My Lais*, pp. 22 4; see also Chaudhuri, *Genocide*, p. 133; yet Bose, "Foodgrain," p. 295.

371 US Consulate Dacca, June 18, 1971, NARA RG59, Gen.Rec., Economic, 1970–73, Box 472, AGR P; *Pakistan News Digest* 19(22), December 1, 1971, XCI, ANA 189/10/7, part 1. Low food stocks were reported by E. Hylton, UNROD, from Rajshahi, Kushtia, and Khulna districts, January 6–12, 1972, AfZ, Nachlass Umbricht, Bangladesh UNROD/UNROB, Information Papers I, Information Paper No. 1.

372 Lifschultz, *Bangladesh*, p. 99; Chaudhuri, *Genocide*, p. 100; Bose, "Foodgrain," p. 301.

373 "Visit to Calcutta and Dacca on 17th/22nd December 1971," Oxfam Archive, AG/2/1–5, Box Bangladesh Consortium of British Charities, file IBRD-FAO ODM.

374 Victor Umbricht, "UNROD in Bangladesh," April 1973, AfZ, Nachlass Umbricht, Bangladesh, UNROD/UNROB Reports, Report SG/Future Assistance/Planning Commission/Various.

375 Curlin *et al.*, "Demographic crisis," pp. 97–8, 103; cf. Chen and Rohde, "Famine," p. 202.

376 UNROD, Information Paper No. 3: Blunt Facts on Relief and Rehabilitation in Bangladesh (Toni Hagen), February 18, 1972, AfZ, Nachlass Umbricht, Bangladesh UNROD/UNROB, Information Papers I, Information Paper No 3/No 11.

377 Curlin *et al.*, "Demographic crisis," pp. 91–2.

378 Tetro to Boerma, April 2, 1972, FAO Archive RG15, FA 6.7, Tetro 1971–72.

379 James Sprague and Stanley Foster, "Second Bangladesh Nutritional Assessment," UNROD, Information Paper No. 21, October 1972,

AfZ, Nachlass Umbricht, Bangladesh UNROD/UNROB, Information Papers I, Information Paper No. 21; cf. Greenough III and Cash, "Post-civil war," pp. 247–8.

380 Australian Embassy Washington, June 3, 1972, ANA 855/2, part 1, p. 164; Australian High Commissioner Dacca, Savingram 7/72, August 28, 1972, same file, p. 234; GDR Embassy Dacca, "Vermerk," September 7, 1972, PA AA MfAA C1044/77, p. 36; Mascarenhas, *Bangladesh*, pp. 19–22; Franda, *Bangladesh*, p. 27. Earlier food riots: Hefley, *Christ*, p. 86.

381 Chaudhuri, *Genocide*, pp. 138–9.

382 S. K. Dey, Bangladesh Today and Tomorrow?, UNROD Information Paper No. 11 [ca. May 1972], 4, AfZ, Nachlass Umbricht, Bangladesh UNROD/UNROB, Information Papers I, Information Paper No. 3/No. 11.

383 Sprague and Foster, "Second Bangladesh Nutritional Assessment," October 1972, tables 4 and 5.

384 See endnote 132 and Ghulam Kabir, *Minority Politics*, Appendix I, for 1961 census figures.

385 N. K. Chandra, "Agrarian classes in East Pakistan (1949–1970)," I, and Asim Makhopadhyay, "Will they return?," *Frontier*, January 8, 1972 and July 31, 1971, in Mamoon, *Media*, pp. 67, 124.

386 Lifschultz, *Bangladesh*, p. 109; Menken and Phillips, "Population," p. 88.

387 Edward J. Clay, "Institutional change and agricultural wages in Bangladesh," *Bangladesh Development Studies* IV(4), 1976, p. 424.

388 Dyson, "Demography," p. 287; Chowdhury and Chen, "Interaction," p. 50; Peter Wheller, UNROB, Confidential report, August 2, 1973, AfZ, Nachlass Umbricht, Bangladesh, UNROD/UNROB, UNROB.

389 Lifschultz, *Bangladesh*, pp. 40–1, 44–6, citing his own 1974 *Far Eastern Economic Review* articles; reports by G. Mazumdar, Indian Border Security Force, January 18 and March 31, 1975, in Dasgupta, *Midnight*, pp. 109, 114; Nurul Islam, "What was it about the 1974 famine?," *Scholars Journal*, October 15, 2005, www.scholarsbangladesh.

com/nurulislam1.php (accessed January 25, 2008). Hindus: Roy, *Genocide*, p. 188. 1971 damage: Alamgir, *Famine*, p. 117.

390 Die Kommunistische Partei von Bangladesh, Zentralkomitee, "Politische Revolution," April 24, 1972, PA AA MfAA C1053/77, p. 13; see also Mascarenhas, *Bangladesh*, p. 7.

391 Aminul Islam, *Victorious Victims*, esp. pp. 102–5. For similar developments in West Pakistan, also including nationalizations, see Noman, *Pakistan*, pp. 75–7, 104.

392 As did the National Awami Party (Bhashani) in 1973: Maniruzzaman, *Bangladesh*, p. 193, n. 19. See Jacques Weber, "La guerre du Bangladesh vue de France," *Guerres mondiales et conflits contemporains* 49(195), 1999, p. 92.

393 Dasgupta, *Midnight*, pp. 44–5; Mascarenhas, *Bangladesh*, p. 47; Australian High Commissioner Dacca, Savingram 3/72 and 9/72, July 4 and September 26, 1972, ANA 855/2, part 1, pp. 189, 243; Maniruzzaman, "Bangladesh," pp. 122–3.

394 Mascarenhas, *Bangladesh*, pp. 26–8.

395 "The greed of the few and the misery of the many," *EPW* 7(18), April 29, 1972, pp. 870–1.

396 Mascarenhas, *Bangladesh*, p. 129.

397 For corruption in Pakistan: Mascarenhas, *Rape*, pp. 29–33; Sisson and Rose, *War*, p. 17; radio broadcast by Mujib, March 10, 1971, in Tewary, *War*, p. 106; after 1971: Blood, *Cruel*, p. 337.

398 Oette (Redress), Torture, p. 7, n. 18.

399 The best analysis is Alamgir, *Famine*, pp. 101–45, esp. pp. 140–3; see Amartya Sen, *Poverty and Famines* (Oxford: Clarendon Press, 1981), pp. 131–54; Gerlach, "Versuch," pp. 81–8; and the data in Chowdhury and Chen, "Interaction," pp. 49–52; Dyson, "Demography," pp. 287, 291; Radheshyam Bairagi, "Food crisis, nutrition, and female children in rural Bangladesh," *Population and Development Review* 12(2), 1986, p. 311.

400 Sen, *Poverty*, pp. 134–41; Alamgir, *Famine*, pp. 242–4, 273; Islam, "What?"; US agricultural attaché, "Bangladesh: Quarterly grain and feed report," May 1, 1974, NARA RG 166, 170/73/18/6–7,

FAS Agricultural Attaché and Counselor Reports 1971–84, Box 36, BD Bangladesh 1974.

401 Quote: Donald McHenry and Kai Bird, "Food bungle in Bangladesh," *Foreign Policy* 27, summer 1977, p. 75.

402 The impact of the flooding on Rangpur district was medium and on Dinajpur low. "Estimate of flood damages," PA AA MfAA C1047/77, esp. p. 33; Islam, "What?"

403 IBRD, Bangladesh: The Current Economic Situation and Short-Term Outlook, May 2, 1975 (Report N. 710a-BD), p. 6.

404 Chowdhury and Chen, "Interaction," p. 50; Martin Ravallion, "The performance of rice markets in Bangladesh during the 1974 famine," *The Economic Journal* 95(377), March 1985, pp. 15–29; Muni Quddus and Charles Becker, "Speculative price bubbles in the rice market and the 1974 Bangladesh famine," *Journal of Economic Development* 25(2), 2000, pp. 155–75; Jenneke Arens and Jos van Beurden, *Jhagrapur: Poor Peasants and Women in a Village in Bangladesh* (New Delhi: Orient Longman, 1980), p. 115.

405 Calculated from IBRD, Bangladesh, table 9.6. September to November were traditionally lean months.

406 Hartmann and Boyce, *Quiet Violence*, pp. 189, 192.

407 M. Ameerul Huq (ed.), *Exploitation and the Rural Poor* (Comilla: Bangladesh Academy for Rural Development, 1976), esp. pp. 93, 107–8, 117 (quote), 154–5.

408 W. B. Reddaway and Md. Mizanur Rahman, "The scale of smuggling out of Bangladesh," *EPW*, 11(23), June 5, 1976, pp. 843–9; Islam, "What?"; other view: Alamgir, *Famine*, pp. 233–9.

409 Muqeem Khan, *Pakistan's Crisis*, p. 10; Ghulam Kabir, *Minority Politics*, pp. 5, 14–15, 62–3; "Friendship, not fish or poultry," *EPW* 7(24), June 10, 1972, pp. 1141–2; G. Mazumdar, Indian Border Security Force, January 18, 1975, in Dasgupta, *Midnight*, p. 109.

410 Islam, "What?"; cf. Gerlach, "Versuch," p. 88; McHenry and Bird, "Food bungle," p. 82; World Food Programme, Bangladesh, Foodgrain Forecast, July 1 to October 31, 1975, NARA, RG166, Ag.Att. Reports, Box 47, BD Bangladesh 1975.

411 Lifschultz, *Bangladesh*, pp. 44–6 (citing 1974 articles).

412 Joseph Collins and Frances Moore Lappé, *Vom Mythos des Hungers* (Frankfurt a.M.: Fischer Taschenbuch, 1978), pp. 32–4; Lifschultz, *Bangladesh*, p. 46 (citing his November 15, 1974 article); Sen, *Poverty*, p. 151; Alamgir, *Famine*, pp. 137, 161–2, 182–5. For increased mortgaging and land conflicts, Arens and van Beurden, *Jhagrapur*, pp. 136–7, 141, 160–7.

413 Alamgir, *Famine*, p. 135.

414 Lifschultz, *Bangladesh*, pp. 7–8.

415 Viktor Umbricht, handwritten conversation note, August 5, 1974, AfZ, Nachlass Umbricht, Bangladesh General I, file General VI.

416 Lifschultz, *Bangladesh*, pp. 46–7.

417 Tajuddin Ahmed, "To the people of Bangladesh," broadcast by Swadhi Bangla Desh Betar Kendra, April 11, 1971, PA AA B37/583; Bose, "Foodgrain," p. 303; Ellis, "Bangladesh," p. 329.

418 McHenry and Bird, "Food bungle," p. 74; Islam, "What?"; M. Syedazzamen, Secretary, Bangladesh Planning Commission, to US Ambassador, May 14, 1974, NARA RG 166, Ag. Att. Reports, Box 36, BD Bangladesh 1974; Habibul Haque Khondker, "Governmental Response to Famine: A Case Study of the 1974 Famine in Bangladesh" (Ph.D. thesis, University of Pittsburgh, 1984), pp. 4, 140–2.

419 Lifschultz, *Bangladesh*, pp. 45–6, 82–3; Khondker, "Response," p. 85; Gerlach, "Versuch," pp. 85–6; Tony Loftas, "'Save us' plea by Bangladesh," *PAN* 7, November 12, 1974, p. 1; see *PAN*, November 15, 1974, p. 7, Oxfam Archive; van Schendel, *Peasant Mobility*, p. 67; Sen, *Poverty*, pp. 131, 146 (for the wage–rice exchange rate); Nasreen, *Girlhood*, pp. 226–32; Alamgir, *Famine*, pp. 128, 135; flood in Rangpur district: Alamgir, *Famine*, pp. 124–5.

420 Sen, *Poverty*, pp. 131, 146–7; Gerlach, "Versuch," pp. 85–6.

421 Alamgir, *Famine*, p. 128; Mascarenhas, *Bangladesh*, pp. 43–4; Khondker, "Response," pp. 5, 90–1; Joiner, *Gloria*, p. 65.

422 Chowdhury and Chen, "Interaction," p. 52; Bairagi, "Food crisis," p. 311.

423 Dyson, "Demography," p. 288.

424 Sen, *Poverty*, pp. 142–4, 151; Alamgir, *Famine*, pp. 157–8.

425 Alamgir, *Famine*, pp. 154, 166–7.

426 Chowdhury and Chen, "Interaction," p. 53; Bairagi, "Food crisis," p. 311; Stan D'Souza and Abbas Bhuiya, "Socioeconomic mortality differentials in a rural area of Bangladesh," *Population and Development Review* 8(4), 1982, pp. 753–69.

427 Greenough and Cash, "Post-civil war," p. 244.

428 "Land of despair," *Wall Street Journal*, November 27, 1974; Lifschultz, *Bangladesh*, p. 45.

429 Hence it may be not by accident that the proportion of Hindus in Rangpur district decreased from 16 percent in 1961 to 5 percent in 1974 (van Schendel, *Peasant Mobility*, p. 51, n. 11). Probably more than 100,000 Bangladeshis fled to India in 1975 and 42,000 were rejected by India's Border Security Force from January to July 1975, 70 to 90 percent of whom were Hindus: Franda, *Bangladesh*, pp. 128–9.

430 Mascarenhas, *Bangladesh*, esp. pp. 8–9.

431 Noman, *Pakistan*, pp. 64–7, 123, 192–206.

432 Bernd Pieschel (GDR Embassy Dacca), "Parlamentswahlen in Bangladesch," February 17, 1973, PA AA MfAA C1047/77, p. 133; reports by G. Mazumdar, Indian Border Security Force, November 25, 1974 and January 18, 1975 in Dasgupta, *Midnight*, pp. 107, 109; Mascarenhas, *Bangladesh*, pp. 22–3, 37; "Bangladesh: Political gangsterism" and "Bangladesh: War against Maoists," *EPW* 8(38), September 1973, p. 1712, and 8(46), November 17, 1973, p. 2033. Quote: Franda, *Bangladesh*, p. 154 (in a 1973 article). There were 5,978 murders reported in 1972, 2,571 in 1973, and 2,782 in 1974: Alamgir, *Famine*, p. 139.

433 Mascarenhas, *Bangladesh*, pp. 16, 89.

434 Kumar Datta, *Land*, pp. 219–20; see also Mascarenhas, *Bangladesh*, p. 173, for 1981.

435 Australian High Commissioner Dacca, Savingrams 5/72 (quote) and 7/72, July 31 and August 28, 1972, ANA 855/2, part 1, pp. 216, 234; Lifschultz, *Bangladesh*, pp. 41, 124; Dasgupta, *Midnight*, p. 80; Mascarenhas, *Bangladesh*, pp. 37, 44.

436 Mascarenhas, *Bangladesh*, pp. 45, 61.

437 Mascarenhas, *Bangladesh*, p. 37.

438 Jahan, "Genocide," p. 385.

439 Australian High Commissioner Dacca, Savingram 8/72, September 12, 1972, ANA 855/2, part 1, p. 243.

440 "The work of the voluntary relief agencies in Bangladesh," 1972, AfZ, Nachlass Umbricht, Bangladesh UNROD/UNROB, Information Papers II.

441 Hartmann and Boyce, *Quiet Violence*, pp. 147–8.

442 Mascarenhas, *Bangladesh*, pp. 104, 128; Franda, *Bangladesh*, pp. 263–4.

443 Mascarenhas, *Bangladesh*, pp. 103–17; Lifschultz, *Bangladesh*, pp. 9–10.

444 Lifschultz, *Bangladesh*, pp. 50, 52; Neil O'Sullivan, "Bangladesh report," March 22, 1976, Oxfam Archive, Project Files, Box 1009, BD59; similar figures for 1977 in Roy, *Genocide*, pp. 59, 67; Mascarenhas, *Bangladesh*, p. 131, gives a figure of 15,000 for 1978; "Bangladesh: The people: Enemies of the government," *EPW* 9(9), March 2, 1974, p. 361 already spoke of 20,000 leftist political prisoners.

445 Oette (Redress), Torture.

446 Mascarenhas, *Bangladesh*, pp. 137–83; Lifschultz, *Bangladesh*, p. 150, n. 1; Dasgupta, *Midnight*, pp. 94–9.

447 Singh, "Foreword," p. ix; for the initial December 10, 1971 order Dasgupta, *Midnight*, pp. 86–7.

448 See Report on the Findings of the People's Inquiry Commission; Jahan, "Genocide," p. 386.

449 Bangladesh Groep Nederland, "The road to repression: Aspects of Bengali encroachment in the Chittagong Hill Tracts 1860–1983," in Wolfgang Mey (ed.), *"They Are Now Burning Village After Village": Genocide in the Chittagong Hill Tracts, Bangladesh* (Copenhagen: IWGIA, 1984), p. 24.

450 Sabyasachi Basu Ray Chaudhury, "Uprooted twice: Refugees from the Chittagong Hill Tracts," in Samaddar, *Refugees*, pp. 254–5;

Wolfgang Mey, "Opposed and linked: The fallacy of symbiosis," in Mey, *They*, pp. 102, 105, n. 1. Riots: "Chittagong tribals up in arms," *Statesman*, May 3, 1980 and Paresh Saha, "Move to uproot Chakmas from their homes," *Amrita Baxa Patrika*, April 20, 1980, in Roy, *Genocide*, pp. 121, 133.

451 Jyoti Prakash Dutta and Mohammed Mazifur Rahman, "Insurgency in Chittagong Hill Tracts: Its origin and impact on economy and environment," *Asian Profile* 26(4), 1998, pp. 313, 320; Syed Nazmul Islam, "The Chittagong Hill Tracts in Bangladesh: Integrational crisis between center and periphery," *Asian Survey* 21(12), 1981, p. 1216; Syed Aziz-al Ahsan and Bhumitra Chakma, "Problems of national integration in Bangladesh: The Chittagong Hill Tracts," *Asian Survey* 29(10), 1989, p. 964.

452 Mark Levene, "Why is the twentieth century the century of genocide?," *Journal of World History* 11(2), 2000, p. 327.

453 Al Ahsan and Chakma, "Problems," p. 964.

454 Chaudhury, "Uprooted twice," p. 254.

455 Nazmul Islam, "Chittagong Hill Tracts," p. 1219.

456 A. B. Chakma, "Look back from exile: A Chakma experience," in Mey, *They*, pp. 42, 47, 53, n. 8; Muhith, *Bangladesh*, p. 228; Aftab Ahmed, "Ethnicity and insurgency in the Chittagong Hill Tracts region: A study of the crisis of political integration in Bangladesh," *Journal of Commonwealth & Comparative Politics* 31(3), 1993, p. 40. For the mass resettlement of Mizos in anti-guerrilla warfare in India, see Chapter 5 of this volume.

457 Chaudhuri, *Genocide*, p. 48; Chakma, "Look," p. 46.

458 "Chittagong tribals up in arms," *Statesman*, May 3, 1980, and Saha, "Move," in Roy, *Genocide*, pp. 121, 135; Chaudhury, "Uprooted twice,", p. 270; Chakma, "Look," p. 50; Bangladesh Groep Nederland and Wolfgang Mey, "The road to resistance: Policies in the Bloody Triangle," in Mey, *They*, pp. 125–7.

459 Chakma, "Look," p. 52, with n. 7; Nazmul Islam, "Chittagong Hill Tracts," p. 1216; al Ahsan and Chakma, "Problems," p. 968.

460 Presidents A. S. Sayeem and Ziaur also received autonomy demands: "Chittagong tribals up in arms," *Statesman*, May 3, 1980,

in Roy, *Genocide*, p. 121; Chakma, "Look," p. 58; Bangladesh Groep Nederland and Mey, "Road," p. 127; Ahmed, "Ethnicity," pp. 41–2. See a 1970 Mujib speech in *Bangla Desh Documents*, p. 110.

461 Wolfgang Mey, "Soil use and land rights in the Chittagong Hill Tracts," in Mey, *They*, p. 84.

462 Maniruzzaman, *Bangladesh*, p. 205.

463 Wolfgang Mey, "Introduction," in Mey, *They*, p. 7; Chittagong Hill Tracts Commission, *"Life is not ours": Land and Human Rights in the Chittagong Hill Tracts, Bangladesh*, update 4 (Amsterdam: IWGIA, 2000), pp. 16, 71, 84.

464 Mark Levene, "The Chittagong Hill Tracts: A case study in the political economy of 'creeping' genocide," *Third World Quarterly* 20(2), 1999, pp. 355–6.

465 S. K. Dutta Ray, "Buddhists struggle for survival, troubles in Rangamati," April 25, 1980, in Roy, *Genocide*, p. 127. Ahmed, "Ethnicity," p. 44, dates a systematic settlement policy as far back as the Mujib administration.

466 Bangladesh Groep Nederland and Mey, "Road," pp. 150–6; Prajnalankar Bhikkhu, "Demographic invasion, militarization and human rights violations in the Chittagong Hill Tracts," in Paliwal, *Islamism*, p. 25.

467 Prakash Dutta and Mazifur Rahman, "Insurgency," p. 312. This was a decrease of 43,329 Bengalis and an increase of 31,116 Jummas, compared to 1991: Chaudhury, "Uprooted twice," pp. 250, 280, n. 20.

468 Prakash Dutta and Mazifur Rahman, "Insurgency," p. 318.

469 Willem van Schendel, "The invention of the 'Jummas': State formation and ethnicity in southeastern Bangladesh," *Modern Asian Studies* 26(1), 1992, pp. 120–1.

470 Chaudhury, "Uprooted twice," pp. 258–77; Bangladesh Groep Nederland and Mey, "Road," pp. 150–6. The data in Chittagong Hill Tracts Commission, "Life," pp. 28, 45, 48, however, suggest that people returning from India had a higher chance for getting all their land back than 128,000 internally displaced families.

471 Chittagong Hill Tracts Commission, "Life," pp. 16, 20; al Ahsan and Chakma, "Problems," pp. 969–70.

472 Mey, *They*, pp. 155, 176. Levene, "Chittagong," pp. 339–69, esp. pp. 356, 360 portrays the settlers rather as stooges of the military.

473 Bangladesh Groep Nederland and Mey, "Road," pp. 132–3.

474 Bangladesh Groep Nederland and Mey, "Road," pp. 136–7, 140.

475 Chittagong Hill Tracts Commission, "Life," pp. 13, 41–2.

476 Bangladesh Groep Nederland and Mey, "Road," pp. 12–13; Franda, *Bangladesh*, p. 235.

477 See also Bose, "Anatomy." There is little evidence for violence by East Pakistani Hindus.

478 Van Schendel, *Peasant Mobility*, esp. pp. 183–90, 248, 251, 254. See also Franda, *Bangladesh*, p. 196.

479 Quoted in Saikia, "Beyond," p. 278.

480 Account in Firdousi, *Year*, p. 40.

481 Mukherji, "Great exodus," I; Reginald Prentice, in *New Statesman*, July 16, 1971, in *Bangla Desh Documents*, p. 570; Heß, *Bangladesch*, pp. 81–2.

5 Sustainable violence

1 The cases discussed below, as far as each dominant insurgent group is concerned, could be attributed to a Maoist approach (Malaya, Indochina, Portuguese Africa, Thailand, Guatemala, Peru), other communist (Soviet Union, Greece), leftist–nationalist (Algeria, Rhodesia, Turkish Kurdistan, East Timor), and non-leftist nationalist currents (Manchuria, Kenya, Chittagong Hill Tracts of Bangladesh, Mizoram in India). Counter-insurgency 'specialists' often ascribe the occurrence of such movements to Maoism alone.

2 54 percent of Africans were resettled in Niassa, 47 percent in Cabo Delgado and 42 percent in Tete districts: Brendan F. Jundanian, "Resettlement programs in counterinsurgency in Mozambique," *Contemporary Politics*, 6(4), 1974, pp. 522, 524. Cf. Michel Cornaton, *Les camps de regroupement de la guerre d'Algérie* (Paris and Montreal: Harmattan, 1998 [first ed. 1967]), p. 125.

3 Kerim Yildiz, *The Kurds in Turkey: EU Accession and Human Rights* (London and Ann Arbor: Pluto, 2005), p. 77; Nadire Mater (ed.), *Voices from the Front: Turkish Soldiers on the War with the Turkish Guerrillas* (New York and Basingstoke: Palgrave Macmillan, 2005), p. 312. Cf. C. Nunthara, *Impact of the Introduction of Grouping of Villages in Mizoram* (New Delhi: Omsons, 1989), pp. 5–6, 48.

4 Benjamin Valentino, *Final Solutions: Mass Killing and Genocide in the 20th Century* (Ithaca and London: Cornell University Press, 2004), pp. 81–4, lists at least 10 million deaths as a result.

5 A point stressed for indigenous people by John D. Leary, *Violence and the Dream People: The Orang Asli in the Malayan Emergency 1948–1960* (Athens, GA: Center for International Studies, Ohio University, 1995), esp. pp. 71–95.

6 One could include the events in the Hukbalahap rebellion in the Philippines 1946 to 1954 and in the 1970s, and forced relocations in Sabah and Sarawak (Malaysia) between 1963 and 1967, as well as those by the South African regime in northern Namibia in the late 1970s. In Laos, US authorities backed a Hmong counter-insurgency against the dominating Pathet Lao rebels in northern Laos from 1960–75. 17,000 Hmong fighters were killed, at least 200,000 civilians lost their homes, and many their lives. Ian Beckett, *Modern Insurgencies and Counter-Insurgencies: Guerrillas and their Opponents since 1750* (London and New York: Routledge, 2000), pp. 99, 104–9; Jane Hamilton-Merritt, *Tragic Mountains: The Hmong, the Americans, and the Secret War for Laos, 1942–1992* (Bloomington and Indianapolis: Indiana University Press, 1993), esp. pp. 121–2, 137–8, 334.

7 In conjunction with resettlements of (parts of) ethnic groups in the Soviet Union from the 1920s through the 1940s, the government wanted to maintain a state monopoly on military power. Socialist communal villages in Mozambique were planned since 1975, before the start of the civil war, and though a number of them later assumed a military function, the socialist government for fear of warlordism refused to set up local militias as suggested by Cuban military advisors. See William Finnegan, *A Complicated War: The Harrowing of Mozambique* (Berkeley *et al.*: University of California Press, 1992), pp. 114, 223.

8 Such militias were allowed for in some cases by the USA among indigenous peoples. I am grateful for this information to Peter Karsten.

9 David McDowall, *A Modern History of the Kurds* (London and New York: I. B. Taurus, 1996), pp. 402–9; Edgar O'Ballance, *The Kurdish Revolt: 1961–1970* (Hamden, CT: Shoe String Press, 1973), pp. 19–20.

10 John L. Tone, *War and Genocide in Cuba, 1895–1898* (Chapel Hill: University of North Carolina Press, 2006), pp. 210–17.

11 Anthony James Joes, *America and Guerrilla Warfare* (Lexington: Kentucky University Press, 2000), pp. 110–11; Anthony James Joes, *Resisting Rebellion: The History and Politics of Counterinsurgency* (Lexington: Kentucky University Press, 2004), p. 125; Valentino, *Final Solutions*, pp. 203, 205; John J. McCuen, *The Art of Counter-Revolutionary Warfare* (London: Faber and Faber, 1966), pp. 172, 211–13; Charles Townshend, *Britain's Civil Wars: Counterinsurgency in the Twentieth Century* (London and Boston: Faber and Faber, 1986), p. 179. For population losses, see Frank Schumacher, "'Niederbrennen, plündern und töten sollt ihr': Der Kolonialkrieg der USA auf den Philippinen (1899–1913)," in Thoralf Klein and Frank Schumacher (eds.), *Kolonialkriege: Militärische Gewalt im Zeichen des Kolonialismus* (Hamburg: Hamburger Edition, 2006), p. 114. For 1920s and 1930s British experiments with mass resettlement in counter-insurgency in Ireland and Burma, see Tim Jones, "The British Army, and counter-guerrilla warfare in transition, 1944–1952," *Small Wars and Insurgencies* 7(3), 1996, p. 266.

12 Alf Andrew Heggoy, *Insurgency and Counterinsurgency in Algeria* (Bloomington and London: Indiana University Press, 1972), pp. 213–27.

13 The influential book by Roger Trinquier, *Modern Warfare: A French View of Counterinsurgency* (New York and London: Praeger, 1964), pp. 69–73, sketches this procedure as "gridding." For the practice in Guatemala see Carol A. Smith, "The militarization of civil society in Guatemala: Economic reorganization as a continuation of war," *Latin American Perspectives* 17(4), 1990, pp. 15–16.

14 Finn Stepputat, "Politics of displacement in Guatemala," *Journal of Historical Sociology* 12(1), 1999, pp. 54–80, esp. p. 66, is among the few critical attempts to theorize on this.

15 Christian Gerlach, *Kalkulierte Morde: Die deutsche Wirtschafts- und Vernichtungspolitik in Weissrussland 1941 bis 1944* (Hamburg: Hamburger Edition, 1999), pp. 1018–36; Valentino, *Final Solutions*, p. 212; Jennifer Schirmer, *The Guatemalan Military Project* (Philadelphia: University of Pennsylvania Press, 1998), p. 55. The latter terminology was also suggested by David Galula, *Counterinsurgency Warfare: Theory and Practice* (New York *et al.*: Praeger, 1966), p. 70.

16 Robert Jackson, *The Malayan Emergency: The Commonwealth's Wars 1948–1966* (London and New York: Routledge, 1991), p. 22; Townshend, *Britain's Civil Wars*, p. 205; Caroline Elkins, *Imperial Reckoning: The Untold Story of Britain's Gulag in Kenya* (New York: Henry Holt, 2005), pp. 62–90, 109.

17 Thompson's memo to Diem, September 1962, in his *Defeating Communist Insurgency: The Lessons of Malaya and Vietnam* (New York and Washington: Praeger, 1966), p. 132.

18 Pierre Bourdieu, *The Algerians* (Boston: Beacon, 1962), pp. 166–7; Keith Sutton, "Army administration tensions over Algeria's *Centres de Regroupement*, 1954–1962," *British Journal of Middle Eastern Studies* 26(2), 1999, p. 250.

19 Carmel Budiardjo and Liem Soei Liong, *The War Against East Timor* (London *et al.*: Zed, 1984), p. 64; Lincoln Li, *The Japanese Army in North China 1937–1941: Problems of Political and Economic Control* (Tokyo *et al.*: Oxford University Press, 1975), p. 167.

20 Gerlach, *Kalkulierte Morde*, pp. 899–904; John A. Nagl, *Counterinsurgency Lessons from Malaya and Vietnam: Learning to Eat Soup with a Knife* (Westport and London: Praeger, 2002), p. 172; David Elliott, *The Vietnamese War: Revolution and Social Change in the Mekong Delta 1930–1975* (Armonk and New York: M. E. Sharpe, 2003), p. 1162; Agnes Smedley, "The red phalanx" and Jean-Philippe Talbo-Bernigaud, "Steamroller in Kabylia," in Gérard Chaliand (ed.), *Guerrilla Strategies* (Berkeley *et al.*: California University Press, 1982), pp. 61, 274; anonymous letter to Jacques Vergès in Patrick Kessel and Giovanni Pirelli (eds.), *Le peuple Algérien et la guerre: Lettres et témoignages 1954–1962* (Paris: L'Harmattan, 2003 [first edition 1962]), p. 388; Thomas H. Henriksen, "Portugal in Africa: Comparative notes on counterinsurgency," *Orbis* 21(2), 1977, p. 399; Angeliki E. Laiou, "Population movements in the Greek countryside during the

civil war," in Lars Baerentzen *et al.* (eds.), *Studies in the History of the Greek Civil War 1945–1949* (Copenhagen: Museum Tusculanum Press, 1987), p. 75; Norma J. Kriger, *Zimbabwe's Guerrilla War: Peasant Voices* (New York: Cambridge University Press, 1992), p. 35; for Sirnak in Eastern Anatolia in the summer of 1990, see McDowall, *History*, p. 428.

21 Jackson, *Malayan Emergency*, pp. 65–107 (quote p. 70); Leary, *Violence*, pp. 85–6; John Newsinger, "Minimum force, British counter-insurgency and the Mau Mau rebellion," *Small Wars and Insurgencies* 3(1), 1992, p. 49; Susan Carruthers, *Winning Hearts and Minds: British Governments, the Media and Colonial Counter-Insurgency 1944–1960* (London and New York: Leicester University Press, 1995), p. 172; *Chega! Report by the Commission for Reception, Truth and Reconciliation in East Timor (CAVR)* (Dili: CAVR, 2006), ch. 7.3, pp. 43–9, www.cavr-timorleste.org/chegaFiles/finalReportEng/07.3-Forced-Displacement-and-Famine.pdf (accessed May 11, 2008); about the importance of airpower generally Trinquier, *Modern Warfare*, and Douglas S. Blaufarb, *The Counterinsurgency Era: U.S. Doctrine and Performance 1950 to the Present* (New York and London: Free Press/ Collier Macmillan, 1977).

22 For example Mario Fumerton, "Rondas campesinas in the Peruvian civil war: Peasant-self-defence organisations in Ayacucho," *Bulletin of Latin American Research* 20(4), 2001, p. 483.

23 Bruce Berman, *Control and Crisis in Colonial Kenya* (London *et al.*: James Currey *et al.*, 1990), p. 356; Daniel Branch, "Imprisonment and colonialism in Kenya, c. 1930–1952: Escaping the Carceral Archipelago," *International Journal of African Historical Studies* 38(2), 2005, p. 245; John P. Cann, *Counterinsurgency in Africa: The Portuguese Way of War, 1961–1974* (Westport and London: Greenwood, 1997), p. 143; Gerald J. Bender, "The limits of counter-insurgency: An African case," *Comparative Politics* 4(3), 1972, p. 352; Jundanian, "Resettlement," p. 526; Ronald Suleski, "Northeast China under Japanese control: The role of the Manchurian Youth Corps, 1934–1945," *Modern China* 7(3), 1981, pp. 351–77; Jackson, *Malayan Insurgency*, p. 24.

24 McDowall, *History*, p. 440.

25 Fabian Klose, "Zur Legitimation kolonialer Gewalt: Kolonialer Notstand, antisubversiver Krieg und humanitäres Völkerrecht im kenianischen und algerischen Dekolonialisierungskrieg," *Archiv für Sozialgeschichte* 48, 2008, pp. 251–8, 268–9; Hartmut Elsenhans, *Frankreichs Algerienkrieg 1954–1962* (Munich: Carl Hanser, 1974), pp. 418–39.

26 Amikan Nachmani, *International Intervention in the Greek Civil War: The United Nations Special Committee on the Balkans, 1947–1952* (New York *et al.*: Praeger, 1990), pp. 95–6; higher estimates: Dominique Eudes, *The Kapetanios: Partisans and Civil War in Greece, 1943–1949* (London: NLB, 1972), p. 354; C. M. Woodhouse, *The Struggle for Greece 1941–1949* (Chicago: Ivan R. Dee, 2002 [first edition 1976]), p. 245.

27 David Anderson, *Histories of the Hanged: The Dirty War in Kenya and the End of Empire* (New York and London: W. W. Norton, 2005), p. 353; Carruthers, *Winning*, p. 175; Heggoy, *Insurgency*, p. 241; for Rhodesia, Tony Hodges, "Counterinsurgency and the fate of rural blacks," *Africa Report*, September–October 1977, p. 20.

28 Hodges, "Counterinsurgency," p. 19; Carruthers, *Winning*, p. 172; Kessel and Pirelli, *Peuple*, p. 413.

29 Polymeris Voglis, "Becoming communist: Political prisoners as a subject during the Greek civil war," in Philip Carabott and Thanasis D. Sfikas (eds.), *The Greek Civil War* (Aldershot and Burlington: Ashgate, 2004), pp. 143, 147; Nachmani, *International Intervention*, p. 96; Eudes, *Kapetanios*, pp. 260 (the left claimed 84,931 government arrests from February 1945 to March 1946), 302.

30 Richard Hunt, *Pacification: The American Struggle for Vietnam's Hearts and Minds* (Boulder *et al.*: Westview, 1995), p. 5.

31 Townshend, *Britain's Civil Wars*, pp. 164–5; Kumar Ramakrishna, "'Transmogrifying' Malaya: The impact of Sir Gerald Templer (1952–1954)," *Journal of Southeast Asian Studies* 32(1), 2001, pp. 82, 87.

32 Anderson, *Histories*, pp. 5, 69, 356; Carruthers, *Winning*, p. 276; Elkins, *Reckoning*, pp. xiii, 58, 140–1, 226–8, 283.

33 Elsenhans, *Frankreichs Algerienkrieg*, p. 439, n. 483.

34 Blaufarb, *Counterinsurgency Era*, pp. 119, 185; Mustafa Dhada, "The liberation war in Guinea-Bissau reconsidered," *Journal of Military History* 62(3), 1998, p. 582; Bender, "Limits," p. 340; Constancio Pinto and Matthew Jardine, *East Timor's Unfinished Struggle: Inside the Timorese Resistance* (Boston: South End Press, 1997), pp. 62–3; Budiardjo and Liem, *War*, p. 35. For Greece, see Jones, "The British Army, and counter-guerrilla warfare in transition, 1944–1952," p. 281.

35 Monika Schlicher, *Osttimor stellt sich seiner Vergangenheit: Die Arbeit der Empfangs-, Wahrheits- und Versöhnungskommission* (Aachen: Internationales Katholisches Missionswerk, 2005), p. 62.

36 Richard Brace and Joan Brace, *Algerian Voices* (Princeton: D. Van Nostrand, 1965), p. 200; Keith Sutton, "Population resettlement – Traumatic upheavals and the Algerian experience," *Journal of Modern African Studies* 15(2), 1977, p. 287. This policy seems to have been applied on a large scale since 1956: Kessel and Pirelli, *Peuple*, p. 42.

37 For the burning of woods in Guatemala, Grupo de Apoyo a Refugiades Gualtemaltecos, *La constrainsurgencia y los refugiades Gualtemaltecos* (Mexico: n.p., 1983), p. 83. Quote: Eudes, *Kapetanios*, p. 310.

38 Maureen Sioh, "An ecology of postcoloniality: Disciplining nature and society in Malaya, 1948–1957," *Journal of Historical Geography* 30, 2004, p. 736; Phillip Deery, "Malaya, 1948: Britain's 'Asian Cold War'?," Working Paper #3, The Cold War as Global Conflict, International Center for Advanced Studies, New York University, www.nyu.edu/gsas/dept/icas/PhillipDeery.pdf, p. 28; Jackson, *Malayan Emergency*, 102–3; Leary, *Violence*, pp. 86–9; Beckett, *Modern Insurgencies*, p. 103; Donald L. Barnett and Karari Njama, *Mau Mau from Within* (New York and London: Monthly Review Press, 1966), quoted in Chaliand, *Guerrilla Strategies*, p. 161.

39 Ian F. W. Beckett, "Robert Thompson and the British Advisory Mission to South Vietnam, 1961–1965," *Small Wars and Insurgencies* 8(3), 1997, p. 60, n. 16; cf. Elliott, *Vietnamese War*, p. 1220; Blaufarb, *Counterinsurgency Era*, p. 119.

40 Bender, "Limits," p. 345; Jundanian, "Resettlement," p. 539; Kay Warren, "Interpreting la violencia in Guatemala: Shapes of Mayan

silence & resistance," in Warren (ed.), *The Violence Within: Cultural and Political Opposition in Divided Nations* (Boulder *et al.*: Westview, 1993), p. 32; Pinto and Jardine, *East Timor*, p. 259, n. 1; John Taylor, *East Timor: The Price of Freedom* (London *et al.*: Zed, 1999), p. 85; Budiardjo and Liem, *War*, pp. 35–6.

41 Luise White, "Poisoned food, poisoned uniforms, and anthrax: Or, how guerrillas die in war," *OSIRIS* 19, 2004, pp. 220–3.

42 Keith Sutton and Richard Lawless, "Population regrouping in Algeria: Traumatic change and the rural settlement pattern," *Transactions of the Institute of British Geographers*, New Series 3(3), 1978, p. 342, sum up the literature.

43 Thompson, *Defeating*, pp. 125, 152; McCuen, *Art*, pp. 161–2; Leary, *Violence*, esp. pp. 44–8, 217 (suggests a mortality of 8 to 12 percent in certain camps within several months); John Coates, *Suppressing Insurgency: An Analysis of the Malayan Emergency, 1948–1954* (Boulder *et al.*: Westview, 1992), pp. 92, 202; Simon C. Smith, "Gerald Templer and counter-insurgency in Malaya: Hearts and minds, intelligence and propaganda," *Intelligence and National Security* 16(3), 2001, p. 69; T. N. Harper, *The End of Empire and the Making of Malaya* (Cambridge *et al.*: Cambridge University Press, 1999), pp. 269–72. Similar death rates were found among resettled hill tribespeople in South Vietnam in 1971: Louis Wiesner, *Victims and Survivors: Displaced Persons and Other War Victims in Viet-Nam, 1954–1975* (New York: Greenwood, 1988), p. 250.

44 Barnett and Njama, *Mau Mau*, pp. 209–10, 439–40 (insurgency staff officer Njama also gave guerrilla losses at 22,000, double the British official figure). Cf. Anderson, *Histories*, pp. 4, 319–20; Tabitha Kanogo, *Squatters and the Roots of Mau Mau 1905–1963* (London: James Currey, 1987), p. 139; Caroline Elkins, "Detention, rehabilitation & the destruction of Kikuyu society," in E. S. Atieno Odhiambo and John Lonsdale (eds.), *Mau Mau and Nationhood: Arms, Authority & Narration* (Oxford *et al.*: James Currey, EAEP and Ohio University Press, 2003), pp. 216–17; Elkins, *Reckoning*, pp. 234, 249–51, 255–65; an eyewitness report is Charity Waciuma, *Daughter of Mumbi* (Nairobi: East African Publishing House, 1969), pp. 111–39.

45 Michel Rocard, "Note sur les Centres de regroupement" in Rocard, *Rapport sur les camps de regroupement et autres textes sur la guerre*

d'Algérie (n.p.: Mille et Une Nuits, 2003), p. 126, cf. p. 133, n. 127; for other sources see Brace and Brace, *Algerian Voices*, pp. 22, 85, 89–90, 131–2, 186; Mahfoud Bennoune, "French counter-revolutionary doctrine and the Algerian peasantry," *Monthly Review* 25(7), 1973, p. 55; Charles-Robert Ageron, "Une dimension de la guerre d'Algérie: les 'regroupements' de populations," in Jean-Charles Jauffret and Maurice Vaisse (eds.), *Militaires et guérilla dans la guerre d'Algérie* (Paris: Editions Complexe, 2001), pp. 331–2, 338, 345–6; Cornaton, *Camps*, pp. 96–7, 114. For the extension see Sutton, "Army administration," p. 257. Guy Pervillé, "La guerre d'Algérie: Combien de morts?," in Mohamed Harbi and Benjamin Stora (eds.), *La guerre d'Algérie* (Paris: Hachettes, 2004), esp. pp. 698, 700, 713, ignores victims of the regroupment camps.

46 J. K. Cilliers, *Counter-Insurgency in Rhodesia* (London *et al.*: Croom Helm, 1985), p. 92, cf. pp. 81, 85, 97, 242; cf. A. K. H. Weinrich, "Strategic resettlement in Rhodesia," *Journal of Southern African Studies* 3(2), 1977, p. 227.

47 Nandini Sundar, "Interning insurgent populations: The buried histories of Indian democracy," www.yale.edu/agrarianstudies/pages/22sundar.pdf (accessed May 7, 2009), pp. 23–5; Nunthara, *Impact*, pp. 4, 7, 9.

48 Weinrich, "Strategic resettlement," p. 219; Budiardjo and Liem, *War*, pp. 74, 82.

49 Peter Niggli, "Äthiopien: Deportationen und Zwangsarbeitslager," *Dokumentation Evangelischer Pressedienst* 25, 1985, May 28, esp. pp. 10, 12, 16–21, 30–2.

50 Ricardo Falla, *Massacres in the Jungle: Ixcán, Guatemala 1975–1982* (Boulder *et al.*; Westview, 1994), pp. 155–6; Ricardo Falla, "Struggle for survival in the mountains: Hunger and other privations inflicted on internal refugees from the Central Highlands," in Robert Carmack (ed.), *Harvest of Violence: The Maya Indians and the Guatemalan Crisis* (Norman: University of Oklahoma Press, 1988), pp. 235–55; Arzobiscopado de Guatemala, Officina de Derechos Humanos, *Guatemala: Nunca Mas, vol. 2: Impactos de la Violencia* (Guatemala: Arzobiscopado de Guatemala, Officina de Derechos Humanos, 1999), pp. 3, 51–3, 66, 88; Grupo de Apoyo, *Constrainsurgencia*, pp. 81–6; Joe Fish and Cristina Sganga, *El*

Salvador: Testament of Terror (New York: Olive Branch Press, 1988), pp. 54–67, 79–87, esp. p. 82.

51 Benetech Human Rights Data Analysis Group of the Commission on Reception, Truth and Reconciliation of Timor-Leste (Romesh Silva and Patrick Ball), The Profile of Human Rights Violations in Timor-Leste, 1974–1999, February 9, 2006, pp. 1–2, http://hrdag. org/resources/Benetech-Report-to-CAVR.pdf (accessed December 6, 2007); CAVR Report, chapter 7.3, pp. 29–31, 38–42, 52–68, www.cavr-timorleste.org/chegaFiles/finalReportEng/07.3-Forced-Displacement-and-Famine.pdf (accessed May 11, 2008); Budiardjo and Liem, *War*, pp. 76–87; Schlicher, *Osttimor*, p. 61; Pinto and Jardine, *East Timor*, pp. 46, 259, n. 2; Taylor, *East Timor*, pp. 90, 97–8. For deaths caused by a government food blockade in Greece: Laiou, "Population movements," p. 64; "excess mortality" refers to the deaths over and above those one would have expected on a long-term statistical basis.

52 Quoted in Stephan Malinowski, "Modernisierungskriege: Militärische Gewalt und koloniale Modernisierung im Algerienkrieg (1954–1962)," *Archiv für Sozialgeschichte* 48, 2008, p. 226.

53 Heggoy, *Insurgency*, p. 186; see also survivor accounts in Kessel and Pirelli, *Peuple*, pp. 305, 481.

54 T. A. Bisson, "Aikawa asks for fifty millions," *Amerasia* 2, March 1938, pp. 9–10; Y. Nagano, "Comments on Manchurian protective villages," *Amerasia* 2, February 1939, pp. 549–51; Ray C. Hillam, "Counterinsurgency: Lessons from early Chinese and Japanese experience against the communists," *Orbis*, 12(1), 1968, pp. 237–41; Rana Mitter, *The Manchurian Myth: Nationalism, Resistance and Collaboration in Modern China* (Berkeley: University of California Press, 2000), pp. 112–14, 122–3; Joes, *Resisting Rebellion*, p. 111.

55 Li, *Japanese Army*, pp. 86, 175–6, 189, 193–5, 201–4, 208–11.

56 Jon V. Kofas, *Intervention and Underdevelopment: Greece During the Cold War* (University Park and London: Pennsylvania State University Press, 1989), pp. 95, 130–1; D. George Kousoulas, *Revolution and Defeat: The Story of the Greek Communist Party* (London: Oxford University Press, 1965), p. 259.

57 Nagl, *Counterinsurgency*, p. 66; Jackson, *Malayan Emergency*, p. 20; Francis Loh Kok Wah, *Beyond the Tin Mines: Coolies, Squatters*

and New Villagers in the Kinta Valley, Malaysia, c. 1880–1980 (Singapore *et al.*: Oxford University Press, 1988), pp. 106–10, 124.

58 Anthony Short, *The Communist Insurrection in Malaya 1948–1960* (London: Muller, 1975), pp. 173, 391, n. 1.

59 Curtis Peoples, "The use of the British village resettlement model in Malaya and Vietnam," April 2002, www.tamil-nation.org/tamileelam/ armedstruggle/thompson.htm (accessed January 26, 2007), p. 3; Peter Paret, *French Revolutionary Warfare from Indochina to Algeria* (New York *et al.*: Praeger, 1964), p. 43.

60 Thompson, *Defeating*, pp. 122, 129, 138; Milton Osborne, *Strategic Hamlets in South Viet-Nam* (Ithaca: Southeast Asia Programme, Cornell University, 1965), pp. 32–3.

61 Nagl, *Counterinsurgency*, p. 128; Blaufarb, *Counterinsurgency Era*, pp. 115, 120, 207–8.

62 In addition, hundreds of thousands fled to the big Algerian cities, to neighboring countries, or to France: Paret, *French Revolutionary Warfare*, pp. 34, 44–5; McCuen, *Art*, pp. 130, 239; Mohand Hamoumou, *Et Ils Sont Devenus Harkis* (Paris: Fayard, 1993), pp. 193–4; Heggoy, *Insurgency*, pp. 213–17.

63 Brian Egan, "'Somos de la tierra': Land and the Guatemalan refugee return," and Gisela Gellert, "Migration and the displaced: Guatemala City in the context of a flawed national transformation," both in Liisa North and Alan Simmons (eds), *Journeys of Fear: Refugee Return and National Transformation in Guatemala* (Montreal *et al.*: McGill & Queen University Press, 1999), pp. 98, 119.

64 Richard Clutterbuck, *Conflict and Violence in Singapore and Malaysia 1945–1983* (Boulder *et al.*: Westview, 1985), p. 177.

65 Wiesner, *Victims*, pp. 47, 50, 347 (estimates that 20 percent of strategic hamlet inmates were resettled, however somewhat understating the number of strategic hamlets); Philip Catton, *Diem's Final Failure* (Lawrence: University of Kansa Press, 2002), pp. 97, 131, 172–4, 177; Elliott, *Vietnamese War*, p. 354. Plans stated that 50 percent would require only "minor regrouping" of a few houses, 30 percent "major regrouping" of about half the families, 15 percent "complete regrouping" of most buildings, and 5 percent entirely new sites (Thompson,

Defeating, p. 122; Thompson himself recommended not to regroup more than 20 to 25 percent of the peasants: Peter Busch, "Killing the 'Vietcong': The British Advisory Mission and the Strategic Hamlet Programme," *Journal of Strategic Studies* 25(1), 2002, p. 147).

66 Wiesner, *Victims*, pp. 127–298, 346–7; for the responsibilities for displacement mostly lying with US forces and the South Vietnamese authorities pp. 66–9, 104–10, 195, 220, 242–3, 349. See also Elliott, *Vietnamese War*, pp. 407, 425, 875; Hunt, *Pacification*.

67 Gerlach, *Kalkulierte Morde*, pp. 1040–55; Bourdieu, *Algerians*, p. 173; Bennoune, "French counter-revolutionary doctrine," p. 50; Heggoy, *Insurgency*, p. 215; Rocard, "Note," pp. 128–30. In Mizoram the distance was often 5 to 15 kilometers. See Nunthara, *Impact*, p. 16.

68 Displacement over a distance of up to three kilometers in Cambodia 1951–54 (Cornaton, *Camps*, p. 37) probably enabled most peasants to work their land.

69 Cilliers, *Counter-Insurgency*, p. 98.

70 Kernial Singh Sandhu, "The saga of the 'squatter' in Malaya: A preliminary survey of the causes, characteristics and consequences of the resettlement of rural dwellers during the Emergency between 1948 and 1960," *Journal of Southeast Asian History* 5, 1964, p. 173; Ramakrishna, "Transmogrifying," p. 91; Victor Purcell, *Malaya: Communist or Free?* (Stanford: Stanford University Press, 1954), p. 80; Nagl, *Counterinsurgency*, p. 75; Joes, *Resisting Rebellion*, pp. 111–12; Paret, *French Revolutionary Warfare*, pp. 45–6; McCuen, *Art*, p. 102 (for Algeria); Bourdieu, *Algerians*, p. 182; Basil Davidson, "Angola in the tenth year: A report and an analysis, May–July 1970," *African Affairs* 70(278), January 1971, pp. 47–8.

71 Loh, *Tin Mines*, pp. 225–8, 267.

72 Bender, "Limits," p. 356; Jundanian, "Resettlement," p. 539.

73 More details about ethnic aspects in Gerlach, "Sustainable violence: Mass resettlement, strategic villages, and militias in anti-guerrilla warfare," in Richard Bessel and Claudia Haake (eds.), *Removing Peoples: Forced Removal in the Modern World* (Oxford *et al.*: Oxford University Press, 2009), pp. 361–92. See Kernial Singh Sandhu,

"Emergency resettlement in Malaya," *Journal of Tropical Geography* 18, 1964, pp. 165, 174; Henriksen, "Portugal," p. 406; Jundanian, "Resettlement," pp. 523–5; Aranya Siriphon, "Local knowledge, dynamism and the politics of struggle: A case study of the Hmong in Northern Thailand," *Journal of Southeast Asian Studies* 37(1), 2006, pp. 68–9; Eric Wakin, *Anthropology Goes to War: Professional Ethics and Counterinsurgency in Thailand* (Madison: Center for Southeast Asian Studies, University of Wisconsin, 1992), p. 141; Joes, *America*, p. 174.

74 Frank Furedi, "Britain's colonial wars: Playing the ethnic card," *Journal of Commonwealth & Comparative Politics* 26(1), 1989, pp. 80, 85; Frank Furedi, "Britain's colonial emergencies and the invisible nationalists," *Journal of Historical Sociology* 2(3), 1989, pp. 247–50, 261; Frank Füredi, *Colonial Wars and the Politics of Third World Nationalism* (London and New York: I. B. Taurus, 1994).

75 Furedi, "Wars," p. 76; cf. Anderson, *Histories*, p. 352.

76 For example, Karl Hack argues that ethnic Chinese in Malaya were fragmented by conflicts between orientations toward Malaya versus China, Communists versus Guomindang, ideological organizations versus traditional communally organized clans, those educated in Chinese and in English, new immigrants versus old Peranakan, and both a large worker and middle-class faction. Karl Hack, "'Iron claws on Malaya': The historiography of the Malayan emergency," *Journal of Southeast Asian Studies*, 30, 1999.

77 David Stoll, *Between Two Armies in the Ixil Towns of Guatemala* (New York: Columbia University Press, 1993); Elkins, *Reckoning*, pp. 171–7, 298–303; Stuart A. Herrington, *Silence Was a Weapon: The Vietnam War in the Villages* (Novato: Presidio, 1982), pp. 24–5, 36.

78 See Gérard Chaliand, *Armed Struggle in Africa: With the Guerrillas in 'Portuguese' Guinea* (New York and London: Monthly Review Press, 1969), pp. 12, 26; Joes, *Resisting Rebellion*, p. 127; Dhada, "Liberation war," pp. 586, 589; Henriksen, "Portugal," p. 406; Gerlach, *Kalkulierte Morde*, pp. 1052–5; A. Roy, *Genocide of Hindus and Buddhists in East Pakistan–Bangladesh* (Delhi: Kranti Prakashan, 1981); McCuen, *Art*, p. 99.

79 Georgios Niarchos and Kevin Featherstone, "The 'enemy' that wasn't yet: The strategy of the Greek government toward the Muslim minority in Western Thrace, 1946–49," paper presented to the Modern Greek Studies Association Conference, New Haven, October 2007, p. 8.

80 The Vietnam war of independence against France in the early 1950s was an exception which finally allowed the Viet Minh to defeat the colonial power in open battle. Still, by 1953, 330,000 Vietnamese fought on the French side compared to 300,000 Viet Minh fighters: Joes, *Resisting Rebellion*, pp. 134–5.

81 Thompson, *Defeating*, pp. 44, 48; Jackson, *Malayan Emergency*, pp. 14, 115.

82 Cann, *Counterinsurgency*, pp. 7–8; Joes, *America*, p. 215.

83 Joes, *Resisting Rebellion*, pp. 125–44.

84 See Douglas L. Wheeler, "African elements in Portugal's army in Africa (1961–1974)," *Armed Forces and Society* 2(2), 1976, pp. 233–50, and Douglas L. Wheeler, "The Portuguese army in Angola," *Journal of Modern African Studies* 7(3), 1969, pp. 425–39; Cann, *Counterinsurgency*, pp. 10, 87–8; for French troop levels in Algeria: Heggoy, *Insurgency*, pp. 73, 79, 157.

85 Hua Wu Yin, *Class and Communalism in Malaysia: Politics in a Dependent Capitalist State* (London: Zed, 1983), p. 97; Jackson, *Malayan Emergency*, pp. 18–19; cf. Anthony Clayton, *The Wars of French Decolonization* (London and New York: Longman, 1994), p. 74.

86 For Algeria: Paret, *French Revolutionary Warfare*, p. 44.

87 Cann, *Counterinsurgency*, p. 103.

88 Henri Barkey and Graham Fuller, *Turkey's Kurdish Question* (Lanham *et al.*: Rowan & Littlefield, 1998), p. 147. The Truth Commission in El Salvador attributed 20 percent of "serious acts of violence" to members of military escorts and civil defense units and 10 percent to Death Squads. The Truth Commission in Guatemala attributed 18 percent of human rights violations 1962–96 to Civil Defense Patrols, the bulk in 1981–83. El Salvador: "From madness to hope," part four, chapter one, www.usip.org/library/tc/doc/reports/

el-salvador/tc_es_03151993_casesA.html (accessed October 5, 2007).
Marcia Esparza, "Post-war Guatemala: Long-term effects of psychological and ideological militarisation of the K'iche Mayans," *Journal of Genocide Research* 7(3), 2005, p. 383.

89 Wangari Maathai, *Unbowed* (New York: Alfred Knopf, 2006), pp. 65–6; cf. Berman, *Control*, p. 372, n. 8; for Guatemala: Linda Green, *Fear as a Way of Life: Mayan Widows in Rural Guatemala* (New York: Columbia University Press, 1999), pp. 31–2; Simone Remijnse, "Remembering Civil Patrols in Joyabaj, Guatemala," *Bulletin of Latin American Research* 20(4), 2001, p. 463.

90 Elkins, *Reckoning*, pp. 118, 147; Elkins, "Detention," p. 207; Charles Allen, *The Savage Wars of Peace: Soldiers' Voices 1945–1989* (London: Michael Joseph, 1990), pp. 125, 133; Wunyabari Maloba, *Mau Mau and Kenya: An Analysis of a Peasant Revolt* (Bloomington and Indianapolis: Indiana University Press, 1993), p. 90; Daniel Branch, "Loyalism During the Mau Mau Rebellion in Kenya, 1952–1960," Ph.D. thesis, University of Oxford, 2005.

91 Anderson, *Histories*, pp. 56–7, 127–31; M. P. K. Sorrenson, *Land Reform in the Kikuyu Country* (Nairobi *et al.*: Oxford University Press, 1967), pp. 100–1; for the British authorities preempting armed revolt, see John Newsinger, "Revolt and repression in Kenya: The 'Mau Mau' rebellion, 1952–1960," *Science & Society* 45(2), 1981, pp. 168–9; Füredi, "Colonial wars," p. 154.

92 Joan Gillespie, *Algeria: Rebellion and Revolution* (Westport: Greenwood, 1976 [first edition 1960]), pp. 122, 150; Alistair Horne, *A Savage War of Peace: Algeria 1954–1962* (New York: Viking, 1977), p. 135; Heggoy, *Insurgency*, p. 305, n. 33; Elsenhans, *Frankreichs Algerienkrieg*, pp. 154–5.

93 David Hoile, *Mozambique, Resistance and Freedom* (London: Mozambique Institute, 1994); Terence Ranger, *Peasant Consciousness and Guerrilla War in Zimbabwe: A Comparative Study* (London: James Currey, 1985), p. 276, n. 8; Fumerton, "Rondas campesinas," p. 482.

94 Hamoumou, *Et Ils Sont*, p. 61, cites some Algerian officers and high functionaries as exceptionally francophile.

95 The pro-Portuguese African Forces Militia in Guinea Bissau included many dissidents from the liberation front PAIGC: Dhada, "Liberation war," p. 585.

96 Ponciano del Pino, "Tiempos de guerra y de dioses: Ronderos, evangélicos y senderistas en el valle de río Apurímac," in Carlos Iván Degregori *et al.*, *Las rondas campesinas y la derrota de Sendero Luminoso* (Lima: IEP, 1996), pp. 119, 173–6; Schirmer, *Project*, p. 97.

97 Joes, *Resisting Rebellion*, p. 135; Ogot according to Anderson, *Histories*, p. 242; cf. Berman, *Control*, p. 357. Branch, "Loyalism," tries to revise the picture that Kenyan Home Guards were for the most part wealthy. While many rank-and-file were not rich, they were above average in terms of literacy.

98 Marshall S. Clough, *Mau Mau Memoirs: History, Memory & Politics* (London: Lynne Rienner, 1998), p. 48.

99 Behrooz Morvaridi, "Resettlement, rights to development and the Ilisu Dam, Turkey," *Development and Change* 35(4), 2004, p. 731; see David Kowalewski, "Counterinsurgent paramilitarism: A Philippine case study," *Journal of Peace Research* 29(1), 1992, p. 75.

100 Hamoumou, *Et Ils Sont*, pp. 153–88; Charles-Robert Ageron, "Les supplétifs Algériens dans l'armée Française pendant la guerre d'Algérie," *Vingtième Siècle* 48, 1995, p. 12; Branch, "Loyalism"; Schlicher, *Osttimor*, pp. 22–4. In uncritically portraying French auxiliaries in Algeria only as victims, Hamoumou's study is insufficient to trace motivations, namely by avoiding the issue of elite building among militia members.

101 Elkins, *Reckoning*, p. 71; Hamoumou, *Et Ils Sont*, p. 17. For the changing payment practice in Guatemala see Schirmer, *Project*, pp. 87–91.

102 Anderson, *Histories*, p. 242, again in reference to Ogot. In this light, Branch's argument that a pro-British stand in Kenya only paid off after 1954 is unsurprising. See Daniel Branch, "From Home Guard to Mau Mau: Ambiguities and allegiances during the Mau Mau Emergency in Kenya, 1952–1960," p. 17, www.ascleiden.nl/pdf/paper2005-02-17.pdf (accessed December 30, 2006).

103 Human Rights Watch, *Civil Patrols in Guatemala* (New York and Washington: Human Rights Watch, 1986), p. 70; Beatriz Manz, *Refugees of a Hidden War: The Aftermath of Counterinsurgency in Guatemala* (Albany: State University of New York Press, 1988), pp. 54, 75–6.

104 Del Pino, "Tiempos," pp. 167–70; Mater, *Voices*, pp. 310–11. For similar tendencies in Guatemala, see an interview with a special forces (G-2) soldier in Schirmer, *Project*, pp. 291–2.

105 Ranger, *Peasant Consciousness*, p. 274; Weinrich, "Strategic resettlement," pp. 224–5.

106 Waciuma, *Daughter*, p. 113; Elkins, *Reckoning*, p. 242.

107 Waciuma, *Daughter*, p. 116; Barnett and Njama, *Mau Mau*, p. 189; Remijnse, "Remembering," p. 458; Matilde Gonzalez, "The man who brought the danger to the village: Representations of armed conflict in Guatemala from a local perspective," *Journal for Southern African Studies* 26(2), Special Issue, June 2000, p. 326.

108 Füredi, *Colonial Wars*, pp. 180–1; Gerlach, *Kalkulierte Morde*, pp. 1049–50.

109 Orin Starn, "Villagers at arms: War and counterrevolution in the Central–South Andes," in Steve J. Stern (ed.), *Shining and Other Paths: War and Society in Peru, 1980–1995* (Durham and London: Duke University Press, 1998), pp. 240, 247; McDowall, *History*, p. 422.

110 Niggli, "Äthiopien," p. 33.

111 Wheeler, "African elements," p. 242; Paret, *French Revolutionary Warfare*, p. 40; Hamoumou, *Et Ils Sont*, pp. 119–22; Maurice Faivre, "L'Histoire des Harkis," *Guerres mondiales et conflits contemporains* 202–203, 2002, pp. 55–63; Ageron, "Supplétifs," pp. 3–20.

112 Thompson, *Defeating*, pp. 103, 134; cf. for a later period Joes, *Resisting Rebellion*, pp. 114–15; for Thailand: Justus M. van der Kroef, "Guerrilla communism and counterinsurgency in Thailand," *Orbis* 18(1), 1974, pp. 127–9.

113 Cann, *Counterinsurgency*, pp. 159–62; Cilliers, *Counter-Insurgency*, pp. 203–4; for the influence of the settlers in Kenya, see Anderson, *Histories*.

114 For the last point Paret, *French Revolutionary Warfare*, p. 147, n. 12.

115 Jackson, *Malayan Emergency*, p. 17; McCuen, *Art*, pp. 160–1.

116 Vietnam: John C. Donnell, "Expanding political participation – The long haul from villagism to nationalism," *Asian Survey* 10(8), 1970, p. 697; Malaya: Nagl, *Counterinsurgency*, p. 100, and Coates, *Suppressing*, pp. 120–1; for Algeria: McCuen, *Art*, p. 228; Kenya: Berman, *Control*, p. 364; Angola: Bender, "Limits," p. 336.

117 Carlos Iván Degregori, "Reaping the whirlwind: The rondas campesinas and the defeat of Sendero Luminoso in Ayacucho," in Kees Konings and Dirk Kruijt (eds.), *Societies of Fear: The Legacy of Civil War, Society and Terror in Latin America* (London and New York: Zed, 1999), p. 86, n. 33; Starn, "Villagers," p. 232.

118 Woodhouse, *Struggle*, p. 237; Field Marshal Alexander Papagos, "Guerrilla warfare," in Franklin Mark Osanka (ed.), *Modern Guerrilla Warfare: Fighting Communist Guerrilla Movements, 1941–1961* (New York and London: Free Press, 1962), pp. 237, 240; McCuen, *Art*, pp. 111–12.

119 Human Rights Watch, *Civil Patrols*, esp. pp. 2, 26; Green, *Fear*, p. 5, n. 5; Stoll, *Between*, p. 327, n. 7; Remijnse, "Remembering," pp. 456, 459.

120 Quoted in Paret, *French Revolutionary Warfare*, p. 44.

121 Joes, *Resisting Rebellion*, p. 113.

122 Green, *Fear*, p. 61; Human Rights Watch, *Civil Patrols*, esp. pp. 18–21 (quote p. 13).

123 About Vietnam: Philip E. Catton, "Counter-insurgency and nation building: The Strategic Hamlet Programme in South Vietnam, 1961–1963," *International Historical Review* XXI(4), 1994, pp. 929–30.

124 Galula, *Counterinsurgency*, pp. 80, 120, 128–9, 132; Blaufarb, *Counterinsurgency Era*, p. 61.

125 Davidson, "Angola," p. 47; for their role in Kenya: Anderson, *Histories*, esp. p. 3; Waciuma, *Daughter*, pp. 88, 95, 104.

126 North and South Vietnam and Cambodia achieved independence in 1954, Malaya in 1957, Algeria in 1962, Kenya in 1963, Guinea Bissau in 1973, Mozambique and Angola in 1975, and East Timor in 2002. The USSR and China regained full territorial sovereignty from Germany and Japan, respectively, in 1944 and 1945.

127 Furedi, "Emergencies," pp. 240–4, quote p. 252.

128 Purcell, *Malaya*, pp. 98–109; Nagl, *Counterinsurgency*, p. 90 (quote); Jackson, *Malayan Emergency*, p. 11; Coates, *Suppressing*, pp. 119–20.

129 Ramakrishna, "Transmogrifying," p. 86, n. 67.

130 Bourdieu, *Algerians*, p. 170.

131 Purcell, *Malaya*, p. 108; Smith, "Gerald Templer," pp. 65–71.

132 Daniel Branch, "Loyalists, Mau Mau, and the elections in Kenya: The first triumph of the system," *Africa Today* 53(2), 2006, pp. 27–50.

133 McCuen, *Art*, p. 96; Heggoy, *Insurgency*, pp. 188–93. The Algerian Assembly was dissolved in April 1956.

134 Interview of Franz Schultheis with Pierre Bourdieu, June 26, 2001, in Pierre Bourdieu, *In Algerien: Zeugnisse der Entwurzelung* (Graz: Camera Austria, 2003), p. 38.

135 Henriksen, "Portugal," p. 401; Davidson, "Angola," p. 48.

136 Catton, "Counter-insurgency," pp. 926, 930–2; Thompson, *Defeating*, p. 125; Blaufarb, *Counterinsugency Era*, pp. 231, 265.

137 Cilliers, *Counter-Insurgency*, pp. 206–14.

138 Sundar, "Interning," p. 14.

139 Kees Koonings, "Civil society, transition and post-war reconstruction in Latin America: A comparison of El Salvador, Guatemala and Peru," *Iberoamericana* 32(2), 2002, pp. 45–71; Starn, "Villagers," p. 241.

140 However, this is a matter of definition because it implies considering South Vietnam as a state dependent on the USA, disregarding the autonomy of the Saigon governments, listing Rhodesia, a colonial settler state, among empires, and Turkey is not really a post-colonial state.

141 Yet in Malaya and Kenya Britain did succeed in enforcing an extraordinary openness to foreign capital that continues in the successor states to this day.

142 Cornaton, *Camps*, pp. 23–41, one of the few trying to systematically analyze the international experience with resettlement during counter-insurgency, inadequately conceptualized it in 1967 as a measure of colonialism (conquest or decolonization), though he acknowledged the post-colonial cases of Greece and Cambodia.

143 By contrast, the Ethiopian government tried to prove the superiority of the socialist system.

144 Examples for such programs in Green, *Fear*, pp. 5, 174, n. 4; "Massive forced re-settlement in East Timor," *Tapol* 38, March 1980, p. 15; van der Kroef, "Guerrilla Communism," pp. 125–6; Dhada, "Liberation war," pp. 584–8; Thompson, *Defeating*, p. 125; Cann, *Counterinsurgency*, pp. 149–53; for a guidebook: Galula, *Counterinsurgency*, pp. 116, 120.

145 Yildiz, *Kurds*, pp. 80–5, as one of many examples.

146 Schirmer, *Project*, pp. 66–9.

147 Jundanian, "Resettlement," p. 519; second quote: Beckett, *Modern Insurgencies*, p. 137; third quote: Osborne, *Strategic Hamlets*, p. 37. See Raúl Benítez Manaut, *La téoria militar y la guerra civil en El Salvador* (San Salvador: UCA, 1989), pp. 285–90.

148 In 1948, 9 percent of Muslim men and 2.1 percent of Muslim women in Algeria could write. The same was true, around 1980, for 35 percent of El Salvadorans (16 percent of all peasants). In Guatemala, 73 percent of all men and 91 percent of women were still illiterate in the mid-1990s; in 1992, 3 percent of Guatemalans read newspapers, 16 percent had a radio, and only 6 percent a TV set. By the late 1960s, three-quarters of the population in the Kurdish provinces in Turkey did not speak Turkish. Gillespie, *Algeria*, p. 35; Fish and Sganga, *El Salvador*, p. 37; Green, *Fear*, p. 26; Gellert, "Migration," p. 114; Kendal, "Kurdistan in Turkey," in Gérard Chaliand (ed.), *A People Without a Country: The Kurds and Kurdistan* (New York: Olive Branch Press, 1993 [French edition 1978]), p. 75.

149 Thompson, *Defeating*, pp. 124–5; see Purcell, *Malaya*, pp. 74–5.

150 Catton, *Diem's Final Failure*, p. 125.

151 Jyoti Prakash Dutta and Mohammad Mazifur Rahman, "Insurgency in Chittagong Hill Tracts: Its origin and impact on economy and environment," *Asian Profile* 26(4), 1998, pp. 317, 320.

152 Wheeler, "Portuguese army," p. 435.

153 Dirk Kruijt, "Exercises in state terrorism: Counter-insurgency campaigns in Guatemala and Peru," in Konings and Kruijt, *Societies of Fear*, pp. 41, 58, n. 8. Quote: Lewis Taylor, "Counter-insurgency strategy, the PCP-Sendero Luminoso and the civil war in Peru, 1980–1996," *Bulletin of Latin American Research* 17(1), 1998, p. 54, n. 18.

154 Michael Richards, "Cosmopolitan world view and counter-insurgency in Guatemala," *Anthropological Quarterly* 58(3), 1985, esp. pp. 100–2. Quote: Smith, "Militarization," p. 12.

155 Tomomi Kozaki and Yusuke Nakamura, "Human security in post-genocide Guatemala: Toward collective reparation and reconstruction at micro and meso levels," *Comparative Genocide Studies* 2, 2005–2006, p. 74. Second quote: Steputat, "Politics," p. 69. For Gramajo's role see also Schirmer, *Project*, esp. pp. 5–6.

156 Ken Anderson and Jean-Marie Simon, "Permanent counter-insurgency in Guatemala," *Telos* 73, 1987, p. 30.

157 Carol A. Smith, "Destruction of the material bases for Indian culture: Economic changes in Totomicapán," in Carmack, *Harvest*, pp. 215, 218, 227.

158 Bennoune, "French counter-revolutionary doctrine," pp. 50, 54, 56. While selection, supervision, and control served to instill discipline, new clothing, meanings of the human body, and attitudes, we can hardly conclude that abstract "metaphors" took control of economists, "steered the perception of reality," and that economic tools such as work discipline were merely a function of an overriding "education to modernity," as Malinowski, "Modernisierungskriege," pp. 237–41, states.

159 Blaufarb, *Counterinsurgency Era*, pp. 57–9, quoting from Rostow's Fort Bragg speech in July 1961.

160 Examples for mountain areas are the Aurès and Kabylia in Algeria, the highlands in Guatemala, Peru, South Vietnam, eastern Turkey, and

Greece, the jungles in Malaya and Cambodia, the marshes and woods in Belarus, and the Mekong delta in South Vietnam.

161 Horne, *Savage War*, pp. 62–3; Hamoumou, *Et Ils Sont*, p. 191.

162 Nicholas Tapp, *Sovereignty and Rebellion: The White Hmong of Northern Thailand* (Singapore et al.: Oxford University Press, 1989), p. 15.

163 Elliott, *Vietnamese War*, pp. 602, 788, Richards, "Cosmopolitan world view," pp. 93–4; Green, *Fear*, p. 47; Yvon le Bot, *La guerre en terre maya: Commonauté, violence et modernité au Guatemala (1970–1992)* (Paris: Karthala, 1992), p. 128.

164 Alex Vines, *Renamo: From Terrorism to Democracy in Mozambique?* (London and Amsterdam: James Currey, 1996 [second, revised edition]), p. 114.

165 *Neue Zürcher Zeitung*, December 21, 1969, in Martin Stähli et al. (eds.), *Cabora Bassa: Modellfall westlicher Entwicklungspolitik* (Berne: Kandelaber, 1971), p. 35.

166 Townshend, *Britain's Civil Wars*, p. 198; McDowall, *History*, pp. 401, 409; Kendal, "Kurdistan," pp. 64, 79.

167 Morton Abramowitz, "Foreword," in Barkey and Fuller, *Question*, p. xii.

168 T. J. B. Jokonya, "The effects of the war on the rural population of Zimbabwe," *Journal of Southern African Studies* 5(2), 1980, p. 139.

169 Starn, "Villagers," p. 233; Carlos Iván Degregori, "Ayacucho, después de la violencia," in Degregori et al., *Rondas*, p. 22.

170 Cynthia McClintock, *Revolutionary Movements in Latin America: El Salvador's FMLN & Peru's Shining Path* (Washington DC: United States Institute of Peace, 1998), pp. 159, 171, 183, 191. These child mortality figures are dubious because not all of the population was under state control, and those outside of the reach of public administration and statistics suffered heavily.

171 Berman, *Control*, pp. 300–7; Kanogo, *Squatters*, pp. 96–120; Barnett and Njama, *Mau Mau*, p. 34; Christopher Leo, *Land and Class in Kenya* (Toronto et al.: University of Toronto Press, 1984), p. 58; quotes: Newsinger, "Revolt," p. 160.

172 Greet Kershaw, *Mau Mau from Below* (Oxford *et al.*: James Currey, 1997), pp. 226–7, 248–9.

173 Anderson, *Histories*, pp. 82, 185, 345; for people of South Asian extraction, Colin Leys, *Underdevelopment in Kenya* (Berkeley and Los Angeles: University of California Press, 1974), p. 44; for plans, David Throup, *Economic and Social Origins of Mau Mau* (London: James Currey, 1987), p. 47.

174 However, it has been argued that the position of international capital in Kenya's economy was much more important than that of the settlers, resulting in a reconciliation of the interests of such companies with the establishment of a friendly post-colonial regime. Ranger, *Peasant Consciousness*, pp. 100–2; Newsinger, "Revolt," p. 183; Clough, *Mau Mau*, pp. 225–6.

175 Bernard Rivers, "Angola: Massacre and oppression," *Africa Today* 21(1), 1974, pp. 48–50.

176 Cann, *Counterinsurgency*, pp. 9, 148; Wilfred Burchett, *Southern Africa Stands Up: The Revolutions in Angola, Mozambique, Zimbabwe, Namibia and South Africa* (New York: Urizen Books, 1978), p. 191; Bender, "Limits," p. 336; Finnegan, *Complicated War*, p. 28; Henriksen, "Portugal," p. 402; Jundanian, "Resettlement," pp. 527–35. By contrast, the number of Europeans in Algeria stagnated during the war on a high level, and they were largely concentrated in urban places, but much land had been taken away from Muslims before: Elsenhans, *Frankreichs Algerienkrieg*, p. 166.

177 Cann, *Counterinsurgency*, pp. 151–2.

178 Stähli *et al.*, *Cabora Bassa*, pp. 14–15, 41–5, 48–51, 56–7; "Stunde der Wahrheit für den Ilisu-Staudamm," *Neue Zürcher Zeitung*, December 13, 2008.

179 Ranger, *Peasant Consciousness*, pp. 15, 68, 130, 229–30; Jundanian, "Resettlement," pp. 536–7; quote: Joao Paulo Coelho, "State resettlement policies in post-colonial rural Mozambique: The impact of the Communal Village Programme on Tete Province, 1977–1982," *Journal of Southern African Studies* 24(1), 1998, p. 62.

180 Morvaridi, "Resettlement," pp. 719–41, esp. pp. 722–3. In 1993, President Ozal mentioned dams in a memo to Prime Minister Demirel

explicitly as a means to prevent the return of displaced Kurds: Yildiz, *Kurds*, p. 79.

181 See Rivers, "Angola," pp. 51, 54; Stähli *et al.*, *Cahora Bassa*, esp. pp. 14, 52–3; Bender, "Limits," p. 351; skeptical about the size of European settlement plans is Jundanian, "Resettlement," p. 531.

182 Terrance W. Kading, "The Guatemalan military and the economics of La Violencia," *Canadian Journal of Latin American and Caribbean Studies*, 24(47), 1999, pp. 66, 84.

183 See Chapter 4 of this volume.

184 Basil C. Gonneris, "Social dimensions of anticommunism in Northern Greece, 1945–50," in Carabott and Sfikas, *Greek Civil War*, pp. 175–86.

185 Catton, *Diem's Final Failure*, pp. 51–6; Elliott, *Vietnamese War*, pp. 445–8; John Ellis, *From the Barrel of a Gun: A History of Guerrilla, Revolutionary and Counter-Insurgency Warfare, from the Romans to the Present* (London and Pennsylvania: Greenhill and Stackpole, 1995), pp. 224–5; quote: Blaufarb, *Counterinsurgency Era*, pp. 230, 266.

186 Maloba, *Mau Mau*, pp. 147–9; Elkins, *Reckoning*, pp. 125–30; Sorrenson, *Land Reform*, pp. 76–7, 110–98 (quotation p. 118).

187 T. David Mason, "The civil war in El Salvador: A retrospective analysis," *Latin American Research Revue* 34(3), 1999, pp. 189–90; Mario Lungo Uclés, *El Salvador in the Eighties: Counterinsurgency and Revolution* (Philadelphia: Temple University Press, 1996), pp. 96–7; Michael Krämer, *El Salvador: Vom Krieg zum Frieden niedriger Intensität* (Cologne: ISP, 1994), pp. 113–15.

188 Paret, *French Revolutionary Warfare*, p. 43; Bourdieu, *Algerians*, p. 170; Horne, *Savage War*, p. 421; Elsenhans, *Frankreichs Algerienkrieg*, pp. 565–86.

189 Cilliers, *Counter-Insurgency*, p 87.

190 Bourdieu, *Algerians*, p. 178, n. 15. For Mizoram, cf. Nunthara, *Impact*, pp. 11, 28, 31.

191 Geoff Lamb, *Peasant Politics, Conflict and Development in Murang'a* (New York: St. Martin's, 1974), p. 10.

192 Anderson, *Histories*, pp. 240–1; Barnett and Njama, *Mau Mau*, p. 139; Throup, *Origins*, pp. 144–51; Loh, *Tin Mines*, pp. 156–9, 211–12; McDowall, *History*, p. 421; Barkey and Fuller, *Question*, pp. 71–2; Stoll, *Between*, pp. 103–5; Remijnse, "Remembering," pp. 459–61; Human Rights Watch, *Civil Patrols*, pp. 23, 30.

193 Gonzalez, "Man," pp. 319–20; Schirmer, *Project*, p. 93; Remijnse, "Remembering," pp. 454, 459, 464; cf. Human Rights Watch, *Civil Patrols*, p. 77.

194 Catton, "Counter-insurgency," pp. 931, 933–5; Donnell, "Expanding," p. 691.

195 Vines, *Renamo*, p. 116; Coelho, "State resettlement," p. 84.

196 Ponciano del Pino, "Family, culture, and 'revolution': Everyday life with Sendero Luminoso," in Stern, *Shining and Other Paths*, pp. 163, 169; Nelson Manrique, "The war for the Central Sierra," in the same volume, p. 193, n. 5; Taylor, "Counter-insurgency," pp. 49–50; Fumerton, "Rondas campesinas," pp. 479–80.

197 Kriger, *Zimbabwe's Guerrilla War*, pp. 51, 69, 98, 142–9, 170–209, 241.

198 Maloba, *Mau Mau*, p. 68.

199 Ranger, *Peasant Consciousness*, pp. 265–73; Cilliers, *Counter-Insurgency*, p. 97; for leveling of differences in Tete district, Mozambique, see Coelho, "State resettlement," p. 62. For the end of the dominance of elders in Algeria, see Sutton and Lawless, "Population regrouping," p. 336.

200 Shelton Davis, "Introduction: Sowing the seeds of violence," in Carmack, *Harvest*, p. 29; Manz, *Refugees*, p. 75.

201 *Guatemala: Nunca Mas*, vol. 2: *Impactos de la violencia*, p. 126; Carlos Vilas, *Between Earthquakes and Volcanoes: Market, State, and the Revolutions in Central America* (New York: Monthly Review Press, 1995), pp. 17–18.

202 Fumerton, "Rondas campesinas," pp. 491–4.

203 Bourdieu, *Algerians*, esp. pp. 141–3, 163–86. See also Cornaton, *Camps*, pp. 109–18, 194–220.

204 Quotes from Bourdieu, *Algerians*, pp. 166, 172, 178, 179. Some similar observations in Fish and Sganga, *El Salvador*, pp. 64, 82–5; Jonathan Randal, *After Such Knowledge, What Forgiveness? My Encounters with Kurdistan* (New York: Farrer, Straus & Giroux, 1997), p. 266.

205 Bennoune, "French counter-guerrilla doctrine," p. 56.

206 Cilliers, *Counter-Insurgency*, p. 97.

207 See, in general terms, Sutton, "Population resettlement," esp. p. 283.

208 Jokonya, "Effects," pp. 134, 140, 145.

209 Cf. Adrian Bailey and Joshua Hane, "Population in motion: Salvadoran refugees and circulation migration," *Bulletin for Latin American Research* 14(2), 1995, pp. 180–3, 190, and figures for refugees abroad in Table 5.1, this volume.

210 Bourdieu, *Algerians*, p. 178, n. 15.

211 Sutton, "Population resettlement," pp. 279–300, esp. p. 283.

212 Examples for the last point are Jundanian, "Resettlement," pp. 525–7; Bender, "Limits," p. 350; and Nunthara, *Impact*, pp. 28, 30, 42–3, 54–5.

213 Loh, *Tin Mines*, p. 89; Newsinger, "Revolt," pp. 164, 168, 173, 175 (argues that the labor movement was the backbone of the rebellion in Nairobi); Clough, *Mau Mau*, p. 102; Steputat, "Politics," p. 60; Susanne Jonas, *The Battle for Guatemala* (Boulder *et al.*: Westview, 1991), pp. 124–5, 148. Inside France, up to 70,000 Algerians, mostly urban workers, were detained in 1957: Kessel and Pirelli, *Peuple*, p. 135.

214 Bender, "Limits," pp. 338–9, 348–9; Rivers, "Angola," p. 54; Laiou, "Population movements," pp. 89, 102.

215 Laiou, "Population movements," p. 86; Sutton, "Population resettlement," p. 287; Cornaton, *Camps*, pp. 92–3, 112–13; Budiardjo and Liem, *War*, p. 85; Bender, "Limits," pp. 344, 353.

216 Richard Clutterbuck, *The Long Long War: Counterinsurgency in Malaya and Vietnam* (New York and Washington: Praeger,

1966), p. 28; Coates, *Suppressing*, p. 16; Peoples, "Use," p. 1; Short, *Insurrection*, pp. 32, 72–3, 118; ethnic aspect: Thompson, *Defeating*, p. 18.

217 Similarly, forced resettlement in the late 1960s made Mizoram the most urbanized state in India: Sundar, "Interning", p. 36 with note 89.

218 The same goes for expanding coffee and other plantations worked by forced resettlers in East Timor 1976–77 and 1982–83: Budiardjo and Liem, *War*, pp. 103–6.

219 See especially the material in Singh Sandhu, "Saga," esp. pp. 164–5, 169–70 (rubber productivity decreased by 10 to 15 percent), and in his "Emergency resettlement," esp. pp. 167–9, 179; Short, *Insurrection*, p. 127; Loh, *Tin Mines*, pp. 66–74, 142. Rubber workers' real wages, in relation to 1939 = 100, developed as follows: 77 (1949), 94 (1950), 96 (1951), 80 (1952), 79 (1953). Cf. Purcell, *Malaya*, p. 148; Füredi, *Colonial Wars*, p. 48. For the longer fight of planters against squatters, whose numbers declined from 400,000 (1945) to 300,000 (1948) and 150,000 (1950), see Harper, *End*, pp. 99–114, 173–4.

220 Cf. Phillip Deery, "The terminology of terrorism: Malaya, 1948–1952," *Journal of Southeast Asian Studies* 34(2), 2003, p. 237; Carruthers, *Winning*, p. 77.

221 Coates, *Suppressing*, p. 62.

222 See David Tucker, "Labor policy and the construction industry in Manchukuo: Systems of recruitment, management, and control," and Ju Zhifen, "Northern Chinese laborers and Manchukuo," both in Paul Kratoska (ed.), *Asian Labor in the Wartime Japanese Empire* (Armonk and London: M. E. Sharpe, 2005), pp. 25–57, 61–78; Li, *Japanese Army*, p. 155.

223 See Bourdieu, *Algerians*, p. 174; cf. Hamoumou, *Et Ils Sont*, pp. 192, 194; Benítez Manaut, *Téoria*, p. 322; Wiesner, *Victims*, pp. 140–1, 282–3.

224 Waciuma, *Daughter*, pp. 99–100; recorded employment of males of working age rose from 25.1 percent (1953) to 27.6 percent (1957): Gavin Kitching, *Class and Economic Change in Kenya: The Making of an African Petite-Bourgeoisie* (New Haven and London: Yale University Press, 1980), p. 376.

225 Taylor, *East Timor*, pp. 122–7.

226 Pinto and Jardine, *East Timor*, p. 260, n. 3 and 5; Taylor, *East Timor*, pp. 157–8; Budiardjo and Liem, *War*, pp. x, 74.

227 Jonas, *Battle*, p. 97; Taylor, *East Timor*, p. 109; McDowall, *History*, p. 401; Mater, *Voices*, p. 312; Bourdieu, *Algerians*, pp. 208, 215, 310, n. 64; Samuel Huntington, "The bases of accommodation," *Foreign Affairs*, 46(4), 1968, p. 648, but cf. Wiesner, *Victims*, p. 68, for Saigon; José Corronel, "Violencia política y respuestes campesinas en Huanta," in Degregori *et al.*, *Rondas*, p. 34; Bender, "Limits," p. 349.

228 Huntington, "Bases," p. 652.

229 Kanogo, *Squatters*, p. 164; quote of a colonial officer after Branch, "Loyalists," p. 28, cf. pp. 43–4.

230 Leo, *Land*, p. 61.

231 Leo, *Land*, p. 57; Branch, "Loyalists," pp. 43–4.

232 Kanogo, *Squatters*, p. 75; Clough, *Mau Mau*, pp. 51, 218.

233 Kanogo, *Squatters*, p. 164.

234 Clough, *Mau Mau*, pp. 225–6; Kanogo, *Squatters*, p. 164; similar argument for Greece in Kofas, *Intervention*, esp. p. 123.

235 Wade Markel, "Draining the swamp: The British strategy of population control," *Parameters* 36(1), p. 41; Newsinger, "Revolt," p. 182.

236 Max Manwaring and Court Prisk, *El Salvador at War: An Oral History* (Washington: National Defense University Press, 1988), p. 228; Fish and Sganga, *El Salvador*, p. 94.

237 Thompson, *Defeating*, pp. 112–13; for practice in Borneo 1963, see Allen, *Savage Wars*, pp. 81–2.

238 South Vietnam: Clutterbuck, *Long Long War*, p. 67, and Blaufarb, *Counterinsurgency Era*, pp. 217–18; Guatemala: Stoll, *Between*, pp. 157–8, Smith, "Militarization," p. 21, and Manz, *Refugees*, pp. 107–12; Algeria: M. Lesne, "Une expérience de déplacement de population: les centres de regroupement en Algérie," *Annales de Géographie* 71, 1962, p. 587; Sutton and Lawless, "Population regrouping," p. 334; Sutton, "Army administration," p. 267 (French

authorities in 1960 regarded 60 percent of the resettled as being in substandard places); Elsenhans, *Frankreichs Algerienkrieg*, p. 660 (the growth of the number of Muslim school students slowed down during the war); Kershaw, *Mau Mau*, p. 336; many schools in Kenya closed: Barnett and Njama, *Mau Mau*, p. 130. See Peter Sollis, "Displaced persons and human rights: The crisis in El Salvador," *Bulletin of Latin American Research* 11(1), 1992, p. 49; Yildiz, *Kurds*, p. 162, n. 21; Loh, *Tin Mines*, pp. 137–9, for Malaya.

239 Nunthara, *Impact*, pp. 19–21; Catton, *Diem's Final Failure*, p. 68; Weinrich, "Strategic resettlement," pp. 216, 222; Sorrenson, *Land Reform*, p. 110; Niggli, "Äthiopien," pp. 40–1.

240 Throup, *Origins*, pp. 19–20, 25, 140–4.

241 Joes, *Resisting Rebellion*, p. 110; Richard Stubbs, *Hearts and Minds in Guerrilla Warfare: The Malayan Emergency 1948–1960* (Singapore *et al.*: Oxford University Press, 1989), pp. 18 (quote), 81; Singh Sandhu, "Saga," p. 152; Loh, *Tin Mines*, p. 139; Deery, "Malaya, 1948," pp. 5, 10–11 (in 1947, the US received 371,000 of 727,000 tonnes of Malayan rubber and 155,000 of 158,000 tonnes of Malayan tin exports). However, Short, *Insurrection*, pp. 347–8, suggests higher costs of the 'Emergency.' Total revenue from duties and taxes on Malayan export goods was around UK£55 million in 1951 and UK£92 million in 1952, which compared to the costs of the "Emergency" US$51.15 million and US$69.3 million, respectively (calculated on the basis of Malayan $8 being the equivalent of UK£1: Leary, *Violence*, p. 116).

242 Jackson, *Malayan Emergency*, p. 20; see David Percox, "Mau Mau & the army of the state," in Odhiambo and Lonsdale, *Mau Mau*, pp. 130, 135; David Percox, "British counter-insurgency in Kenya, 1952–56: Extension of internal security policy or prelude to decolonisation?," *Small Wars and Insurgencies* 9(3), 1998, pp. 59, 67; Newsinger, "Revolt," p. 182.

243 See Thomas Mockaitis, "The origins of British counter-insurgency," *Small Wars and Insurgencies*, 1(3), December 1990, p. 210; C. C. Chin and Karl Hack (eds.), *Dialogues with Chin Peng: New Light on the Malayan Communist Party* (Singapore: Singapore University Press, 2005), p. 162.

244 Jundanian, "Resettlement," pp. 528, n. 33, 531; cf. Rivers, "Angola," p. 54.

245 Leary, *Violence*, pp. 43, 54–5 (based on the assumption that the total number of Orang Asli resettled was 50,000); lower figures in Loh, *Tin Mines*, pp. 123, 136–7 (M$67 million 1950–52). According to Singh Sandhu, "Saga," p. 162, the expenses for a New Village were M$300 per capita; similar for the State of Kedah by Short, *Insurrection*, p. 395, n. 3.

246 Joes, *America*, p. 227; McCuen, *Art*, pp. 211–13.

247 Davidson, "Angola," p. 49; Ellis, *Barrel*, p. 212; McCuen, *Art*, p. 259.

248 Cann, *Counterinsurgency*, pp. 6, 9–10, 190–1; quote: interview with José de Sousa, who left Portugal in 1967, in "Expat lives: A different rhythm," *Financial Times*, US edition, May 5–6, 2007, House and Home, p. 11.

249 Kriger, *Zimbabwe's Guerrilla War*, p. 112; Coates, *Suppressing*, pp. 123–4.

250 Barkey and Fuller, *Question*, pp. 140, 152, n. 15; Randal, *After*, pp. 257–8.

251 Jonas, *Battle*, pp. 168–9; Anderson and Simon, "Permanent counterinsurgency," pp. 9–11, 13, 20; Kading, "Guatemalan military," pp. 76, 83; Smith, "Militarization," pp. 37–8, n. 3. Britain gave financial assistance to suppress the Kenyan insurgency from June 1954 as settlers resisted higher taxes – their tax burden being much lower than in the motherland: Percox, "Counter-Insurgency," p. 88.

252 Joes, *America*, pp. 165, 206.

253 Kofas, *Intervention*, pp. 22, 123, 130; Eudes, *Kapetanios*, p. 299; Woodhouse, *Struggle*, pp. 203, 247. From 1945 to 1947, the US had provided three-quarters of $416 million of UNRRA funds (more than half of this contribution in food).

254 Papagos, "Guerrilla warfare," p. 238.

255 McCuen, *Art*, p. 260.

256 Blaufarb, *Counterinsurgency Era*, pp. 243, 269.

257 Jenny Pearce, "From civil war to 'civil society': Has the end of the Cold War brought peace to Central America?," *International Affairs* 74(3), 1998, pp. 594–5; interview with Guillermo Ungo, in Manwaring and Prisk, *El Salvador*, p. 390.

258 Rolf Steininger, "Grossbritannien und der Vietnamkrieg 1964/65," *Vierteljahrshefte für Zeitgeschichte* 45, 1997, p. 593.

259 Bailey and Hane, "Population," pp. 179, 181, 187; Krämer, *El Salvador*, pp. 117–18.

260 Smith, "Militarization," pp. 23–4; Victor Montejo, *Voices from the Exile: Violence and Survival in Modern Maya History* (Norman: University of Oklahoma Press, 1999), p. 251, n. 1; Manz, *Refugees*, pp. 119–20; Budiardjo and Liem, *War*, pp. 90, 109; Cilliers, *Counter-Insurgency*, p. 140; Siriphon, "Local knowledge," p. 70; Wakin, *Anthropology*, pp. 117, 120–1.

261 Kading, "Guatemalan military," pp. 57–91; Smith, "Militarization," pp. 13–14.

262 Stoll, *Between*, pp. 85–6; Egan, "Somos," p. 109, n. 4; Falla, *Massacres*, p. 19; Clark Taylor, *Return of Guatemala's Refugees: Reweaving the Torn* (Philadelphia: Temple University Press, 1998), p. 6.

263 Human Rights Watch, *Civil Patrols*, p. 90; Richards, "Cosmopolitian world view," pp. 96–7; Valentino, *Final Solutions*, p. 208.

264 Gonzalez, "Man," p. 320.

265 Green, *Fear*, p. 34; Gellert, "Migration," pp. 112–29, esp. pp. 118, 122–6 (though with contradictory figures); Smith, "Militarization," pp. 21–3.

266 Manz, *Refugees*, pp. 53–5, 59–60, 74, 82–3, 136, 143; Bailey and Hane, "Population," p. 190.

267 However, only 15 to 20 percent were completely landless. Smith, "Militarization," pp. 22–32.

268 This would seem different from Schirmer, *Project*, an ethnography based on interviews with Guatemalan military officers and their publications without drawing their perceived omnipotence into question.

269 Bender, "Limits," esp. pp. 340–6; Cann, *Counterinsurgency*, p. 145; Manz, *Refugees*, pp. 42–3, 209–10.

270 Elliott, *Vietnamese War*, esp. pp. 4–5, 158, 437, 451, 465, 787, 920–1, 1242.

271 494 of those who surrendered were born in Malaysia, 694 in Thailand. Deery, "Malaya, 1948," p. 29; Peter Taaffe, "End of empire: Memoirs of a Malaysian communist guerrilla leader," *Socialism Today* 91, April 2005, www.socialismtoday.org/91/malaya.html.

272 Hua, *Class*, esp. p. 158.

273 In 1999, up to 280,000 East Timorese and Indonesian transmigrants left the country due to the pro-Indonesian violence and then out of fear of repression for having supported integration into Indonesia. By 2005, 30,000 still remained in Indonesian West Timor. In the 1999 referendum, 21.5 percent of voters had opted for integration: Taylor, *East Timor*, pp. xii, xxvii–xxix; Schlicher, *Osttimor*, pp. 6, 20; Irena Cristalis, *Bitter Dawn: East Timor, a People's Story* (London and New York: Zed, 2002), pp. 151–8.

274 Faivre, "L'Histoire," p. 59; Hamoumou, *Et Ils Sont*, pp. 46, 242, 246–8; Charles-Robert Ageron, "Le Drame des Harkis: Mémoire ou Histoire?," *Vingtième Siècle* 68, October–December 2000, pp. 3–15. The term 'harki' originally applied only to members of specific armed formations but has become an umbrella term for all former French auxiliaries in Algeria.

275 Hamilton-Merritt, *Mountains*, esp. pp. xvii, 337–478.

276 Figures cited are inconsistent: 50,000 to 70,000 Algerian Muslims came to France until the end of 1963 (only a minority of them seem to have been former armed loyalists), whereas the numbers of Algerian Muslim emigrants in France for 1974 ranged from 200,000 to 600,000. Hamoumou, *Et Ils Sont*, p. 123; Faivre, "L'Histoire," p. 60.

277 Finnegan, *Complicated War*, esp. pp. 32, 63, 70, 278; Vines, *Renamo*, esp. pp. 73–119; from a pro-Renamo point of view: Hoile, *Mozambique*.

278 "Kenia – Brennender Hass," *Tagesspiegel*, March 26, 2009; "Schwierige Rückkehr für Kenias Vertriebene," *Neue Zürcher Zeitung*, May 21, 2008.

279 Gonneris, "Social dimensions," p. 183; Woodhouse, *Struggle,* p. 209.

280 See Ranger, *Peasant Consciousness,* pp. 284–7, 300–8, 314–15, 334–5; Smile Dube, "Genocide in Matabeleland and Midlands in Zimbabwe: A failed transition to democracy and ethnic co-existence," in Alexandre Kimenyi and Otis L. Scott (eds.), *Anatomy of Genocide: State-Sponsored Mass-Killings in the Twentieth Century* (Lewiston: Edwin Mellen, 2001), pp. 79–110 (albeit this is a confused and heavily partisan contribution); "Bannstrahl gegen das Regime in Harare," *Neue Zürcher Zeitung,* April 5, 2007.

281 Pearce, "From civil war," p. 590; North and Simmons, "Fear and hope," pp. 22, 24; "Guatemals schwacher Staat im Griff der Drogenmafia," *Neue Zürcher Zeitung,* March 5, 2010, p. 9.

282 Green, *Fear,* pp. 55–79 (chapter "Living in a state of fear"); Manuel Angel Castillo, "Exodus and return with a changing migration system," in North and Simmons, *Journeys of Fear,* p. 135.

283 Pearce, "From civil war," p. 590; "Ex-Generalstaatsanwalt ermordet," Spiegel online, October 12, 2007.

284 Finnegan, *Complicated War,* pp. 97, 308, n. 21/2; see Hoile, *Mozambique,* pp. 96–101, and Vines, *Renamo,* pp. 97–100.

285 Kershaw, *Mau Mau,* pp. 226, 241; Branch, "Imprisonment," pp. 248, 254–6; Maloba, *Mau Mau,* pp. 33–4, 41–3; Throup, *Origins,* pp. 10, 171–3, 190; Gillespie, *Algeria,* p. 146; Stubbs, *Hearts,* pp. 15, 45; Jackson, *Malayan Emergency,* pp. 9–10; Harper, *End,* pp. 158–60; Mitter, *Manchurian Myth,* pp. 105–6, 191 (quote); cf. Suleski, "Northeast China," p. 366; Michael Gunter, *The Kurds and the Future of Turkey* (New York: St. Martin's, 1997), pp. 54–7; Barkey and Fuller, *Question,* pp. 29–34.

286 Hagen Fleischer, *Im Kreuzschatten der Mächte: Griechenland 1941–1944* (Frankfurt a.M. *et al.*: Peter Lang, 1986), p. 135.

287 German counter-insurgency in Belarus, especially from 1943 to 1944, is an exception; most murdered at that time were women and children while men were sought for forced labor: Gerlach, *Kalkulierte Morde,* pp. 1001–3.

288 Cilliers, *Counter-Insurgency*, p. 207; Green, *Fear*, pp. 31–2, 176, n. 12; Bender, "Limits," p. 341, n. 29; Elkins, *Reckoning*, pp. 244–52.

289 Bourdieu, *In Algerien*, p. 72.

290 Elkins, *Reckoning*, p. 208.

291 Singh Sandhu, "Emergency resettlement," p. 161.

292 Bender, "Limits," p. 348; Heggoy, *Insurgency*, p. 214; Sutton, "Population resettlement," p. 289; Cornaton, *Camps*, pp. 80–7.

293 For Peru: Starn, "Villagers," p. 240; for Kenya: Waciuma, *Daughter*, pp. 128, 139; for Malaya: photo in Allen, *Savage Wars*, fourth page after p. 98.

294 Starn, "Villagers," p. 240 ("The people got macho"); for Guatemala: Human Rights Watch, *Civil Patrols*, p. 74; Green, *Fear*, pp. 83–4; Esparza, "Post-war Guatemala," p. 383.

295 Bourdieu, *In Algerien*, p. 72; Monika Schlicher, "'Die Soldaten nehmen ihnen jegliche Würde': Gewalt gegen Frauen als Mittel der Kriegführung," in Klemens Ludwig (ed.), *Osttimor: Der zwanzigjährige Krieg* (Reinbek: rororo, 1996), p. 62; Manz, *Refugees*, p. 92.

296 Singh Sandhu, "Emergency resettlement," esp. pp. 166, 175; Singh Sandhu, "Saga," esp. pp. 144, 168; Loh, *Tin Mines*, pp. 178–84, 192–8, 248–50, 270–1; Jackson, *Malayan Emergency*, p. 20; Thompson, *Defeating*, p. 125. For Algeria: Sutton, "Population resettlement," p. 294.

297 Coelho, "State resettlement," pp. 61–91, esp. pp. 62–8, 91, n. 89.

298 Sutton, "Population resettlement," pp. 289–94; Keith Sutton, "The influence of military policy on Algerian rural settlement," *Geographical Review* 71(4), 1981, pp. 382–5, 390; Sutton and Lawless, "Population regrouping," p. 339; Cornaton, *Camps*, pp. 119–31.

299 Figures indicative of this fluctuation in Cornaton, *Camps*, pp. 156, 162, 171, 178, 184.

300 Sutton, "Influence," pp. 386–7, 390; Keith Sutton, "Algeria's socialist villages – a reassessment," *Journal of Modern African Studies* 22(2), 1984, p. 225; for inquiry responses about most urgent desires, Cornaton, *Camps*, pp. 158–61, 166, 176, 187, 231–2.

301 Sorrenson, *Land Reform*, pp. 147–50, 162–4.

302 Degregori, "Ayacucho," p. 22.

303 Yildiz, *Kurds*, p. 162, n. 25.

304 Sundar, "Interning," p. 16.

305 Nunthara, *Impact*, pp. 10, 21, 50.

306 Laiou, "Population movements," esp. pp. 79–81, 88–102.

307 Sollis, "Displaced," p. 53.

308 See Sutton, "Army administration," p. 267.

309 Bernard Fall, "A portrait of the 'Centurion'," in Trinquier, *Modern Warfare*, p. xviii.

310 Deery, "Terminology of terrorism," esp. pp. 236, 240; Gerlach, *Kalkulierte Morde*, p. 925; Gérard Chaliand, "With the guerrillas in 'Portuguese' Guinea," in Chaliand, *Guerilla Strategies*, p. 209.

311 Chin and Hack, *Dialogues*, pp. 360, 375, n. 39.

312 Tim Jones, "The British Army, and counter-guerrilla warfare in Greece, 1945–49," *Small Wars and Insurgencies* 8(1), 1997, p. 100.

313 Jones, "The British Army, and counter-guerrilla warfare in Greece, 1945–49," pp. 88–106, esp. p. 99; Jones, "The British Army, and counter-guerrilla warfare in transition, 1944–1952," pp. 268, 274; veiled reference to Germany in Beckett, *Modern Insurgencies*, pp. 91, 93.

314 Jones, "The British Army, and counter-guerrilla warfare in transition, 1944–1952," pp. 275–6.

315 Cf. Mark Mazower, *Inside Hitler's Greece: The Experience of Occupation, 1941–1944* (New Haven and London: Yale University Press, 2001), pp. 155–89. Troops: Woodhouse, *Struggle*, p. 191. In March 1945, there were 96,000 British troops in Greece: Jones, "The British Army, and counter-guerrilla warfare in Greece, 1945–49," p. 89 (see also p. 94); references to Germany: p. 94.

316 Kousoulas, *Revolution*, p. 259; Jones, "The British Army, and counter-guerrilla warfare in Greece, 1945–49," pp. 96–9.

317 Nagl, *Counterinsurgency*, pp. 65–6, 71; Townshend, *Britain's Civil Wars*, p. 158; Jackson, *Malayan Emergency*, pp. 19, 23, 29;

Beckett, *Modern Insurgencies*, p. 100; Jones, "The British Army, and counter-guerrilla warfare in transition, 1944–1952," pp. 278–81, 289 (quotation p. 280).

318 Allen, *Savage Wars*, p. 129; Jackson, *Malayan Emergency*, p. 44; Rhodesian units also fought in Malaya (Leary, *Violence*, pp. 195–8).

319 Jones, "The British Army, and counter-guerrilla warfare in transition, 1944–1952," pp. 290, 291

320 Sundar, "Interning," p. 11.

321 Antonio Varsori, "Britain and US involvement in the Vietnam War during the Kennedy Administration, 1961–63," *Cold War History*, 3(2), January 2003, pp. 83–112, esp. pp. 86–9, 94–7; Beckett, "Robert Thompson," pp. 41–63; Catton, "Counter-insurgency," p. 924. For a different view of Thompson's "Delta plan": Busch, "Killing," pp. 135–62, esp. pp. 139–46.

322 Busch, "Killing," p. 137; Joes, *America*, p. 220. Lansdale had been active with the anti-Japanese guerrillas in the Philippines in World War II, then in the Joint US Military Advisory Group in the Philippines since 1950, since early 1954 with the CIA in Saigon, and 1965–66 as chief of the Revolutionary Development Program in South Vietnam: Beckett, *Modern Insurgencies*, p. 109; Nagl, *Counterinsurgency*, pp. 164–5.

323 Nagl, *Counterinsurgency*, p. 125.

324 Mockaitis, "Origins," p. 209.

325 Gene Z. Hanrahan, *Japanese Operations Against Guerrilla Forces* (Chevy Chase: Operations Research Office, Johns Hopkins University, 1954), pp. 1–2, quote 1 (a confidential study for the Operations Research Office, Johns Hopkins University); for the German side, "Richtlinien zur Bandenbekämpfung," February 26, 1943, Nuremberg Document NO-475, BA Film 44297.

326 See Wakin, *Anthropology*, esp. pp. 67, 90, 117, 120–1; cf. van der Kroef, "Guerrilla communism," pp. 127–8. For the role of anthropologists in combating the Malayan insurgency see Leary, *Violence*, pp. 54, 56.

327 Blaufarb, *Counterinsurgency Era*, pp. 182–3.

328 Weinrich, "Strategic resettlement," p. 207.

329 Gabriel Aguilera Peralta, "Terror and violence as weapons of counterinsurgency in Guatemala," *Latin American Perspectives* 25/26, spring and summer 1980, VII(2–3), p. 98; Blaufarb, *Counterinsurgency Era*, pp. 282, 285; Richards, "Cosmopolitan world view," p. 95; Kruijt, "Exercises," p. 40. See Kendal, "Kurdistan," pp. 71, 78; and Martha Huggins, "U.S. supported state terror: A history of police training in Latin America," *Crime and Social Justice* 27, 1987, pp. 149–71. For the influence from the Inter-American Defense College, an OAS-affiliated institution in Washington DC, on Peruvian military doctrine, see Enrique Obando, "Civil–military relations in Peru, 1980–1996: How to control and coopt the military (and the consequences of doing so)," in Stern, *Shining and other Paths*, p. 386.

330 Steputat, "Politics," p. 61; Richards, "Cosmopolitan world view," p. 94. However, for the limited learning effect, see Schirmer, *Project*, p. 43.

331 Frédéric Guelton, "The French Army 'Centre for Training and Preparation in Counter-Guerrilla Warfare' (CIPCG) in Arzew," in Martin S. Alexander and J. F. V. Keiger (eds.), *France and the Algerian War, 1954–62: Strategy, Operations and Diplomacy* (London and Portland: Frank Cass, 2002), pp. 35–53; Heggoy, *Insurgency*, pp. 176–82; Bennoune, "French counter-revolutionary doctrine," pp. 46–7; Cann, *Counterinsurgency*, pp. 40–2. Peru: Obando, "Civil–military relations," p. 388.

332 Elsenhans, *Frankreich Algerienkrieg*, p. 60, n. 265.

333 Taylor, "Counter-insurgency," p. 36.

334 Catton, *Diem's Final Failure*, pp. 90–1.

335 Smith, "Militarization," p. 12; see Schirmer, *Project*, p. 59.

336 Mario Enrique Morales quoted in Smith, "Militarization," p. 13.

337 Dhada, "Liberation war," p. 584; Henriksen, "Portugal," p. 401; Rivers, "Angola," p. 53.

338 Cann, *Counterinsurgency*, p. 37.

339 Ellis, *Barrel*, p. 213; Brace and Brace, *Algerian Voices*, p. 121.

340 Davidson, "Angola," pp. 37–49.

341 "Fence-of-legs" means that civilians, controlled by soldiers, move alongside and close to each other toward a suspected insurgency area in order to spot and capture guerillas or refugees. Jamie Davidson and Douglas Kammen, "Indonesia's unknown war and the lineages of violence in West Kalimantan," *Indonesia* 73, April 2002, pp. 84, 86. However, this technique was largely used only in 1980–81: Budiardjo and Liem, *War*, pp. 41–2.

342 Guelton, "French Army," pp. 39, 49; in general terms cf. Jean-Marc Marill, "L'Héritage Indochinois: adaptation de l'armée française en Algérie (1954–1956)," *Revue historique des armées* 2, 1992, pp. 26–32. Quote: Bourdieu, *Algerians*, p. 164.

343 Mockaitis, "Origins," pp. 222–3; cf. Thomas Mockaitis, "The British Experience in Counterinsurgency, 1919–1960," Ph.D. thesis, University of Wisconsin, 1988, esp. pp. 277–280, 393, which contradicts Jones, "The British Army, and counter-guerrilla warfare in transition, 1944–1952," p. 294; cf. Elkins, *Reckoning*, pp. 103, 105, 409, n. 3. The learning effects from Malaya for the design of 'rehabilitation' camps in Kenya were limited too: Luise White, "Separating the men from the boys: Constructions of gender, sexuality and terrorism in Central Kenya, 1939–1959," *International Journal of African Historical Studies* 23(1), 1990, p. 19. Caroline Elkins argues that certain British colonial officials wanted to adopt strategies from Malaya and Greece only selectively: Caroline Elkins, "The struggle for Mau Mau rehabilitation in late colonial Kenya," *International Journal of African Historical Studies* 33(1), 2000, p. 36.

344 Mockaitis, "Origins," pp. 209–25, esp. pp. 213, 221–2; Mockaitis, "British Experience," pp. 377–406; Beckett, *Modern Insurgencies*, pp. 44, 91; Frank Furedi, "Kenya: Decolonisation through counter-insurgency," in Anthony Gorst *et al.* (eds.), *Contemporary British History 1931–1961* (London and New York: Pinter, 1991), pp. 142–3; Cann, *Counterinsurgency*, p. 55; Jones, "The British Army, and counter-guerrilla warfare in transition, 1944–1952," pp. 265–307.

345 Joes, *America*, p. 109.

346 See Heggoy, *Insurgency*, pp. 78, 183; Coates, *Suppressing*, pp. 86–7; Stubbs, *Hearts*, p. 73; Cann, *Counterinsurgency*, p. 118. Quote: Steputat, "Politics," p. 69.

347 Kenneth Matthews, *Memories of a Mountain War: Greece: 1944–1949* (London: Longman, 1972), p. 180.

348 This resembles detention facilities in British Kenya run by European settlers or loyalist chiefs: Elkins, *Reckoning*, p. 151.

349 Paret, *French Revolutionary Warfare*, p. 43; Bourdieu, *Algerians*, p. 164; Heggoy, *Insurgency*, pp. 214, 222; Lesne, "Expérience," pp. 570–6, 603; Cornaton, *Camps*, pp. 42–54, 80–1; Sutton, "Army administration," pp. 244, 247–8, 252, 257 (French quote: p. 252); Cann, *Counterinsurgency*, p. 74. For English quote and earlier efforts, see Sutton, "Influence," pp. 380–1.

350 Purcell, *Malaya*, pp. 74–5; Smith, "Gerald Templer," pp. 62–3; Harper, *End*, p. 175; Singh Sandhu, "Saga," pp. 155–9; Jones, "The British Army, and counter-guerrilla warfare in transition, 1944–1952," pp. 283–4, 287; and see the sources listed in note 346.

351 Osborne, *Strategic Hamlets*, p. 13, n. 13.

352 Ranger, *Peasant Consciousness*, pp. 168, 250.

353 Joseph J. Zasloff, *Rural Resettlement in Viet Nam: An Agroville in Development* (University of Pittsburgh, August 1962); Peoples, "Use"; Donnell, "Expanding," p. 695.

354 Catton, "Counter-insurgency," pp. 918–40; Catton, *Diem's Final Failure*; in the same vein, based on British, US, and Australian documents, Osborne, *Strategic Hamlets*, pp. 25–30; Blaufarb, *Counterinsurgency Era*, pp. 102–9, 120–2; Busch, "Killing," pp. 136–45.

355 Fall, "Portrait," p. viii.

356 Joes, *Resisting Rebellion*, p. 115; Nagl, *Counterinsurgency*, pp. 157–8.

357 Krämer, *El Salvador*, pp. 51–2, 59, 79; Manwaring and Prisk, *El Salvador*, pp. 225–6; Hugh Byrne, *El Salvador's Civil War* (Boulder and London: Lynne Rienner, 1996), p. 109.

358 A contrary view can be found in Mark Mazower, "Violence and the state in the twentieth century," *American Historical Review* 107(4), 2002, p. 1172.

359 Davidson, "Angola," p. 47; Wheeler, "Portuguese army," pp. 433–5; Bender, "Limits," pp. 346–50.

360 Leroy Vail and Landeg White, *Capitalism and Colonialism in Mozambique: A Study of Quelimane District* (Minneapolis: University of Minnesota Press, 1980), p. 399; Weinrich, "Strategic resettlement," p. 225.

361 Del Pino, "Family," pp. 163–9; Starn, "Villagers", Degregori, "Rondas campesinas," pp. 235, 239; Manrique, "War," p. 193, n. 5; Joes, *Resisting Rebellion*, p. 117; Corronel, "Violencia," pp. 61, 83, 96; Degregori, "Ayacucho," pp. 24, 27; Fumerton, "Rondas campesinas," pp. 470–97.

362 Human Rights Watch, *Civil Patrols*, pp. 15, 23, 25, 36–7; Montejo, *Voices*, p. 66; Schirmer, *Project*, pp. 36–8, 83.

363 Anderson, *Histories*, pp. 124, 240–1; Kershaw, *Mau Mau*, p. 327; Maloba, *Mau Mau*, p. 89.

364 Loh, *Tin Mines*, p. 166, n.; Beckett, *Modern Insurgencies*, p. 102. François-Xavier Hautreux, "L'engagement des harkis (1954–1962)," *Vingtième Siècle* 90(2), 2006, p. 34, notes that the first auxiliary groups in Algeria were formed without official directives.

365 Newsinger, "Minimum force," pp. 47–57, repudiating theses by Tim Jones; another uncritical supporter of the "minimum force" claim is Mockaitis, "British Experience," esp. pp. 36–129.

Note to Table 5.1

Yukio Ishida, "Die japanischen Kriegsverbrechen in China 1931–1945," in Wolfram Wette and Gerd R. Ueberschär (eds.), *Kriegsverbrechen im 20. Jahrhundert* (Darmstadt: Wissenschaftliche Buchgesellschaft, 2001), p. 338; Christian Gerlach, *Kalkulierte Morde: Die deutsche Wirtschafts- und Bevölkerungspolitik in Weissrussland 1941 bis 1944* (Hamburg: Hamburger Edition, 1999), pp. 899–904, 955–8, 1040–55; Angeliki E. Laiou, "Population movements in the Greek countryside during the civil war," in Lars Baerentzen *et al.* (eds.), *Studies in the History of the Greek Civil War 1945–1949* (Copenhagen: Museum Tusculanu Press, 1987), pp. 55–103, esp. pp. 59, 73; Jon V. Kofas, *Intervention and Underdevelopment: Greece During the Cold War* (University Park and London: Pennsylvania State University Press, 1989), p. 131 (more than one million evacuated); C. M. Woodhouse,

The Struggle for Greece 1941–1949 (Chicago: Ivan R. Dee, 2002 [first ed. 1976]), pp. 237, 266, 286; Dominique Eudes, *The Kapetanios: Partisans and Civil War in Greece, 1943–1949* (London: NLB, 1972), p. 354; Michel Cornaton, *Les camps de regroupement de la guerre d'Algérie* (Paris and Montreal: Harmattan, 1998 [first ed. 1967]), pp. 36–8, about French Indochina and Cambodia, and p. 123 about Algeria; Curtis Peoples, "The use of the British village resettlement model in Malaya and Vietnam," April 2002, www.tamil-nation.org/tamileelam/armedstruggle/thompson.htm (accessed January 26, 2007), p. 3; Kernial Singh Sandhu, "Emergency resettlement, in Malaya," *Journal of Tropical Geography* 18, 1964, pp. 157–83, esp. pp. 164, 174; Singh Sandhu, "The saga of the 'squatter' in Malaya: A preliminary survey of the causes, characteristics and consequences of the resettlement of rural dwellers during the emergency between 1948 and 1960," *Journal of Southeast Asian History* 5, 1964, pp. 143–77; Robert Jackson, *The Malayan Emergency: The Commonwealth's Wars 1948–1966* (London and New York: Routledge, 1991), p. 115; John D. Leary, *Violence and the Dream People: The Orang Asli in the Malayan Emergency 1948–1960* (Athens, GA: Center for International Studies, Ohio University, 1995), pp. 44–8; Donald L. Barnett and Karari Njama, *Mau Mau from Within* (New York and London: Monthly Review Press, 1966), pp. 439–40; David Anderson, *Histories of the Hanged: The Dirty War in Kenya and the End of Empire* (New York and London: W. W. Norton, 2005), p. 241; Caroline Elkins, *Imperial Reckoning: The Untold Story of Britain's Gulag in Kenya* (New York: Henry Holt, 2005), pp. xvi, 366, 429, n. 366; Alistair Horne, *A Savage War of Peace: Algeria 1954–1962* (New York: D. Van Nostrand, 1977), pp. 14, 538; Richard Brace and Joan Brace, *Algerian Voices* (Princeton *et al.*, 1965), p. 19; Mohand Hamoumou, *Et Ils Sont Devenus Harkis* (Paris: Fayard, 1993), pp. 193–4; M. Lesne, "Une expérience de déplacement de population: les centres de regroupement en Algérie," *Annales de Géographie* 71, 1962, p. 573, n. 1; Ian Beckett, *Modern Insurgencies and Counter-Insurgencies: Guerrillas and their Opponents since 1750* (London and New York: Routledge, 2000), pp. 54, 192; Douglas S. Blaufarb, *The Counterinsurgency Era: U.S. Doctrine and Performance 1950 to the Present* (New York and London: Free Press/Collier Macmillan, 1977), pp. 120, 270; Louis Wiesner, *Victims and Survivors: Displaced Persons and Other War Victims in Viet-Nam, 1954–1975* (New York *et al.*: Greenwood, 1988), pp. 346–7; John C. Donnell, "Expanding political participation – The long haul from villagism to nationalism," *Asian Survey* 10(8), 1970, p. 697; Bernd Greiner, "Die Blutpumpe: Zur Strategie und Praxis des Abnutzungskrieges in Vietnam 1965–1973," in Greiner *et al.* (eds.), *Heiße Kriege im Kalten Krieg* (Hamburg: Hamburger Edition, 2006), pp. 169–70, 223–4; John P. Cann, *Counterinsurgency in Africa: The Portuguese Way of War, 1961–1974* (Westport and London: Greenwood, 1997), pp. 155–6; Thomas H. Henriksen, "Portugal in Africa: Comparative notes on counterinsurgency," *Orbis* 21(2), 1977, p. 395; Gerald J. Bender, "The limits of counterinsurgency: An African case," *Comparative Politics* 4(3), 1972, pp. 333, 336; Mustafa Dhada, "The liberation war in Guinea-Bissau reconsidered," *Journal of Military History* 62(3), 1998, p. 580; Anthony James Joes, *Resisting Rebellion: The History and Politics of Counterinsurgency* (Lexington: Kentucky University Press, 2004), pp. 114, 117; for Indonesia see Chapter 2 of this volume; C. Nunthara, *Impact of the Introduction of Grouping of Villages in Mizoram* (New Delhi: Omsons, 1989), pp. 5–6, 67–71; Norma J. Kriger, *Zimbabwe's Guerrilla War: Peasant Voices* (New York *et al.*: Cambridge University Press, 1992), pp. 4, 47, 228; Benetech Human Rights Data Analysis Group of the Commission on Reception, Truth and Reconciliation of Timor-Leste (Romesh Silva and Patrick Ball), "The Profile of Human Rights Violations in Timor-Leste, 1974–1999," February 9, 2006, pp. 1–2, http://hrdag.org/resources/Benetech-Report-to-CAVR.pdf (accessed 6 December 6, 2007); "Massive forced re-settlement in East Timor," *Tapol* 38, March 1980, p. 15; Kevin Lewis O'Neill, "Writing Guatemala's genocide: Truth and Reconciliation Commission reports and Christianity," *Journal of Genocide Research* 7(3), 2005, p. 334; Liisa L. North and Alan B. Simmons, "Fear and hope: Return and transformation in historical perspective" and Gisela Gellert, "Migration and the displaced: Guatemala City in the context of a flawed national transformation," in North and Simmons (eds.), *Journeys of Fear: Refugee Return and National Transformation in Guatemala* (Montreal *et al.*: McGill & Queen University Press, 1999), pp. 3, 12, 17, 119–20 (there were up to 1.5 million Guatemalan exiles in the USA in 1998); Dirk Kruijt, "Exercises in state terrorism: Counter-insurgency campaigns in Guatemala and Peru," in Kees Konings and Dirk Kruijt (eds.), *Societies of Fear: The Legacy of Civil War, Society and Terror in Latin America* (London and New York: Zed, 1999), p. 49; David Stoll, *Between Two*

Armies in the Ixil Towns of Guatemala (New York: Columbia University Press, 1993), pp. xxiv–xxv, 156, 334, n. 20; Benjamin Valentino, *Final Solutions: Mass Killing and Genocide in the 20th Century* (Ithaca and London: Cornell University Press, 2004), p. 203; Max Manwaring and Court Prisk, *El Salvador at War: An Oral History* (Washington: National Defense University Press, 1988), pp. 336–8; David McDowall, *A Modern History of the Kurds* (London and New York: I. B. Taurus, 1996), pp. 421–8, 438; Nadire Mater (ed.), *Voices from the Front: Turkish Soldiers on the War with the Turkish Guerrillas* (New York and Basingstoke: Palgrave Macmillan, 2005), pp. 309–16; Siegwart-Horst Günther and Burchard Brentjes, *Die Kurden* (Vienna: Braumüller, 2001), pp. 83–93, cite higher figures (five million displaced, high additional mortality due to diseases and land mines, 95,000 village guards by 1998). Peru: Carlos Iván Degregori, "Reaping the whirlwind: The rondas campesinas and the defeat of Sendero Luminoso in Ayacucho," in Kees Konings and Dirk Kruijt (eds.), *Societies of Fear: The Legacy of Civil War, Society and Terror in Latin America* (London and New York: Zed, 1999), pp. 72–3; Orin Starn, "Villagers at arms: War and counterrevolution in the central-south Andes," in Steve J. Stern (ed.), *Shining and Other Paths: War and Society in Peru, 1980–1995* (Durham and London: Duke University Press, 1998), pp. 227, 247; Carlos Iván Degregori, "Ayacucho, después de la violencia", in Degregori *et al.* (eds.), *Las rondas campesinas y la derrota de Sendero Luminoso* (Lima: IEP, 1996), p. 24; dead for Peru include victims of pro-government forces only while the guerrillas, unusually, killed a higher number of people: Hildegard Willer, "Peru kennt die Wahrheit und tut sich schwer damit," *Neue Zürcher Zeitung* online, October 22, 2008. For Bangladesh, see Chapter 4 of this volume.

6 What connects the fate of different victim groups?

1 From 1941 to 1945, 4–4.5 percent of the Greek population perished, which was one of the highest rates in Europe behind Poland, the Soviet territories under German rule, and Yugoslavia.

2 Protective custody report of Buchenwald concentration camp, December 15, 1944, in Romani Rose (ed.), *Der nationalsozialistische*

Völkermord an den Sinti und Roma (Heidelberg: Dokumentations-und Kulturzentrum Deutscher Sinti und Roma, 2003), pp. 192–3.

3 This may even be so for German camps in general. Concentration camps were just one distinct category of camps organized by one particular SS administration.

4 Dieter Pohl, *Verfolgung und Massenmorde in der NS-Zeit 1933–1945* (Darmstadt: Wissenschaftliche Buchgesellschaft, 2003), p. 153, and my own estimates.

5 Aside from about 600 Soviet POWs, about 250 sick camp prisoners were killed in the first murder with gas, including some Jews: Kazimiersz Halgas, "Die Arbeit im 'Revier' für sowjetische Kriegsgegangene in Auschwitz," in *Die Auschwitz-Hefte*, vol. 1 (Weinheim and Basel: Beltz, 1987), pp. 167–72; Reinhard Otto, *Wehrmacht, Gestapo und sowjetische Kriegsgefangene im deutschen Reichsgebiet 1941/42* (Munich: Oldenbourg, 1998), pp. 190–1.

6 Out of about six million Jews murdered, circa 165,000 were Germans and 65,000 Austrians: Pohl, *Verfolgung*, p. 109; lower figures in Raul Hilberg, *Die Vernichtung der europäischen Juden* (Frankfurt a.M.: Fischer Taschenbuch, 1994), p. 1300.

7 Of the 12 to 14 million non-combatants who perished, about 500,000 were Germans, including 180,000 disabled people, 165,000 Jews, 50,000 so-called asocials (overlapping with 15,000 Sinti and Roma), and perhaps 25,000 Germans among those executed after being sentenced by civilian or military courts.

8 Two-thirds of Jewish Germans as of early 1933 survived (and close to half of those Jews still in Germany in mid-1939), compared to only 20 percent survivors among all Jews who came within the German sphere of influence.

9 Even inside one of the few German settlement areas in Ukraine, actual occupation policies were mostly shaped by issues other than German settlers: Wendy Lower, "A new ordering of race and space: Nazi colonial dreams in Zhytomyr, Ukraine, 1941–1944," *German Studies Review* 25(2), 2002, p. 243.

10 Götz Aly, *Hitler's Beneficiaries: Plunder, Racial War and the Nazi Welfare State* (New York: Metropolitan Books, 2006), p. 30, and

German version, Aly, *Hitlers Volksstaat* (Frankfurt a.M.: S. Fischer, 2005), p. 314.

11 Mark Mazower, *Inside Hitler's Greece: The Experience of Occupation, 1941-1944* (New Haven and London: Yale University Press, 2001), pp. xi, 20, 155, 39–41, with contradictory figures about starvation deaths; statistics in Isaac Matarasso, "'...and yet not All of Them Died': The destruction of Salonika's Greek Jews during the German occupation" [1948], in Steven Bowman (ed.), *The Holocaust in Salonika: Eyewitness Accounts* (n.p.: Sephardic House, 2002), pp. 170–1; Bea Lewkowicz, *The Jewish Community of Salonika: History, Memory, Identity* (London and Portland; Vallentine Mitchell & Co., 2006), p. 69; Joshua Eli Plaut, *Greek Jewry in the Twentieth Century, 1913–1983: Patterns of Jewish Survival in the Greek Provinces before and after the Holocaust* (Madison: Fairleigh Dickinson University Press, 1996), pp. 54–7.

12 Mazower, *Inside*, p. 36.

13 Hagen Fleischer, "Deutsche 'Ordnung' In Griechenland 1941–1944," in Loukia Droulia and Hagen Fleischer (eds.), *Von Lidice bis Kalavryta – Widerstand und Besatzungsterror: Studien zur Repressalienpraxis im Zweiten Weltkrieg* (Berlin: Metropol, 1999), pp. 151–224. Cf. also Mazower, *Inside*, pp. 201–18.

14 Quoted in Hagen Fleischer, *Im Kreuzschatten der Mächte: Griechenland 1941–1944* (Frankfurt a.M.: Peter Lang, 1986), p. 455.

15 Mazower, *Inside*, pp. 23–4, 58, 215–18; Aly, *Hitler's Beneficiaries*, pp. 245–8; diary entry MacVeagh, May 10, 1941, in John O. Iatrides (ed.), *Ambassador MacVeagh Reports: Greece, 1933–1947* (Princeton: Princeton University Press, 1980), p. 361; later example in Feldkommandantur 1042 Peleponnes, "Lagebericht," December 31, 1943, in Martin Seckendorf *et al.* (eds.), *Die Okkupationspolitik des deutschen Faschismus in Jugoslawien, Griechenland, Albanien, Italien und Ungarn (1941–1945)* (Berlin and Heidelberg: Hüthig Verlagsgemeinschaft, 1992), p. 295.

16 Report of May 24, 1941, in Iatrides, *Ambassador MacVeagh*, p. 368; Christos Hadziiossif, "Griechen in der deutschen Kriegsproduktion," in Ulrich Herbert (ed.), *Europa und der 'Reichseinsatz': Ausländische Zivilarbeiter, Kriegsgefangene und KZ-Häftlinge in Deutschland 1938–1945* (Essen: Klartext, 1991), pp. 210–11.

17 Some have claimed that a deliberate deindustrialization strategy, especially regarding the dyes and textile industry, was another factor: Janis Schmelzer and Martin Seckendorf, "IG Farbenindustrie und deutsche Okkupationspolitik in Griechenland: Ein bisher nicht beachtetes Dokument vom 21. April 1941," *1999* 20(2), 2005, pp. 33–48.

18 US Ambassador MacVeagh to President Roosevelt, November 6, 1940 (quote), MacVeagh's report of November 9, 1940, and his May 7 and 8, 1941 diary entries, in Iatrides, *Ambassador MacVeagh*, pp. 242, 245, 359–60; cf. Mazower, *Inside*, pp. 27, 34; Stavros B. Thomadakis, "Black markets, inflation and force in the economy of occupied Greece," in John O. Iatrides (ed.), *Greece in the 1940s: A Nation in Crisis* (Hanover and London: New England University Press, 1981), p. 71.

19 Fleischer, *Kreuzschatten*, p. 116.

20 Mazower, *Inside*, pp. 46–8; May 24, 1941 entry, in Iatrides, *Ambassador MacVeagh*, p. 368. The Greek government had purchased 350,000 tons of Australian and Soviet wheat in early 1941 and included a clause in the contract that the grain would be delivered even if Greece were occupied by a foreign power. Nonetheless, the British authorities confiscated the shiploads and used the wheat for their own troops. Fleischer, *Kreuzschatten*, p. 122.

21 Mazower, *Inside*, pp. 28, 33, 49, 55; Thomadakis, "Black markets," p. 65; Steven Bowman, *Jewish Resistance in Wartime Greece* (London and Portland: Vallentine Mitchell, 2006), p. 66.

22 Mazower, *Inside*, p. 28.

23 This included textile, leather, glass, and tobacco industries. Plaut, *Greek Jewry*, p. 41; cf. Thomadakis, "Black markets," p. 68.

24 Hadziiossif, "Griechen," p. 219.

25 Thomadakis, "Black markets," p. 75.

26 Mazower, *Inside*, p. 57; for women establishing Child Centers for the starving, see memories by Nausika Flenga-Papadaki in Eleni Fourtoni (ed.), *Greek Women in Resistance: Journals – Oral Histories* (New Haven: Thelphini Press, 1986), pp. 32, 43–5.

27 Mazower, *Inside*, pp. 57–61; Kostas Vergopoulos, "The emergence of the new bourgeoisie, 1944–1952," in Iatrides, *Greece*, pp. 302–3.

28 Mazower, *Inside*, pp. 37, 40; Fleischer, *Kreuzschatten*, p. 117; Martin Seckendorf, "Verbrecherische Befehle: Die Wehrmacht und der Massenmord an griechischen Zivilisten 1941 bis 1944," *Bulletin der Berliner Gesellschaft für Faschismus- und Weltkriegsforschung* 13, 1999, p. 10. There is no clear picture of how the famine affected Jewish communities: see Yomtov Yacoel, "In the anteroom of Hell" (1943), in Bowman, *Holocaust*, and Matarasso, "... and yet," pp. 27, 134; Bowman, *Jewish Resistance*, p. 28, n. 7.

29 Hadziiossif, "Griechen," p. 220; Mazower, *Inside*, p. 108.

30 Testimony by Toula Mara-Mihalakea, in Fourtoni, *Women*, pp. 29, 31; Thomadakis, "Black markets," pp. 78–9.

31 Mazower, *Inside*, pp. 75–8; Hadziiossif, "Griechen," pp. 224–6; Mark Spoerer, *Zwangsarbeit unter dem Hakenkreuz: Ausländische Zivilarbeiter, Kriegsgefangene und Häftlinge im Deutschen Reich und im besetzten Europa 1938–1945* (Stuttgart and Munich: Deutsche Verlags-Anstalt, 2001), p. 70.

32 Hadziiossif, "Griechen," p. 226. In the Larissa Jewish community, there had been deaths "from lice, cold and hunger" in 1941–42, and when warned of imminent deportation in 1943, 235 Jews stayed so as not to lose their International Red Cross food rations: Plaut, *Greek Jewry*, pp. 64–6.

33 Yacoel, "Anteroom," pp. 41–4, 51; Bowman, *Jewish Resistance*, p. 28, n. 8; Lewkowicz, *Jewish Community*, p. 133; Hadziiossif, "Griechen," p. 216 (5,000 recruited).

34 See Hans Safrian, *Eichmann und seine Gehilfen* (Frankfurt a.M.; Fischer Taschenbuch, 1997), p. 229, and letter Suhr (RSHA) to Rademacher, August 18, 1942, in Seckendorf, *Okkupationspolitik*, p. 204 (quote).

35 Yacoel, "Anteroom," pp. 51–3 (3 percent died, i.e. about 100; Yacoel was part of a group that visited the workers and reported on the conditions); Bowman, *Jewish Resistance*, pp. 55, 58; Lewkowicz, *Jewish Community*, p. 133 (400 died); Steven Bowman, "Salonikan memories," in Bowman, *Holocaust*, p. 16 ("hundreds died").

36 Yacoel, "Anteroom," pp. 47–76 (who was involved in the committee and negotiations). According to him, the payment was not made in gold (see esp. p. 66), opposed to Aly, *Hitler's Beneficiaries*,

pp. 254–5. For previous sales of community real estate: Yacoel, "Anteroom," p. 30.

37 Aly, *Hitler's Beneficiaries*, p. 255; Hadziiossif, "Griechen," pp. 216–17; Yacoel, "Anteroom," pp. 52–5; Matarasso, "...and yet," p. 159. The "malumore" of non-Jews is mentioned in a report by the Italian Consulate General, October 22, 1942, in Daniel Carpi (ed.), *Italian Diplomatic Documents on the History of the Holocaust in Greece (1941–1943)* (Tel Aviv: Tel Aviv University, 1999), pp. 115–16.

38 Aly, *Hitler's Beneficiaries*, p. 248; cf. Thomadakis, "Black markets," p. 69; Hadziiossif, "Griechen," pp. 216–17.

39 Fundamental: Thomadakis, "Black markets," pp. 73–5; Mazower, *Inside*, p. 54; see a British intelligence report of August 25, 1943 for the importance Greeks put on expectations of a British-led invasion, in Richard Clogg (ed.), *Greece 1940–1949: Occupation, Resistance, Civil War: A Documentary History* (Basingstoke and London: Palgrave Macmillan, 2002), p. 114.

40 Hadziiossif, "Griechen," p. 223.

41 Minna Rozen, "Jews and Greeks remember their past: The political career of Tzevi Koretz (1933–1943)," *Jewish Social Studies* 12(1), 2005, pp. 126–7; Fleischer, *Kreuzschatten*, p. 167.

42 Pathbreaking: Aly, *Hitler's Beneficiaries*, pp. 254–67, 282; for labor incentives: Hadziiossif, "Griechen," pp. 217, 226; for recovering real incomes: Thomadakis, "Black markets," p. 72.

43 Mazower, *Inside*, p. 242, overlooks this. Between 22 and 24 percent of the Salonikan Jews were selected for forced labor in Auschwitz, but most died within 18 months from horrible treatment and conditions. Mazower, *Inside*, pp. 244, 267; cf. Lewkowicz, *Jewish Community*, p. 147. The offers by the Salonika Jewish council to hand over half of the Jewish movable property and real estate and to concentrate all Greek Jews on one island at their own expense did not prevent the deportations: Mentes M. Molho, "Assets of Jews of Salonika," in Bowman, *Holocaust*, pp. 245, 247.

44 Loring M. Danforth, *The Macedonian Conflict: Ethnic Nationalism in a Transnational World* (Princeton: Princeton University Press, 1995), p. 77.

45 Safrian, *Eichmann*, p. 228; for the deportations in general, see pp. 225–60.

46 Letter of March 23, 1943, in Clogg, *Greece*, pp. 104–6, and Bowman, *Jewish Resistance*, pp. 77–8. At some point, all three Prime Ministers under the occupation – Georgios Tsolakoglou, Logothetopoulos, and Ioannis Rallis – protested against the persecution of Jews, though not forcefully enough. Fleischer, *Kreuzschatten*, p. 367.

47 Yacoel, "Anteroom," p. 105.

48 Yacoel, "Anteroom," pp. 34–5; reports by the Italian Consulate General, February 20 and 28 and March 14, 1943, in Carpi, *Documents*, pp. 126–7, 130, 137.

49 "Proclamation," June 9, 1944, in Clogg, *Greece*, p. 103; Fleischer, *Kreuzschatten*, p. 366. But Bishop Methodios in charge of Corfu protested: Rozen, "Jews," p. 127.

50 Mazower, *Inside*, p. 55; Molho, "Assets," pp. 222–4; Rozen, "Jews," p. 127; report by Italian Consulate General, March 20, 1943, in Carpi, *Documents*, p. 140.

51 Matarasso, "...and yet," pp. 142, 165; Mazower, *Inside*, p. 247; cf. Molho, "Assets," pp. 219–20.

52 Lewkowicz, *Jewish Community*, pp. 133–4, 143, n. 6.

53 Plaut, *Greek Jewry*, p. 57; different figures in Aly, *Hitler's Beneficiaries*, pp. 231–3; Greek exiles: Konstantin Loulos, "Vergeltungsmaßnahmen der Besatzungsorgane und 'endogene' Repressalien in Griechenland 1941–1944," in Droulia and Fleischer, *Lidice*, pp. 139–40.

54 Plaut, *Greek Jewry*, pp. 62, 68–9. Over 90 percent were killed, except for Jews from Athens and mainland towns in the Italian zone (as opposed to the islands).

55 Plaut, *Greek Jewry*, pp. 51, 83–5 (2.3% of business and 4% of homes); Molho, "Assets," pp. 229–30 (8.6% of businesses and 2.7% of homes in Salonika), see also p. 227; Yacoel, "Anteroom," p. 73; Lewkowicz, *Jewish Community*, pp. 190–6 (quote p. 192).

56 Hadziiossif, "Griechen," p. 217.

57 John Sakkas, "The civil war in Evrytania," in Mark Mazower (ed.), *After the War Was Over: Reconstructing the Family, Nation,*

and State in Greece, 1943–1960 (Princeton and Oxford: Princeton University Press, 2000), p. 189; Mazower, *Inside*, p. 131. British officers could drive by car in these zones for hours without meeting any Germans or Italians: Report by Major D. J. Wallace, August 29, 1943, in Clogg, *Greece*, p. 118.

58 Mazower, *Inside*, pp. 113, 120 (for anti-guerrilla operations generally, see pp. 155–200); Bowman, "Salonikan memories," p. 18.

59 Mazower, *Inside*, pp. 155–201, esp. pp. 155, 183–5, 48–9; Droulia and Fleischer, *Lidice*. See Chapter 5 in this volume.

60 Hadziiossif, "Griechen," pp. 217, 228–9; Mazower, *Inside*, p. 345.

61 Hadziiossif, "Griechen," pp. 217, 226–7.

62 Mazower, *Inside*, p. 54.

63 Fleischer, *Kreuzschatten*.

64 Loulos, "Vergeltungsmaßnahmen," pp. 137–50; Mazower, *Inside*, pp. 322–54.

65 Stathis N. Kalyvas, "Red terror: Leftist violence during the occupation," in Mazower, *After the War*, pp. 142–83.

66 Mazower, *Inside*, pp. 344–51.

67 In Athens, some police officers issued forged identity cards for Jews and some priests baptized Jews or certified Jewish–non-Jewish marriages: Safrian, *Eichmanns Gehilfen*, pp. 270–1.

68 Examples in Bowman, *Jewish Resistance*, esp. pp. xxii, 42; Plaut, *Greek Jewry*, pp. 66, 95. There were only 440 surviving orphans, pointing to a low number of children surviving with Christian families. Most returnees from Germany were young unmarried adults (see "Census of Jewish population of Salonika in July 1946," in Matarasso, "…and yet," p. 174.

69 Christian Gerlach and Götz Aly, *Das letzte Kapitel: Realpolitik, Ideologie und der Mord an den ungarischen Juden* (Stuttgart and Munich: Deutsche Verlags-Anstalt, 2002), pp. 438–9; Aly, *Hitler's Beneficiaries*, pp. 268–75; Safrian, *Eichmanns Gehilfen*, pp. 275–83.

70 "Panevvoikon Vima," May 6, 1943, quoted after Mazower, *Inside*, p. 56.

71 Danforth, *Macedonian Conflict*, pp. 53–4.

72 Fleischer, *Kreuzschatten*, p. 84, mentions that 90,000 leftists were forced to renounce their party affiliation from 1936 to 1941.

73 Sometimes even restraint was displayed; for example, influential parts of the Greek political elites were reluctant to enter World War I. Greece could only be coerced into it in 1917 under pressure generated by a British naval blockade, British, French, Serbian, Russian, and Italian troops entering the country, and a British-staged coup.

74 Cf. Georgios Niarchos, "Between Ethnicity, Religion and Politics: Foreign Policy and the Treatment of Minorities in Greece and Turkey, 1923–1974," Ph.D. thesis, London School of Economics and Political Science, 2005.

75 The following paragraph is largely based on Plaut, *Greek Jewry*, pp. 22–103, esp. p. 69.

76 Most Jews of Salonika were repeatedly at odds with Greek foreign policy: after 1908, their loyalty remained first with the Ottoman Empire, and in World War I, many advocated siding with Germany since it was Russia's enemy and championed international propaganda against anti-Semitism. Plaut, *Greek Jewry*, pp. 31–2.

77 In Salonika, home of more than half of Greek Jews, further local developments exacerbated this, such as the 1917 fire that destroyed Jewish neighborhoods, the 1929 stock market crash, and the civil disturbances of the 1920s and 1930s: Bowman, *Jewish Resistance*, p. 21.

78 The population of Evrytania (central Greece) declined from 53,471 in 1940 to 24,307 in 1991, that of Florina and Kastoria districts in western Greek Macedonia from 156,000 (1941) to 116,000 in 1951 and 105,000 in 1981. Sakkas, "Civil war," p. 205, n. 1; Danforth, *Macedonian Conflict*, p. 78, n. 25.

79 Xanthippi Kotzageorgi-Zymari with Tassos Hadjianastassioni, "Memories of the Bulgarian occupation of Eastern Macedonia: Three generations," in Mazower, *After the War*, p. 280. By 1971, close to 395,000 Greeks worked in West Germany: Ulrich Herbert, *Geschichte der Ausländerbeschäftigung in Deutschland 1880–1980* (Bonn: Dietz, 1986), p. 188.

80 Danforth, *Macedonian Conflict*, pp. 73–4.

81 Nicos C. Alivizatos, "The 'Emergency Regime' and civil liberties, 1946–1949," in Iatrides, *Greece*, pp. 222–8 (quotes); Polymeris Voglis, "Between negation and self-negation: Political prisoners in Greece, 1945–1950," in Iatrides, *Greece*, p. 77; Aphrodite Mavroede-Pandeleskou, "Trikeri 1951: The Makronissos Journal," in Fourtoni, *Women*, pp. 178–80; cf. p. 185 in the same volume.

82 Vergopoulos, "Emergence," in Iatrides, *Greece*, pp. 298–318, puts much emphasis on the 1941–44 period. He argues that almost all industrial firms existing in 1961 had only gone into business within the previous twenty years (p. 311).

83 Bowman, *Jewish Resistance*, p. 6.

84 Niarchos, "Ethnicity," offers a long-term approach from 1923 to 1974, but largely concentrates on Greek–Turkish issues with much emphasis on Turkish policies.

7 The ethnization of history

1 Ziauddin Ahmed, "The case of Bangladesh: Bringing to trial the perpetrators of the 1971 genocide," in Albert Jongman (ed.), *Contemporary Genocides* (Leiden: PIOOM, 1996), p. 99 (Ahmed shares the cited view). For Ward Churchill, *A Little Matter of Genocide: Holocaust and Denial in the Americas 1492 to the Present* (San Francisco: City Lights Publishers, 1997), p. 4, the "American holocaust was and remains unparalleled, both in terms of its magnitude and the degree to which its goals were met, and in terms of extent to which its ferocity was sustained over time by not one but several participating groups." Cf. Alan Rosenbaum (ed.), *Is the Holocaust Unique?* (second edition, Boulder and London: Westview, 2001). Yehuda Bauer, "Comparison of genocides," in Levon Chorbaijan and George Shirinian (eds.), *Studies in Comparative Genocide* (London and New York: Macmillan and St. Martin's, 1999), pp. 31–43, distinguishes "Holocaust" and "genocide" based on a qualitative difference. Only one starts with a capital letter.

2 Ahmed Sharif *et al.* (eds.), *Genocide '71: An Account of the Killers and Collaborators* (Dhaka: Muktijuddha Chetana Bikash Kendra, 1988), p. 13.

3 Leo Kuper, *Genocide: Its Political Uses in the Twentieth Century* (New Haven and London: Yale University Press, 1981), p. 186.

4 Benetech Human Rights Data Analysis Group of the Commission on Reception, Truth and Reconciliation of Timor-Leste (Romesh Silva and Patrick Ball), The Profile of Human Rights Violations in Timor-Leste, 1974–1999, February 9, 2006, pp. 1–2, http://hrdag.org/resources/ Benetech-Report-to-CAVR.pdf (accessed December 6, 2007).

5 Households in Conflict Network, University of Sussex, The Bosnian Book of the Dead: Assessment of the Database – Full Report (Patrick Ball *et al.*), June 17, 2007, www.hicn.org/research_design/rdn5.pdf; see "Das bosnische Totenbuch," *Frankfurter Allgemeine Zeitung*, June 21, 2007; "Bosnia war dead figure announced," BBC, June 21, 2007, http://news.bbc.co.uk/2/hi/europe/6228152.stm (all accessed May 7, 2008). A number of 102,622 dead (54 percent unarmed civilians) had earlier been presented by the Demographic Unit of the Prosecutor, International Tribunal for the Former Yugoslavia: Manus Midlarsky, *The Killing Trap: Genocide in the Twentieth Century* (Cambridge *et al.*: Cambridge University Press, 2005), p. 26.

6 R. J. Rummel, *Death by Government* (New Brunswick and London: Transaction Publishers, 1994) arrives at exaggerated death figures for most "democides" by so-called bracketing; instead of primary research, he takes the mean of available published estimates, mostly out of works of general character and therefore secondary quality, and from scholarly and journalistic accounts, to determine mortality. An exception seems to be an assumed number of 6,000 Vietnamese killed by US troops between 1960 and 1972 (and 10,000 by French troops before – Algeria is not even mentioned, according to the index), a figure that can hardly have come as the mean of all available estimates and that compares to over 1.6 million alleged killed in Vietnamese communists' actions 1945–1987 (pp. 4, 243, 267–7). Positive references to Rummel's numbers or similar works in Eric Hobsbawm, *The Age of Extremes: A History of the World* (New York: Vintage, 1996), p. 12; Jacques Semelin, *Purify and Destroy: The Political Uses of Massacre and Genocide* (New York: Columbia University Press, 2007), p. 109; Israel Charny, "Toward a generic definition of genocide," in George Andreopoulos (ed.), *Genocide* (Philadelphia: University of Pennsylvania Press, 1994), p. 92, n. 1 ("marshaled systematic evidence"); Helen

Fein, *Genocide: A Sociological Perspective* (London *et al.*: Sage, 1993), pp. xii–xiii ("very stark empiricism").

7 Dinah Spritzer, "Holocaust numbers spark row," *Jewish Telegraphic Agency*, April 16, 2007, http://jta.org/news/article/2007/04/16/101189/auschwitzmuseumcontroversy (accessed January 4, 2009).

8 See also Alexandra Goujon, "'Genozid': A rallying cry in Belarus: A rhetoric analysis of some Belarusian nationalist texts," *JGR* 1(3), 1999, pp. 353–66.

9 Such vocabulary is, for example, a feature common to Soviet Extraordinary Commission Reports about Nazi crimes from 1944–46.

10 Lucid analysis in Daniel Feierstein, *El genocidio como práctica social* (Buenos Aires: Fondo de Cultura Económica, 2007), p. 205.

11 Cf. Jacques Sémelin, "Extreme violence: Can we understand it?," *International Social Science Journal* 44(4), 2002, p. 434.

12 See Feierstein, *Genocidio*, pp. 146–50, 168–9.

13 Donald Beachler, "The politics of genocide scholarship: The case of Bangladesh," *Patterns of Prejudice* 41(5), 2007, pp. 467–92.

14 Frank Chalk and Kurt Jonassohn (eds.), *The History and Sociology of Genocide* (New Haven and London: Yale University Press, 1990), p. 397. In fact, other victim groups also won national independence or state leadership in the wake of mass violence, such as in the cases of the Armenians, Bosnia and Herzegovina, or the Rwandan Patriotic Front (RPF) in Rwanda. The Soviet Union and Poland "won out over" Nazi Germany, etc.

15 Alexander Laban Hinton, "The dark side of modernity: Toward an anthropology of genocide," in Hinton (ed.), *Annihilating Difference: The Anthropology of Genocide* (Berkeley *et al.*: University of California Press, 2002), p. 5.

16 Michael Wildt, "Biopolitik, ethnische Säuberungen und Volkssouveränität," *Mittelweg 36* 15(6), December 2006, p. 105.

17 In the tradition of Benedict Anderson, *Imagined Communities: Reflections on the Origin and Spread of Nationalism* (second edition, London and New York: Verso, 1991).

18 Mark Levene, "Why is the twentieth century the century of geno-cide?," *Journal of World History* 11(2), 2000, p. 329.

19 These problems cannot be addressed by simply setting "Jew" consistently in quotation marks as practiced by Tim Cole. See his "Constructing the 'Jew': Writing the Holocaust: Hungary 1920–45," *Patterns of Prejudice* 33(3), 1999, pp. 19–27.

20 Hinton, "Dark side," p. 5.

21 Raphael Lemkin, *Axis Rule in Occupied Europe* (Washington: Carnegie Endowment for International Peace, 1944), p. 91.

22 Hinton, "Dark side," pp. 4, 6.

23 Vinay Lal, "The concentration camp and development: The pasts and future of genocide," *Patterns of Prejudice* 39(2), 2005, p. 223.

24 Mark Mazower, "Violence and the state in the twentieth century," *American Historical Review* 107(4), 2002, p. 1168. A cautiously for-mulated example is Eric Weitz, *A Century of Genocide: Utopias of Race and Nation* (Princeton: Princeton University Press, 2003), esp. pp. 73, 84, 98.

25 Neither in Dinah Shelton (ed.), *Encyclopedia of Genocide and Crimes Against Humanity*, 3 vols. (Detroit *et al.*: Thomson Gale, 2005) nor in Israel Charny (ed.), *Encyclopedia of Genocide*, 2 vols. (Santa Barbara: ABC-CLIO, 1999) does one find entries on "Vietnam" or "Indochina." Also, 'intent' is a convenient vehicle to define away the extermination of indigenous peoples and even to con-trast 'Western' to Nazi and other mass slaughters: for Australia, Dirk Moses, "Genocide and settler society in Australian history," in Moses (ed.), *Genocide and Settler Society* (New York and Oxford: Berghahn, 2004), pp. 18–20; for Paraguay and Brazil, Jared Diamond, *The Third Chimpanzee: The Evolution and Future of the Human Animal* (New York: HarperCollins, 1992), p. 288.

26 Midlarsky, *Killing Trap*, p. 86.

27 Fein, *Genocide*, p. 17.

28 Proclamation of Independence Order, April 10, 1971, in *Bangla Desh Documents* (Madras, n.y. [1971]), pp. 281–2; Rafiq ul Islam, *A Tale of Millions* (Dacca: Bangladesh Books International, 1981),

reproduction of a Mukti Bahini poster before Appendix A ("struggle to avenge the genocide of our people"); Asim Mukhopadhyay, "Facts, hopes, and doubts", April 24, 1971, citing Dr. Ashabul Huq, Commander of the Southwest Sector of the Mukti Fouz, in Muntassir Mamoon (ed.), *Media and the Liberation War of Bangladesh, vol. 2: Selections from the* Frontier (Dhaka: Centre for Bangladesh Studies, 2002), p. 98.

29 Martin Adeney, "Heavy fighting and burning in Chittagong," *Guardian*, March 31, 1971, for the Bangla Desh Students' Action Committee in Britain; Rehman Sobhan, "Prelude for an order for genocide," *Guardian*, June 5, 1971, in *Bangla Desh Documents*, pp. 277–9.

30 Statement by Prime Minister Tajuddin, *Hindustan Standard*, April 18, 1971, in I. N. Tewary (ed.), *War of Independence in Bangla Desh* (New Delhi: Navachetna Prakashan Varanasi, 1971), p. 167.

31 Speech by Abu Sayeed Chowdhury, Royal Commonwealth Society, London, June 8, 1971, in Fazlul Quader Quaderi (ed.), *Bangla Desh Genocide and World Press* (Dacca: Begum Dilafroz Quaderi, 1972 [second, revised edition]), p. 107.

32 Information Service of India/Indian Embassy in Bonn, "Nachrichten aus Indien," "UN's Intervention for Stopping Genocide in East Pakistan Sought," and "India Draws Attention of UN Members to Genocide," March 30 and April 1, 1971, PA AA B37/626.

33 *Hindustan Standard*, March 11, 1971, in Tewary, *War*, p. 125; FRG Consulate-General Dacca, telegram March 12, 1971, PA AA B 37/630; Islam, *Tale*, p. 52.

34 See Mamoon, *Media*, p. 3.

35 Kalyan Chaudhuri, *Genocide in Bangladesh* (Bombay *et al.*: Orient Longman, 1972), pp. 205, 210.

36 John Bowen, "Culture, genocide, and a public anthropology," in Hinton, *Annihilating Difference*, p. 390.

37 Omer Bartov and Phyllis Mack (eds.), *In God's Name: Genocide and Religion in the Twentieth Century* (New York and Oxford: Berghahn, 2001), esp. their "Introduction," p. 2; Thomas Scheffler, "Einleitung: Ethnizität und Gewalt im Vorderen und Mittleren Orient," in Scheffler

(ed.), *Ethnizität und Gewalt* (Hamburg: Deutsches Orient-Institut, 1991), p. 11.

38 For Bosnia: Weitz, *Century*, p. 203; "not many scholars have looked [...] at the religious aspect of modern genocide": Bartov and Mack, "Introduction," p. 1.

39 Nathan Glazer and Daniel Patrick Moynihan, "Introduction," in Glazer and Moynihan (eds.), *Ethnicity: Theory and Experience* (Cambridge, MA: Harvard University Press, 1975), pp. 1–26, quote p. 18.

40 A transition described by Maud Mandel, "Faith, religious practice and genocide: Armenians and Jews in France following World War I and II," in Bartov and Mack, *In God's Name*, pp. 283–316. However, the experience of mass violence can also solidify religious identity (as the Shiite remembrance of the battle of Kerbela shows) or a move back from nationalism with a secular to a religious background (as Palestinians' shifting memory of the two expulsions of 1948 and 1967 indicates). See Thomas Scheffler, "Ethnizität, symbolische Gewalt und internationaler Terrorismus im Vorderen Orient," in Scheffler, *Ethnizität*, pp. 223–4.

41 Samuel Totten and William S. Parsons, "Introduction," in Samuel Totten *et al.* (eds.), *Genocide in the Twentieth Century: Critical Essays and Eyewitness Testimony* (New York and London: Garland, 1995), p. xxix.

42 For the latter, Jan Gross, *Neighbors: The Destruction of the Jewish Community in Jedwabne, Poland* (Princeton and Oxford: Princeton University Press, 2001).

43 Wolfgang Reinhard, *Geschichte der Staatsgewalt* (Munich: C. H. Beck, 1999), pp. 517–25.

44 Jacques Sémelin, "From massacre to genocidal process," *International Social Science Journal* 54(4), 2002, p. 433.

8 Conclusions

1 For example in Roger W. Smith, "Human destructiveness and politics: The twentieth century as an age of genocide," in Isidor Wallimann

and Michael N. Dobkowski (eds.), *Genocide and the Modern Age* (New York *et al*.: Greenwood, 1987), p. 23.

2 Helen Fein, *Genocide: A Sociological Perspective* (London *et al*.: Sage, 1993), p. 48; Jacques Semelin, *Purify and Destroy: The Political Uses of Massacre and Genocide* (New York: Columbia University Press, 2007), p. 10.

3 For an interpretation of the 'Mau Mau' conflict integrating pauperization, but not reduced to it, see David Throup, *Economic and Social Origins of Mau Mau* (London *et al*.: James Curry, 1987), esp. pp. 140–64.

4 European rule in colonial Latin America until 1800 can also be understood as the self-imposition of new European elites, who negotiated their rule and manipulated the indigenous people, but without totally controlling processes among the latter. Michael A. McDonnell and Dirk Moses, "Raphael Lemkin as historian of genocide in the Americas," *JGR* 7(4), 2005, p. 522.

5 So far, Robert Melson's argument that revolution is a necessary condition for so-called total domestic genocide is largely based on thoughts about state power, political systems, and parties. In terms of social mobility, Melson has only referred to the rise of a Jewish bourgeoisie and educated middle class in Germany at the end of the nineteenth century, but he has paid no attention to social mobility (also of other groups) from World War I to the 1940s. While Melson's general thesis appears questionable (from the Holocaust as total "domestic" genocide through his generalization from only two cases), it would seem worthwhile to inquire deeper into the relationships between mass violence on the one hand and social shifts involved in revolution on the other hand. Cf. Robert Melson, *Revolution and Genocide: On the Origins of the Armenian Genocide and the Holocaust* (Chicago and London: University of Chicago Press, 1992). However, this would require an understanding of revolution beyond a mere top-down act of manipulation by communist groups as put forward in Eric Weitz, *A Century of Genocide: Utopias of Race and Nation* (Princeton: Princeton University Press, 2003).

6 While there were always many rural dwellers responsible for direct violence as a result of such processes, rural victimhood appears to me as a much graver historical fact, unlike in Semelin's view of the Bosnian conflict (*Purify*, p. 219).

7 Ben Kiernan, "Twentieth-century genocides: Underlying ideological themes from Armenia to East Timor," in Robert Gellately and Ben Kiernan (eds.), *The Spectre of Genocide* (Cambridge *et al.*: Cambridge University Press, 2003), pp. 39–46.

8 Leo Kuper, *Genocide: Its Political Uses in the Twentieth Century* (New Haven and London: Yale University Press, 1981), p. 50.

9 Concerning Jews: Kuper, *Genocide*, pp. 13–14, 42–3.

10 However, the fact that far from all belonged to elites does not invalidate the middlemen minority concept for me, as it does for Mark Levene, *The Meaning of Genocide* (London: I. B. Tauris, 2005), p. 125.

11 For such an attempt: Walter Zenner, "Middlemen minorities and genocide," in Wallimann and Dobkowski, *Genocide*, pp. 253–81, esp. pp. 262, 274.

12 Frank Bajohr, *Parvenüs und Profiteure: Korruption in der NS-Zeit* (Frankfurt a.M.: Fischer, 2001), esp. pp. 13–14; Franz O. Gilles, *Hauptsache sparsam und ordnungsgemäß: Finanz- und Verwaltungskontrolle in den während des Zweiten Weltkrieges von Deutschland besetzten Gebieten* (Opladen: Westdeutscher Verlag, 1994); Rainer Weinert, *"Die Sauberkeit der Verwaltung im Kriege": Der Rechnungshof des Deutschen Reiches 1938–1946* (Opladen: Verlag für Sozialwissenschaften, 1993); Christian Gerlach, *Kalkulierte Morde: Die deutsche Wirtschafts- und Vernichtungspolitik in Weißrußland 1941–1944* (Hamburg: Hamburger Edition, 1999), pp. 176–7, 227–9, 678–83. A scholar who recently emphasized the egalitarian aspect of Nazi violent redistribution in a state-centered analysis downplays corruption and does not list Bajohr's, Gilles's, or Weinert's books in his bibliography: Götz Aly, *Hitler's Beneficiaries: Plunder, Racial War and the Nazi Welfare State* (New York: Metropolitan Books, 2006).

13 Similarly, a view in which revolutions are merely perceived as staged by manipulative elites (as in Weitz, *Century*) appears to be disregarding the fact that radical social change has also been actively appropriated by social groups.

14 Aly, *Hitler's Beneficiaries*, pp. 94–155; similar effects are described in passing by Martin Shaw, *War and Genocide* (Cambridge: Polity,

2003) p. 93, and in vague terms by Weitz, *Century*, p. 6, for the persecution of Armenians in 1915 ("crowds," "Turkish population").

15 Cf. Johan Galtung, *Strukturelle Gewalt: Beiträge zur Friedens- und Konfliktforschung* (Reinbek: Rowohlt, 1975).

16 For the following see my contribution "Famine and mass violence" at the conference under the same title, Youngstown State University, September 7, 2008.

17 Such as those in Roger W. Smith, "Scarcity and genocide," in Michael N. Dobkowski and Isidor Wallimann (eds.), *The Coming Age of Scarcity: Preventing Mass Death and Genocide in the Twenty-first Century* (Syracuse: Syracuse University Press, 1998), pp. 199–219.

18 Distinctions between these forms of confinement are fruitful, but they all are often discussed together too narrowly under the single heading of 'camps,' as in Joel Kotek and Pierre Rigoulet, *Das Jahrhundert der Lager* (Berlin and Munich: Propyläen, 2001).

19 Similar points are made by Shaw, *War*, p. 49; Mark Levene, "The changing face of mass murder: massacre, genocide, and post-genocide," in George Andreopoulos (ed.), *Genocide* (Philadelphia: University of Pennsylvania Press, 1994), p. 444; Daniel Feierstein, *El genocidio como práctica social* (Buenos Aires: Fondo de Cultura Económica, 2007), p. 69, n. 43.

20 Shaw, *War*, p. 49 (genocide "can never be uncontested"). But note that isolated groups with little cohesion have not waged collective physical resistance, for example the disabled in Nazi Germany.

21 Similar points have been made by Levene, *Meaning*, p. 96; Alex Alvarez, *Governments, Citizens, and Genocide: A Comparative and Interdisciplinary Approach* (Bloomington and Indianapolis: Indiana University Press, 2001), p. 20; James Waller, *Becoming Evil: How Ordinary People Commit Genocide and Mass Killing* (Oxford et al.: Oxford University Press, 2002), pp. 94–123.

22 Frank Chalk and Kurt Jonassohn, "Introduction," in Chalk and Jonassohn (eds.), *The History and Sociology of Genocide* (New Haven and London: Yale University Press, 1990), pp. 16, 23–24, call only "one-sided killing" "genocide," which includes, however, "situations in which an objectively powerless group resists genocide"; the "very

hopelessness" of their uprisings is interpreted as underscoring their helplessness. Such distinctions appear normative and arbitrary.

23 For instance, the Soviet Union between 1929 and 1939 and Cambodia from 1975 to 1979 were not at war, but their leaderships perceived the country to be threatened by foreign powers, they had been relatively recently occupied by foreign troops in combination with civil wars, and both countries were in fact invaded again in 1941 and 1979, respectively.

24 As opposed to the genocide approach that asks questions primarily about one target group and (predominantly) state authorities organizing the persecution.

25 In Guatemala, for another example, 54.2 percent of all farms had a size of less than 1.5 hectares in 1979, and 79 percent of the population were below the poverty line in 1980. Yvon le Bot, *La guerre en terre maya: Commonauté, violence et modernité au Guatémala (1970–1992)* (Paris: Karthala, 1992), p. 48; Susanne Jonas, *The Battle for Guatemala* (Boulder *et al.*: Westview, 1991), p. 177.

26 See Mark Levene, "Why is the twentieth century the century of genocide?," *Journal of World History* 11(2), 2000, esp. pp. 308, 319.

27 The degree of internal repression does not account for external violence, including that by parliamentary democracies. With regard to socialist countries, class differences (intertwined with notions of ethnicity or religion) that accounted for fault lines seem to have persisted in little-industrialized regions not only in the early phase of socialism, but also during its dissolution, as in Chechnya, Nagorny Karabach, or Kosovo.

28 Eric Wolf, "Killing the Achés," in Richard Arens (ed.), *Genocide in Paraguay* (Philadelphia: Temple University Press, 1976), p. 53.

29 Vinay Lal, "The concentration camp and development: The pasts and future of genocide," *Patterns of Prejudice* 39(2), 2005, p. 237.

30 With reference to the likely socioeconomic status of genocide victims, Helen Fein listed working class, middle class, educated class, middlemen-minority, "strangers," and hunting and gathering people – but no peasants or sharecroppers! Fein, *Genocide*, p. 30.

31 Michael Mann, *The Dark Side of Democracy: Explaining Ethnic Cleansing* (Cambridge: Cambridge University Press, 2005), p. 475,

notes that 96 percent of all political violence registered in India – except for Kashmir – is urban.

32 This especially refers to the forced labor of French and Belgian women in World War I and the German forced labor program in World War II; the deportation of the Belgian and French populace from certain areas in World War I, the expulsions from Alsace-Lorraine by Germany and from the Sudetenland by Czechoslovakia in and after World War II, as well as the internment of some of the Japanese Americans; the British naval blockade against Germany in World War I; and the air attacks in World War II, most notably by the British and US air forces against Japan and Germany. German massacres in Belgium in 1914 claimed thousands of lives, and in France and Italy during World War II, German collective violence in the context of anti-resistance warfare killed several tens of thousands.

33 Among these were about 180,000 disabled, 165,000 Jews, and numerous other groups including social outsiders ('asocials'), Sinti and Roma, so-called professional criminals, deserters or alleged defeatists, and political opponents.

34 An exception is Leo Kuper, "Theoretical issues relating to genocide: Uses and abuses," in George Andreopoulos (ed.), *Genocide* (Philadelphia: University of Pennsylvania Press, 1994), p. 34.

35 The conflicts in South Vietnam and Bangladesh can be considered cases in between.

36 See my discussion with Christopher Browning, who emphasizes quasi-colonial conquest, about the timing and circumstances of Hitler's decision to exterminate all European Jews: cf. Christopher Browning, *Nazi Policy, Jewish Workers, German Killers* (Cambridge *et al.*: Cambridge University Press, 2000), pp. 26–57, and Christian Gerlach, *Krieg, Ernährung, Völkermord: Deutsche Vernichtungspolitik im Zweiten Weltkrieg* (Zurich and Munich: Pendo, 2001), pp. 235–75.

37 This effect was less pronounced in the case of the incorporation (full annexation) of a new territory.

38 I shall explore the dynamics of imperialist violence for the society from which it emanates in my next book, *The Extermination of European Jews: Mass Destruction in Extremely Violent Societies*.

39 Cf. the volume by Robert Gellately and Nathan Stolzfus (eds.), *Social Outsiders in Nazi Germany* (Princeton and Oxford: Princeton University Press, 2001) that virtually exclusively asks questions about Germany itself; not all would apply to occupied countries in the same way.

40 As for technology, it was solely the murder of about 3.5 million people by gas (half of all Jews killed and maybe one-quarter of all non-combatant victims) that was unique, and not deportations, resettlement, the uses of starvation, or anti-partisan warfare strategies.

41 Except for political opponents and 'gypsies' (Sinti and Roma), most other groups mentioned were primarily persecuted if they were German. About 180,000 of a quarter of a million murdered disabled people were Germans.

42 Contrary to the suggestion by Birthe Kundrus, "Entscheidung für den Völkermord? Einleitende Überlegungen zu einem historiographischen Problem," *Mittelweg 36*, 15(6), 2006, esp. pp. 13–14.

43 For Cambodia: Weitz, *Century*, p. 187.

44 Shaw, *War*, pp. 4–6, 19–21, 26 (quotes pp. 19, 26).

45 Weitz, *Century*, pp. 15, 251–2; see also John R. Bowen, "Culture, genocide, and a public anthropology," in Alexander Laban Hinton (ed.), *Annihilating Difference: The Anthropology of Genocide* (Berkeley: University of California Press, 2002), pp 382–3.

46 Quotes from Mark Mazower, "Violence and the state in the twentieth century," *American Historical Review* 107(4), 2002, p. 1159. On pp. 1176–7, Mazower calls Nazism one of the "decontextualized European examplars" of state violence.

47 See also Christian Gerlach and Nicolas Werth, "State violence – Violent societies," in Sheila Fitzpatrick and Michael Geyer (eds.), *Beyond Totalitarianism: Stalinism and Nazism Compared* (Cambridge et al.: Cambridge University Press, 2008), pp. 133–79.

48 Jacques Sémelin, "Elemente einer Grammatik des Massakers," *Mittelweg 36* 15(6), 2006, p. 20; Mazower, "Violence," p. 1177.

49 Dirk Moses, "Genocide and settler society in Australian history," in Moses (ed.), *Genocide and Settler Society* (New York and Oxford: Berghahn, 2004), p. 24; Mazower, "Violence," pp. 1165–6.

50 Weitz, *Century*, pp. 190–235; Semelin, *Purify*, pp. 215–18.

51 See Taner Akçam, *A Shameful Act: The Armenian Genocide and the Question of Turkish Responsibility* (New York: Metropolitan Books, 2006), pp. 133–41; Taner Akçam, *From Empire to Republic: Turkish nationalism and the Armenian Genocide* (London and New York: Zed, 2004), pp. 159–61; Ugur Ü. Üngör, "'A Reign of Terror': CUP Rule in Diyarbekir Province, 1913–1918," M.A. thesis, University of Amsterdam, 2005, pp. 46–53, 71; Hans-Lukas Kieser and Dominik Schaller, "Völkermord im historischen Raum," in Kieser and Schaller (eds.), *The Armenian Genocide and the Shoah* (Zurich: Chronos, 2002), pp. 25, 67, n. 63; Hilmar Kaiser, "'A scene from the inferno': The Armenians of Erzurum and the genocide, 1915–1916," in Kieser and Schaller, *Armenian Genocide*, p. 164; Guenter Lewy, *The Armenian Massacres in Ottoman Turkey: A Disputed Genocide* (Salt Lake City: University of Utah Press, 2005), pp. 82–8.

52 For example in Shaw, *War*, who theoretically appreciates war as socially organized, but in practice very much emphasizes state organization.

53 Another example of contradictory interests and actions in the El Salvadoran armed forces in 1979–80 is provided by William Stanley, *The Protection Racket State: Elite Politics, Military Extortion, and Civil War in El Salvador* (Philadelphia: Temple University Press, 1996), pp. 186–7.

54 Mazower, "Violence," p. 1170.

55 Compare my *Kalkulierte Morde* with my article "The Wannsee Conference, the fate of German Jews, and Hitler's decision in principle to exterminate all European Jews," *Journal of Modern History* 70(4), 1998, pp. 759–812.

56 See also Sémelin, "Elemente," pp. 29–30.

57 Pierre Bourdieu and A. Sayad, "Paysans déracinés, bouleversements morphologiques et changements culturels en Algérie," quoted in Pierre Bourdieu, *In Algerien: Zeugnisse der Entwurzelung* (Graz: Edition Camera Austria, 2003), p. 180, about displaced rural dwellers.

58 Fein, *Genocide*, p. 77.

59 Feierstein, *Genocidio*, esp. pp. 13, 83, 104–5, 139, 202–3.

60 For two credible accounts on the last point in the Armenians' deportations, see Mae M. Derdarian, *Vergeen: A Survivor of the Armenian Genocide. Based on a Memoir by Virginia Meghrouni* (Los Angeles: Atmus Press, 1996), pp. 125–6; description by Eitan Belkind, in Yair Auron, *The Banality of Indifference: Zionism and the Armenian Genocide* (New Brunswick and London: Transaction, 2001), p. 184.

61 *Guatemala: Nunca Mas*, vol. 2: *Impactos de la Violencia* (Guatemala: Arzobispado de Guatemala, Oficina de Derechos Humanos, 1999), pp. 11–13.

62 See also Alexander Laban Hinton, "Zündstoffe: Die Roten Khmer in Kambodscha," *Mittelweg 36* 15(6), 2006, pp. 71, 73; Ervin Staub, *The Roots of Evil: The Origins of Genocide and Other Group Violence* (New York *et al*.: Cambridge University Press, 1989), pp. 13–23; Levene, *Meaning*, p. 172; Sémelin, "Elemente," p. 23; quote: Alain Bertallo, "Von der Ethnisierung zum Genozid: Mechanismen der Mobilisierung Unbeteiligter zu Akteuren kollektiver Gewaltexzesse," in Schaller *et al.*, *Enteignet*, p. 69; an example in Throup, *Origins*, pp. 190–1.

63 Hinton, "Zündstoffe," pp. 71, 72, and Zygmunt Bauman, *Modernity and the Holocaust* (Cambridge: Polity, 1993), pp. 91–2, emphasizing a higher degree.

64 J. A. C. Mackie, "Anti-Chinese outbreaks in Indonesia, 1959–1968," in Mackie (ed.), *The Chinese in Indonesia* (Honolulu: University Press of Hawaii, 1976), p. 80, refers to such mechanisms.

65 Semelin, *Purify*, pp. 49–50.

66 See also the contributions in Martin Zimmermann (ed.), *Extreme Formen von Gewalt in Bild und Text des Altertums* (Munich: Herbert Utz, 2009) which show how rulers in antiquity used demonstrative cruelty and arbitrary torturous 'punishments' to foster their power.

67 Semelin, *Purify*, p. 294. Quotation from Kuper, *Genocide*, p. 102.

68 Sémelin, "Elemente," p. 21.

69 See also Scott Strauss, *The Order of Genocide: Race, Power and War in Rwanda* (Ithaca and London: Cornell University Press, 2006), pp. 88: "Killing Tutsis, in short, became a source of legitimacy and power in the context of acute crisis."

70 For a different interpretation emphasizing "rituals" and bonding experiences, see Weitz, *Century*, pp. 132–40, 175–85, 222–9.

71 Here I concur with the overview in Birgit Beck, *Wehrmacht und sexuelle Gewalt: Sexualverbrechen vor deutschen Militärgerichten* (Paderborn *et al.*: Schöningh, 2004), pp. 13–62. There are opposite assertions in some recent scholarship on the topic, for example in Alexandra Stiglmayer (ed.), *Mass Rape: The War against Women in Bosnia-Herzegovina* (Lincoln and London: University of Nebraska Press, 1994). In such narratives there is a tendency to view every mass rape as an attack on the nation – and every 'genocide' as a rape of the nation. An example is Ronit Lentin, "(En)Gendering Genocide: Die Feminisierung der Katastrophe," *Zeitschrift für Genozidforschung* 1(1), 1999, pp. 70–93, esp. p. 80.

72 Sexual abuse by anti-communists against 'communist' women in Indonesia in 1965 and by loyalist militia members against women in resettlement villages in Kenya in the 1950s seems to fall into this category.

73 Tassoula Vervenioti, "Left-wing women between politics and family," in Mark Mazower (ed.), *After the War Was Over: Reconstructing the Family, Nation, and State in Greece, 1943–1960* (Princeton and Oxford: Princeton University Press, 2000), p. 105.

74 Weitz, *Century*, pp. 186–7.

75 Sémelin, "Elemente," p. 33; Jared Diamond, *Collapse: How Societies Choose to Fail or Succeed* (New York: Viking Press, 2005), pp. 322–4. For a much broader, though controversial, thesis and treatment regarding the connections between the "youth bulge" and violence, see Gunnar Heinsohn, *Söhne und Weltmacht: Terror im Aufstieg und Fall der Nationen* (Zürich: Orell Füssli, 2003).

76 See Raul Hilberg, *Perpetrators, Victims, Bystanders: The Jewish Catastrophe, 1933–1945* (New York: Aaron Asher, 1992).

77 Peter du Preez, *Genocide: The Psychology of Mass Murder* (London and New York: Marion Boyars, 1994), p. iii. Levene, *Meaning*, p. 9, makes a similar argument with reference to the existing world system.

78 On the other hand, the chapters on Indonesia and anti-guerrilla warfare in this book have demonstrated that there are also limits on

the ability of intervening foreign powers to induce violence in other countries or to keep such violence under control.

79 Lal, "Concentration camp," p. 243. Dirk Moses and Mark Levene also see "genocide" as "part of a single process" or to be "understood within a single frame of reference," spreading from the so-called West to twentieth-century contenders and then post-colonial polities. However, they put most emphasis on the emergence of the nation-state (Levene, *Meaning*, pp. 4–7, 205).

80 A similar point is made by Mazower, "Violence," p. 1158. Despite all the criticism it drew for allegedly denouncing bourgeois democracy, Michael Mann's book *The Dark Side of Democracy* describes murderous "ethnic cleansing" as a transitional phenomenon, a perversion that will go away once all countries have become democracies in a form "appropriate" to their plural character (pp. 522–9, quotation p. 529).

81 Levene, *Meaning*, p. 41, holds that "liberal-democratic" regimes can commit "genocide" on the basis of the performance of their nineteenth-century colonialism.

82 Shaw, *War*, p. 74.

INDEX